THE PAPERS OF

WOODROW WILSON

VOLUME 44

AUGUST 21–NOVEMBER 10, 1917

SPONSORED BY THE WOODROW WILSON
FOUNDATION
AND PRINCETON UNIVERSITY

THE PAPERS OF

WOODROW WILSON

ARTHUR S. LINK, *EDITOR*

DAVID W. HIRST, *SENIOR ASSOCIATE EDITOR*

JOHN E. LITTLE, *ASSOCIATE EDITOR*

FREDRICK AANDAHL, *ASSOCIATE EDITOR*

MANFRED F. BOEMEKE, *ASSISTANT EDITOR*

PHYLLIS MARCHAND AND MARGARET D. LINK,

EDITORIAL ASSISTANTS

Volume 44

August 21–November 10, 1917

PRINCETON, NEW JERSEY
PRINCETON UNIVERSITY PRESS
1983

INTRODUCTION

THE opening of this volume finds Wilson in the last stages of the preparation of his reply to Pope Benedict XV's peace appeal of August 1, 1917. Reports from American ambassadors in the Allied capitals make it clear that there is no possibility of a joint American-Allied reply; indeed, these reports reveal that the French, Italian, and Russian governments think that the Pope is acting on behalf of Austria-Hungary and that they have no intention of answering his note. Hence Wilson decides that he will have to reply on his own. In an eloquent note dated August 27, 1917, Wilson expresses warm agreement with the Pope's lofty desire for peace. But, Wilson says, a lasting peace cannot be made with a ruthless military autocracy bent upon dominating the world. The United States, Wilson adds, repudiates the notion of "punitive damages, the dismemberment of empires, the establishment of selfish and exclusive economic leagues." It only awaits evidence of the will and purpose for a just and lasting peace on the part of the German people themselves. Wilson's reply is the opening salvo in what will become his ideological battle against the German military regime. A few days after dispatching his note, Wilson asks Colonel House to assemble a group of experts and scholars to ascertain what peace terms the Allies would insist upon "in order that we may formulate our own position either for or against them."

Eighteen days later, Wilson receives a long personal letter from the British Prime Minister, David Lloyd George, urging him to send representatives to a forthcoming inter-Allied council in London to make war plans for 1918; indeed, Lloyd George bluntly asks Wilson to abandon his stance of aloofness from all inter-Allied discussions and to send delegates to all inter-Allied councils. Wilson agrees (he is under pressure from numerous other persons to do so) and asks House to arrange for the recruitment of the members of the American mission to what Wilson and House call "the peace conference."

Meanwhile, although American mobilization is getting into high gear, numerous other problems challenge Wilson's leadership at home. He easily fends off a movement in Congress to establish a joint congressional committee to oversee war expenditures. However, the labor situation continues to be dangerously volatile, and Wilson becomes personally drawn into the settlement of all major strikes. Moreover, he appoints what is called the President's Mediation Commission to survey the labor situation in general and to deal with several potentially dangerous situations in particular. As this volume ends, the commission, headed by Secretary William B. Wilson, is in Arizona and reports on the labor situation in the copper districts of that state and on the earlier Bisbee deportations.

All through the period covered by this volume, Lansing, under Wilson's watchful eye, continues discussions with the special Japanese envoy, Viscount Ishii, looking toward a comprehensive Japanese-American understanding on the Far East. Unable to agree on details, Lansing and Ishii sign, on November 2, 1917, an ambiguous statement in which Japan reaffirms her allegiance to the principles of the Open Door and the United States acknowledges that Japan, because of her propinquity to China, has "special interests" in that country.

There are numerous other concerns which require Wilson's attention and decision. For example, he sets the minimum price of wheat on August 30, 1917. He is embarrassed when suffragettes, put into jail for picketing the White House, go on a hunger strike. He intervenes decisively when Secret Service agents harass the former German propagandist, William Bayard Hale. The documents in this volume abundantly reveal Wilson's concern about these and a hundred other problems of a country at war.

"VERBATIM ET LITERATIM"

In earlier volumes of this series, we have said something like the following: "All documents are reproduced *verbatim et literatim*, with typographical and spelling errors corrected in square brackets only when necessary for clarity and ease of reading." The following essay explains our textual methods and review procedures.

We have never printed and do not intend to print critical, or corrected, versions of documents. We print them exactly as they are, with a few exceptions which we always note. We never use the word *sic* except to denote the repetition of words in a document; in fact, we think that a succession of *sics* defaces a page.

We usually repair words in square brackets when letters are missing. As we have said, we also repair words in square brackets for clarity and ease of reading. Our general rule is to do this when we, ourselves, cannot read the word without stopping to determine its meaning. Jumbled words and names misspelled beyond recognition of course have to be repaired. We correct the misspelling of a name in the footnote identifying the person.

However, when an old man writes to Wilson saying that he is glad to hear that Wilson is "comming" to Newark, or a semiliterate farmer from Texas writes phonetically, we see no reason to correct spellings in square brackets when the words are perfectly understandable. We do not correct Wilson's misspellings unless they are unreadable, except to supply in square brackets letters missing in words. For example, for some reason he insisted upon spelling "belligerent" as "belligerant." Nothing would be gained by correcting "belligerant" in square brackets.

We think that is very important for several reasons to follow the rule of *verbatim et literatim*. Most important, a document has its own integrity and power, particularly when it is not written in a perfect literary form. There is something very moving in seeing a Texas dirt farmer struggling to express his feelings in words, or a semiliterate former slave doing the same thing. Second, in Wilson's case it is crucially important to reproduce his errors in letters which he typed himself, since he usually typed badly when he was in an agitated state. Third, since style is the essence of the person, we would never correct grammar or make tenses consistent, as one correspondent has urged us to do. Fourth, we think that it is very important that we print exact transcripts of Charles L. Swem's copies of Wilson's letters. Swem made many mistakes (we correct them in footnotes from a reading of his shorthand books), and Wilson let them pass. We thus have to assume that Wilson did not read his letters before signing them, and this, we think, is a significant fact. Finally, printing typed letters and documents *verbatim et literatim* tells us a great deal about the educational level of the stenographic profession in the United States during Wilson's time.

We think that our series would be worthless if we produced unreliable texts, and we go to some effort to make certain that the texts are authentic.

Our typists are highly skilled and proofread their transcripts carefully as soon as they have typed them. The Editor sight proofreads documents once he has assembled a volume and is setting its annotation. The Editors who write the notes read through documents several times and are careful to check any anomalies. Then, once the manuscript volume has been completed and all notes checked, the Editor and Senior Associate Editor orally proofread the documents against the copy. They read every comma, dash, and character. They note every absence of punctuation. They study every nearly illegible word in written documents.

Once this process of "establishing the text" is completed, the manuscript volume goes to our editor at Princeton University Press, who checks the volume carefully and sends it to the printing plant. The volume is set in Linotype by a typographer who has been working on the Wilson volumes for years. The galley proofs go to the proofroom, where they are read orally against copy. And we must say that the proofreaders at the Press are extraordinarily skilled. Some years ago, before we found a way to ease their burden, they used to query every misspelled word, absence of punctuation, or other such anomalies. Now we write "O.K." above such words or spaces on the copy.

We read the galley proofs three times. Our copy editor gives them a sight reading against the manuscript copy to look for remaining typographical errors and to make sure that no line has been dropped. The Editor and Senior Associate Editor sight read them against documents and copy. We then get the page proofs, which have been corrected at the Press. We check all the changes three times. In addition, we get *revised* pages and check them twice.

This is not the end. Our indexer of course reads the pages word by word. Before we return the pages to the Press, she comes in with a list of queries, all of which are answered by reference to the documents.

Our rule in the Wilson Papers is that our tolerance of error is zero. No system and no person can be perfect. We are sure that there are errors in our volumes. However, we believe that we have done everything humanly possible to avoid error; the chance is remote that what looks at first glance like a typographical error is indeed an error.

Beginning with this volume, we will, for reasons of economy of space, usually print foreign-language documents only in translations and not in their original texts. Any person who desires to do so is welcome to examine our copies of the original documents.

This is the last volume in *The Papers of Woodrow Wilson* to be set in Linotype. We take this opportunity to pay our tribute and to express our thanks to Ray O'Grady and Eddie Machos, the two men who have set in Linotype most of our volumes to this point. We also thank our editor at Princeton University Press, Judith May, for continuing invaluable help and Professors John Milton Cooper, Jr., William H. Harbaugh, and Richard W. Leopold for reading the manuscript of this volume and for being, as always, constructively critical.

THE EDITORS

Princeton, New Jersey
March 15, 1983

CONTENTS

The Papers, August 21-November 10, 1917
Wilson Materials

News reports
Interviews

Collateral Materials

Political correspondence, reports, memoranda, and aide-mémoire

ILLUSTRATIONS

Following page 294

ABBREVIATIONS

ALI	autograph letter initialed
ALS	autograph letter signed
ASB	Albert Sidney Burleson
ASBhw	Albert Sidney Burleson handwriting, handwritten
CC	carbon copy
CCL	carbon copy of letter
CCLS	carbon copy of letter signed
CLS	Charles Lee Swem
CLSsh	Charles Lee Swem shorthand
EBW	Edith Bolling Wilson
EMH	Edward Mandell House
FKL	Franklin Knight Lane
FLP	Frank Lyon Polk
FR	*Papers Relating to the Foreign Relations of the United States*
FR-WWS 1917	*Papers Relating to the Foreign Relations of the United States, 1917, Supplement, The World War*
FTC	Federal Trade Commission
HCH	Herbert Clark Hoover
Hw, hw	handwriting, handwritten
HwCL	handwritten copy of letter
HwCLS	handwritten copy of letter signed
HwLS	handwritten letter signed
HwS	handwritten signed
JD	Josephus Daniels
JPT	Joseph Patrick Tumulty
JRT	Jack Romagna typed
L	letter
MS	manuscript
MSS	manuscripts
NDB	Newton Diehl Baker
PS	postscript
RG	record group
RL	Robert Lansing
RLhw	Robert Lansing, handwriting, handwritten
T	typed
TC	typed copy
TCL	typed copy of letter
TCLS	typed copy of letter signed
TI	typed initialed
TLS	typed letter signed
TS	typed signed
TWG	Thomas Watt Gregory
WBW	William Bauchop Wilson
WCR	William Cox Redfield
WGM	William Gibbs McAdoo
WHP	Walter Hines Page
WJB	William Jennings Bryan
WW	Woodrow Wilson
WWhw	Woodrow Wilson handwriting, handwritten

WWhwLI   Woodrow Wilson handwritten letter initialed
WWsh   Woodrow Wilson shorthand
WWT   Woodrow Wilson typed
WWTL   Woodrow Wilson typed letter
WWTLI   Woodrow Wilson typed letter initialed
WWTLS   Woodrow Wilson typed letter signed
WWTS   Woodrow Wilson typed signed

ABBREVIATIONS FOR COLLECTIONS
AND REPOSITORIES

Following the National Union Catalog
of the Library of Congress

AFL-CIO-Ar	American Federation of Labor-Congress of Industrial Organizations Archives
AGO	Adjutant General's Office
CtY	Yale University
CtY-D	Yale University Divinity School
DLC	Library of Congress
DNA	National Archives
FFM-Ar	French Foreign Ministry Archives
FO	British Foreign Office
GFO-Ar	German Foreign Office Archives
IEN	Northwestern University
InNd	University of Notre Dame
HPL	Hoover Presidental Library
IOR	India Office Records
JDR	Justice Department Records
KHi	Kansas State Historical Society
KyU	University of Kentucky
MH-Ar	Harvard University Archives
NHpR	Franklin D. Roosevelt Library
NNC	Columbia University
OClW	Case Western Reserve University
PRO	Public Record Office
RSB Coll., DLC	Ray Stannard Baker Collection of Wilsoniana, Library of Congress
SDR	State Department Records
VtU	University of Vermont
WC, NjP	Woodrow Wilson Collection, Princeton University
WDR	War Department Records
WP, DLC	Woodrow Wilson Papers, Library of Congress

SYMBOLS

[September 4, 1917]	publication date of a published writing; also date of document when date is not part of text
[*October 22, 1917*]	composition date when publication date differs
[[October 20, 1917]]	delivery date of speech if publication date differs
**** ***	text deleted by author of document

THE PAPERS OF

WOODROW WILSON

VOLUME 44

AUGUST 21–NOVEMBER 10, 1917

THE PAPERS OF
WOODROW WILSON

A Press Release

The White House. 21 August, 1917.

The following scale of prices is prescribed for bituminous coal at the mine in the several coal producing districts.[1] It is provisional only. It is subject to reconsideration when the whole method of administering the fuel supplies of the country shall have been satisfactorily organized and put into operation. Subsequent measures will have as their object a fair and equitable control of the distribution of the supply and of the prices not only at the mines but also in the hands of the middlemen and the retailers.

The prices provisionally fixed here are fixed by my authority under the provisions of the recent Act of Congress regarding administration of the food supply of the country, which also conferred upon the Executive control of the fuel supply. They are based upon the actual cost of production and are deemed to be not only fair and just but liberal as well. Under them the industry should nowhere lack stimulation.   Woodrow Wilson

WWTS MS (WP, DLC).

[1] The mimeographed press release, Aug. 21, 1917 (WP, DLC), included a list of prices (f.o.b. mine) for twenty-nine mining districts in twenty-two states. Costs for "Run of Mine" coal varied from $1.90 to $3.25 per ton; for "Prepared Sizes," from $2.15 to $3.50; and for "Slack or Screenings," from $1.65 to $3.00. Prices were lowest in the Big Seam district of Alabama and highest in Oklahoma and Washington State.

To Robert Lansing, with Enclosures

My dear Mr. Secretary: The White House 21 August, 1917

Here are some very interesting papers which I have just received from a Princeton classmate of mine[1] and I am sending them to you with the suggestion that you be kind enough to have them very carefully examined in order that we may presently discuss the question of what action on our part is desirable.

Cordially and sincerely yours,   Woodrow Wilson

[1] In W. R. Wilder to WW, Aug. 17, 1917, TLS (SDR, RG 59, 860C.01/53, DNA).

ENCLOSURE I

From George Jan Sosnowski

Dear Mr. President: New York. August 8, 1917.

By cementing the ties between the German people and the crown, the German Government has achieved a great victory, not only in their internal politics, but over the Allies. The staged parliamentary revolution in the Reichstag and the peace resolution passed by it, as well as the strategical benefits derived by Germany through the complete collapse of Russia are placing the United States and the Allies in a most precarious position.

In the very near future it is probable that the entire Rumanian Army, with a goodly part of the Russian Army, will surrender, resulting in a break of the Russian-Rumanian front, opening for German occupation the fertile lands of Russia as far east as the Azoff Sea and the fall of Kieeff and Odessa within a few months' time.

Owing to a misconception of the slavic question, the Allies have committed the most unfortunate political and strategical blunders since the Russian Revolution. It would seem as if the statesmen of the Allies are laboring under the wrong impression, that the German Government at this time is working for universal peace. Two or three months ago this was no doubt so, but not today. The Allies let the best opportunity slip from their hands. The situation is now in the control of the Kaiser and he has the Allies on the hip and his only concern is the leadership of the United States, which he fears.

The peace resolution was passed by the Reichstag solely as a sop to Russia, and it will do its work shortly, unless the Allies change their tactics in dealing with the problem of the East front. The German propaganda today controls Russia and Russian democracy is still looking for a man to lead her to ultimate freedom.

Under present conditions, Russia cannot survive through the coming winter. She will be hors de combat before winter sets in. The few Russian patriots are helpless before the ignorant masses, and even the leaders of the Russian socialists have lost control. The Russian Socialists are not preaching patriotism, but war on the possessing classes of Russia, who are looking for salvation not to the Allies, but to Germany. The result of this will not be the fault of the Russian democracy or of the other Slav nations who are thus being pushed under the German yoke by the Allies' ignorance of the Slavic question. Even the learned mind of Mr.

Balfour was confused when he made the statement to the whole World through the Associated Press that the Poles are "a medley of nationalities," for the Poles are the purest Slavic race, the "medley of nationalities" being Russia, which explains why nobody ever heard of Russian pariotism and why the Poles are known as the most patriotic people among the Slavs. Why does Mr. Balfour expect the peoples of Russia, who are without Russian patriotism and real Russian nationality, to fight for something they never possessed or aspired to? Poles, Lithuanians and Ruthenians, the most powerful of all nationalities, composing Russia, surely cannot be expected to fight for Russian sovereignty over them. The only way the Allies can secure the unstinting cooperation of those nationalities is to cooperate with the United States in putting into effect the Wilson doctrine.

Today the Poles in Europe are the actual leaders of all the Slavic peoples of Austro-Hungary and partly so of the Lithuanians and Ruthenians. It is still within the reach of the Poles to insure a victory for the Allies.

The Slavs have unbounded confidence in the United States and in your leadership; their confidence in the Allies has been lost, and the situation is entirely in your hands. In proof of this I am enclosing a memorandum drawn up by the Polish National Defense Committee,[1] which memorandum expresses the opinion of the Polish socialists (90% of whom are Polish nationalists, not internationalists) and of the Austrian Poles, who play an important part in Polish politics, but who are not and never were a deciding power, nor entrusted with the inner secrets of Polish politics. But they are at present an interesting factor should the formation of a Polish army be contemplated, as some of the Poles in the Russian army are already contaminated by ill-considered Russian socialistic ideals, and these Poles will be most effectually controlled by the Polish national socialists.

I differ with the Polish National Defense Committee on many points, but mostly concerning the method of bringing about the declaration of independence of Poland and the immediate formation of a Polish Government outside of Poland, and a Polish army made up of Poles in the Russian army and in Russia.

The recognition of the independence of the former Republic of Poland and the formation of a Polish army as described by me in my previous letters to you and to Secretary Lansing, are the only means of averting the greatest disaster to the Allies that has yet befallen them.

The unsettled Polish question is of constant danger to the Allies as will appear from the following: Some weeks ago some of the Polish leaders, through German socialistic channels, were approached with a proposition to agree with Russia on a certain frontier line between Poland and Russia and to conclude a treaty by which Russia would guarantee to Poland that the Russians would not invade Polish territory no matter what circumstances might develop during this war. At the same time it was said that Germany would withdraw her lines behind the rivers Bzura, Rafka and Narev in Western Poland, thereby evacuating the greater part of Russian Poland, and that Austria would evacuate Galicia. Had the Poles agreed to this proposition all the German forces on the Eastern front would have been available for use on the Western front and Austria would have been able to concentrate all of her forces against the Italians.

For the present the danger is averted, thanks to the loyalty of the Poles, but is there any assurance that this same scheme will not be worked again in the near future, and with better results for the Germans?

I am, Your Excellency,

Most respectfully,   G. J. Sosnowski.

1 That is, the following document.

ENCLOSURE II

From Alesander Debskí[1] and Bronislaw D. Kulakowski

Mr. President: [New York, c. Aug. 8, 1917]

The entrance of the United States into the war had a fundamental influence upon the course of events. The voice of the great Western Democracy resounded powerfully, drowning the voices of the belligerent powers, from which the oppressed peoples could not expect the longed for liberty in spite of all promises to that effect.

For the first time since over a century the Polish nation heard on January 22, 1917 words not of hope only but of certainty, words from a source in which it has implicit confidence—the Chief Executive of the people of the United States.

Your name, Mr. President, occupies a place of honor in the thoughts and the sentiments of the entire Polish nation.

Your voice encouraged the aspirations of the Independence Party in Poland.

Struggling for the Polish state, the Independence Party endeavored to take advantage of the victories of the Central

Powers and the friendliness of Austria in order to build up on the territories abandoned by the Russians, Polish life which for over a hundred years was trampled down and persecuted. The Polish nation now raises its head and turns even against the powerful German Empire.

A new stage in the work of liberation is approaching. At a convention of Poles from all the three parts of Poland and from foreign countries, held at Stockholm in May 1917, there were laid foundations for the future policy of Poland, corresponding to the changes which have occurred of late.

The undersigned, Alexander Dembski, a United States citizen, took part in these debates and begs to inform the President of the United States that all Poles expect a betterment of their lot from the action of the United States and that they wish to express their deep gratitude and their sincere friendship for the United States of America.

Living up in our estimation to our duty to the democracy of the United States and of Poland as well, we beg to submit the present memorandum in the name of the Polish National Defense Committee.

We have endeavored to present the Polish question impartially and to show the desire of the Poles for the establishing of a permanent modus of communicating with the American nation.

In your hands, Mr. President, rests the fate of an entire nation.

As soldiers of liberty we put ourselves and the services of our organization at your disposal.

Accept, Mr. President, the expressions of our deepest respect.

> Alesander Debskí
> Bronislaw D. Kulakowski
> for the POLISH NATIONAL DEFENSE COMMITTEE

TLS (SDR, RG 59, 860C.01/53, DNA).

[1] Alexander Debskí, or Alexander Dembskí, a mechanical engineer of New York, was a senior member and leader of the Union of Polish Socialists, an organization formed in New York in 1890. See Piotr S. Wandycz, *The United States and Poland* (Cambridge, Mass., 1980), pp. 97-102.

To Samuel Isett Woodbridge[1]

My dear Woodbridge: The White House 21 August, 1917

You may be sure that your letter of July sixth[2] was greatly enjoyed and I am sorry I have to return to it so meager an answer, but I am sure you will understand in all the circumstances how impossible it is for me to write letters.

Will you not say to the ladies who represent the American Woman's Club of Shanghai how deeply gratified I was by their generous message? It was indeed delightful to hear such a voice of loyalty and friendship from across the seas.

You may be sure we are watching developments in China, so well as we can from this distance, with the greatest solicitude. I hope with all my heart that in the providence of God some permanent and beneficent result may be worked out.

With warmest regards from us all,

Faithfully yours,   Woodrow Wilson

TLS (WC, NjP).
1 Presbyterian missionary in Shanghai. His wife, Janie Wilson Woodrow Woodbridge, was a first cousin of Woodrow Wilson.
2 It is missing.

To Newton Diehl Baker, with Enclosure

My dear Mr. Secretary: [The White House] 21 August, 1917

In the matter of the enclosed memorandum, my heart pulls one way (namely, in the direction of Governor Harrison's recommendation) and my head in the other, in the direction of your own judgment. I suppose I must follow my head in this case, and I would be very much obliged to you if you would confer with the Attorney General as to the best selections that can be made.[1]

Cordially and faithfully yours,   Woodrow Wilson

TLS (Letterpress Books, WP, DLC).
1 Wilson followed Baker's suggestion and earlier advice by Gregory [TWG to WW, July 2, 1917, TLS (WP, DLC)] and appointed a Filipino, Ramon Avanceña, on October 4, and an American, Frederick Charles Fisher, on November 17.

E N C L O S U R E

From Newton Diehl Baker

My dear Mr. President,   [Washington] August 17, 1917.

On July 28th, Governor General Harrison cabled:

"Supreme Court wish to renew my recommendation contained in my telegram June 12th, that two Filipinos be appointed, and would be gratified if my views may be laid before the President."

to which the Chief of the Bureau of Insular Affairs sent this reply:

"*Confidential.* Referring to telegram from your office of 28th instant, Supreme Court, after your recommendation was laid before President, he decided that in the filling of the vacancies created there should be appointed one American and one Filipino and so advised the Resident Commissioners. Do you now desire to re-open this question?"

Governor General Harrison now cables as follows:

"Referring to telegram from your office of 30th ultimo, I earnestly request that the following be laid before the President: Secretary of Justice Victorino Mapa, on behalf of the Cabinet, states as follows:

'The cabinet sincerely believes that the appointment of a majority of Filipinos to the Supreme Court would be a just recognition of the capacity invariably demonstrated by Filipino judges in the efficient and impartial administration of justice, and a logical step under the present organization of the insular government. The Cabinet is entirely convinced that such a step, so anxiously desired by the Filipino people, would leave assured, as well as may be possible, at the present time, the due protection of the rights of all the inhabitants of the Philippines.' The Chief Justice gives following opinion: 'Filipinization of the Supreme Court is an important part of the President's own general policy regarding the Philippines, and the judicial system is ready for this forward step.' I heartily concur with the above and renew my recommendation that a Filipino majority be appointed."

In transmitting Governor General Harrison's views to you, I regret that I am not able to concur in the opinion he expresses. The United States has decided not to withdraw from the Philippine Islands at this time, as to the dominant government of these islands, and I am satisfied that, until such time as we are ready to give independence to the island, a majority of the supreme court should be Americans. The representation which the Filipino people have in that Court of a substantial minority seems to me as full a recognition of the capacity for self-government of the people as under the circumstances is either wise or necessary.

I understand there are two vacancies and if you so direct, I will take up with the Attorney General the selection of suitable names for presentation for consideration.

Respectfully yours,   Newton D. Baker

CCL (WDR, RG 94, AGO-Misc. File, No. 2638715, DNA).

To Newton Diehl Baker, with Enclosure

Dear Baker,   [The White House, c. Aug. 21, 1917]

I would very much fear the results of this (*if* it is true) because of Blease[1] and the passions he would rejoice to raise.

W.W.

ALI (N. D. Baker Papers, DLC).
  [1] Coleman Livingston Blease, Governor of South Carolina, 1911-1915, a violent anti-Negro demagogue.

E N C L O S U R E

AltaPass, N. C. Aug. 20-21, 1917.

Hon. D. F. Houston, Dept. Agrl. Washn.

Report negro and Portorican troops to be stationed at Camp Jackson at Columbia. the enemies of administration and me personally would want no bigger club. it would be almost fatal. the blame would be put upon me. I protest earnestly against it. see President for me and explain the situation. it must not be done.

A. F. Lever.

T telegram (N. D. Baker Papers, DLC).

Three Letters to William Cox Redfield

My dear Mr. Secretary: [The White House] 21 August, 1917

I know that you will understand what I mean when I say that I think it would be very unwise to let it appear even to Mr. Shapiro that I had made any suggestion in this matter, but I entirely agree with your own attitude about it. I think such a resolution very ill-timed and very unfortunate.[1]

Cordially and faithfully yours,   Woodrow Wilson

  [1] Nathan D. Shapiro, a lawyer and Republican assemblyman of Brooklyn, had proposed that the Assembly of the State of New York adopt a resolution calling upon Wilson to proclaim that the American people were willing to make peace with any enemies who would accept an honorable and lasting settlement, with reductions in armaments and no annexations or indemnities. Shapiro had sent a copy of his resolution on August 4 to Redfield, who had replied that he doubted the wisdom of such a resolution; Redfield added that he thought that talk of peace at this juncture was "premature" and "positively embarrassing" to Wilson. Shapiro replied on August 14 that his intention was not to talk peace but to persuade Wilson to define the war aims of the United States in order to counter requests for exemptions from the draft. Many such requests, Shapiro said, were based on a patriotism or military spirit that was somewhat half-hearted, and, in his words, "justly so." Redfield sent this correspondence to Tumulty and asked whether Wilson had any suggestions for a further reply to Shapiro. WCR to JPT, Aug. 16, 1917, TLS (WP, DLC). The enclosures were returned to Redfield, but the White House staff had prepared a summary. White House Staff to WW, c. Aug. 20, 1917, T MS (WP, DLC).

Shapiro also wrote directly to Wilson: N. D. Shapiro to WW, Aug. 16, 1917, TLS (WP, DLC). Shapiro favored abolishing "the gruesome and colossal militarism of Germany" and noted that Russian militarism had come to an end. However, he thought that many Americans who were called under the selective draft were "unalterably opposed to shedding one drop of their blood for any of the ambitions of either England, Italy or even France." In view of current uncertainties, Shapiro urged Wilson to state clearly and definitely how he would go about "making the world safe for democracy." Moreover, Shapiro added, Wilson should enter into peace talks and work for disarmament. "I believe that such a move on your part will meet with universal support and that the service you will thereby render may even be greater than the service rendered by Christ, for he preached civilization when people were not ready to accept it; you, on the other hand, can preach it at a time when all are crying for it." This letter was shown to Wilson, and it was acknowledged on August 22.

My dear Mr. Secretary: [The White House] 21 August, 1917

I think I shall always feel uneasy when I act contrary to your judgment;[1] but the conviction has grown upon me that we began wrong in our arrangements for the administration of the control of exports,—as I explained to you the other day,—and I believe that the only solution is to entrust the whole action and detail of administration in that matter to one instrumentality, the instrumentality already created, namely, the Exports Board.

I am accordingly signing an Executive Order to that effect; but I shall not publish it. The Exports Board, like the Exports Council, is my own executive agency, and this administrative readjustment concerns only the action of this agency.

May I not say again how sincerely and deeply I appreciate your own generous and loyal attitude towards my decisions in such matters?

Cordially and faithfully yours,   Woodrow Wilson

[1] See WCR to WW, Aug. 18, 1917 (first letter of that date), Vol. 43.

My dear Mr. Secretary: [The White House] 21 August, 1917

Thank you for your suggestion about considering the Enemy Trading Act in connection with the export arrangement.[1]

With regard to Mr. Thurman's reference to Section 9 of the Act of March 4, 1909, let me say that it seems to me that that section is not applicable. Inasmuch as Congress has authorized me to exercise the powers with regard to the limitation of exports through such agencies as I may designate, I feel that the way is cleared in this legislation from all obstacles such as Mr. Thurman suggests in this case.

I know that Mr. McCormick was going to confer with you about this important matter which I am so anxious to arrange in the best possible way, and I am going to see him today and learn the result of his conference with you.

In haste, with warm regard,

Faithfully yours,   Woodrow Wilson

TLS (Letterpress Books, WP, DLC).
    1 WCR to WW, Aug. 18, 1917 (second letter of that date), Vol. 43.

To Amos Lawrence Lowell

My dear President Lowell: The White House 21 August, 1917

May I not acknowledge in this way the receipt of your telegram of August eighteenth,[1] transmitting to me the resolution of the Executive Committee of the League to Enforce Peace concerning the peace proposals of His Holiness, Pope Benedict, and say how sincerely I appreciate such messages?

Cordially and sincerely yours,   Woodrow Wilson

TLS (A. L. Lowell Papers, MH-Ar).
    1 A. L. Lowell to WW, Aug. 18, 1917, Vol. 43.

To John Cardinal Farley

[The White House] August 21, 1917.

Your telegram has been received.[1] The Secretary of War tells me that Colonel Hine had been transferred to the command of the Sixty-ninth before your telegram came.

Woodrow Wilson.

T telegram (Letterpress Books, WP, DLC).
    1 J. Card. Farley to WW, Aug. 15, 1917, printed as an Enclosure with WW to NDB, Aug. 16, 1917 (third letter of that date), Vol. 43.

To Henry Noble Hall

My dear Mr. Hall: [The White House] 21 August, 1917

I am obliged to you for your letter of the fifteenth.[1] It expresses not a little of my own concern and I hope sincerely that the matter you refer to is now being more wisely and more successfully handled.

Cordially and sincerely yours,   Woodrow Wilson

TLS (Letterpress Books, WP, DLC).
    1 H. N. Hall to WW, Aug. 15, 1917, Vol. 43.

To John Franklin Fort

My dear Governor: [The White House] 21 August, 1917

Thank you warmly for your letter of August eighteenth.[1] I very carefully discussed the whole coal situation yesterday with two of your colleagues, Davies and Colver, and your letter came, therefore, as a very opportune contribution to the conference. It is a tough question and I am by no means confident that I have struck the right judgment.

I am sorry that you have been ill and beg that you will take care of yourself.

In haste   Faithfully yours,   Woodrow Wilson

TLS (Letterpress Books, WP, DLC).
[1] J. F. Fort to WW, Aug. 18, 1917, Vol. 43.

To Jacques A. Berst

My dear Sir: [The White House] 21 August, 1917

I have your letter of August eighteenth.[1]

I have no inclination, of course, to do anything that will be injurious to the Exchange, but I think you will realize how critically important it is at this juncture in the affairs of the nation that no instrumentalities which create international ill feeling should be permitted to affect the feelings and the opinions of the people of the country, particularly when they affect them most unjustly toward the particular foreign nation concerned. I hope that it will be possible very promptly, therefore, to comply with my suggestions concerning the film play "Patria."

Very truly yours,   Woodrow Wilson

TLS (Letterpress Books, WP, DLC).
[1] He meant J. A. Berst to WW, Aug. 16, 1917, Vol. 43.

To Edward Nash Hurley, with Enclosure

My dear Hurley: [The White House] 21 August, 1917

Is not this a matter in which the Shipping Board is vitally interested? If it is and any practical suggestions occur to you, I would be very much obliged if you would personally confer with the members of the War Industries Board to see what if anything will be effective to meet the situation which Governor Lister here anxiously outlines.

Cordially and sincerely yours,   Woodrow Wilson

TLS (Letterpress Books, WP, DLC).

ENCLOSURE

Olympia, Washington, 6 pm., August 18, 1917.

For some weeks there has been a most unsatisfactory condition existing in the lumber industry in the northwest. Many of the logging camps and lumber mills are closed and thousands of men are unemployed as a result of the strike now going on. The State Council of Defense aided by many public spirited citizens, has endeavored to bring about an adjustment, without success. The Secretary of War, speaking for the Council of National Defense, has suggested a solution which has not been accepted. On Thursday last I presented a plan of settlement and find that it does not meet with the approval of the operators. It is claimed by the operators that a sufficient number of plants are running to supply Government demands. They state, however, that this demand does not exceed seven and one half per cent of the normal output of the plants. I personally feel that during this crisis we are not performing our full degree of duty unless we also operate the mills and camps to supply the ninety two and one half per cent general demand. Every plan thus far suggested to bring about an adjustment of the differences has failed and I am writing to suggest the appointment of a commission by you to make a complete investigation covering the lumber industry of the States of Washington, Idaho, and Oregon. This commission to have the power to call for information relating to the cost of operation, wages paid to employes, living conditions of employes, the price now being obliged for lumber, sales condition on competitive territory, in fact, to cover all lines of investigation that might furnish information which would result in obtaining a proper investigation again bringing about normal conditions in this industry. If the plan suggested appeals to you a joint federal and state commission might be appointed with one member representing each of the States of Oregon, Idaho and Washington, the representative member from each State to be appointed by the Governor of the State period. I suggest the above plan to you only after it appears that every other possible method of bringing about a settlement of the differences has been tried and failed. Should the plan meet with your approval, may I suggest early action. If present conditions continue the situation is certain to become grave.   Ernest Lister.

TC telegram (E. N. Hurley Papers, InNd).

To Ernest Lister

[The White House] 21 August, 1917

Permit me to express appreciation of your telegram of August eighteenth and to say that I shall further bestir myself to see what can be done in the situation through existing instrumentalities, preserving your interesting suggestion for later consideration.   Woodrow Wilson.

T telegram (Letterpress Books, WP, DLC).

To Waddill Catchings

My dear Mr. Catchings: [The White House] 21 August, 1917

I am in receipt of your telegram[1] and appreciate your splendid offer to act in any manner that I may think best in the interests of the country in these times in connection with the labor situation in Alabama.

To avoid a stoppage of work in the Alabama coal fields it is necessary that conditions be arranged which will not only be acceptable to the coal operators but which will also be acceptable to the miners. It is with the hope of being able to work out such an arrangement that the Secretary of Labor has secured separate conferences with the Alabama operators and miners in Birmingham, Alabama, on the twenty-third instant. I feel strongly the necessity of continuing these operations uninterruptedly and urge your earnest cooperation with the Secretary towards the accomplishment of that purpose.

Sincerely yours,   Woodrow Wilson[2]

TLS (Letterpress Books, WP, DLC).
   [1] W. Catchings to WW, Aug. 17, 1917, Vol. 43.
   [2] This letter repeated a draft enclosed in WBW to CLS, Aug. 21, 1917, TLS (WP, DLC).

From John R. Mott

Mr. President: Washington August 21, 1917.

A few days ago, when you received our Special Diplomatic Mission, you requested us to prepare and submit to you a statement, outlining the plans we would propose for promoting an effective educational campaign in Russia, and for raising the morale of the Russian soldiers. Senator Root appointed a group of our number to prepare this statement. This we have done, in collaboration with him. He and I are hoping that you may be able to see us, with reference to this important matter, possibly tomorrow, Wednesday, should this prove to be convenient to you.

At the suggestion of Mr. Lansing, I am sending this statement to you, in order that you may have opportunity to examine it in advance. Mr. Root thought that it would be well to have it printed, so as to facilitate your reading it.[1]

With highest regard,

Faithfully yours,   John R. Mott

TLS (WP, DLC).
    [1] See G. Creel to WW, Aug. 20, 1917, n. 1, Vol. 43.

From Edward Mandell House, with Enclosure

Dear Governor: Magnolia, Massachusetts. August 21, 1917.

I am sending you a copy of a cable which Lord Northcliffe has received and enclosed to me. He adds in his letter: "The enclosed addendum to the submarine report has reached me. The situation is an annoying and anxious one. This memorandum does not agree with the optimistic speech to which I referred."

The speech to which he refers is the one recently made by Lloyd George.[1]   Affectionately yours,   E. M. House

TLS (WP, DLC).
    [1] Lloyd George had addressed the House of Commons on August 16 on food and shipping. The British government, he said, had concluded that, "with reasonable economy," there was "no chance of starving out the population of these Islands." He also stated that the Germans were exaggerating the success of their submarine campaign. Actually, he said, at the current rate, the British were losing only one third of the tonnage that the Germans claimed to be sinking. "The losses are diminishing, the building is increasing." Antisubmarine measures were becoming more effective, and the construction of new tonnage was quickening. Looking ahead, the Prime Minister concluded: "Our difficulties will diminish, and our power will increase; their difficulties will increase, and their power will diminish—and they know it." *Parliamentary Debates: Commons,* Fifth Series, Vol. 97, cols. 1471-84.

E N C L O S U R E

Extract of telegram received by Lord Northcliffe, August 14, through Foreign Office.

Lord Northcliffe should also be informed that on August 9 the War Cabinet decided owing to the need of maintaining tonnage so far as is possible to devote to the construction of vessels all the steel plates which can be used in spite of the fact that this will involve a reduction in the output of shells. It was also decided to release men from Munition Works and from the Army for the necessary labour. The Prime Minister feels that the speedy turning out of tonnage is to-day absolutely the first war need.

T MS (WP, DLC).

From Thomas Watt Gregory

Dear Mr. President: Washington, D. C. August 21, 1917.

Mr. Tumulty referred to me this morning copy of a wire sent to you from San Francisco on the 17th by Mr. George L. Bell,[1] in which he says that the Governors of eight western states resent the continued publicity from the federal departments concerning I.W.W. matters and complain of the lack of cooperation by these departments because they are not informed of the announced intention of action on the part of the federal government or consulted in regard to it.

This department has given out no statement whatever in regard to I.W.W. activities during the past week, nor can I recall that any have been given out since Mr. Bell was in Washington. I have repeatedly declined to make any statement, and have given general notice to the various branches of this department that they should make none, either here or in the far west. I do not believe they have given out anything with the exception of an interview the assistant district attorney in San Francisco was reported to have given some three weeks ago. On hearing of this I wired strict instructions to the district attorney at that point to enforce the rule of this department, and it then developed that the assistant had done some imprudent talking in the absence of the district attorney.

You know of the intended action I have in mind with respect to the I.W.W.[2] This is being developed through the usual channels, and I have not considered it advisable to reveal my plans to any of these western governors, though this will undoubtedly be done a little later.

Every representative of this department in the west is under specific instructions to cooperate with the state authorities and especially to give them all information bearing on violations of state laws.

While I have no knowledge of anything having been given out by any representative, except as above indicated, I have today wired all United States District Attorneys, Marshals and agents in charge of investigation work in the states of California, Washington, Arizona, Utah, Montana, New Mexico, Minnesota,

Nebraska, Oregon and Idaho that the governors of these states have earnestly urged that nothing be given out by government officials on the subject of the I.W.W. and instructed them to see that this request is observed. This I have done merely as an additional precaution.

I, of course, cannot control irresponsible newspaper utterances which may have appeared in western papers.

Under the facts as stated, I cannot help but consider Mr. Bell's wire as impudent, but I will not trouble you by commenting on that phase of it.

Faithfully yours,   T. W. Gregory

TLS (WP, DLC).

¹ It had been summarized in a file memorandum and the telegram had been sent to Gregory. White House memorandum, Aug. 21, 1917, T MS (WP, DLC).

² That is, to arrest and try the leaders of the I.W.W. for interference with the war effort and for criminal conspiracy to block industrial production and incite draft evasion, desertion, and insubordination in the armed forces. Gregory had issued instructions on July 17 to United States district attorneys to collect all information about the I.W.W. which might be useful to the Justice Department in determining what action might be taken under the various criminal statutes of the United States or that might be useful to state authorities. Seven weeks later, on September 5, agents of the Bureau of Investigation raided I.W.W. headquarters in thirty-three cities. In these and subsequent raids, they arrested dozens of persons and seized five tons of material as evidence. The Justice Department arranged to centralize the main prosecution of the case in Chicago, where 166 officers, organizers, and secretaries of the I.W.W. were indicted on September 28. *U. S. v. W. D. Haywood et al.* was set to begin in the spring of 1918. See H. C. Peterson and Gilbert C. Fite, *Opponents of War. 1917-1918* (Madison, Wisc., 1957), pp. 61-64; William Preston, Jr., *Aliens and Dissenters: Federal Suppression of Radicals, 1903-1933* (Cambridge, Mass., 1963), pp. 118-24; and Melvyn Dubofsky, *We Shall Be All: A History of the Industrial Workers of the World* (New York, 2d end., 1975), pp. 405-409.

From Robert Lansing, with Enclosure

My dear Mr. President: Washington August 21, 1917.

Before writing you a letter on the Pope's appeal to the belligerents I prepared some comments upon the communication, which I enclose.   Faithfully yours,   Robert Lansing.

TLS (WP, DLC).

E N C L O S U R E

August 19, 1917.

Comments on the Pope's Peace Appeal.

As to the motives which inspired the Pope to make this appeal, I believe that the following may be assumed:

1st. *A sincere desire for the restoration of peace.*

The only doubt which may be cast upon this motive is that the Pope did not speak when Belgium was lawlessly invaded and the Belgian people were atrociously treated. In fact no effort was made by him till the possibility of victory by the Central Powers seemed remote.

2d. *An earnest wish to preserve the Empire of Austria-Hungary from dismemberment.*

This menace to Austria-Hungary is very real because of the jealousies and dislikes of the various nationalities composing the Dual Empire. The spirit of separation, which was checked by fear of Russia, has, since the overthrow of the Czar and the practical elimination of the territorial greed of the former Russian Government, became [become] much stronger and threatens to disrupt the present political union.

The keen interest and sympathy of the Pope for Austria-Hungary arises from the fact that that Empire has been the main support of the Vatican for half a century; and has been always faithful to the doctrine of temporal power.

3d. *A desire to preserve monarchy from the increasing danger of socialism and the irreligious tendencies of socialistic doctrine.*

It is not so much democracy as socialism that the Roman Church fears, although both are more or less antagonistic to hierarchical government, and equally so in the denial of temporal power to the church.

4th. *The preservation, if not the increase, of the influence of the Roman Church.*

It is significant in this connection that the restoration of Belgian territory and of Belgian sovereignty and recreation of the Catholic monarchy of Poland are particularly mentioned, while the Slavic states of Serbia and Montenegro are not referred to in the bases proposed.

The reasons for making an appeal at this particular time would seem to be largely due to Austro-Hungarian influence. Though there is no direct evidence the presumption is very strong as shown by the following facts:

The people of Austria-Hungary are suffering greatly and peace is their supreme desire.

There is danger of disorders and insurrections unless the Austrian Government takes steps toward peace. This the Em-

peror appreciates and has been active in encouraging efforts
to that end.

If the war is carried through until one side or the other
triumphs, Austria-Hungary will, whoever conquers, be in a worse
pass than if peace were made before a decision was reached.
In the one case, disintegration of the Empire would almost certainly follow; in the other, Austria-Hungary would be practically
a vassal state of Germany. For the preservation of the integrity
of the Empire with substantially its present boundaries peace
should come as soon as possible.

Possibly the final defeat of the Central Powers appears more
certain, now that it is evident that the United States intends to
exert all its resources against its enemy.

Further evidence of Austrian influence is to be found in the
appeal itself. While the evacuation of Belgium by Germany is
mentioned, no mention is made of the restoration of Serbia,
Montenegro and Roumania by Austria. The Italian claims and
the questions relating to the Balkan States are postponed for
negotiation.

It is known that Germany and Austria have been making
special efforts toward peace at the present time. The intrigues in
Russia, the Stockholm Conference, the propaganda in this country and in neutral countries, all belong to one general plan of
seeking peace while victorious on land and while submarine warfare appears successful. The Pope, probably unwittingly, was induced to make his appeal at this time so that another influence
would be brought to bear on the Entente and the United States.

When the terms proposed are analyzed they divide themselves
into two parts:

1st. Terms relating to perpetuation of peace.

2d. Terms relating to boundaries.

The first series of terms embracing disarmament, arbitration
and freedom of the seas depends upon the good faith of the
powers and upon their ability to agree as to the provisions. As to
the good faith of the German Government as it is now constituted
there cannot be two opinions. The German rulers cannot be
trusted. They unhesitatingly broke the treaty neutralizing
Belgium; they violated the Hague Treaties by which they were
morally, if not legally, bound; they broke their word as to submarine warfare; and they have constantly deceived, intrigued
and lied.

To depend upon the good faith of a Government so utterly discredited and so evidently lacking in regard for moral obligation

would be to invite new aggressions as soon as opportunity offered to pursue its ambitions of dominion.

Until the Government of Germany becomes trustworthy it would be folly to rely upon its treaty promises.

The second series of terms, relating to territory, practically restores the *status quo ante bellum*, although in certain particulars it may be considered favorable to Austria-Hungary.

Primarily the territories of the principal powers are left intact except as to the territories "forming *part* of the old kingdom of Poland." It is noted that "part" of Poland is to be erected into an independent state, thus leaving the question of *what* territory uncertain. Presumably it refers to Russian Poland. If the proposal had embraced the whole of ancient Poland it would give the kingdom a position on the Baltic coast now Prussian and a considerable section of Galicia. It would appear therefore that the word "part" was used designedly to exclude these areas.

The disputed territories, such as Alsace-Lorraine, the Trentino and Dalmatian coast, are left to negotiation.

There is no proposal that the Balkan States shall be restored. The whole subject is to be examined in a "spirit of equity and justice." Thus Serbia's former possessions are not even assured.

In the same way the future of Armenia is left to the determination of the negotiators.

There is no reference to Turkey, to the internationalization of the Dardanelles or the free use of waterways. Armenia is to be discussed.

Except in the restoration of Belgium and the return of the German colonies, everything is left to future negotiation. The proposal, therefore, amounts practically to no more than the German proposal of December 12, 1916. It means that the belligerents meet and discuss the territorial questions and the measures necessary to preserve future peace. *That is identically the object which the German Government sought last December*. It is true it names certain subjects to be discussed at the council board and suggests certain principles which should be applied in reaching an agreement, but it does not name all the subjects of dispute nor does it advocate any definite principle save condon[e]ment in relation to crimes committed against Belgium and Serbia. It practically asks these two countries not to ask or expect any restitution of their shattered fortunes or any recompense for the wanton destruction of life and property although it holds out a vague suggestion that if there are reasons against condonement in certain cases they should be weighed in justice and equity.

All that the Central Powers seek is to get the Allied Powers at a conference where, relying on the differences in interest between them, they may hope to break up the alliance and avoid paying the penalty for the evil which they have wrought.

T MS (SDR, RG 59, 763.72119/792½, DNA).

From Robert Lansing

My dear Mr. President: Washington August 21, 1917.

The Russian Ambassador called to see me Monday afternoon to ask me as to the attitude of this Government toward the Pope's appeal. I told him that the communication was still under consideration and I did not feel warranted in expressing an opinion at the present time. He said that he was disappointed because his Government had telegraphed to ask him to inquire, because it was desirous to act in a similar way if possible.

I agreed that similar but independent action seemed wise, and asked him if his Government had indicated its views as to the appeal. He said that it had and that the terms proposed were unsatisfactory as they provided for a peace with the military autocracy of Germany, the overthrow of which was the supreme object of the war and the essential thing for perpetual peace and the safety of democracy. He then asked me to convey this information to you.   Faithfully yours,   Robert Lansing.

TLS (WP, DLC).

William Bauchop Wilson
to Joseph Patrick Tumulty

My dear Mr. Tumulty: Washington August 21, 1917.

Referring to the telegram from Judge Chambers relative to the Georgia, Florida and Alabama Railroad, which you inclosed,[1] I know of no way in which the Federal Government can compel a change from the seemingly arbitrary attitude taken by the officials of this railroad. The Georgia, Florida and Alabama Railroad is a so-called independent line running from Richland, Georgia, to Carrabelle, Florida, with a branch line to Quincy, Florida, and total mileage of 192 miles. Its gross earnings in 1916 were $573,627.

I do not know of the nature of the telegram sent by Stone,

Shea, Sheppard and Dodge to Senator Hollis, but while the contest is of vital importance to men who are engaged in it and to them it is presumably the one big thing in existence, I do not believe there need be any fear that the four brotherhood chiefs will convoke the 600 general chairmen in a meeting at Washington for the purpose of dealing with this proposition. If the road were a part of some great general system, there might be fear of such a movement being undertaken. But being a local road, controlled principally by local capital, Mrs. Cora B. Williams of Atlanta, Georgia, being president of it, any general movement inaugurated to influence these local parties would simply result in penalizing people who are in no way responsible for the trouble and who have no means of influencing its adjustment. No one knows this better than the brotherhood chiefs themselves, and I shall be greatly surprised if a conference of the general chairmen is called for this purpose.

There has been some dissatisfaction among the members of the brotherhoods because they have not been represented on the transportation committees of the Council of National Defense, and there is greater likelihood of a conference of the general chairmen to consider this matter than there is for the consideration of a dispute on a local road in Georgia and Florida.

There is no way that I know of in which the situation can be handled by the Federal Government beyond the point where Judge Chambers has gone, unless influences can be brought to bear on the local owners of the property to induce them to accept the good offices of the Board of Mediation.

I am inclosing herewith a list of the officers and directors of the company,[2] and also the telegram from Judge Chambers.

Cordially yours,   W B Wilson

TLS (WP, DLC).

[1] W. L. Chambers to WW, Aug. 20, 1917, Vol. 43.
[2] This enclosure not printed.

Walter Hines Page to Robert Lansing

London. Aug. 21, 1917.

6996. My 6990 of today.[1] Following is the text of the cipher telegram which Mr. Balfour has just despatched to Count Deselis,[2] the British Minister to the Holy See: "You should take a convenient opportunity of pointing out to the Cardinal Secretary of State that we have not yet had an opportunity of consulting our Allies on the subject of the Pope's note and are therefore not in a position to say what reply if any could usefully be sent to his suggestion as to the terms on which a durable peace might best be assured. You should add that in our opinion no progress is likely to be made until the Central Powers and their Allies have officially announced the objects for which they are carrying on the war the measure of restoration and reparation which they are prepared to concede and the methods by which the world may be effectively guaranteed against any repetition of the horrors from which it is now suffering. Even as regards Belgium where they have owned themselves a great wrong we have no clear intimation of their intention either to restore its complete independence or to repair the injuries which they have inflicted upon it. His Eminence will doubtless have present to his mind the statements which the Allies made in reply to President Wilson's note. No corresponding statements have been issued either by Austria or Germany and it seems to us useless to attempt to bring the belligerents into agreement until we know clearly the points on which they differ. I assume that you have a copy of the joint reply of the Allies to President Wilson and of the despatch on the same subject which I wrote on January seventh. If not I will at once send you copies for "convenience of reference."   Page.

T telegram (SDR, RG 59, 763.72119/748, DNA).
   1 It is missing in the files of the Department of State.
   2 John Francis Charles, Count de Salis. He was the son of a French countess.

William Graves Sharp to Robert Lansing

Paris. Aug. 21, 1917.

2407. Confidential. Your circular of August 18, 4 P.M.[1] In a conversation with Mr. Ribot, at which Mr. Cambon was present, I was informed that instructions had been cabled over to Mr. Jusserand at Washington to ascertain the President's attitude upon the peace communication of the Pope and that this request had been repeated a second time.

Mr. Ribot started out by saying that the French Government felt that, before expressing its own views, the British Government should be first sounded as to its attitude and that the latter might in fact, in the position to be taken by it, be regarded as representing the views of the European Allies upon that question.

We expressed further the belief that the Pope's communication was so lacking in specific recommendations, not alone in so far as France was concerned as to the restoration of Alsace and Lorraine, but also as to the question of reparation for losses, that a good deal of thought would have to be given to its answer.

In any event it was the opinion of both Mr. Ribot and Mr. Cambon that there should be a complete accord among the Allies in making their answer. They say that they would appreciate very much if I would express their desire that the President would first communicate his own views to them so that there might follow an exchange of opinion between them to the end that such accord might be arranged. Mr. Ribot said that it was obvious that even among the European Allies there might result some difference of opinion upon some of the points that might be made in answer on account of the different interests, that he could see that this might be especially true in the present as it applied to the opinion of the United States compared to the views of some of the Allies.

Notwithstanding this view of the matter the question was presented as to whether it might be possibly thought best for the Allies to join together in making their answer.

I gather from the attitude of both Mr. Ribot and Mr. Cambon that they felt it especially desirable to get each of the Allies' views before the formal declaration by anyone of them should be made. Mr. Ribot was rather cautious and reserved in expressing his own views However, on seeing Mr. Cambon alone this afternoon, he stated that since seeing me, in reference to the communication of the Pope, he had had word from the Chargé d'Affairs of the French Government in London² stating that Mr. Balfour had just informed him that, inasmuch as the German Chancellor at Berlin, Dr. Michaelis, was expected today to discuss the subject before the Reichstag, he thought it would be wise to wait until that speech had been made before undertaking to formulate their own reply. Mr. Cambon who has always been quite free in frankly expressing his own views to me upon various matters discussed between us from time to time, told me that he felt quite confident that the Pope was not alone actuated by a desire to help Austria in issuing the communication, but that it was primarily to strengthen his own power and that of the Catholic Church. Incidentally in that connection he expressed the opinion that the Pope's authority as well as the cause of Catholicism would be rather strengthened by the severance of relations between the State and the Church, such as existed in both the United States and France.

Mr. Cambon further asserted that the French Government could not favorably consider the Pope's appeal. This attitude is certainly voiced by substantially all the papers in Paris which characterize the communication as not only too vague in its declarations but as unjust in denying reparation for the great damage wrought by Germany upon the territory of the Allied countries which its armies have invaded.   Sharp.

T telegram (SDR, RG 59, 763.72119/752, DNA).
  [1] RL to All Diplomatic Missions in Allied Countries, Aug. 18, 1917, Vol. 43.
  [2] Aimé-Joseph de Fleurian, Counselor of Embassy.

Peter Augustus Jay[1] to Robert Lansing

Rome. August 21, 1917.

1062. Department's confidential circular regarding Pope's Peace note received today via Paris. Confidential. Have just had interview with the Minister for Foreign Affairs whom I informed of President's desire and that his views would be considered confidential. Baron Sonnino said substantially as follows: Note should not be taken too seriously. Italian Government thinks less hurry (?), waiting to see trend of public opinion in Italy and elsewhere and if a reply must be given will previously consult Allies. Move evidently instigated by Germany and carried to Vatican through Austria, Empress of Austria[2] being friend of Pope. Pope himself is possibly unconsciously being made use of. Note is vague and gives no basis of negotiation with Italy. Austrian press now allowed to declare Austria can (?) mutual interest. Note creates difficulty with Catholic party in Italy which is steadily taking greater part in internal affairs, and is also an attempt to steal effect of possible socialist success in Stockholm peace move and to depress public towards inevitable winter campaign. Question of reply especially difficult for Italy in view of her relations with Vatican.

Baron Sonnino has the personal impression that a good firm reply drawn up by President sent in advance of the other Allied replies would greatly impress public opinion especially in view of our previously well known desire for peace.

I asked him twice if I could telegraph the above paragraph regarding our replying first. He agreed repeating they were his personal views.   Jay.

T telegram (SDR, RG 59, 763.72119/749, DNA).
  [1] Counselor of the American embassy in Rome, at this time Chargé d'Affaires.
  [2] Zita, Princess of Bourbon and Parma, Empress of Austria and Queen of Hungary.

To George Lewis Bell

[The White House] 22 August, 1917

I am at a loss to understand your telegram of the seventeenth.[1] After careful inquiry it develops that no statement whatever in regard to I.W.W. activities has been authorized or made by representatives of the federal government since your visit to Washington. I of course do not know what the newspapers may have stated.   Woodrow Wilson.

T telegram (Letterpress Books, WP, DLC).
 [1] That is, the telegram described in TWG to WW, Aug. 21, 1917.

To John R. Mott

My dear Doctor Mott: The White House 22 August, 1917

Thank you very much for the memorandum which you and Mr. Root have prepared for me about publicity in Russia. I want and intend to help and would have liked to discuss the matter with you yesterday but had to ask the Secretary of State to act as my substitute in the matter because it was physically impossible to add another item to the day's work.

In great haste

          Cordially and sincerely yours,   Woodrow Wilson

TLS (J. R. Mott Papers, CtY-D).

To Newton Diehl Baker

My dear Mr. Secretary: The White House 22 August, 1917

I am warmly obliged to you for having let me see the enclosed.[1] Lippmann is always not only though[t]ful but just and suggestive.

          Cordially and sincerely yours,   Woodrow Wilson

TLS (N. D. Baker Papers, DLC).
 [1] W. Lippmann to NDB, Aug. 20, 1917, printed as an Enclosure with NDB to WW, Aug. 20, 1917 (first letter of that date), Vol. 43.

From William Cox Redfield

My dear Mr. President: Washington August 22nd, 1917.

I have your favors of the 21st and note the signing of the Executive Order placing the administration of Export Licenses under the Exports Board. I accept the order in what I trust is a loyal spirit. I cannot conceal from you, however, that quite apart from the thing done, the manner of its doing has deeply hurt me.

I assume your thoughtful suggestion about not publishing the order to be meant in kindly courtesy to me. I think, however, publication of it is unavoidable. A pending request for an appropriation of $384,000. for carrying on the work through the rest of the fiscal year is before the Appropriations Committtee of the House of Representatives. This must be cancelled and I assume the new organization will wish to take it over.

Doubtless also, the Exports Board will require funds from you to carry themselves along temporarily. Otherwise they will have none. The funds in our possession for this work are to some extent obligated for bills not yet received and to replace supplies advanced from our Department stock. Details of this I have asked our Disbursing Officer to arrange with Mr. McCormick. The unobligated and unexpended balance of the money transferred to this Department from your National Defense Fund will be returned to the Treasury to the credit of that fund as soon as the amount thereof is determined.

We are receiving many letters each day which it will be necessary to answer by pointing out that the power has been placed in other hands and that the Department of Commerce is not the proper place to address hereafter.

I assume there is no direct authority of law for the employees of the Department of Commerce in the cities of Boston, New York, Chicago, St. Louis, New Orleans, San Francisco and Seattle, to act for the Exports Board. If, however, you will send me a request that they do so pending the formation of a separate force on the part of the Exports Board in each of these cities, I will accept that as sufficient authority for the purpose. It will, of course, not be possible to continue permanently the arrangement whereby the officers of the Department of Commerce do this work in these various cities now that the matter has been transferred to another organization.

You may be quite sure that whatever I can do to facilitate the matter will be done.

Yours very truly, William C. Redfield

TLS (WP, DLC).

From William Gibbs McAdoo

PERSONAL.

Dear "Governor":   Washington August 22, 1917.

I am glad to see that you have fixed the price of bituminous coal. I do hope that you intend to fix the price quickly of anthracite, as well. There is no more extortionate trust in this country than the anthracite trust, nor one which grinds the people—the poor people particularly—more by its extortions than this trust. It is given a monopoly in the great cities by the laws and ordinances which compel the use of smokeless coal, and it takes advantage of that fact to extort the utmost from those who are compelled to use its product. For the great masses of poor people on the Eastern seaboard it is more important to control the price of anthracite than of bituminous. Each is, however, vitally important.   Affectionately yours,   W G McAdoo

TLS (WP, DLC).

From Newton Diehl Baker

Dear Mr. President: Washington. August 22, 1917.

President Sharpless,[1] who is doubtless well known to you, called on me yesterday to present the inclosed memorial[2] which the Society of Friends of Philadelphia had asked him to make sure actually reached you. I told him I would place this copy in your hands.

General Crowder and I are both giving earnest thought to the subject of conscientious objectors and hope to be able to work out a plan which will be considerate of the embarrassment under which these people find themselves but will not encourage a simulation of conscientious objection on the part of others.

                    Respectfully,   Newton D. Baker

TLS (WP, DLC).

[1] Isaac Sharpless, Dean of the T. Wistar Brown Graduate School of Haverford College.

[2] I. Sharpless and J. H. Bartlett, for the Representative Meeting of the Society of Friends of Philadelphia and Vicinity, to WW, c. Aug. 21, 1917, TS MS (WP, DLC). The memorial noted, first, that the President had not yet declared what sort of noncombatant service was to be performed by conscientious objectors, and, second, that a recent order by General Crowder had directed such persons, when exempted by the local boards, to mobilize with other conscripted persons. This seemed "to violate the intent of the Act" and would undoubtedly result in a number of Friends and probably others declining to obey. The memorial asked Wilson not to include as noncombatant service any work to be performed under military orders. It also said that the Friends were loyal and helpful servants of the government, but that, "by history and conviction," they were "prevented from taking any military part in the present emergency." The memorial con-

cluded by quoting Abraham Lincoln's remarks to a delegation of Friends in similar circumstances.

From Edward Mandell House, with Enclosures

Dear Governor: Magnolia, Massachusetts. August 22, 1917.

Here are two despatches that have just come and which I am hastily sending.

I hope they will adopt Sir William's suggestion, and it looks from Balfour's cable that they will. I am sorry the one word lacking should be an important one. I take it that it means Russia.

Affectionately yours,   E. M. House

TLS (WP, DLC).

E N C L O S U R E   I

London, August 22, 1917

No. 771. I am in fullest sympathy with the President's line of thought as expressed in your telegram received August 20th.[1]

I have telegraphed our British Minister at the Vatican saying we have had no opportunity of consulting with the Allies and therefore are not in a position to say what answer if any should be sent to the Pope. But that in our opinion it was time for the Central Powers to make a statement of their policy. This had already been done by the Entente Powers. Next move should be made by enemy. United States Ambassador here is telegraphing full text. I hope this step will meet with the President's approval.

First thought of the (Russian Govt?) is that a reasonable reply on behalf of all the Allies should be sent. First thought of the French Government is that no answer is at present necessary. For my own part, I greatly dread idea of any joint endeavor of composing elaborate document dealing with complex problems necessarily looked at from somewhat different angles by each belligerent. Drafting difficulties alone seem to render task impossible.   A. J. Balfour.

[1] See the extract from the House Diary printed at Aug. 18, 1917, Vol. 43.

ENCLOSURE I I

London, August 22, 1917.

No. 773. I have seen the President's message to Mr. Balfour[1] and the reply. Mr. Balfour appreciates the President's courtesy in cabling his views.

If the President replies to the Pope's message I shall urge the British Government to make no answer excepting to state they entirely agree with what the President has to say.

William Wiseman.

TC telegrams (WP, DLC).
[1] EMH to A. J. Balfour, Aug. 18, 1917, TC telegram (E. M. House Papers, CtY), which repeated the first six paragraphs of WW to EMH, Aug. 16, 1917, Vol. 43.

From Edward Mandell House

Dear Governor: Magnolia, Mass. August 22, 1917.

The missing word in Balfour's despatch is "Russian Government."   Affectionately yours,   E. M. House

TLS (WP, DLC).

From Thomas Watt Gregory

Dear Mr. President: Washington, D. C. August 22, 1917.

I have read Dr. Cleveland Moffett's letter to you transmitted with your letter of the 17th inst.[1]

It seems to me that the nature of your answer would depend upon whether or not you would consider it wise to ask Congress to legislate with regard to public utterances of the kind so righteously complained of by Dr. Moffett. If you have no present intention of asking for such action by Congress, probably the best thing to say to Dr. Moffett is that you have referred his letter to this Department for consideration. As a matter of fact, such utterances, without more, I am quite sure do not come within the reach of any existing federal statute.

I am keeping for my files a copy of the letter written to you by Dr. Moffett and am returning herewith the original.

Faithfully yours,   T. W. Gregory

TLS (WP, DLC).
[1] C. L. Moffett to WW, Aug. 16, 1917, and WW to TWG, Aug. 17, 1917, both in Vol. 43.

To Teachers and School Officers

The White House, August 23, 1917.

The war is bringing to the minds of our people a new appreciation of the problems of national life and a deeper understanding
of the meaning of the aims of democracy. Matters which heretofore have seemed commonplace and trivial are seen in a truer
light. The urgent demand for the production and proper distribution of food and other national resources has made us aware of
the close dependence of individual on individual and nation on
nation. The effort to keep up social and industrial organizations
in spite of the withdrawal of men for the army has revealed the
extent to which modern life has become complex and specialized.

Those and other lessons of the war must be learned quickly,
if we are intelligently and successfully to defend our institutions.
When the war is over we must apply the wisdom which we have
acquired in purging and ennobling the life of the world.

In these vital tasks of acquiring a broader view of human
possibilities the common school must have a large part. I urge
that teachers and other school officers increase materially the
time and attention devoted to instruction bearing directly on the
and attention devoted to instruction bearing directly on the
problems of community and national life.

Such a plea is in no way foreign to the spirit of American
public education, or to existing practices. Nor is it a plea for a
temporary enlargement of the school program appropriate merely to the period of the war. It is a plea for a realization in public
education of the new emphasis which the war has given to the
ideals of democracy and to the broader conceptions of national
life.

In order that there may be definite material at hand with
which the schools may at once expand their teaching, I have
asked Mr. Hoover and Commissioner Claxton[1] to organize the
proper agencies for the preparation and distribution of suitable
lessons for the elementary grades and for the high school classes.
Lessons thus suggested will serve the double purpose of illustrat-
ing in a concrete way what can be undertaken in the schools
and of stimulating teachers in all parts of the country to formulate new and appropriate materials drawn directly from the communities in which they live.

Sincerely yours,   Woodrow Wilson.

TCL (WP, DLC).

[1] That is, Herbert Hoover and Philander Priestly Claxton, United States Commissioner of Education.

To Edward Mandell House, with Enclosure

My dear House, The White House. 23 August, 1917.

Here is a first draft of a reply to the Pope. Please tell me exactly what you think of it.

I am sure that it should be as brief as possible. I centre it, therefore, on one point: that we cannot take the word of the present rulers of Germany for anything.

I have tried to indicate the attitude of this country on the points most discussed in the socialistic and other camps. I have not thought it wise to say more or to be more specific because it might provoke dissenting voices from France or Italy if I should,—if I should say, for example, that their territorial claims did not interest us.

I shall await you[r] comments with the deepest interest, because the many useful suggestions you have made were in my mind all the while as I wrote.

My own feeling is that we should speak at the earliest possible moment now, and I hope with all my heart that the British and other associated governments will adopt Sir William Wiseman's suggestion and say ditto to us.

I think of you every day with the greatest affection. I am doing now daily just about twice as much as I can do, and the pace is telling, but I hope that when our organizations (for example our coal organization, at the head of which I am going to put Harry Garfield) are in working order I shall be able to get to sea for a day or two of real freedom and rest. Faith I need it!

All join in affectionately [affectionate] messages.

Faithfully Yours, Woodrow Wilson

WWTLS (E. M. House Papers, CtY).

E N C L O S U R E

Every heart that has not been blinded and hardened by this terrible war must be touched by this moving appeal of His Holiness the Pope, must feel the dignity and force of the humane and generous motives which prompted it, and must fervently wish that we might take the path of peace he so persuasively points out. But it would be folly to take it if it does not in fact lead to the goal he proposes. Our response must be based upon the stern facts and upon nothing else. It is not a mere cessation of arms he desires; it is a stable and enduring peace. This agony must not be gone through with again, and it must be a matter of very sober judgment what will insure us against it.

His Holiness in substance proposes that we return to the *status quo ante bellum*, and that then there be a general condonation, disarmament, and a concert of nations based upon a general acceptance of the principle of arbitration; that by a similar concert freedom of the seas be established; and that the territorial claims of France and Italy, the perplexing problems of the Balkan states, and the restitution of Poland be left to such conciliatory adjustments as may be possible in the new temper of such a peace, due regard being paid to the aspirations of the peoples whose political fortunes and affiliations will be involved.

It is manifest that no part of this programme can be successfully carried out unless the restitution of the *status quo ante* furnishes a firm and satisfactory basis for it. The object of this war is to deliver the free peoples of the world from the menace and the actual power of a vast military establishment controlled by an irresponsible government which, having secretly planned to dominate the world, proceeded to carry the plan out without regard either to the sacred obligations of treaty or the long established practices and long cherished principles of international action and honor; which chose its own time for the war; delivered its blow fiercely and suddenly; stopped at no barrier either of law or of mercy; swept a whole continent within the tide of blood,— not the blood of soldiers only, but the blood of innocent women and children also and of the helpless poor; and now stands balked but not defeated, the enemy of four-fifths the world. This power is not the German people. It is the ruthless master of the German people. It is, no doubt, no business of ours how that great people came under its control or submitted with temporary zest to the domination of its purpose; but it is our business to see to it that the history of the rest of the world is no longer left to its handling.

To deal with such a power by way of peace upon the plan proposed by His Holiness the Pope would, so far as we can see, involve a recuperation of its strength and a renewal of its policy; would make it necessary to create a permanent hostile combination of nations against the German people, who are its instruments; would result in abandoning the new-born Russia to the intrigue, the manifold subtle interference, and the certain counter-revolution which would be attempted by all the malign influences to which the German Government has of late accustomed the world. Can peace be based upon a restitution of its power or upon any word of honor it could pledge in a treaty of settlement and accommodation?

Responsible statesmen must now everywhere see, if they never saw before, that no peace can rest securely upon political or economic restrictions meant to benefit some nations and cripple or embarrass others, upon vindictive action of any sort, or any kind of revenge or deliberate injury. The American people have suffered intolerable wrongs at the hands of the Imperial German Government, but they desire no reprisal upon the German people, who have themselves suffered all things in this war, which they did not choose. They believe that peace should rest upon the rights of peoples, not the rights of governments,—the rights of peoples great or small, weak or powerful,—their *equal* right to freedom and security and self-government and to a participation upon fair terms in the economic opportunities of the world,—the German people of course included, if they will accept equality and not seek domination.

The test, therefore, of every plan of peace is this: Is it based upon the faith of all the peoples involved or merely upon the word of an ambitious and intriguing government, on the one hand, and of a group of free peoples, on the other? It is a test which goes to the root of the matter; and it is the test which must be applied.

The purposes of the United States in this war are known to the whole world,—to every people to whom the truth has been permitted to come. They do not need to be stated again. We seek no material advantage of any kind. We believe that the intolerable wrongs done in this war by the furious and brutal power of the Imperial German Government ought to be repaired, but not at the expense of the sovereignty of any people,—rather in vindication of the sovereignty of those that are weak and of those that are strong as well. Punitive damages, the dismemberment of empires, the establishment of selfish and exclusive economic leagues, we deem childish and in the end worse than futile, no proper basis for a peace of any kind, least of all for an enduring peace. That must be based upon justice and fairness and the rights of mankind.

We cannot take the word of the present rulers of Germany as a guarantee of anything that is to endure, *unless explicitly supported by such conclusive evidences of the will and purpose of the Garman [German] people themselves as the other peoples of the world would be justified in accepting. Without such guarantees*[1] treaties of settlement, agreements for disarmament, covenants to set up arbitration in the place of force, territorial adjustments, reconstitutions of small nations, if made with ⟨them⟩ *the German government*, no man, no nation could now depend on. We must await some new evidence of the purposes of the great peoples of the Central Empires. God grant it may be given soon and in a way to restore the confidence of all peoples everywhere in the faith of nations and the possibility of a covenanted peace.[2]

CC MS (WP, DLC).
[1] Words in angle brackets deleted by Wilson; words in italics added by him.
[2] There are WWsh and WWT drafts of this document in WP, DLC.

To Benjamin Franklin Battin

[The White House]
My dear Professor Battin: 23 August, 1917

It is with the sincerest grief that I learn of the death of your wife,[1] and I hope that you will permit me to send you this line of very deep sympathy. It is very grievous that you should be thus left alone.

Cordially and sincerely yours,   Woodrow Wilson

TLS (Letterpress Books, WP, DLC).
[1] Sarah Ellen Williams Battin, Swarthmore 1893, had died in Philadelphia on August 20.

From Herbert Clark Hoover, with Enclosure

Dear Mr. President: Washington August 23, 1917.

I attach herewith copy of a letter which has been circulated in large numbers, and certainly to the whole of the agricultural press of the country, by Senator Reed. I may also mention that Senator Gronna and Congressman Young[1] have both been telegraphing to their constituents in North Dakota making misrepresentations as to the objectives of the Food Administration and encouraging farmers to withhold their wheat from sale, despite the fact that North Dakota is fully represented on the Fair Price Committee under Dr. Garfield.

This attempt to stir up the agricultural sections of the country against our efforts to secure an equitable position between the producer and consumer will, if it is successful, absolutely break down the whole question of food administration and thereby seriously imperil the whole problem of feeding the Allies and protecting our own people over the coming winter.

I beg to remain,

Your obedient servant,   Herbert Hoover

TLS (WP, DLC).
[1] George Morley Young, Republican of North Dakota.

ENCLOSURE

UNITED STATES SENATE   August 15, 1917.

Letter sent to AMERICAN SWINEHERD:

Dear Sir:

It seems to me the interests of the farmer are being seriously jeopardized.

His market has been destroyed.

He is at the mercy of one man.

Is is not the business of all men and newspapers interested in the farmers' welfare to give attention to the present situation?

I venture to inclose some remarks I made in the Senate which you may possibly find of interest.

Very respectfully,   JAS. REED.

T MS (WP, DLC).

From Abram Isaac Elkus

Dear Mr. President: [New York] August 23, 1917.

The following may be already known by you and if so you will, I beg, pardon my bothering you.

In the Pope's Peace Note nothing is said about the future of Turkey or its peoples. This circumstance, of itself, may not be of the greatest importance, but I have learned from conversations with Von Kuhlmann and other German officials, that Germany will be satisfied with Turkey, as her return for the war, Turkey to remain nominally, perhaps as an Independent Power, but in reality a German province. Germany may partially recoup her losses in Turkey and its possibilities.

It is significant, that besides the hundreds of thousands of Armenian *Protestant* Christians in Turkey, there are also many thousand *Roman Catholic* Armenians with their separate Patriarch in Constantinople, who have been substantially undisturbed during the war.

Again, the Pope has been permitted, since Italy declared war against Turkey, to maintain a Papal Legate at Constantinople, Cardinal Dolchi,[1] with semi-diplomatic powers and who is well informed as to Turkish-German plans.

May I venture to hope that this information may be of some slight service, and with kindest regards, beg to remain,

Very sincerely yours,   Abram I Elkus

TLS (WP, DLC).
[1] The Most Rev. Angelo Maria Dolci, Archbishop of Amalfi, Apostolic Delegate to Constantinople since 1914.

To the President of the National Council Assembly at Moscow[1]

Washington, August 24, 1917.

I venture to take the liberty to send to the members of the Great Council now meeting in Moscow the cordial greetings of their friends, the people of the United States, to express their confidence in the ultimate triumph of ideals of democracy and self-government against all enemies within and without, and to give their renewed assurance of every material and moral assistance they can extend to the government of Russia in the promotion of the common cause in which the two nations are unselfishly united.   Woodrow Wilson.

T telegram (SDR, RG 59, 861.00/474, DNA).

[1] Aleksandr Feodorovich Kerenskii presided at the conference, which met from August 25 to 29. Phillips, in recommending that Wilson send an encouraging message, wrote that about 1,000 members would be present. These would include all members of the four Dumas as well as representatives of the peasant councils, the Committee of Workmen and Soldiers, the zemstvos (village councils), the municipal governments, educational and scientific institutions, industry, and commerce. The assembly had been called more to provide support for the Provisional Government than to debate its program, but the Russian embassy in Washington had said that some changes might result. Phillips described the meeting as the government's first attempt to go to the country and said that it was "vitally important" to give every possible support to this effort. Lansing discussed Phillips' letter with Wilson on August 24. W. Phillips to RL, Aug. 24, 1917, TLS (SDR, RG 59, 861.00/474, DNA).

To Herbert Clark Hoover

My dear Mr. Hoover: The White House 24 August, 1917

Thank you for letting me see Senator Reed's letter. Of course, it is perfectly outrageous, but I think that Senator Reed and those who are like him have already tarred themselves so distinctly with the same brush that their influence will be negligible if they will only be kind enough to attach their names always to what they write.

Cordially and faithfully yours,   Woodrow Wilson

TLS (H. Hoover Papers, HPL).

To Robert Lansing, with Enclosure

My dear Mr. Secretary: [The White House] 24 August, 1917

There are some impressive representations made in the enclosed and I send it in order that you may have the benefit of the suggestions it conveys.

Cordially and faithfully yours,   [Woodrow Wilson]

CCL (WP, DLC).

ENCLOSURE

William English Walling

Sends a statement by Mr. Henry Slobodin,[1] a Russian Socialist.

Mr. Slobodin's theme is an American propaganda in this country as active and intelligent as the German propaganda, in order
to show the American side of the war to the foreign population.
He says in dealing with the widespread opposition to the war
the United States has "shown a lack of knowledge and training
in the science of government.

"I have particularly in mind that part of the foreign-born
population of this country which speaks and reads other languages than English—millions of them. It may be taken for
granted that they are accessible to argument * * * but no arguments were used for the American side of the question. The
Germans and pro-Germans pour millions of dollars into a campaign of education for the purpose of arousing discontent against
the American Government and the war. The Americans rely
upon big-feeted detectives and policemen's clubs to hold the
foreign population in check. They do nothing to gain and hold
the allegiance of the foreign population."

Says the foreign population would prefer to support the government. We must show them that we are just as much for peace
as they are—through the foreign papers, etc. This must be backed
by the authority and prestige of the Government. There are many
Germans in this country of high intelligence who are true Americans. They have written and spoken for America, and have
received no support. They should be utilized.

Advocates same policy of education with regard to the Jews,
who are now "misled by a bastard idealism of peace."

Says there are many Russians in America well known and
of high repute in Russian revolutionary circles and pro-Ally,
who should have been sent at once to Russia as emissaries of
the American side. Mentions a Dr. C. Shidlovsky (Ph.D.)[2] who
is a personal friend of Kerensky, Breshkowskaya[3] and others.
"But the Americans were too self-sufficient. They sent the Root
commission which was lost in Russia like babes in the woods. I
am convinced that had America taken advice and acted with
intelligence and energy, it could have saved the eastern Russian
debacle."

Mr. Slobodin is strongly pro-Ally.

T MS (WP, DLC).
[1] Henry (or Harry) Leon Slobodin, a lawyer, had for many years been chair-

man of the Socialist party of New York State, and, before that, national secretary of the Socialist Labor party. Slobodin was born in Rostov, Russia, in 1866
and had emigrated to the United States in 1890. He was graduated from the
New York University Law School in 1896. For a further statement of his views,
see H. L. Slobodin, "The Russian Revolution," *International Socialist Review*,
XVII (May 1917), 645-47.
   2 Unidentified.
   3 Ekaterina Konstantinovna Breshko-Breshkovskaya, called "Babushka" and
"Little Grandmother of the Revolution."

To Joseph Patrick Tumulty

Dear Tumulty: [The White House, c. Aug. 24, 1917]
   I would be very much obliged if you would write to Mr. Brand[1]
that he may be sure that none of us will do anything to interfere
unnecessarily with the law of supply and demand in the cotton
market; and he may also be sure that we have the interests of
that industry as much at heart as he has.[2] We shall be obliged
to be governed by military and other considerations, but will
act as conservatively as possible.   The President.

TL (WP, DLC).
   1 Charles Hillyer Brand, Democratic congressman from Georgia.
   2 C. H. Brand to WW, Aug. 22, 1917, TLS (WP, DLC).

To Abram Isaac Elkus

                                        [The White House]
My dear Mr. Ambassador: 24 August, 1917
   Thank you sincerely for your letter of August twenty-third and
the light it throws on an important matter.
   In great haste, with warm regard,
                         Sincerely yours,   Woodrow Wilson

TLS (Letterpress Books, WP, DLC).

From Edward Mandell House, with Enclosure

Dear Governor: Magnolia, Mass. August 24, 1917.
   You have again written a declaration of human liberty.
   I endorse every word of it. I am sure it is the wise, the states-
manlike and the right way to answer the Pope's peace overtures.
England and France will not like some of it, notably, where on
page three you say that "no peace can rest upon political or economic restrictions meant to benefit some nations and cripple
others, upon vindictive action of any sort, or any kind of revenge
or deliberate injury."

And again on page four where you say: "Punitive damages, the dismemberment of empires, the establishment of selfish and economic leagues, we deem childish etc." But you have the right of it, and are fully justified in laying down the fundamentals of a new and greater international morality.

America will not and ought not to fight for the maintenance of the old, narrow and selfish order of things. You are blazing a new path, and the world must follow, or be lost again in the meshes of unrighteous intrigue.

I am cabling Balfour expressing my personal hope that England, France and Italy will accept your answer as also theirs.

I am, with an abiding affection,

Your devoted,   E. M. House

TLS (WP, DLC).

ENCLOSURE

Magnolia, Mass. August 24, 1917.

The President has composed an answer to the Pope's peace overture and will probably send it within a few days.

It will serve, I think, to unite Russia and add to the confusion in Germany.

If the Allied governments could accept it as their answer to the Pope it would, in my opinion, strengthen their cause throughout the world. If the United States are to put forth their maximum effort, there must be a united people, and the President has struck the note necessary to make this possible.

CC MS (WP, DLC).

From Newton Diehl Baker, with Enclosure

[Washington, c. Aug. 24, 1917]

For the information of The President   Baker

ALS (WP, DLC).

ENCLOSURE

Ft. Sam Houston, Texas Aug. 24, 1917.

Number 5876. Following report just received from Commanding Officer Battalion twenty fourth infantry[1] doing guard duty at

Camp Logan Houston, Texas quote   Serious clash has occurred between approximately one hundred fifty 24th Infantry men and civilian population[2]   Have utilized all troops to quiet riot   Have situation in hand at present 24th Infantry Camps quiet but approximately 150 men still out   Have 400 Illonois troops after them   Will keep you advised of situation   From 9 to 12 casualties so far   unquote Nothing further known as to cause of trouble   In name of Secretary War I have ordered Coast Artillery Companies from Galveston to proceed to Houston by interurban railroad as promptly as possible taking extra supply of ammunition Governor[3] has declared Martial Law   Have placed General Hulen[4] an excellent officer who saw service in the Phillipine insurrection in command   Have also ordered Colonel Waltz[5] with Battalion 19th Infantry proceed from Ft. Sam Houston to Houston as promptly as rail transportation can be provided.

Will send additional Companies of that regiment later if reports show such action necessary. Shall disarm battalion 24th infantry and return them to Columbus, N. M.   Parker[6]

T telegram (WP, DLC).

[1] The Third Battalion of the Twenty-fourth Infantry Regiment, which consisted of eight white officers and 654 black enlisted men, had arrived in Houston from Columbus, N. M., on July 28. Major Kneeland S. Snow had assumed command of the battalion at Camp Logan, in the San Felipe district of Houston, on about August 20. Robert V. Haynes, *A Night of Violence: The Houston Riot of 1917* (Baton Rouge, La., 1976), pp. 60, 91.

[2] Severe tension had developed during August between black soldiers and white police officers and other civilians in the Houston area. There had been several violent clashes, and, on August 23, the rumor spread that a black corporal had been shot and killed by the police. That same evening, several black soldiers at Camp Logan armed themselves with Springfield rifles and ammunition and resisted or evaded efforts by their officers to have the weapons collected. At this point, it was rumored that a white mob was approaching the area, and much wild shooting broke out. At 8:50 P.M., Sergeant Vida Henry led about 100 armed black men on a march from the camp toward San Felipe, and more shots were fired. Other incidents occurred about the same time. Meanwhile, white civilians had begun to arm themselves, some by breaking into hardware stores, and nearby troops of the Illinois National Guard were organized into a riot-control force. During the evening, fifteen whites and three blacks were killed or mortally wounded; another black, Sergeant Henry, committed suicide; and there were several other serious injuries. Order was gradually restored by the Illinois and Texas National Guard troops and civil authorities. The Third Battalion was disarmed and confined, and, on August 24, a sheriff's posse and four Illinois companies searched the black community and arrested soldiers suspected of rioting or mutiny. On the following morning, two trains carrying the Third Battalion, guarded by two companies of the Nineteenth Infantry, left Houston for Columbus, N. M. A military investigation continued. *Ibid.*, pp. 115-92.

[3] James Edward Ferguson.

[4] Brig. Gen. John A. Hulen of the Texas National Guard.

[5] Col. Millard Fillmore Waltz.

[6] Maj. Gen. James Parker, commanding general of the Southern District, U. S. Army.

From William Graves Sharp

Paris. Aug. 24, 1917.

Confidential for the President. Further referring to the Department's circular of eighteenth instant and my 2407 of the 21st instant, Concerning the Pope's peace offering. At the Foreign Office yesterday afternoon, I was informed by Mr. de Margerie,[1] director of political affairs, that a telegram had been received from French Ambassador Petrograd[2] to the effect that Tereschenko, the Minister for Foreign Affairs, had just announced to him his disapproval of the communication of the Pope and had referred to it in most bitter terms. That this, the French Government, is very unfavorable to it the chief reasons being that the Pope in no instance recognizes the difference, from a moral standpoint between the aggressor and those who have been so greviously [grievously] wronged and that to accept a peace on the general principles proposed by the Pope would be to allow an enemy to remain substantially in full possession of his (army?) and resources which would offer the temptation at an opportune moment to renew hostilities against the weakened countries of the smaller and less powerful Allies.

The fact that so much was left unsaid in the appeal as to defining and confirming the rights of these smaller powers also condemned it. The opinion was expressed that the overture was chiefly made through the solicitation of the Austrian Government; that the Emperor and Empress are very devoted Catholics and would naturally feel an additional interest in having the Pope make an intercession in addition to the fact that the very serious economic conditions of that country were well known. The opinion was further expressed that the German Government would never offer any definite terms of peace until forced by arms to do so, but, that consistent with its practice in the past, it would seek to draw out expressions from the Allied Powers, from which course it might gain some possible advantage.

Incidentally much importance is attached to the recent publication of the white book at Athens[3] in which is quoted the message of the Kaiser to King Constantine showing that as early as August fourth[4] an understanding and alliance had been made by Germany with Turkey. In this connection Mr. de Margerie told me that he had in his possession a letter from the Turkish Minister then in Paris[5] under date of August (fourteenth?) as I remember stating that his Government would observe strictest neutrality and enter into no hostile alliances. A Paris press report from Zurich says that "the new Chancellor's statement repudiating the peace resolution of July nineteenth[6] caused a foreboding sensation in Parliamentary circles. There is some talk about a new (ministerial) crisis. The Chancellor is accused of being an extreme reactionary and of having insulted the Reichstag after duping the party leaders who had entered into negotiations with him upon the subject of the peace resolution."

Very bitter comments by the Berlin press are reported in that dispatch. Judging from their character, I would say that the new Chancellor's career will be anything but wise and helpful to Germany.

The following quotations from leading Paris newspapers upon the German Chancellor's speech before the Reichstag, may be taken as fairly typical of the sentiments of the French people. LE TEMPS: Behind closed doors Mr. Michaelis said yesterday that he approved of the Vatican's action but even behind closed doors he refrained from defining his conception of peace. He intimated that he had not had time to confer with the Bulgarians and the Turks yet their opinion on the liberation of Belgium for instance is not needed nor will his remarks about Asia Minor compensate for his equivocal silence on what he terms "The material content" of the pontifical document. The Chancellor was addressing the most highly qualified representatives of all the parties in Parliament; none save the delegate of the dissident socialists asked for a single precision once again. The debate was stifled last winter. Manoeuvers are being repeated these last days. A statement by the Chancellor about Alsace Lorraine was announced from Germany [that] the Imperial Government would grant complete autonomy to the annexed provinces recognizing to them all the rights of a confederate state. This declaration was not made yesterday but the prospect of it will continue to be held out. It is indeed but a decoy.

LA LIBERTE: We are quite willing to believe that Berlin did not suggest the action of Benoit XV but Berlin likes to send its Vienna Ally on errants [errands] allowing for hand washing in case of failure. When Mr. Gerard was in Berlin Bethmann would urge him to offer American mediation and when that diplomat asked questions about Germany's peace conditions he would receive answers whose extravagence was terrifying.

LE JOURNAL: There was a very singular sentence in the first version of Mr. Michaelis' declarations. It spoke of the Central Powers as unable, in spite of all their efforts, to agree on the reply to the Pope. This sentence does not appear in the revised version because it was intended solely for domestic consumption. Its interest is no less because of this. The allusion is perfectly clear. Austria is meant. It is no secret that Vienna and Berlin see the solution of the war under different angles and the end is not yet. A further initiative of Benoit XV is already talked of. The Entente has never made a secret of its war aims, notably in the Orient. The reply of Mr. Wilson clearly specified the expulsion of the Turks from Europe and the liberation of oppressed nations.

LE FIGARO: In spite of the prophecies of the German press Doctor Michaelis had no information to give the Reichstag and was content with declaring himself vaguely satisfied with the Pope's initiative but the Chancellor could not help making an avowal which is of capital importance to us. He acknowledged that Germany's enemies still showed no sign of wanting peace and this reduces to nothing Hindenburg's boa[s]ts which were once more *resolved* [resorted] to in order to revive the confidence of Parliament.[7] It is doubtful whether the Marshal's persistent reiteration of his confidence in the success of submarine warfare can bear much conviction in Germany. The limit he had first allowed for reducing England and France to complete submission and starvation by stopping all navigation has long since been doubled and Germany's enemies are so far from being reduced to submission that Mr. Michaelis himself declares he sees among them no desire for peace. He might have added that everywhere even in Russia the desire to win and the certainty of winning are more deeply rooted than ever.

LE MATIN: The Chancellor made no direct reply to the note of the Pope beyond announcing that it has been impossible, due to lack of time, for the Allies of Germany to come to an agreement as to the reply to be made. In truth the Bulgarians are not in accord with the German Socialists as their ideas of conquest are still very strong. Austria is a strong adherent of the principle of no annexation in order to save her empire. If he could not reply directly to the note he could say that his entire sympathy was with it. At the same time this is only natural as the note is favorable to Germany. French people have no need of being worried as to the allusions of the Chancellor concerning the aims of the Allies.

LE GAULOIS: Those who thought that the Chancellor was at last to give some idea of the war aims of Germany were again deceived. It is difficult to believe that after three years it would be so hard for Germany and her Allies to come to an agreement, such as the reply to be given to the note from the Pope as to peace. The truth is that he is trying to shift the burden to the side of the Allies. He pretends that he is able to publish certain facts as to the bad faith of the Allies. These facts cannot matter to us. We have published our aims and our conscience is clear.

JOURNAL DES DEBATS: Mr. Michaelis merely said that he had not yet been able to reach and [an] understanding with his Allies about the attitude to be adopted towards the Pope's note.

The Chancellor seems to have tried particularly to denounce the spirit of conquest which he detects among the Entente Powers. These are the same tactics which he adopted when he came into power. The tresis [thesis] of a defensive war imposed upon Germany is needed by the Berlin Government as a vindication before the public to offset the disappointments which have resulted from the adventure. So the old tresis [thesis] is now served up anew but brought back to a position easier to defend. Such a revival should not make any dupes. It will suffice to recall that the Allies whose "war aims" are now denounced, had no more war aims on August 1st, 1914, than a belated wayfarer assaulted by a bandit at a street corner.

Germany wants to avoid committing herself. She is reserving all her chances as in her vague note of December twelfth[8] but today as then, she seeks occasion for vague but public talk about peace. Therefore she could not fail to make use of the Pope's note. This is a danger which the allied governments and especially President Wilson must avert by their attitude in replying to Benoit XV.   Sharp.

T telegram (SDR, RG 59, 763.72119/767, DNA).

[1] Pierre de Margerie.

[2] Joseph Noulens.

[3] Ministère des Affaires Étrangères de Grèce, *Documents diplomatiques 1913-1917: Traité d'alliance gréco-serbe; Invasion germano-bulgare en Macédoine* (Athens, 1917). These documents (in French and Greek) were presented to the Greek parliament on August 18. London *Times*, Aug. 20, 21, and 24, 1917. For an English translation of the documents, see *American Journal of International Law*, XII (1918), Supplement, 86-174.

[4] That is, August 4, 1914.

[5] Presumably Rifaat Pasha, at that time the Turkish Ambassador to France.

[6] For the text of Michaelis' statement of August 21 to the Main Committee of the Reichstag, see *Schulthess' Europäischer Geschichtskalender* (1917) I, 755-59. Michaelis said, among other things, that the Pope's appeal for peace had come from the latter's "spontaneous initiative." Germany had not elicited it but was sympathetic and was consulting its allies about a reply. For documents relating to the response of the Central Powers, see Wolfgang Steglich, ed., *Der Friedensappell Papst Benedikts XV. vom 1. August 1917 und die Mittelmächte* (Wiesbaden, 1970).

[7] Michaelis had read to the Main Committee a telegram in which Hindenburg had called attention to the Entente's heavy loss of shipping and had said that Germany's military situation at the beginning of the fourth year of war was better than ever before. *Schulthess'* (1917) I, 756-57.

[8] That is, the German peace note of Dec. 12, 1916, about which see RL to WW, Dec. 14, 1916, Vol. 40.

From Samuel Gompers

Sir: Washington, August 24, 1917.

As chairman of the American Alliance for Labor and Democracy,[1] and by authority of the Advisory Board thereof, I beg to have the honor to respectfully invite you to deliver an address at the national conference called by the Alliance to be held at Minneapolis, Minnesota, September fifth, sixth, and seventh.

May I as briefly as possible recite a few incidents which have lead to the call for this national conference?

On Friday evening, June 29th, having been invited to deliver an address before the New York Central Federated Union, I accepted and performed that service. It is not necessary that I should dwell upon that which I communicated to my fellow workers of New York. Suffice it to know that as a result of that meeting the New York Central Federated Union, being the representatives of the organized labor movement of New York and vicinity, and affiliated to the American Federation of Labor, adopted a resolution expressing appreciation of the service which I had rendered; determined upon a large campaign for the more thorough Americanization of the labor movement of New York and vicinity (that is as far as its jurisdiction went) and it appointed a committee to cooperate with me for the purpose of putting that declaration into effect.

For some time there has been in existence a labor publicity bureau in New York. I called and held a conference to discuss ways and means by which the resolution of the New York Central Federated Union might become most effective. Several conferences were held in New York thereafter, in which a constantly growing number of persons participated. It was decided to organize a body of active men and women and to invite the cooperation of organizations of labor and the following title was adopted as the name of that organization,—

AMERICAN ALLIANCE FOR LABOR AND DEMOCRACY.

At one of the earliest conferences, the following was adopted as a declaration of its purposes:

IT IS THE SENSE OF THIS CONFERENCE THAT IT IS THE DUTY OF ALL THE PEOPLE OF THE UNITED STATES, WITHOUT REGARD TO CLASS, NATIONALITY, POLITICS OR RELIGION, FAITHFULLY AND LOYALLY TO SUPPORT THE GOVERNMENT OF THE UNITED STATES IN CARRYING THE PRESENT WAR FOR JUSTICE, FREEDOM AND DEMOCRACY TO A TRIUMPHANT CONCLUSION, AND WE PLEDGE OURSELVES TO EVERY HONORABLE EFFORT FOR THE ACCOMPLISHMENT OF THAT PURPOSE.

This declaration has been and will be our guide in the activities in which we may be engaged or the services we may be called upon to render.

The alliance has established headquarters at 280 Broadway, New York City, and has a competent force of writers and speakers and a clerical force. We have conducted a campaign of publicity in the printed and spoken word, and much has already been accomplished in disseminating information and securing the cooperation of many, so that there shall be the greatest possible solidarity in spirit and action among the working people and all the people, so that the Republic of the United States and the democracies of the world may be triumphant in this great world struggle to make an accomplished fact what you have so well declared,—that the world may be made safe for democracy.

To more thoroughly disseminate the principle and purpose for which our movement stands, to bring the message home to those who may have the opportunity of hearing and visualizing the cause for which our country has entered this titanic war, the American Alliance for Labor and Democracy has called a national conference to be held at Minneapolis, Minnesota, for the three days beginning September 5th, 1917.

Conscious of the tremendous responsibilities devolving upon you and the inconvenience which you might experience in undertaking the trip, if you will accept our invitation and deliver an address to our national conference at Minneapolis I am of the opinion that there is not any one act which would be of greater importance and of such far-reaching influence upon all our people, our country and the great cause in which we are engaged under your leadership.

Very respectfully yours,   Saml. Gompers.

TLS (S. Gompers Letterpress Books, AFL-CIO-Ar).

¹ The A.A.L.D. was formed primarily to counter the People's Council of America for Democracy and Peace, about which see the Diary of Josephus Daniels, entry for July 13, 1917, n. 3, Vol. 43. The People's Council had announced that it would hold a national conference in Minneapolis on September 1 which would be "truly representative of labor and would reflect the real mind of labor." *Ibid.*, entry for Aug. 17, 1917, n. 1, Vol. 43. Gompers later wrote that there was "one way to refute that claim once and for all time, and I accepted the challenge." He called a national conference of the A.A.L.D. to meet at the same time in the same city. "I had no official authority for my course in organizing the Alliance and serving as its president," Gompers added, "but I had the intrinsic authority arising out of great national need and opportunity to serve." Samuel Gompers, *Seventy Years of Life and Labor: An Autobiography* (2 vols., New York, 1925), II, 382. For further information, see Bernard Mandel, *Samuel Gompers: A Biography* (Yellow Springs, Ohio, 1963), 389-94, and Frank L. Grubbs, Jr., *The Struggle for Labor Loyalty: Gompers, the A.F. of L., and the Pacificists, 1917-1920* (Durham, N. C., 1968).

As it turned out (again, see the note to the second entry from the Daniels diary, just cited), the Minnesota authorities forbade the People's Council to

meet in Minneapolis, whereupon it met in Chicago. About the meeting of the
A.A.L.D., see M. Hale to WW, Sept. 7, 1917, n. 3.

From George Creel

Memorandum for The President:

My dear Mr. President: [Washington] August 24, 1917.
    Attached memorandum explains itself. Put this plan in opera-
tion, and I feel certain that all criticism will be ended. I would
be glad if you said nothing of my connection in the matter, but
handled the suggestions as coming from a Committee.
                            Respectfully,   George Creel

    Appointing a new Asst. P.G. to care for objectionable matter
going through mails[1]

TLS (WP, DLC).
 [1] CLShw.

From the Diary of Josephus Daniels

                                        August Friday 24 1917
        Cabinet. Is war popular? President said you usually obtained
popular sentiment from his point of view. B said Kenyon was
quoted as saying $\frac{2}{3}$ people did not favor war & President said he
did believe K— had said it. 100 years ago French people would
not tolerate idea that Paris represented France. If N. Y. taken,
Iowa would be glad. Race prejudice. Fight in Houston, Texas.
Negro in uniform wants the whole sidewalk.
    Pres. story of nicely dressed white lady, colored boy, poorly
dressed, carried her bag in car. She gave him some money, then
turned and kissed him several times on lips, & as he shambled
out she sat in seat and cried. Why? The observer wondered.

Hw bound diary (J. Daniels Papers, DLC).

From Edward Mandell House

Dear Governor: Magnolia, Massachusetts. August 25, 1917.
    May I suggest that you substitute some other word for "child-
ish" in the sentence beginning "Punitive damages, dismemberment of empires etc."
    This sentence may cause dissention, and to apply the term
"childish" to the group advocating these things would add fuel to

the fire. Of course, what you say is true, but sometimes the truth hurts more than anything else.

Affectionately yours,   E. M. House

I am deeply concerned about what you say about yourself, and I hope you will get to sea at once for a real rest.

TLS (WP, DLC).

From Newton Diehl Baker, with Enclosure

Dear Mr. President: Washington. August 25, 1917

I do not know whether the Secretary of Labor's office sent you a copy of the inclosed dispatch or not, but I think you will be glad to see it.   Respectfully yours,   Newton D. Baker

TLS (WP, DLC).

E N C L O S U R E

Seattle Wn., August 21, 1917.

The agricultural division and the industrial division of the I.W.W. organization called strike for Monday the twentieth   On Sunday the nineteenth the military authorities arrested the secretary[1] of the industrial division in Spokane together with twenty six others   They are all held as military prisoners   Sunday evening the secretary of the industrial division called off the strike We have kept in close touch with the conditions in the agricultural district of the State and find that no appreciable number of laborers have quit in answer to the call for a strike   This strike call seems to be a complete failure   There is plenty of labor in the agricultural districts and the men are satisfied generally with the conditions   Fear of I.W.W. activity in this State is fast declining.   White & Snyder[2]

T telegram (WP, DLC).

[1] James Rowan. He and the twenty-six others were arrested by a company of federalized Idaho National Guardsmen from Fort Wright, under command of Maj. Clement Wilkins. *New York Times*, Aug. 20, 1917. For additional information, see Dubofsky, *We Shall Be All*, p. 403, and Robert L. Tyler, *Rebels of the Woods: The I.W.W. in the Pacific Northwest* (Eugene, Ore., 1967), pp. 133-35.

[2] Henry Middleton White, a lawyer of Bellingham, Wash., had been appointed by Wilson in 1913 as Commissioner of Immigration at the Port of Seattle. Edgar Callender Snyder had been Washington correspondent of the Omaha *Bee* since 1895. White and Snyder at this time were serving as Commissioners of Conciliation for the Department of Labor.

From Newton Diehl Baker, with Enclosure

Dear Mr. President: Washington. August 25, 1917.

I inclose a confidential cablegram which has just come from General Pershing. Unfortunately the underscored words seem to be faultily transmitted by cable and it usually takes more than a day to have them serviced for correction. I send this only for your information.

The third paragraph of this cablegram deals with rather frequent requests which come to me from Mr. Tardieu that I organize all sorts of ancillary troops to be used back of the French lines until we need them. General Pershing apparently has reached the conclusion that the French would rather have us work for them than fight for them. I am adhering rigidly to the policy of getting our own Army organized, and find it sufficiently difficult to get the large bodies of technical troops necessary for our own full equipment.

Respectfully,   Newton D. Baker

TLS (WP, DLC).

ENCLOSURE

Paris, August 24, 1917.

Number 119. August 23, 7:00 P.M. For the Chief of Staff. Confidential.

Paragraph 1. Reference my numbers 69, 74 and 101 and proposed meeting of shipping representatives of Allied powers London September 4th, American representative will be confronted with questions of shipping required by United States and should be strongly supported in demands upon Allies for sufficient commercial shipping to carry out army program outlined your confidential cablegram number 57 if not already assured. Any consideration of less tonnage should be opposed by our representatives. As indicated in former cablegram, the British and especially the French have reached absolute limits of man power and any augmentation their military forces can not be expected. Imperative hasten our organization and training so that we will have the troops contemplated your project in Europe ready for active service by May. Military activity of Allies on land should be strongly reinforced by combined navies and destruction U-boat bases accomplished if possible. High British army officers confidentially condemn waiting policy British Admiralty, and regard British Navy management as extremely inefficient and totally lacking in initiative. In view of gravity of shipping question recommend our government insist upon aggressive policy by combined British and American navies. Generally conceded that our energy saved the Allies from defeat. Hence our position in this war very strong and *should* [solid?]. Hence to dictate policy of Allies in the future. Allies now fully realize dependence upon our cooperation and we need not hesitate demand both aggressive naval policy and full share all high commercial shipping. Recommend American representative shipping conference *be instructed* accordingly.

Paragraph 2. Confidential report to French General Staff indicates further domestic troubles in Russia. French expect to aid Russian army by sending French officers to help organize army. Considerable store placed in assistance of Americans in reorganizing railroads. Reported here that America will aid in this work.

Paragraph 3. Cable from High Commissioner Tardieu to French Prime Minister obtained through confidential sources indicates French pressure to divert United States from program of using all available shipping to land and supply and [an] army in France. He reports difficulty in persuading Secretary of War to send units other than those destined for the Army and that he is obliged Quote *act with* caution Unquote implying that further demands are to be made on us for men. This constant pressure for units outside of military requirements seems to be reversion to the original plans Aenivelle [Gen. Nivelle][1] which contemplated our participation in the war should be to furnish laborers and technical troops. Suggest such requests receive very careful consideration and that our own military requirements be given full weight. Attention invited to first paragraph this cable on necessity of using shipping for landing and supplying army. *With reference to* a review memorandum of May 25th from Major General Tasker H. Bliss to Secretary Baker as to deliberate desire of French and English.[2] My observations in France have confirmed impression stated in that memorandum.

Pershing

T telegram (WP, DLC).
  [1] For a description of General Nivelle's views in this regard, see André Kaspi, *La France et le Concours Américain, Février 1917-Novembre 1918* (3 vols., Lille, 1975), I, 94.
  [2] Bliss' memorandum is printed as an Enclosure with NDB to WW, May 27, 1917, Vol. 42.

From Jouett Shouse

My dear Mr. President: Washington, D. C. August 25, 1917.

It was a source of regret to me and to them that you were unable to see the Kansas committee who were here this week, but I fully understood the circumstances which prevented an appointment with them. They had some interesting facts to present concerning the labor situation in Kansas. I hope you may talk over with Mr. Hoover the conditions they outlined to him.

The exemption boards in Kansas, both local and district, seem to feel it is contrary to the instructions of the Provost Marshal General, and hence contrary to their duty under those instructions, to relieve from the operation of the draft men actually engaged in farming and live stock raising. No doubt the same condition applies in other sections of the country. The result is that in our state, so largely dependent upon agricultural pursuits, the labor situation on the farms is becoming serious in the extreme. Unless there is some relief, production will inevitably suffer.

Our young farmers are patriotic. They are willing to serve their country. Many of them feel it a disgrace to ask for exemption and will not do so. I have no sympathy in the world with the slacker who has sought or who may seek to escape the draft through a sudden attempt to transform himself into a farmer. But I feel very earnestly that the actual, bona fide, skilled farmer, in almost every instance, can render a greater service just now by remaining at hard work on the farm than by going into the army.

Therefore I urged upon the committee from Kansas that they suggest to Mr. Hoover the following plan and I am taking the liberty of submitting it to you: that a proclamation be issued by you personally or by you through the Provost Marshal General, exempting from the operation of the draft all men now actually engaged in farming who were so engaged on the first of March last. The date thus specified was more than a month before the declaration of war, more than two and a half months before the selective draft bill became a law. Those who were engaged in farming then were *real* farmers. Unless they have subsequently changed their avocations they are still *real* farmers. Their places in the army can be taken by others without injury to the army; their places on the farm cannot be filled by unskilled and inexperienced labor without real loss in production at a time when we can ill afford such loss.

The farmers of the country today are in competition with the munitions makers, the steel manufacturers and other large employers for the labor necessary to produce and harvest their crops. Judge Towner of Iowa[1] told me last night that in his state a wage of five dollars per day is being offered for corn cutters, and even at such a cost it is difficult to procure hands. Unless the young men who have been and who are actual farmers shall be allowed to continue to pursue their accustomed avocations, the volume of our farm products must inevitably decrease. And unless exemption is provided by definite proclamation to apply generally, and thus remove the implication of disgrace in claiming exemption, a serious menace to American agriculture cannot be averted.

As you know, I believe thoroughly in the selective draft law. I believe every citizen owes the definite obligation of service to his government. I would simply urge that provision be made that each may serve where he can be of greatest value, and that such provision be so definite that it shall not depend upon the judgment of a local board or be subject to varied interpretation in different sections of the country. Each state must fill its quota in the National Army. But men should be sent who can best be spared, not those vitally needed at home. May I, therefore, be permitted to impress upon you very earnestly the suggestion contained in this letter?

With genuine esteem and respect, believe me,

Sincerely yours,   Jouett Shouse

TLS (WP, DLC).
[1] Horace Mann Towner, Republican congressman from Iowa.

From Josephus Daniels

Dear Mr. President: Washington. Aug. 25. 1917.

I do not know whether you see Mr. Bryan's paper. If not you will be interested and pleased, I am sure, to read the two marked brief editorials in the last issue of the Commoner.[1]

Sincerely   Josephus Daniels

ALS (WP, DLC).
[1] The clipping is attached to JD to WJB, Aug. 29, 1917, CCL (J. Daniels Papers, DLC). In the first editorial, "Resisting the Draft," Bryan wrote: "War is a last resort—it is a reflection upon civilization that it still reddens the earth—but so long as nations go to war the citizens cannot escape a citizen's duty. . . . If a few are permitted to resist a law—any law—because they do not like it, government becomes a farce. The law must be enforced—resistance is anarchy." In the second editorial, "Abusing Free Speech," Bryan wrote that, once the country was committed to war, no sympathy should be wasted on those who were arrested for attacking the government or aiding the enemy under the cloak of free speech. He concluded as follows: "There are only two sides to a war—every American must be on the side of the United States." *The Commoner*, XVII (Aug. 1917), 1.

From Jessie Woodrow Wilson Sayre

Dearest Father,   Siasconset, Massachusetts. Aug. 25, 1917

Your beautiful long letter made me so happy![1] I have been feeding on it ever since. It was so wonderful of you to take the time in all these appallingly busy days to write me.

We have had a very pleasant summer. It is really delightful here. The purity of the air is something to marvel at and on the hottest days there is a breeze. To speak of *hot* days to any one living in Washington is absurd for even on our so-called *hot* days I have needed two blankets at night.

Our protector, Dr. Naylor, turned out to be [an] exceptionally congenial person. He fitted admirably into our little circle. He is travelled, well read, and considerate and helpful in all matters large and small. We were really blessed in discovering him. He is now in France doing Y.M.C.A. work too.

Frank's letters are not very detailed. We know that he is in Paris at headquarters on the executive committee but what that involves is left largely to our common sense to imagine. He has been away to visit the British work in the war zone but I do not believe has been at all near the trenches or in any particular danger. Letters are miserably slow in coming. Nearly four weeks on the average!

Our house here looks out across a meadow to the ocean and thence to France. The children play on the sand every afternoon and love it. You ought to see how brown and well they are!

It is an ideal place. It is good to be away from all the Williamstown people and their everlasting talk! We have found pleasant entertaining people here who seem to take things more normally and sanely and yet the war touches them as closely. Perhaps its because I'm not intimate enough with them to see inside. Any way its a relief.

Nell was up here for two days. It was wonderful to have her and now Margaret is coming, at last, for about the same length of time. My visit to the Vreelands[2] was given up because of Mr. Brown's[3] illness. He is not expected to live.

As he has been out of his head and suffering greatly for a long time, it seems as if it might be a blessed relief.

I was mighty glad to get all the gossip about Annie from Nell. What a lot of conversation that poor child has always provided us with! I hate divorce and remarriage, but if she is really happy and off *your* mind at last I shall be profoundly thankful. It really is intensely amusing from beginning to end. I mean all this last business.

I am enclosing a letter[4] to me from a man whom you have met but whom you probably don't remember. Frank has the highest regard for him so when his first letter came I offered to do as the enclosed letter indicates. I am sending him a note also to you though of course you may be far too busy to pay any further attention to the matter. I merely thought that he might be just the kind of a man you might be looking for for any number of the million things you have to get done.

Darling Father, how I admire and love you, how wonderful and God-sustained you seem in all these intricate affairs to be, how undeviatingly *right*. I am so proud of you and I love you so dearly, dearly.

Give my most affectionate love to dear Edith. I wish I could send you both some of this pure air to rest and refresh you!

Ever devotedly your daughter   Jessie

ALS (WC, NjP).
  [1] WW to Jessie W. W. Sayre, July 21, 1917, Vol. 43.
  [2] That is, the Williamson Updike Vreelands of Princeton.
  [3] The father of Alice May Brown (Mrs. Williamson Updike) Vreeland, of Brooklyn.
  [4] It is missing.

Sir William Wiseman to Edward Mandell House

New York. August 25, 1917.

44444 99999 FOLLOWING FOR HOUSE FROM ROBERT CECIL:

BALFOUR is on a holiday and I am acting for him. It is proposed to ask LORD READING to go to Washington in connection with financial situation. I gather you approve of this suggestion and in itself it seems excellent. But I am fearful lest it should complicate still further our representation in the U. S. unless indeed it were part of some general re-arrangement. It is on this point that I should greatly value your advice. A complete understanding between our two countries is of such vital importance to both of them and even to the whole world that I am venturing to hope that you may feel able to tell me quite candidly and fully what you think. May I ask you bluntly whether you think our present Ambassador with all his great merits exactly the right man for the post. Does he command the complete confidence of the President for after all that is the essential point. If not is there anyone else barring BALFOUR who could not I think be spared who would do better. Then about NORTHCLIFFE. Should he remain and if so in what position. Lastly what powers should READING have and how should they be made to fit in with the position of the Ambassador and Northcliffe if he remains. I know I have no right to ask you for this service but I also know that whether you feel able to advise me or not you will forgive me in view of the vast importance of the interests at stake. I realize that you were kind enough to express your views very fully on these matters to Mr. Balfour, Drummond and Wiseman, but circumstances have so much changed that I have ventured to ask you for a fresh expression of them.

T telegram (W. Wiseman Papers, CtY).

To Walter Hines Page

Washington, August 27, 1917.

Please decipher the following communication and send two copies of it to Mr. Balfour, asking him to retain òne for himself and to be good enough to transmit as soon as possible the other to His Holiness the Pope, for the President, as there is no Papal Legate accredited to the United States. Please expedite.

The following is the full text: Quote

(See text of note attached.)   Lansing

To His Holiness
Benedictus XV.
     Pope.   August 27, 1917.

In acknowledgment of the communication of Your Holiness to the belligerent peoples, dated August 1, 1917, the President of the United States requests me to transmit the following reply:

Every heart that has not been blinded and hardened by this terrible war must be touched by this moving appeal of His Holiness the Pope, must feel the dignity and force of the humane and generous motives which prompted it, and must fervently wish that we might take the path of peace he so persuasively points out. But it would be folly to take it if it does not in fact lead to the goal he proposes. Our response must be based upon the stern facts and upon nothing else. It is not a mere cessation of arms he desires; it is a stable and enduring peace. This agony must not be gone through with again, and it must be a matter of very sober judgment what will insure us against it.

His Holiness in substance proposes that we return to the *status quo ante bellum*, and that then there be a general condonation, disarmament, and a concert of nations based upon an acceptance of the principle of arbitration; that by a similar concert freedom of the seas be established; and that the territorial claims of France and Italy, the perplexing problems of the Balkan states, and the restitution of Poland be left to such conciliatory adjustments as may be possible in the new temper of such a peace, due regard being paid to the aspirations of the peoples whose political fortunes and affiliations will be involved.

It is manifest that no part of this programme can be successfully carried out unless the restitution of the *status quo ante* furnishes a firm and satisfactory basis for it. The object of this war is to deliver the free peoples of the world from the menace and the actual power of a vast military establishment controlled by an irresponsible government which, having secretly planned to dominate the world, proceeded to carry the plan out without regard either to the sacred obligations of treaty or the long established practices and long cherished principles of international action and honor; which chose its own time for the war; delivered its blow fiercely and suddenly; stopped at no barrier either of law or of mercy; swept a whole continent within the tide of blood, not the blood of soldiers only, but the blood of innocent women and children also and of the helpless poor; and now stands balked but not defeated, the enemy of four-fifths of the world. This power is not the German people. It is the ruthless master of the German people. It is no business of ours how that great people came under its control or submitted with temporary zest to the domination of its purpose; but it is our business to see to it that the history of the rest of the world is no longer left to its handling.

To deal with such a power by way of peace upon the plan proposed by His Holiness the Pope would, so far as we can see, involve a recuperation of its strength and a renewal of its policy; would make it necessary to create a permanent hostile combination of nations against the German people, who are its instruments; and would result in abandoning the new-born Russia to the intrigue, the manifold subtle interference, and the certain counter-revolution which would be attempted by all the malign influences to which the German Government has of late accustomed the world. Can peace be based upon a restitution of its power or upon any word of honor it could pledge in a treaty of settlement and accommodation?

Responsible statesmen must now everywhere see, if they never saw before, that no peace can rest securely upon political or economic restrictions meant to benefit some nations and cripple or embarrass others, upon vindictive action of any sort, or any kind of revenge or deliberate injury. The American people have suffered intolerable wrongs at the hands of the Imperial German Government, but they desire no reprisal upon the German people, who have themselves suffered all things in this war, which they did not choose. They believe that peace should rest upon the rights of peoples, not the rights of governments,—the rights of peoples great or small, weak or powerful,—their *equal* right to freedom and security and self-government and to a participation upon fair terms in the economic opportunities of the world,—the German people of course included, if they will accept equality and not seek domination.

The test, therefore, of every plan of peace is this: is it based upon the faith of all the peoples involved or merely upon the word of an ambitious and intriguing government, on the one hand, and of a group of free peoples, on the other? This is a test which goes to the root of the matter; and it is the test which must be applied.

The purposes of the United States in this war are known to the whole world, to every people to whom the truth has been permitted to come. They do not need to be stated again. We seek no material advantage of any kind. We believe that the intolerable wrongs done in this war by the furious and brutal power of the Imperial German Government ought to be repaired, but not at the expense of the sovereignty of any people,—rather a vindication of the sovereignty both of those that are weak and of those that are strong. Punitive damages, the dismemberment of empires, the establishment of selfish and exclusive economic leagues, we deem inexpedient and in the end worse than futile, no proper basis for a peace of any kind, least of all for an enduring peace. That must be based upon justice and fairness and the common rights of mankind.

We cannot take the word of the present rulers of Germany as a guarantee of anything that is to endure, unless explicitly supported by such conclusive evidence of the will and purpose of the German people themselves as the other peoples of the world would be justified in accepting. Without such guarantees treaties of settlement, agreements for disarmament, covenants to set up arbitration in the place of force, territorial adjustments, reconstitutions of small nations, if made with the German Government, no man, no nation could now depend on. We must await some new evidence of the purposes of the great peoples of the Central Powers. God grant it may be given soon and in a way to restore the confidence of all peoples everywhere in the faith of nations and the possibility of a covenanted peace.

Robert Lansing, Secretary of State of the
United States of America.

T telegram (SDR, RG 59, 763.72119/726, DNA).

To Samuel Gompers

My dear Mr. Gompers: The White House 27 August, 1917

You may be sure that if I could get away to do anything of the kind, I would be glad to speak at the national conference called by the American Alliance for Labor and Democracy for September fifth, sixth, and seventh. I know the attitude of that alliance, the fine action they have taken in these days of stress, and I should like for every reason to be present and to speak, but each day convinces me more and more that it is my bounden duty to remain close to my desk here and to say anything that I must say from time to time from Washington. I am sure that you will believe that only the firmest convinction [conviction] based upon experience leads me to this conclusion, when I would prefer another.

Cordially and sincerely yours,   Woodrow Wilson

TLS (S. Gompers Papers, AFL-CIO-Ar).

To Thomas Watt Gregory

The White House
My dear Mr. Attorney General: 27 August, 1917

I wish you would be kind enough to look at the enclosed.[1] Do you think there is anything we could do to this wretched creature, Hannis Taylor, or is he too small game to waste powder on?

Faithfully yours,   Woodrow Wilson

TLS (T. W. Gregory Papers, DLC).

[1] It was a clipping from the *New York American*, Aug. 12, 1917, of an article by Taylor, an international lawyer of New York, under the headline, "Hannis Taylor, Legal Authority, Says Supreme Court Will Forbid Sending Militia or Conscripts Abroad." Taylor stated that he favored prosecuting the war vigorously with American sea power, financial power, and "all other legal and constitutional means," but that he deplored "the unhappy and entirely meretricious afterthoughts" which were being assigned as reasons for participation in the war. He also objected to the "bacchanalian revel of illegality" which was imperiling the very life of the Constitution. Taylor cited legal precedents to support his argument that Wilson's proclamation of July 9, 1917, which called the National Guard into the military service of the United States, was "unconstitutional and void." If this action was allowed to stand, Taylor asserted, there would be "a military dictatorship pure and simple," and the republic would be "Prussianized."

To Josephus Daniels

My dear Mr. Secretary: The White House 27 August, 1917

Thank you for letting me see the two editorials from the Commoner. I am not fortunate enough to see the paper regularly, and am particularly glad to see these editorials. They show a fine spirit and a very high principle, as I should have expected.

Cordially and sincerely yours,   Woodrow Wilson[1]

TLS (W. J. Bryan Papers, DLC).
[1] Daniels sent this letter to Bryan as an enclosure with JD to WJB, Aug. 29, 1917, TLS (W. J. Bryan Papers, DLC).

To Jouett Shouse

My dear Mr. Shouse: The White House 27 August, 1917

I have your letter of August twenty-fifth and realize the very grave importance of the matter you broach. I cannot see my way, however, to making so wide and sweeping a class exemption as you suggest. The matter of leaving the farmers on the farms has been given the most careful and sympathetic attention by the War Department, and I have before me a letter from the Secretary of War from which I quote the following sentence:

"General Crowder had foreseen the practical need of enabling men in agricultural work to remain at their tasks until the close of the harvest season, and has ingeniously arranged the details of calling to the colors so that the men on the farms will practically all fall within the last group and will, therefore, not have to report for military service until on or about October first."[1]

I feel that a class exemption would lead to many difficulties and to many heartburnings, much as I should personally like to see all the genuine farmers left at their indispensable labors.

Cordially and sincerely yours,   Woodrow Wilson

TLS (J. Shouse Papers, KyU).
[1] NDB to WW, Aug. 22, 1917, TLS (WP, DLC).

To Vira Boarman Whitehouse, with Enclosure

My dear Mrs. Whitehouse: [The White House] 27 August, 1917

I thought that my former letter[1] in its closing sentence expressed just what you feel that I omitted. I am very sorry to have expressed myself so unsuccessfully and beg that you will let me substitute the enclosed.

In great haste, with sincere regard,

Cordially yours,   Woodrow Wilson

[1] WW to Vira B. Whitehouse, Aug. 14, 1917, Vol. 43.

ENCLOSURE

To Vira Boarman Whitehouse

My dear Mrs. Whitehouse: [The White House] 27 August, 1917

I am greatly gratified to learn that it is your impression that there is a growing sentiment in the State of New York in favor of woman suffrage, and I shall look forward with the greatest interest to the results of the state conference you are planning to hold in Saratoga the latter part of this month. May I not express the hope that the conference will lead to a very widespread interest in your campaign and that your efforts will be crowned with the most substantial and satisfactory success? I hope that the voters of the State of New York will rally to the support of woman suffrage by a handsome majority. It would be a splendid vindication of the principle of the cause in which we all believe.

   Cordially and sincerely yours, Woodrow Wilson

TLS (Letterpress Books, WP, DLC).

To Albert Sidney Burleson

My dear Burleson: [The White House] 27 August, 1917

Will you not generously read and generously judge the enclosed?[1] I think the suggestion is a very helpful one and may be of great relief to you.

  Always   Faithfully yours, Woodrow Wilson

TLS (Letterpress Books, WP, DLC).
 [1] Creel's memorandum enclosed in G. Creel to WW, Aug. 24, 1917. The Editors have been unable to find the memorandum.

To Newton Diehl Baker, with Enclosure

My dear Mr. Secretary: The White House 27 August, 1917

The sender of the enclosed message[1] is a perfectly truthful man and I think it wise to send you this account from him of the trouble at Houston. He says, you will notice, that he speaks from personal knowledge and observation.

 In haste
   Cordially and faithfully yours, Woodrow Wilson

TLS (WDR, RG 94, AGO-Misc. File, No. 2638715, DNA).
 [1] Joe Henry Eagle, Democratic congressman from Houston.

ENCLOSURE

Houston, Texas, August 24, 1917.

Dear Mr. President: From my personal knowledge and observation I report to you on race riot here last night. Cause of trouble was that yesterday afternoon two negro troopers resented arrest of negro woman by local police which resulted in violence but no deaths. News spread to camp of negro troops of regular army who all afternoon manifested restive condition, so much so that watermelon feast planned for them last night was abandoned and they were ordered by their superior officers not to leave camp. Last night however, after dark a few hundred negro regulars mutinied, broke into arsenal and procured guns and ammunition and went on rampage of indiscriminate slaughter of police and citizens any one regardless of age or sex, also, while they literally ran amuck firing volleys at lights in houses and shooting any white person in sight on streets or in residence. They went out to "Get" the police and broadened their activities to include all white persons. Then followed a night of terror and anarchy with citizenship terrified and enraged at barbarism in uniforms as monster of death at their doors. Fortunately the twenty fourth Illinois National Guard were in camp who in local parlance "rounded up" some of the outlaws and then gathered as a net around that portion of the city in which the remaining two hundred outlaws were known to be located, gradually tightening the net until all were caught. Since they were thus arrested they are guarded in camp by Illinois National Guard whose gallant captain these outlaws slaughtered by shooting, by stabbing with bayonets, by battering his head into pulp and by cutting his throat and these worthy national guard have held infuriated armed citizens at bay from wreaking vengeance upon the outlaw negro soldiers. This in brief is the story.

It conclusively proves tragic blunder committed in ordering negro troops to Southern camps. Besides this tragedy the presence of negro troops here has largely demoralized local negro feeling and conduct. Unless all these negro troops are sent away quickly my opinion that last night's tragedy is but a prelude to a tragedy upon enormous scale. If not that at least incessant trouble so as to destroy all army efficiency in camp. It is an utterly impossible situation to rectify in any other way than the prompt removal of all negro troops who are here and rescinding any order for others to come and in this hour of our tragedy it is indisputably clear that the fault and responsibility and blame do not rest upon the citizenship of Houston.

Very respectfully,   Joe H. Eagle, M.C.

T telegram (WDR, RG 94, AGO-Misc. File, No. 2638715, DNA).

To Bernard Mannes Baruch

My dear Baruch: [The White House] 27 August, 1917

Here is a report on the cost of the production of copper which I have just received this morning from the Federal Trade Commission.[1] I wish that you and your colleagues of the Purchasing Commission would be kind enough to look the memorandum and the attached tables over preliminary to conferring with me about the prices to be put upon copper. I shall wish to move very considerately in this big matter and hope that this memorandum will be serviceable to you and your colleagues in determining what advice you give me.

Cordially and faithfully yours,   Woodrow Wilson

TLS (Letterpress Books, WP, DLC).
[1] "Memorandum on the cost of production of copper in 1917," n.d., T MS (F.T.C. General, RG 122, DNA).

To Thomas James Walsh

My dear Senator: [The White House] 27 August, 1917

I have just heard with the greatest distress of the illness of your wife.[1] Apparently my necessary absorption nowadays in the business of the hour keeps even news of this tragical sort away from me.

May I not express to you my very deep sympathy? My heart goes out to you, my dear Senator, in this day of your trial and distress, and I hope that you will not think it an intrusion on my part for me to tell you so.

Cordially and sincerely yours,   Woodrow Wilson

TLS (Letterpress Books, WP, DLC).
[1] Elinor Cameron McClements Walsh.

To Jessie Woodrow Wilson Sayre

                                        The White House.
My precious Little Girl,   27 August, 1917.

This is just a love message for your birthday. I wonder if the letter I wrote you from the MAYFLOWER just after dear Frank left for France reached you all right? My heart was very full of thoughts of your loneliness then and has been full of you ever since. I have not seen Nell since she was with you. I am very eager to get driect [direct] news of you and the darling little ones.

We are all well, and Edith joins me in messages of warmest love. I am beginning to feel the strain, of course, and have to admit that I am very tired, and envy each one of my colleagues that gets off for a week's or ten days rest. They seem to me the most fortunate of men! This does not mean, however, that there is the last thing the matter with me. The strain is, of course, more on my mind than on my body,—comes rather from the things that I have to decide than from the things that I have to do,—the things that I have to decide and the things that I have to see that others do as they should be done. I take exercise every day and sleep like a top whenever I get the chance; I should only like to get more chances!

Take care of yourself, my darling girlie, and when you get a moment sit down and tell me what Frank's plans are about coming back, and what the plans are for the autumn and winter. I am going to keep Garfield down here probably the greater part of the winter. I have put him in charge of the fuel supply of the country, as Hoover is in charge of the food supply. He is talking of leasing a small apartment and bringing Mrs. Garfield down when the cool weather permits. Will all of this interfere with what you and Frank had planned to do, I wonder?

Helen has been out with Marion Erskine,[1] you know, on Georgian Bay, but she is in Chicago on her way back now and may be here again any time, I imagine, though we have had no definite news.

With a heart full of love, and Many, Many Happy Returns,
Your devoted Father

WWTLS (WC, NjP).
[1] Helen Bones had been visiting Marion Brower (Mrs. Albert DeWolf) Erskine, daughter of Marion McGraw Bones Brower. See WW to Jessie Sayre, July 21, 1917, Vol. 43.

From Robert Lansing

My dear Mr. President: Washington August 27, 1917.

I have read the enclosed papers with very great interest indeed and consider that they present a phase of the situation in this country to which we have possibly given too little attention.

Would it not be well to show Henry Slobodin's statement to Mr.

Creel in order that he may consider the means of meeting the suggestions made?   Faithfully yours,   Robert Lansing

TLS (WP, DLC).

From Robert Lansing, with Enclosure

My dear Mr. President: Washington August 27, 1917.

I enclose to you a letter which I received from Doctor Mott, explaining the report which he and Mr. Root submitted to you.

I have telegraphed Doctor Mott, Mr. Root and Mr. Cyrus H. McCormick that they have an appointment with you at two-thirty Thursday afternoon, August 30th.

Faithfully yours,   Robert Lansing.

TLS (WP, DLC).

E N C L O S U R E

John R. Mott to Robert Lansing

Mr. Secretary: Washington, D. C., August 22, 1917.

Referring to your question as to whether the "Plans for American Coöperation to Preserve and Strengthen the Morale of the Civil Population and the Army of Russia," recommended by our Special Mission, do not appear to be more American than Russian, we would call attention to the fact that the printed memorandum which we prepared for the President was designed primarily to exhibit the American part of the project. With this in mind, the memorandum was entitled "American Coöperation." For the sake of brevity, the description of Russia's part in the undertaking was omitted, although, in all our thinking and constructive suggestions, we have had this constantly in mind. We are agreed as to the first importance of having all that is done, done so far as possible under Russian leadership and supervision. On the Russian side of the shield, the whole activity will be presented as the activity of the Russians. The organization will be Russian, the language will be Russian, the teachers and speakers will be almost entirely Russians, the writing will be done by Russians, and the institutions and societies through which American help is to be rendered are Russian.

Before we left Russia, definite steps had been taken to organize a National Committee or Council, to have entire supervision of the placing and equipping of the proposed buildings, the organizing of the activities to be conducted in them, the locating and coaching of the secretaries, including the American workers, and the close supervision of all that is to be done. This Committee was being constituted entirely by important Russian citizens whom we had discovered in the different centers as most intelligent with reference to all the problems involved and as most interested in their solution. They were proceeding carefully in the building up of the Committee. The day before we left Petrograd, they told us they were thinking of inviting Prince Kropotkin[1] to serve as Chairman, as he seemed to be the most popular and influential man for the position, from the point of view of both the soldiers and officers. While the Russians may decide to appoint one or two Americans on their Committee, virtually the entire membership will be Russian. The activities in each of the buildings at the front, in the training-camps, and in the garrison cities will be conducted under the supervision of local committees composed entirely of Russians. The experiments which we tried so successfully and to which reference was made in the memorandum were all conducted on this plan.

So far as the proposed educational campaign among the civil population, as well as among the soldiers, is concerned, our thought from the beginning has been that the five principal agencies mentioned by us would be conducted in the main by the Russians. For example, the Bureau of Speakers and Teachers would be guided by Russian committees; all of the hundreds of speakers and teachers would be Russians; the pamphlets, leaflets, and poster advertisements would be prepared by Russian scholars and writers; and such material as might have been produced in America or other countries would be translated and, where necessary, supplemented by this corps of Russian writers. We omitted to state, in this connection, that there would be a committee of Russians to help choose as well as edit this material. In connection with the film service, we would utilize the Russian[s] and Russian lecture and educational societies, as well as the buildings erected for serving the soldiers. The reason why we called particular attention to American films is the fact that the Russians themselves whom we consulted expressed to us the strong desire that large use be made of American films. They deem it very important that we acquaint the Russian civil and military population with American life and that we bring vividly before them America's part in this War and that we seek to assure them that America has identified herself with them in the great struggle. We would suggest that an American manager for this film service is desirable because of the far greater efficiency of the American film services. The proposed news service contemplates news from America and it must be managed at this end by Americans. The publication at the other end would be arranged by Russians. The object here, as in the case of the film service, is to promote among the Russians a right understanding of America and, therefore, a much closer and more sympathetic coöperation.

In the budget which we have submitted, there is one item entitled "Helping Certain Russian Agencies such as the Soldiers' Newspaper." Our investigation revealed here and there the existence of certain Russian societies and committees which are in a position to help multiply points of helpful contact with and to give larger access to both the civil and military population. All of these are doing a very restricted work through lack of funds; so, quite apart from helping them along lines indicated in the other features of the budget, we thought it would be a wise use of money to make grants directly to these agencies for the enlargement of their regular work. There is one society, for example, which organizes the maimed and invalided Russian exchanged prisoners and sends them among the bodies of troops to raise their fighting spirit. We were in a position to observe the helpful effect of its work and believe that it would be wise to give it financial help.

Let us reiterate the point developed in the paragraph at the middle of page five of the memorandum which we left with the President, namely, the paragraph which calls attention to the fact that the Russians heartily welcome American coöperation through such agencies as the Association in its practical ministry among the soldiers. First and last we conferred with scores of the wisest leaders of Russian opinion and action and not one of them exhibited any reservation on this point. They clearly need our help and earnestly desire it.

Since Mr. Root and I saw you this morning, we have been in conference with Mr. Putnam, of the Congressional Library, with reference to the project of the American Library Association to furnish books to the American soldiers in the various cantonments and have been much impressed by the fact that the various activities which are being introduced in the American Army for keeping up the morale of the troops are substantially the same as the Russians desire in this critical moment for their own soldiers.

Could you not kindly arrange with the President for us to see him next Thursday or, failing that, on Wednesday? Mr. Root will gladly return from Clinton, New York, and I will likewise be glad to come out of the Canadian woods for this most important purpose. Mr. Root tells me that it will be impossible for him to come to Washington any time during the period from September 1st to 9th, owing to other engagements. Please send word to Mr. Root at Clinton, Oneida County, New York, and to me at my office, 124 East Twenty-eighth Street, New York City.

With sincere regard,

Faithfully yours,   John R. Mott

P.S. You will be interested to know that a few days ago I received a cablegram from France indicating that the French leaders desire that America send over immediately five hundred American Association secretaries, to extend the Y.M.C.A. work throughout the French Army. General Pershing has cabled that this should be done immediately and that it is the greatest single service which America can render just now to the French Army. I have taken luncheon today with one of the leading representatives of France now in Washington and he strongly endorses this appeal. I must speak to the President on this point when we meet. Moreover, since reaching Washington I have received a communication from Italy, indicating that the Italian leaders, including prominent Roman Catholics, in view of what they have seen of the American Association work in France as a means of strengthening the morale and occupying usefully the spare time of the soldiers, desire that we send a number of American secretaries to Italy, in order to introduce in the Italian Army the same helpful methods. Furthermore, I received last week a belated cablegram from an influential Bishop of the Russian Orthodox Church—the Bishop of Tomsk,[2] a garrison city with 50,-000 soldiers, where we made one of our experiments with the help of an American secretary taken from the prison camp work, —urging that America spread this agency quickly throughout the Russian Army and that we send American workers for this purpose. J.R.M.

TLS (WP, DLC).

[1] Prince Petr Alekseevich Kropotkin (1842-1921), a geographer, author, revolutionist, and social philosopher.

[2] Bishop Anatoly.

From Edward Mandell House, with Enclosures

Dear Governor: Magnolia, Massachusetts. August 27, 1917.

I suppose you have received this letter of Balfour's to Page from another direction, but I think it important enough to call to your attention.

The difficulty confronting us which they do not appreciate is Denman and the anti-British element here.

Balfour agreed with Denman, as you will remember, that these ships could be taken over, and if the new Shipping Board adopts a different course, Denman will probably make an attack. It is a pity, however, that it is necessary for this Government to take any course other than is customary among nations. Could not the decision be postponed until the war is over?

Tardieu also sends me a memorandum, which he has submitted to the Shipping Board, in which he protests most vigorously against France being placed in the same category as Great Britain. He seems willing to have the English ships taken, but cannot see why we should treat France in the same way.

Affectionately yours,　E. M. House

TLS (WP, DLC).

ENCLOSURE I

Extracts from letter from Lord Northcliffe, August 25, 17.

"Our people are evidently very agitated about this most delicate and difficult question of the British ships now building here. The Censor is wisely stopping reference to it in the English newspapers, but that it will be raised in Parliament is very obvious. That it will create a very bad impression in Europe is equally obvious. Is there not some possible compromise?

This morning, among a number of communications that I received is one from Mr. Balfour in which he says that he presented to Mr. Page a letter, dated August 16th, a copy of which I enclose.

My instructions are to point out that my Government will keenly feel the blow, which will be a very serious one to England, if these ships are taken over by your Government. In the belief that the ships would not be transferred, public statements have been made by the Prime Minister in which these ships have been included in his estimates of British tonnage.

My Government places itself entirely in the hands of the President."

ENCLOSURE II

Copy of letter sent by Mr. Balfour to Mr. Page on August 16th, 1917.

"When I was in U. S. the question was raised as to whether Shipping under construction in American yards on British account should be taken over by U.S.G. or should remain in ownership of country for which it was being built.

Mr. Denman at that time head of Shipping Board raised this point in the course of a conference at which both he and General Goethals were present. Mr. Denman made somewhat a grievance of course which British Government had adopted: his line of argument being that British orders occupied all yards in U. S.; that American labour and American capital were absorbed in construction of British shipping; and that with their assistance Britain would find herself at the end of the war possessed of great Mercantile Marine which U. S. had built but did not own.

I took the liberty of pointing out to Mr. Denman in reply that in ordering these ships before America entered the war Great Britain took the only course open to her and one which, however question of ownership was ultimately decided, must be to the advantage of all Powers fighting against Germany. It was of first necessity that the whole world's resources in shipbuilding open to the Allies should be used in construction of mercantile ships and as America was not then among belligerents it was only by British Government that necessary arrangements could at that time be made with private owners of shipyards in U. S. I added that under no circumstances would the British Government enter into controversy with State Department on the question of ownership and that we placed complete reliance upon justice and goodwill of authorities in Washington.

To this policy we still adhere. If U.S.G. after surveying all circumstances of the case think ships that we have ordered in their yards should belong to them we shall not think of making any protest, nor are we of opinion that, if ships on completion are used in war work of the Allies, question of ownership has any material bearing upon conduct of war.

It may however be worth observing that if our own policy towards our Allies were taken as a precedent there would be no change of ownership in case of British ships now under construction in American yards. We always drew sharp distinction between ships building for Allies in our yards and ships building for neutrals; the latter were brought under British flag and retained in allied services for the period of the war; work on the former was dealt with exactly as if ships were being built for British owners and when finished they were handed over without reserve to the country on whose account they had been ordered. There was as far as I could ascertain only one exception to this general practice and in this particular case satisfactory arrangements were made.

From the very nature of the case largest losses in mercantile shipping have been borne by Great Britain. It is on Great Britain in the main that the Allies have relied for maintenance of sea borne traffic on which not merely their capacity for fighting but their very existence depends; it is on Great Britain that the full brunt of submarine campaign has fallen. Our losses have been heavy and unless we obtain ships now under construction for us in America we cannot easily tide over critical period which must elapse before our own extended shipbuilding programme bears its full fruit.

We should therefore feel much gratification if U.S.G. thought it consistent with the claims of their own national interests to allow ships now building for us in America to remain in their present ownership; though for the reasons given above we shall not press the point. We rely (as I said at Washington) on their justice and goodwill."

ENCLOSURE III

Extracts of letter from Norman Hapgood, July 28, 1917.

"I have just come back from an interesting trip in Lorraine. It is only the governing class here that keeps the people in the war, and it is no easy job to keep up the army morale. The French soldier is a great soldier, but he hates this war. It has lasted too long for him. Also he has figured out that France will not have men enough after the war to get on her feet.

Unless the dictatorship works surprisingly well in Russia next year's fighting will have to be mostly by the British supplemented by the Americans. But the British hang on ∗ ∗ ∗ ∗ "

T MSS (WP, DLC).

From Herbert Clark Hoover

Dear Mr. President: Washington August 27, 1917.

Delegations from several parts of the country have been to see me in connection with the exemption of a certain class of agriculturalists under the draft, and I have, in addition, had the advantage of a conference in Chicago with two hundred odd editors of agricultural publications from all over the country on this and other subjects.

It does appear to me that a serious situation is arising from the operation of the draft law against men who may be styled "key men" in agriculture, that is, men of the foreman, manager and ownership type, the draft of whom will certainly diminish the food production.

From all quarters I have found no disposition of a desire to diminish the quotas of the states in question, but a desire that some definite form of exemption should be initiated towards men of this character, and a larger proportion of the draft thrown upon the purely laboring and town classes.

A difficulty also lies in that a great many of the "key men" in question have too much patriotism to themselves make application for exemption.

I regard the matter as one of extreme importance to our whole food supply, and that these men should receive even greater consideration than "key men" in industrial establishments.

It does not appear that any action can be taken without inspiration from you, and I sincerely hope you may be able to give it consideration.

If it seems desirable to you that this class should be exempted, it would be very desirable to have, in addition to instructions to this effect, some expression from you that such men are as much in the service of the nation as men at the front, in order that the patriotic scruples of many should be overcome.

I beg to remain

Your obedient servant,   Herbert Hoover

TLS (WP, DLC).

From Bernard Mannes Baruch

My dear Mr. President: Washington, D. C. August 27, 1917.

I am in receipt of your esteemed favor of August 27th, together with report of the Federal Trade Commission, which I will promptly present to my colleagues of the Purchasing Commission.

After examination and study, I will acquaint you of our readiness to report.

Cordially and Faithfully yours,   Bernard M Baruch

TLS (WP, DLC).

From Frank Irving Cobb

Dear Mr. President,   New York, August 27, 1917.

The afternoon papers print a dispatch from Washington stating that evidence is in the possession of the State Department showing that Germany planned to make war against the United States after crushing France and Great Britain. Secretary Lansing is reported to have confirmed the statement of Lord Robert Cecil that there had been such a plot. If such evidence is in the State Department its publication would have an enormous effect upon the public sentiment in this country, both in breaking down opposition to the war and spurring the public to new endeavors. Will you permit me to suggest that it ought to [be] printed as soon as possible and that all other evidence in the archives of the State Department showing a policy of settled hostility to the United States on the part of Germany be made public.

Sincerely yours,   Frank I. Cobb.

T telegram (WP, DLC).

From Newton Diehl Baker, with Enclosure

My dear Mr. President: Washington. August 27, 1917

When I received your letter of August 16th, inclosing the letter to you from Mr. Rufus M. Jones,[1] I was obliged to delay until I could discover something about the Friends Reconstruction Unit to which Mr. Jones refers. I now find that work to be closely associated with the activities of the Red Cross. It does not seem to me that it will be wise now to designate this work of reconstruction as the sort of non-combatant service contemplated for religious objectors, chiefly for the reason that any definition of that sort of work at this time may have the effect of encouraging further "conscientious" objecting. On this whole subject my belief is that we ought to proceed with the draft and after the conscientious objectors have been gotten into the camps and have made known their inability to proceed with military work, their number will be ascertained and a suitable work evolved for them. I am therefore taking the liberty of inclosing a suggested reply for you to send to Mr. Jones.

Respectfully yours,   Newton D. Baker

TLS (WP, DLC).
   [1] See WW to NDB, Aug. 16, 1917 (second letter of that date), n. 1, Vol. 43.

ENCLOSURE

My dear Mr. Jones: August 28, 1917

I have received your letter of August 15th, with regard to the work of the reconstruction unit for relief and reconstruction work in the devastated war zones in northern France.

The Secretary of War informs me that there will be no difficulty about the securing of passports for members of the unit, unless they are of draft age and included in the first draft, the rule being that any man who is not to be called in the first draft may leave the country upon the understanding that he will return should his services be later required.

The question as to whether the work of these reconstruction units can be designated as non-combatant service for conscientious objectors cannot now be determined. The varieties of conscientious objection developed in the application of the selective conscription law have been so numerous as to make it necessary to delay the establishment of a policy until we can be sure that we have both satisfied the requirements of the law and gone just as far as we can justly go in the recognition of the rights of individual conscience in such a matter. When the total number of persons interposing conscientious objection to military service has been ascertained, I hope to be able to work out with the Secretary of War a plan which will give the nation the benefit of the service of these men without injustice to the great company of young men who are free to accept their country's call to military duty.

In the meantime, I am sure you will permit me to express my deep appreciation of the reconstruction work proposed, and my happiness that it is being carried out in association with the Red Cross which is already doing a great work in France to express the heart of America.   Cordially yours,[1]

CC MS (WP, DLC).
[1] Wilson sent this letter as WW to R. M. Jones, Aug. 28, 1917, TLS (Letterpress Books, WP, DLC).

From William Graves Sharp

Paris. August 27, 1917.

For the President. This afternoon I have received the following communication from Mr. Pashirech [Pashitch] Minister for Foreign Affairs of the Serbian Government now resident in Paris:[1] "The Chargé D'Affaires of the Government of the United States having communicated to me the desire of the President of the United States to be informed of the opinion of the Servian Government relative to the recent papal peace communication, I hasten to send you the inclosed note requesting that you kindly to forward it to His Excellency the President." Translation of the note accompanying the above letter reads as follows: "The appeal of His Holiness the Pope for the conclusion of peace between the belligerents could not in our opinion serve as basis of discussion of conditions for a future peace for the following reasons: His Holiness the Pope makes no distinction between those who provoked this horrible and disastrous war and those who are its victims. Similarly His Holiness the Pope makes no mention of the principle of liberty and of the right of each nation to dispose of its own lot[,] a principle which would allow peoples oppressed and entangled under the yoke of dynasties either by matrimonial combinations or by the toiling of international conventions to liberate themselves and to live freely. The stability of future peace could be assured only by the liberty and equality of all peoples and by a real sanction of the decision of an international tribunal which should watch over the safety of the entire world. Servia and the Servian people who were unjustly attacked by Austria-Hungary the advance guard of Germany in her penetration towards the orient, were not even mentioned in the Pontifical appeal, which deals however with other questions, very interesting and useful from the international point of view, but having a lesser importance.

Again, the peace proposition of His Holiness passes under silence all Yugoslavs other than the Serbs; nor does it mention the Tzheks and the Slovaks, Servian peoples enslaved to the interests of the Hapsburg dynasty and thereby to the interests of Germany in her policy of imperialism and conquest.

For all these considerations, the Servian Government and people, who gave so many proofs of their pacifism and their great love for peace at the time of the Austrian ultimatum, when they accepted all the conditions laid down by Austria-Hungary which were compatible with the dignity of an independent state, find it impossible to give their consent to the last Pontifical note.["]

Sharp.

T telegram (SDR, RG 59, 763.72119/776, DNA).
[1] Nikola P. Pašić.

To George Foster Peabody

My dear Mr. Peabody: The White House 28 August, 1917

My heartfelt thanks for your generous letter of this morning![1] You know how to give comfort and cheer and a sense of generous support when they are most needed, and I am certainly your debtor, for in these days every friendly voice is of incalculable value.

I am delighted to know that you are here helping the Secretary of War. He has my entire confidence and has proved a really wonderful addition to our strength and our wise counsels.

Cordially and sincerely yours,   Woodrow Wilson

TLS (G. F. Peabody Papers, DLC).
[1] It is missing.

To Joseph Patrick Tumulty

Dear Tumulty: [The White House, c. Aug. 28, 1917]

The reasoning of this memorandum[1] would be very convincing if, as a matter of fact, I had ever succeeded in getting the "emotional power" into my voice when speaking into a phonograph. As a matter of fact, I sound like a machine and I should hate to have the address so read given any perpetuity.

I none the less warmly appreciate the motives and purpose of Mr. Falck.   The President.

TL (WP, DLC).
[1] JPT to WW, Aug. 25, 1917, TL (WP, DLC). Tumulty endorsed a proposal by Edward Frederick Falck of the Aeolian Company of New York that Wilson "make a phonographic record of his Momentous Flag Day Address." (This address is printed at June 14, 1917, Vol. 42.) Falck wrote that it was universally considered in this country and abroad as "the great message of the war and one of the greatest in the English language," and he urged that it be made available in Wilson's own voice for "each fire-side in the country" and also for posterity. E. F. Falck to JPT, Aug. 24, 1917, TLS (WP, DLC).

From Newton Diehl Baker

Dear Mr. President: Washington. August 28, 1917.

I have just received your note of the 27th inclosing a very informing telegram to you from Mr. Eagle with regard to the cause of the outbreak at Houston.

I am having a careful investigation of that whole situation made and have sent the Inspector General of the Army there to insure its thoroughness and fairness. All told, I think the people of Houston are to be warmly praised and congratulated for their fine behavior under these trying circumstances. Undoubtedly, some part of their moderation can be attributed to the presence of the Illinois National Guard who seemed to have behaved with great composure and effectiveness; but when all the allowance is made which is properly due to this restraining cause, these people still deserve credit for having remained calm, refrained from any sort of attack upon the colored people of their own community and generally not to have permitted an East St. Louis riot to arise out of a very provoking and tragic situation.

Respectfully,   Newton D. Baker

TLS (WP, DLC).

From Louis Paul Lochner

Minneapolis, Minn., Aug. 28, 1917.

On behalf of the organizing committee of the People's Council, I desire to protest against the following proclamation just issued by the Governor of Minnesota:

"WHEREAS, An organization designating itself as the People's Council of America has announced that it will hold a national convention and public meetings in the City of Minneapolis, from September 1st to September 6th, 1917, and

WHEREAS, An order was issued by me to the Sheriff of said Hennepin County, on August 27th, 1917, directing said sheriff to prevent the holding of said convention and said meeting of the same would be likely to hinder the Federal Government in the prosecution of the war, and disturb the public peace, and

WHEREAS, The Sheriff of said County has this day, in accordance with said order, personally appeared and advised me that said convention and meeting, if held, in his opinion would result in bloodshed, rioting and loss of life, and

WHEREAS, Said convention and meetings can, in my opinion, under the circumstances have no other effect than aiding and abetting the enemies of this country; now, therefore I, J. A. Burnquist, Governor of the State of Minnesota, do hereby order that the holding of said convention and meetings within the county of Hennepin, or elsewhere in the State of Minnesota be and the same is hereby prohibited, that the peace office[r]s of the City of Minneapolis and the County of Hennepin and elsewhere in the State of Minnesota are hereby charged with the enforcement of this order and are directed to use all means at their command to secure obedience thereto and that if additional forces are required they are hereby directed to call on me therefor."

The organization committee consists of the following citizens: Victor Berger, James J. Bagley, William O. Hart, Judah L. M[a]gnes, Winter Russell, Emily Green[e] Balch, Edward T. Hartman, James H. M[a]urer, Benjamin Schlesinger, Joseph D. Cannon, Amy Mali Hicks, Duncan McDonal[d], Joseph Schlossberg, H. W. L. Dana, Morris Hillquit, Rose Schneiderman, Eugene V. Debs, Richard W. Hogue, Patrick Nagle, Western Starr, Mary Ware, Bennett Bishop, Paul Jones, Scott Nearing, Frank Stephens, Crystal Eastman, Jenkin Lloyd Jones, James Oneal, Sidney Strong, Max Eastman, Lindley M. Keasbey, Jacob Panken, Arthur Lesuer, Edmond C. Evans, Daniel Kiefer, Elsie Clews Parsons, Mrs. William I. Thomas, Fola La Follette, Charles Kruse, Max Pine, Irwin St. John, Tucket P. Geliebler, Algernon Lee, A. W. Ricker, John D. Works; treasurer David Starr Jordan, and is prepared to assume full responsibility for the orderly and lawful conduct of the meeting. Delegates from various states are already en route for Minneapolis. Is there no way in which the rights of speech and peaceful assembly, guaranteed under the Constitution, can be secured for them. We appeal to you for aid.

Louis P. Lochner

T telegram (WP, DLC).

From Vira Boarman Whitehouse

Sir: New York Aug. 28th, 1917.

It is difficult to adequately express our appreciation of your kindness in again writing to me and further amplifying your very kind message to the Conference, which the suffragists of New York State are about to hold in Saratoga. The additional sentence leaves nothing to be desired, and those few words, we are confident, will do an infinite amount to help us win our campaign.

At present, we are suffering from the very general disapproval of the course of the pickets, over whom, of course, we have no control and whose methods we deeply deplore. Your message should help as much as anything to show the voters of New York State the fair attitude to take.

Yours very gratefully and respectfully,
Vira Boarman Whitehouse (Mrs. Norman deR.
Whitehouse, chairman.)

TLS (WP, DLC).

Hugh Leo Kerwin[1] to Joseph Patrick Tumulty

My dear Mr. Tumulty: Washington August 28, 1917.

In connection with the threatened tie-up of the entire Alabama coal field, involving upwards of 25,000 workmen, I am quoting herewith, for the information of the President who was very much concerned over the situation, a telegram just received which is self-explanatory:

"Secretary Wilson left Birmingham seven thirty-five this morning en route for Washington. Will arrive in morning seven thirty. Through Secretary's efforts settlement has been effected between Alabama coal operators and miners; threatened strike averted."

I may add that a telegram received this morning from Commissioners White and Snyder representing the Department in the State of Washington states that all shipyards in the Northwest are now at work.   Sincerely yours,   H. L. Kerwin.

TLS (WP, DLC).
    1 Private secretary to William B. Wilson.

Sir William Wiseman to the Foreign Office

[New York] Aug. 28th. '17.

No. 62. Following from Northcliffe to Phillips for BALFOUR and CH. of E.:[1]

No. 212. Re Inter-Allied Council. I have pressed for United States representation on the Inter-Allied Council both to McA. and Col. H. The President without giving any reason objects. Am writing H. again to-day. Let me remind you that McA. was very insistent on the status of our representatives. He specially demanded "a distinguished statesman and a distinguished soldier," people who are known on this side of the Atlantic. I hope I have made it clear that he regards the Inter-Allied Council as one of his lines of defence against critics who accuse him of spending the Nation's money recklessly.

T telegram (W. Wiseman Papers, CtY).
    1 That is, the Chancellor of the Exchequer, Andrew Bonar Law.

From the Diary of Josephus Daniels

August Tuesday 28 1917

W.W. read his reply to Pope at meeting of Cabinet. It leads all nations. Believed England wished us to lead off. L knew Italy did. France had said nothing. It made peace talk impossible until the German Imperial Gove[rnme]nt had given place to government by the people.

Baker told good story. Went to Norfolk on Sylph. His flag was flying when he went ashore. English ship signalled "Who went ashore?" "Secretary of War." "Thanks awfully." "Don't mention it," said Martin[1] in American slang. "We will be careful not to do so" said English ship. Good example of English ignorance of American slang.

New Orleans German wishes to contribute to German Red Cross. No. England & France would not agree. Senator Hitchcock wanted a German woman, whose father a German officer, sent home. Engl[an]d & France would not grant safe conduct. H wished this Govnt to compel. She lived with H in his summer home.

One Maryland man had 5 sons, 4 volunteered & 5th drafted. Last one was needed to cultivate crop. One Mormon Elder had 11 out of 16 sons drafted.

Wilson's private secretary said "Mr. W cannot come because he is in Birmingham." Pres. amused: "Man cannot in person take degree because he is in Europe.["]

B said Pres. ought to make a speech. People did not know what they were fighting for. Princeton man asked WW "How many times can you make the same speech varying the form[?]" "I do not know—have not reached my limit yet[."]

[1] A signalman on U.S.S. *Sylph*.

Two Letters to Newton Diehl Baker

My dear Mr. Secretary: The White House 29 August, 1917

There is a point worth considering in the enclosed telegrams.[1] I did not have in mind the other day when I recommended the appointment of such a committee by the Council of National Defense any investigation which would have the I.W.W.'s as a special object of inquiry, but rather a commission to take under review the circumstances which were causing unrest and dissatisfaction on the part of organized labor. I agree with the Governors whose telegrams I am sending that the I.W.W.'s would welcome and profit by the publicity and advertisement of an investigation which put them at the center of the stage, but I take it for granted that that can be avoided.

Cordially and sincerely yours,   Woodrow Wilson

[1] Telegrams dated Aug. 28, 1917, from Governors James Withycombe, Re-

publican, of Oregon; Moses Alexander, Democrat, of Idaho; and Emmet Derby Boyle, Democrat of Nevada. Summarized and recorded as "Referred to Sec'y of War." White House memorandum, Aug. 29, 1917, T MS (WP, DLC). There was a similar telegram from William Dennison Stephens, Republican, Governor of California: W. D. Stephens to WW, Aug. 29, 1917, T telegram (WP, DLC).

My dear Mr. Secretary: The White House 29 August 1917

Thank you warmly for remembering to send me Conrad's "Typhoon."[1] I shall look forward with the greatest pleasure to reading it, and I thank you for your kindness.

In haste   Faithfully yours,   Woodrow Wilson

TLS (N. D. Baker Papers, DLC).
  [1] Joseph Conrad, *Typhoon* (Garden City, N. Y., 1916). The copy is in the Wilson Library, DLC.

To Robert Bruce Coleman and Thomas Samuel Hawes[1]

[The White House] August 29, 1917

With regard to the controversy between your company and its absent employees I beg to inform you that the United States Board of Mediation and Conciliation and William L. Chambers, United States Commissioner of Mediation and Conciliation, are my personal representatives and to request that their offer of mediation as made by Judge Chambers be accepted. In the present circumstances of the country I have the right to expect that this request be fully complied with and the most cordial cooperation be accorded Judge Chambers.

Woodrow Wilson

T telegram (Letterpress Books, WP, DLC).
  [1] They were, respectively, general manager and general counsel of the Georgia, Florida and Alabama Railway, with headquarters in Bainbridge, Ga.

To Allen Schoolcraft Hulbert

My dear Allen: [The White House] 29 August, 1917

The enclosed letter, which is the result of my writing to the Secretary of Agriculture, shows that they do not quite catch your point[1] (Houston may catch it when he comes back). I shall write them that as I understand it what you want is to be put into touch with them so that you can cooperate with them and get the benefit of their advice. In the meantime, I send you Mr. Harrison's letter.[2]

I conferred with the War Department and think that you can

rely on being exempted if you ask again, as I think you ought, for it is entirely justified by the circumstances.

Cordially and sincerely yours,   [Woodrow Wilson]

CCL (WP, DLC).
¹ See A. S. Hulbert to WW, Aug. 16, 1917, Vol. 43.
² Wilson's letter to Houston and the reply by Floyd Reed Harrison, Assistant to the Secretary of Agriculture, are missing. Wilson's letter to Harrison is WW to F. R. Harrison, Aug. 29, 1917, TLS (Letterpress Books, WP, DLC).

From George Foster Peabody

Dear Mr President   Washington Aug 29 1917

This is a great day in history for the "moving of the waters" of the mind of the world, yea even I dare believe the mind of the German people, which will be reckoned as having been observed in connection with your wonderful message in reply to the Pope.

Of course it is related to your other powerful truth presentations, but it can and will stand by itself as the most comprehensive as well as terse putting of a world situation—a condition existing.

I cannot express my profound sense of the presence of the all informing mind of Deity as I read this evidence that America has been given the Master Mind of the World in this crisis.

I have faith to believe that it demonstrates the power as well as the sincerity of your prayers to the overruling Power of God —who ever works through men.

I thank you as I take heart of courage for a strengthened hope.

I am now in receipt of your most honoring response to my previous word but I cannot refrain from telling you of my deep response to and faith in your noble reply to the Pope, and German imperialism.

Sincerely Yours   George Foster Peabody

ALS (WP, DLC).

From Edward Mandell House

Dear Governor: Magnolia, Massachusetts. August 29, 1917.

The reception given to your answer to the Pope by the press and, indeed, by the people of America, is spontaneous and enthusiastic beyond expectation. Even the Providence Journal, that is so pro-ally that it forgets to be American, joins the generous chorus.

Spring-Rice comes in the morning, and I shall have an opportunity to get his mind. If he accepts it, we need not fear but that it will be welcomed everywhere.

Affectionately yours,   E. M. House

TLS (WP, DLC).

Two Letters from Robert Lansing

PERSONAL AND CONFIDENTIAL:

My dear Mr. President: Washington August 29, 1917.

I enclose to you two telegrams which the Italian Ambassador confidentially communicated to me this afternoon in response to inquiries which I had made of him three or four days ago.[1] After reading them will you please return them to me for my confidential file?   Faithfully yours,   Robert Lansing.

TLS (WP, DLC).
[1] They were rough translations of Italian diplomatic messages which reported that the Pope's appeal for peace had come as an unwelcome surprise to the Spanish government, which had said that the move was "inopportune." However, the Spanish government would probably endorse it "without enthusiasm." T MSS (SDR, RG 59, 763.72119/854A, DNA).

My dear Mr. President: Washington August 29, 1917.

In connection with Mr. Tumulty's suggestion that Mr. Whitlock be permitted to write articles about Belgium which he made in his letter of May 31st,[1] I ought to say that before I received your letter enclosing Mr. Tumulty's a representative of EVERYBODY'S MAGAZINE asked me whether I would be willing for him to make a contract with Mr. Brand Whitlock to write a series of articles for the magazine. I told him that I thought it would be improper for Mr. Whitlock to do so while in the diplomatic service.

In making this reply I had two things in mind, first, the invariable rule against a diplomatic officer to write for publication, and, second, the slowness with which articles would appear in a monthly magazine.

It is my opinion that, in view of the little service which can be rendered by a Minister near the Belgian Government it might be well for Mr. Whitlock to resign, return to this country, and devote himself to publicity work in presenting Belgium's case. His presence and oral presentation would have great influence on the people, and he would at the same time have the opportunity to use his pen in a way that would be more valuable than by writing for a monthly publication.

I know of no way in which Whitlock could perform a greater service to the country at the present time. Later, when the war is over, he might be appointed again in the diplomatic service.

Faithfully yours,   Robert Lansing.

TLS (R. Lansing Papers, DLC).
  [1] See JPT to WW, May 31, 1917, Vol. 42.

From John Fox

My dear Mr. President: New York August 29, 1917.

The American Bible Society has just made an agreement at the earnest request of the Y.M.C.A. to furnish them free of all charge with one million Testaments which they are to distribute among the soldiers and sailors of the United States.

Our own presses, running sixteen hours a day, cannot keep up with the demand so we have had to make a contract for $180,000 with outside firms to make these books quickly, and we have used up our reserve funds.

Besides this we must furnish other Scriptures, Bibles; single Gospels, some with French and English in parallel columns; pulpit Bibles for chaplains, etc., and have already issued or are issuing three quarters of a million copies.

We are, therefore, asking the public for $400,000 to cover these expenses and the Y.M.C.A. heartily endorses this appeal. Will you endorse it also?

The arrangement with the Y.M.C.A. will largely obviate the confusion and waste that comes from several organizations playing more or less at cross purposes. We will furnish the books, the Y.M.C.A. will distribute them.

Under these circumstances could you not let us have a few lines heartily commending this appeal? Inasmuch as the Y.M.C.A. has been sanctioned by the Government as an auxiliary to the Service it would seem a natural thing to have you commend this singularly important service which we will render, and commend our appeal for $400,000. I enclose herewith what may fairly be called a precedent. It may interest you to know that Mr. Cleveland, then living in Princeton, helped me to write this appeal for funds and sent me to Chief-Justice Fuller with a message from him, Mr. Roosevelt being then President.[1] Your address at our Centennial[2] makes any words from me unnecessary as to the national aspect of our work in general, and this work in particular.

In behalf of the Board of Managers I have the honor to be,

Very sincerely yours,   John Fox

TLS (WP, DLC).

1 T. Roosevelt, G. Cleveland, M. W. Fuller, W. J. Bryan *et al.*, *A National Appeal* (1904), printed flyer (WP, DLC).
2 Printed at May 7, 1916, Vol. 36.

From Henry Fountain Ashurst

Dear Mr. President: Washington. August 29, 1917

Herewith I hand you a telegram from reputable citizens of Jerome, Arizona. For your information, I submit to you a copy of my reply thereto.[1]

With great esteem,   Respectfully,   Henry F. Ashurst

TLS (WP, DLC).

1 Thomas A. Miller and Henry Clark Smith, the president and the secretary of the Industrial Peace League of Jerome, Ariz., had sent Ashurst a resolution adopted by the league. It requested Wilson to proclaim the I.W.W. an "outlaw organization" which would not be tolerated during the war, and also to declare that leaders of the I.W.W., "along with other radical antigovernment propagandists," would be "considered enemies of the government and treated accordingly as they were at Spokane." The league further stated that it did not believe in vigilance committees or mob rule but favored legal action to protect the public safety and interest. Moreover, the league favored high wages and satisfactory working conditions and was not unfriendly to organized labor. It called upon all loyal citizens to cooperate for industrial peace. T. A. Miller and H. C. Smith to H. F. Ashurst, Aug. 28, 1917, T telegram (WP, DLC). Ashurst replied that he shared the league's view with regard to the I.W.W. and would render every assistance in his power. He had laid the matter before the President. H. F. Ashurst to T. A. Miller and H. C. Smith, Aug. 29, 1917, T telegram (WP, DLC).

From George Lewis Bell

San Francisco, Calif., August 29, 1917.

Replying your telegram of twenty second, I have just returned from conference with Judge Covington at Portland, Oregon, where I went in response to telegram from him saying you wished us to confer. I submitted entire matter to him and will also send you a written report explaining situation referred to in my telegram to you on August seventeen.[1]   George L. Bell.

T telegram (WP, DLC).

1 G. L. Bell to WW, Aug. 16, 1917 (second telegram of that date), Vol. 43.

Sir Eric Campbell Geddes to David Lloyd George, with Enclosure

My dear Prime Minister,   [London] 29th August 1917.

You will recollect that Admiral Mayo, the Commander-in-Chief of the United States Atlantic Fleet, has come over here with his Staff to talk things over at a Naval Officers' Conference with the

Allies. The French and Italians are sending Naval representatives next week.

Admiral Mayo has had a thorough talk with the First Sea Lord[1] and with Sir David Beatty[2] who has met him in London. He has described on the attached memorandum the purpose of his visit, and we hope very much that it will bear fruit.

The Naval Conference is to take place next week, and then Admiral Mayo and his Staff are going to the Grand Fleet to soak in all the information that they can.

I thought you would like to know what was being done, and I will let you know the result of the Naval Conference at which I and the First Sea Lord are of opinion that it will be suitable if I take the Chair, although the Conference was called at the suggestion of Admiral Mayo, and all the Foreign representatives are Naval Officers.

I propose that we should entertain the Members of the Conference and their Ambassadors at a luncheon next week, and I feel that it would be very much appreciated if you could possibly manage to attend the luncheon. It is impossible as yet to fix a date, but I will let you know as soon as possible in the hope of being able to get you to come.

Admiral Mayo tells me that he has come over with the instructions of President Wilson that he is to ascertain in what possible way the Americans can more fully come into Naval warfare, and that President Wilson has told him that in discussing the co-operation of the American Naval Forces with the Allies he is not to be too much influenced by the fear of running risks. He told me that President Wilson's words were—that you cannot make omelettes without breaking eggs, and that war is made up of taking risks; so that we hope to be able to get more co-operation from them both now and in the future.

Yours sincerely,   E Geddes[3]

TLS (F/17/6/8, D. Lloyd George Papers, House of Lords Record Office).

[1] Admiral Sir John Rushworth Jellicoe, First Sea Lord and Chief of the Naval Staff.

[2] Vice-Admiral Sir David Beatty had succeeded Jellicoe in 1916 in command of the British Grand Fleet.

[3] Hereinafter referred to as Sir Eric Geddes.

ENCLOSURE

ADMIRAL MAYO'S NOTES ON THE PURPOSE OF HIS VISIT.

The purpose of the present visit of the Commander-in-Chief of the United States Atlantic Fleet is, in general terms, as follows:

(1). To learn more fully what has happened, and what has been done.

(2). To get more closely in touch with what is being done; and then

(3). To discuss what it is proposed to do.

The above outline is indicated in order that the United States, first having full information as to past and present plans, may then more clearly appreciate proposals looking to future operations; all to the end that the United States may more intelligently and effectually employ its strength and resources in co-operation with the Allies to win the war.

T MS (F/17/6/8, D. Lloyd George Papers, House of Lords Record Office).

To John Burke

My dear Governor Burke: [The White House] 30 August, 1917

The subject matter of your letter of yesterday[1] was already very much on my mind and has given me a great deal of trouble. I have just this moment come from an interview with Mr. Hoover about it.

It is a very perplexing thing to know what to do. In the first place, of course, you understand that the Government is not "fixing the price": it is merely determining the price it will offer for wheat in the purchases it must make for itself and on behalf of other governments, and there is nothing in the law that obliges the farmer to sell at that price if he can get a better. In the second place, I take it to be impracticable to fix one price for one part of the country and another for another part, and that the best that we can do if we pay the regard we are in duty bound to pay to the consumer is to fix a price as nearly fair to all as possible. The difficulty in my mind is that in the regions you refer to there have been short crops both this year and the last, and it would be almost impossible to provide compensation for the losses thereby entailed without making the price oppressive to the country at large.

I set these matters forth merely that you may know how difficult I am finding it to come to a just conclusion and yet how anxious I am to do so.

Cordially and sincerely yours,   Woodrow Wilson

TLS (Letterpress Books, WP, DLC).

[1] Burke, a Democrat whom Wilson had appointed Treasurer of the United States in 1913, had been Governor of North Dakota from 1907 to 1913. He had written to Tumulty to warn that the price of wheat was likely to be set too low for the farmers of North Dakota and that this would "hurt the administration beyond repair with the farmers," especially in the Northwest. Burke noted

that they were "the fellows who elected the President in the last election." Burke expressed the hope that his message could reach Wilson promptly "and prevent a great injustice to the Northwest." J. Burke to JPT, Aug. 29, 1917, TLS (WP, DLC).

A Statement[1]

The White House, August 30, 1917.

Section 11 of the food act provides, among other things, for the purchase and sale of wheat and flour by the Government, and appropriates money for the purpose. The purchase of wheat and flour for our allies, and to a considerable degree for neutral countries also, has been placed under the control of the Food Administration. I have appointed a committee to determine a fair price to be paid in Government purchases. The price now recommended by that committee—$2.20 per bushel at Chicago for the basic grade—will be rigidly adhered to by the Food Administration.

It is the hope and expectation of the Food Administration, and my own also, that this step will at once stabilize and keep within moderate bounds the price of wheat for all transactions throughout the present crop year, and in consequence the prices of flour and bread also. The food act has given large powers for the control of storage and exchange operations, and these powers will be fully exercised. An inevitable consequence will be that financial dealings can not follow their usual course. Whatever the advantages and disadvantages of the ordinary machinery of trade, it can not function well under such disturbed and abnormal conditions as now exist. In its place the Food Administration now fixes for its purchases a fair price, as recommended unanimously by a committee representative of all interests and all sections, and believes that thereby it will eliminate speculation, make possible the conduct of every operation in the full light of day, maintain the publicly stated price for all, and, through economies made possible by stabilization and control, better the position of consumers also.

Mr. Hoover, at his express wish, has taken no part in the deliberations of the committee on whose recommendation I determine the Government's fair price, nor has he in any way intimated an opinion regarding that price.[2]

Woodrow Wilson.

Printed in the *Official Bulletin*, I (Aug. 31, 1917), 1-2.

[1] Wilson had appointed a special commission, headed by Harry A. Garfield, which included representatives of farm organizations and of consumers, to advise him on the price to be set for wheat. The commission met until 6:30 P.M. in Washington on August 29 but could not come to any agreement because the

representatives of the consumers said that they would not agree to set the price at a penny higher than $2 a bushel. That same afternoon, at 4:30 P.M., Senators Thomas Sterling of South Dakota, Porter J. McCumber of North Dakota, and Knute Nelson and Frank B. Kellogg of Minnesota called on Wilson at the White House and showed him numerous messages from their constituents which demanded a price higher than $2 a bushel. *New York Times*, Aug. 30, 1917; Head Usher's Diary, T MS (WP, DLC), Aug. 29, 1917.

The commission, by a unanimous vote on August 30, recommended that the price of wheat be set at $2.20 a bushel. Hoover presumably reported the recommendation when he saw Wilson at 11:30 A.M. on August 30, and Wilson then issued this statement. *New York Times*, Aug. 31, 1917; Head Usher's Diary, Aug. 30, 1917.

² Hoover undoubtedly wrote the foregoing statement. For one thing, there is no copy of it in WP, DLC; for another thing, Wilson never used the term "Allies" when he referred to the cobelligerents of the United States. In fact, he reprimanded Hoover for using the term "Allies." See WW to HCH, Dec. 10, 1917.

To Thomas Watt Gregory

[The White House]

My dear Mr. Attorney General: 30 August, 1917

I would be very much obliged if you would have the enclosed papers¹ carefully examined by somebody of judgment in your department. I have telegraphed to the Manager and General Counsel of the Georgia, Florida & Alabama Railway Company at Bainbridge, Georgia, requesting them to accept the mediation suggested by Judge Chambers, asking them to regard Judge Chambers as my personal representative and saying that the general circumstances of the country justify me in expecting a full compliance with my request, but, of course, it is possible that they will not comply. In that case, it is my purpose, unless your department sees serious obstacles, to proceed to take charge of the road and operate it inasmuch as there are supplies on its line which are necessary to be governed [the government]. This is a drastic remedy but it might be wholesome by way of example in other quarters if I were to adopt it, and I should like to know what the law in the matter may be interpreted to be.

Cordially and sincerely yours,   [Woodrow Wilson]

CCL (WP, DLC).
¹ Undoubtedly all the materials relating to the negotiations with the managers of the Georgia, Florida and Alabama Railway Co.

To Robert Lansing

My dear Mr. Secretary: [The White House] 30 August, 1917

It seems to me that the suggestions which Fletcher makes in the enclosed are something more than interesting. They are important and so far as I can judge from this single presentation of the matter I should think they ought to be acted on.¹

Cordially and faithfully yours,   [Woodrow Wilson]

CCL (WP, DLC).

1 The State Department, on August 22, had requested Fletcher's advice on certain measures which had been proposed to counter German propaganda in Mexico. These included, first, an embargo on the shipment of newsprint paper to Mexico from the United States, and, second, an arrangement for increased advertising by the American, British, and French mercantile communities in various anti-American newspapers. This second measure was expected to create a basis for protests against obnoxious stories, or even for the threat to withdraw, en bloc, the advertising. A third proposal was for the State Department to provide a motion-picture film for Mexico along the lines of the one already prepared for Russia. It would have pictures of "typical American scenes, pertaining to war preparations, school activities, life of the American workman and scenes showing activities of various Departments of this Government." RL to H. P. Fletcher, Aug. 22, 1917, T telegram (SDR, RG 59, 862.20212/580, DNA).

Fletcher replied on August 28 that the scheme for advertising by the local mercantile communities in the hostile press was impractical and would have little effect because of the existing German subsidies. He thought that the motion-picture scheme was excellent; it had already been adopted in Mexico by all the other leading belligerents. Instead of the imposition of a strict embargo on newsprint paper, Fletcher recommended that the embassy control its importation in order to limit slanderous and malicious attacks against the United States. "My experience in Latin-America," he wrote, "leads me to believe that the intelligent public opinion of these countries in a time of great crisis like the present respects more a vigorous and direct policy, in defense of national prestige, than hesitating and overscrupulous regard for Latin-American susceptibilities which in many cases exist only on the surface." H. P. Fletcher to RL, Aug. 28, 1917, T telegram (SDR, RG 59, 862.20212/581, DNA).

To Thomas Lincoln Chadbourne, Jr.[1]

My dear Mr. Chadbourne: [The White House] 30 August, 1917

Please say to the men on September fourth how entirely my heart is with them and how my thoughts will follow them across the sea with confidence and also with genuine envy, for I should like to be with them on the fields and in the trenches where the real and final battle for the independence of the United States is to be fought, alongside the other peoples of the world struggling like ourselves to make an end of those things which have threatened the integrity of their territory, the lives of their people, and the very character and independence of their governments. Bid them Godspeed for me from a very full heart.

Cordially and sincerely yours,   Woodrow Wilson

TLS (Letterpress Books, WP, DLC).

1 Wilson was replying to T. L. Chadbourne, Jr., to WW, Aug. 28, 1917, TLS (WP, DLC). Chadbourne was chairman of the Mayor's Committee on National Defense of New York, which had arranged various events to honor the men who had been drafted into the National Army.

From the President of the National Council Assembly at Moscow

Russian Embassy Washington August 30, 1917.

"The message of greeting of the President of the United States to the Moscow State Council being read in conference on August

27th, the Council has manifested by enthusiastic cheers its gratitude for the wishes formulated by the President, emphasizing that the feeling of the great American Democracy and its faith in the common triumph of the Allies for the sake of justice and liberty are shared by all the people of Russia."

T MS (WP, DLC).

From William Gibbs McAdoo

Dear "Governor":   Washington August 30, 1917.

Mr. Kitchin tells me that the bill for insurance on the lives of enlisted men in the Army and Navy may come before the House tomorrow, or, in any event, the next day, Saturday. Both he and Judge Adamson think a letter from you to the Judge would be extremely helpful. The bill as reported to the House reduces from $10,000, as proposed in the bill you approved, to $5,000, the amount of life insurance which the officers and enlisted men are privileged to take. I think this is a great mistake. I am told that the $10,000 limit will probably be restored upon the floor of the House. I think it would be wise if you would express the hope that this may be done.

I wish I could send you a tentative draft of a suitable letter, but I really never feel that I can suggest anything for you, as you can always do the job so much better than anyone else.

If you can find the time to read the enclosed article[1] (altogether too long, I am sorry to say) which I have prepared for publication in the Sunday papers of September 9th, it will give you a general idea of the provisions of the bill and the angle from which I view it. Perhaps this may be helpful.

The letter to Judge Adamson should reach him before noon Friday. I enclose an opening paragraph which may be serviceable to you in identifying to Judge Adamson the bill concerning which you write.[2]   Affectionately yours,   W G McAdoo

TLS (WP, DLC).
    [1] It is missing, but it presumably included much of the same information in a memorandum by McAdoo which appeared in the *Official Bulletin*, I (Aug. 30, 1917), 12.
    [2] McAdoo's draft was the basis for the first and last paragraphs of WW to W. C. Adamson, Sept. 1, 1917. WGM to WW, with WW pencil emendations, Aug. 30, 1917, T MS (WP, DLC).

From Cleveland Hoadley Dodge

Dear Mr President   New York August 30th, 1917

I wish that I had the wonderful gift which you have, of expressing your meaning in words. I would like to tell you what I think of you, but I can very feebly express what I want to say. I have for good reasons kept away from Washington this Summer, but you have constantly been in my thoughts and I thank God that, if what I hear is true, you are standing the awful strain so well.

A man who has just returned from Canada, told me today that he had met a prominent Canadian official who said to him, that this awful war had only produced one great man & that was President Wilson. Reckon he is right. Men who have been your bitterest enemies politically have gone out of their way yesterday & today, to let me know how highly they thought of your letter to the Pope. You have won the whole American people to a remarkable degree. All party lines seem to have been forgotten, & it is a joy to realize how you are making use of the best talents of the country, regardless of party lines or affiliations. Isn't it glorious to realize how wonderfully the great American people, under your leadership, have proved themselves to be thoroughly sound at heart.

Many well informed men in New York think that the war will be over this Winter, but whether that proves true or not, it hardly seems possible that the Austrians and Germans can hold out much longer, & if your great letter can only reach their hearts and minds, the inevitable effect will come.

We have had my married daughter Julia Rea & her four children[1] with us all Summer & they have been a great joy. We have good news of Bayard & his family[2] at Beirut & of Elizabeth[3] at Constantinople, but all the recent reports from Turkey & Syria indicate that the suffering of the peoples there are indescribably awful. The Turks are treating the Americans very well.

Pray forgive this long letter & believe me with warm regards from all of us to all of you

Ever affectionately   Cleveland H Dodge

ALS (WP, DLC).
[1] That is, Julia Parish Dodge (Mrs. James Childs) Rea and William Holdship Rea, Cleveland Dodge Rea, Grace Dodge Rea, and Ruth Rea.
[2] That is, Bayard Dodge.
[3] That is, Elizabeth Wainwright Dodge (Mrs. George Herbert) Huntington.

From John R. Mott

Mr President,   On train, August 30th, '17

On my way home I am constrained to write you to express my sincere appreciation of the sympathetic consideration you have given to the proposals which we presented today[1] as well as to the printed memorandum.

The reason we recommended that, in addition to the $2,200,-000. for the educational campaign in Russia, $4,000,000. be devoted to the vitally important work of strengthening the morale and cheering and raising the spirit of the three armies ($2,000,-000. to the Russian Army, $1,000,000. to the French, $1,000,000. to the Italian), instead of devoting $3,300,000. to this work in the Russian Army only, is that while the situation in France and Italy is not critical in the sense that it is in Russia, nevertheless our help in these two countries is imperatively needed. The next few months are the period of greatest strain to which the soldiers of France and Italy are likely to be subjected. The military, civil and religious leaders of these countries recognize the need of our help and have taken the initiative in earnestly requesting our cooperation. If the full $4,000,000. could be allocated now to the three armies, it would meet the emergency in each country promptly, quietly and effectively. This would enable us to meet the great opportunity and at the same time give us time to enlist gifts before additional funds are needed. We question whether any money will be spent which will prove to have been more highly-multiplying.

There would be some advantages in having Mr Dodge serve as Treasurer of the entire fund. He is accessible and is immediately related to the work in all the countries concerned, and, I need not add, has a realizing sense of what is at stake and a real heart interest in the plan.

Permit me to reiterate my sense of the unique and very great service you have rendered in your reply to the Pope. It has done more than any individual or collective action since the War began to clarify men's minds on the central issue, to unify and concentrate the will of the peoples associated with us and to prepare the way for the larger understanding which must be the precursor of the enduring peace.

With highest regard,

                    Faithfully yours   John R. Mott

ALS (WP, DLC).
   [1] Wilson conferred with Root, Mott, and Cyrus H. McCormick at the White House during the afternoon of August 30.

A Draft of a Letter to Samuel Gompers[1]

c. Aug. 31, 1917

Mr. Samuel Gompers,
    President, American Federation of Labor,
        Washington, D. C.

My dear Mr. Gompers:

I ~~beg you to believe that~~ *am sure that you understand that* my inability to accept the invitation to address the Minneapolis conference of the American Alliance for Labor and Democracy is due to *only* official necessity, and not in any degree to ~~inappreciation~~ *lack of* of the occasion' importance *of the* The cause you and your fellow patriots uphold is one with the cause we are defending with arms. While our soldiers and sailors are doing their manful ~~all~~ *work* to hold back reaction in its most brutal and aggressive form, we must oppose at home the organized and individual efforts of those dangerous elements who hide disloyalty behind a screen of specious and evasive phrases.

~~It is with pride indeed that~~ *with real pride* I have read the names of the men and women who are to take part in the Minneapolis conference. Not one but has a record of devoted service to fundamental democracy; not one but has fought the long, hard fight for equal justice, braving every bitterness that the humblest life might know a larger measure of happiness.

[1] The following document (WP, DLC) was drafted by George Creel and edited by Wilson.

With all my heart I want them to feel that their devotion
to country is in no wise a betrayal of principle, and that in serving
America today they are serving their cause no less faithfully than in
the past. I myself have had sympathy with the fears of the workers
of the United States; for the tendency of war is toward reaction, and
too often military necessities have been made an excuse for the destruction of laboriously erected industrial and social standards.
These fears, happily, have proved to be baseless. With quickened
sympathies and appreciation, with a new sense of the invasive and
insidious dangers of oppression, our people have not only held every
inch of ground that has been won by years of struggle, but have added
to the gains of the Twentieth Century along every line of human betterment. Questions of wages and hours of labor and industrial readjustment
have found a solution which gives to the toiler a new dignity and a new
sense of social and economic security. I beg you to feel that my
support has not been lacking and that the Government has not failed at
any point in granting every just request advanced by you and your
associates in the name of the American worker.
No one who is not blind can fail
~~How blind indeed is he who fails~~ to see that the battle line
of democracy for America stretches today from the fields of Flanders
to every house and workshop where toiling, upward striving men and women
~~by the light of hope are~~ counting the ~~threatened~~ treasures of the rights
and justice and liberty which are being threatened

meant
By our enemies.

~~and liberties of mankind.~~ Yet there are those who, under the guise

of various organizations, are setting up false lights along our course.

They talk much of peace, labor and democracy and would pervert our pur-

poses by draping the propaganda of Berlin in phrases that thinly conceal

the selfsame spirit which recently intrigued openly against our lives

and national safety. It is the misfortunes of some of the well meaning

and worthy among us that they have followed this false leading and have

not recognized that the new machinery of sedition is driven by the old

motive force.

I have read with care the programs of these chameleon organi-

zations as they have taken colour in exact consonance with the aims of

the forces which now, in fear and faltering, are attempting to consoli-

date the gains of reaction in a peace with plunder.

It has not been a matter of surprise to me that the leaders

certain
in ~~these~~ groups have sought to ignore our grievances against the men

~~who~~ have equally misled the German people. Their insistence that a

grossly
nation whose rights have been violated, whose citizens have been foul-

ly murdered under their own flag, whose land has been made the haven

of intrigue and conspiracy, whose neighbors have been invited to join

makes conquest of its territory,
in ~~its territorial conquests,~~ whose patience in pressing the claims of

justice and humanity has been met with the most shameful policy of

truculence and treachery; their insistence that a nation so outraged

does not know its own mind, that it has no ~~easily~~ comprehensible reason

or
for defending itself, ~~and~~ for joining with all its might in maintaining

a free future for itself and its ideals, is of a piece with their deafness to the oft repeated statement of our national purposes.

Time and again the aims of America have been set forth clearly and explicitly, and that your conference may be able to deal decisively with this portion of the enemy propaganda, a re-statement may have importance:

Recognition of the rights and liberties of small nations.

Freedom of the seas.

The limitation of armaments on land and sea.

Recognition of the principle that government derived its power from the consent of the governed.

Reparation for wrongs done and the erection of adequate safeguards to prevent their being committed again.

No indemnities except as payment for manifest wrongs.

No people to be forced under sovereignty under which it does not wish to live.

No territory to change hands except for the purpose of securing those who inhabit it a fair chance of life and liberty.

No readjustments of power except such as will tend to secure the future peace of the world and the future welfare and happiness of its peoples.

A genuine and practical cooperation of the free peoples of the world in some common covenant that will combine their forces to secure peace and justice in the dealings of nations with one another.

The guarantee of inviolable security of life, of worship, and of industrial and social development to all peoples who have lived hitherto under the power of governments devoted to a faith and purpose hostile to their own.

~~It is ~~~~the poss~~~~~~ phivivi~~~~~~ of our war aims.~~ Is
it, perhaps, that these forces of antagonism have not yet learned to
know the voice of that America we love and serve? ~~Is it because they
are grounded in a state policy which measures national gains and purposes in terms of annexation and the terrorization and control of
peaceful neighbors, and conceives its triumphs of its own lust for
power as a sanctifying commerce with a higher culture!~~ It may well
be that those among us who stand ready to forward the plans of aggression bred in secret do not understand the language of democracy when it
proclaims the purposes of war in terms of a peace ~~of~~ ^{for} the peoples that
shall be untroubled by ~~the machinations of~~ those to whom men are but
the pawns in their struggle for power and gain. But true Americans,
those who toil here for home and the hope of better things, whose lifted
eyes have caught the vision of a ~~liberal~~ _{liberated} world, ~~these it is who~~ have said
that of the policy of blood and iron there shall be an end and that equal
justice which is the heart of democracy shall rule in its stead.

    I can not conclude without at least a word of tribute to you
as a citizen and as a chosen and trusted leader of labor. Your courage
and devotion have not only strengthened the nation but equally have they
protected and advanced the cause to which you have given your life.
America owes much to you and the workers of America even more. The
history of these years will acclaim you the embodiment of that vision

—6—

and devotion with which the American laboring men have ranked themselves against the possibility of world wide oppression.

     May not those who toil and those who have made common
cause of the larger hope for the masses of mankind, take renewed
heart as they think on these days when America has taken its stand
for the rights of humanity and the fellowship of social and international justice.

                 (Signed) Woodrow Wilson

To Samuel Gompers

My dear Mr. Gompers: The White House 31 August, 1917

I am sure that you understand that my inability to accept the invitation to address the Minneapolis conference of the American Alliance for Labor and Democracy is due only to official necessity, and not in any degree to lack of appreciation of the importance of the occasion. The cause you and your fellow patriots uphold is one with the cause we are defending with arms. While our soldiers and sailors are doing their manful work to hold back reaction in its most brutal and aggressive form, we must oppose at home the organized and individual efforts of those dangerous elements who hide disloyalty behind a screen of specious and evasive phrases.

I have read with real pride the names of the men and women who are to take part in the Minneapolis conference. Not one but has a record of devoted service to fundamental democracy; not one but has fought the long, hard fight for equal justice, braving every bitterness that the humblest life might know a larger measure of happiness.

With all my heart I want them to feel that their devotion to country is in no wise a betrayal of principle, and that in serving America today they are serving their cause no less faithfully than in the past. I myself have had sympathy with the fears of the workers of the United States; for the tendency of war is toward reaction, and too often military necessities have been made an excuse for the destruction of laboriously-erected industrial and social standards. These fears, happily, have proved to be baseless. With quickened sympathies and appreciation, with a new sense of the invasive and insidious dangers of oppression, our people have not only held every inch of ground that has been won by years of struggle, but have added to the gains of the Twentieth Century along every line of human betterment. Questions of wages and hours of labor and industrial readjustment have found a solution which gives to the toiler a new dignity and a new sense of social and economic security. I beg you to feel that my support has not been lacking and that the Government has not failed at any point in granting every just request advanced by you and your associates in the name of the American worker.

No one who is not blind can fail to see that the battle line of democracy for America stretches today from the fields of Flanders to every house and workshop where toiling, upward striving men and women are counting the treasures of right and justice and liberty which are being threatened by our present enemies.

It has not been a matter of surprise to me that the leaders in certain groups have sought to ignore our grievances against the men who have equally misled the German people. Their insistence that a nation whose rights have been grossly violated, whose citizens have been foully murdered under their own flag, whose neighbors have been invited to join in making conquest of its territory, whose patience in pressing the claims of justice and humanity has been met with the most shameful policy of truculence and treachery; their insistence that a nation so outraged does not know its own mind, that it has no comprehensible reason for defending itself, or for joining with all its might in maintaining a free future for itself and its ideals, is of a piece with their deafness to the oft-repeated statement of our national purposes.

Is it, perhaps, that these forces of antagonism have not yet learned to know the voice of that America we love and serve? It may well be that those among us who stand ready to forward the plans of aggression bred in secret do not understand the language of democracy when it proclaims the purposes of war in terms of a peace for the peoples that shall be untroubled by those to whom men are but the pawns in their struggle for power and gain. But true Americans, those who toil here for home and the hope of better things, whose lifted eyes have caught the vision of a liberated world, have said that of the policy of blood and iron there shall be an end and that equal justice which is the heart of democracy shall rule in its stead.

May not those who toil and those who have made common cause of the larger hope for the masses of mankind take renewed heart as they think on these days when America has taken its stand for the rights of humanity and the fellowship of social and international justice?

Sincerely yours,   Woodrow Wilson

TLS (photostat in RSB Coll., DLC).

To Thomas James Walsh

[The White House] August 31, 1917

My heart goes out to you in your great sorrow.[1] May God comfort and console you.   Woodrow Wilson

T telegram (Letterpress Books, WP, DLC).
[1] Mrs. Walsh had died on August 30.

From William Graves Sharp

Paris. Aug. 31, 1917.

For the President. May I heartily commend your answer to the Pope's peace note published in the Paris press today. It has met with general approval not only in editorial comment but in the expression of opinion of the people. There is a common accord that the views therein expressed are thoroughly representative of those held by the Allied Powers, and they are especially welcomed at this time as forecasting the nature of conditions upon which a satisfactory and permanent peace can only come.

The strength of the document lies in the fact that all the assertions made are unassailable in their absolute truth, and to those, like myself, who have lived for the past three years within the sound of their cannon, the indictment against the brutality of the German hosts lashed on by fear of disobedience to the imperial command is no less true than it is justly merited. The entire frankness with which the attitude of our Government is expressed towards the Pope's appeal and the rare discernment with which you have laid bare the real situation which exists in war-cursed Europe should make a deep impression upon those whose compassionate desire for peace has blinded them to the dangers which you so clearly point out as inevitably to follow unless its foundations be established in freedom and justice. Indeed, it is my prophecy that by your words of yesterday you have rendered an inestimable service to mankind in not only pointing the way but hastening the day of the accomplishment of this universally desired end. To those who will but see, the doorway has been left wide open.

The answer is altogether admirable both in its felicity of expression and the comprehensive way in which the great questions involved are discussed.   Sharp.

T telegram (SDR, RG 59, 763.72119/794, DNA).

From William Bauchop Wilson

My dear Mr. President: Washington August 31, 1917.

Referring to our conversation yesterday concerning the disturbed situation in the Northwest and Southwest with regard to I.W.W. activities and other labor difficulties, the general purpose of a commission created in accordance with the suggestion of Mr. Gompers and approved by the Council of National Defense is admirably set forth in a statement made by Secretary Baker to the Council of National Defense, as follows:

"To inquire into the real causes of this discontent on both sides, meeting in each instance the Governor of the State, telling him they were there as representatives of the national Government and of the President with a view to lending sympathetic counsel and aid to the State government in the development of a better understanding, and also to deal with employers and employees in a conciliatory spirit, seeking to compose differences and allay misunderstanding, and to foster a feeling that the national Government is actively interested in the situation."

As a specific line of action I suggest:

(1) The creation of a commission composed of five persons, namely: The Secretary of Labor; Colonel J. L. Spangler, of Pennsylvania; Verner Z. Reed, of Colorado (representatives of employers); John H. Walker, of Illinois; E. P. Marsh, of Washington (representatives of labor).[1] I suggest also the appointment of Felix Frankfurter as secretary of the commission.

(2) That the commission visit, first, those States whose industries are most seriously affected, interview the governors and secure their cooperation. Call conferences of employers and employees whenever it is deemed advisable and endeavor to work out a mutual understanding between them which will insure the continued operation of the industry on a basis acceptable to both sides. The industrial conferences in the most important cases could be arranged for in advance by the representatives of the Department of Labor already on the ground, thus saving the time of the commission. The members of the commission should have an interview with the President, not only for the purpose of getting his instructions at first hand but also because of the beneficial effect it would have upon the minds of the people with whom they are to come in contact.

(3) The commission should report to the President from time to time and at the conclusion of its work.

(4) It is suggested that while the compensation may be paid by the Department of Labor it would be advisable to have the expenses paid from the special funds of the President. Minor details can be worked out by the commission as it proceeds with its work.   Faithfully yours,   W B Wilson

TLS (WP, DLC).

[1] Col. Jackson Levi Spangler, of Bellefonte, Pa., a retired coal-mine operator, whose National Guard rank was awarded for his services in relief work following the Johnstown flood of 1889; Verner Zevola Reed, of Denver, Colo., an author, capitalist, and student of American Indian myths and folklore; John Hunter Walker, who had headed the Illinois state organization of the United Mine Workers for several years and was currently president of the Illinois Federation of Labor; and Ernest P. Marsh, president of the Washington State Federation of Labor.

From Edward Mandell House, with Enclosure

Dear Governor: Magnolia, Massachusetts. August 31, 1917.

Mr. Miller,[1] Gordon's partner, told me what Arthur Richmond Marsh[2] had said about your note and, because of his fine literary discrimination, I asked Miller to put it in writing so I might send it to you. He says he sends it because its praise is in a different key from most others.

Karl Weigand writes me:

"It is to my mind the greatest step that has yet been taken towards peace. Its effect will be splendid in Germany. The psychological tactics will avail the President more in attaining the end he has aimed at than many corps on the front. It gives the German liberals every assurance they have wanted. It confirms everything that Harden has been writing about Mr. Wilson. It is a wonderful document."

Affectionately yours,   E. M. House

TLS (WP, DLC).

[1] That is, David Hunter Miller, of the New York law firm of Miller and Auchincloss.

[2] Marsh, Harvard 1883, had been Assistant Professor of English Literature at the University of Kansas and Professor of Comparative Literature at Harvard before beginning a business career in 1899. He was vice-president and president of the New York Cotton Exchange from 1908 until 1911, when he became editor of *The Economic World; A Weekly Chronicle of Facts, Events and Opinions.*

E N C L O S U R E

David Hunter Miller to Edward Mandell House

Dear Colonel House: New York August 30, 1917

Last evening I happened to meet Mr. Arthur Richmond Marsh who talked to me about The President's note to the Vatican. Mr. Marsh said that he thought that this note was the greatest state paper that had ever been written; that The President had shown himself to be not only the leading statesman of this age but of any age, and that he was the only man who had ever had the opportunity of speaking to the entire world and at the same time had shown himself equal to such opportunity. The President, he said, had achieved the impossible or, at least, what anyone would have said before reading his note to have been impossible; that while the Pope had used with extraordinary ability the only weapon left to the Vatican, namely, the weapon of an idea, The President had answered with the same kind of weapon and had written an answer that was itself unanswerable.

In speaking of what Mr. Marsh called the impossibility of

The President's achievement, or in other words, its impossibility from an antecedent point of view, he said that The President had divided the world into two classes—on the one side the Prussian autocracy and on the other side the rest of humanity.

Mr. Marsh believes that the one thing in the world that the German oligarchy really fear is the compelling force throughout the world of the will and ideas of The President, and he believes that the note will create a visible upheaval in German opinion.

Mr. Marsh's last words to me on the subject were

"Since reading The President's note my head is in the clouds and I can think of nothing else."

Sincerely yours,   David Hunter Miller

TLS (WP, DLC).

From Robert Bruce Coleman and Thomas Samuel Hawes

Bainbridge, Ga., August 31, 1917.

Your message received, and answer delayed account absence Mr. Hawes. Every train on our line is operating on schedule time and we have no troubles with any of our employees. About forty of our former employees resigned August second and third but new men thoroughly competent have taken their places and we are under contract with the new men for twelve months. There is absolutely no danger of a strike or other interference with transportation on our line. Many of our new men resigned good positions to accept employment with us and if we discharge them and take back men who resigned it would be unfair to the new men and subject us to damage for breach of contract. Several of those who resigned have accepted employment elsewhere as shown by applications to this company for service letters from other lines and we have given them good references. Two have applied to us for reinstatement. We feel that we are morally and legally right in all that we have done but the dignity of your request is such that we cannot take the responsibility of declining it, still we have no authority to comply with it at this time. Therefore we respectfully request that you grant us two weeks in which to answer. This request is based on the fact that the President of this Company and most of the Directors and stockholders are absent and we desire to present the matter to them personally and obtain authority to act. We assure you that if we can give an answer before the two weeks are up that we will do so gladly.   R. B. Coleman, General manager,

T. S. Hawes, General Counsel.

T telegram (WP, DLC).

From Herbert Clark Hoover

Dear Mr. President: Washington August 31, 1917.

Would you advise me whether you think Mr. Carter Harrison, of Chicago, would be a man of balanced mind and equanimity to handle such situations as Dr. Garfield has gone through with during the past week?

I especially want to suggest to you a committee to consider the whole question of conservation in connection with brewing, as to whether we should interfere with the brewing trade in any fashion, and I want some gentleman of prime importance and open fairness of mind to assist in assembling such a committee and to act under direction from you, if it pleases you to inaugurate such a measure.   Yours faithfully,   Herbert Hoover

TLS (WP, DLC).

From the Diary of Josephus Daniels

1917 Friday 31 August

Cabinet—President said a Georgia State Judge had issued an injunction against any employes striking or thinking about striking or almost looking at another man or quitting if another did. A DF[1] Judge WW said to a Georgia Congressman as his private opinion. Gregory said the Judge had issued second order that it should remain in effect until passed on by a jury.

I brought up request of Gov. Stewart of Montana,[2] requesting secret service men to go there to get evidence against I.W.W. 50 could do it. All copper mines closed & men who wish to work are terrified. If evidence could be had to put 25 in jail the others would submit. Gregory said: "Why do they not come to me? We have trails out & must have evidence.["]

I asked WW: Are you going to march in parade.[3] With a twinkle in his eye he said, "I understand they wished good-looking men & so I agreed."

He spoke of the Peace League,[4] who wishes to hold meetings as "Eminent cranks and others who have sense in normal times"

Mrs. W— named the ships we received from Germany. I was about to name them for all the Presidents.

[1] "Damned fool."
[2] Samuel Vernon Stewart, a Democrat.
[3] The parade in Washington on September 4 to honor the District of Columbia contingent of the National Army. Wilson led the parade and reviewed the 28,000 marchers. *Washington Post*, Sept. 5, 1917.
[4] That is, the People's Council of America.

To Newton Diehl Baker, with Enclosure

My dear Mr. Secretary: U.S.S. MAYFLOWER, 1 September, 1917

I have, to speak plainly, very little confidence in the Member of the House who writes this letter, but the charge he refers to being a serious one I would be very much obliged if you would have the enclosed letter read as confidentially as possible by someone who is in a position to judge the question whether we should take the matter up or not. I do not quite feel at liberty to let it pass.   Cordially and faithfully yours,   Woodrow Wilson

TLS (N. D. Baker Papers, DLC).

E N C L O S U R E

From Charles August Lindbergh

                          Little Falls, Minnesota, August 27, 1917.
Your Excellency: An Open Letter.

As I happened to be in the City of Washington at the time of the recent rioting that took place near the Executive Mansion[1] and was an eye witness of the illegal and indefensible acts performed by mobs composed principally of soldiers and sailors wearing the uniform of the United States and civil service employees from nearby executive offices in attacking defenseless women, I, as a plain citizen, desire to acquaint you with some of the things which I saw and heard and the impressions made upon my mind then, and since gathered from conversations with numbers of my fellow citizens who have not hesitated to express their honest sentiments concerning these things.

On the 14th day of August, in this year of 1917, I was riding on a street car passing the White House grounds when I observed a crowd of people filling the street opposite the Cameron House. From the noise and excited action, it was plain that the gathering was a mob of some kind and I left the car to see what it was about. In the mob were a large percentage of men wearing uniforms of the Army, Navy and Marine Corps of the United States. As nearly as I could ascertain, a large proportion of the remainder were clerks from the executive departments of the State, War, Navy and Treasury Departments near by, who had just been dismissed from their work as it was about half past four in the afternoon. I saw a young man climb up the front of

[1] About this and related incidents, see also H. N. Hall to WW, Aug. 15, 1917, Vol. 43.

the Cameron House and endeavor to pull down certain flags that were there—one of them the stars and stripes of our country. I saw that violence was used in many ways directed at the exterior of the building and its occupants within. I saw that the police who were present in sufficient numbers to have easily dispersed the mob had they been so disposed, did nothing whatever to stop the mob violence but actually encouraged it by rough-handling anyone who tried to protect the women or, in any way sympathized with those who were being attacked without warrant of law.

On this occasion, I got to see only a part of the mob performance. But from certain circumstances which came under my personal observation, I came to the conclusion that there were just enough designing persons in this mob to give it direction and positive purpose. Their directive control could have been as plainly observed by any intelligent person in authority as by myself. It was plain enough to cause me to suspect that the real designers would encourage a repetition of these unlawful performances and the presence of the government employees led me also to suppose that, if there was a repetition, it would take place about the same time on the following day. At the same time, I considered it almost unthinkable that the authorities would permit a recurrence of such disgraceful scenes within the Nation's capital. Yet, notwithstanding my hope and expectation that law and order would be preserved, the impression that I had received in regard to a recurrence was so strong that I went there at the same hour the next day.

Sure enough, the mob again assembled and began abusing, choking, striking and dragging through the streets, several of the women who carried flags and banners. Following this second day's scenes of mob violence, I visited the women against whom the actions of the mob had been directed, at their headquarters in the Cameron House. Several of them showed wounds and contusions on their arms, necks and heads, as a result of the violence that had been practiced upon them. As before, the mob had been composed principally of persons wearing the uniform of the United States and clerks from the nearby executive offices of the government; as before, the activities of the police had been directed in opposition to anyone who tried to protect defenseless women and, as before, there were circumstances which compelled me to conclude that, if someone in authority did not exercise a restraining hand, there would be repetitions of such outrages indefinitely.

On the 16th, at the same hour as before, I went again to the same locality within sight and sound of your official residence. And again the same things occurred. The many violences enacted are common knowledge now, so I shall not recite their sickening details. My purpose was to study the situation in order that I might be able to help, if any fair and sane way appeared, to prevent the continued recurrence [of] such scenes in the very heart of our country. I came to the conclusion from what I saw, that mob violence was being used as a brutal subterfuge to avoid a fair and square test of the question of the Right of Petition in the form that "picketing" takes.

You have certainly read of the fight made in the House of Representatives by one of your illustrious predecessors to preserve to the people that right guaranteed them by the Constitution. John Quincy Adams fought in debate for several days single handed and alone for the right of even slaves to petition Congress. He won, you remember. The Constitution of the United States either gives to citizens the right to petition the President and Congress for redress of grievances or it does not; these women are either lawfully exercising that supposed right or they are not. The Constitution itself and the laws of the land provide lawful, peaceful and orderly methods of testing these questions. It is not my purpose herein and now, to discuss the question whether the women who are picketing the White House grounds have pursued the best, or even a proper, method of presenting their petition for redress of grievances. Neither do I intend to discuss the righteousness of their cause nor whether they have grievances to redress. It ought to be sufficient for all purposes that they apparently think they have. The courts are fully competent to decide these questions when the facts are brought to their attention and there is no lack of means and opportunity to bring them there. I am simply exercising the privilege as an American citizen of protesting to the authorities against mob rule and the arrest and farcical conviction of citizens upon the false and trumped-up charge of committing offenses such as obstructing the street, which they did not commit, while employees of this government including men wearing its uniform, are left to go scot free after the commission of the gravest crimes against decency and the very foundations of democracy itself.

On not one of the three occasions when I was an eye witness of what actually occurred, did the police make an earnest effort to hinder or stop the mob in its violence or to arrest its leaders and instigators. Instead of that, they have arrested the women[2]

[2] Mrs. Lavina Dock of Fayetteville, Pa.; Edna A. Dixon of Washington, D. C.; Catherine Mary Flanagan of Hartford, Conn.; Lucy Ewing and Madeline M. (Mrs. William Upton) Watson of Chicago; and Natalie Hoyt Gray of Colorado Springs, Colo. *Washington Post*, Aug. 18 and 19, 1917.

on what I believe to be a false charge. They never did obstruct the streets and the actual culprits on this charge are those who have been opposing them, even to the extent of exercising mob violence for which there is no warrant or justification in law, whatever.

In support of my own evidence of what occurred on the three days in question, I am going to insert here the testimony of another eye witness, Miss Beulah Amidon, daughter of a Judge of a United States Court,[3] who has related her experiences for publication in the Fargo, N. Dak. Courier-News: Miss Amidon says:

"I have stood perfectly quiet and empty handed on Pennsylvania Avenue, 'The proudest street in the proudest city in the world, and seen a police officer laugh while a crowd of hoodlums snatched at me, and a sailor in the uniform of the United States doubled up his fist and hit me deliberately in the chest.

I have seen a woman who weighed less than a hundred pounds knocked down by another sailor in uniform and dragged twenty feet by the ribbon around her neck.

I have seen three sailors in uniform climb to the second story of a private house and tear down the stars and stripes while two police officers stood by and made no attempt at interference.

I have seen the hole made in a pane of glass and the ceiling of a room by a bullet fored [fired] through a lighted window at which three women were sitting.

I have seen a girl knocked down by two negro messenger boys and the young army officer in uniform who came to her assistance locked up for 'disorderly conduct,' while her assailant looked on and jeered.

I have seen a newspaper man fined twenty-five dollars in the 'Courts of Justice' in the Nation's Capital because he struck a man who had knocked down two girls who were walking quietly down the street.

I have seen six policemen, a police woman and a plain clothes man, snatch a woman's property from her hands, cruelly twisting her arm as they did so.

These things did not happen in 'Old Russia.' They were merely incidents in a few days of rioting which occurred in the Capital of the United States during the last week.

Since January, the President of the United States has refused to see the women who came to him asking him to use his influence to secure political liberty for 20,000,000 American citizens."

It is impossible to see, Mr. President, how you could escape

[3] Charles Fremont Amidon, United States judge for the District of North Dakota since 1896.

from direct responsibility for these things even if you desired to do so. I am persuaded that you do not desire escape from such responsibility. In a sense that cannot be compared with any other president, you have assumed an attitude of leadership in this country that approaches the absolute. One word of command from you would have dissipated those mobs, yet they continued for three days in their mad work uninterrupted. Even if you had not assumed the authority which you have, as Commander-in-Chief, you could have prevented soldiers from disgracing the uniform of the United States and could have brought troops to clear the streets when the police failed to do their duty. It would take little more than a nod from you to induce the authorities of the District and the City to bring such charges against the picketers as would bring their cause and their offense—if they have committed any—to a prompt and effective adjudication. Yet you did not speak that word, you did not exercise that authority and you withheld the nod.

Having been convinced by what I heard and saw take place on these three days within sight and sound of your office windows, that neither you nor the city authorities intended to do anything to cause these lamentable proceedings to cease, it was clear that unless Congress could be induced to take some action, they were due to continue indefinitely. On the evening of the third day of the riots, there happened to be a meeting in Washington of certain members of the Non-Partisan League. The proceedings which I have tried to describe were discussed and as a result of that meeting the following Resolution was introduced in the House by John M. Baer,[4] a Representative from North Dakota:

"66th Congress,
1st Session. H. RES. 130.
"Whereas in the City of Washington, District of Columbia, about three hundred feet from the White House premises, is a building known as the Cameron House, in which is located headquarters and main offices of a women's organization, at which is continually congregated women of character, courage and intelligence, who come from various sections of the United States; and

Whereas on three successive days, to-wit, the fourteenth, fifteenth and sixteenth days of August, nineteen hundred and seventeen, on said days immediately following the closing of day's work by the clerks and employees in the executive departments, hundreds of these clerks and employees, acting with

---

[4] John Miller Baer, the first Nonpartisan member elected to Congress. He took his seat on August 10, 1917.

sailors, then and now in the service of the United States Navy and in uniform at the time, and soldiers then and now in the service of the United States Army, also in their uniforms at the time—all these clerks, employees, sailors, soldiers and others, formed themselves into mobs and did deliberately, unlawfully, and violently damage the said headquarters and offices of the said women's organization by pelting rotten eggs through the doors and windows, shooting a bullet from a revolver through a window, and otherwise damaging said Cameron House, and also violently and unlawfully did strike, choke, drag, and generally mistreat and injure and abuse the said women when they came defenseless upon the streets adjoining, as well as when they were in the said building; and

Whereas the organized police of the City of Washington, District of Columbia, made no attempt to properly safeguard the property and the persons of the said defenseless women, but on the contrary, said police even seemed to encourage the lawless acts of the mob; and

Whereas such lawlessness [occurred] in the capital of the United States and within a few hundred feet of the Executive Mansion and Offices of the President of the United States; and

Whereas these attacks upon defenseless women are not only an outrage and crime in themselves that prove the perpetrators and those lending aid to the same, to be miserable cowards, but, in addition, create through the world contempt for the United States and set a vicious example to the people throughout the United States and the world at large, of lawlessness and violence, and encourage designing cowards and manipulators everywhere to form mobs to molest the innocent and defenseless under any pretext whatever; and

Whereas there seems to be no activity or any attempt on the part of anyone in authority in the City of Washington, District of Columbia nor by the government officials of the United States, to apprehend, arrest, or punish those perpetrating the violence, or to prevent the daily repetition of this violence, on account of which the same may recur indefinitely unless Congress acts in the premises; and

Whereas the legal status upon the premises stated would excuse the occupants of the Cameron House, if they were so disposed, in firing upon the mobs aforesaid and thus create a state of greater violence and outlawry to further injure the prestige and good name of the United States for maintaining law and order and the institutions of democracy: Therefore Be It

RESOLVED, That the Speaker appoint a Committee of seven

members to investigate into all the facts relating to the violent and unlawful acts aforesaid and make the earliest possible report upon the conditions, with the purpose in view of purging the Army and Navy of the United States and other official departments, of all lawless men who bring disgrace upon the American flag by participating in mob violence, and also inquire regarding the conduct of all government employees and the police of the City of Washington, District of Columbia, with a view to maintaining law and order."

This resolution was introduced at the opening of the daily session of the House, at noon on the 17th day of August, 1917. Congress did not have time to act in any manner in the premises before it produced results. The disturbances abruptly ceased. There was no mob in front of the White House grounds at half past four on the afternoon of that day and there has been none since.

There are some people in this country, who affect to deplore the existence of Congress as a co-ordinate branch of our system of government and are wont to rail in the newspapers against certain members of that branch as "wilful objectors" at certain times. This evidence that I have just given of the power and effectiveness of public opinion as it is reflected in Congress, in protecting the constitutional rights of even the humblest and the weakest of our citizens, should give such persons pause to reflect. If the founders of our government were wise in giving us a president to act as the executive head, they were still more wise in giving us a legislative department to make the laws and control the manner of their execution. And, indeed, if those who drafted the constitution intended to give one branch precedence in power and authority over another, it was the legislative branch that received that distinction rather than the executive, because they placed the power in the hands of Congress to impeach and remove the president, himself, and every member of the Judiciary, while the president has no power to remove any member of Congress. In the light of what has just occurred, let any man, sane, sober and uninfluenced by blind prejudice, ask himself what would have happened to the Right of Petition, had there been no Congress, on the 17th of August, 1917.

Among all your illustrious predecessors, Mr. President, the two most often selected by your partisan admirers to compare you with, are Thomas Jefferson and Abraham Lincoln. Would Thomas Jefferson, the exponent of democracy, refuse, as Miss Amidon charges you have done, "to see the women who came to him asking him to use his influence to secure political liberty for twenty million American citizens"? Would he tolerate, in the capital of the Nation over which he had the honor to preside, the arrest of citizens on a false and trumped-up charge in order to avoid a judicial decision involving the Right of Petition for redress of grievances? To ask these questions is to answer them. For Thomas Jefferson, such a course would have been unthinkable.

And how about Abraham Lincoln? During the Civil War between the states, the term "copperhead" which we are just now hearing so much about was applied to the bulk of the Democratic party in the North. In July, of 1864, that party held its national convention at Chicago. It denounced Abraham Lincoln as a tyrant, in its platform declared the war a failure and nominated as its candidate for president, a man who might have been the hero of that war, but was not. During that war, the cause of democracy and human freedom had been in greater danger of destruction than it has ever been since. Certain unthinking advisers of Abraham Lincoln wanted him to take official cognizance of disloyal utterances which were rife during the succeeding political campaign in which his acts for the preservation of the Union were the chief topics of embittered adverse discussion. But he, Great Soul, believed that to destroy the right of free speech in a democracy would be a greater danger to the Republic than rebellion itself and refused to avail himself of a power which he could easily have obtained to fill the northern jails with his calumniators. Ten months afterwards, the war was won and the soul of Lincoln has come down to us as that of a man who dared to risk his reputation, his political success, the chance to win a war and even life itself, rather than sacrifice one jot or tittle of the democracy he loved.

Twelve years later, one of the most prominent delegates of that 1864 convention lacked but one electoral vote of being chosen as the President of the United States and some members of the party that denounced Lincoln as a tyrant have had some influence with the government on an occasion or two since. Abraham Lincoln could see that the objectors of to-day, in a representative form of government, may be the rulers of to-morrow and that, unless there is absolute freedom of expression in all questions of government, there is and can be, no such thing as a democracy.

Ah no, Mr. President. Your admirers are wrong. You resemble neither Jefferson nor Lincoln unless your actions greatly belie your heart. If Jefferson and John Quincy Adams were right in upholding the Right of Petition, then you are dead wrong in denying the same. If Abraham Lincoln was right in allowing the utmost freedom of discussion of his official acts in the midst of the greatest war the world had ever seen up to his time, then every act of your administration, wherein you seek to destroy freedom of thought and conscience, is wrong because diametrically opposed to the course which Lincoln pursued.

In conclusion, allow me as an intense lover and believer in the democracy of Lincoln, Adams and Jefferson and as a plain citizen of the Republic, to beg for justice to the women who are petitioning at your door. They have been misrepresented in the public press and hounded by hoodlums enough. Things have come to such a pass in this country that no one either can or will give them justice but you. If they are violating the law of the land in their manner of presenting their petition may they not, at least have a fair and impartial trial on charges that will properly present the issues involved before a court of some degree of respectability which will hear and determine those issues in harmony with the great principles of democracy upon which our government is founded?

Very respectfully yours,   C. A. Lindbergh

TLS (WP, DLC).

To William Charles Adamson

My dear Judge: U.S.S. MAYFLOWER, 1 September, 1917

May I not express to you and through you to the Committee on Interstate and Foreign Commerce of the House my sincere gratification at the favorable report the Committee has just made on the bill granting family allowances, indemnities and life insurance for the officers and enlisted men of the Army and Navy; and the hope that the proposed measure may receive the prompt approval of the Congress?

There are so many arguments for the bill that I do not know which to put forward as the most imperative. No doubt you have assembled them in your own mind in their most effective order. But what principally appeals to me about the bill is that it takes into consideration the whole obligation of the soldier not only, but the whole obligation of the Government,—the obligations of justice and humanity both to the soldier and to his family. It is one of the most admirable pieces of legislation that has been proposed in connection with the war and I cannot too earnestly urge its adoption.

I observe with regret that the limit of life insurance available to the officers and men in the service has been reduced from

$10,000 to $5,000. I earnestly hope that the $10,000 limit may be restored.

Cordially and sincerely yours,   Woodrow Wilson

TLS (Letterpress Books, WP, DLC).

To Thomas Staples Martin

My dear Senator: u.s.s. MAYFLOWER, 1 September, 1917

Information has come to me through the public prints and otherwise that a fresh attempt is to be made, this time in connection with the revenue measure, to saddle me with a legislative committee with the professed purpose of assisting me to control the vast expenditures of the Government, and I am writing to ask if I may not have your active cooperation in preventing such a burden being put upon me, for an additional authority put alongside of me in this already tremendous task of directing the administrative activities of the Government is just the thing which would create confusion and make my task twice as complex as it is. The burden of responsibility is already all but too great to carry, and to have the responsibility shared would embarrass me without lightening it.

I am very anxious that my friends in the Senate should understand how serious this is. I am writing to you not because I for a moment doubt your attitude in the matter but in order that, if you care to do so, you may cite my feeling about it.

Cordially and faithfully yours,   Woodrow Wilson[1]

TLS (Letterpress Books, WP, DLC).
[1] Wilson wrote identical letters to Senators James and Simmons: WW to O. M. James and WW to F. M. Simmons, both Sept. 1, 1917, TLS (Letterpress Books, WP, DLC).

To John Sharp Williams

My dear Senator: u.s.s. MAYFLOWER, 1 September, 1917

I know what your attitude is towards the proposal to constitute a Congressional Committee to assist in some way in controlling the expenditure of the vast sums of money which Congress has appropriated and is about to appropriate, and I feel sure that you will do your utmost to prevent the creation of any such body, but I am very anxious that my friends in the Senate should all know how serious the matter is. It would constitute a very great added difficulty and burden so far as I am concerned in the administration of the war. The great impediment to an effective control on my part as things stand is that there are so many consultative bodies and so many instrumentalities upon which I must keep my eye at the same time. Fortunately, the instrumentalities which now exist are under my authority. To have another authority put over them or any body which might be conceived of as exercising an independent authority would be fatal to the unity of the administration and to the very kind of control which the proponents of such a committee have in mind. I have taken the liberty of writing this to you in order that I might have your cooperation, which I know you will generously give, in preventing what would undoubtedly be a practical blunder of the gravest sort.   Cordially and faithfully yours,   Woodrow Wilson

TLS (J. S. Williams Papers, DLC).

To Frank Irving Cobb

Personal.

My dear Cobb: U.S.S. MAYFLOWER, 1 September, 1917
    Unfortunately, there are no documents in the State Department which could be said to establish the thing mentioned in your telegraphic message to me of August twenty-seventh. After receiving your telegram, I conferred with the Secretary of State and found that the statements he had made were based, and I think very reasonably based, upon documents and evidences no one of which plainly declare the fact. In short, it was a conclusion, and no conclusion, however well founded in inference, can be established by evidence. I wish it could be.
                Cordially and faithfully yours,   Woodrow Wilson

TLS (IEN).

To John Fox

My dear Doctor Fox: U.S.S. MAYFLOWER, 1 September, 1917
    I am glad to have an opportunity to endorse the effort of the American Bible Society to procure a fund of $400,000 to cover the expenses of supplying the men in the National Army with Bibles. This is an object which I am sure all Christian people will wish to see accomplished. I hope that it may be, for the sake of the men who are going to the front. They will need the support of the only book from which they can get it.
                Cordially and sincerely yours,   Woodrow Wilson

TLS (Letterpress Books, WP, DLC).

To Thomas Lincoln Chadbourne, Jr.

U.S.S. MAYFLOWER,

My dear Mr. Chadbourne: 1 September, 1917

May I not drop you just a line to say how much I personally appreciate your generosity in coming down to Washington and giving up your time to act as Counselor for the Exports Board? I am sure they appreciate it as much as I do, but I wanted to give myself the pleasure of telling you personally how much and how sincerely I admire your action.

Cordially and sincerely yours, Woodrow Wilson

TLS (Letterpress Books, WP, DLC).

To Cleveland Hoadley Dodge

My dear Cleve: U.S.S. MAYFLOWER, 1 September, 1917

You always think of me at the right time and always send me the sort of message my heart is waiting for. Whenever I write anything like the reply to the Pope my first and greatest desire is to know what men whose judgment I trust think of it, because I never entirely trust my own instinct and conclusion. A letter like yours, therefore, brings me not only the message of friendship which my heart desires, but also the reassurance which my mind craves, and I thank you for it out of a full heart.

It cheers me to hear that your loved ones are safe. I think of them very often and am grateful to God that at least some element of prudence towards America has been planted in the heart of the Turk.

Always Affectionately yours, Woodrow Wilson

TLS (WC, NjP).

From Thomas Watt Gregory

Dear Mr. President: Washington, D. C. September 1, 1917.

I acknowledge receipt of yours of August 27th enclosing a page from the issue of the NEW YORK AMERICAN of August 12th containing an article by Hannis Taylor, alleged to be an argument against the sending of the newly levied troops abroad.

Of course, a complete answer to the whole thing is that these troops are no longer state militia as contemplated by the Constitution and are now a part of the army of the United States.

I do not believe it is worth while to make any reply, as this would be just what Taylor would like and it would unduly magnify the discreditable utterances involved. Another reason for not paying any attention to it is that the partial publication was made almost three weeks ago and the few people who saw it have doubtless forgotten about it.

Faithfully yours,   T. W. Gregory

TLS (WP, DLC).

From Newton Diehl Baker

My dear Mr. President: Washington. September 1st, 1917.

I have received the telegrams from the Western Governors with regard to the probable stimulating affect [effect] upon I.W.W. activities of an announcement that the Commission of Secretary Wilson is appointed to investigate that society. Secretary Wilson, I am sure, is aware of the possibilities in this regard, and will center the work of his Commission upon general labor conditions tactfully. In the meantime, I have suggested to Secretary Wilson that Felix Frankfurter be taken along as Secretary on his Committee. While this has not been definitely determined, it seems likely, and I have suggested to Felix the possibility pointed out by the Governors as one to be carefully avoided.

Respectfully yours,   Newton D. Baker

TLS (WP, DLC).

To Edward Mandell House

My dear House,   [U.S.S. Mayflower] 2 September, 1917.

I am delighted that you thought the reply to the Pope what it should be and that it has, on the whole, been so well received. I did not dare to submit it to our Associates across the sea more than twenty-four hours before I made it public. I felt morally certain that they would wish changes which I could not make. I was confirmed in that view when Jouserand the next day went up in the air because it seemed to exclude economic punishment of Germany after the war. It will work out as well this way as any. The differences of opinion will be less embarrassing now than they would have been if I had invited them beforehand.

I am beginning to think that we ought to go systematically to work to ascartain [ascertain] as fully and precisely as possible just what the several parties to this war on our side of it will be inclined to insist upon as part of the final peace arrangements, in order that we may formulate our own position either for or against them and begin to gather the influences we wish to employ,—or, at the least, ascertain what influences we can use: in brief, prepare our case with a full knowledge of the position of all the litigants. What would you think of quietly gathering about you a group of men to assist you to do this? I could, of course, pay all the bills out of the money now at my command. Under your guidance these assistants could collate all the definite material available and you could make up the memorandum by which we should be guided.

Have you had a talk with Frankfurter? If you have not, I wish you would have. He knows what some of the other governments are doing to get their cases ready and their pipes laid, and he might be able to give you a lead as to doing what I am here suggesting.

I am writing from the MAYFLOWER at Hampton Roads. Next week I shall try to get away for a longer time. Do not be alarmed about my health. I need rest, and am growing daily more conscious that I do; but I am fit and all right.

All join in affectionate messages.

Affectionately Yours,   Woodrow Wilson

WWTLS (E. M. House Papers, CtY).

From Scott Ferris

Dear Mr. President: [Washington] September 2, 1917.

I hope I may not in your eyes assume the role of a tale-bearer. I hope I may not in your eyes assume the role of a trouble-maker.

But I have felt it my duty to mail you the enclosed 3-page circular letter which is being circulated promiscuously over our State.[1] I do not suppose you will have time, with the awful pressure that must weigh on you, to wade through this 3-page letter or to weigh its consequences. But I am wondering if you will not deem it of sufficient importance to let some clerk make a digest of its contents, pointing out the salient features to you.

The part that seems so unjust to me is where he reiterates over and over again a pretended quotation from you, "that we had gone into this war with no special grievance of our own."[2] I know that has been explained by you; I know it was never said by you; I know it is almost treasonable to misquote you in times like these, and I know our people will not give heed to such conduct.

I think every paper in the State, unless it be a few Socialistic or Anarchistic papers, are denouncing him for this conduct. A large portion of the towns have adopted resolutions demanding his resignation. Our two million people of the bright new State resent this most keenly and I was quite anxious you know that our people do not approve of his conduct, and that you be informed of what was going on.

I have just returned from the State after three weeks vacation and find our people very much wrought up over this matter.

I think it is so necessary that Congress adjourn and let the Congressmen go home to their districts and explain that the war was thrust upon us; that the causes of the war were greater than we had ever suffered before as a provocation for war; that your two and a half years of pleadings for neutrality were in vain, and I believe all phases of the situation ought to be presented forcefully to the people. Again, our conduct of the war ought to be explained; our various Acts of Congress ought to be explained, and third, the third, [sic], the villainous results that would have ensued had we followed a course of submission. I believe all these things ought to be presented to the end that disloyal and unpatriotic citizens both in and out of Congress should not be allowed to have their nefarious doctrines take root and find lodgment in the minds of the good people who have heard but one side and who are unacquainted with the real situation.

Upon my return to Washington I had thought of asking for an engagement to come down and say a word to you regarding conditions out there, but knowing the pressure that must be on you, I have refrained from doing it and have resorted to this letter.

With great respect and friendship, I am

Very sincerely yours,   Scott Ferris

TLS (WP, DLC).

¹ T. P. Gore to A. Melton, Aug. 23, 1917, mimeographed L (WP, DLC). In this letter, Gore responded to a telegram from Alger Melton, chairman of the Democratic State Committee of Oklahoma, about Gore's amendment to the war revenue bill to forbid the use of the funds appropriated to send drafted men abroad without their consent. Melton had requested Gore either to represent the people of the state or to resign as United States senator. Gore retorted that he did represent the people of Oklahoma, who were in favor of peace and against war; indeed, Wilson had been reelected because he had kept American sons out of the slaughter pens of Europe. Gore offered to resign if other members of Congress would do so, so that all might go to the country and ask for a vote of confidence. Gore also said, however, that he would support every measure "calculated to make this a short and successful war and to speed an early, honorable and lasting peace." The American contribution should be, not men, but money and munitions. Gore favored a declaration of acceptable terms of peace so that "our boys may know exactly what they are dying for." He warned against overvaluing "all this cloth-of-gold, peacock-feather, rainbow rhetoric about carrying democracy to people who would rather be dead than democrats." Gore concluded by calling on Melton to protect "the sacred and inalienable right to the freedom of thought and to the freedom of speech."

² What Wilson said in his address (printed at May 12, 1917, Vol. 42) was: "We have gone in with no special grievance of our own, because we have always said that we were the friends and servants of mankind. . . . We go because we believe that the very principles upon which the American republic was founded are now at stake and must be vindicated."

From Newton Diehl Baker

Dear Mr. President: Washington. September 2, 1917.

I have by reference from you a letter dated August 27th from Mr. Hoover which I take the liberty of returning with a memorandum or comment made by General Crowder[1] in which I find myself constrained to concur.

Of course Mr. Hoover's interest is keen and justified, but both General Crowder and I are daily asked by all sorts of interests to urge upon you the making of regulations or the issuance of instructions to Boards which will have the effect of increasing the exemptions of particular classes. Mine owners, railroad and steamship operators, ship builders, steel makers, and representatives of many other industries vital to the national situation are among this number and, if we should start, I don't know where we could stop with such special instructions. The total number of men to be taken by this draft is, of course, not large as compared with the total number of men available to carry on the industry and business of the country and I am persuaded that the effect of the draft upon any industry will be less serious than many people suppose.

On the whole, I am clear that it is wiser to allow the district boards to exercise the discretion which the law seems to have intended they should have and then, after the draft is made and if we find an intolerable or bad situation anywhere, resort can be had to your plenary power as Commander in Chief to discharge men for the interest of the Government and in that way we ought to be able to redress any difficulty which is peculiar and unnecessarily burdensome.

Respectfully,   Newton D. Baker

TLS (WP, DLC).

[1] E. H. Crowder to NDB, Aug. 30, 1917, TLS (WP, DLC).

From Walter Lowrie

Bobbio Pellice, Prov. di Torino.
Dear Mr. President: September 2, 1917.

Today in this little alpine village the local deputy to parliament gathered the people in the square to hear from him a patriotic speech. He had much to say about the noble and encouraging example of America and about the clear words of President Wilson. The enclosed translation of your Decoration Day speech was then distributed to his electors.[1]

It is likely you know how very great an effect, not only the intervention of the United States, but more particularly your messages and speeches have had here in Italy, especially upon the peasant folk. Our intervention assured them of victory: your words helped them to have a good conscience. In my opinion, these two factors, or these two phases of one fact, have an importance which cannot be exaggerated, for they have availed to preserve the moral unity of this people and to fortify them to continue this war unto the end.

It seemed superfluous to tell you this. But the little incident here in this village represents so concretely what is going on all over Italy that I make bold to impart it to you.

I also take this occasion to say that now when America is in such favor and when every one is lauding Woodrow Wilson I have reason to be glad that in my humble post as preacher in Rome I have ever been loyal not only to my country but to its President. Only this I do confess, that one day at dinner, when none but members of the Embassy were present, and when the Ambassador was inclined to tease me, I turned the tables on him by reciting some of your most famous and hardest sayings —as part of a collection I was making of P. H. Wilson's Maxims.[2] But that was only to chagrin the Ambassador,—who stands up so straight for his Chief that he leans over backwards. Now, happily, neither the Ambassador nor I have to do any standing up. And I express my verriest thought when I say that never in my day has the power of the spoken word appeared so great as when you have spoken. You have a rare advantage in being spokesman for a great country; but the country is fortunate in having such a spokesman—while most other rulers are dumb. To speak to the whole world, and by the clearness and cogency of words to frame the thoughts of all peoples (including our enemies), represents a degree of greatness which no ruler has hitherto attained and few have dreamed of.

I have felt lonely as an exile over here—but now no more since you are sending, or are about to send, so many of my fellow countrymen to join me. You have in many ways contributed to making my lot happier, and though all this is an undesigned consequence of larger plans and purposes, I am nevertheless grateful and shall be eager to see you and thank you when the war is over and I can return home. I reckon it as my only title to fame that I was once, in a sort of a way, your pastor.[3] I was one year too early to be your pupil.

Respectfully and devotedly yours,   Walter Lowrie.

TLS (WP, DLC).

[1] He meant Wilson's Flag Day speech of June 14, 1917, printed at that date

in Vol. 42. It was translated and printed as *Mentre si lotta per la giustizia e per la libertà: L'intervento dell'America: Discorso pronunciato dal Presidente Wilson celebrando il Giorno della Bandiera, 14 giugno 1917* (Milan, 1917). There is a copy in WP, DLC.

[2] This seems to refer to the selections from "Pudd'nhead Wilson's Calendar" at the head of each chapter of Mark Twain's *Pudd'nhead Wilson*.

[3] He had been summer pastor of a small church in Keene, N. Y., when the Wilsons were vacationing in Keene Valley in 1907.

From David Lloyd George[1]

Private and Personal

                        10, Downing Street,

Dear Mr President   Whitehall, S.W.   3rd. Sept. 1917.

I am taking advantage of the visit of Lord Reading to Washington to lay in front of you certain views about the conduct of the war which I have formed in the light of my experience during the last three years. We are approaching a very difficult period in which it will be necessary to take far reaching decisions which will be of the utmost importance as regards our future campaign —decisions which will be of vital moment to all the armies in the field. In arriving at these decisions I think it is essential that the heads of the British and the United States Governments should fully understand one another's views. I avail myself of this method of communication because I do not wish my remarks to have an official character. I am only anxious that you should, as far as that is possible without direct conversation, be in full possession of my views.

First of all as to the general strategy to be followed in the prosecution of the war during the winter of 1917-18 and the spring and summer of 1918. The hard fact which faces us to-day is that in spite of the efforts of the Allies to raise and equip armies and to manufacture munitions, in spite of their superiority in men and material and the perfection to which they have brought their offensive arrangements, the Germans at the end of 1917 as at the end of each of the previous years' campaign, find themselves in possession of more and not less Allied territory. By the end of 1917 the Allies had confidently expected to have produced very serious results on the German military power even if they did not succeed in overthrowing it altogether. Their failure is, of course, mainly attributable to the military collapse of Russia. It is also true to say that in every other respect, politically and economically, the Germanic combination is far weaker than it has ever been. But I am convinced from my experience of the last three years that the comparative failure of

[1] Lord Reading handed this letter to Wilson on September 20, 1917.

the Allies in 1917 is also in some measure due to defects in their mutual arrangements for conducting the war.

As compared with the enemy the fundamental weakness of the Allies is that the direction of their military operations lacks real unity. At a very early stage of the war Germany established a practically despotic dominion over all her allies. She not only reorganised their armies and assumed direction of their military strategy but she took control also over their economic resources, so that the Central Empires and Turkey to-day are to all intents and purposes a military Empire with one command and one front. The Allies on the other hand have never followed suit. The direction of the war on their side has remained in the hands of four separate Governments and four separate General Staffs (namely those of France, Great Britain, Italy and Russia) each of which is possessed of complete knowledge only of its front and its own national resources, and which draws up a plan of campaign which is designed to produce results mainly on its own section of front. The defects of this system have not been lost sight of. From time to time and of late with greatly increased frequency, there have been International Conferences to discuss the Allied war plans. But up to the present these Conferences have done little more than attempt to synchronise what are in reality four separate plans of campaign. There has never been an Allied Body which had knowledge of the resources of all the Allies and which could prepare a single co-ordinated plan for utilising those resources in the most decisive manner, and at the most decisive points, looking at the front of the Central Powers as a whole and taking into account their political, economic and diplomatic as well as their military weaknesses.

At the forthcoming Conferences, which will assemble as soon as the results of the present offensives have become clear, I shall urge the imperative importance of establishing more effective unity in the Allied strategy. The policy we have pursued hitherto has been to concentrate all our attacks on Germany, on the ground that Germany is the mainspring of the hostile alliance, & that it is therefore sound policy to try and knock out her army first, even though it is the strongest with which we are confronted, because if we succeed, all the rest will collapse with it. In consequence, for more than three years, the armies of the main Allies have been engaged each summer in a series of terrific and most costly offensives against the strongest part of the enemy line—offensives which have never yet produced any decisive results in breaking down the enemy military organisation. He still opposes a solid and hitherto impenetrable defence. That this policy was a sound policy at the outset of the war I have no doubt. But that we have continued to pursue it so long despite the great changes which have come over the general character of the war, is, I believe, mainly due to the fact that there has been no Body in existence on the Allied side which could consider the military problem as a whole, regardless of the traditions which have grown up in each army, and of the national prejudices and prepossessions of the several Allies, in the use of their forces.

Before committing ourselves to a repetition of these frontal assaults, I feel that we are bound to study the position especially with a view of determining whether there is not an alternative plan of campaign. For some time past it has seemed to me that we ought to consider very carefully whether we cannot achieve decisive results by concentrating first against Germany's allies. In favour of this latter policy it can be urged that the opposing armies are now on parallel lines from one end of every front to the other, and that the war is now practically a siege of the Central Empires, to which must be applied the principles of siege warfare. In a siege you do not seek out the strongest part of the enemy line but the weakest, in the hope that if you break down the defence there, the position as a whole will be turned. To-day the weakest part of the enemy line is unquestionably the front of Germany's allies. They are weak not only militarily but politically. They are also very anxious for peace, so that a comparatively small success might produce far reaching results. Moreover, just inasmuch as their armies have been controlled and their resources organised by Germany as part of the defence of their new Empire of Mittel-Europa, to attack them is to strike at Germany to a far greater extent than was the case in the early days of the war. It is to knock away the props upon which the German military power now increasingly depends. If this were once done, if the inability of the Prussian military machine to defend its allies were thus proved, and the dream of Eastern dominion thus destroyed by the defection of one of these allies, the whole enemy military edifice might fall rapidly in ruins.

There is another aspect of the case. In Northern Europe it is only possible to carry on an intense campaign for six or at most seven months of the year. It so happens that these winter months are the best campaigning season in South Eastern Europe and Turkey in Asia. It seems to me doubtful if we have ever made really adequate use of the Allied forces to achieve decisive results in the South Eastern theatre during the period when they could not be employed on the main fronts.

I need not go further into the strategical questions at issue. What I have said will be sufficient, I think, to make it clear that if we are to make the best possible use of the forces at the disposal of the Allies, it is of supreme importance to establish more effective unity in the direction of the war on the Allied side. If we are to avoid wasted effort and wasted loss of life those who draw up the plan of campaign must have full knowledge of the resources of all the Allies, not only in men, and munitions, but in shipping, railway material and so forth, so as to determine how they can best be employed against the enemy organisation. In my opinion it will be necessary to establish some kind of Allied joint Council, with permanent military and probably naval and economic staffs attached, to work out the plans for the Allies, for submission to the several Governments concerned.

This brings me to the second question to which I would like to draw your attention. It relates to the representation of the United States at the Councils of the Allies. I fully appreciate the objections which the American people feel to being drawn into the complex of European politics. The British people have always attempted to keep themselves aloof from the endless racial and dynastic intrigues which have kept Europe so long in a state of constant ferment, and even to-day their main desire is to effect a settlement which will have the elements of peaceful permanence in itself, and so free them and the rest of the world from the necessity of further interference. These feelings must naturally be far stronger in America. I have not, therefore, the slightest desire that the United States should surrender the freedom of action which she possesses at present.

At the same time, there are, in my opinion, very strong reasons why the United States should consider whether they ought not to be represented at the Conferences of the Allies. To begin with I think the presence of a representative of the United States at the Conferences which will determine the future strategy of the war, would be of the utmost value to the Allied cause. I do not say this merely because the decisions will vitally affect the American army in Europe. I attach great importance to it for this reason. But another reason weighs still more strongly with me. I believe that we are suffering to-day from the grooves and traditions which have grown up during the war, and from the inevitable national prejudices and aspirations which, consciously or unconsciously, influence the judgment of all the nations of Europe. I believe that the presence at the deliberations of the Allies of independent minds, bringing fresh views, unbiassed by previous methods and previous opinions, might be of immense value in helping us to free ourselves from the ruts of the past, and to avoid having our armies drawn into a strategy which is bound to be immensely costly, and which may not be that calculated to give us the best results.

There is another reason. We have now reached a point when it is becoming more and more difficult to maintain, not only the national unity of each of the Allies, but unity among the Allies themselves, in the vigourous prosecution of the war. Every nation in Europe is becoming exhausted. The desire for peace in some quarters is becoming almost irresistible. The argument that any kind of peace is better than a continuation of the present suffering and carnage is daily increasing its appeal. At the same time people are beginning to ask themselves whether victory is obtainable at all and this question will be asked with all the greater insistence in a few weeks time if the end of the campaigning season shows that the whole campaign of 1917, has made no decisive impression upon the German military position. There is no question that victory is within our power. It may be nearer than any of us can reasonably calculate. But if it is to be obtained, it will only be because the free nations exhibit greater moral unity and greater tenacity in the last desperate days than the servants of autocratic power. The preservation of that moral unity and tenacity will be our principal task during the forthcoming winter, and I believe that it depends more and more upon the British Commonwealth and the United States. This does not mean, of course, that our Allies are not fighting as vigourously and as valiantly as ever. It rather means that for one reason or another they have mobilised their national resources to the utmost point of which they are capable without having overthrown the enemy, and that consciously or unconsciously they rely upon the British and the Americans to supply that additional effort which is necessary in order to make certain of a just, liberal and lasting peace. As you may be aware the appearance of the vanguard of the American army has produced a tremendous effect, especially in France. I would ask you to consider, therefore, whether it is not of the utmost importance that the purpose and ideals as well as the wisdom of America should be manifested in the Council Chamber as well as on the battle field, if we are to preserve unshaken during this difficult winter season the resolution of the Allies to go on with the war until Prussian military despotism over Germany and her allies is broken, by revolution from within or defeat from without. I recognise, of course, that there are grave difficulties in the way. But I feel that I ought to put in front of you the immense importance to the success of our cause which I believe attaches to the manifestation at the Conferences of the Allies of the determination of America to prosecute the war with her whole strength and of her confidence in ultimate victory.

In conclusion may I say how much we all here have appreciated the speeches you have made about the war. If you will permit me to say so I believe that your statements have been not the least important of the contributions which America is making to the cause of human freedom. They have not only been a profound and masterly exposition of the Allied case. They have recalled to many the ideals with which they entered upon the war, and which it is easy to forget amid the horrors of the battlefield and the overtime and fatigue in munition shops. They have given to the bruised and battered peoples of Europe fresh courage to endure and fresh hope that with all their sufferings they are helping to bring into being a world in which freedom and democracy will be secure, and in which free nations will live together in unity and peace.   Ever sincerely   D Lloyd George

TLS (WP, DLC).

From Walter Hines Page

Dear Mr. President: London, Sep. 3. 1917

As I promptly telegraphed you and as, of course, you have heard through many channels, your reply to the Pope received a most enthusiastic welcome here not only because it meets with universal approval: there's a deeper reason than that. It expresses definitely the moral and the deep and clear political reason for the war—the freeing of the world, including the German people, from the German military autocracy; and it expresses this better and with more force than it has ever been expressed by anybody on this side the world. You have made acceptable peace-terms clearer not only to the enemy but also to the Allies than they have ever before been made known. All these nations here have so many relatively unimportant and so many purely selfish aims that their minds run on. Here you come setting forth the one big thing worth fighting for—the one big moral and political aim—no revenge, no mere boundary rectifications, no subsidiary thing to confuse the main purpose. This gives moral leadership to the whole war, and the British *know* and feel this.

Some time ago in a general conversation Mr. Balfour said something like this to me: "There is universal admiration and wonder at the American energy and earnestness in getting into the war, wh. has no parallel. But there are people who privately express a certain fear lest your ardour may cool with the first wave of war-weariness. What shd. one say to them? Mind you, I have no such fear myself, but I am sometimes met with the necessity to allay it in weaker minds."

I replied: "To put it in good American, the real answer to any such person is, 'Go to hell!' But the judicious answer is, 'Who is going to cool American ardour and how will he go about it? The dam is burst and the flood is come. Will you do me the favour to refer all such persons to me?' " I haven't seen any such yet. But such doubt, wh. I have no doubt, was felt in ignorant quarters, is forever laid by your letter to the Pope. And the leadership of the war is now definitely and confessedly transferred to you, in British opinion.

The acknowledgment of this took many forms even before this letter. Several of your speeches, notably your speech asking for a declaration of war, have been reprinted in dozens of forms for wide distribution. There's hardly a reading household in the Kingdom but has a copy. The proposed treaty between the Allied naval Powers, binding everyone to give help if any one were attacked for four years after the war, Mr. Balfour tells me you regard as now unnecessary. "I agree with the President," he remarked; "but, so far as I am concerned, I'd make such a treaty, if it be wanted, for 4 or 40 or 400 years." As for Japan, our coming into the war—so it looks here—has settled any danger that may have lurked in that quarter. The British treaty with Japan counts as nothing compared with the British feeling towards us. One was a matter of convenience. The other is a force of nature as well as a creature of necessity.

The telegrams and other documents, telegraphed to you, which show the customary insincerity & cold-blooded willingness to murder, touching the Argentine Republic,[1] it is here hoped, will, if you have published them, bring the Argentine Government into the war. It is hoped, too, that the proof of Sweden's using her Ministers and pouches in Germany's behalf may cause a change of Government in Sweden. The smuggling that has been done through Sweden is the most helpful to Germany of all her channels of supply; and the large quantity of iron ore that has gone from Swedish mines is, perhaps, the most valuable help from outside that Germany has got since the war began.

Admiral Mayo's coming has given the whole Government and especially the Admiralty great satisfaction. As soon as he came I invited the chief Admiralty officers and British admirals to dinner to meet him, and they have shown him continuous atten-

tion since. He told me to-day that they are showing him everything that he cares to see and are answering all his questions.
The naval Conference (British, French, Italian, and American)
begins tomorrow. Immediately after the conference ends, Admiral Mayo will visit the Grand Fleet. The submarine activity
continues (as I regard it) to be a most serious thing. Convoyed
ships have come safely, wh. seems to point to success in our
getting troops and supplies to France. But the toll that the submarines continue to take of unconvoyed freight ships is making
the trouble of shipping very great. All ships will have to be convoyed.

This Government is most anxious for a number of our Representatives and Senators to make a visit to England and France,
not really for any specific legislative conference, although the
invitation may take that form, but for personal interchanges of
experience. It is a common saying in England that even no Englishman can really understand the war and its problems who has
not made a visit to France. I recall that I was forcibly struck with
Bryce's confession to this effect, after he had come back from
France. It is on this principle—that it is well for American legis-
lators to get as vivid an idea as possible—that the British are eager
for a number of them to come. I agree with them.

The abandonment of Riga, it is feared here, will mean the
German occupation of Petrograd and that will mean the getting
of more supplies from Russia and the getting of men, too, for all
sorts of labor—will mean, in fact, the prolongation of the war.
The German spirit, in spite of hunger, can be kept up by such a
land-victory and by the continued submarine success for—Heaven
knows how long; and these German successes seem to point to
the slow and murderous necessity of whipping the German army,
lock, stock, and barrel. That, with our help, is only a question of
time. But, within that time, the sickening loss of life will continue. But for the falling down of Russia and the psychological
effect of the submarine campaign, I shd. have a very lively hope
of the German collapse before the coming winter is gone. The
public and the Government here set high expectations on your
Embargo.

Take your actions all together from the Conscription-act to the
Embargo—what a record that is! Of course it has saved the Allied
cause, which wd. otherwise have been lost—in great measure if
not wholly. And the British know that and freely say so. This in
itself is a conquest over British "arrogance" wh. makes us henceforth the masters of the English-speaking world.

Lord Reading again goes to the United States—on the ship that carries this. He goes on a general financial errand, the details of wh. I do not know—further than the necessity of coming to some concrete understanding. So far as I can find out, the British use their money well (allowing, of course, for the waste of war from wh. every nation suffers); but they seem to me to be awkward and careless and then suddenly panic-stricken in their large dealings with us to procure money. The financial conferences to wh. they have invited me seemed to me like a voyage through mist till you suddenly come to a great fall. I have prayed them to be definite before they become panic-stricken. "The Ambassador is quite right," exclaims the Prime Minister. We then adjourn till the next scare comes; and then the same journey is taken again—to the same Nowhere.

I fear, Mr. President, that my recent letters have been duller than they might have been; but I have seen little use in repeating what I have very fully telegraphed, and all important things have gone by wire. And one week pushes another so quickly in these over-busy days that mail-day comes before I know it. We now have three buildings for offices—the Embassy, the Army, and the Navy; and even admirals and generals take much of my time— properly. The working-adjustment of our plans and methods, in many Departments of the Government, with the British—mere details as most of them are—require constant work by my staff and me; and an admirable staff it is. We are happy to serve to the very best of our ability.

Yours faithfully,   Walter H. Page

T. P. O'Conner,[2] who has gone to the U. S. to solicit money for his party wishd. me to give him an introduction to you. I didn't; but no doubt you'll see him—as, no doubt, it wd. be well. He's an Irishman—a professional Irishman and an M.P.—of somewhat the better sort; if there be any better sort of Professional Irishman. When Lloyd George proposed the plan of an Irish convention, "T. P." said to me: "That's a good move—all right; but, of course, we've got to object—got to play hell and do our fireworks." They are all insincere. They don't want Home Rule—the Professional Irishman doesn't; for, if they had Home Rule, his Profession of agitating for it wd. be gone. The agitation has made long & conspicuous careers for them. Home Rule achieved, their careers wd. end. This is what O'Conner himself tells me. What need his party has for a large fund isn't apparent. But raising money is a conventional job they all have. God didn't bless me with enough wisdom to see the end of this Irish question. Think of this: a Count Plunkett[3] was recently elected to Parliament by an Irish constituency, as a Sinn Feiner. The Church at Rome now puts into the calendar of Saints the Bishop Plunkett, who was Primate of Ireland 400 years ago! Subtle? Yes, and effective.

But this much seems certain: The English, after 300 years of mismanagement, are making a sincere effort to settle the Irish question—with what success time only can tell. This Government now understands its importance not only to themselves, as they have never understood it before, but also as affecting American-British relations.

In general—in this war-world where I have seen the wisest men guess wrong and some of the strongest men break down and waves of opinion flow strong in all directions at once, nobody catches me making prophecies; but I venture this: whenever we can drive the submarines from the ocean, we shall quickly see the end of the war. And in a time of great war-ships and of fantastic inventions, who shall say that their defeat may not at last be accomplished by the American ocean-going tugs that tow coal-barges from Virginia to Massachusetts—perhaps the humblest craft that ever cut the waves?

Sincerely yours,   Walter H. Page

ALS (WP, DLC).
    [1] About these documents, see W. Phillips to WW, Sept. 3, 1917.
    [2] That is, Thomas Power O'Connor, not O'Conner, popularly known as "Tay Pay," the Irish journalist and nationalist leader; an M.P. since 1885. About his views during his visit to the United States, see "T. P. Talks of Obstacles in Home Rule Fight: Nationalist Party, Seeking Autonomy, Is Trying to Keep Ireland from Committing Suicide—Futility of Sinn Fein's Hopes," *New York Times Magazine*, July 1, 1917. Senator Phelan introduced O'Connor and his colleague, Richard Hazleton, M.P., to Wilson on July 5. O'Connor expressed to Wilson the thanks of his party for the sympathy which Wilson had shown for the Irish cause. *New York Times*, July 6, 1917.
    [3] George Noble Plunkett, created a papal count in 1884. He was elected to the House of Commons on February 4, 1917, and, under pressure from the Sinn Fein, refused to take his seat.

From George Wylie Paul Hunt

Phoenix, Arizona,
September 3, 1917.

My dear Mr. President:

On the 1st instant I telegraphed you as follows:

"I have just returned from Columbus, New Mexico, where the men deported from Bisbee July 12 are camped. The impressions of that visit, resulting from careful inquiry designed to disclose the mental attitude of these men, their processes and course of reasoning, the quality of their loyalty to the government, and their hopes and aspirations for the future, coupled with my natural repugnance for an act so unamerican, so autocratic, as that which forced them from their homes, constrain me to urge that you insist upon an early recognition of their constitutional rights and a resumption of American justice in this State. I am deeply mindful of the cares which so heavily weigh upon you at this time, and I will gladly relieve them in any way or degree within my power, but I am convinced that it is vital to the maintenance of this Union's proud boast of democracy, to which your utterances and acts so eloquently testify, and to the restoration of confidence in the efficacy of the federal constitution, that these men be returned to their homes under ample federal protection, there to answer in the constituted courts of justice any charges of unlawful conduct that may be regularly placed against them. I am writing you more fully and in my capacity as conciliator submitting a formal report to the Secretary of Labor."[1]

In amplification of the above telegram I wish to explain that on the afternoon of the 19th ult., acting upon the suggestion and advice of Conciliator John McBride, of the Department of Labor, with whom I had been cooperating in an effort to bring about a settlement of the labor disputes in the Globe-Miami copper district, I left Globe for Columbus, New Mexico, where between 900 and 1,000 of the men deported from Bisbee on July 12 are still encamped. The visit to the Columbus refugees was not paid with any idea that it would or could result in a settlement or compromise of the difference between the particular men affected and the companies by whom they were formerly employed, for not only has the relationship of employer and employe ceased to exist, but the undesirable though not extraordinary status of operator and striker were terminated by means so abrupt and so violent that it was not reasonable to suppose there remained any basis of reconciliation as between the principal parties.

Nevertheless, in pursuance of your summons to me to do what I could to act as conciliator and mediator in this State, it had been my intention to go to Bisbee from Globe, but before the situation in the latter place justified my departure every striker and practically every strike sympathizer in the Warren District was deported, through the medium of a large armed force of so-called deputies under the leadership of Sheriff Harry Wheeler of Cochise county, and there remained in the Warren District no one to whom I could appeal for a settlement of existing differences. The workingmen were gone, and it is not to be presumed that the operators, successful and defiant in their stupendous act of usurpation of the functions of the law, or of lawlessness, were in a frame of mind to listen to appeals to their fairness. There remained only the possibility that by contact with the deported

[1] G. W. P. Hunt to WW, Aug. 31 (not Sept. 1), 1917, T telegram (WP, DLC).

men there might be gained, not an explanation or defense of the
grievances which led them to strike—for in view of the act which
occurred the original differences are forgotten—but an insight
into the mental processes and course of reasoning through which
they justify their efforts, during the existing emergency, to secure
economic reforms; into the depth of their realization of the responsibilities resting upon them as citizens of or as men claiming
the protection of a nation at war in a great cause, and of their
sense of loyalty to that nation; into the intimate phases—the
psychology, as it were—of their attitude toward employers of labor
in general; toward mankind in general; toward the vital problems
of mankind which wait upon the outcome of the present struggle; toward the war itself. Such an insight—not profound, to be
sure, but such a partial insight as I might gain, it seemed to me
would likely shed a little light upon the causes of labor's unrest,
and so far as this country is affected, or at least so far as the
metal industry is affected, might possibly aid in the formulation
of a plan for dispelling the discontent and suspicion prevailing,
and for remedying a condition that constitutes so great a menace
to many necessary industries.

Of particular interest was the chance of learning whether or
not the sinister influences of the enemies of this country were at
work among the deported men. Numerous suggestions—in fact,
broad statements—that they were have emanated from those who
defend the deportation.

I spent five days in camp, talking to the refugees, singly and
in groups, receiving their confidences and learning their views,
judiciously questioning them when necessary to ascertain their
real frame of mind. From first to last I talked to as many as a
third of the camp's population. A considerable number of them,
who have for many years resided, in Bisbee, some with, some
without families, I have been personally acquainted with. I feel
that I acquired, with reasonable accuracy, the information I
sought.

There was not to be found the slightest evidence of German
influence or the work of German money, now or heretofore. That
charge, emanating from the defenders of the deportation, I am
satisfied was a hoax pure and simple.

There are a considerable number of I.W.W.'s—more than there
were at the time the deportation occurred, which is a perfectly
logical effect of such a method—probably constituting one-half of
the men in the camp. About one-third are affiliated with labor
unions in no wise connected with the I.W.W., while approximately one-third belong to no labor organization. I found no

line of cleavage, so far as it related to their views on any subject other than the technical one of membership, between the union men and the unaffiliated men. The I.W.W.'s were frequently distinguishable for unfortunate utterances, but more among them are men without convictions than is true of those who carry no red card.

These men—speaking of them by and large—are not unpatriotic. Just now, to be sure, their spirits are not exuberant, and their expressions do not disclose any excesses of patriotism, but nothing appears to be further from their thoughts than feelings or sentiments of disloyalty. They are just ordinary human beings, struggling in their own ways and according to their own lights for a betterment of the conditions which they expect will be their lot through life—hardly so much evidence of an aspiration for better things, in order that all mankind might be the gainer, as one could wish for, but forward-looking men with a rather personal outlook upon affairs. There are few extreme radicals among them. I talked with no one who struck me as being unamenable to reason.

The situation to them seems very simple and practical, and they are wholly unable to comprehend why their strike should be associated with the war, or held by anyone to be an act of unfaithfulness to the government in its emergency. The fact that the war is the direct cause of the enormous profits being realized by copper producers they understand, but the point they hold to is that these tremendous additional profits are being realized, and that they are entitled to a share. Instead of receiving the share which they hold to be just, however, they point out that they are unable to buy, with their present wage, as many of the necessaries of life as they could a few years ago with a wage considerably lower in dollars and cents. They cannot understand why the war should be so one-sided in its effect upon capital and labor, as to justify extraordinary gain to the former while denying to the latter the right of organized action to secure a living wage. They are unable to fathom the depths of that reasoning which upholds the operator who says that rather than divide profits with the miner he will close down his mines while condemning the men, and branding them as traitors, for demanding bare justice, and laying at their door the serious charge of curtailing an industry essential to the successful prosecution of the war. Why, they ask, is the charge of curtailment so limited in its scope that it reaches, and that without trial, but one side to the controversy.

But as I said before, it is not now the merit or justice of their demands upon the companies which interests the men. That is a closed incident, so far as they are personally concerned. The one great passion of their daily life is the hope that their constitutional rights may be restored—that they may be returned, in an honorable way, to the place and the homes from which they were taken in humiliation, without warrant or process of law, by force of arms. And it may be said that, although the time which has elapsed has been very trying to their faith, they still cling to the confidence they have had from the first that the guarantees of the American constitution, as they understand those guarantees, will prove to be realities. It is not that the men are determined to live in the town from which they were expelled. In fact, they appear without exception to realize that under any circumstances life would be made, in one way or another, unendurable for them in Bisbee, and it is altogether likely that even those with established homes would soon move away, rather than endure the persecution which they are confident would be their lot; but they want to return to their homes; to hold their heads up among their fellow men; to enjoy the experience of protection in the rights guaranteed by the fundamental law of the land, at the hands of the government which calls upon them to uphold it in the hour of a great trial.

This is why they remain, with few defections, at the refugee camp. They are at liberty to go—not, indeed, where they will, for certain near-by cities have their doors barred to the refugees—but they want to be taken back to Bisbee, under the government's protection. They are not remaining at Columbus because they want to live off the government, for they are not lazy men, nor men seeking lives of idleness; neither is their present life, in unprotected tents, on a bleak and barren desert, ideal so far as it concerns creature comforts. They want their liberty, and the right to support themselves and their families, but they want that liberty to be restored where it was taken from them. They appreciate the kindness of the government in relieving the physical distress in which their deportation placed them, but while the one great act of justice which absorbs their minds is lacking all other kindnesses will be insufficient.

Mr. President, I cannot escape agreement with these men in those fundamental principles with which we are now chiefly concerned. Whether or not there are individuals among them who are undeserving; whether or not there are some without whom any community were better off, collectively they have suffered a great wrong, but what should be of greater concern, the most sacred principles of human liberty upon which our government is founded, and for the preservation and further establishment of which, throughout the world, we are now preparing to pour out the life-blood of our young men, have been shockingly violated, and I cannot but feel that it would be destructive of the patriotic ardor which burns in every true American's breast if it should be demonstrated that there exists a class of men in this country so powerful, so influential, that they can disregard the laws of society, take the administration of justice into their own hands and within the borders of a State of this Union set up an autocracy, defying both State and Federal authority.

With the many ruthless incidents of the deportation I shall not weary you. Doubtless you are sufficiently familiar with them to give you a fair idea of the details of the outrage. Suffice it to say that these incidents are still occurring, and there has appeared no hand able or willing to adequately check them. I am possessed of the firm conviction—a conviction supported by the scarcely veiled utterances of the mining companies' chief spokesmen—that these incidents are manifestations of a determination entered into by the great copper mine operators of Arizona to crush organized labor in this State, and that, while employing the "camouflage" of patriotic protestations they are in reality using the nation's extremity to serve their selfish ends, and they are going about their enterprise in a manner that would shame the Prussian autocracy.

I desire to renew my offer to assist in any way within my power to relieve the great burdens weighing upon you. Please call upon me whenever there is any way in which I may serve the nation or yourself.

Very sincerely yours,   Geo. W. P. Hunt

TLS (WP, DLC).

From William Phillips, with Enclosure

Dear Mr. President: Washington Sept. 3 [1917].

I am sending you four telegrams of intense interest. The first telegram explains the following three messages.

Two more messages of the same character have been received this morning and are now being deciphered, but as they are very long, I doubt whether I shall be in a position to send them to you until late this afternoon or this evening.

Respectfully yours   William Phillips

ALS (WP, DLC).

E N C L O S U R E

London, August 31, 1917.

7064. Most secret. For the President.

Admiral Hall, director of intelligence department of the Admiralty, has given me a number of documents comprising German cipher messages between German diplomatic officers and the Berlin Foreign Office chiefly relating to the Argentine and definitely implicating the Swedish Government.

In view of the negotiations now going on between Germany and Argentina, the British Government hope that you will immediately publish these telegrams, asking that their origin be kept secret as in the case of the Z telegram.[1] I have the cipher originals and am sending them to you by a trustworthy messenger[2] personally known to you who will deliver them into your hands about September twelfth, fifteenth.

These telegrams also prove that Sweden has continuously used her Legations, and her pouches, and her code, to transmit official information between Berlin and German diplomatic officers.

I am following this with five separate messages numbered one to five, telegraphing the text of the five principal documents.[3]

Page

T telegram (WP, DLC).

[1] The Zimmermann telegram, about which see WHP to WW, Feb. 24, 1917, Vol. 41.

[2] That is, Wiseman.

[3] The five T telegrams, WHP to RL, dated Aug. 31, Sept. 1, and Sept. 2, 1917, are in WP, DLC. The first three (Nos. 7065, 7066, and 7067) included English translations of telegrams of May 19, July 3, and July 9, 1917, from Count Karl-Ludwig von Luxburg, the German Chargé d'Affaires in Buenos Aires, to the German Foreign Office. These messages had been transmitted from the Swedish legation in Buenos Aires as its own official messages to the Swedish Foreign Office. They referred to Argentine ships en route to Europe. Luxburg's telegram of July 9 included these sentences: "As regards Argentine steamers, I recommend either compelling them to turn back, sinking them without leaving any traces, or letting them through. They are all quite small." For the texts of these three messages, which were made public by the State Department on September 8, 1917, see FR-WWS 1917, I, 322-23.

The fourth telegram, No. 7068, transmitted a memorandum prepared by Admiral Hall in August 1917. Hall described the Swedish communication system available to German diplomats in various countries and suggested the possible political benefits to be gained by exposing it. On the other hand, he pointed out, exposure would entail the loss by the Allies of "supremely valuable intelligence."

The fifth telegram, No. 7069, was a translation of an intercepted cipher letter from Heinrich von Eckhardt, the German Minister to Mexico, dated March 8, 1916, to Theobald von Bethmann Hollweg. Eckhardt had recommended that Folke Cronholm, the Swedish Chargé in Mexico City, be secretly awarded a "crown order of the second class" for his many services to the German legation.

From the Diary of Colonel House

[Magnolia, Mass.] September 3, 1917.

Franklin Bouillon, the French radical,[1] came over from Washington to see me concerning his international parliament plan. He wishes the United States to join with the French, British and Italians at their next meeting in November. He has seen the President and did not find him sympathetic.[2] The President told him, so he says, that he was afraid if our members of Congress went over to such a conference, they would come back full of ideas as to the prosecution of the war, which might seriously hamper the plans he has made.

The truth is, the President is something of an autocrat by nature. He does not desire any interference. Even when he knows and feels the necessity of going forward, his nature rebels at any interference. This is not unusual in public men. They know the right path and they can describe it vividly for others to take, but when it comes to using it themselves, it is a different story.

I am not sure Bouillon's plan is a good one, but at the moment, I can see no objection to our considering it. Anything that will promote a better understanding between nations should be encouraged. But the President is set against commissions either going from this country or coming from abroad. He believes in a one man authority. A benevolent dictatorship, under intelligent direction, is undoubtedly the most effective and benign government in the world, but it is dangerous in the extreme and should not be countenanced. It is better to lose something of efficiency in order to retain that which is of more value.

T MS (E. M. House Papers, CtY).

[1] Henri Franklin Bouillon was president of the Radical party, the largest group in the Chamber of Deputies, and chairman of a forthcoming interparliamentary conference. He had come to the United States to invite both houses of Congress to nominate delegates and to join the group, which sought closer cooperation among the Allies. For accounts of his views, see the *New York Times*, June 16 and July 7, 1917. Bouillon addressed the France-America Society in New York on September 6 at a meeting to commemorate the double anniversary of the birth of Lafayette and the Battle of the Marne. *Ibid.*, Sept. 7, 1917. A week later, it was announced that he would be "Minister for Missions Abroad" in a new cabinet to be organized by Paul Painlevé. *Ibid.*, Sept. 15, 1917.

[2] Wilson saw Bouillon on August 30. On his return to Paris to take up his new post, Bouillon told reporters of the great satisfaction which he felt over the results of his visit. The Paris newspapers gave particular prominence to his description of his leave-taking with Wilson. With a final shake of his visitor's hand, said Bouillon, Wilson had said to him: "To the last man, to the last dollar, the whole force of the United States is at your service." *Ibid.*, Sept. 28, 1917.

A Message

[Sept. 4, 1917]

To the Soldiers of the National Army:

You are undertaking a great duty. The heart of the whole country is with you. Everything that you do will be watched with the deepest interest and with the deepest solicitude not only by those who are near and dear to you, but by the whole nation besides. For this great war draws us all together, makes us all comrades and brothers, as all true Americans felt themselves to be when we first made good our national independence. The eyes of all the world will be upon you, because you are in some special sense the soldiers of freedom. Let it be your pride, therefore, to show all men everywhere not only what good soldiers you are, but also what good men you are, keeping yourselves fit and straight in everything and pure and clean through and through. Let us set for ourselves a standard so high that it will be a glory to live up to it and then let us live up to it and add a new laurel to the crown of America. My affectionate confidence goes with you in every battle and every test. God keep and guide you![1]

T MS (C. L. Swem Coll., NjP).
[1] There is a WWsh draft of this message in the C. L. Swem Coll., NjP.

Three Letters to George Creel

My dear Creel: The White House 4 September, 1917

Here are some papers which I wish you would read.[1] If you should have anything to suggest after you have read them, I know I need not tell you that I shall be delighted to cooperate with you.

Cordially and sincerely yours,   Woodrow Wilson

[1] They were undoubtedly the "proposals" which Mott, Root, and McCormick had left with Wilson on August 30. The Editors have not found them, but Mott summarized and commented on them in J. R. Mott to WW, Aug. 30, 1917.

My dear Creel: The White House 4 September, 1917

Here is a suggestion about the rural districts which may add a small element to our consideration of the problem that you and I are so much interested in.[1]

Faithfully yours,   Woodrow Wilson

[1] The enclosure is missing, but the White House staff had summarized it as follows:
"Senator Joe T. Robinson, of Arkansas, encloses a letter from Mr. Hugh D. Hart, of Little Rock. Senator Robinson says Mr. Hart is one of the brainiest

men in Arkansas, a refined gentleman, thoroughly devoted to the cause of the Government and the Administration.

"Mr. Hart, a general insurance agent, states that reports from his men throughout the State show a great deal of dissatisfaction over America's entrance into the war. An expression used very generally is that it is simply a rich man's war. Mr. Hart does not attribute this unsatisfactory feeling to inherent disloyalty but thinks it is due to lack of information as to the cause of the war. The average man in the interior of Arkansas (and this is true of other Southern States and many of the Northern and Western) does not read the New York Times of [or] the Saturday Evening Post and has had no adequate means of learning the vital facts. Mr. Hart is of the opinion that if these people are properly instructed there can be found in America no more enthusiastic or loyal class of citizens. The purpose of his letter is to suggest the advisability of having the Federal Government inaugurate a Nation-wide campaign for the enlightenment of the rural people. He suggests the enlistment as a branch of the National Army of patriotic men and women who are ineligible for military service to devote their time to the holding of meetings throughout the rural districts and to disseminate literature for the purpose of informing them on the vital meaning of this war." White House memorandum, Sept. 4, 1917, T MS (WP, DLC).

My dear Creel: The White House 4 September, 1917

I forgot to suggest to you the other day that Mr. Basil Miles,[1] who went with our Commission to Russia as its Secretary, is in town and I should say would be a capital man to use in making our plans for the enlightenment of Russia. I think it would be worth your while to consult with him and to use him.

Faithfully yours,   Woodrow Wilson

TLS (G. Creel Papers, DLC).
[1] Miles had served from 1905 to 1908 in the American embassies in St. Petersburg and Berlin. After resigning from the diplomatic service, he became superintendent of the foreign mails division of the Post Office Department and then head of the Washington office of the United States Chamber of Commerce. He returned to the embassy in Petrograd in 1916, and, in January 1917, was appointed special assistant to the Ambassador with the rank of minister plenipotentiary. Miles was assigned temporarily to the State Department on October 16, 1917.

To Robert Lansing

My dear Mr. Secretary: The White House 4 September, 1917

I have myself received intimations of the feeling on the part of the men at the head of the news-gathering associations and of some of the leading editors of the country, to which you refer in your letter of September first.[1] It is based upon a complex of misunderstandings (many of which are now being removed) and of jealousies which I can expound to you some time, but the net result of my impressions is that it would be safest not to call them into systematic conference. They are a difficult lot to live with. They do not agree among themselves.

Cordially and sincerely yours,   Woodrow Wilson

TLS (SDR, RG 59, 811.911/26½, DNA).
[1] RL to WW, Sept. 1, 1917, TLS (WP, DLC).

To Harry Augustus Garfield

My dear Garfield: The White House 4 September, 1917

Here is a matter which indirectly touches your own labors[1] and I am sending it to you to form an element in your thought.

Cordially and faithfully yours,   Woodrow Wilson

TLS (H. A. Garfield Papers, DLC).

[1] J. R. Kennamer and J. L. Clemo to WW, Aug. 29, 1917, TLS, enclosing W. B. Wilson, "Memorandum to the Representatives of the Mine Workers of Alabama," T MS, both in WP, DLC. Kennamer and Clemo were president and secretary, respectively, of the United Mine Workers of America, District Twenty, Birmingham, Ala. They informed Wilson that, out of "profound deference to our Government in this crisis" and to "the judgment of Secretary Wilson," they had been constrained to accept the latter's proposals, even though these would postpone indefinitely consideration of wages and hours of labor. The reason given for postponement was that "the Government recently had fixed selling prices F.O.B. mines so low that they could do nothing that would have a tendency to increase the cost of production." The U.M.W. officials understood, however, that the mine operators were appealing to the President for readjustment of the prices, and they accordingly requested that, if an increase was granted, it be large enough to give the miners some relief on wages and working conditions. A miners' convention in Birmingham voted on September 7 to defer action on the proposed agreement but not to strike for the time being. *United Mine Workers Journal*, XXVIII (Sept. 13, 1917), 5.

To J. R. Kennamer

My dear Mr. Kennamer: [The White House] 4 September, 1917

I am in receipt of your very interesting memorandum which you were kind enough to send me under date of August twenty-ninth and you may be sure that it will have my most serious consideration. I hope and believe that I need not assure you that such matters as it presents are constantly in my thoughts and that it is my desire to do everything that it is possible to do in the circumstances to safeguard the interests of labor and to secure to all classes of laborers the benefit they are entitled to.

Cordially and sincerely yours,   Woodrow Wilson

TLS (Letterpress Books, WP, DLC).

To Deborah Knox Livingston[1]

[The White House]

My dear Mrs. Livingston: 4 September, 1917

May I not express through you my very great interest in the equal suffrage campaign in Maine? The pledges of my party are very distinct in favor of granting the suffrage to women by state action and I would like to have the privilege of urging all Democrats to support a cause in which we all believe.

Cordially and sincerely yours,   Woodrow Wilson

TLS (Letterpress Books, WP, DLC).

1 Deborah Knox (Mrs. B. F.) Livingston was an active lecturer before women's groups and a leader in the Women's Christian Temperance Union. As chairman of the Maine State Suffrage Campaign Committee, she had sent a telegram from Bangor requesting an endorsement for woman suffrage for Maine similar to the one which Wilson had given to the New York suffrage campaigners. Deborah K. Livingston to WW, Aug. 30, 1917, T telegram (WP, DLC).

To Robert Bruce Coleman and Thomas Samuel Hawes

[The White House] 4 September, 1917

Absence from Washington delayed my seeing your telegram of August thirty-first. I am at a loss to understand why you request two weeks longer to decide the question of mediation which has been before you since February. Your recent action in disregard of federal jurisdiction in matters of interstate commerce has created an impression which I take it for granted you will wish to remove very promptly and I renew my request that you do so now.   Woodrow Wilson.

T telegram (Letterpress Books, WP, DLC).

To Scott Ferris

My dear Mr. Ferris: [The White House] 4 September, 1917

I thank you sincerely for your letter of September second with its enclosure, which I think you are entirely justified in sending me. It is very hard to handle such things without action of any sort, but I suppose that action would only lend importance to it.

I heartily agree with you that it would be of the greatest service to the country if the members of Congress might soon return to their constituents and give them the benefit of the full light upon the war and its objects and the circumstances which they would be so fully able to give. I hope with all my heart that the business of Congress may make this possible.

With warm regard,

Cordially and sincerely yours,   Woodrow Wilson

TLS (Letterpress Books, WP, DLC).

To Herbert Clark Hoover

My dear Mr. Hoover: [The White House] 4 September, 1917

On the whole, I think that Mr. Carter Harrison of Chicago is rather too much of a politician to be entrusted with such matters as you had in mind when you wrote your letter of August thirty-first.

After you suggested a certain college president to me,[1] I was thinking over the men available of that kind and two men occurred to me whom I think you would find satisfactory in every respect. One is President Meiklejohn of Amherst; the other, Professor Henry B. Fine of Princeton.

I wish I knew someone to suggest for the function you had in mind for Mr. Harrison. On the whole, I think for the present we had better leave the brewing trade alone until the situation develops more clearly.

Cordially and sincerely yours,   Woodrow Wilson

TLS (Letterpress Books, WP, DLC).
[1] Ray Lyman Wilbur, M.D., President of Stanford University who served with Hoover first as a volunteer in the Food Administration and then as chief of its conservation division and assistant to the Food Administrator.

To John Hessin Clarke

The White House
My dear Mr. Justice Clarke: 4 September, 1917

That my reply to the Pope should meet with your unqualified approval affords me very deep gratification.[1] There never was any debate in my mind as to what the reply should be. After all, though the issues of the war look complex, they are in fact simple, and our own experience in attempting to deal with the German Government shows how futile the acceptance of any pledge from it would be.

It gratifies me very much indeed to find the Press of the allied countries accepting the answer with so much heartiness. It would help things mightily if there might be a single united voice in this transcendent matter.

Cordially and sincerely yours,   Woodrow Wilson

TLS (J. H. Clarke Papers, OClW).
[1] Clarke's letter is missing.

To John Joseph Fitzgerald

My dear Fitzgerald: [The White House] 4 September, 1917

I understand that the latest plan of the Republicans is to tack on the espionage committee as a rider to the Deficiency Bill. If they do, of course I cannot sign it, and yet that would lead to the most undesirable delay in the repassage of the measure, and I am writing this line to ask for your active cooperation to prevent any such tactics from succeeding. You have already told me how you feel in this matter and I know I have the acquiescence of your judgment in my opinion, but I thought I would give myself the pleasure of telling you how I am counting on you to out-maneuver these gentlemen who are doing their best to get their hand on the steering apparatus of the Government.

Cordially and sincerely yours,   [Woodrow Wilson]

CCL (WP, DLC).

To Albert Sidney Burleson

My dear Burleson: The White House 4 September, 1917

I must admit that I haven't been able to read all of the en-closed,[1] but you know that I am willing to trust your judgment after I have once called your attention to a suggestion.

Cordially and faithfully yours,   Woodrow Wilson
Espionage Act Creels suggestions rejected.[2]

TLS (A. S. Burleson Papers, DLC).
[1] "Rules of procedure for the exclusion of illegal matter from the mails under the Espionage Act." White House memorandum, Sept. 4, 1917, T MS (WP, DLC).
[2] ASBhw.

To William Phillips

My dear Mr. Phillips: [The White House] 4 September, 1917

Of course, if Mr. Tardieu insists upon a personal interview with me about the matter of the ships, I shall appoint a time, but I wish very much that Mr. Tardieu might be given politely to understand that I have several times conferred with the Chair-man of the Shipping Board about this matter and am convinced that as much progress is being made in determination of our policy as it is possible in the present circumstances to make. I am sure that the desire of the Shipping Board is as genuine as mine to help France in every possible way, but we must not do the thing by bits, we must do it as part of a well-considered policy which takes into consideration the whole difficult question. I do not see anything to be gained by a conference with Mr. Tardieu because I know what he has to say and I have a full memorandum from the Shipping Board as to their point,[1] and I could only return again after such a conference to the Board and repeat the circle.

    Cordially and sincerely yours, Woodrow Wilson

TLS (Letterpress Books, WP, DLC).
 [1] E. N. Hurley to RL, Aug. 29, 1917, CCL (WP, DLC). This letter is printed in Edward N. Hurley, *The Bridge to France* (Philadelphia, 1927), pp. 331-33. It was in effect a reply to Balfour's letter to W. H. Page of August 16, printed as Enclosure II with EMH to WW, Aug. 27, 1917. Hurley records (p. 34) that he took up with Wilson the whole question of ship ownership.

To Robert Goodwyn Rhett

My dear Mr. Rhett: [The White House] 4 September, 1917

 I need not tell you how sincerely I appreciate the desire and the intelligent efforts of the Chamber to render useful patriotic service in connection with the present war, or that the matter with which your letter of September first[1] deals has been very much in my thoughts.

 It has been so much in my thoughts that I have come to some very definite conclusions about it. The work of the Committee on Public Information in the matter of propaganda is being very simply done through existing means and is quietly and rapidly spreading through one channel and another, and my conviction is that it would be a public mistake to create an instrumentality exclusively for the purpose of propaganda. I think the objects of such a body would be misunderstood, and the misunderstanding would be taken advantage of by those who are trying to make mischief. It would be said that the Government was finding itself in desperate need of assistance in order to clear up the thing which they pretend to consider obscure, namely, the objects of the United States in entering the war. Definite propaganda of this sort is generally futile in this country, while the very simple means of explanation and discussion which the Committee on Public Information is using is familiar to everybody and has nothing unusual about it.

 It may be that my judgment in this matter is not the right one, but it has been very maturely arrived at, and I am sure that your colleagues will understand that in stating it so definitely I am not intending to convey the least intimation of anything but very genuine appreciation of the proposal and offer the Chamber has so generously made.

Cordially and sincerely yours,   Woodrow Wilson

TLS (Letterpress Books, WP, DLC).

¹ R. G. Rhett to WW, Sept. 1, 1917, TLS (WP, DLC). Rhett suggested a new agency to supplement the work of the Committee on Public Information. The new agency would have nothing to do with censorship, the *Official Bulletin*, or the public announcement of news as such. Rather, it was "frankly to be a propaganda bureau which would, in our opinion, be justified in war where it could not, for obvious reasons, be tolerated in peace times." Rhett added that the Chamber of Commerce of the United States wished Wilson's views on the plan so that they and he would not work at cross purposes.

From Edward Mandell House

Dear Governor: Magnolia, Mass. September 4, 1917.

In your letter of September 2nd you mention one of the things I have had in mind for a long while, and about which I intended to talk with you upon my first visit to Washington.

I have been trying to do in a quiet and not very efficient way, what you have suggested as wanting me to do systematically and thoroughly. I shall be delighted to undertake the work and will go about it at once.

Frankfurter has been here, and many others interested in the subject, and there will be no difficulty in bringing together a group that will be able to get the data and information you desire. At my suggestion, Buckler has been informing himself on the Balkan situation, but he has been handicapped by working only in London.

What would you think of putting a man on each of the most complicated problems and, if necessary, sending them to Europe?

I believe your reply to the Pope is the most remarkable document ever written, for surely there was never one approved throughout the world so universally and by every shade of political opinion. It is having a[n] enormous effect in Germany, and I do not believe that Government will be able to stem the tide that will soon set in against them.

If the Pope will now have the good sense to say that you have not closed the door to peace, but have shown the way to open it wide, Austria and Catholic Germany will become clamorous for the needed reforms. I have seen this thought as to the Pope's action suggested in the press, and I have myself called it to the attention of several Catholics hoping that it might reach him.

Lord Robert Cecil cables as follows:

"We are being pressed here for a declaration of sympathy with the Zionist movement, and I should be very grateful if you felt able to ascertain unofficially if the President favors such a declaration.

We greatly admire the Note and it has been received with much satisfaction by our Press. I am very grateful for the advice you have given. Both Balfour and I appreciate in the highest degree your kindness in allowing us to trouble you with these matters."

Wiseman is sailing today and is bringing with him data and information regarding the Polish question. They hope no decision of policy by the U. S. Government will be announced until this information arrives.

We are breaking up here on the 14th.

Affectionately yours,   E. M. House

TLS (WP, DLC).

From Newton Diehl Baker

Dear Mr. President: Washington. Sept. 4, 1917.

I have your letter of Sept. 1st, enclosing a letter from Mr. Shouse, with regard to the effect of the draft upon agricultural production. Of course, Mr. Shouse is right in believing that, even with the postponed call to agriculturalists, there will be some disturbance of agricultural production, but I am afraid he has set his eye on that and closed it to every sort of importunity which comes to us in favor of such classes as mine workers, transportation workers, millers, bread bakers and so on. I am clear that it would be impossible by any sort of regulation now made to bring about a wise adjustment of the draft burden upon the several callings and industries. After the drafted men are actually called into the field, we shall know from the appeals perfected from the District Boards to you as President just where the worst difficulties are, and, at least, will have the data for a better solution than could now be worked out by forecast.

Respectfully yours,   Newton D. Baker

TLS (WP, DLC).

From Thomas Staples Martin

Dear Mr. President: Washington, D. C. September 4, 1917.

I have just this moment received your letter. I am in thorough accord with the views you express about the unwisdom of having a legislative committee charged with any duty in connection with the expenditure of the moneys appropriated by Congress. I am very glad indeed to have this statement from you, as it will strengthen my hands in the earnest efforts I will make to prevent the enactment of any law providing for such a committee.

Very sincerely yours,   Thomas S. Martin

TLS (WP, DLC).

From Ollie Murray James

My dear Mr. President: Washington, D. C. September 4, 1917

I received your letter this morning, expressing your opposition to the creation of a war committee, and you may rest assured that I shall do all I possibly can against it as I have done in the past. I think no greater folly could be indulged in, and I shall be pleased to bring to the attention of my colleagues your intense opposition to this action.

Hope you will call on me at any time I can be of service.

With kind regards,   Your friend,   Ollie M James

TLS (WP, DLC).

Two Letters from Thomas Watt Gregory

Personal and Confidential

Dear Mr. President: Washington, D. C. September 4, 1917.

I had expected to see you at Cabinet meeting today and tell you that I had arranged to leave Washington tonight to be gone about three weeks. As there is no Cabinet meeting, I write you this note.

Some days ago Dr. Grayson advised me to take as much as three weeks or a month in the woods, and I am convinced that it is wise to follow his advice. He said that he had mentioned the matter to you and that you had approved. Under these circumstances, I feel justified in leaving without speaking to you personally about it.

The Solicitor General[1] will return on the seventh and be here from then until I get back. In the meanwhile, Mr. Todd[2] will be Acting Attorney General, and you will find both of them exceptionally reliable and satisfactory.

I feel a bit mean about leaving at this time, but believe that doing so will be safer in the long run.

Faithfully yours,   T. W. Gregory

[1] That is, John William Davis.
[2] That is, George Carroll Todd.

Dear Mr. President: Washington, D. C. September 4, 1917.

I herewith present for your consideration copies of two telegrams received today from United States District Attorney Anderson at Boston.[1]

I intended to bring the matter up at Cabinet meeting today, but as none is to be held and as I am leaving Washington tonight to be gone two or three weeks, I feel that the situation referred to by Mr. Anderson should be called to your attention for such action as you think proper.

I am also sending copies of these telegrams to the Secretary of War and the Secretary of Labor.

Faithfully yours,   T. W. Gregory

TLS (WP, DLC).
[1] G. W. Anderson to TWG, Sept. 4, 1917, two TC telegrams (WP, DLC). Both telegrams dealt with a recently begun strike of mechanics and repairmen of the Boston & Maine Railroad, which threatened to disrupt the transportation of troops and war supplies. Anderson urged that some means be found to get the men back to work pending a review of the case either by a federal court or by a federally appointed fact finder.

From John Fox

My dear Mr. President: New York September 4th, 1917.

We are deeply indebted to you for your note of September first.

Before publishing it I am reluctantly obliged to trouble you for an interpretation. Your letter reads "to cover the expense of supplying the men in the National Army with Bibles." Does this mean to exclude the Navy? I hardly suppose so. Does it mean to restrict the supply of Scriptures to any part of the Army as distinguished from the whole? We understand it to mean the Army in the inclusive sense of the Army and Navy, including all men whether in the National Guard, the drafted men, or the regular Army.

If this is what is meant would it be proper for us to change the wording so as to say "supplying the Army and Navy with Bibles"?[1]

Please pardon this additional burden.

I have the honor to be,

Very sincerely yours,   [John Fox]

TL (WP, DLC).
[1] "Please write to Doctor Fox that his interpretation of my letter is right and that I hope he will alter the language so that it will be clear." WW to JPT, c. Sept. 5, 1917, TL (WP, DLC).

Sir Cecil Arthur Spring Rice to the Foreign Office

Washington 4 Sept. 1913 [1917]

2558 French Ambassador had audience with President and pointed out dangers likely to result from certain expressions in his answer to Pope. President said that regard must be paid to public opinion here which was in some respects lukewarm. French Ambassador was not consulted or informed with regard to President's answer and is struck by very independent attitude assumed by President throughout.

Recent elections have turned badly for democratic party[1] and President may be somewhat alarmed at accusations made against him for having been elected on a peace platform and then repudiating it. ⟨Best general opinion seems to be that he is not likely to change his policy.⟩ French Ambr. is impressed by danger of Germany assuming a democratic mask and making apparently moderate peace offers which might cause revulsion of public feeling here. The President's military measures show that he is determined on action of a serious character and he must have anticipated public reception of his last note in Germany. The general impression is that he means business but no doubt he would be much affected by a serious change in public opinion.

Hw telegram (FO 115/2264, p. 57, PRO).

[1] Spring Rice probably had in mind the election on July 10 of John Miller Baer, the candidate of the Nonpartisan League, to the House of Representatives to replace Henry Thomas Helgeson, Republican of North Dakota, who had died on April 10. Although Baer had urged the prosecution of the war with all possible vigor and had endorsed the draft, his election was widely viewed as a victory for the socialist and antiwar elements. Robert L. Morlan, *Political Prairie Fire: The Nonpartisan League, 1915-1922* (Minneapolis, 1955), pp. 130-33. Six other men had been elected to fill vacancies since the beginning of the Sixty-fifth Congress; in five cases a member of the same party as the previous incumbent had been chosen; in the sixth, in Pennsylvania, Earl Hanley Beshlin, a Democrat, had succeeded a Republican.

To Jouett Shouse

My dear Mr. Shouse: The White House 5 September, 1917

I am sure that you will read the enclosed copy of a letter I have just received from the Secretary of War[1] with appreciation of its frankness and of the cogency of the arguments which it urges.

Cordially and faithfully yours,   Woodrow Wilson

TLS (J. Shouse Papers, KyU).
[1] NDB to WW, Sept. 4, 1917.

To Thomas Staples Martin

My dear Senator: [The White House] 5 September, 1917

It is cheering and delightful to get such a reply as yours of yesterday and I am sincerely your debtor for it.

Cordially and faithfully yours,   Woodrow Wilson

TLS (Letterpress Books, WP, DLC).

To Ollie Murray James

My dear Senator: [The White House] 5 September, 1917

Thank you warmly for your note of yesterday which I deeply appreciate.   Faithfully yours,   Woodrow Wilson

TLS (Letterpress Books, WP, DLC).

To Azel Washburn Hazen

My dear Friend: [The White House] 5 September, 1917

Your letter of September first[1] has made my heart very full. In these days of excessive strain the voice of a valued friend not only makes the heart beat quicker but also steadies it and makes it more fit for service. I thank you with all my heart and beg to send Mrs. Hazen also my warmest messages of friendship.

Cordially and faithfully yours,   Woodrow Wilson

TLS (Letterpress Books, WP, DLC).
[1] It is missing.

From Frank Irving Cobb

Dear Mr. President: New York. September 5, 1917.

This comes from Victor Ridder, of the Staats-Zeitung, who may or may not be acting in good faith.

Certain influential German-Americans in New York, who profess to believe that Germany is beaten in the war and that the German people themselves would realize it if they knew what the United States is actually doing and what it intends to do, think that an enormous effect would be produced in Germany if the facts could be presented directly to the leaders of German liberalism. They have a plan to send a committee to Copenhagen and from there get in touch with men like Scheidemann and Harden and present the case. They say this could be done if the United

States Government permitted them to go without official knowledge or responsibility for their undertaking and they say that it would have an immediate influence in furthering peace.

Whether this is a new manifestation of the Stockholm Conference, I do not know; but they are very anxious to get their idea to you. They may or may not be sincere. Personally, I think they realize that Germany is at the end of her rope. If you care to consider the matter at all, I could easily find out what kind of a committee they propose to send to Copenhagen. The names and records could be investigated and that might throw light on the good faith of the undertaking. In supping with this particular devil, a very long spoon is necessary and, of course, neither you nor Secretary Lansing could have any official knowledge of the purposes of such a committee. At best, its members could be allowed to go only as other American citizens are allowed to go abroad, on personal business. It may be merely another instance of Greeks bearing gifts, but if you would like a more thorough investigation made of the matter, we can easily do it for you.

There is no doubt that your reply to the Vatican has made a most extraordinary impression upon the minds of the German-Americans. They see in it the only ray of hope for the German people. My own guess is that, inasmuch as all German minds are more or less alike, it is bound to have the same effect over there as here, except as the reaction may be delayed by the obstacles interposed by the German Government.

With sincere regards,   As ever yours, Frank I. Cobb.

TLS (WP, DLC).

From John Sharp Williams

My dear Mr. President: [Washington] Sept. 5, 1917.

I have yours written on the "Mayflower" under date of Sept. 1st. I agree with you perfectly about the so-called "Committee to supervise expenditures," which would soon become a "committee upon the conduct of the war." When a committee came to supervising expenditures, it might agree that Pershing was a failure and that money devoted to paying him was unwisely spent, and insist that somebody else be substituted; or that some Admiral couldn't command a fleet, and they would, therefore, advise Congress that he be not paid. There is no telling where the thing would end.

There never was a war conducted in the world that was conducted with any sense, by a parliamentary Congressional committee. The "Long Parliament" tried it. Until Cromwell and Iredell and a few other real soldiers, who carried on war without paying much attention to the "Long Parliament,"—and finally abolished the Long Parliament itself,—came into power, the "Long Parliament" had been most ineffectual, its committee had been stupidly intermeddling all the time, and with bad results notwithstanding the infinitely less resources of the King.

I shall undoubtedly use what influence I possess in defeating any such folly. War, above all things, is the one thing which most requires undivided supreme authority. Even the executive ought not to interfere with the actual campaigns, at the front, except by noting the efficiency and inefficiency of the men vested with the responsibility and, in case of a conclusion that one of them was inefficient, ruthlessly removing him, no matter who he was, and putting somebody else in his place, believed to be efficient. Even that could be carried too far, as Abraham Lincoln's mistakes early in the War Between the States abundantly prove. The strength of the Confederacy consisted very largely in the fact that Jefferson Davis would stand by men like Albert Sidney Johnston and Robt. E. Lee, notwithstanding the fact that both were harshly criticised at the beginning,—so harshly criticised that Albert Sidney Johnston, early in the war not long before his death, suggested to Mr. Davis that perhaps he had better be removed, and Lee, later, after Gettysburg, sent his resignation in. Davis superbly refused to act upon either suggestion.

Even if we had a Republican President in,—unless I regarded him as a fool and unless I regarded him as absolutely incompetent; or unless I doubted his earnestness in the war,—I would not hear for a moment to anything like Congressional interference with what ought to be executive functions. Possessing, as I do, the utmost confidence in your earnestness, and your intelligence, I will, of course, still more bitterly oppose that sort of thing now.

I am, with every expression of regard,
                    Very truly yours,   John Sharp Williams

TLS (WP, DLC).

From William Phillips

My dear Mr. President: Washington September 5 ,1917.

I had a talk this morning with Mr. Gillet,[1] who is one of Mr. Tardieu's right-hand men, and explained fully your anxiety to help France in every possible way, that you were in close touch with the Shipping Board on the subject of Mr. Tardieu's memorandum, and that I felt that there was nothing to be gained at the present moment by a further conference between you and Mr. Tardieu. I am sure that Mr. Tardieu will fully understand your position and will not urge for an interview at this time.[2]

Mr. Gillet said that their real anxiety was for a decision on our part; that if there was a decision in the negative it would at least put them in a position to proceed on their own account. He expressed Mr. Tardieu's fear that there would be no decision one way or the other, and that this would give rise to a very embarrassing position for France in view of the extreme urgency for additional shipping.

With assurances of respect, etc., I am, my dear Mr. President,
Faithfully yours,   William Phillips

TLS (WP, DLC).
[1] He cannot be further identified. However, according to André Kaspi, the preeminent authority on Franco-American relations during the First World War, Gillet was not "one of Mr. Tardieu's right-hand men." A. Kaspi to the Editor, Oct. 10, 1981.
[2] Tardieu did not insist upon having the interview.

From the Diary of Colonel House

September 5, 1917.

The Attorney General stopped off on his way to Maine and spent the day. He had but little of interest to tell. I asked him when the Cabinet knew about the President's reply to the Pope. He said not until the afternoon of the 28th at the Cabinet meeting. The note had already been coded and cabled abroad and had been given to the foreign ambassadors. Gregory said there was no dissention concerning it. It was too late to make any changes since it had already been put out. The first proof of the message had in it the word "childish," but after receiving my second letter on the subject, the President evidently called in the first issue and eliminated that word. Gordon tells me that the British Ambassador told him that Jusserand "jumped the bars" when he first read it before the elimination of "childish" was made, and was happy at the change.

From Newton Diehl Baker, with Enclosure

Dear Mr. President: Washington. September 6, 1917.

I inclose a telegram which came to me today from Herbert S. Bigelow, who is doubtless known to you as a single tax exponent and reformer of radical tendencies. I have answered his telegram[1] and you need give it no attention, but I thought you would be interested in the statement inclosed in red[2] as showing the effect of the answer to the Pope on at least one very outspoken and prominent leader of radical opinion.

Respectfully,   Newton D. Baker

TLS (WP, DLC).
    [1] Baker was a friend and admirer of Bigelow. He urged Bigelow to "stress the democratic and unselfish reason for the American entry into the war." Daniel R. Beaver, *Newton D. Baker and the American War Effort, 1917-1919* (Lincoln, Neb., 1966), p. 236.
    [2] The sentence beginning "I believe that President Wilsons answer . . . " to the end of the telegram.

E N C L O S U R E

Chicago, Sep. 5, 1917

I am invited to speak in Milwaukee Friday night under auspices of Socialist party   In view of Government action at National Socialists Headquarters in Chicago today[1] I request information as to the Governments intention with reference to the Milwaukee meeting   I do not approve of the so called majority report of the Socialist party on the war. I believe that President Wilsons answer to the Pope satisfies american public opinion and that the war should be prosecuted on that basis but I think that most socialists are misunderstood and that the suppression of their press and meetings prevents that reconciliation to the war program which would rapidly develope if they were free to talk their hearts out about it   I ask for them as well for myself the right to be judged after we speak and not before   If however the Government is going to interfere with the Milwaukee meeting I request notification of it as I do not wish to be put in the position of conflict with the Government   Will you kindly address a reply tomorrow if possible to the Grand Pacific Hotel Chicago.   Herbert S. Bigelow.

T telegram (WP, DLC).
    [1] The Department of Justice, on September 5, carried out its carefully coordinated series of raids, not only on the headquarters of the I.W.W. throughout the United States, but also on the national headquarters of the Socialist party in Chicago.

From John Joseph Fitzgerald

My dear Mr. President: Washington, D. C., September 6, 1917.

Upon my return I find your favor of the fourth instant relative to the proposal to provide for a special joint committee on expenditures in the Deficiency Bill. As I informed you in our recent conversation the theory of the proposed committee is indefensible and I shall do everything in my power to prevent its establishment.

In the consideration of the Deficiency Bill I intend to discuss the question and to contrast the advantages of our system with the British system which is so much misunderstood. A recent discussion in the House of Commons is highly illuminating on this subject.

Permit me to assure you that no such provision will be incorporated in any bill which is under my control and I shall do my best to prevent the enactment of any law which provides for the creation of such a committee.

Very sincerely yours,   John J. Fitzgerald

TLS (WP, DLC).

From Mary Bird Whiteway

Dear President Wilson,   Liverpool, 6th Septr. 1917.

So many letters have been lost that I am writing again to thank you very much for the handsome pair of binoculars which you sent to be presented to my husband, William Keen Whiteway, for the part he took in saving the lives of the crew of the Alexander Anderson, at sea, on 1st October, 1916, when he was second officer of the S.S. "Sagamore"; he would have been so proud of the gift had he been here to receive it and would have written to thank you himself.

It is just six months since the "Sagamore" was torpedoed, since which time my husband has been missing, only two out of the crew of 60 have returned home sound and whole, five more were saved but they have all lost their feet through gangrene and then amputation; their sufferings were terrible, they were 10 days in the ship's little boat, and 10 died of exposure while 7 were picked up when the boat was found: they had been five days without water and the weather was dreadful, with 25° of frost, on the 3rd March, when they were torpedoed.

We are so thankful that you have joined the Allies, it will bring the War to a successful ending so much more quickly and so save many lives.

To think that people who call themselves Christians should have caused such world wide misery is dreadful to comtemplate: we must all make it impossible for such a thing ever to be repeated, as soon as the war is ended, or Germany will begin again to prepare for another war as soon as she thinks no one is watching her—the self-righteous and arrogant Germans will be most difficult to convict of sin.

How can they say they did not cause this war? They had a railway timetable printed & distributed which was to be substituted for the existing one 48 hours after war was declared; I know that for a positive fact!

This generation is willingly laying down its lives but it is for us to see that it shall never happen to a future generation.

My other letters written to America at the time I wrote to you must have been lost therefore,[1] for fear you should not have received my letter, I am writing again.

We have seen numbers of American soldiers in our streets on their way to the Front & it makes our hearts ache for them & those they have left at home in anxiety for their safety, the suspense is dreadful. I believe every English family is bereaved.

With kind regards hoping Germany will soon have to give in,
          Yours faithfully,   Mary Bird Whiteway.

ALS (WP, DLC).
    [1] Her earlier letter is missing.

To Herbert Clark Hoover

My dear Mr. Hoover: The White House 7 September, 1917

I have been very much interested in your letter of September fourth about the hog supply in the United States.[1] I was discussing the matter this afternoon with the Secretary of Agriculture, since it so directly affects the matter of production, and found his observations and suggestions so interesting that I am going to take the liberty of asking you if you will not avail yourself of an early opportunity to see him and match your views with his in this important matter.

          Sincerely yours,   Woodrow Wilson

TLS (H. C. Hoover Papers, HPL).
    [1] H. C. Hoover to WW, Sept. 4, 1917, TLS (WP, DLC). Hoover proposed a plan to increase the production of hogs by organizing the producers and packers. His letter is printed in Francis William O'Brien, ed., *The Hoover-Wilson Wartime Correspondence, September 24, 1914 to November 11, 1918* (Ames, Ia., 1974), pp. 77-79.

To John Joseph Fitzgerald

My dear Fitzgerald: [The White House] 7 September, 1917

I deeply appreciate your letter of yesterday and thank you for it very warmly. It is fine to have such support.

Faithfully yours,   Woodrow Wilson

TLS (Letterpress Books, WP, DLC).

From Newton Diehl Baker, with Enclosure

Dear Mr. President: Washington. September 7, 1917.

I said to you in a note some days ago that I had suggested to Secretary Wilson that Felix Frankfurter act as secretary of the proposed board to examine into labor conditions throughout the troubled sections of the West and South-west. Frankfurter, who is a very thoroughgoing and thoughtful fellow, has handed me the inclosed memorandum which I submit for your information.

Respectfully yours,   Newton D. Baker

TLS (WP, DLC).

E N C L O S U R E

Washington. September 4, 1917.

MEMORANDUM for the Secretary of War:

SUBJECT: Plan for dealing with so-called I.W.W. strikes and western labor troubles.

In order to adopt any plan of meeting and allaying the disorders and difficulties in the western labor field certain general facts and tendencies must be kept in mind:

1. The number of I.W.W.'s is probably very small and a great mistake may result from the popular confusion of all labor movements, not sanctioned by the A. F. of L., with the I.W.W. The identification of all recalcitrant labor with the I.W.W. is encouraged by employers and employers' associations who are opposed to labor unions in general, but this identification is all too frequently acted upon by the western authorities, both civil and military.

2. Scientific students of the labor movement are in agreement that the number of the radicals in the labor movement has grown steadily in the last fifteen years. These radicals have generally been socialists whether inside or outside the A. F. of L. The A. F. of L. has taken a definite stand against this group and voted

down, in the A. F. of L. convention, all measures they propose. For example, such legislation as the eight-hour day, minimum wage, old age pension, etc., have been largely opposed by the present leadership of the A. F. of L. on the theory that such benefits must be secured by organization rather than by legislation. The radical group believes in both methods.

3. The workers in the industries fundamentally important in the prosecution of the war, for example, the steel mills, stockyards, mines, needle trades, etc., are largely non-English speaking. Many of the leaders who are able and responsible are socialists dissatisfied with the prevailing policy of the A. F. of L. They are even more opposed to the I.W.W. recognizing as they do that violent movements will injure the cause of the workers. But both leaders and workers are alarmed by the fact that, apparently, the Government and the more enlightened employers seem to be compelling them to choose between the I.W.W. and the A. F. of L.

4. Unfortunately the A. F. of L. has shown itself thus far unable to organize and direct the policy of the workers, these non-English speaking workers, in the industries affected. It is immaterial to go into the causes for this, the fact is incontestable.

In the light of the foregoing background the needs of the situation become clear:

1. It is necessary to separate the constructive and responsible radicals from the I.W.W. and to endeavor to deal with them. Specifically we must sift the I.W.W. from unorganized immigrant labor, from the radical wing of the A. F. of L. who are opposing Mr. Gompers' leadership, from labor that is organized but not associated with the A. F. of L., such as the Amalgamated Clothing Workers of America, whose organization numbers about 80,000 members.

2. In all this the devoted, patriotic services of Mr. Gompers are not minimized. His leadership is recognized as indispensable. But it will be fatal to the handling of the labor situation to assume that Mr. Gompers controls all labor or even all organized labor with which the Government should deal, or to assume that all those who are not for Mr. Gompers are for the I.W.W. On the contrary, the Government must distinguish between radicalism in the labor movement and the destructive policies of the I.W.W. The Government in the United States, as the governments in England and France have done, must in some way seek to utilize the leaders of such movements and not repress them or drive their following into methods of violence.

3. It is to be remembered that these leaders, in general, sup-

ported Mr. Wilson in the last campaign because of the Administration's legislative labor policy, and the general friendliness towards just industrial aspirations. These leaders, without question, can be enlisted in the effective support of the Administration, but they are in danger of being permanently alienated, and surely their following will be, if some recognition of their view-point is not sought. It will be found that their view-point can be fairly met if the right currents of good-will are generated between the Administration and them.

4. To this end a more intimate knowledge of the factors of the western field and a more discriminating analysis of the various forces at work are indispensable. For that object a public commission would be the least likely instrument. Such public commission would be too much identified with the authorities and the employing interests which have thus far shown only negative hostility towards this radical but non-I.W.W. movement. It would be an ineffective agency of inquiry. More than that, it would intensify the difficulties by dignifying the violent I.W.W. elements, it would be perverted as capital for them, no matter how skillfully it was managed. It could not escape being regarded as the Administration's recognition of the I.W.W. movement, and thus serve as an intensification of the line of cleavage between the Government and Western labor radicalism.

5. The objection is to publicity, at present; the need is for a quiet inquiry, such as was pursued in the case of the Mesaba unrest last Spring.[1] What is needed now is a quiet, authoritative gathering of knowledge and the opening of a relation of confidence between the administration and responsible leaders in the Western labor world. The education of state authorities and of employers in a wiser tolerance towards labor will come much better after the foundation of knowledge is thus laid.

Recommendations:

In view of the foregoing it is suggested that some one, either in behalf of the President or the War Department be sent out quietly:

(a) To determine the extent of the I.W.W. in the discontented groups;

(b) To seek out responsible leaders who can be counted on for constructive work; and

(c) To help these leaders in the formulation of reasonable plans which could be submitted to some organ of the administration here, or to an official commission which might later deal with the situation publicly.

In carrying out this recommendation experienced and responsible men who are trusted by the radicals, who are out of the A. F. of L. and yet thoroughly loyal to the Administration would be of great assistance. Such a man, for instance, is Sidney Hillman, of the A. C. W. of A.,[2] whose organization is not recognized by the A. F. of L., but who is one of the leading forces in responsible labor movements. The mere enlistment of such a man would go a long way towards remedying the situation. Of course, in an inquiry such as herein suggested, the help of the A. F. of L. would be brought into cooperation.

The foregoing views have the support of Mr. Justice Brandeis and several of the most disinterested students of the labor movement now in the Government service.   F.F.

TI MS (N. D. Baker Papers, DLC).
   [1] Mesaba is a small village at the eastern end of the Mesabi Range in St. Louis County, Minnesota. Frankfurter referred to a strike of iron-ore miners and surface workers which began on June 3, 1916, chiefly over the issues of wages and the contract-labor system prevalent in the Mesabi region. By the end of June, two thirds of the work force of the iron region, some 10,000 men in all, were estimated to be on strike. The I.W.W. seems not to have been involved at first, but its organizers soon appeared and set up a union local on the range. The mining companies refused to negotiate and used every means, including the employment of private armed police forces, to break the strike. The strikers and local public officials appealed in July to William B. Wilson for federal mediation. Wilson sent Hywel Davies and W. R. Fairley on July 21 to investigate the situation and to attempt to arrange mediation. The employers still refused to negotiate, but Davies and Fairley made a thorough report. The miners called off their strike on September 17. No face-to-face negotiations had taken place, but many of the mining companies did increase wages and improve working conditions in the wake of the strike. Dubofsky, *We Shall Be All*, pp. 319-31.
   [2] Hillman was president of the Amalgamated Clothing Workers of America.

From Edward Mandell House

Dear Governor: Magnolia, Massachusetts. September 7, 1917.

I hope you will think well to give the United Press the new expose which has just come through.[1] They have a much better service to South America than the Associated Press, and also serve as many papers in the United States. The revelations are of such a character that every paper will carry them. I mention this merely because the A.P. were given the Zimmermann note and several other coups, although they have never been over friendly to your Administration.

Wiseman should arrive with the proofs on Wednesday or Thursday of next week.

And this reminds me that in one of Cecil's cables he said: "It would be hard to overestimate the value of Wiseman's services."

I understand that General Scott will retire this month and that General Sharp,[2] Quartermaster General, will also retire soon. The importance of filling these two places with the best possible material cannot be overestimated. If a scandal comes in the Army, it always develops in the Quartermaster's Department, and I have been told that there were indications of the present organization breaking down in certain directions. It is an enormous undertaking and calls for the best people the country affords.

Have you made up your mind regarding what answer you will make to Cecil concerning the Zionist Movement? It seems to me that there are many dangers lurking in it, and if I were the British I would be chary about going too definitely into that question.   Affectionately yours,   E. M. House

TLS (WP, DLC).
   ¹ See n. 3 to WHP to WW, Aug. 31, 1917, printed as an Enclosure with W. Phillips to WW, Sept. 3, 1917. Lansing gave copies of the telegrams to the press on September 8. See, e.g., the *New York Times*, Sept. 9, 1917.
   ² Maj. Gen. Henry Granville Sharpe, Quartermaster General since 1916.

From Matthew Hale

Dear Mr. President: Boston September 7, 1917.

In accordance with my promise of Wednesday,¹ I am sending you Ickes' name and address: Harold L. Ickes,² 1916 Harris Trust Building, Chicago, Illinois.

Since talking with you I find that he has accepted the position of Chairman of the Executive Committee of the State Council of Defense for Illinois. I do not think he is entirely satisfied with the work, but he feels so anxious to get in and help somewhere that he does not want to wait until something more satisfactory turns up. His starting in on this position would give you a very opportune chance of asking him to come on for a short talk in regard to the situation in Illinois in connection with the war sentiment. The whole idea of his Illinois work, to quote his own language, is as follows:

   "My idea is to start a state wide organization and campaign along patriotic lines with a view to educating the people on the war issue and bringing them, if possible, to a more enthusiastic support of the war."

You will therefore see that he is in full sympathy with your program. I think that a letter from you and a short talk with him, would have a really great effect, not only on him, but on the large following that he has among Progressive Republicans in Illinois. I certainly hope that you will write to him.

In regard to the other matter of which I spoke to you, namely, the existence among certain liberals of a feeling that the administration has shown a tendency to interfere with free speech, free assembly, and a free press, I have been thinking the situation over very seriously since seeing you. Your position as outlined to me is so clear and so convincing that I do hope from the bottom of my heart that you will make an opportunity between now and our liberal conference the first of October to take the people of the country into your confidence and to outline in more detail your general position in regard to these fundamental principles upon which we are all really agreed. It seems to me that such an utterance on your part would not only have the effect of restoring the confidence of those liberals who are really anxious to support you, but would also have the effect of lessening the danger of an indignant majority abusing the rights of the minority by creating riots or otherwise interfering with their constitutional rights.

The advantages from such a course would, in my opinion, more than offset any danger there might be in the public utterances of these pacifists, in fact I think these pacifists really become dangerous in proportion as they are suppressed and compelled to use secret methods. I do not think that resolutions passed by a few scattered pacifists' assemblies (particularly where the use of German money can be shown) can have any really serious effect upon public opinion in Russia. Would not resolutions like those passed by the recent Labor Alliance in Minneapolis[3] more than offset the others?

Of course I appreciate the strength of what you said, that you "could not just bat balls up into the air." I do agree with you fully that you have got to have a proper occasion for making this kind of a statement, but I also feel that such an occasion will surely arise between now and October 1st and I sincerely hope that you will see your way clear toward doing this.

It is needless, perhaps, to say that if it were not for my firm conviction that you feel about all these things just as strongly if not more strongly than I do, I should not be bothering you with any suggestions as to how to overcome this opposition which I am perfectly sure exists and which I am afraid is growing, among people who ought normally to be your strongest advocates and supporters.

                        Very sincerely yours,   Matthew Hale

TLS (WP, DLC).
  [1] Hale saw Wilson at the White House on September 5.
  [2] Harold LeClair Ickes, lawyer and political reformer of Chicago, a leader of the Progressive party in Illinois.
  [3] The convention of the American Alliance for Labor and Democracy met in Minneapolis on September 5-7. The delegates, on September 6, adopted resolutions which affirmed their support for the war aims set forth by Wilson in his addresses of January 22, April 2, and June 14, 1917, and in his notes to the Russian Provisional Government of May 26 and to the Pope of August 27. The resolutions summarized the main points which Wilson had made on each of

these occasions and declared that, collectively, they set forth a clear program of war aims which the A.A.L.D. could and did wholeheartedly support. The resolutions are printed in *Cong. Record*, 65th Cong., 1st sess., pp. 6737-38. See also Grubbs, *The Struggle for Labor Loyalty*, pp. 66-69.

From Dudley Field Malone

Dear Mr. President: New York September 7, 1917.

Last autumn, as the representative of your Administration, I went into the Woman Suffrage States to urge your reelection. The most difficult argument to meet among the seven million women voters was the failure of the Democratic Party, throughout four years of power, to pass the Federal Suffrage Amendment looking toward the enfranchisement of all the women of the country. Throughout those States, and particularly in California, which ultimately decided the election by the votes of women, the women voters were urged to support you even though Judge Hughes had already declared for the Federal Suffrage Amendment, because you and your Party, through liberal leadership, were more likely nationally to enfranchise the rest of the women of the country than were your opponents. And if the women of the West voted to reelect you, I promised them I would spend all my energy, at any sacrifice to myself, to get the present Democratic Administration to pass the Federal Suffrage Amendment. But the present policy of the Administration, in permitting splendid American women to be sent to jail in Washington, not for carrying offensive banners nor for picketing, but on the technical charge of obstructing traffic, is a denial even of their constitutional right to petition for, and demand the passage of the Federal Suffrage Amendment. It therefore now becomes my profound obligation actively to keep my promise to the women of the West.

In more than twenty States it is a practical impossibility to amend the State Constitutions; so the women of those States can only be enfranchised by the passage of the Federal Suffrage Amendment. Since England and Russia in the midst of the great war have assured the national enfranchisement of their women, should we not be jealous to maintain our democratic leadership in the world by the speedy national enfranchisement of American women? To me, Mr. President, as I urged upon you in Washington two months ago, this is not only a measure of justice and Democracy, it is also an urgent war measure. The women of the nation are, and always will be, loyal to the country, and the passage of the Suffrage Amendment is only the first step towards their national emancipation. But unless the Gov-

ernment takes at least this first step towards their enfranchisement, how can the Government ask millions of American women
educated in our schools and colleges, and millions of American
women in our homes, or toiling for economic independence in
every line of industry, to give up by conscription their men and
happiness to a war for Democracy in Europe, while these women
citizens are denied the right to vote on the policies of the Government which demands of them such sacrifice? For this reason,
many of your most ardent friends and supporters feel that the
passage of the Federal Suffrage Amendment is a war measure
which could appropriately be urged by you at this session of
Congress. It is true that this Amendment would have to come
from Congress, but the present Congress shows no earnest desire
to enact this legislation for the simple reason that you, as the
leader of the Party in power, have not yet suggested it. For the
whole country gladly acknowledges, Mr. President, that no vital
piece of legislation has come through Congress these five years
except by your extraordinary and brilliant leadership. And millions of men and women to-day hope that you will give the Federal Suffrage Amendment to the women of the country by the
valor of your leadership now. It will hearten the mothers of the
nation, eliminate a just grievance, and turn the devoted energies of brilliant women to a more hearty support of the Government in this crisis.

As you well know, in dozens of speeches in many States I
have advocated your policies and the war: I was the first man
of your Administration, nearly five years ago, publicly to advocate preparedness, and helped to found the first Plattsburg
Training Camp. And if, with our troops mobilizing in France,
you give American women this measure for their political freedom, they will support with greater enthusiasm your hope and
the hope of America for world freedom.

I have not approved all the methods recently adopted by
women in the pursuit of their political liberty; yet Mr. President,
the Committee on Suffrage of the United States Senate was
formed in 1883 when I was one year old; this same Federal
Suffrage Amendment was first introduced in Congress in 1878;
brave women like Susan B. Anthony were petitioning Congress
for the suffrage before the Civil War, and at the time of the
Civil War men like William Lloyd Garrison, Horace Greeley,
and Wendell Phillips assured the suffrage leaders that if they
abandoned their fight for suffrage, when the war was ended the
men of the nation "out of gratitude" would enfranchise the
women of the country. And if the men of this country had been

peacefully demanding for over half a century the political right or privilege to vote, and had been continuously ignored or met with evasion by successive Congresses, as have the women, you, Mr. President, as a lover of liberty, would be the first to comprehend and forgive their inevitable impatience and righteous indignation. Will not this Administration, reelected to power by the hope and faith of the women of the West, handsomely reward that faith by taking action now for the passage of the Federal Suffrage Amendment?

In the port of New York during the past four years, billions of dollars in the export and import trade of the country have been handled by the men of the Customs Service, their treatment of the traveling public has radically changed, their vigilance supplied the evidence for the Lusitania note, the neutrality was rigidly maintained, the great German fleet guarded, captured and repaired, substantial economies and reforms have been concluded, and my ardent industry has been given to this great office of your appointment. But now I wish to leave these finished tasks, to return to my profession of the law and to give all my leisure time to fight as hard for the political freedom of women as I have always fought for your liberal leadership.

It seems a long seven years, Mr. President, since I first campaigned with you when you were running for Governor of New Jersey. In every circumstance throughout those years I have served you with the most respectful affection and unshadowed devotion. It is no small sacrifice now for me, as a member of your Administration, to sever our political relationship. But I think it is high time that men in this generation, at some cost to themselves, stood up to battle for the national enfranchisement of American women. So in order effectively to keep my promises made in the West, and more freely to go into this larger field of democratic effort, I hereby resign my office of Collector of the Port of New York, to take effect at once, or at your earliest convenience.

Yours respectfully, Dudley Field Malone

TLS (WP, DLC).

From Max Eastman

My dear President Wilson: New York September 8th, 1917

I want to express my appreciation of your letter to the Pope. It has surprised as well as delighted me, for I took your negative response to the Russian proposal of peace terms as final.[1] I thought you had adopted the entire animus of the allied war on

Germany, and I was dismayed in my hope of a "scientific peace."

Now you have declared for substantially the Russian terms—no "punitive damages," no "dismemberment of empires," "vindication of sovereignties," and by making a responsible ministry in Germany the one condition of your entering into negotiations, you have given a concrete meaning to the statement that this is a war for democracy. The manner in which you have accomplished this—and apparently bound the allies to it into the bargain—has my profound admiration. I am encouraged by this renewed assurance of your faith in democracy to lay before you two matters in which I believe that democracy is suffering at home more than the exigencies of military organization demand.

The first is the matter of the right of free speech and assemblage for the minority.

A week ago Tuesday I went to Fargo, North Dakota, to speak in favor of the very peace terms which on Wednesday were made public as your own in the letter to the Pope. I had not spoken for five minutes when an entire company of United States soldiers in their uniforms (Company B, I believe) burst into the hall, took possession of the platform, began to put out the lights, ordered all ladies to leave the building, and openly threatened me with violence. After a futile attempt to address them, I stepped down from the platform, and on the advice of persons in the audience made my escape from a side door while they were celebrating their victory. I went to the house of a friend, where I was called up on the telephone and told that the soldiers were hunting for me and intended to lynch me. I armed myself and left town in an automobile, leaving my bags at the hotel. The soldiers formed a cordon around my hotel stopping everyone who came in or out, and openly declared their intention to hang me. This continued until midnight when they learned that I had left town. These facts were published in full in the Fargo morning paper, but they were not sent out by the Associated Press.

My friend in Fargo whose name I can furnish privately, informed me that officers were present at the meeting, including a colonel. I cite this only as one example of the wanton violations of constitutional right which are being perpetrated in the name of the war for democracy, and perpetrated by soldiers in your command. Is there not grave danger to our civil liberties in these hundreds of thousands of armed men, if in the name of patriotism they are allowed with impunity to degenerate into gangs of marauders?

The other principle of democracy which I believe is being violated beyond the necessities of military efficiency, and illegally violated too by officers of your appointment, is the freedom of the press. As I think you know, I edit a monthly magazine, THE MASSES.[2] In that magazine I have endeavored to state my full opinions about the war policy, as far as the statement of them did not violate the law. I have not violated any law, nor desired to violate any law. Nevertheless, the Post Office department declared the August issue of my magazine unmailable. I appeared before Judge Learned Hand, in the 2nd district court of New York, and asked for a court order compelling the Post Office to receive the magazine. It was granted, Judge Hand ruling not only that my magazine was mailable under the law, but that there was not even a question whether it was mailable or not, as on such a question the Postmaster General would have power to decide. The post office, however, secured from Judge Hough of the Circuit Court of Appeals a stay of this order pending appeal to that court, which will probably convene in October. He also put the Post Office under a bond of $10,000 to secure me of my damage in case the appeal was lost. Meanwhile, however, the Postmaster General has revoked my mailing privilege altogether, on the ground that the continuity of mailing of my periodical has been interrupted—it having been interrupted only tentatively, and that at the request of the Post Office, by a stay of execution, pending an appeal which should determine whether it was to be interrupted or not. It is not necessary for you to consider what is in the magazine in order to be assured that this action is beyond the powers that a republic should depute to an appointed bureaucracy even in war-time. For I have repeatedly requested the post office to inform me what specific things or kinds of things in my magazine they consider unmailable, so that I might make up the magazine in such a way as to be mailable in the future, and they have stubbornly and contemptuously refused. Moreover the Postmaster General, in endeavoring to justify the suppression of the MASSES to the Senate, stated that it was denied the mails because it is a part of an organized propaganda to promote resistance to the draft. This accusation of crime is absolutely false.

I am informed by my attorneys that in ordinary times they could proceed against the Postmaster General and the Secretary of Treasury and Solicitor Lamar of the Post Office, for conspiracy to destroy my magazine, and win the case without difficulty. At least it is a fact that I am ready to make my magazine conform to the laws, if it does not. I have so stated to the Post Office, and I have been unable to extract any response from them but this grim and underhanded act of bureaucracy which I have described.

You know that the powers which would like to kill the propaganda of socialism are mighty, and you also know that this propaganda will surely play a great part in the further democratizing of the world. I ask you whether it is with your authority that an appointee of yours endeavors to destroy the life of one of the three growing Socialist magazines in this country, as a war measure in a war for democracy—and to do this without even giving its editor the opportunity which he has demanded to alter it or mould it somewhat to meet the exigencies of a military situation?

I believe that the support which your administration will receive from radical-minded people the country over, depends greatly on its final stand on these two critical matters of free speech and assemblage and the freedom of the Press.

Yours sincerely,   Max Eastman

TLS (WP, DLC).
¹ A puzzling statement. Wilson had returned no such negative response to the Provisional Government.
² About the case of *The Masses*, see n. 2 to the Enclosure printed with WW to ASB, July 13, 1917, Vol. 43.

From Richard Stephens and W. R. Davis

Clifton, Ariz., Sept. 8, 1917.

Citizens Committee has prevailed upon striking labor unions in this district to accept as final the rulings of Board of Arbitration, one member to be appointed by President Wilson, one to be appointed by President Gompers and the other selected by the operators in this district. This action officially endorsed by all crafts. This would dissolve existing deadlock. As business men, tax payers and patriotic Americans, we call upon you to lend your aid and influence in bringing about an immediate settlement. We consider this an inopportune time to reject any reasonable and honest proposition to bring about harmonious conditions. Citizens and strikers in honestly presenting this reasonable method of settlement. Operators while not rejecting have not held out any hopes of accepting terms offered. We rely upon you to help us bring to bear the influence of the government. Ex-Governor Hunt would not be acceptable as one of arbitrators, to either citizens or operators, hence would deem his appointment ill-advised;

must be disinterested and absolutely neutral party. There are many such. Citizens Committee,

Richard Stephens, Chairman;

W. R. Davis, Secretary.[1]

T telegram (WP, DLC).

[1] "Dear Tumulty: Please convey the substance of the Secretary of Labor's letter to these gentlemen in reply to their telegram. The President." WW to JPT, c. Sept. 8, 1917, TL (WP, DLC). Wilson referred to WBW to WW, Aug. 31, 1917.

Paul Henry Bastedo to William Sowden Sims

Queenstown, Ireland September 9, 1917.

From: Lieutenant P. H. Bastedo, U.S.N., U.S.S. Melville
To: Vice Admiral W. S. Sims, U.S.N.
Subject: Conversation with Dr. and Mrs. Grayson, U.S.N. with regard to the President's views on the submarine situation.

1. In compliance with your letter of September 7, 1917 I have to submit the following account. Endeavor has been made to set down the facts as closely as they can be remembered and to go into detail as much as possible that all attending information may be known.

2. I have known both Dr. and Mrs. Grayson well for several years. They are both in each others complete confidence. I have on occasion talked freely with the doctor and he has talked in the same manner to me. For over two years in addition to my duty in the Bureau of Steam Engineering I have been an aide at the White House.

3. On the afternoon of August 7, 1917 I saw Mrs. Grayson at tea at the White House. She said that she had had luncheon there during which she had heard I would be coming in and that she had waited to say good bye. I had called on Dr. and Mrs. Grayson a day or two previously to say good bye but they had not been at home. She knew I was leaving Washington but apparently did not know on what duty. At tea I told her that I was going abroad to report to Vice Admiral Sims for such duty as might be assigned and that I expected it would be in connection with radio work.

4. Upon leaving the White House she offered to drive me home. I thanked her but could not go at the time as I had an engagement at the Navy Department so we drove around there. During the drive she said she wished we could take a ride and have a talk. Evidently there was something on her mind. As we sat outside the Navy Department she finally said there was something she wanted to tell me but she did not know whether she

should or not. She then told me that the President had said in her presence that he would like to see any plan put into effect that Admiral Sims believed would effectively do away with the submarine menace, regardless as to whether the plan were favored by the British Admiralty or our Navy Department.

4. [sic] I believe that what she said was given on the spur of the moment and only with the idea of being of some assistance to Admiral Sims.

5. Dr. Grayson then came up and I told them both good bye and went over to the Navy Department. He did not know at the time what Mrs. Grayson had just said.

6. About 7:30 p.m. the same day Dr. Grayson called me up on the telephone in the appartment where I was living and said that he would like to have a talk that evening, that he would be in a little after eleven as he was going to the theatre with the President's party.

7. Dr. Grayson called at the appartment where I was living about eleven thirty that night and told me that Mrs. Grayson had become frightened at what she had said that afternoon and that he had come in to confirm what she had said as he had been present when she had heard the President talking. He confirmed what Mrs. Grayson had said in the afternoon in regard to the submarine problem. He also said that the President had known Admiral Sims to be ever a man of original ideas which produced results and that the President would like to see what might be called "Sims ideas" now applied to the submarine problem. He said that the President would like to see the submarine menance [menace] done away with speedily, that the President had given him to understand the British had fallen into a rut. I asked doctor Grayson what I should do only in the event that Admiral Sims said his hands were tied and that he could not carry out his plans due to the fact that he could not get desired action out of the Navy Department. Doctor Grayson told me in this event to cable him the word "safe" and that upon receipt of this message the President would investigate the Department's action to date i.e. send for the complete record of correspondence between Admiral Sims and the Navy Department with information showing what action had been taken by the Navy Department. Dr. Grayson said he had told the President that Admiral Sims was the man to send abroad and that from the time when Admiral Sims took command Dr Grayson had continually told the President that Admiral Sims is the man to handle the submarine question. Dr. Grayson said that Admiral Mayo

and others would be going abroad from time to time but that he believed no one would tell Admiral Sims of the President's private views on the submarine question and that Admiral Sims would like to know what these views were. Dr Grayson also told me that were I diverted by any officer from reporting direct to Admiral Sims, I was to tell that officer I had an important message and that it would be best I go direct to Admiral Sims. Dr. Grayson and I then went outside to the curb where Mrs. Grayson had been waiting in their car. I told them both good night and good bye.

8. By chance I met Dr. and Mrs. Grayson on the train going from Washington to New York, but as I remember, the matter was not discussed, neither was it discussed when I had luncheon with them in New York, Sunday, August 12th. I naturally thought of the matter each time when I saw them but as Dr. Grayson apparently had nothing more to say I kept quiet.

9. I have discussed the above with no one except Lieut Gilmore[1] as has been previously stated. He was not told the contents of the message but was consulted as to delivery of the part with reference to cabling the word "safe." In accordance with your instructions I have not since and will not mention anything of the above to anyone.   P. H. Bastedo.

HwS MS (W. S. Sims Papers, DLC).
[1] Lt. Reginald Everett Gillmor, not Gilmore, a member of Admiral Sims' staff.

From the Diary of Colonel House

September 9, 1917.

Last night around seven o'clock two secret service men called to say that the President had sent them from Washington to tell me he would be here tomorrow on the Mayflower. No one knows of his visit, not even the Cabinet or his own household. The President and Mrs. Wilson left by the rear entrance of the White House, escaping notice until they reached New York where they boarded the Mayflower. He gave there an indefinite statement as to their cruise.

Around eleven o'clock the Navy Yard of Boston called me over the telephone to say they had a wireless for me stating that the Mayflower would be in Gloucester Harbour at two o'clock.

Loulie and I went over to meet the boat, boarded it and got the President and Mrs. Wilson and motored along the shore for two hours or more. We stopped first at our cottage and then went over to Mrs. T. Jefferson Coolidge's[1] house to look at her prints, china, etc. which have been inherited from Thos. Jefferson. We dined on the Mayflower.

Before dinner the President and I had an intimate talk of perhaps an hour and again for an hour and a half after dinner. He came, he said, to talk about the advisability of asking for Lansing's resignation. He said that every time he wrote a note, or put out a statement, Lansing followed it with a conservative construction. Then when the President objected, he would correct it, thereby making endless confusion and largely nullifying the effect of the note. He thought Lansing was not well, and that he led a life to tax a strong man, much less a sick one. Lansing is out every night attending dinners, returning home to work until two o'clock or after, and is in his office at nine in the morning. He consumes an infinite number of cigarettes and black coffee between times. The President thought the character of people with whom he goes is not conducive to a broad outlook as they are mostly society folk and reactionaries.

I argued against asking for his resignation as I doubted whether he could do better. I asked whom he had in mind to replace him. He said there were one or two members of his Cabinet he thought would be better, Baker being one, although he felt Baker could not be spared from the War Department. I said, "I suppose Houston is the other man you have in mind"; to which he tentatively assented. I expressed the belief that it would be a serious mistake to put Houston in the State Department. I considered him a man of good judgment, but without diplomacy and that he would be very hard to work with. The President said he had never found Houston at all obstinate in taking advice. My reply was that Houston's department was one in which the President had taken no active interest, but he would find if he came in contact with him as often as it would be necessary if he were Secretary of State, a different story would have to be told. I thought, too, it would be impossible for me to work with him, friends though we have always been.

I thought if he took Baker, he should make Polk Secretary of War. The President seems to have a distaste for most of the State Department personnel. I argued strongly for Polk and also for Lansing, suggesting that he allow Lansing to remain until he fell ill again, and then use that as an excuse, thus saving his sensibilities.

The President suggested sending Lansing as Chairman of the Commission which is to go to Brazil.[2] I did not consider this commensurate with his position and urged an ambassadorship.

He said there were none vacant. I replied "you could make a vacancy at London. That between hurting the sensibilities of Page and Lansing, there was less reason for sparing Page." I thought if he would promise Lansing a place on the peace commission he would be willing to accept London. The President demurred. He did not think him fit for a peace commissioner; that he would give out statements at that congress just as he does in Washington, thereby nullifying his, the President's, work.

We left the subject with a tentative agreement that he would speak to Lansing when he returned to Washington and offer him London. I also suggested that he mention the work he had asked me to do regarding the peace congress. I think, however, I shall qualify this for if he asked for his resignation, it would be better not to bring me in, directly or indirectly, because Lansing might use that as an excuse to resign himself, giving my activities in his department as an excuse. I shall caution the President about this. I insisted again that he appoint Polk to the War Department in the event Baker is transferred to the State Department. I practically guaranteed Polk's successful administration of the War Department.

We discussed Root in relation to the peace conference.

The President spoke quite caustically against the Catholics in their endeavor to control the Government through appointments. He said he was never so fully awake to is [it] as now. This came about when we were discussing the appointment of a new Chief of Staff and Quartermaster General. I mentioned General Barry.[3] The President thought well of him, but was unwilling to put an Irish Vatholic [Catholic] in that place because his experience with them was that they never recommended anyone for office excepting fellow Catholics, which brought about an undesirable state of affairs.

He told me of the talk he made to the naval officers when he inspected the fleet at Hampton Roads not long ago.[4] He spoke to all of them, including ensigns, and said about this: "None of you have had any experience in modern warfare, therefore, the least of you knows as much as the highest, and I would like suggestions from any officer in the Navy, no matter how humble his rank, regarding the conduct of our war at sea. These suggestions will be received by the Navy Board, and if you find they are not noticed, then send them to me direct." The President said he noticed the Admirals squirm under this sort of talk.

He is sending a commission to England which I recommended at the suggestion of Arthur Pollen and others, and he told the members before they left that he wished them to go over and find a way to break up the hornets nest, and not try to kill individual hornets over a forty acre lot. He said he was willing to risk the loss of half our Navy if there was a commensurate gain.

We discussed the question of capital ships. I told him our minds diverged on this subject. He admitted it, but, after I had made an argument in favor of capital ships, he refused to discuss it further, declaring that no matter whether I was right or he was right, it was impracticable to make an arrangement with Great Britain at this time looking to our securing some of her capital battleships after the war in consideration of our abandoning our shipbuilding program of capital ships in order to build submarine destroyers. He thought the only thing that could be binding on Great Britain would be a treaty, and a treaty must necessarily go to the Senate for confirmation. He did not believe this country was prepared for a treaty of that sort with Great Britain. Anything less than a treaty, he thought footless because the present Administration might change and the British Government might change, and what would a verbal agreement amount to under new administrations. I argued that an arrangement could be made which would meet the approval of our people. He, in turn, said if the British Government wanted to do this after the war, they would do it anyway, and if they did not want to do it, we had no means of making them short of a treaty.

I disagree entirely with this conclusion. He has not accepted their offer, therefore Great Britain will be in no way bound to give us her battleships in the event we need them. The truth of it is, he does not believe in capital battleships; therefore, he is not interested in working out a plan by which they might be secured. In this I think he is making a mistake. I cannot see how he can think otherwise than that they are necessary to the maintenance of the supremacy at sea. The fact that they are now bottled up in harbours seems to impress him greatly, although I pointed out that they could come forth whenever they pleased by throwing a proper screen around themselves, and that they could destroy an enemy's fleet if inferior, and leave themselves in command of the seas.

We talked a great deal about the Chief of Staff and the Naval Board, and an infinite number of minor matters.

During the afternoon we were discussing Lincoln. We agreed that Washington would continue in history the greater man. I repeated what Sedgwice [Sedgwick][5] said when he lunched with me Saturday, i.e. that a Massachusetts historian had made the statement that Lincoln would never have been great by his deeds; but it was what he had written that had impressed the world and had given an insight into his mind that otherwise would never have been unfolded. The President did not agree with this. He thought Lincoln's deeds entitled him to greatness as well as what he wrote. He thought that his environment was, to a certain extent, limited and that by lack of wider education he did not have the outlook he might otherwise have had. Yet he thought his judgment would have been equal to any situation that might have confronted him.

[1] Clara Amory Coolidge. Her late husband, Thomas Jefferson Coolidge, Jr. (1863-1912), had been a great-great-grandson of Thomas Jefferson and a collector of Jeffersoniana. The Coolidge home in Magnolia was a partial replica of Monticello.

[2] As has been noted (see D. da Gama to WW, June 25, 1917, n. 1., Vol. 43), Wilson had it in mind to send a special mission to Brazil "to arrange for a greater co-ordination of forces and the closest possible co-operation of the two Governments." The mission was to embark within a month or six weeks and would include both Latin-American specialists and military men. On August 11, the *New York Times* reported that the administration had "under consideration" the appointment of a special mission to Brazil "to promote the community of sentiment . . . respecting this country's war aims." The mission, whatever its exact objective, never materialized.

[3] Maj. Gen. Thomas Henry Barry, at this time commander of the Central Department of the Army, with headquarters in Chicago.

[4] It is printed at August 11, 1917, Vol. 43.

[5] That is, Ellery Sedgwick, editor of the *Atlantic Monthly*.

From Robert Lansing, with Enclosure

My dear Mr. President: [Washington] September 10, 1917.

Will you be good enough to give me your views in regard to the enclosed memorandum, which was handed to me by the British Ambassador today? It deals with the proposed military conference to be held in Paris toward the close of this month.

Faithfully yours,   Robert Lansing.

CCL (SDR, RG 59, 763.72/6868½, DNA).

ENCLOSURE

Handed me by British
Amb. Sept 10/17

MEMORANDUM.

The Russian Minister of Foreign Affairs suggested to the British Ambassador in Petrograd that as a military conference is to be held in Paris towards the end of September, the suggested conference which Russian Ministers were to attend might conveniently meet a little later in London. Monsieur Terestchenko proposed to take with him Prince Lvov and Monsieur Konovaloff,[1] who is an economic expert. Sir George Buchanan observed that such a conference would have the great advantage of giving opportunity for a frank exchange of views between the Russian Government and the other Allies as regards Russia's part in the war and material assistance to her from the Allies. It was difficult for the Allies to decide how far they could continue to despatch war material to Russia without personal contact with members of the Russian Government. This was all the more necessary in view of recent events on the Russian front, the economic and financial crisis, and the renewed activity of the Maximilists.[2]

Monsieur Terestchenko agreed and expressed the hope that an American representative would be invited to attend the conference, especially as financial questions would figure largely in the discussions.

He also said that deplorable as the loss of Riga was, he did not believe Petrograd would be in real danger except from air attacks, and vigorous defensive measures were being taken. The Government did not wish to go to Moscow except as a last resort.

Sir George Buchanan expressed the hope that attention would not be distracted from the military crisis by the rumours about counter-revolution and the arrest of the two Grand Dukes.[3] Monsieur Terestchenko replied that cypher messages and letters from the wife of the Grand Duke Paul had been found of a highly compromising nature, but the arrest of the Grand Dukes would probably not be prolonged and was only domiciliary.

British Embassy,
Washington
September tenth 1917.

T MS (SDR, RG 59, 763.72/6868½, DNA).
[1] Aleksandr Ivanovich Konovalov, formerly, and soon to be again, Minister of Trade and Industry in the Provisional Government.
[2] That is, the Bolsheviks.
[3] The Grand Dukes Pavel (Paul) and Mikhail Aleksandrovich, uncle and brother, respectively, of Nicholas II, were placed under house arrest by the Provisional Government in late August because of rumors that they were involved in a monarchist plot. They were released within a few days when no evidence was found against them. William Henry Chamberlin, *The Russian Revolution, 1917-1921* (2 vols., New York, 1935), I, 201.

From Robert Lansing, with Enclosure

Dear Mr. President: Washington September 10, 1917.

I beg to send you enclosed a copy of a telegram from the Minister of Foreign Affairs of Russia to the Russian Ambassador in

Washington, which was handed to the Department by the Ambassador a few days ago.

With assurances of respect, etc., I am, my dear Mr. President,
Faithfully yours,   Robert Lansing

TLS (SDR, RG 59, 763.72119/855½ A, DNA).

ENCLOSURE

RUSSIAN EMBASSY Washington.
"Petrograd 21st August 3rd September.

"President Wilson's reply to the Peace Note of the Pope was met in Russia with the greatest sympathy, and has been commented in that spirit by the whole press, except only by the extremist organs.

"The Provisional Government notices with the sincerest gratification that the principles on which the President's answer was based fully coincide with the precepts adopted by the new Russia in her exterior policy. In this unity of ideas existing between ourselves and the great American Republic, we see the valuable pledge to our mutual cooperation in elucidating the aims of the present war, as well as in adopting a common political course.

"Kindly transmit this first impression to the Government to which you are accredited, and also convey that at the present moment we are elaborating the project of a declaration in which will be stated the solidarity of the Provisional Government with the ideas expressed in the President's note.

Terestchenko.["]

T MS (SDR, RG 59, 763.72119/855½ A, DNA).

From Walter Hines Page

Dear Mr. President: London. 10, Sep. '17

Admiral Hall, chief Intelligence Officer of the Admiralty, is, the man who gave us the Zimmermann telegram about Mexico, and the telegrams, publishd. today, about Sweden's transmitting official German documents and about the German insult to the Argentine Government. It is he who has served us 1,000 good turns ever since the war began. Mr. Bell, of my staff, who has daily dealings with him, keeps this channel of information open most admirably.

Admiral Hall's service is so helpful that it has occurred to me that possibly you may think it worthy of some special mark of appreciation. We have no Orders or Decorations to bestow—thank Heaven; and you cd. not, in good etiquette, write to the subject of another Government. But if you wd. send me a message of appreciation that I might give to him, you wd. please one of the best and ablest servants that any Government has and a man who is as ardently American as any foreigner can be. Bell, too, deserves much credit for the way in which he handles all this delicate business.

Yours Sincerely,   Walter H. Page

Hall is, within himself, a Big Department of the British War Government.

ALS (WP, DLC).

A Telegram and a Letter from Arthur Charles Townley[1]

St Paul, Minn., Sept. 10, 1917.

The National Non-partisan League in cooperation with other organizations of farmers and organized labor will have a delegation in Washington representing over one million voters on Wednesday and request privilege of brief interview with you regarding pending revenue bill to urge your cooperation in securing higher excess profits and income taxes to carry out your noble assertion that profits and patriotism can not be used in the same sentence.[2]   National Non-partisan League,

per A. C. Townley, Prest.

T telegram (WP, DLC).
    [1] One of the founders and, at this time, president of the National Nonpartisan League.
    [2] Wilson did not see the delegation. He spent the period from September 8 to September 15 vacationing aboard the presidential yacht, *U.S.S. Mayflower*.

Mr. President: St. Paul, Minn. September 10, 1917.

A monster mass convention of producers and consumers will be held at St. Paul, Minnesota, in the Municipal Auditorium that accommodates about fourteen thousand people. We expect to have it full. The convention will run for three days, 18th, 19th and 20th of September. This convention will be held under the auspices of the National Nonpartisan League, co-operating with other organizations of farmers, also with organizations of laboring men and consumers.

We shall discuss the necessary limitations and difficulties of governmental price fixing and the feasibility of Federal acquisition upon a fair basis, and Federal operation of natural resources, natural monopolies, such as railroads, and basis [basic] industries, and sale of services and products thereof at cost. We realize, with you, the necessity for the successful conduct of the war, of a strong and contented population, assured that the financial sacrifice involved in this conflict shall be equal, and that the war shall not inure to the selfish advantage of any.

The League is in hearty accord with your statement that patriotism and profits should not be mentioned in the same breath. We are willing and anxious to aid you in crystallizing public sentiment behind this principle; and believe that this conference will be a long step towards organizing public sentiment for a fair revenue law that will reach the tremendous reservoirs of wealth and profits of the United States for our use in the conduct of our war, and at the same time make for justice in producing that revenue.

I take great pleasure in asking you to favor us with a message to the American People through this conference, in person if you can, and by a written message, if not in person; or through any representative that you may choose to send.

With deep assurance of our loyalty in this time of stress and danger, I beg to remain

Most sincerely yours,   A. C. Townley

TLS (WP, DLC).

Hugh Leo Kerwin to Joseph Patrick Tumulty

My dear Mr. Tumulty: Washington September 10, 1917.

In the absence of Secretary Wilson who has been ill for the past few days I desire to inform you that the strike of the mechanical department of the Boston & Maine Railroad involving some 3800 men was satisfactorily adjusted on Saturday evening by Honorable Rowland B. Mahany,[1] Commissioner of Conciliation of the Department of Labor, cooperating with Honorable Henry B. Endicott, Chairman of the Massachusetts Committee on Public Safety. This is the matter that the President called to the attention of Secretary Wilson on September 5th at which time he transmitted to this Department letter from the Attorney General and copies of telegrams received from United States Attorney Anderson of Boston, which I am returning herewith.

Sincerely yours,   H. L. Kerwin.

TLS (WP, DLC).
[1] Rowland Blennerhassett Mahany.

From the Diary of Colonel House

September 10, 1917.

I called for the President at half past nine and motored with him and Mrs. Wilson to the Essex Count[r]y Club where I turned them over to Mona, Randolph[1] and Hugh and Mrs. Wallace. I returned home to do some necessary work.

The President and Mrs. Wilson lunched with us at half past one o'clock. There was no one present besides ourselves excepting Mona and Randolph. After lunch the President and I went to my study where we talked for an hour. The main discussion was of peace terms and the collating of data necessary for intelligent dealing with the subject. I showed him Felix Frankfurter's brief suggesting what he considered necessary information for dealing with a single country, and taking Germany as an example.[2] The President thought as I did that it was absurd to prepare such comprehensive data. He declared that if anyone started such a metaphysical and historical discussion that he could easily brush it aside and bring him down to the real business of peace making.

I called his attention to the necessity of not broaching this subject when he took up with Lansing the matter of their differences. I thought he should bring up the question of my directing the peace conference work immediately, and leave the personal questions relating to Lansing until later. I had two reasons for this. One was that it would give me more time to try and straighten out Lansing through Frank Polk and Gordon, or through Lansing directly.

I told the President I was afraid he was making a mistake in contemplating a change, and I hoped he would first have a frank talk with Lansing and insist upon his leaving statements to the press, either to his press representative or to Polk. The President agreed to do this, but thought it might cause Lansing to tender his resignation. If this should happen, I thought it would be better to have it come that way rather than to ask for it. I have in mind getting Polk to prime Lansing and get him in a frame of mind to accept the President's rebuke kindly.

I told the President that I trusted Polk's discretion thoroughly and what I had in mind to do. I make it a rule never to keep anything back from the President. He knows the whole story as far as I am concerned. In this connection, I told him of Dudley's recent indiscretion in his talk with Monsignor Dunn and the message sent to the Papal Delegate.[3] In talking of this, we agreed that Dudley was not himself or he would not have made such a blunder. The President wondered if it would "involve us" in any way. I thought not, and stated why.

In discussing Dudley, he seemed to feel keenly the action he took on the suffrage question, and declared that Dudley was one of the last men he would have suspected of disloyalty to him. I excused Dudley by saying he was not himself—an excuse which he seemed ready to accept.

I showed him President Eliot's proposal for a conference of the belligerents.[4] He had not seen it. I am sometimes startled by the President's lack of information concerning current happenings. He looked over Eliot's statement casually, criticised it severely, and put it down remarking that it was "nothing better than the mewlings of an old man." He is mistaken in this, and if he had read it carefully he would not have had this opinion, although he would not have agreed with Eliot.

He said he was growing tired of Jusserand's excitable impertinence and wondered whether we could not have him recalled in a way not to hurt French sensibilities. What angered him was Jusserand's criticism of his reply to the Pope—a criticism which came to him almost immediately after Jusserand made it.

Once or twice during the conversation I threw the President off his line of thought by interpolations, and he found it difficult to return to his subject. He smiled plaintively and said: "You see I am getting tired. This is the way it indicates itself." I noticed later, too, that he had forgotten that the Swiss Legation was representing the German Government at Washington. He had forgotten what government had taken over their interests. I am glad he is taking this rest "for faith, he needs it." No man has ever had deeper or graver responsibilities, and no one has met them with more patience, courage and wisdom.

When we went back on the veranda, we found a large gathering of newspaper men and photographers on the lawn, and one of the secret service men asked permission for them to come and see the President. They asked no questions but he and I, at their request, were photographed together. The President, Mrs. Wilson and I motored the entire afternoon. I left them at their landing at six o'clock and returned home to attend to some pressing work. Mona, Ran and I dined with them on the Mayflower. The evening was entirely social and so was the ride.

We tried to keep him in as merry a mood as possible. He seemed to thoroughly enjoy his visit, and it was arranged that I should come to Washington either next week or the beginning of the week following for further discussion.

During lunch the President spoke of his nervousness when

speaking in public. I had thought that he was entirely free from it, and yet he said if he had to walk across a crowded stage, with an audience in front of him, he always wondered whether he would drop before he reached the speakers stand.

While driving, he described himself as "a democrat like Jefferson, with aristocratic tastes." Intellectually, he said, he was entirely democratic, which in his opinion was unfortunate for the reason that his mind led him where his taste rebelled.

I sent today the following cable to Lord Robert Cecil:

"The President has been here with me for two days and I used this occasion to ask him concerning your inquiry regarding the Zionist Movement. In his opinion, the time is not opportune for any definite statement further perhaps than one of sympathy, provided it can be made without conveying any real commitment. Things are in such a state of flux at the moment that he does not consider it advisable to go further. I am glad Wiseman has proved so serviceable and has justified my confidence in him."[5]

[1] That is, Mona House Tucker and Randolph Foster Tucker, House's daughter and son-in-law.

[2] It is missing in all collections.

[3] House discussed this incident in his diary entry of September 4. It involved a letter which Mgr. John Joseph Dunn, chancellor of the Archdiocese of New York and director of the New York branch of the Society for the Propagation of the Faith, had sent to the Apostolic Delegate in Washington, Archbishop Giovanni Bonzano, following a conversation with Dudley F. Malone, which, in turn, was based upon an earlier discussion between Malone and House. "What I asked Dudley to do," House wrote, "was to suggest to the Papal Delegate at Washington that the Pope answer any inquiry concerning the President's reply to his peace message by saying that he did not believe the President had closed the door to peace, but rather had indicated a way by which it might be opened wide. I cautioned Dudley about mentioning my name, either directly or indirectly, and also about giving an impression that the suggestion had any significance whatever beyond his own personality. It was to be merely a thought of his own which he desired to convey to the Papal Delegate so if he thought fit, he in turn might convey it to the Vatican. My purpose was two-fold: First to unite Austria and Catholic Germany in favor of the legislative reforms which the President made as a requirement for peace negotiations. Second, to leave the door open for further discussion in the event it seemed necessary. What Dudley did was to convey the impression that he was in some way acting for the President. It is an extraordinary indiscretion. It seemed a simple thing to do and it never occurred to me that it could be distorted. It has taken me the greater part of the day telephoning to New York . . . to get the situation measurably composed. Fortunately, the Papal Delegate refused to take an anonymous suggestion and transmit it to the Vatican, therefore the matter stands just where it was before, excepting Dudley's conversation with Monsignor Dunn and Dunn's letter to the Papal Delegate."

[4] Charles W. Eliot, "Is a Peace Conference Now Possible?" *New York Times*, Aug. 27, 1917. Eliot suggested that, while none of the belligerents was yet ready for an armistice, much less a final peace settlement, the present stalemate in the war might be conducive to an informal gathering of representatives of the warring governments to exchange views. The delegates would be chosen by the respective belligerents but would be uninstructed and would have no powers except to make public reports of their findings. Eliot proposed a detailed agenda for such a conference under two broad headings: "1. The means of so organizing the civilized world that international war can be prevented—by force when

peaceable means have failed. 2. The removal or remedying in good measure of the public wrongs, injustices, and distrusts which contributed to the outbreak of the present war, or have been created during its course—wrongdoings and passions which will cause future wars unless done away with."

[5] E. M. House to R. Cecil, Sept. 10, 1917, T telegram (W. Wiseman Papers, CtY).

From Robert Lansing, with Enclosures

My dear Mr. President: Washington September 11, 1917.

I think you will be interested to know the present situation with reference to the efforts of this country and the countries associated with this country in the war, looking to the support of Polish independence.

On August 27th, after I had consulted informally with the Secretary of War, I sent a cable to London, asking for a statement of the British Government, with reference to this question. A reply to this cable was received on September 5th, and on the same date the British Ambassador handed me a memorandum on this subject. Copies of these papers I herewith enclose for your consideration.

I shall be very grateful if you would kindly indicate whether you desire to recognize the National Polish Committee, sitting in Paris, and if so, what form you think this recognition should take.   Faithfully yours,   Robert Lansing.

TLS (SDR, RG 59, 860C.01/22½ E/B, DNA).

ENCLOSURE I

MEMORANDUM

His Majesty's Government have received official notification of the constitution of a National Polish Committee the seat of which is to be in Paris.

The Committee propose to undertake:

1. The representation of Polish interests in Great Britain, the United States and Italy and any other country in which Polish interests may render this necessary.

2. To deal with political questions arising out of the recent constitution of a Polish Army to fight on the side of the Allies.

3. The protection of persons of Polish nationality in allied countries.

Among the members of the Committee are:

Tiltz,[1] Seyda, Sobaski, Zamoyski and Paderewski.

His Majesty's Government are inclined officially to recognize this Committee but would be glad of the views of the United States Government on the proposal, before they take any action, in view of a recent suggestion by the United States Ambassador at London that His Majesty's Government should recognize a Polish Provisional Government in the United States.

(Signed) Cecil Spring Rice,
BRITISH EMBASSY
WASHINGTON
September 3, 1917.

T MS (SDR, RG 59, 860C.01/21, DNA).
1 Actually, Erazm, or Erasme, Piltz.

E N C L O S U R E   I I

AMEMBASSY LONDON.   Washington, August 27, 1917.

Department has been considering for several months means looking to the support of the Polish people in their efforts to obtain their freedom and to restore Poland as an independent nation. It has been suggested that a great stimulus might be given to the Polish cause, and, indirectly to the general cause against Germany, by the establishment in this country of a Polish Provisional Government to be recognized by this Government and the allied governments as the government of an independent Poland. Upon such recognition this Government could legally loan the government so set up funds for military purposes secured by Polish bonds underwritten by this country and the Allies. The further suggestion has been made that such a government thereupon recruit Poles resident in this country and if naturalized Americans either above or below the draft age, and if aliens, of any age. The army so recruited to be trained in Canadian camps supplied by the English and when trained to be transported to Europe on English transports. This army to be commanded by an American or Polish General under either the American or Polish flag and to fight in conjunction with American troops in France.

You are requested informally and orally to sound the British Government, ascertaining whether the present time is considered opportune for action as above suggested. In the event that the British Government is favorably inclined to this proposition, please report any suggestions it may have as to the method to be adopted to secure proper representation of the Polish people in any government to be established in this country. You may suggest, informally, that it might be possible by a proclamation of the President, accepted by the Allies, to offer the Polish people the assistance of this country toward the formation of a Provisional Government and the establishment of a military force to be used in conjunction with the armies already fighting Germany.

CONFIDENTIAL. There seems to be a rather varied opinion among the Poles as to the method to be adopted in the premises. Apparently, however, the majority of them feel that the initiative in any such project must be taken by this country. As you probably know, there is already established in France an autonomous Polish army, fighting under the generalship of the French and recruited from Poles now residing in France. It does not seem altogether practicable, however, further to recruit this army from Poles resident in this country.

Report on this matter by cable as soon as possible.

Lansing.

TC telegram (SDR, RG 59, 860C.01/21a, DNA).

ENCLOSURE III

London. September 4, 1917.

7098. Your 5344, August 27, 4 P.M.

A committee of Poles representing all parts of the country German, Russian, and Austrian Poland has been organized in Paris to do practically what the proposed Provisional Government in the United States would do and this committee is represented to the British Government as being more completely representative than any other and as having working relations with bodies of Poles in Poland. With his present knowledge of that committee and of the plan proposed by you Lord Robert Cecil is disposed to see what the committee can accomplish before committing himself to the approval of your plan. In spirit however he heartily agrees with your purpose, and would welcome further information.

He thinks well of the raising a Polish army in the United States. What help the British Government can give he can determine only after a more definite plan is submitted. And he would like to see a plan of what you think can be done. Concerning transporting such an army he reserved an opinion till he can be informed how large it is likely to be, hinting he could then consult the Admiralty. In general he falls in with the plan to raise such an army and awaits further information.

TC telegram (SDR, RG 59, 860C.01/22, DNA).

To Dudley Field Malone

U.S.S. MAYFLOWER,
My dear Mr. Collector: 12 September, 1917

Your letter of September seventh reached me just before I left home and I have, I am sorry to say, been unable to reply to it sooner.

I must frankly say that I cannot regard your reasons for resigning your position as Collector of Customs as convincing, but it is so evidently your wish to be relieved from the duties of the office that I do not feel at liberty to withhold my acceptance of your resignation. Indeed, I judge from your letter that any discussion of the reasons would not be acceptable to you and that it is your desire to be free of the restraints of public office. I, therefore, accept your resignation, to take effect as you have wished.

I need not say that our long association in public affairs makes me regret the action you have taken most sincerely.

Very truly yours,   [Woodrow Wilson]

CCL (WP, DLC).

To Frank Irving Cobb

Personal.

My dear Cobb: U.S.S. MAYFLOWER, 12 September, 1917

I am very much obliged to you for your letter of September fifth, and beg that you will pardon my delay in replying to it. I have sneaked off from Washington and am trying to get a little rest, and am glad to say that I am succeeding.

I would suggest that, if possible, you go into the suggestion of Mr. Victor Ridder's a little further and ascertain what particular German-Americans in New York they have it in thought to send abroad on the errand you refer to. I feel pretty sure that in any case it would be unwise even to wink at such an errand, but I would feel the more certain of my judgment if I knew the men and their affiliations. It is very generous of you to offer to make this inquiry for me. It would be serviceable in many directions.

Cordially and faithfully yours,   [Woodrow Wilson]

CCL (WP, DLC).

To William Bauchop Wilson

U.S.S. MAYFLOWER,

My dear Mr. Secretary: 12 September, 1917

After receiving your letter of August thirty-first, I had an interview with Judge Covington upon his return from his Western trip, and upon hearing what he had to say asked him to see you and lay before you certain considerations which he thought important and which I think important about the proposed commission of inquiry. I have, therefore, delayed in expressing a judgment about the programme you submit in your letter of August thirty-first, and write now to ask if you feel inclined to modify your suggestions in view of what Judge Covington has to report.

Cordially and sincerely yours,   Woodrow Wilson

TLS (LDR, RG 174, DNA).

Herbert Clark Hoover to Joseph Patrick Tumulty

Dear Mr. Tumulty: Washington, D. C. September 12, 1917.

Please find enclosed herewith a telegram[1] from one of our people, which explains itself.

Various Northwestern Congressmen have called upon me and I explained to them that the prices laid down by the Committee could not be altered, but apparently the farmers have been advised that the matter is still under consideration. It is therefore most desirable that the President should send out some word, settling this one way, or another.

A further situation arises because of mass meetings being held by the North Dakota farmers,—apparently with a good deal of anti-war sentiment,—demanding that they shall have a higher price for their wheat, and something of the same kind is being done in Oklahoma. The net result of these activities is that the farmers over the country are getting the idea that if they hold out long enough they can get more money, and the arrivals of wheat in the market are very low.

The whole question is whether or not the consumer is to pay another $5.00 or $6.00 per barrel for flour in order to please a lot of malcontents, and if they are to pay this higher price, the problem will arise at once whether we can maintain tranquillity in the large industrial centers during this winter.

Even with the reduction effected by the Food Administration plan, the price of flour is 125 percent over normal. The Commission that fixed the prices, as you know, was in itself a majority of the farmers.

Under the circumstances, it seems to me that it is necessary for the President to send some word to the Oregon and Washington delegates that no change will be made, and after the President returns, I need badly to have a discussion over the entire situation.　　　　　Yours faithfully,　Herbert Hoover[2]

TLS (WP, DLC).
　[1] T. B. Wilcox to H. C. Hoover, Sept. 11, 1917, TC telegram (WP, DLC). Writing from Portland, Oregon, Wilcox reported that farmers in that area would "sell nothing" so long as hope remained for a higher price than that set by the Food Administration. He urged that Hoover "prevail upon" Wilson to settle the question promptly.
　[2] "Dear Tumulty: Please find out from Mr. Hoover what form he thinks my statement which he here suggests ought to take. The President." WW to JPT, c. Sept. 17, 1917, TL (WP, DLC).

From John William Davis

Dear Mr. President:　　Washington, D. C. September 13, 1917.

Pursuant to the request made in your letter of August 17, 1917, I have examined the charges made by the Union Against Militarism in their "Memorandum on Invasion of Constitutional Rights."[1]

According to the allegations of the memorandum the evidence submitted covers (1) the arbitrary denial of the right of free speech and assemblage by local officials, (2) illegal arrest and search by local police and Federal authorities, (3) lawless assumption of power by members of the military forces, (4) unfounded complaints of over-zealous Federal district attorneys, and (5) arbitrary action of postmasters in denying the use of the mails.

Of the five charges made, therefore, the first relates to matters falling under the jurisdiction of the States, and the third and fifth to matters falling under the jurisdiction of the War, Navy and Post Office departments.

The exhibits submitted in support of the charges consist of (a) three photographs of the Boston Peace Parade Riots and five affidavits relating to this parade, (b) a copy of an ordinance adopted by the City of Indianapolis, (c) three affidavits relating to an alleged attempt upon the part of Federal officials to break up the Socialist organization in Indianapolis, and (d) seven affidavits relating to alleged unconstitutional behavior upon the part of Federal officials in Chicago.

The photographs and affidavits relating to the Boston Peace

Parade all concern alleged misconduct upon the part of soldiers, sailors, and State or city officials.

The affidavits relating to the alleged attempt upon the part of Federal officials to break up the Socialist organization in Indianapolis are in conflict with the Department's reports, which show that this charge is unfounded.

The affidavits relating to the alleged unconstitutional behavior upon the part of Federal officials in Chicago refer chiefly to the alleged breaking up of a meeting of "conscientious objectors" by F. S. Townley,[2] who it is charged was under the influence of liquor at the time.

I am advised that the statements in the affidavits concerning the alleged breaking up of a meeting through the disorderly conduct of Townley and his associates are untrue, and that Townley was not under the influence of liquor.

The "Memorandum on Invasion of Constitutional Rights" also makes a number of complaints not specifically covered in the supporting affidavits. It refers to twelve persons indicted in Grand Rapids for distributing literature in opposition to the draft. This case was called to the attention of the Department of Justice by the United States Attorney, was promptly investigated, and was dropped upon the conclusion that the indictments were not good.

The memorandum refers to another case in which a man in Syracuse, New York, was proceeded against for writing on his registration blank in the State military census that he was opposed to participation in this war. In this case United States Judge Ray[3] swore out a warrant against the man and instructed the United States Attorney to present the case to the grand jury. The United States Attorney presented the case to the grand jury as instructed, but asked them to return no bill.

Complaint is also made in a general way that charges of treason have been preferred against certain persons for the sole offense of criticising the Government's war policies. There have been no such prosecutions for treason instituted against persons with the authority of this Department. On the contrary, in every case where this Department's attention has been called to cases of prosecution for treason under the circumstances referred to in the memorandum of the Union Against Militarism this Department has instructed the United States Attorney not to prosecute for treason.

Complaint is also made that in some cases persons unable to produce their registration cards upon demand were held for investigation pending such production. While this method of enforcing the registration provision of the draft law was not specifically authorized by this Department, it was no doubt considered by police officers as being in accordance with the spirit and purpose of section 62 of the registration regulations, reading as follows:

All persons registered will be furnished a registration certificate. Since all police officers of the Nation, States, and municipalities are required to examine the registration lists and make sure that all persons liable to registration have registered themselves, much inconvenience will be spared to those who are registered if they will keep these certificates always in their possession. All persons of the designated ages must exhibit their certificates when called upon by any police officer to do so.

The United States Attorneys are charged with the duty of prosecuting all delinquents within their respective districts for crimes and offenses cognizable under the authority of the United States. They necessarily and properly have a wide discretion in the performance of this duty. There is nothing in the data submitted by the Union Against Militarism to show that they have abused this discretion.

Without going into further detail, it suffices to say that while some few isolated instances of excess of zeal are shown, the charges made by the Union Against Militarism, in so far as they relate to matters coming under the jurisdiction of this Department, are without substantial merit.

For your convenience I enclose a memorandum setting forth the charges relating to the War, Navy and Post Office Departments, with references to the data submitted in support of the charges.[4]

I also return herewith the letter to you from the American Union Against Militarism of August 10, 1917, and the documents submitted to you in connection with that letter.

Respectfully,   Jno. W. Davis

TLS (WP, DLC).
[1] WW to TWG, Aug. 17, 1917, and Lillian D. Wald *et al.* to WW, Aug. 10, 1917, both printed in Vol 43.
[2] He cannot be further identified.
[3] George Washington Ray.
[4] This memorandum, not printed, quoted, without comment, the protests made in Miss Wald's letter against the attack upon the Boston peace parade on July 1 and the alleged invasion of constitutional rights by officials of the Post Office Department.

From William Gibbs McAdoo

Dear Mr. President: Washington September 13, 1917.

With your approval, I addressed under date of July 18, 1917, a communication to representatives of the Allied Governments in this city, urging the establishment of an Inter-Ally Council sitting in Europe, with a view to making to the Secretary of the Treasury and to the Purchasing Commission recently established recommendations as to the requirements of the Allies and the priorities to be observed between them.

In one form or another, all of the representatives concerned have advised me of their general and cordial acceptance of the plan thus presented to them. Informally or formally, all have advised that, in their judgment, American representatives should make a part of the proposed Council. Lord Northcliffe, head of the British War Mission, says on this point:

His Majesty's Government observe with much regret that the United States Government appear disinclined to appoint an authoritative representative of their own upon the proposed Inter-Allied Council. They earnestly trust that this decision may be reconsidered. They would press upon the United States Government the difficulty in which the Council will constantly find itself in coming to any decision. It is inevitable that the representative of each Ally will tend to be mainly concerned with making good the claims of his own government, and will often be without authority to abate those claims. No one of the Allies will be in a position to deal with the claims of the others, and the council can hardly proceed by the method of vote. The Council may be therefore unable in certain cases to arrive at any joint recommendation and in such an event, it would be very desirable for the United States Government to be represented at the discussions by a high authority competent to report to them the opinion he had formed on the basis of what had passed.

In the experience of His Majesty's Government in spheres where ultimate questions of supplies of commodities, of tonnage, or of finance, depended on them, they have found no option but to form their own judgment after hearing the views of each of the Allies. Guided by this experience, His Majesty's Government consider that the presence of a representative of the United States Government on the Inter-Allied Council is indispensable to its efficient working.

The French Government, through its High Commissioner, Mr. Tardieu, has expressed itself on this point as follows:

The French Government consider that, in order that the Inter-Allied Council in Europe, in which each country will have, as representatives, specially able men, in military, economical and financial matters, should have its decisions considered at their full value by the American Government and the Congress, it is necessary that the United States Government be directly kept informed of the work of this Council, and this could not be done in a more efficient way than by having the United States Government sharing in the Council's transactions.

I am continually impressed, as our relations with the Allied Governments develop from day to day, that if we are to employ intelligently and to the best purpose and effect the credits we are authorized to extend to foreign governments, we must of necessity have a more intimate knowledge of their needs as related to the military objects and methods adopted by them from time to time for the conduct of the war. The operation of an Inter-Ally Council without American representation would meet the necessities of the case in part only. The Allied Governments in Europe are perhaps unable to avoid a certain particularism of view in regard to war measures. There is, indeed, a common cause binding them together, but, in the negotiations with them relating to loans there is also apparent a constant tendency to subordinate consideration of the war *as a whole* to considerations of the war as it affects particularly each of these governments, and as it is viewed by their respective general staffs. Obviously, the special requirements presented to us, even though somewhat competitively, by the borrowing Governments, are necessary elements in our study of the general situation; but, as a corrective of the errors that must inhere in such unrelated propositions, I see no recourse whatever except that American influence should be exerted in order to encourage, as much as possible, a study of true *relative* values among the various elements of our problem.

That some such coordinated investigation of Allied needs is beginning to be realized by our own War Department as a matter of importance, is indicated in the following citations, the first of which appears in the report made by General Scott, Chief of Staff, on the Roumanian situation; and the second of which is an excerpt from correspondence between the Secretary of War and Colonel Lassiter,[1] our military attache in London.

Excerpt from General Scott's Report.

Should it be decided to accede to the request of the Roumanian Government for military supplies, I recommend that the annexed list showing in order of urgency the things most needed be examined by the Board which, since I left home, has doubtless been organized at the War Department for dealing with the question of supplies for our own and the Allied armies.

Excerpt from Colonel Lassiter's cable of August 21, 1917,
to Secretary Baker.

I hope to put this matter on a slightly better footing by negotiations made yesterday, whereby certain important authorities agreed to help, but I expect difficulties to continually recur, and believe only solution is to have a supplies and shipping commission sitting in Paris or London which can view the whole situation and decide how space shall be allotted on ships, what stores are most essential to move first, and what allotment shall be made of the stores available in different countries.

Excerpt from Secretary Baker's letter of September 1st,
to the Secretary of the Treasury.

I assume that the object suggested by Colonel Lassiter would be accomplished by the Inter-Ally Purchasing Board which you have suggested should be established either in Paris or London.

While these citations refer in one case to a council presumed to sit in America, and in the other to a council presumed to sit in Europe, they both present the idea of American cooperation in the study of the military plans of ourselves and our associates, since these plans, to be most effective, must have a measure of Unity which is now lacking.

By reason of the conditions heretofore existing, it did not seem prudent to assure to any of the Allies Governments sums of money to cover their expenditures for more than a few weeks at a time. This method of dealing with the matter is of course highly objectionable, both from their point of view and from our own. They should have, as nearly as we can give it, a financial program covering a period of several months. And on our part it would be equally desirable that the disposition of the available funds should not continue to be the subject of competitive efforts on the part of the Allies, with the possibility of irritations among them—an irritation which may extend to the lender who can not possibly satisfy the demands of all. In order to make a prudent decision concerning advances to be made during a period of from three to six months, it is particularly desirable that the war situation *as a whole* should be carefully considered and that recommendations concerning the needs for such a period should be laid before us.

I am entirely satisfied that the important objectives to be gained by associating American representation with an Inter-Ally Council can be had without in any way endangering that independence of political position which I well know it is your desire to maintain. It will certainly be possible to give to representatives of the Treasury and War Department, if you should approve both, such instructions as would prevent any political complications arising from their consultative activities concerning purely military problems.

I have not supposed that the role thus indicated for our representatives would be in any way that of arbiter in the deliberations of the proposed Inter-Ally Council.

Their useful function would be: (a) To encourage a greater unity of purpose with respect to the use of our resources than seems now to obtain among the allies; (b) to report more fully than would otherwise be known to us, the reasons for agreement or disagreement among the European members of the Council, thus largely increasing the knowledge made available to us for rendering final decisions upon the respective applications of the Allied Governments for assistance.

In conclusion, I have the honor to recommend specifically that the Allied Governments who have been addressed in this matter should now be notified that one or more American representatives will be named to sit in consultative capacity in the Inter-Ally Council, which is about to be organized. If this recommendation meets your general approval, the details of the matter will then be laid before you for further consideration.

Cordially yours,   W G McAdoo

TLS (WP, DLC).
1 William Lassiter.

From Josephus Daniels

Washington. Sept 13, 17

Secretary Baker desires you to know that the Georgia railroad controversy is settled by the Company agreeing to accept mediation. Judge Chambers and his associates are now recognized by both sides as conciliators. We both feel this information will be gratifying to you. Secretary Baker brought it about in a manner that will win your approval and congratulations.

Daniels.

T radiogram (J. Daniels Papers, DLC).

To Thomas Staples Martin

[*U.S.S. Mayflower*, Sept. 14, 1917]

Am greatly cheered to hear of the passage by the House of the Insurance Bill. In view of the great and immediate importance which I attach to this measure I venture to express the hope that it may be acted upon at the earliest possible time by the Senate. My sincere regards.   Woodrow Wilson.

T radiogram (WP, DLC).

To William Judson Hampton[1]

My dear Sir,   U.S.S. MAYFLOWER. 15 September, 1917.

I am sure that you will not have misunderstood my long delay in replying to your letter of the twenty-third of July last.[2] It has been due to an extraordinary pressure of public business not only, but also to a feeling that I really did not know how to write an adequate answer. It is very hard for me to speak of what my mother was without colouring the whole estimate with the deep love that fills my heart whenever I think of her; but, while others cannot have seen her as I did, I am sure that everyone who knew her at all must have felt the extraordinary quiet force of her character, must have felt also the charm of her unusual grace and refinement, and must have been aware of the clear-eyed, perceiving mind that lay behind her frank grey eyes. They were not always grey. They were of that strange, changeable colour which so often goes with strong character and varied ability. She was one of the most remarkable persons I have ever known. She was so reserved that only those of her own household can have known how lovable she was, though every friend knew how loyal and steadfast she was. I seem to feel still the touch of her hand and the sweet steadying influences of her wonderful character. I thank God to have had such a mother!

Very sincerely Yours,   Woodrow Wilson[3]

Photographic reproduction of WWTLS printed in Vernon Boyce Hampton, "In the Footsteps of Joseph Hampton and the Pennsylvania Quakers," *Bucks County Historical Society Papers*, VIII (1940), 256.

[1] Pastor of the Methodist Episcopal Church of Butler, N. J.

[2] It is missing.

[3] A WWsh draft of this letter is in WP, DLC.

From Dudley Field Malone

Dear Mr. President,   New York. Sept. 15th 1917.

Thank you sincerely for your courtesy, for I knew you were on a well-earned holiday and I did not expect an earlier reply to my letter of Sept. 7th 1917.

After a most careful re-reading of my letter, I am unable to understand how you could "judge that any discussion by you of my reasons for resigning would not be acceptable to me," since my letter was an appeal to you, on specific grounds, for action by the Administration on the Federal Suffrage Amendment.

However, I am profoundly grateful to you for your prompt acceptance of my resignation.

Yours respectfully   Dudley Field Malone.

ALS (WP, DLC).

From the Diary of Colonel House

New York, September 16, '17.

Sir William and I had a most interesting conversation on our motor trip to Plymouth, and from there to New London, where to [he] took the train for New York.

His Government took my estimate of him and each in turn gave him their confidential views. He says his Government think we are peculiar to pick him out as the medium for our most confidential negotiations, but if we are satisfied, they are. The fact that we do this indicates the character of representatives the British have in the United States. Of course, Wiseman, even with his ability, would not be so essential if the British Foreign Office had used good judgment.

The most startling thing Sir William told was that Lloyd George invited him and Lord Reading down to his country place, Walton Heath, and told them in the strictest confidence what he had in mind to do. He had not even yet communicated this to the War Cabinet.

The war on the western front, in his opinion, bids fair to be a stalemate despite the fact that the military leaders continue to assert they will eventually obtain a decision there. George said they first asked for more munitions. When these were supplied, it was the weather that prevented, and then it was the Russian collapse. He believes that another way out must be found and he has in mind the smashing of Turkey, or the smashing of Austria through the Italian front.

There is to be an Allied Conference in October or the first of November and Lloyd George wishes the President to send a representative, preferably me—to take part in it and to father the idea as to Turkey and Austria. He explained that he could not do this himself without risking his influence at home and in the Allied countries, but the United States could do it with impunity. That if the proposal was made by us and insisted upon, that he, George, would yield to our arguments and help force the other Allies into line.

Wiseman was instructed to bring this word to me, and Reading was instructed to take it to the President. No one else was to know of it. Reading was also directed to ask the President to name me as the representative from the United States, because "they trusted me and had no secrets from me." I hope it can be arranged for someone else to go for I do not desire to work in even a semi-official capacity.

I tried to impress Sir William with the idea that it was of more importance to have Russia become a virile democracy than it was to beat Germany to her knees. He is to send my views to his Government. He thought his people were beginning to look upon Russia as a hopeless problem. It may be that she is, but I am not yet willing to give her up.

I thought if conditions became worse in Russia, the conservative element would welcome German intervention in order to compose the situation. The people generally would soon desire order, even if it were German order, rather than what they seem to be drifting into. I outlined with considerable detail what I thought could be done to help compose Russia. One thing which is lacking is an agreement among the Allies as to policy.

Wiseman is to cable his Government that their present proposal to attack Germany from the south was what I suggested to them nearly two and a half years ago. Lloyd George told Wiseman that he thought it necessary for the German military oligarchy to have some symbol of defeat before it would be safe to undertake peace making. Here, again, I interposed to say, that after the Battle of the Marne they had this symbol of defeat, and that I tried to get the Entente to consent to open peace negotiations at that time.

Germany had counted up the men and economic power of the Entente and had felt that she would be beaten in a further trial of strength. She did not realize, as indeed the Allies did not realize themselves, that Germany was not overmatched, because the Allied strength was separated, largely disorganized, and could not be altogether coordinated. On the other hand, Germany had her 120 millions of people in a compact body and organized for war down to the last button. If we had been permitted to open negotiations at that time, we could have forced Germany to have done what we felt was necessary. If she had refused, the President would have been willing to throw the strength of the United States against her. The result of these negotiations would probably have meant peace, and they would probably have meant the overthrow of the present German Government, perhaps, the Dynasty itself.

History, I hope, will censure the Entente Governments for refusing to listen to our proposal for peace at that propitious time.

Wiseman said he met some people who thought Lloyd George is striving for a republic in England with himself as in the chief role. In Wiseman's and Milner's presence, a discussion was started concerning the powers of the President of the United States, which they assumed was practically that of a dictator when our country was at war. Milner said: "As a matter of fact you (meaning Lloyd George) are practically Great Britain's dictator." Something was then said of the King. Lloyd George replied: "He does not count. We cut off the head of one king for interfering." Wiseman said if George had not been Prime Minister, he would have resented this remark by leaving the conference.

He says the English realize that the war has reduced itself to a contest between Prussia, on the one hand, and Great Britain and the United States on the other. We discussed the tragedy of having a reactionary Cabinet in England at this period of the war. Curzon and Carson can hardly be matched in that direction, while Bonar Law and Lloyd George are anything but progressive at the moment. It is a pity that a man like Grey is not in supreme command. The entire British Government is honey-combed with reactionaries.

Sir William said the Government had decided to accept my advice given in a recent cable. Following my suggestion, they had already sent Reading, and are recalling Spring-Rice just as soon as they can find someone to take his place. The post at Washington is considered the great prize at this time, and there is keen opposition to Grey because of his relations with Asquith and the old Government. They also considered Grey too much of a pacifist. Still they will send him if it can be brought about. Each faction desires its own particular man. It may result in their keeping Lord Reading here.

Today I lunched with the President on board the Mayflower.

We had a talk before lunch. I told him of Wiseman's report and of Lloyd George's desire that a representative from the United States be sent to the Inter-Allied Conference, and of his desire that I should come. I indicated a willingness to go in the event the President wished me to do so. Mrs. Wilson, who was present during that part of the conversation, hoped I would remain in the United States because of the important work I was doing, and also because of the danger of crossing.

The President thought he could not go much further toward meeting Lloyd George's wishes than to express a feeling that something different should be done in the conduct of the war than had been done, and to say that the American people would not be willing to continue an indefinite trench warfare. He thought it would be inadvisable to commit himself further, and to this I agreed.

The difficulty is, Lloyd George's methods and purposes are not always of the highest. It is unfortunate not to have a government there composed of such men as Grey, Balfour and Cecil. International dealing is easy when such men are in comand. It is not pleasant when one is unable to receive statements of policy at their face value.

I left the Mayflower with the President at three o'clock, but came directly home instead of going with him to the Pennsylvania Station. I saw Wiseman in the late afternoon and we discussed plans for the immediate future. We have the greatest difficulty in keeping the Ambassador, Reading and Northcliffe on amicable terms.

To Edward Mandell House, with Enclosure

My dear House: The White House 17 September, 1917
I wish you would read the letter which Tumulty has attached to the enclosed correspondence and give me your judgment about it. I feel that there is a great deal of force in what Tumulty urges, but I am anxious to have your judgment on his argument before I form a final conclusion.

It was a great pleasure to see you.

In desperate Monday haste

Faithfully yours,   Woodrow Wilson

TLS (E. M. House Papers, CtY).

E N C L O S U R E

Joseph Patrick Tumulty to Albert Sidney Burleson

Dear General: The White House 15 September 1917.

Since talking with you yesterday with reference to the Massachusetts political situation, I have thought a great deal about it and must confess that there are certain phases of it that I think we ought to discuss before finally placing the matter before the President with the idea of procuring a statement from him such as has been suggested.

Of course, the filling of the state ticket in Massachusetts is a party necessity and the failure to do so would have a bad effect psychologically on the Democracy of the Nation.

But what I wish to advert to now is the effect on the whole country of a statement by the President such as is suggested; namely, that "sooner or later the forward-thinking men of the Nation must unite regardless of party to carry into effect those progressive principles which are so vital to the people of this country." The wisdom of the President's making a statement of this kind at this time is what troubles me.

These thoughts are in my mind: A statement of this kind issued at this time means the beginning of a great movement in this country for the wielding [welding] together of the liberal forces in both the Democratic and Republican parties. My fear is that the Democratic election in Massachusetts is not a proper stage upon which to exploit this idea. Therefore, I doubt the wisdom of it very much. The election of Mr. McCall, the Republican candidate,[1] is inevitable to my mind and if we went into this fight with the announcement of this principle, the whole country would accept it as a test, and failure would be disastrous. It would be better in these circumstances to let the Massachusetts election go by default than that we should go forward in this thing and meet with failure. In my opinion, therefore, we should await the opportunity which the Congressional elections of next year will offer us, to forward this character of campaign.

Another objection to it is this,—if the President at this time interferes, he will be charged with injecting partisan politics into a local contest at a time when the whole attitude of Congress and the country is really non-partisan. I have been in close touch with the Massachusetts situation, reading every day the editorial and news comment on the political situation there from the leading papers, particularly the Springfield Republican, the Boston Post, and the Boston Globe. Frankly, the difficulty with the Massachusetts situation is the effort of our generous Irish friends there to "hog" the situation as far as the State situation is concerned, and it is because of the utter disgust of the Democrats of the State that Mr. Mansfield[2] was allowed to take the field without opposition. Wouldn't it be better to allow Mr. Mansfield to be beaten that [than] that we should buttress him and support his campaign by surrounding him with such fine men as Hale and Olney?[3] Why not reserve these fine men and this announcement for the campaign of next year when no charge of injecting partisan politics can be made against the President?

I think, therefore, that the logic of the situation demands that the kind of campaign suggested should be reserved for the Congressional elections of next year. My suggestion, therefore, is that we get the best ticket we can in Massachusetts now and keep the President wholly out of the fight at this time.

However, if the President decides to do as you suggest, I think the statement should take the form of a letter to Mr. Hale himself, congratulating him upon the unselfish character of his service, then saying, "Sooner or later the forward-thinking men, etc., etc."   Sincerely yours,   J P Tumulty

TLS (J. P. Tumulty Papers, DLC).
 [1] Samuel Walker McCall, Republican candidate for governor.
 [2] Frederick William Mansfield, Democratic candidate for governor.
 [3] That is, Matthew Hale and Richard Olney (1871-1939), Democratic congressman from Massachusetts. Olney was a nephew of the late former Secretary of State, Richard Olney.

To Louis Freeland Post

My dear Mr. Post: [The White House] 17 September, 1917

Now that I have returned to my desk and am looking over the reports on the matters of last week, may I not send you a line to express the very sincere appreciation and admiration I feel for the effective conciliatory action of the department in the Boston & Maine strike[?]   Telegraphic news of it cheered me while I was away.

Cordially and sincerely yours,   Woodrow Wilson

TLS (Letterpress Books, WP, DLC).

To Joseph Patrick Tumulty, with Enclosures

Dear Tumulty:　　　　　　　[The White House, Sept. 17, 1917]

I hope with all my heart that Colver will go. They want him and I think he would do the thing admirably.

The President.

Phoned Mr. Colver 9/17/17.

TL (WP, DLC).

E N C L O S U R E　　I

William Byron Colver to Joseph Patrick Tumulty

My dear Mr Tumulty,　　　　　　Washington 11 Sept 1917

It is up to me to reply to this. I do not want to make the long journey unless it is my duty. I could suggest any other speaker you might care to name.

The situation in the Northwest is most unpleasant and I think the administration should not let the loose talk that they will indulge in go unanswered.

Most of those people mean well but they are being dreadfully misled. What is your pleasure or that of the National Committee.

Yours　　W. B. Colver.

ALS (WP, DLC).

E N C L O S U R E　　I I

St Paul Minn 1917 Sep 10

The National Non Partisan League in cooperation with other farm organizations and organized labor holding monster high cost living conference here St Paul September eighteenth to twentieth　Will be at least six thousand delegates　Will you speak conference supporting Presidents opposition to excessive profits　Will pay your expenses　Wire collect letter.[1]

Natl Nonpartisan League per Benj C. Marsh.

T telegram (WP, DLC).

[1] Colver did attend and speak at the conference.

To Joseph Patrick Tumulty

Dear Tumulty: [The White House, c. Sept. 17, 1917]

I would be very much obliged if you would have a form letter written to the following effect, to use in answer to all requests for special messages, unless they are of such an extraordinary character and interest that you think an exception might be made:

"The President directs me to say in reply to your letter of * * * that the pressure of public duties is so great upon him at present that he feels it is literally impossible for him to send special messages such as you suggest. He would not be willing to write them offhand, and it would not be possible for him to take the time to consider them in a way he should wish to consider them if he sent them upon so important an occasion. He feels confident that you will understand and will pardon a man whose days are not long enough for the tasks assigned to him."   The President.

TL (WP, DLC).

To Robert Lansing

My dear Mr. Secretary,   The White House. 17 September, 1917.

Thank you very much for having let me see the enclosed.[1] It is very satisfactory. I hope that they will see that it is not necessary for them to make any reply.

Faithfully Yours,   W.W.

WWTLI (SDR, RG 59, 763.72119/856½, DNA).
[1] The Enclosure printed with RL to WW, Sept. 10, 1917 (second letter of that date).

To David Franklin Houston

My dear Mr. Secretary: [The White House] 17 September, 1917

Here is a letter from a young friend of mine enclosing a plan about hogs.[1] I would be very much obliged if you would tell me what you think I ought to answer.[2] I know that he is acting in the most genuine spirit of helpfulness.

Faithfully yours,   Woodrow Wilson

TLS (Letterpress Books, WP, DLC).
[1] From Allen S. Hulbert. Hulbert's letter is missing.
[2] A White House memorandum, Sept. 25, 1917, T MS (WP, DLC), reveals that Houston replied to Wilson's letter on September 24. Wilson forwarded Houston's letter and some enclosed papers to Hulbert on September 25, with the following comment: "I wish with all my heart that something more definite and more directly helpful could be done, but I dare say you appreciate the reasons." WW to A. S. Hulbert, Sept. 25, 1917, TLS (Letterpress Books, WP, DLC).

From Joseph Patrick Tumulty

Dear Governor: The White House. 17 September 1917.

I learned from a confidential source that Mr. Lovett does not look with favor upon the proposed selection of Mr. Baruch as chairman of the War Industries Board, and that he intends to resign if this selection is made.

I think if you sent for him and had a little talk, you could persuade him from taking such a step.

Sincerely yours,   The Secretary

TL (WP, DLC).

From William Gibbs McAdoo

Dear Mr. President: Washington September 17, 1917.

I think Mr. Malone's resignation as Collector of the Port of New York should be accepted to take effect upon the appointment and qualification of his successor. It would be very unwise to accept the resignation to take effect immediately, because it would involve the execution of a large bond by the Deputy Collector and certain inconveniences in an administrative way which may as well be avoided.

As you know, I have felt for a long time that it was important to put a man in this office who would give it his personal attention. Aside from the regular duties of the office, the embargo on exports and the probable embargo on some imports under the pending trading with the enemy act, to say nothing of other matters developing from time to time and requiring the attention of the Collector in New York, make it of essential importance that a man of character, ability and industry, who will give his entire time and attention to the office, should be appointed. Such a man should also have knowledge of general Treasury administration.

The man best fitted for this position is Mr. Byron R. Newton, Assistant Secretary of the Treasury. He has had a wide experience in the Department, and is unusually qualified in temperament, character and ability for this responsible position. He is a New Yorker, is well known in the newspaper world particularly throughout the State, has not been identified with any of the factions in New York City, and is thoroughly loyal to the Administration and to the service. My sole objection to his appointment is the fact that I shall lose him as Assistant Secretary of the Treasury, but in the circumstances I feel that he can render a greater service at New York than at Washington.

I think the nomination should be made promptly, and hope this recommendation will meet with your approval.[1]

Cordially yours,   W G McAdoo

TLS (WP, DLC).

[1] Wilson appointed Newton on September 18; the Senate confirmed the nomination on October 1.

From Edward Nash Hurley

Dear Mr. President: Washington September 17, 1917.

On August 23rd Secretary Lansing sent me a copy of a despatch received from our Embassy at London quoting a personal letter from Mr. Balfour to Mr. Page, and asked me for my views thereon.[1] I replied on August 29th as per the attached copy,[2] and Secretary Lansing has replied stating that he had telegraphed my letter of August 29th in full prefaced by a statement that the views contained therein were those of this government. I also wish particularly to call your attention to my recent letter of September 14th to Secretary Lansing outlining the views of the Shipping Board in connection with our future action.[3] I am very anxious to discuss the matter with you further at your convenience.   Very faithfully yours,   Edward N. Hurley

TLS (WP, DLC).

[1] See A. J. Balfour to WHP, Aug. 16, 1917, printed as an Enclosure with EMH to WW, Aug. 27, 1917.

[2] E. N. Hurley to RL, Aug. 29, 1917, TCL (WP, DLC). Hurley stated that the primary responsibilities of the United States, as far as its own shipping resources were concerned, were the transport and maintenance of the American army in France. There were a great many uncertainties as to how much shipping would ultimately be required for these purposes, such as the total number of American troops who would ultimately go to France, the exact amounts of many kinds of supplies which they might need, and, above all, the number of American ships which might be sunk by German submarines in the course of the war. Therefore, it was impossible to state at the present time how much of the shipping being built for foreign nations in American shipyards might have to be taken over by the United States for its own purposes. Hurley believed that the administration should move slowly and cautiously in this matter. The only reassurance that he was willing to give to the Allies was that any shipping which might be taken over by the United States would be used exclusively in the service of the American army in France and in that of the Allies as well.

[3] E. N. Hurley to RL, Sept. 14, 1917, TCL (WP, DLC). Hurley here reiterated the arguments in his letter of August 29. However, he clarified the position of the Shipping Board by stating that it had reached a conclusion concerning foreign-owned ships in American shipyards: "For the present at least, it is deemed vitally essential not merely to the successful conclusion of the war, but to the actual safety of our military forces, to retain control of all ships built by American labor in American yards."

Sir Horace Plunkett to Arthur James Balfour

My dear Arthur,   [Dublin] 17th September, 1917.

I am sorry to worry you in your retreat but I am in rather a difficulty over a small matter which may have some importance.

Wilson sent me a personal message by Sir William Wiseman to the effect that he was deeply concerned for the success of the Irish Convention and asked me to keep him confidentially informed as to its progress and prospects. Far the best (and, incidentally, much the easiest) way to do this would be to send him my Secret Report to The King, which you may or may not have seen. I enclose as much of it as I have in print. A further instalment is in the printers' hands. I do not myself think there could be any objection to letting him see the document, and I am quite certain he could be relied upon to keep it secret. Of course, I should send it through the F.O. who, I presume, would have it personally handed to the President by Spring-Rice or the *Chargé d'Affaires* at Washington.

As far as I can judge, we are not likely to break up without coming to some agreement, and the longer we fight over it inside the Convention, the better chance there is of producing a scheme which will be acceptable North and South and possible for the Government to adopt. The country, even in the portions where Sinn Fein has completely routed the Parliamentary Party, is longing for a settlement and quite ready for any reasonable compromise. The difficulty is, of course, with Ulster, but even there things are moving satisfactorily.

If you see no objection to my sending this report to the President, perhaps you would kindly have a wire sent to me and get your Secretary to give the necessary authority to the F.O. to have my letter delivered.[1]   Yours ever,   Horace Plunkett

TLS (A. J. Balfour Papers, FO 800/211, PRO).
  [1] There is no evidence that Plunkett's report was sent to Wilson.

To Max Eastman

My dear Mr. Eastman: [The White House] 18 September, 1917

I thank you very warmly for your generous appreciation of my reply to the Pope, and I wish that I could agree with those parts of your letter which concern the other matters we were discussing when you were down here.[1] I think that a time of war must be regarded as wholly exceptional and that it is legitimate to regard things which would in ordinary circumstances be innocent as very dangerous to the public welfare, but the line is manifestly exceedingly hard to draw and I cannot say that I have any confidence that I know how to draw it. I can only say that a line must be drawn and that we are trying, it may be clumsily but genuinely, to draw it without fear or favor or prejudice.

Cordially and sincerely yours,   Woodrow Wilson

TLS (Letterpress Books, WP, DLC).
¹ Neither the Head Usher's Diary nor the Executive Office Diary records this meeting.

Two Letters to Robert Lansing

My dear Mr. Secretary,   The White House. 18 September, 1917.

So far as I understand the objects of the conference here re-ferred to,¹ I think that we could with advantage take part in it; but I must say that it is very vaguely forecast. Have we any other sources of information concerning it?

Faithfully Yours,   W.W.

WWTLI (SDR, RG 59, 763.72/6869½, DNA).
¹ See RL to WW, Sept. 10, 1917 (first letter of that date) and its Enclosure.

My dear Mr. Secretary,   The White House. 18 September, 1917.

Before I form a final opinion on this matter¹ I would very much like to know the feeling of the leading Poles in this country about it,—the men associated with Mr. Paderewski. Is there not some way in which we could learn it,—some way they would appreciate as showing our reliance on their judgment? I think they would have reason to feel badly if we were to act without consulting them, and I would be very much obliged it [if] you would ar-range to see them.   Faithfully Yours,   W.W.

WWTLI (SDR, RG 59, 860C.01/22½ E/B, DNA).
¹ See RL to WW, Sept. 11, 1917, and its Enclosures.

To Edward Nash Hurley

My dear Mr. Chairman: [The White House] 18 September, 1917

I have read the letters you spoke of when you were here last evening about the commandeering of the ships now building in our yards, and want to say that I think the necessities and policy of the case could not have been better stated.

Cordially and sincerely yours,   Woodrow Wilson

TLS (Letterpress Books, WP, DLC).

To Newton Diehl Baker

My dear Baker: The White House 18 September, 1917

If you have any opportunity to exercise a guiding hand in this matter, don't you think you could bring about the selection of some outsider such as Mr. Scott was in the case referred to in the enclosed memorandum, or perhaps steer the matter towards Judge Lovett himself? I do not know whether Tumulty's impression stated in the enclosed[1] is well founded or not, but in any case I think my suggestion is worth making.

Cordially and faithfully yours,   Woodrow Wilson

TLS (N. D. Baker Papers, DLC).
[1] JPT to WW, Sept. 17, 1917.

To Joseph Wright Harriman

Personal.

My dear Mr. Harriman: [The White House] 18 September, 1917

I appreciate very much your full and frank letter of September eighth[1] and most sincerely wish that I knew just how to act upon the suggestion which it conveys.

I feel confident that the tremors and uneasiness of the business world will presently pass and I think what we do down here will steady it more than anything I can say. I have tried to make it clear in what I have said about profits and the business processes of the Government that we intended to do full justice, but I also meant to make it clear that we did not think that large profits were justifiable in the circumstances. I think this is a time when everybody must make the utmost sacrifice for the common objects we have in view in this great struggle, and I am sure that is your own feeling and judgment also. If the endeavor to restrict profits within some reasonable limit unsteadies the business world, I am afraid I can give it no assurance which will steady it again.

But you may be sure, nevertheless, that whenever I have an occasion to say anything I will seek to keep your advice in mind and find means of reassurance, for there certainly is no justification for discouragement or pessimism of any kind or degree.

May I not express my very profound appreciation of the advertisement of which you send me a copy? It is more generous, I take the liberty of saying, than just, for I do not deserve it, but as an evidence of your feeling it gratifies me very deeply.

Cordially and sincerely yours,   Woodrow Wilson

TLS (Letterpress Books, WP, DLC).
[1] It is missing.

From Edward Mandell House

Dear Governor: New York. September 18, 1917.

After thinking the matter over I find myself not altogether trusting Lloyd George's plan which Reading is to present to you.[1] The English naturally want the road to Egypt and India blocked, and Lloyd George is not above using us to further this plan. He is not of the Grey-Balfour type and in dealing with him it is well to bear this in mind.

The Premier of New South Wales[2] called today. He is anxious that you make an exception of the fourteen small ships (3500 tons each) that are being built in this country. He says Australia would consider it a mark of great friendship.

I had a talk with Roland Morris today. I hope you will see him for ten or fifteen minutes before he leaves for Japan next Tuesday, in order to give him your viewpoint as to Far Eastern questions. I think he has the right view himself and, if you agree with it, he will understand in what direction to proceed.

We cannot meet Japan in her desires as to land and immigration, and unless we make some concessions in regard to her sphere of influence in the East, trouble is sure, sooner or later to come. Japan is barred from all the undeveloped places of the earth, and if her influence in the East is not recognized as in some degree superior to that of the Western powers, there will be a reckoning.

A policy can be formulated which will leave the open door, rehabilitate China, and satisfy Japan. Morris sees this clearly but needs your sanction, if, indeed, such a policy has your sanction.   Affectionately yours,   E. M. House

TLS (WP, DLC).
[1] That is, the general military strategy suggested in D. Lloyd George to WW, Sept. 3, 1917.
[2] William Arthur Holman.

From William Bauchop Wilson, with Enclosure

My dear Mr. President: Washington September 18, 1917.

I am sending you herewith a memorandum to the Secretary of Labor proposing the appointment of a commission along the lines of our discussion this afternoon. I have read the memorandum to Mr. Gompers over the telephone and it meets with his approval.

May I again suggest that it would give added influence to the commission to have its members meet you immediately before proceeding to the working end.

Faithfully yours,   W B Wilson

TLS (WP, DLC).

E N C L O S U R E¹

MEMORANDUM FOR THE SECRETARY OF LABOR.

I am very much interested in the labor situation in the mountain region and on the Pacific Coast. I have listened with ⟨the closest⟩ attention ⟨to the⟩ and *concern to the numerous* charges of misconduct and injustice that ⟨have been made against each other by⟩ representatives *both* of employers and *of* employees *have made against each other*. I am not so much concerned, however, with the manner in which they have treated each other in the past as I am desirous of seeing some kind of a working arrangement arrived at for the future, particularly during the period of the war, on a basis that will be fair to all parties concerned. To assist in the accomplishment of that purpose, I have decided to appoint a commission to visit ⟨the mountain and Pacific Coast states⟩ *the localities where disagreements have been most frequent* as my personal representatives. The commission will consist of William B. Wilson, Secretary of Labor; Colonel J. L. Spangler, of Pennsylvania; Verner Z. Reed, of Colorado; John H. Walker, of Illinois; and E. P. Marsh, of Washington. Felix Frankfurter of New York will act as Secretary of the commission.

It will be the duty of the commission to visit in each instance the Governor of the state, advising him that they are there as the personal representatives of the President with a view to lending sympathetic counsel and aid to the state government in the development of a better understanding *between laborers and employees*, and also *themselves* to deal with employers and employees in a conciliatory spirit, seek to compose differences and allay misunderstanding, and ⟨to foster a feeling that⟩ *in any way that may be open to them show the active interest of* the national Government ⟨is actively interested in the situation⟩ *in furthering arrangements just to both sides*. Wherever it is deemed advisable conferences of employers and employees should be called with the purpose of working out a mutual understanding between them which will insure the continued operation of the industry on conditions acceptable to both sides. The commission should also endeavor to learn the real causes for any discontent which may exist on either side, not by the formal process of public hearings but by getting into touch with workmen and employers by the more informal process of personal conversation. I would be pleased to have the commission report to me from time to time such information as may require immediate attention.

President.[2]

T MS (WP, DLC).
[1] Words in angle brackets deleted by Woodrow Wilson; words in italics added by him.
[2] President Wilson issued the revised statement on September 19.

Herbert Clark Hoover to Joseph Patrick Tumulty

Dear Mr. Tumulty: Washington September 18, 1917.

With regard to your note of the 17th on the subject of the Pacific Northwestern protest as to the differentials affecting the Government purchase of the Northwestern wheat, I inclose a memorandum[1] which I sent on the 8th to several of the senators and congressmen of the Northwest and which seems to me to cover the situation. I understand they are coming to see the President,[2] and this will inform you of the matter as far as we are concerned.

I would add that the average yield in the Pacific Northwest was some twenty-four bushels to the acre as against only fourteen or fifteen bushels in the Mississippi Valley points, so it is quite evident that the farmers in the Pacific Northwest will make more money than those in the Mississippi Valley, even with a freight differential against them.

Yours faithfully,   Herbert Hoover

TLS (WP, DLC).
[1] It is missing in both the Hoover and Wilson Papers.
[2] Senator Chamberlain brought a delegation of twenty-two persons representing the wheat growers to the White House on September 20 for a meeting of half an hour. A transcript of the Swem shorthand notes of this meeting (C. L. Swem Coll., NjP) reveals that the representatives of the northwestern wheat growers appealed to Wilson to set a price for northwestern wheat which would take into account the additional freight rates incurred on account of the long distance of the region from its markets. Wilson replied that, should the northwestern wheat growers withhold their crops, the Allied governments would simply divert their purchases to Argentina and Australia. "What I am afraid of, therefore," Wilson continued, "is that if . . . the farmers hold their wheat, the bottom will presently drop out of the price entirely and . . . our surplus will go begging, and, with the going begging of the surplus, will come the depression of the price of what we are consuming at home."

From the Diary of Josephus Daniels

1917   Tuesday 18   September

Cabinet—The President back from his trip on the Mayflower. . . . He felt encouraged by news from France. Spoke highly of Ambassador Sharp's telegram. Before Kornelof revolted,[1] Sharp had quoted a man returning from Russia predicting it would happen & that he would win

[1] An abortive and bloodless attempt at a coup against the Provisional Government in early September, led by the right-wing general, Lavr Georgievich Kornilov, then commander in chief of the Russian armies. The attempted coup served chiefly to reveal how weak the Provisional Government really was. For a full discussion of the affair, see Chamberlin, *The Russian Revolution*, I, 192-222.

To Newton Diehl Baker

My dear Mr. Secretary: The White House 19 September, 1917

Here is another snag. The gentlemen who sign this memorandum as conscientious objectors belong to a church which keeps the seventh day as the Sabbath and therefore they don't want to work on Saturday.[1] Could it be arranged to have them work on Sunday?   Faithfully yours,   Woodrow Wilson

TLS (WDR, RG 94, AGO-Misc. File, No. 2638715, DNA).
[1] S. W. Mentzer *et al.* to WW, c. Sept. 17, 1917, TLS (WDR, RG 94, AGO-Misc. File No. 2638715, DNA). The signers, an executive committee of the "Church of God," also asked that any of their members who might be drafted be employed in agricultural work.

To William Bauchop Wilson

My dear Mr. Secretary: The White House 19 September, 1917

I am very glad to accept the enclosed memorandum.[1] I am in hope that you will act upon it.

In haste

Cordially and sincerely yours,   Woodrow Wilson

TLS (LDR, RG 174, DNA).
[1] Wilson enclosed a typed copy of the revised statement printed as an Enclosure with W. B. Wilson to WW, Sept. 18, 1917.

To Edward Mandell House, with Enclosure

My dear House,   The White House. 19 September, 1917.

Lansing is not only content that you should undertake the preparation of data for the peace conference but volunteered the opinion that you were the very one to do it, and I promised him

I would send you the enclosed memorandum, which he had drawn up. Of course we shall have to define the studies of our assistants with as much precision as possible or they would all be as thorough and exhaustive (and therefore as useless) as Frankfurter would be if he went to the depths he proposed.

In great haste,

With affectionate messages from us all
Faithfully,   W.W.

WWTLI (E. M. House Papers, CtY).

ENCLOSURE

CONFIDENTIAL MEMORANDUM ON PREPARATORY WORK FOR PEACE CONFERENCE.

September 15, 1917.

It is impossible in selecting negotiators to represent this Government at the Peace Conference to find men who possess the full knowledge to deal with the numerous and complex questions which will arise. It is important, therefore, that they should be furnished beforehand with information and data in a condensed form upon which they can rely in the discussion of questions even though they may not be participants in all the discussions.

To accomplish this purpose experts on the various probable subjects of negotiation should be invited, with or without compensation, to prepare brief, though comprehensive articles on these subjects, explaining to the writers that the purpose is for the use of the representatives of the United States at the Peace Conference and that, therefore, their work must be kept secret.

The subjects in general would fall under the heads of History, Commerce, and International Law. *History* would naturally be divided under the various countries and could be developed along political, commercial, industrial and military lines. Possibly it would be found advantageous to group certain countries together in treating of their history, while colonial possessions would require special treatment. *Commerce* would be in a measure statistical but would involve the careful study of exports and imports, markets and trade routes. *International Law* would cover a wide range of subjects, relating to peace and war, such as maritime law, rules of war, neutralization of land communication, internationalization of waterways, extent of territorial waters, &c.

Outside of these subjects which fall under the three heads named, there are others which should be considered, such as disarmament, international guaranties and their enforcement, arbitration, &c. Possibly, too, it would be advisable to have the constitutions and political institutions of the countries carefully analyzed and commented upon.

Following out this general plan, which, if adopted, ought to be elaborated with great care in order that the experts engaged would understand the exact limits of their respective studies, a selection should be made from the historians, political economists and jurists in this country, who are especially qualified to deal with particular subjects. Each should prepare a pamphlet of not to exceed 10,000 or 15,000 words on the topic assigned to him and these pamphlets after being submitted to the person or persons having general charge of the work of gathering information for the negotiators should be secretly printed and carefully indexed for use when occasion arises.

In addition to these condensed articles it would probably be advisable to have a collection of documents, statistics, quotations, &c., which would form appendices to the articles, but which should be indexed so that they could be readily referred to. These appendices should also be secretly printed.

Full instructions should also be prepared for each writer engaged on this work explaining the method of treatment of the subject assigned to him.

The division of subjects, the selection of writers, the issuance of instructions, the examination of articles and collected data, and the direction of printing and indexing should be in the hands of one man, who should have such assistants as he may require.

Queries

How far should the United States take part in the determination of European boundaries?

How far should the United States take part in the redistribution of colonial possession[s]?

Should the United States go further than to approve or disapprove an agreed boundary on any other ground than that it contains an element of future discord?

Should the basis of territorial distribution be race, language, religion or previous political affiliation?

Where two or more countries have political claims to a particular territory, as in Macedonia, what should be the basis of settlement? If it is determined that the preponderance of a particular nationality in the population is controlling *prima facie*, how far should conquest or enforced colonization affect such basis? (This might apply to Alsace-Lorraine, Schleswig-Holstein and the region about Dantzig.)

Should colonial possessions be guaranteed to the power holding them without a limitation as to the character of the government, commercial freedom, and economic opportunity to other nations?

T and Hw MSS (SDR, RG 59, 182/1, DNA).

From Newton Diehl Baker, with Enclosure

Dear Mr. President,   Washington. September 19, 1917.

The enclosed memorandum was made for me by Lippman[n], who has evidently been in conference with Mr. Gompers. I of course, know of the memorandum of agreement referred to, and it was brought to your attention at the time of Mr. Macey's appointment.

I have no further knowledge of subsequent proceedings, but it would seem that as we have appointed a board for the adjustment of difficulties of this kind, very grave difficulties would be created, were the Government to repudiate its action.

I am sending this with the thought that perhaps Mr. Hurley has taken the matter up with you. If he has not, and you desire it, I will take it up at once with the Secretary of Labor and get him to get all the facts, for submission to you, so that you may communicate with Mr. Hurley in the matter.

I have had a somewhat similar arrangement with regard to the cantonment construction, and have insisted on living absolutely up to its terms, so that labor has at no point had a chance to charge us with any lack of fidelity to the understanding. The result is that the cantonments have been completed in record-breaking time, and under conditions which I think justify the wisdom of an understanding of this kind with labor.

Respectfully yours,   Newton D. Baker

TLS (WP, DLC).

E N C L O S U R E

MEMORANDUM for the Secretary of War: Sept. 19, 1917.

SUBJECT: Adjustment of labor disputes in private shipyards.

1. About August 20th a memorandum agreement for the adjustment of labor disputes in private ship building plants, where the shipping board and navy are having construction carried on, was signed between the Secretary of the Navy, Mr. Hurley,

Chairman of the United States Shipping Board, Admiral Capps, General Manager of the Emergency Fleet Corporation, on the one hand, and Mr. Gompers, and 12 International Presidents of Metal Trades' Unions on the other hand.[1] The President appointed the member of the adjustment board representing the public, V. Everit Macy,[2] and the board was organized about September 3rd.

2. This agreement for adjustment between the Government and Organized Labor is the foundation on which must rest any future agreements for adjusting labor disputes incident to production of munitions and supplies. If the Government should be placee [placed] in the position of evading this agreement we can hardly expect that the union leaders can be induced to accept further voluntary arrangements; and the necessity of compulsory arbitration laws will be presented to the Administration.

3. Mr. Hurley and Admiral Capps in letters about two weeks ago to Mr. Macy, Chairman of the Adjustment Board, following conversations with Mr. Macy, took the general position that the Shipping Board could not submit labor disputes to such adjustment unless the Adjustment Board would limit any advances in wages to figures set by Admiral Capps. This has stopped all activities of the Adjustment Board; and Mr. Macy is only waiting from day to day to put his resignation into the hands of the President. In the meantime the Pacific Coast conditions, which were being held in check by the Adjustment Board's efforts, have broken out dangerously.

4. Mr. Hurley and Admiral Capps now maintain that the ship builders will be in collusion with the workers and that their local representative in voting as associate member on the Adjustment Board would conspire with the ship workers' local representative on the Board. The Shipping Board's contracts provide that the United States Shipping Board must bear the burden of wage increases.

5. Because of pressure that has been brought upon Mr. Hurley in the past few days it is probable that Mr. Hurley's position has changed somewhat, and that he would maintain that he is now mainly interested in preventing the functioning of the Adjustment Board until the ship builders have agreed to stand all or part of the wage increase on commandeered ships which constitute over one third of the tonnage now under construction. It would seem that this question could well be left to arbitration and should not be allowed to interfere with the adjustment of the strikes which are causing incalculable harm to the Government's war program.

6. Mr. Hurley while taking care of the pennies as against his ship builders is playing with dynamite; he is jeopardizing the honor of the Government in its dealings with organized labor. If the President does not at once bring the adjustment memorandum back into full life there will, according to Mr. Gompers' own statement, be an irreparable estrangement between the Government and labor.   WL

TI MS (N. D. Baker Papers, DLC).

[1] This agreement created the Shipbuilding Labor Adjustment Board, about which see V. E. Macy to WW, Sept. 20, 1917. The standard history of the board is Willard E. Hotchkiss and Henry R. Seager, *History of the Shipbuilding Labor Adjustment Board, 1917 to 1919*, Bulletin of the United States Bureau of Labor Statistics No. 283 (Washington, 1921).

[2] Valentine Everit Macy, at this time president of the National Civic Federation, best known for his reform work as Commissioner of Public Welfare of Westchester County, N. Y.

From Newton Diehl Baker

Dear Mr. President: Washington. September 19, 1917.

I don't want the inclosed[1] to be too encouraging, because, of course, it represents only our experience with the first five percent of the men called under the draft, but it does not seem from this first survey as though our problem was going to be unmanagably large, or so large that a very generous and considerate mode of treatment would be out of the question.

I feel quite sure that our policy of not announcing in advance the course to be taken has limited the number of these objectors to those who actually do entertain scruples of that kind.

Respectfully yours,   Newton D. Baker

TLS (WP, DLC).

[1] "Conscientious Objectors Reported at Cantonments," T MS (WP, DLC). Of ten training camps surveyed on the subject, seven had reported no conscientious objectors, one had two, another six, and a third had "3/10 of 1 per cent." There were four camps yet to be heard from.

From Edward Mandell House

Dear Governor: New York. September 19, 1917.

I am returning the correspondence concerning the Massachusetts situation.

I am not hopeful of success there, but I see no harm in your sending at the proper time a message to Hale showing that you have an interest in the progressives getting together.

Hale telephoned me last night and read a telegram from Burleson which indicated that you had already made up your mind to write such a letter, and in consequence he has decided to go on the ticket.

I do not think a letter of that kind will commit the Administration to such an extent that the defeat of the ticket will be considered a defeat of the Administration. Neither do I think that you can say that kind of thing too often. It may be said now and again next year, and with as much more emphasis as the occasion requires.   Affectionately yours,   E. M. House

TLS (WP, DLC).

From Robert Lansing

My dear Mr. President: [Washington] September 19, 1917.

I have just learned that Lord Reading is the bearer of a personal letter to you from the Prime Minister and that he has cabled to know whether the letter had been delivered yet.

I believe it would be very advisable if you could see Lord Reading—not for an interview but simply for the purpose of delivering the letter—tomorrow or next day; and then let the interview which you have arranged for next Monday remain and see him then. I make this suggestion in view of the fact that it may cause embarrassment if the letter is not promptly delivered as evidently Lloyd-George is very anxious to have it in your hands at the earliest possible moment.

Will you please have Mr. Forster let me know your decision in the matter and I will communicate with Lord Reading if you can arrange for a five-minute appointment with him as suggested.[1]
                    Faithfully yours,   Robert Lansing.

TLS (Lansing Letterpress Book, SDR, RG 59, DNA).
    [1] Wilson saw Reading for a half hour on September 20. The appointment for September 24 was canceled.

From Robert Scott Lovett

My dear Mr. President: Washington September 19, 1917.

I enclose a statement approved by my associates which correctly states the agreement of the War Industries Board with the copper producers; and pursuant to your request of this afternoon, we have endeavored to put it in a form which we would suggest for your consideration as suitable for publication.
                    Very respectfully,   Robert S. Lovett

TLS (WP, DLC).

William Bauchop Wilson to Joseph Patrick Tumulty

My dear Mr. Tumulty: Washington September 19, 1917.

I am in receipt of your letter of the 10th instant, inclosing a telegram from Richard Stephens, Chairman, and W. R. Davis, Secretary, of the Clifton, Arizona, Citizens' Committee, proposing the settlement of the strike at Clifton by submission to arbitration.

The telegram clearly states that the operators have not accepted the proposition to arbitrate, and until the President has such assurance, it would be useless for him to undertake to name an arbiter. Should the commission now under consideration by the President be finally determined upon, it is possible that it may be able to work out an adjustment of the difficulty, not only at Clifton but at other points in Arizona.

I am returning the telegram herewith.

Cordially yours,   W B Wilson

TLS (WP, DLC).

To Robert Scott Lovett, with Enclosure

My dear Judge Lovett: [The White House] 20 September, 1917

Thank you for your letter of yesterday enclosing the statement approved by yourself and your associates with regard to the agreement of the War Industries Board with the copper producers. I am taking pleasure in making it public at once.

Cordially and sincerely yours,   Woodrow Wilson

TLS (Letterpress Books, WP, DLC).

E N C L O S U R E[1]

After investigation by the Federal Trade Commission as to the cost of producing copper, the President has approved an agreement made by the War Industries Board with the copper producers fixing a price of twenty-three and one-half cents per pound f.o.b. New York, subject to revision after four months. Three important ⟨considerations⟩ *conditions* were imposed by the Board. First, that the producers would not reduce the wages now being paid; ⟨notwithstanding the reduction in the price of copper, which would involve a reduction in wages under the "sliding scale" so long in effect in the copper mines⟩; Secondly, *that* the operators ⟨shall⟩ *would* sell to the Allies and *to* the public copper at the same price paid by the Government, and ⟨will⟩ take the necessary measures, under the direction of the War Industries Board, for the distribution of the copper, ⟨and⟩ to prevent it from falling into the hands of speculators, who would increase the price to the public; and third, *that* the operators pledge themselves to exert every effort necessary to keep up the production of copper to the maximum of the past, so long as the war lasts.

The War Industries Board felt that the maintenance of the largest production should be assured, and that a reduction in wages should be avoided. The stipulation that the present wages shall not be reduced compels the maintenance of the highest wages ever paid in the industry, which without such stipulation would, *with the reduction made in the price of copper*, be reduced under the sliding scale ⟨with the reduction made in the price of copper⟩ *so long in effect in the copper mines*. Within this year copper has sold as high as 36 cents per pound, and the ⟨present⟩ market price would *now* be higher than it is had it not been well known for some weeks that the Government would fix the price.

The principal copper producers throughout the country have evinced ⟨a most patriotic⟩ *an admirable* spirit and for weeks have promptly supplied every request of the Government for copper, without awaiting decision as to price, and agreeing to accept the price which the Board should ultimately fix. The proper departments of the Government will be asked to take over the mines and plants of any producers who fail to conform to the arrangement and price, if any such there should be.

T MS (WP, DLC).
    [1] Words in angle brackets deleted by Wilson; words in italics added by him.

To Newton Diehl Baker

My dear Mr. Secretary: The White House 20 September, 1917

Thank you for sending me the enclosed memorandum.[1] I had a talk with Hurley and hope that the best that is possible in the circumstances is being made out of a bad situation.

    Cordially and faithfully yours,   Woodrow Wilson

TLS (N. D. Baker Papers, DLC).
    [1] That is, the Enclosure with NDB to WW, Sept. 19, 1917 (first letter of that date).

Two Letters from Newton Diehl Baker

My dear Mr. President: Washington. September 20, 1917.

I have your note of the 19th,[1] enclosing a letter of the 18th by the chairman of the National Advisory Committee for Aeronautics with regard to the operation of the draft upon men in the spruce logging and lumbering industry. I feel that I ought to take this matter up with the Secretary of Labor before attempting to express an opinion. As you know, there has been difficulty with labor in the spruce field, and, while it might be necessary for us to organize under some military form a regiment or other unit of foresters to go into the forests and get the spruce we need, I feel very sure that in the interest of the whole labor situation that course ought not to be taken except as a last resort. The Secretary of Labor has been constantly in touch with this lumber strike, and the last report I had on the subject was so favorable that I assumed it needed no further attention from me. I will, therefore, get into communication with Secretary Wilson and bring my own information down to date.

I do not see how in any event a remedy could be provided by any sort of directions, even from Washington, to the District Exemption Boards in the matter of exemption of individuals. If, when the draft is completed, it is found that serious inroads have been made upon the number of men engaged in this industry, we can use your power to discharge men from the military service to correct the difficulty; but no anticipatory action of that kind could be taken.   Respectfully yours,   Newton D. Baker

[1] WW to NDB, Sept. 19, 1917, TLS (Letterpress Books, WP, DLC).

My dear Mr. President: Washington. September 20, 1917.

I have your letter enclosing the petition of the gentlemen who observe Saturday as the Sabbath. It will give me pleasure to keep this point of view in mind when we come to arrange non-combatant service for conscientious objectors.

I am beginning to feel that nothing short of a comprehensive knowledge of Professor James's book on "Varieties of Religious Experience"[1] will ever qualify a man to be a helpful Secretary of War.   Respectfully yours,   Newton D. Baker

TLS (WP, DLC).
[1] He of course referred to William James, *The Varieties of Religious Experience* (New York and London, 1902).

From Edward Mandell House

Dear Governor: New York. September 20, 1917.

Thank you for your letter of yesterday enclosing Lansing's memorandum as to what preparatory work he thinks necessary for the peace conference. He has done it very well and his ideas are not far from mine.

I have the matter of organization pretty well outlined in my own mind, subject to your approval. I think it will be necessary to have three men working closely with me here, besides those studying special problems.

Among those here, I had thought tentatively of Mezes and Lippman[n]. Mezes to be my confidential man and Lippman to be secretary. The objection to Lippman is that he is a Jew, but unlike other Jews he is a silent one. The small group around me must be in thorough sympathy with your purposes.

The City College, I am sure, will be glad to give Mezes indefinite leave of absence if you approve his selection. Could he be objected to because he is Mrs. House's brother-in-law? He is one of the ablest men I know, has a broad progressive outlook, is well grounded in both political and economic history, speaks French and German and understands Italian and Spanish.

Thanks to Frankfurter, quite a number of people know that you have this owrk [work] in mind for me to do, and David Lawrence has already mentioned it in his dispatches. However, this is not important for the reason that the other belligerents are well advanced in such work.

Lansing's attitude is just what I expected. I have never found the slightest trace of petty jealousy in him as far as I am concerned.   Affectionately yours,   E. M. House

TLS (WP, DLC).

From Valentine Everit Macy

Sir: Washington, D. C., September 20, 1917.

On August 20th, 1917, an agreement was signed by Mr. F. D. Roosevelt, as Acting Secretary of the Navy, the Chairman of the United States Shipping Board, the General Manager of the Emergency Fleet Corporation, Mr. Samuel Gompers, and the Presidents of the International Unions of the workmen engaged in the building and repairing of ships. The agreement provided for the establishment of a Board to which should be referred "disputes concerning wages, hours or conditions of labor in the construction or repair of shipbuilding plants or ships in shipyards," and it further provided that the "decisions of said Board will, in so far as this agreement may be capable of achieving such result, be final and binding on all parties." The Board was to be composed of three permanent members: The Chairman, to be appointed by yourself, one member by the Fleet Corporation, and one by Samuel Gompers. In addition there were to be two "Associate Members, one to be designated by the owner or owners of local plants in which a dispute had arisen, and one by the majority of the workers in the particular craft or crafts directly interested in the disputed matters."

On August 25th, you did me the honor to appoint me as Chairman of the Board established under this agreement. Since your appointment of me to that position, I have been advised that Hon. Josephus Daniels, Secretary of the Navy, Admiral Capps and Mr. Hurley for the Shipping Board and all the representatives of the labor organizations united in recommending me to you for such appointment.

On August 28th, I reached Washington and met Mr. A. J. Berres,[1] who had been appointed a member of the Board by Mr. Gompers. Upon the arrival, on September 1st, of Mr. E. F. Carry,[2] the appointee of the Fleet Corporation, the members met and the Board was organized.

From the above date until September 10th, the Board held daily sessions and conferred with shipyard owners and their employes from New York, Wilmington and Seattle, where strikes were in progress or were threatened. In addition, the Board communicated with employers and employes in Texas, Boston, Portland, Oregon, and San Francisco.

Several conferences were held with the Chairman of the Shipping Board, the General Manager of the Fleet Corporation[3] and Assistant Secretary Roosevelt. From these interviews, two facts developed:

First, that the local shipyard owners were unwilling to appoint an Associate Member to the Board as provided in the agreement, without first being assured that the Fleet Corporation would assume all increased costs that might result from any decisions rendered by the Board; and

Second, that the Chairman of the Shipping Board and the General Manager of the Fleet Corporation were loath to have the final decision as to wage scales, and consequently part of the labor cost of constructing ships, taken out of their hands and placed in the Board.

The Board was being pressed for action from many sources,

and in order to have the situation clearly understood, addressed a memorandum (copy of which is enclosed) to the Chairman of the Shipping Board and the General Manager of the Fleet Corporation.[4]

There seems to be a disposition to place the Board in the position of having urged that the ship yard owners should be guaranteed any increase[d] cost by reason of wage adjustment or awards by our Board; when as a matter of fact the purpose the Board had in mind in sending the memorandum was to have the Emergency Fleet Corporation determine definitely what part, if any, the government or the owners should bear.

It was necessary to know that the increased cost, if any, occasioned by an award of wages by our Board was taken care of, for if that were to remain indefinite it would have confused the situation materially and rendered ineffective the findings and destroyed the usefulness of the Board.

The question of how any increased cost resulting from the findings of the Board was to be met was a matter to be settled between the Fleet Corporation and the yard owners, for as a judicial body our only consideration should be what was a just wage scale or proper conditions of labor. For the above reasons, it became impossible for the Board to function as contemplated by the agreement of August 20th.

On the 10th, letters were received from Mr. Hurley and General Manager Capps (which are enclosed).[5]

The following morning, the 11th, the Board met with these gentlemen, and Mr. Carry, the representative of the Fleet Corporation, believing that his services were no longer required, presented his resignation which was immediately accepted by Mr. Hurley. For the past ten days, therefore, it has been impossible to make operative the agreement of August 20th, and there seems to be no prospect of so doing.

As you know, in the meantime serious situations have arisen, particularly in the ship building and repairing industry on the Pacific coast, impairing the facility for ship construction and repair.

I am in consequence sending you this report and am awaiting your pleasure with reference to the further action which you may desire me to take as your appointee. Should you think best, please consider my resignation as chairman of the Labor Adjustment Board in your hands.

Allow me to express my deep appreciation of the honor conferred upon me by your appointment and to assure you of my willingness and desire to serve in any capacity at any time that you may believe to be in the public interest.

Very respectfully yours,   V. Everit Macy.[6]

TLS (WP, DLC).

[1] Albert Julius Berres, secretary of the metal trades department of the American Federation of Labor.

[2] Edward Francis Carry, president of the Haskell & Barker Car Co., Inc., of Michigan City, Ind.

[3] That is, Admiral Capps.

[4] V. E. Macy to E. N. Hurley and W. L. Capps, Sept. 7, 1917, CC MS (WP, DLC). Macy explained that the Shipbuilding Labor Adjustment Board could accomplish little or nothing until the Emergency Fleet Corporation decided whether or not it would compensate ship-yard owners for increases in the wage scales instituted by the board. Macy also pointed out that the owners had not been a party to the agreement which had established the board. Some of them, he added, were now refusing to abide by any decision of the board until a settlement of the question of who should pay for increased wages had been reached.

[5] W. L. Capps to E. N. Hurley, Sept. 10, 1917, and E. N. Hurley to V. E. Macy, Sept. 10, 1917, both TLS (WP, DLC). Capps argued that the Emergency Fleet Corporation, if it acted with due regard for the public interest, simply could not assume a blanket responsibility for any wage increases to be granted either at present or in the future. Even in agreements or contracts already made or about to be made, a 10 per cent increase in wages would cost the government an estimated $50,000,000 if such a policy was followed. The only equitable policy was for the Emergency Fleet Corporation to determine carefully in the case of each ship yard what portion of the cost of wage increases it might reasonably be expected to bear. Capps admitted that such a policy might require a considerable modification in the functions of the Labor Adjustment Board. Hurley's letter was largely an endorsement of Capps' conclusions on the subject.

[6] Wilson wrote to Tumulty about this letter as follows: "Here is something which, like Mr. Gompers' letter you were showing me the other day, will probably be reconsidered when the real position of affairs is known. Will you not hold it pending that outcome?" WW to JPT, c. Sept. 24, 1917, TL (WP, DLC). Tumulty replied: "This controversy has been settled. I would suggest that you allow me to acknowledge Mr. Macy's letter, telling him that I have called it to the attention of the President." Wilson noted: "OKeh W.W." JPT to WW, Sept. 24, 1917, TL (WP, DLC). See the following correspondence on this subject, especially JPT to WW, Sept. 23, 1917.

Edward Mandell House to Robert Lansing

Dear Mr. Lansing: New York. September 20, 1917.

The President tells me of your conference with him yesterday as far as it related to me, and the work which you both have in mind for me to do.

I expect to be in Washington next week and I hope we may have an opportunity to talk it out, so I may have the benefit of your views and wide experience.

The memorandum which you gave the President, and which he in turn sent me, is in every way admirable and will be helpful in planning an organization.

Sincerely yours,   E. M. House

TLS (SDR, RG 59, 182/2, DNA).

Sir William Wiseman to Sir Eric Drummond

[New York] Sept. 20, 1917.

No. 12. (A). Situation here is better than when I left. MCADOO is more inclined to be helpful because he now realises the very serious responsibility which he would assume if Allied finance collapsed through any petty action of his. Of course, he still has his political difficulties and there are serious financial problems unsolved, but Reading is approaching them in the right spirit, and is very acceptable person to all the Administration. HOUSE, as usual, is very helpful, and I believe we are now tackling situation properly.

(B). While I cannot say there is any popular enthusiasm for the war, there is a very solid determination to carry on with all the resources of the country until the German military power is crushed. The position of the President remains very strong. Feeling towards the British is improving, but the administration is becoming impatient with the French.

(C.) The President learns from confidential sources that French morale is very bad, and that they may not hold together through the winter. He is alarmed about this, and he would do anything in reason to safeguard the situation. For example, he might put U. S. troops into the line earlier than at present intended.

(D). For your private information only, I believe it would be possible to persuade the President to send HOUSE or BAKER, War Minister, on official visit to London and Paris to confer. Do you think this would be desirable?

(E). Reference CECIL's cable to House regarding blockade cooperation:[1] In principle his suggestions are acceptable, and I think matter can be arranged if you would let me know precisely what you want done.   W.

T telegram (W. Wiseman Papers, CtY).
   [1] It is missing. However, it undoubtedly adhered closely to the policy outlined in a memorandum of the British embassy in Washington dated August 27, 1917, T MS, enclosed in C. Barclay to W. Wiseman, Sept. 30, 1917, TLS, both in W. Wiseman Papers, CtY. Both the memorandum and Barclay's letter stressed the necessity of close and continuous consultation between the British and American governments on blockade policy as well as trade policy toward the neutral nations in general. Each government would continue to follow an independent policy, but those policies would have to be closely coordinated. To that end, the memorandum specifically proposed "a recognised method of continual consultation" both in London and Washington. "These two sets of conferences," the memorandum continued, "would not be Allied Councils with joint powers of decision, but meetings of friendly associates for the purpose of mutual information on which each may base his own independent recommendations to his Government. The information and recommendations would relate to two main classes of subjects: (1) Applications by exporters for licenses to ship goods to the Northern neutrals and applications for free passage of goods to these neutrals through the naval patrols. (2) Requests received from the Northern

neutrals for facilities for the importation of supplies and proposals put forward by them or by any of the Governments associated in the war against Germany as to the conditions upon which such requests might be granted."

To Joseph Wright Harriman

[The White House]
My dear Mr. Harriman: 21 September, 1917
Thank you for writing again.[1] I did somewhat misunderstand your argument. I quite agree with you that delay is very disadvantageous and I can assure you that I have been trying to prevent it in every possible instance. I am pressing everybody all the time. We had lacked materials for some of the necessary decisions, but have been pressing the inquiries just as fast as we had the men through which to press them.

Cordially and sincerely yours,   Woodrow Wilson

TLS (Letterpress Books, WP, DLC).
   [1] Harriman's letter is missing.

To Newton Diehl Baker

[The White House] 21 September, 1917
My dear Mr. Secretary:

I can see nothing in the enclosed papers which would justify me in dissenting from the findings of the District Board No. 1, State of Indiana.[1]

I want to discuss with you some time soon your opinion as to whether we should regard teaching in general as one of the indispensable occupations in connection with the draft. I have heard of one or two teachers who are really indispensable where they are, and if their occupation is indispensable, then they ought to be exempted. We will take this up some time soon.

In haste   Faithfully yours,   Woodrow Wilson

TLS (Letterpress Books, WP, DLC).
   [1] The papers are missing but a White House memorandum, T MS, Sept. 12, 1917 (WP, DLC), reveals that they dealt with the claim of exemption from the draft of one Emmet W. Arnett of Tippecanoe County, Ind. They were referred to the Secretary of War.

Two Letters to Joseph Patrick Tumulty

Dear Tumulty: [The White House, c. Sept. 21, 1917]
Is Mr. Macfarland still in Washington? and is he waiting for a decision of this Patria business?[1] I confess myself very much

mixed up about it. I am afraid there are a number of things still in the film which are objectionable, but it is true that they could hardly be eliminated now without destroying the whole thing, and I am inclined to think that we cannot fairly insist upon more than has been done. What is your own judgment?

The President.

TL (WP, DLC).
[1] Wilson's question was inspired by G. S. Macfarland to WW, Sept. 21, 1917, ALS (WP, DLC), which, in fact, did not mention the *Patria* affair. The letter was written on the stationery of the New Willard Hotel, Washington.

Dear Tumulty: [The White House, c. Sept. 21, 1917]

I must say I am surprised that Mrs. Rinehart should intervene in this matter.[1] We are proceeding upon very definite information and a very clear-cut principle in Costa Rica. Won't you be kind enough to acknowledge her letter for me and say that it has been brought to my attention?   The President.

TL (WP, DLC).
[1] Mary R. Rinehart to WW, Sept. 18, 1917, TLS (WP, DLC). Mary Roberts (Mrs. Stanley Marshall) Rinehart, the popular novelist, mystery-story writer, playwright, and war correspondent, protested against the refusal of the Wilson administration to recognize the regime of Federico Tinoco Granados in Costa Rica. She insisted that his predecessor, Alfredo González Flores, had been pro-German and was now living in New York on German money, whereas the Tinoco government was pro-American and wished to offer the United States the use of its excellent harbors.

To Newton Diehl Baker

My dear Mr. Secretary: The White House 21 September, 1917

I remember our conversation about the Chief of Staff and I would be very much obliged if you would make the announcement.[1]

In great haste
    Cordially and faithfully yours,   Woodrow Wilson

TLS (N. D. Baker Papers, DLC).
[1] That is, the announcement of the retirement of Hugh L. Scott as Chief of Staff on September 22 and his replacement by Tasker H. Bliss.

From Newton Diehl Baker

Dear Mr President: Washington September 21, 1917

I have your note.[1] Mr Scott will not resign until it is convenient and meantime we can find a suitable person.

I fancied the Judge had some feeling of the kind suggested from what he said to me when he first came about the publicity of the information of the War Industries Board, in which Mr Baruch was named first.

Respectfully   Newton D. Baker

ALS (WP, DLC).
  [1] WW to NDB, Sept. 18, 1917.

From Samuel Gompers

Sir: Washington, D. C. September 21, 1917

Several days ago[1] I felt impelled to respectfully call your attention to the action of the Emergency Fleet Corporation and the United States Shipping Board in repudiating and annulling the agreement into which they entered together with the Secretary of the Navy, the responsible officers of 15 organizations of labor, including the undersigned.

This morning Mr. V. Everit Macy, Chairman of the Board, permitted me to see a copy of the letter he addressed to you yesterday in which the situation was more fully set forth.

The purpose of my writing now is to call your attention to the fact of the very precarious position in which the action of the Fleet Corporation and the Shipping Board has placed the representatives and responsible men of the organized labor movement of the country, in annulling the terms of the agreement entered into August 20th.

First the interpretation placed by the Corporation and the Shipping Board upon the Agreement of August 20th is wholly wrong and more than likely unintentionally does the other signators to the agreement an injustice. There is no good reason why the Corporation and the Shipping Board should not determine what part of any award which the adjustment board would make should be borne by the ship yard owners, or by the Government, or by both.

But quite aside from all these considerations, this one fact stands out conspicuously,—that the Secretary of the Navy with the representatives of the Corporation and of the Shipping Board, Mr. Hurley and Admiral Capps, signed the agreement. If there was any provision in the agreement to which they objected they ought to have withheld their signatures until it conformed to their views as to the needs of the Government. But within fifteen days after signing the agreement, important agencies of the Government, the United States Shipping Board and the Emergency Fleet Corporation, nolens volens, broke a solemn agreement. In other words, they have treated is [it] as "a scrap of paper."

You can readily understand the effect and influence of this action upon the minds and actions of the working people of the country. I am free to say that I have grave apprehensions as to the consequences, and I earnestly hope that you may see your way clear to impress upon the Board and the Corporation the need of revising their course and to reinstate Mr. Carey as their representative [and] that Mr. Macy your own appointee and Mr. Berres the man whom I recommended, be brought in to resume their functions under the terms of the August 20th agreement.

Very respectfully yours,   Saml. Gompers.

TLS (WP, DLC).
¹ On September 17, when he saw Wilson at the White House.

From Edward Nash Hurley, with Enclosure

Dear Mr. President: Washington September 21st 1917.

I am hopeful that the inclosed letter to Mr. Gompers, which is the result of careful consideration, will end the controversy which has given us so much concern.

As you are aware, there has not been at any time a dispute between the Emergency Fleet Corporation and Labor. The whole question has been between the shipyard owners and the Government; the former trying to escape all financial responsibility for wage increases.

Mr. Gompers himself has been most helpful. He promptly recognized the difficulties of the situation and his comments have greatly assisted in clarifying the questions involved.

Very respectfully yours,   Edward N. Hurley

TLS (WP, DLC).

E N C L O S U R E

Edward Nash Hurley to Samuel Gompers

My dear Mr. Gompers: [Washington] September 21, 1917.

After the most careful consideration of all the issues involved in the present controversy as to whether the Government should bear all the burden of wage increases or whether an equitable proportion of the burden should be borne by the shipyard owners, Admiral Capps and I have reached the conclusion that the interests of the nation will be protected by an interpretation of the contract which will not permit the employer to escape financial responsibility.

The main question which has been in our minds, as clearly set forth in our letters to the Adjustment Board and in our interview with you, has been whether the Emergency Fleet Corporation should bear the entire burden of such increases as may be awarded in justice to labor, upon whose patriotism I have always relied. We have held an open mind upon the precise meaning of the agreement with respect to the manner in which the necessary wage increases shall be met. The careful consideration which we have given to the problem—to your views and the views of those who have argued the case of the employers—has led Admiral Capps and me to believe that after justice has been done to the labor that is spending its energy in the great and righteous war in which our country is engaged, the Emergency Fleet Corporation and the Shipping Board can determine what part of the wage awards can be borne by the Emergency Fleet Corporation, leaving the remainder to be borne by the shipyard owners.

We are happy in finding our views in this respect in agreement with your own because I believe the logical result of giving effectiveness to them will be to bring a prompt settlement of all labor troubles in connection with the shipbuilding program, which is so vital to the success of the nation in war. By this solution, justice to labor will not wait upon the settlement of questions relating to the responsibility of employers.

The discussion we have had, I feel confident, has clarified the views of all of us. As I have said before, I have complete faith in the patriotism of the men who were originally selected for membership in the Wage Adjustment Board, and, with the atmosphere cleared, I would like to see the Board start functioning at once.

Our interpretation of the agreement, like yours, has brought us to the conclusion that the great necessity of the hour is to have justice done immediately in the establishment of an adequate standard of wages.

We all agree likewise that no injury must be done to the employers, but the interest of the government demands that they must bear their due proportion of the sacrifices all of us must make. They cannot expect to escape their portion of the responsibility for financing the war. We are all partners in the greatest enterprise in which democracy has ever been forced to engage.

In reaching this decision, I cannot fail to commend the splendid patriotism that has animated your consideration of the issues involved. No argument that you have made has been without consideration for the interest of the entire nation, and I am confident that employers and employees will join in meeting us in the spirit with which we approach them.

Sincerely yours,   [Edward N. Hurley]

CCL (WP, DLC).

From Allen Bartlit Pond

Dear Sir: Chicago Sept. 21st, 1917.

The War Committee of the Union League Club of Chicago,—following up the suggestion that you made in your letter to me under date of 17 July,[1]—had a conference with Mr. Nieman of Milwaukee and subsequently with Mr. Clabaugh[2] representing the Department of Justice in Chicago. In pursuance of the policy determined upon in consonance with your suggestions and the above conferences, the Committee is causing to be printed in three German-language Chicago newspapers, three times a week each, a series of carefully prepared articles dealing with pertinent truths involved in the present international situation.

I enclose herewith English original drafts of the first three articles of the series—appearing Monday, Wednesday and Friday of this week. Under separate enclosure I am transmitting marked copies of the German papers in question, namely, the Staats Zeitung, the Presse and the Abendpost.[3]

We are proposing to extend the work by running a series of articles, somewhat differently shaped, in certain pro-German Swedish papers published in Chicago and vicinity.

Just what the re-action will be to the articles cannot now be forecast, but we are in hopes to insert the thin edge of a wedge in some perverse and heretofore tightly closed minds.

Has your attention been called to the fact that our "Bill" has suffered a sudden change of heart?[4] He can hardly be said to have experienced a change of mind—owing to the absence of any such organ in his make-up. Poor Thompson! Nature did badly by him when she put him together; and a freak of Providence—a sort of cosmic political accident—thrust him, all barren of wit, into a position where his ineptitude is pitiful. Now that he has changed his tune he will dribble patriotism daily and "grandfather's sword" will feebly carve the circumambient ether.

Respectfully yours,   Allen B Pond

TLS (WP, DLC).

¹ WW to A. B. Pond, July 17, 1917, Vol. 43.
² Hinton Graves Clabaugh, head of the Chicago office of the Division of Investigation (formerly the Bureau of Investigation) of the Department of Justice.
³ These enclosures are all missing.
⁴ William Hale Thompson, the anti-British Mayor of Chicago who had strongly opposed American participation in the war, on September 19 issued a proclamation on the occasion of the departure of new army recruits from the Chicago area for training camp. Thompson called upon all Americans to stand behind the army and navy in any conflict with a foreign power. He further requested them to pray for the soldiers and sailors. *New York Times,* Sept. 20, 1917. As it turned out, this action did not represent any permanent change of heart on Thompson's part in regard to American foreign policy.

From the Diary of Josephus Daniels

September Friday 21 1917

Cabinet—WW: It is a good idea to watch how some men vote & vote the other way. Told story of Dr West—"You fool didn't you see how West voted?" said a pro-Wilson member of faculty who had voted against WWs policies. "If you don't understand a question, ncvcr vote as West votes." Good rule in Congress.

Lansing's news about Bernstorff getting money caused me to call him old Sherlock Holmes

Lord Reading to the War Cabinet

Washington. 21st September 1917.

Secret. No. 2784.

Q 12. From Lord Reading for War Cabinet.

Have had interview with President who received me cordially, and explained there had been some regretable delay owing to mistake about arranging appointment on our part. I mention this merely to account for delay.

I explained report of Committee on position of Northern Neutral Countries and placed in his hands for his own personal perusal only.¹ I mentioned War Cabinet thought it desirable that American troops should not only be sent to France as quickly as possible, but should take their place on some parts of line as and when ready without waiting completion of American Army, to take over a portion of line. I explained French moral[e] required encouragement and there would be some disillusionment on their part if they had to wait until next Spring for active cooperation from Americans in the field. President was inclined to agree with our views and said that any suggestion of a settled policy was not authentic. President was anxious to have more particulars as to present aspect of submarine warfare. I said that I had latest information and would give him any particulars he wished. I stated that Cabinet was very desirous of whole-hearted and close cooperation of America with us Allies and he expressed himself guardedly, but sympathetically, but there was some danger of American representative on any British or Allied Board losing independent judgment which had already happened in some cases. Conversation to be resumed later.

Administration is proceeding vigorously although there has been delay in some respects particularly in regard to ship-building programme.

Everything depends on President and I am convinced that it is highly important that he should be kept as fully informed as possible, and that he should feel assured that nothing is being kept from him by us. I have impressed on him that it is wish of British Cabinet to give him every information.

T telegram (FO 371/3112, No. 184454, PRO).
[1] About this memorandum, see W. Wiseman to E. Drummond, Sept. 20, 1917, n. 1.

To Edgar Palmer

My dear Mr. Palmer: [The White House] 22 September, 1917

I am sincerely sorry about the outcome of the recent legislation as it affects yourself.[1] It was legislation of which personally I disapproved. I can only say that you have acted in an admirable spirit and that I thank you for your whole attitude in the matter.

Cordially and sincerely yours,   Woodrow Wilson

TLS (Letterpress Books, WP, DLC).
[1] E. Palmer to WW, Sept. 20, 1917, TLS (WP, DLC). Palmer informed Wilson that, in view of the Attorney General's opinion interpreting Section 3 of the Lever Food and Fuel Act, he had, on the advice of his own lawyers, submitted his resignation as chairman and member of the zinc committee of the Advisory Commission of the Council of National Defense.

Section 3 of the Lever Act barred any agent of the government from soliciting contracts in which he had any personal interest but allowed him to recommend a contract if he first disclosed in writing any interest he had in it. In no case, however, could such an agent actually award the contract. Gregory's advisory opinion on Section 3 served only to increase the ambiguity of its language. In view of "the narrow margin of difference" between "recommending" on the one hand, which was legal with a full disclosure, he said, and *"inducing, soliciting,* or *awarding"* on the other hand, which was not legal even with a disclosure, "it would be well as a practical matter for such persons to exercise great caution as to the kind of *recommendations* they shall make." Confronted with this opinion, numerous members of the various commodity boards of the Advisory Commission submitted their resignations. See Robert D. Cuff, *The War Industries Board: Business-Government Relations during World War I* (Baltimore, 1973), pp. 108-109, 150-52.

To Newton Diehl Baker

My dear Mr. Secretary: The White House 22 September, 1917

Apropos of our conversation just after Cabinet yesterday, you will be interested, I think, in the enclosed.[1]

Cordially and sincerely yours,   Woodrow Wilson

TLS (N. D. Baker Papers, DLC).

[1] Herbert Howland Sargent, "Memorandum on the General Strategy of the Present War Between the Allies and the Central Powers," Sept. 6, 1917, T MS (N. D. Baker Papers, DLC). Sargent, a retired army major who had been recalled to active duty and was about to become Professor of Military Science and Tactics at Princeton University, argued that the war on the western front had reached a total stalemate which neither side could break: massive attacks produced only minor alterations in the line of trenches, with staggering casualties to the attackers. Therefore, it was futile to pour American troops into western Europe. Sargent believed that the only hope for a breakthrough lay in an attack against the Central Powers at a more vulnerable point and to leave the western front with only enough forces to maintain the stalemate. One plan would be for the Allies to attack from the eastern end of the Mediterranean against Turkey south of the Black Sea or, alternatively, to attack from the head of the Aegean Sea against Bulgaria and Turkey west of the Black Sea and north of the Sea of Marmora. This would cut the theater of operations of the Central Powers in two and lead rapidly to the fall of Constantinople. Winston Churchill had had the right idea in the Dardanelles campaign but should have concentrated on an army attack against the Turkish armies rather than the largely naval effort that led to the failure at Gallipoli. Another plan, to which Sargent devoted most of his space, was to send an American army from San Francisco across the Pacific and through the Indian Ocean to the Persian Gulf to cooperate with the English army then near Baghdad in an advance northward against the Turks. He acknowledged that this would require extensive cooperation from Japan but assumed that it would be readily forthcoming.

Two Letters from Newton Diehl Baker

My dear Mr. President: Washington. September 22, 1917.

I have your note of the 12th [22nd], enclosing a copy of Major Sargent's notes on the strategy of the present war. I have already started the inquiry in a formal way which you suggested, and find that the matter has been considered pretty thoroughly, and several discussions are produced in writing. I hope in a few days to have the best thought of the military men on the subject for submission to you.

Respectfully yours,   Newton D. Baker

The President: Washington, September 22, 1917.

I have the honor to acknowledge your communication of the 19th instant,[1] asking that an answer be formulated which can be sent to all letters protesting against the drafting of farmers for the National Army instead of exempting them so that they may remain on the farm and increase the food supplies for the

American people and for the nations with which the United States is cooperating.

In reply, I beg to say that the claims of agriculture have been very carefully considered and a method devised which will enable claims to be allowed which justify exemption, and will, in other cases, leave the farmer and his hands at home to gather the crops before joining the colors.

The Selective Service Act authorizes the President "to exclude or discharge from said selected draft * * * or to draft for partial military service only from those liable to draft as in this Act provided, persons of the following classes: * * * Persons engaged in industries, including agriculture, found to be necessary to the maintenance of the Military Establishment or the effective operation of the military forces or the maintenance of national interest during the emergency."

Exclusive original jurisdiction for the decision on all claims for discharge on the ground of being engaged in an agricultural enterprise has been vested by Congress in what are known as District Boards. There are one or more District Boards for each Federal judicial district. Members of these Boards must reside in the District for which they are appointed and at least one member of each Board is in close touch with the agricultural situation in his district. These Boards are directed to make a survey of the industrial and agricultural conditions in the District under their control, ascertaining as near as may be the labor supply available for necessary industries and for agriculture outside of the men called for military service and to take into consideration all such facts in determining claims for discharge.

Wherever, in the opinion of the District Board the direct substantial material loss to any industrial or agriculture enterprise necessary to the maintenance of the Military establishment or effective operation of the Military forces or the National interest during the war, out weighs the loss that would result from the failure to obtain the military service of any person engaged in such enterprise, the Board will issue a certificate of discharge.

It has been thought not feasible to go beyond this general authorization to the District Boards and make wholesale discharges of farmers as a class upon a mere showing that a claimant for discharge has some color of right to be called a farmer. To do so would let down the bars and release upon a central office the insistent demands of thousands of industries which would have an equal right for consideration.

A method has also been devised whereby farmers and farm

hands are granted special consideration consistent with the letter of the Act and in accordance with its spirit. By this method the Local Board receives from the District Board a list of the men who have presented claims for temporary discharge on the ground of necessity to gather crops. Certificates of discharge will not issue in such cases; but the Local Board, on examining such claims, will be enabled, if it deems fit, to designate such individuals for the contingents to be summoned to report to mobilization camp at later dates fixed by The Adjutant General. Thus the temporary need of leaving those men at the crop work will be satisfied without complicating or diminishing the quotas.

It is to be borne in mind that all branches of industry, and indeed all activities of life, are affected by the draft and we must in many cases rely upon the services of those above and below the draft age. It may be, in many cases, inconvenient but the Nation as well as the individual must be considered. There will be no hardship in the many cases where agricultural claims have been allowed, and in those case[s] where the claims have been disallowed the young men who are serving the country must and can be replaced by those younger or older who cannot serve the country in the army.

Very respectfully yours,   Newton D. Baker[2]

TLS (WP, DLC).
[1] Actually, Tumulty wrote to Baker on September 19, acting on the following direction from Wilson: "Won't you ask them at the War Department to formulate an answer which I can send to all letters of this sort, for they are very numerous? If they would outline a reply, it would be very serviceable to me and I would not have to trouble them with individual protests." WW to JPT, c. Sept. 19, 1917, TL (WP, DLC). Wilson's note was inspired by C. F. Jenkins to WW, Sept. 17, 1917, TLS (WP, DLC).
[2] The reader will note that Wilson repeated most of Baker's letter verbatim in WW to C. F. Jenkins, Sept. 27, 1917.

From William Bauchop Wilson

My dear Mr. President: Washington September 22, 1917.

I have called the members of the Commission to look into the western labor situation to meet in Washington on the 27th to arrange their itinerary. I would be very much pleased if you can arrange to meet them on that date.[1] I expect we will be ready to start about the 28th or 29th.

Faithfully yours,   W B Wilson

TLS (WP, DLC).
[1] Wilson met the commission at the White House on September 27.

To Edward Mandell House

The White House Sept 23 1917
Edith is not well and I would be freer a day or two later Will
send you a later message when I can suggest a time
                                        Woodrow Wilson

T telegram (E. M. House Papers, CtY).

To Joseph Patrick Tumulty, with Enclosure

[The White House, Sept. 23, 1917]
Please make some inquiries about this, so that I may know
more about the strike.   The President.

TL (WP, DLC).

ENCLOSURE

Pittsburg, Pa., September 23, 1917.
The seven thousand men on strike in the Jones and Laughlin
plants at Pittsburgh, Pennsylvania, and members of Steel City
Union affiliated to the American Federation of Labor composed
of 8 nationalities at its mass meeting today instructed us to wire
you that we unanimously pledge our loyal and patriotic support
in the prosecution of the war for the preservation of the world
democracy.
Cal. Wyatt, General Organizer, American Federation
                                        of Labor.
                Clem Wessel, Secy. Steel City, Union.

T telegram (WP, DLC).

From Joseph Patrick Tumulty, with Enclosure

Dear Governor: The White House. September 23, 1917.
Mr. Hurley, Mr. Gompers and Mr. Macy met at my office this
morning with the result that the plan indicated by Mr. Hurley
in the letter I read to you the other day has been accepted and
that the wage adjustment board has already begun its work. Mr.
Gompers suggested that the attached telegram be sent by you at
once to the labor leaders who control the California, Oregon and
Washington labor situations. This telegram is the result of the
conference with Mr. Hurley, Mr. Gompers and Mr. Macy of the

adjustment board. They think it will do much to ease the situation. It will prevent the culmination of a dangerous situation on the Coast.   J.P.T.

TL (WP, DLC).

ENCLOSURE

COPY.

TELEGRAM.   September 23, 1917.

Charles W. Boyle, Labor Temple, Seattle, Washington.
E. J. Stack, 162 Second Street, Portland, Oregon.
John O'Connell, Labor Temple, San Francisco, Calif.
                    or house address.

Mr. Hurley has just informed me that a unanimous agreement has been reached in the San Francisco situation to refer the entire subject matter to the ship building and labor adjustment board. The sole remaining issue is the temporary wage at which the men will agree to return. This point probably will be cleared up today. This is most gratifying as it assures a prompt and satisfactory settlement. Mr. Hurley has also informed me that he has asked the wage adjustment board to make findings in the Seattle and Portland situations as well and with equal promptness. I need not say that this happy solution of the labor trouble on the Pacific Coast would be most gratifying to me as it is a further evidence of the patriotism of labor. In view of it I would ask that no cessation of work occur at Portland or Seattle. The wage board begins functioning at once and will announce its findings with expedition. I count confidently upon the patriotic cooperation of the workmen and their leaders. The men can count upon just and prompt action.   Woodrow Wilson

Copy to Hon. Gavin McNab, San Francisco.[1]

T MS (WP, DLC).
[1] This telegram was sent to the aforementioned persons on September 23, 1917.

From Gavin McNab

San Francisco, Calif., Sept. 23, 1917.

Thank you for your telegram which was most helpful to us in bringing about a conclusion. I am pleased to inform you that the conference committee of labor leaders and employers has just agreed unanimously on a temporary wage scale and a recommendation to the respective labor trades and employing concerns that work be resumed immediately.[1]

Gavin McNab.

T telegram (WP, DLC).
   [1] See also J. O'Connell to WW, Sept. 24, 1917, T telegram (WP, DLC). In response to Wilson's telegram of September 23, O'Connell pledged to do everything in his power "to uphold your hands and to have your request complied with."

From Charles M. Bottomley

Portland, Oregon, Sept. 23, 1917.

With deepest regret we are compelled to inform you that we were unable to comply with request [and] that men in steel plants in mass meeting voted unanimously to strike Monday, September twenty fourth, at ten a.m. This action was felt necessary to protect their interests in view of fact of employers opposition to members belonging to unions and their pursuit of so-called open shop policy. There are three cases in court here where employers have discharged persons for joining unions of their craft; further, they have refused to try to settle differences with us, instead have thrown whole question on shipping Board. The workers in meeting unanimously convey to you their hearty cooperation and support in prosecuting the war with determination to bring it to a successful conclusion.

Chas. M. Bottomley, Secretary,
Metal Trades Council, Executive Committee.

T telegram (WP, DLC).

To Edward Mandell House

My dear House,   The White House. 24 September, 1917.

I do not think that anyone could reasonably criticise your associating President Mezes with you in the work of preparing data for the final settlement, and I should be glad to see you get Lippman[n] too, if he can be spared from the work he is now doing in the War Department. You certainly can do the work best with the assistance of men you know and trust.

I was mighty sorry to head you off from coming down to-day; but Mrs. Wilson is really suffering a great deal, with a severe attack of grippe and every minute I can spare from the work of the day I ought to spend making it easier for her. I am hoping each day that she will be much better, and then I can have a free mind for the many things we must talk over, you and I.

Affectionately Yours,   W.W.

WWTLI (E. M. House Papers, CtY).

To Arthur Brisbane

My dear Mr. Brisbane: [The White House] 24 September, 1917

Thank you for your letter of September twenty-third with its enclosure.[1] You may be sure I shall take pleasure in calling it to the attention of the Postmaster General, who, I believe, is as anxious as I am to do the right thing and to do it carefully and prudently.

Cordially and sincerely yours,   Woodrow Wilson

TLS (Letterpress Books, WP, DLC).

[1] The Editors have not found the letter and its enclosure, but see Burleson's note on the next letter.

To Albert Sidney Burleson

My dear Burleson: The White House 24 September, 1917

I am sure you will read this letter from Mr. Brisbane with its enclosure with interest. It seems very earnest and I hope you will consider it worthy of a very careful weighing.

Faithfully yours,   Woodrow Wilson

Milwaukee Leader and Victor Berger.

Turned down B's request. Prest expressed doubt but yielded. B.

TLS (A. S. Burleson Papers, DLC).

To Walter Hines Page

My dear Page: [The White House] 24 September, 1917

I have your letter of the tenth of September about Admiral Hall and Mr. Bell. I am very glad to fall in with your suggestion and hope that you will some time take some private occasion to assure the Admiral of my very great appreciation of what he has done and the spirit in which he has done it, and Mr. Bell also of my admiration for his part in the work.

I wish I could write a long letter, but you will know why I cannot.

In haste

Cordially and faithfully yours,   [Woodrow Wilson]

CCL (WP, DLC).

To Thomas Watt Gregory, with Enclosure

The White House

My dear Mr. Attorney General: 24 September, 1917

The enclosed letter from House explains itself and I am sending it along with the enclosed editorials[1] in order to ask you if you will not be kind enough to have the investigation suggested by House made with as much thoroughness as possible. We cannot leave any stone unturned to prevent or soften labor troubles.

Cordially and sincerely yours,   Woodrow Wilson

TLS (JDR, RG 60, Numerical File No. 185354/43½, DNA).
   [1] They are undated editorials clipped from the *Boston Journal* and the Boston *Globe* on the Mooney case. Both said that Mooney had been "railroaded" and emphasized the injurious impact of the trial, conviction, and death sentence upon public opinion in Russia.

E N C L O S U R E

From Edward Mandell House

Dear Governor: New York. September 21, 1917.

I have never brought to your attention such matters as that of the death sentence of Thos. J. Mooney of San Francisco, but in this instance I feel it is important for you to give it some personal attention for the reason that it has a bearing on the labor troubles in the West and has excited such nation wide interest.

Federal investigation of the methods employed in securing conviction is all that is asked and that I think, in the circumstances, should be done.

Affectionately yours,   E. M. House

TLS (JDR, RG 60, Numerical File No. 185354/43½, DNA).

From Edward Mandell House

Dear Governor: New York. September 24, 1917.

I am sorry to hear that Mrs. Wilson is not well, but I hope it is nothing serious.

I merely wanted to talk with you about the organization for the peace conference, which I am ready to begin as soon as we have discussed it.

In the event you do not want me to go to Europe just now and decide on sending someone to the Allied War Council, what would you think of McAdoo and Baker? It would not be a bad idea to have both of them visit England, France and Italy at this time and for reasons which are apparent.

Affectionately yours,   E. M. House

TLS (WP, DLC).

From George Luis Baker

Portland, Oregon, September 24, 1917.

About eleven thousand men employed in ship building plants went on strike here today. We understand these yards are all working on Government orders. Please advise me at earliest moment what course the Government intends to take.

Geo. L. Baker, Mayor.

T telegram (WP, DLC).

To Bernard Mannes Baruch

My dear Baruch: [The White House] 25 September, 1917

The suggestion here made by Mr. Hoover I understand to be exactly what we originally intended, is it not?[1] If that is your opinion and that of your colleagues, as it is certainly mine, I shall be very glad to issue the instructions suggested by Mr. Hoover if you will suggest the most desirable form. I would be obliged for an early answer, since the matter seems pressing.

Cordially and faithfully yours,   Woodrow Wilson

TLS (Letterpress Books, WP, DLC).
[1] "Rules and Regulations Governing Licensees for the Importation, Manufacture and Refining of Sugar, Sugar Syrups and Molasses," mimeograph copy (WP, DLC).

To Thomas Watt Gregory

The White House
My dear Mr. Attorney General: 25 September, 1917

I would very much like you seriously to consider whether publications like the enclosed do not form a sufficient basis for a trial for treason.[1] There are many instances of this sort and one conviction would probably scotch a great many snakes. So far as I can see, an indictment could easily be founded upon such utterances as this.

Cordially and sincerely yours,   Woodrow Wilson

TLS (JDR, RG 60, T. W. Gregory Papers, Numerical File No. 9-12/117-1, DNA).
[1] The enclosure is missing, but see TWG to WW, Oct. 6, 1917.

To George Creel

My dear Mr. Creel: [The White House] 25 September, 1917

I heartily approve of the suggestion you have made that through your committee some effort be made to coordinate the work of the various bureaus, departments and agencies interested in presenting from the platform various phases of the national task. With the cooperation of the departments, the Food Administration, the Council of National Defense and the Committee on Public Information it would seem possible to enlist the many state and private organizations who have put the nation's cause above every other issue and stand ready to participate in a speaking campaign that shall give to the people that fullness of information which will enable and inspire each citizen to play intelligently his part in the greatest and most vital struggle ever undertaken by self-governing nations.[1]

Your suggestion of Mr. Arthur E. Bestor,[2] president of Chautauqua Institution, to direct this work is excellent. You are fortunate to be able to enlist one who has been so intimately connected with a great American educational institution devoted to popular instruction without prejudice or partisanship.

Cordially and sincerely yours,   Woodrow Wilson

TLS (Letterpress Books, WP, DLC).
[1] This was the beginning of the Speaking Division of the Committee on Public Information, not to be confused with the previously organized Four Minute Men. Although the two organizations overlapped somewhat in functions and were to merge on September 1, 1918, the Four Minute Men concentrated on providing volunteer speakers on the local level who conformed to a fairly rigid format prescribed by the C.P.I., while the Speaking Division arranged tours of nationally, or even internationally, known figures. See Stephen Vaughn, *Holding Fast the Inner Lines: Democracy, Nationalism, and the Committee on Public Information* (Chapel Hill, N. C., 1980), pp. 116-40.
[2] Arthur Eugene Bestor.

To Newton Diehl Baker

My dear Mr. Secretary: The White House 25 September, 1917

I have your memorandum about labor in the spruce producing industry and think you are quite right about it.

In haste   Faithfully yours,   Woodrow Wilson

TLS (N. D. Baker Papers, DLC).

To Walter Lowrie

My dear Mr. Lowrie: The White House 25 September, 1917

It was certainly very thoughtful of you to send me your letter of September second with its enclosure. It has interested me not only, but cheered me very much. Such incidents as you relate encourage me to believe that influences which I thought might be weak may possibly turn out to be very strong in the direction of an ideal attitude throughout the war and something like an ideal solution after it. I pray with all my heart that this may be so.

I wish I had time for a real letter. I have only time for this line of greeting and gratitude.

Cordially and sincerely yours,   Woodrow Wilson

TLS (W. Lowrie Papers, NjP).

From Robert Lansing, with Enclosures

My dear Mr. President: [Washington] September 25, 1917.

As I informed you yesterday by telephone Viscount Ishii intends to leave Washington on Thursday, the 27th, and I am very anxious before he goes to submit to him a formula for a note relative to the "Open Door" policy.

I enclose memoranda of two interviews I have had with him on the subject—one dated September 6th and the other September 22d. These memoranda will explain the reason for the draft note to him which I enclose.

I hope that you can return these papers to me with your views in order that I may submit a draft to him tomorrow—(Wednesday).   Faithfully yours,   Robert Lansing.

TLS (SDR, RG 59, 793.94/583A, DNA).

E N C L O S U R E   I

MEMORANDUM of Conference with
Japanese Special Ambassador, VISCOUNT ISHII.
September 6, 1917.

The special Ambassador and I conferred this afternoon for an hour and a half at the Department.

During the first part of the conference the subject discussed was to what extent Japan had rendered aid in the war, and how it might cooperate more fully with the Allies and this country.

I told him that I considered the great problem was *transportation*, and that it seemed to me Japan might be able to do more than she had done in this matter.

He replied that Japan was doing a good deal to aid and that they had chartered several hundred tons of shipping to the Allies which was being used in the Mediterranean trade.

He then spoke of the fact that we had embargoed iron and steel and that it was causing not only dissatisfaction but much distress in Japan on account of its absolute need in the shipyards of that country, which have been greatly increased in capacity.

I explained to him that this Embargo had been made necessary by the fact that steel was being used largely in the manufacture of munitions and in the increased output of shipping in this country; that of course we had to look out first for our own interests in that particular; that again transportation entered into the problem in that we had to depend upon scrap steel on the Pacific coast for our shipyards there or else bring it from the east, which was very difficult as our rolling stock was short. I went on to say that possibly some arrangement could be made for the release of a certain amount of steel to Japan, provided Japan would transfer to us some of the ships already constructed, as it was a matter of immediate importance to us to obtain shipping, and it was a matter of immediate importance to Japan to obtain material. I said that while I could not speak with accuracy about these matters I believed that we might be able to supply steel to build vessels which would have a combined greater tonnage than the vessels they would transfer to us.

The Ambassador said he was not sure whether this could be arranged, but he thought it was very well worthy of consideration and that we could take it up more in detail later.

It was very evident that the industrial situation in Japan was chiefly in his mind and I thought the suggestion such as I made appealed to him.

We further discussed the possibility of utilizing Japan's tonnage for the transportation to Russia of railroad material and munitions.

The Ambassador said he felt that this could very well be done and his Government would be glad to aid in the matter. At the same time he said it was a more or less technical matter and he could only speak as an amateur.

I told him I was in very much the same situation and that of course our conversation was entirely informal and tentative.

I asked the Ambassador whether he desired to discuss other questions than those immediately pertaining to the war, because if he so desired I was willing to do so—but I thought the supreme object of both Governments at the present moment should be the winning of the war and an understanding as to how we could cooperate to that end. He said that in view of the fact that he had come here and been so handsomely received by the American people he thought it would be unfortunate not to consider some of the other questions as we had to look forward to a time when the war would be over. He said in the first place he ought to inform me that when he returned to Japan from France, where he was Ambassador in 1915, he stopped in London and saw Sir Edward Grey. Japan at that time had taken Kaio Chau and the German Islands in the South Pacific. He said he told Sir Edward Grey it was the intention of his Government to return Kaio Chau to China, but that no Government in Japan could stand if they did not retain some of the South Sea Islands as "souvenirs" of the war; that it had been a sacrifice for his Government to enter the war, which they were not compelled to do under their treaty of alliance—that is according to the letter of the treaty—but he thought they were according to the spirit. He then went on to say that Sir Edward Grey had practically consented in the readjustment of territory after the war; that the German Islands north of the equator should be retained by Japan, while those south of the equator should go to Great Britain.

I replied that I was glad to know this and appreciated his frankness in telling me, but that I could make no comment on such an agreement at the present time.

I asked him what further questions he wished to discuss and he said to me: "Have you anything to propose in regard to China?"

I replied that I had and while I realized that he would want to consider my proposition before making a reply I would like to present it. I said the proposition was this:

That the co-belligerents against Germany should, jointly or simultaneously, re-declare the "Open Door" policy in a statement which would have a very beneficial effect upon China and I believed upon the world at large, as it was in accord with the principles of commerce to which we all agreed.

The Ambassador seemed a little taken aback by this suggestion and said that of course he should like to consider it and that he appreciated the arguments in its favor although he said he did not know as it was absolutely necessary in view of the fact that Japan had always lived up to the principle.

I replied that Japan had always lived up to any declaration

which she had made; that the good faith of Japan could not be questioned; and that upon that this Government always relied and felt no anxiety once the Japanese Government had passed its word.

The Ambassador replied that he felt that Japan had a special interest on account of its position in regard to China, and while its desire was to have China open and free to all countries he felt there might be criticism if there was a bare declaration of the "Open Door" policy without some mention of Japan's special interest.

I replied to him that we recognized the fact that Japan, from her geographical position, had a peculiar interest in China but that to make a declaration to that effect seemed to me needless as it was the result of natural causes and not political; that any such declaration might be interpreted as a peculiar political interest and I was very doubtful whether it would be wise to include it in a reaffirmation of the "Open Door" policy.

The Ambassador said that his Government was of course in favor of the "Open Door" policy; that they would maintain it as they had in the past, but he was not willing yet to say whether he thought it would be a real advantage to reaffirm it.

I said that the "Open Door" policy was peculiarly advantageous to Japan; that if we should return to spheres of influence in which the various powers had a paramount interest in certain sections of China the advantage which Japan had in geographical position would be destroyed; that Japan, with the industrial advantage which she had by reason of cheap and efficient labor and the short distance which she had to carry her goods to the Chinese markets, benefitted more than any other of the countries by the "Open Door" policy; that so far as this country was concerned it might be considered advisable to reestablish spheres of influence, but that it was entirely contrary to our policy and principle and we were most anxious to preserve the doctrine in dealing with China. I said I hoped he would give the matter very careful consideration and would be prepared to discuss it further at our next conference, which is to take place on Monday, September 10th.

During the course of the early part of the conversation the Ambassador said that through various channels the German Government had three times sought to persuade Japan to withdraw from the Allies and to remain neutral, but that in every case his Government had firmly rejected the suggestion.

I said to him that I could imagine their seeking some such step as they had planned to attempt it through Mexico as was indicated in the Zimmerman[n] note. I further said to him that it was a matter of no concern to this Government, in view of the fact that Japan's loyalty to an ally, and her reputation for good faith was too well established to be even suspected.

[1] Ishii's reports on this conversation conform very closely to Lansing's record. A. Satō to I. Motono, No. 332, received Sept. 8, 1917; A. Satō to I. Motono, No. 336, Sept. 9, 1917, both Hw telegrams (Ishii Mission File, Japanese Foreign Office-Ar).

E N C L O S U R E   I I

MEMORANDUM of Conference with VISCOUNT ISHII
at my Residence.

September 22, 1917.

Viscount Ishii called at 3:00 p.m. by appointment, and after some preliminary remarks he introduced the subject of the "Open Door" and the suggestion that a redeclaration at this time would be advantageous.

He said that he had heard from his Government and that they did not wish to do anything to affect the *status quo* in China and that it would be hard to explain to the Japanese people why a declaration was made at this time if the suggestion was adopted.[1]

I told him that he must realize that in the present state of the world Japan and the United States were the only countries which could furnish money for the development of China's vast resources; that, if we permitted the gradual restoration of the policy of "spheres of influence," which seemed to be going on, the Allied Governments would look upon us as seeking to monopolize the opportunities; and that it seemed to me that we should unite in every possible way to dispel the impression that we would selfishly seek to take advantage of their wasted condition and build up our own fortunes without thought of those who were fighting the battles of this country and of Japan, as well as their own battles. I said that I thought this was a time when Japan and the United States ought to show a magnanimous spirit and say to them, "We will not take advantage of your calamities as we might do. We will seek no special privileges in China. When this war is over and you begin to rebuild your fortunes by commerce and trade, you will find the markets of China and the opportunities in that land as open and free to you as they are to us." If we redeclared the "Open Door" policy, I told him that is what it would mean, and I asked him if it was not worth while to gain the gratitude and confidence of the Allies by an announcement of our purpose to be generous and unselfish in this time when the future must look so dark to them.

The Viscount said that he appreciated all this and that he also realized what I had said before about Japan being the chief beneficiary from the "Open Door" which was manifestly true, but that the Japanese people would be likely to blame the Government if there was nothing said about Japan's "special interest" in China, that the opposition in the Diet would seize upon such an opportunity to attack the Ministry for making a needless declaration, while getting nothing for Japan.

I said to him that if he meant by "special interest" "paramount interest," I could not see my way clear to discuss the matter further; but, if he meant a special interest based upon geographical position, I was not unwilling to take the matter into consideration. I said further that I appreciated his difficulty which pertained to the political situation in Japan and would try and find some formula to satisfy the wishes of his people in case a redeclaration of the "Open Door" policy could be agreed upon in principle.

The Viscount said that he wished I would prepare such a formula first for his consideration and I told him that I would. He seemed to be much impressed with the idea that to redeclare the "Open Door" at this time would be accepted as a generous act by the Allies and strengthen the bond of friendship and confidence between the powers and Japan. He also said that he was convinced that Japan on account of its proximity to China would be especially benefitted by a continuance of the "Open Door" policy, and that the only difficulty of the proposed redeclaration was that it might not appeal to the Japanese public and be used as a pretext to attack the Government.

In this conversation I also said to him that there seemed to be a misconception of the underlying principle of the "Monroe Doctrine"; that it was not an assertion of primacy or of paramount interest by the United States in its relation to other American Republics; that its purpose was to prevent foreign powers from interfering with the sovereign rights of any nation in this hemisphere; and that the whole aim was to preserve to each republic the power of self-development. I said further that so far as aiding in this development this country was on an equal footing with all other countries and claimed no special privileges.

As for China I said that I felt that the same principle should be applied and that no special privileges and certainly no paramount interest in that country should be claimed by any foreign power. I also said that I appreciated the pressure of population in Japan and the need for industrial expansion, and that I believed that Japan had occupied Korea and was developing Manchuria chiefly because of this unavoidable necessity.

The Special Ambassador spoke of Manchuria and said that his country desired the "Open Door" policy to be applied there, that his Government sought no monopoly there, and that even if China was willing to cede the territory to Japan, Japan would not accept it.

I told him that I was glad to hear this frank declaration and I hoped that his view of the application of the "Open Door" policy was the same as mine. My view was that in China foreign commerce and trade should be entirely unhampered. He replied that was his view. I then said that I felt that when a railroad or canal was built in China by the nationals of one country special rates or other privileges should not be given to citizens of that country engaged in trade or industry in China, but that the citizens of all countries should receive identical treatment. The Ambassador assented to this with some hesitation, and seemed desirous to avoid a discussion of the application of the principle of the "Open Door."

We discussed other subjects, but they were of minor importance.[2]

[1] I. Motono to A. Satō and K. Ishii, No. 312, Sept. 18, 1917, Hw telegram (Ishii Mission File, Japanese Foreign Office-Ar).

[2] Ishii's report of this meeting, which conforms to Lansing's record, is A. Satō to I. Motono, No. 371, Sept. 25, 1917, Hw telegram (Ishii Mission File, Japanese Foreign Office-Ar).

ENCLOSURE III

(DRAFT)

Excellency:

I have the honor to communicate herein my understanding of the agreement reached by us in our recent conversations touching the questions of mutual interest to our Governments relating to the Republic of China.

Charges have repeatedly been made of late, some accusing the United States and others Japan of seeking to take advantage of present world conditions to acquire political influence or control in China. The Governments of the United States and of Japan having always recognized China as a sovereign and independent state, and having repeatedly declared that they consider foreign interference in China's domestic political affairs to be violative of Chinese sovereignty, resent such accusations as offensive and as wholly unjustified.

In order to silence such mischievous reports, therefore, it is believed by us that a public announcement once more of the desires and intentions shared by our two Governments with regard to China is advisable.

The Governments of the United States and Japan recognize that territorial propinquity creates special relations between countries; and consequently the United States Government recognizes that Japan has a special relation to China, particularly to that part to which her possessions are contiguous. The territorial sovereignty of China, nevertheless, remains unimpaired, and the Government of the United States has every confidence in the repeated assurances of the Imperial Japanese Government that in the enjoyment of such special relations they have no desire to discriminate against the trade of other nations or to disregard the commercial rights heretofore granted by China in treaties with other Powers.

The Governments of the United States and Japan declare furthermore that they earnestly desire the faithful observance throughout all China of the principle of the so-called "Open Door," or equality of opportunity for participation by the citizens or subjects of all nations having treaty relations with China in the commerce and in the economic and industrial development of that country, and that they will not take advantage of present conditions to seek special rights or privileges in China which would abridge the rights of the citizens or subjects of other friendly States. They furthermore agree to bring this declaration to the attention of other interested Governments and invite those Governments to give their adherence to these declarations.

I shall be glad to have Your Excellency confirm this understanding of the agreement reached by us.

T MSS (SDR, RG 59, 793.94/583A, DNA).

From Valentine Everit Macy

Sir: Washington September 25, 1917.

The Shipbuilding Labor Adjustment Board find from conferences held here with shipyard owners and the employees, that the conditions and matters in dispute on the Pacific Coast are so complicated that the Board cannot reach intelligent conclusions without a personal visit to the Coast to secure full information upon local conditions. The Board believes it important that their findings should be accompanied with such facts that the public will be convinced of the justice of any action taken. Hastily considered decisions could easily cause great injury to employers and employees throughout the country.

The Board will, therefore, leave within ten days for the Pacific Coast to visit the shipyards, unless by so doing they would conflict with your wishes, or the plans of the Commission already appointed by you to study the Labor conditions on the Coast.

Very respectfully yours,   V. Everit Macy.[1]

TLS (WP, DLC).
[1] Wilson wrote to Tumulty about this as follows "Please ascertain from the Secretary of Labor whether he thinks the visit here proposed by Mr. Macy to the Pacific Coast will in any way interfere with or cross wires with the commission of inquiry, and if he does not think so, please apprise Mr. Macy of my entire approval of what he proposes. I take this means as a time-saver." WW to JPT, c. Sept. 26, 1917, TL (WP, DLC). Tumulty replied: "This matter has already been attended to. The Secretary of Labor agrees that the Board should make this trip." JPT to WW, Sept. 26, 1917, TL (WP, DLC).

From William Gibbs McAdoo

Dear Governor,   [Washington] Sep. 25/17

If you can find time, please glance over the enclosed.[1]

You will see that what I feared as the result of carrying the 2nd. class mail matter fight into the Revenue bill is already being realized. It is, in my humble opinion, extremely shortsighted to unnecessarily imperil the Liberty Loan this way. Already I have felt obliged to reduce the next offering to 3 billion dollars instead of the 3½ billion which I regarded as the minimum.

My only point in bringing this to your notice is to impress you with the necessity of my having your support in these matters affecting the finances. The harm already done by the Postmaster General cannot be repaired now but I earnestly hope that we may avoid similar mistakes in the future.

The financial load is very heavy and it cannot be successfully carried by your Secretary of the Treasury if his usefulness is impaired.   Affectionately yours   W G McAdoo

ALS (WP, DLC).
[1] Ralph Smith, "Secretary M'Adoo Withdraws Request for Editor's Help," *Atlanta Journal*, Sept. 23, 1917. This article printed an exchange of telegrams between McAdoo and Horace Edward Stockbridge, editor of the Atlanta *Southern Ruralist* and president of the Farmers' National Congress for 1916-1917. McAdoo, in a telegram to Stockbridge on September 15, had requested the support of the Farmers' National Congress for the second Liberty Loan bond sale. Stockbridge responded on September 21 with a curt refusal and the charge that McAdoo and the administration had supported an increase in second-class mail rates in the war revenue bill which would "ruin" farmers by increasing the cost of farm journals. McAdoo replied on September 22 with a stinging

denunciation of Stockbridge's attitude and the declaration that the government did not need his assistance. McAdoo also stated that he had not approved of the postal rate increase, had believed that this was an inopportune time to raise the issue, and had argued that it had no place in the revenue bill but should have been included in legislation concerning the Post Office Department.

Burleson had urged the inclusion of an increase in second-class mail rates in the war revenue bill since May. The various amendments to the revenue bill designed to attain this end provoked much controversy and many protests to the White House throughout the summer. The War Revenue Act as approved on October 3, 1917, included a series of rate increases for second-class mail to begin on July 1, 1918. It also included zone charges on that portion of a publication consisting of advertising, according to the distance it was sent. 40 *Statutes at Large* 327-28.

From John Aldus McSparran and Others

Mr. President: Washington, D. C., September 25, 1917.

Having given careful consideration to the reply made by you this afternoon in response to our memorial,[1] we desire to emphasize our conviction that the imperative necessity of immediate action to relieve the conditions that threaten an adequate food supply has not as yet been fully apprehended, and we therefore beg leave to add the following brief statement to the memorial now in your possession.

We are convinced that an order from the Government paroling real farmers and experienced farm help whose absence would reduce production from service for such time as they shall continue to work at farming, with the requirement that they shall report from time to time that they are so doing, will restore the conscript law to its primary purpose as regards agriculture and allay the feeling of unrest that arises out of the demand to grow more food and then take away from the farm those who best know how to perform this service. The farmers of the country have this year planted and sowed to the extent of their ability under the distinct understanding that businesses not necessary to the conduct of the war would be used to fill the draft. This has not been done, and while the farmer will do his best in this emergency he cannot be expected to produce food without farmers, and no statement of lack of authority will meet the situation. The case is desperate and the remedy appears simple. We hope that remedy may be applied, but if it is not, the organized farmers feel that they have at least performed a highly patriotic service in calling the attention of the government to the desperate seriousness of the farm labor situation.

Sincerely yours,   John A. McSparran
Master Pa. State Grange

> John C. Ketcham
>   Master Mich. State Grange
> C. S. Barrett, Georgia
>   Pres. National Farmers Union
> W. N. Giles
>   Secy N. Y. State Grange
> A. V. Swift, Oregon
>   Vice Pres. National Farmers
>   Union
> C. T. Davis
>   Master Conn. State Grange
> Geo H Bowles, Virginia
>   Treas. Virginia Farmers Union[2]
> Committee of Allied Farm Organiza-
> tions of the United States.

TLS (WP, DLC).

[1] Actually, Wilson had met with McSparran and a group of farm leaders at the White House at 5 P.M. on September 24. Their memorial is missing in WP, DLC.

[2] Those whose full names are available were John Clark Ketcham, Charles Simon Barrett, and Charles Talcott Davis.

From Henry Lowndes Maury[1]

Your Excellency: Butte, Montana September 25, 1917.

Butte normally produces at least one-fourth of the copper of the United States. Approximately thirty million pounds in May; twenty million in June; twelve million in July; ten million in August; nothing in September of this year.

We are waging a war where copper is one of the essentials to protect the lives of our men fighting for the expansion over the world of the ideas of Jefferson and LaFayette. Furthermore, we are spending thousands of millions of our national wealth during a war which may last for years, and we must increase this wealth, if possible, as we go, to repair the inordinate waste of war. Of gold and silver we have enough, but of copper and corn we must provide. Any thing which prevents the transformation of our latent wealth, the labor power of the United States, into useful articles, is as detrimental at this time, as the acts of our enemies.

Since the 12th day of June, there has been a deadlock between the copper producers in New York and the copper producers under ground in Butte. In May there were approximately fifteen thousand men at work in the Butte mines, and in the smelter city of Anaconda, where Butte ores are reduced, making copper and zinc useful for trade and war. In June, this number suddenly fell by at least eight thousand. The postal authorities state that seven thousand men ordered their mail forwarded from Butte in thirty days after June the 12th. At no time since the 12th day of June have there been as many as sixty-five hundred men working in the mines in Butte and at the smeltery in Anaconda, nor will there be a material increase in this number until the reasons for this are thoroughly analyzed, the true cause understood, *and removed.* I have given it twenty-three years of patient study after preliminary preparation for such work under "Daddy" Holmes and Heath Dabney at the Virginia University.[2]

For twenty years, we had a continuing stream of surplus labor power entering Castle Garden from Europe. It finally increased to much more than one million people per year. In August 1914, it almost ceased and in the last six months our present stock has diminished by at least one million of the best and bravest.

The condition in Montana today is the same as the condition of the labor market in England after the 'Black Death.' Parliament passed laws making it punishable with death to ask for an increase in wages, but, Thorold Rogers,[3] says, that for two generations thereafter wages steadily rose. In short, applying that experience to Butte, there will be no great production of copper from this most concentrated mining field in the world until wages are increased, and until certain conditions under which the men have labored and which enter into the laborers regard for the worth of his job are better. I must explain these to you briefly.

Two systems have arisen here under the Anaconda Copper Mining Company (a branch of the Standard Oil) which are repugnant to democratic government. These two matters are the out-growth of a long continued and preeminently successful attempt on the part of this company to control the shrievalty of this county and even the judiciary, legislature and executive of this state by coercion of its servants at the polls and preparation therefor by a system of espionage carried on through an employment bureau or by means of what is called in the language of the West a 'Rustling Card System.' Every man who seeks employment must give his previous history. He is looked up and if he has shown any political activity, that is not in accord with the will of the masters, he cannot get employment, and there is such a community of interest by other smaller copper producers, that if one is discharged from the employ of the main company he cannot get work in the Butte district. We in Butte have known of hosts of instances where good workmen have been driven from service by means of this system of espionage and into poverty, degradation, and despair, because of adverse political tenets. This system is not necessary for any legitimate mining purposes of this corporation, which mined here with astonishing success for thirty years without any such system. The men say that this system must go, before they will return to work in Butte. The Company answers that the Government of the United States follows such a system with its servants; the men reply that the Company is not the Government, that it only thinks it is, and that the heads of the Government are in their power to change, but the heads of the Company are not within their power to change, if the system is abused. Furthermore, the most successful individual copper miner, ex-Senator W. A. Clark,[4] has never used such a system.

The other cause of hatred in the hearts of the men is the private gunmen of the Company. It is estimated that in the City of Butte and the City of Anaconda the Company employs at least one thousand of these at a price of six dollars per day for Butte, five dollars per day for Anaconda. This item of expense enters into the cost which the Government pays for copper. It is entirely unnecessary, if the Company defended itself with conscious rectitude in its dealings with its men and with the state life of Montana. It justifies its cause by heralding to the world that the people of Butte are lawless, destroyers of lives and property. I, myself, have seen that same little frail old man, W. A. Clark walking our streets at eleven and twelve o'clock at night alone, and in perfect safety, and my ideas brought from Virginia, Your Excellency, against ladies going unattended at night on the streets of any large city have yielded to my experience in Butte. These men hold the office of Deputy Sheriff, appointed by the Company, paid by the Company, and against our Constitutional Provision, that no man shall hold office unless he takes oath that he will not receive any compensation except such as is allowed by law. The men regard this system of the company as being tantamount to an open transfer of the powers of government to individuals in New York. Few good citizens in Butte there are who would not rather tax themselves additionally and pay from the public purse any watchmen necessary to protect the company's coal from being stolen by old women and its brasses being taken away by thieving children. These men are determined to brook no longer a governing power not answerable to the will of the majority at the polls.

I need not repeat to Your Excellency, the long list of abuses to which this private power has been put by this company. The change of your mental attitude towards labor as evidenced by the Adamson act, the appointment of Mr. Brandeis, has lead me to believe that you have read the report of the committee to study

Industrial Unrest[5] and know subjectively at least, the crimes of corporate gunmen. You may cause investigations to be repeated in the Butte situation. The diagnosis for the whole terrible disorganization here can be found in Ricardo's Iron Law, that wages tend to that point (upward as well as downward) which will enable the laborer to live according to his scale and reproduce, and the additional fact that bacon in Butte is fifty cents a pound. The normal scale of twenty years ago was $3.50 per day and bacon was twelve cents a pound.

There will be little copper from Butte produced by married men at a less wage then [than] six dollars per day, and even the heads of the company themselves say that one married man is worth, as a miner, two single men. Furthermore, Butte has had a truly remarkable public school system, where the ideals of democracy are expounded, and the new generation hates a government not answerable to the people's will and hates a master who desires to control a popular expression at the polls.

There are some agitators here, some of the I.W.W. organization. There is no German influence. There is some hostility to draft from the Finns who are unwilling to fight for Russia and the Irish who are unwilling to fight for England, but, it is the truthful boast of the Metal Mine Workers Union, which is conducting the strike, that while there are one hundred sixty, or more, slackers in Butte, (whom my partner, the United States District Attorney here is running down as diligently as he can) yet, not a single member of the Metal Mine Workers Union has been found a slacker. The agitagors [agitators] are but the spark, the powder was here all the time ready to explode with any other spark.

The proper department will have trouble in changing these conditions which I have narrated. It will have to deal with men who, from long use of unchallenged power have gained a stubborn belief in their divine right to exercise it contrary to right and justice equaled only by our ancestors belief in the right of the Caucasians to hold the African in involuntary servitude.

It is not exaggeration to say that the monument which Tamerlane erected to his memory of the skulls of his enemies would not be larger than might be built of the skulls of those who, unredressed at law, have died either violently or by unsanitary conditions in the mines of Butte.

Your Excellency, in closing I must say that while I am of the party of Kerensky and Viviani, normally, yet your first administration compelled my vote for you the second time you sought office, and I realized as keenly as my old preceptor, your schoolmate, Heath Dabney, that it was necessary for America to fight. Perhaps what is true of Butte is true of Arizona and may be true in ninety days of Michigan.

On an investigation of this kind men who seek a swimming hole for life, in the Rubicon are not of much good.

Yours in good faith,   Lowndes Maury

(1) Cabinet Oct. 2.
(2) Hold until Secretary of Labor comes back.[6]

TLS (WP, DLC).
[1] Lawyer of Butte, Montana, partner of the federal district attorney and future United States senator from Montana, Burton Kendall Wheeler.
[2] That is, George Frederick Holmes and Richard Heath Dabney.
[3] James Edwin Thorold Rogers, *Six Centuries of Work and Wages: The History of English Labour* (2 vols., London, 1884), I, 228-42.
[4] William Andrews Clark, Democratic senator from Montana, 1901-1907.
[5] United States. Commission on Industrial Relations, *Final Report of the Commission on Industrial Relations* (Washington and Chicago, 1915).
[6] Transcript of CLSsh on first page of letter.

From Charles W. Boyle

Seattle, Washn., Sept. 25, 1917.

Your telegram of twenty third gratefully received Monday, and in consideration thereof men will work until Saturday morning, awaiting settlement. Refusal of workers to handle any except eight hour labor is keeping industry in turmoil and industry is rapidly becoming of greater moment than wage scale issue.

Charles W. Boyle.

T telegram (WP, DLC).

From the Diary of Josephus Daniels

September Tuesday 25 1917

Cabinet—Price of nitrates gone up very much, doubled—Houston said unwarranted. Navy had supply for 12 months.

Redfield told of bitter dispute between Dem & Rep, the latter being bitter against W.W. Finally he had to admit WW was right, but would not give him personal credit, but said: Wilson is making good only because he is inspired by the Almighty, by God!

Burleson said man in small store in Nebraska had this big sign:
"I have been drafted
Serve Your Country by buying early from me

Isaac Goldberg.

To Robert Lansing

Dear Mr. Secretary   [The White House, Sept. 26, 1917]

Thank you for letting me have these. I spent half an hour with Viscount Ishii.[1] I did most of the talking (to let him see my *full* thought) and he seemed to agree throughout in *principle*.[2]

W.W.

ALI (SDR, RG 59, 793.94/583½, DNA).
[1] Wilson saw Ishii at the White House at 4 P.M. on September 26. Ishii did not submit a written report of this meeting.
[2] Lansing had conferred with Ishii earlier in the same afternoon. They agreed upon further changes in Lansing's draft, which made the draft (undoubtedly approved at some time by Wilson) read as follows:
"Excellency:
"I have the honor to communicate herein my understanding of the agreement reached by us in our recent conversations touching the questions of mutual interest to our Governments relating to the Republic of China.
"Charges have repeatedly been made of late, some accusing the United States and others Japan of seeking to take advantage of present world conditions to acquire political influence or control in China. The Governments of the United States and Japan having always recognized China as a sovereign and independent state, resent such accusations as offensive and as wholly unjustified.
"In order to silence such mischievous reports, however, it is believed by us that a public announcement once more of the desires and intentions shared by our two Governments with regard to China is advisable.
"The Governments of the United States and Japan recognize that territorial propinquity creates special relations between countries; and consequently the United States Government recognizes that Japan has a special interest in China, particularly in that part to which her possessions are contiguous. The territorial sovereignty of China, nevertheless, remains unimpaired, and the Government of the United States has every confidence in the repeated assurances of the Imperial Japanese Government that, while geographical position gives them such special interest they have no desire to discriminate against the trade of other nations or to disregard the commercial rights heretofore granted by China in treaties with other Powers.
"The Governments of the United States and Japan deny that they have any purpose to infringe in any way the independence or territorial integrity of China and they declare furthermore that they always adhere to the principle of the so-called 'Open Door,' or equal opportunity for commerce and industry in China, and that they will not take advantage of present conditions to seek special rights or privileges in China which would abridge the rights of the citizens or subjects of other friendly States. Moreover they mutually declare that they are opposed to the acquisition by any other government of any special rights or privileges that would affect the independence or territorial integrity of China or that would deny to the subjects or citizens of any country the full enjoyment of equal opportunity in the commerce and industry of China.
"They furthermore agree to bring this declaration to the attention of other interested Governments and invite those Governments to give their adherence to these declarations.
"I shall be glad to have Your Excellency confirm this understanding of the agreement reached by us." T MS (SDR, RG 59, 793.94/583½, DNA).
According to Ishii, when he and Lansing agreed to use the phrase "special interest in China," Lansing said: "This official document will amount to a recognition of Japan's Monroe Doctrine toward China, and possesses an important meaning for the political situation in Asia." A. Satō to I. Motono, No. 381, Sept. 28, 1917, Hw telegram (Ishii Mission File, Japanese Foreign Office-Ar).

To Frank Irving Cobb

Personal.

My dear Cobb: The White House 26 September, 1917

Thank you for your letter of September twenty-fifth.[1] I have very little doubt that we came to the right conclusion about the informal mission.

I do not know what further evidence against Judge Cohalan is in the possession of the Department of Justice, but I will try to find out at once.

In haste

Cordially and faithfully yours,   Woodrow Wilson

TLS (IEN).

[1] It is missing. A transcript of a shorthand note on the next letter reads: "Regarding finding additional evidence about complicity of Judge Cohalan of New York in Irish-German plot."

To Thomas Watt Gregory

[The White House]

My dear Mr. Attorney General: 26 September, 1917

I refer the enclosed letter from Mr. Frank I. Cobb of the World to you in the hope that there may be some further evidence in your hands which will enable you to act upon the suggestion contained therein. I think it highly desirable to bring this man to book if it is possible to do so.

Faithfully yours,   [Woodrow Wilson]

CCL (WP, DLC).

To Allen Bartlit Pond

My dear Mr. Pond: [The White House] 26 September, 1917

I am very much obliged to you for your interesting letter of September twenty-first and want to express my sincere appreciation of the unusual efforts you are putting forth to get the right view of the nation's and the world's affairs put before the readers of the German language newspapers.

It is astonishing, as you say, how many people are affecting an eleventh-hour conversion.

In haste

Cordially and sincerely yours,   Woodrow Wilson

TLS (Letterpress Books, WP, DLC).

To Margaret Woodrow Wilson

My dearest Daughter: [The White House] 26 September, 1917

I hate to dictate a note to you but I want to hasten to assure you before I can get the time to write one myself that I have very cheerfully consented to the dedication to me of Mr. Macmillen's and Mr. MacKaye's national hymn.[1] How I would love to hear you sing it!

Poor Edith has been suffering terribly for a week now with a grippe which seems to go uncommonly hard with her, but her general condition is improving and I hope that the awful headaches will presently relax their grip and be done. The rest of us are well and we all unite in messages and dearest love.

Your loving   [Father]

CCL (WP, DLC).
  [1] *American Consecration Hymn* (New York, 1917), music by Francis Macmillen, words by Percy W. MacKaye. Macmillen was best known as a concert violinist and teacher. The words of this song are enclosed in P. W. MacKaye to WW, Sept. 23, 1917, TLS (WP, DLC), which also reveals that MacKaye had written them at Margaret Wilson's suggestion. Wilson's letters of consent to the dedication are WW to F. Macmillen and WW to P. W. MacKaye, both Sept. 24, 1917, TLS (Letterpress Books, WP, DLC).

From Levi Hollingsworth Wood and Others

Brooklyn, N. Y., Sept. 26, 1917.

We beg to register our vigorous protest against that portion of the trading with the enemy bill dealing with the press.[1] It makes possible the practical wiping out of a free press in the United States and completely sets adverse [subverts] constitutional rights. We do not stand for obstructing the war or embarrassing the government in any way, but regard freedom of discussion even of peace and war absolutely essential to preservation of your [our] democractic liberties. Postmaster General's reported attitude means total abolition during war of entire radical and most of the labor press. War power already being used by authorities to stifle legitimate agitation by labor for better conditions. This suppression of fundamental American rights can only encourage resort to secret methods and eventually force. It will arouse widespread distrust and uneasiness which will hamper effective prosecution of the war. We urge your veto of this farreaching and unAmerican proposal.

National Civil Liberties Bureau,[2]
L. Hollingsworth Wood,
John Lovejoy Elliott,

Norman M. Thomas,
John Haynes Holmes,
Amos Pinchot,
Roger H. Baldwin.[3]

T telegram (WP, DLC).

[1] The Senate-House conference committee on the trading with the enemy bill (H.R. 4960) had, on September 19, added a provision to the measure, Section 19, which required all foreign-language newspapers and publications to file with the postmaster of the place of publication an affidavit comprising an exact and full English translation of any news item or editorial which commented on the United States Government or any nation engaged in the war, their policies, international relations, the state or conduct of the war, or any related subjects. Any publication which failed to comply was not only denied the use of the mails but was also forbidden to be distributed in any other manner. The President could, however, issue permits exempting specific publications from the requirement. Despite some objections, the Senate and House accepted the conference report and Wilson approved the bill on October 6. *New York Times*, Sept. 20, 1917; 65th Cong., 1st sess., S. Doc. 110; 40 *Statutes at Large* 425.

[2] The name taken by the Civil Liberties Bureau when it separated from the American Union Against Militarism. The separation became official on October 1. See Donald Johnson, *The Challenge to American Freedoms: World War I and the Rise of the American Civil Liberties Union* (Lexington, Ky., 1963), pp. 23-24.

[3] The signers not heretofore identified were Wood, lawyer of New York, a Quaker active in peace and social-reform groups, and a founder of the American Friends Service Committee; and Elliott, teacher and leader of the New York Society for Ethical Culture and founder of the Hudson Guild, a well-known settlement house on Manhattan's West Side.

From George Creel

Dear Mr. President: Washington, D. C., September 26, 1917.

May I urge that your Industrial Commission be directed to proceed to San Francisco at once to make a thorough investigation of labor's charge that Mooney and other defendants in the case are being made the victims of conspiracy and legal injustice. This Mooney case has assumed a national, as well as international aspect. Russia and the European countries are watching it, and American labor itself is in a very ugly state of mind. It is the duty of the Commission to ascertain the causes of industrial unrest, and this Mooney case is one of the fundamental causes. The very fact that they were proceeding to San Francisco would bring a change, and a report to you on the situation would end the conspiracy that is now going on. As I told you, our upper and middle classes need not cause us any concern. Labor, however, is in an irritated and suspicious frame of mind.

Respectfully,   George Creel

TLS (WP, DLC).

From Bernard Mannes Baruch

My dear Mr. President: Washington, D. C. September 26, 1917.

Referring to your letter of the 25th, which was received this forenoon:

Your understanding of the suggestions made by Mr. Hoover is correct, and such is the understanding of myself and my colleagues, and we so agreed with Mr. Hoover in conference with him some ten days ago.

In addition, we have informally notified the various governments that the purchases should be made by the Food Administrator, and so far as any food products have come before our Commission, we have referred them to Mr. Hoover and shall take such further necessary action to carry out this understanding.

We do not think it necessary for you to issue any further instructions. There are some details in connection with this which we will take up with Mr. Hoover for the protection of the Treasury.   Very sincerely yours,   Bernard M Baruch

TLS (WP, DLC).

From Hester Drayton Boylston[1]

My Dear Mr Wilson   Atlanta, Ga Sept 26th, 1917

Accept my very cordial thanks for the beautiful Roses with which you honored me on my eigthtieth birthday. I do assure you, your thoughtful[ness] is most highly appreciated, and completed the pleasure of a "A perfect Day."
                    Very Sincerely   Hester. D. Boylston

HwCLS (received from Mrs. E. N. Sumrall).
  [1] Mrs. J. Reid Boylston. Wilson had taken his meals at her elegant boarding house in Atlanta from 1882 to 1883. Wilson had sent Mrs. Boylston eighty American Beauty roses.

William Bauchop Wilson to Joseph Patrick Tumulty

My dear Mr. Tumlty: Washington September 26, 1917.

I am in receipt of your letter of the 25th instant, inclosing telegram from George L. Baker, Mayor of Portland, Oregon. Mayor Baker should be advised that the Adjustment Commission of the Shipping Board, of which Mr. Macy is the Chairman, is about to proceed to the Pacific Coast to take up the existing disputes in the shipping industry directly on the ground.

I am returning the telegram herewith.
                    Cordially yours,   W B Wilson

TLS (WP, DLC).

To Charles Francis Jenkins[1]

My dear Mr. Jenkins: [The White House] 27 September, 1917

In reply to your letter of September seventeenth,[2] whose importance I fully appreciate, I beg to say that the claims of agriculture in connection with exemption from the draft have been very carefully and anxiously considered by the Secretary of War and myself and a method has been devised which we believe will enable all claims to be allowed which justify exemption and will in other cases leave the farmer and his help at home to gather the crops before joining the colors.

The Selective Service Act authorizes the President "to exclude or discharge from said selected draft ⁕ ⁕ ⁕ or to draft for partial military service only from those liable to draft as in this Act provided, persons of the following classes: ⁕ ⁕ ⁕ Persons engaged in industries, including agriculture, found to be necessary to the maintenance of the Military Establishment or the effective operation of the military forces or the maintenance of national interest during the emergency."

Exclusive original jurisdiction with regard to the decision of all claims for discharge on the ground of being engaged in an agricultural enterprise has been vested by Congress in what are known as the District Boards, for each federal judicial district. Inasmuch as members of these boards must reside in the district for which they are appointed, a plan has been followed by which at least one member of each board should be in close touch with the agricultural situation in his district. These boards have been directed to make a survey of the industrial and agricultural conditions in the district under their control, ascertaining as near as may be the labor supply available throughout the necessary industries and for agriculture outside of the men called for military service, and to take into consideration all such facts in determining claims for exemption.

Wherever, in the opinion of the District Board, the direct and substantial material loss to any industrial or agricultural enterprise necessary to the maintenance of the Military Establishment or to the effective operation of the military forces or the national interest during the war outweighs the loss that would result from the failure to obtain the military service of any person engaged in such enterprise, the Board will issue a certificate of exemption.

It has not been thought feasible to go beyond this general authorization and make wholesale discharges of farmers as a class upon the mere showing that a claimant for discharge has some color of right to be called a farmer. To do so would be to let down the bars and bring down upon a central office the insistent demands of thousands of industries which would have an equal right for consideration.

A method has been devised, however, whereby farmers and farm hands are to be granted special consideration consistent with the letter of the Act and in accordance with its spirit. By this method it is intended that the Local Board shall receive from the District Board a list of the men who have presented claims for temporary discharge on the ground of the necessity of gathering the crops. Certificates of discharge will not issue in such cases, but the Local Board, on examining such claims, will be enabled if it deems it necessary to designate such individuals for the contingents to be summoned to report at the mobilization camp at later dates, to be fixed by the Adjutant General. Thus the need of leaving the men temporarily at the work of gathering the crops may be satisfied without complicating or diminishing the quotas.

It is to be borne in mind that all branches of industry, and indeed all activities of life, are affected by the draft and we must in many cases rely upon the services of those above and below the draft age. It may in many cases be inconvenient, but the nation as well as the individual must be considered. There will be no hardship in the many cases where agricultural claims have been allowed, and in those cases where the claims have been disallowed the young men who are serving the country must and can be replaced by those younger or older who cannot serve in the Army.

Sincerely yours,   Woodrow Wilson[3]

TLS (Letterpress Books, WP, DLC).
   [1] Coeditor and principal owner of the Philadelphia *Farm Journal*.
   [2] C. F. Jenkins to WW, Sept. 17, 1917, TLS (WP, DLC).
   [3] "The President desires that to all inquiries concerning the exemption of farmers this letter be sent." CLS to JPT, c. Sept. 27, 1917, TL (WP, DLC).

To George Creel

My dear Creel: [The White House] 27 September, 1917

Perhaps since I saw Doctor Mott yesterday[1] he has seen you and conveyed to you my suggestion that instead of drawing a whole million from the Treasury we make such arrangements as the Treasury may suggest for withdrawing portions of it from time to time. This would be very much more convenient for the Treasury, for I have consulted with them in matters of this sort several times. I ought to have thought of it when I consulted with you the other day.

Faithfully yours,   [Woodrow Wilson]

CCL (WP, DLC).
    1 John R. Mott's very cryptic notes of his conversation with Wilson on September 26 (Hw MS [J. R. Mott Coll., CtY-D]) indicate that they spoke of the proposed American propaganda effort in Russia and its relation to the Committee on Public Information. They also discussed the forthcoming Y.M.C.A. fund drive to raise $35,000,000 for its wartime activities among American servicemen and in foreign countries and how this drive could avoid conflict with the second Liberty Loan campaign. They discussed the relationship of Y.M.C.A. field secretaries to army and navy chaplains: how their work could be coordinated and friction between the two groups avoided. There was some discussion of the "exemptions question," presumably the exemption of Y.M.C.A. personnel from the draft. Finally, they spoke about the American Ambassador to Russia, David R. Francis, but there is no hint of what they said about him. About the Y.M.C.A. fund drive and the relations of chaplains and Y.M.C.A. secretaries, see C. Howard Hopkins, *John R. Mott, 1865-1955* (Grand Rapids, Mich., 1979), pp. 524-26, 535-36.

From Joseph Patrick Tumulty, with Enclosure

Dear Governor: [The White House] September 27th [1917].

I hope you will forgive me for sending you this letter but inasmuch as Mr. Villard is asking for a hearing, I don't want to turn him down.   The Secretary.

TL (WP, DLC).

E N C L O S U R E

Oswald Garrison Villard to Joseph Patrick Tumulty

My dear Mr. Tumulty: [New York] September 26, 1917

I am greatly alarmed, in the interest of the Administration, at what is happening in this matter of suppression of the press in the rider to the Trading with the Enemy Act and the action already taken by the Postmaster General. I cannot but feel that if this policy is carried out it will do more to create sedition and disloyalty and anarchy in this country than anything that has taken place. It will drive the extreme radicals and agitators to underground work. Do you know that neither in Germany nor in Russia was so far-reaching an act ever passed? Even in Russia they permitted a review of the actions of the publications and the official suppressing by a court. Nothing of the kind is provided here. There is apparently no appeal from the Postmaster

General, which means his third assistant or some $1,200 clerk who has passed upon the details of the thing.

Today, Mr. Victor Berger came in,—the ex-Congressman,—and told me that the Third Assistant Postmaster General[1] informed him on Saturday that his Milwaukee paper will be suppressed shortly, not because of any single utterance but because of its "general tendency." He asked for details, but got none. He has an investment of $200,000. His political doctrines are not yours, as they are not mine, but he is surely legitimately engaged in presenting the news of the world from the point of view of Socialism. Just think what an impression all this will make in Berlin, where they have allowed the Socialist newspapers in the main to go on unchecked, except occasionally! As you know, they are our hope in bringing about the revolution we want. How can we, in the face of this, hold up our heads and not be accused of the blackest hypocrisy if we go ahead and suppress our Socialist newspapers here in a war avowedly waged for democracy?

I cannot believe that Mr. Wilson will so reverse himself on all his democratic teachings as to sign this bill, if he appreciates what it means. Therefore I am telegraphing you, asking you to appoint a time for a hearing when protestants may be heard before him. The damage, I believe, will be incalculable if this bill becomes a law,—provided it applies to the English language papers, about which there seems to be some confusion,—for it will inevitably drive protestants to underground activities.

I know that you know—from what you have said to me—that the safety of the republic lies in letting the dissatisfied talk; but certainly a republic at war to make a democracy out of an empire cannot go further than either Prussia or Russia ever dared to go, can it?

In the interest of your own cause and of your Administration, I beg of you to help us clear up this situation. And do not let Burleson suppress Berger's paper unless you wish to see 4,000,000 Socialist votes at the next election, see Hillquit come near carrying off the Mayoralty in New York,[2] and generally divide us up into a Socialist and anti-Socialist camp. Cannot Burleson's underlings be made to understand that the Socialist doctrine is now supreme in half a dozen European countries, that it is a perfectly legitimate political propaganda, indeed a model for human living which most of us would be for, because of its essential democracy, if we could but believe that its economic bases were sound?

In the name of free speech and American liberty,
    Faithfully yours,   Oswald Garrison Villard.

TLS (WP, DLC).
  [1] Alexander Monroe Dockery.
  [2] About the mayoralty campaign in New York, see W. Lippmann to WW, Oct. 8, 1917, n. 1.

To Joseph Patrick Tumulty

Dear Tumulty: [The White House, Sept. 28, 1917]

Please say to Mr. Villard that I genuinely regret that the arrangement of such a hearing at present is practically out of the question.   The President.

TL (WP, DLC).

To Albert Shaw

My dear Shaw: The White House 28 September, 1917

Mr. Tumulty has looked over the proof of the messages and state papers which you were so kind as to send us[1] and has formed the opinion that they are very carefully compiled and very accurate. The compilation will certainly prove very valuable to myself amongst others and I am obliged to you for having undertaken it.

    Cordially and sincerely yours,   Woodrow Wilson

TLS (A. Shaw Coll., NjP).
  [1] Albert Shaw, ed., *President Wilson's State Papers and Addresses* (New York, 1917).

To Thomas Staples Martin

My dear Senator: [The White House] 28 September, 1917

I hope that there is no danger that after the passage of the Revenue Bill an adjournment will be taken before the soldiers' insurance bill is acted on. I feel to the full the very great desirability of the adjournment of Congress for the purpose of putting the constituencies all over the country in touch with the thoughts and facts and principles which have governed us here, but I think nevertheless that the effect of failing to pass the insurance bill immediately would be very demoralizing indeed, particularly upon our military forces and, of course, that is a matter of capital concern.

I know that you will understand and pardon the liberty I am taking in writing this note. I feel sure that it chimes with your own instinctive judgment.

Cordially and sincerely yours,   Woodrow Wilson

TLS (Letterpress Books, WP, DLC).

To Frank Irving Cobb

Confidential.

My dear Cobb: [The White House] 28 September, 1917

There is nothing yet in the hands of the Department of Justice which would supplement the evidence in the case you wrote me about, though there seems to be some expectation there that other evidence will presently be forthcoming. I write this just to supplement my last letter.

In haste   Faithfully yours,   [Woodrow Wilson]

CCL (WP, DLC).

To the White House Staff

[The White House, c. Sept. 28, 1917]

Please get this gentleman[1] into communication at once with the Commission of Labor Inquiry which is starting West under the direction of the Secretary of Labor. I have asked that commission to look into this very case.   The President.

TL (WP, DLC).

[1] J. Edward Morgan, a publicist for the International Workers Defense League of San Francisco, who was at this time touring the East Coast on behalf of Thomas J. Mooney. A White House memorandum reveals that Morgan had written to Tumulty on September 28 and requested an interview with Wilson concerning the Mooney case, about which he claimed to know "every detail." He also wanted to discuss the proposed extradition of Alexander Berkman, who had been indicted for his alleged complicity in the Mooney affair. For information on Morgan and his activities at this time, see Richard H. Frost, *The Mooney Case* (Stanford, Cal., 1968), pp. 48, 278-80, 288-89, 298.

From Max Eastman

New York City
My dear President Wilson: September 28th, 1917.

I judge that your letter to me was not meant to be private, but, nevertheless, I want to apologize for its having gotten into the papers without special permission from the White House. Mr.

David Lawrence induced my stenographer to read it to him over the long distance telephone, and as it appeared in a somewhat garbled form in the Evening Post and the reporters came to my office, I thought it was best to give them a correct account of the correspondence.

I hope I am right in thinking this has not caused you any inconvenience.

I appreciate the friendliness of your letter.

Sincerely yours,   Max Eastman

TLS (WP, DLC).

From Grenville Stanley Macfarland

Personal & Confidential

My dear President Wilson,   En Route Sept 28, 1917.

I am much gratified to be able to say to you that since two o'clock this afternoon I have been in charge of the editorial policy of the New York American etc. Mr. Hearst was kind enough to confer this authority upon me by wire today.

If you still have the confidence in my friendship which you were so good as to express at our last conversation,[1] you will I am sure appreciate what this undertaking on my part, imports.

I shall be regularly in Washington to keep in touch with the publicity needs of the government. If I do not succeed in helping you along your difficult way it will not be due to any want of heart in the effort, for I most heartily believe in you and in your course. Of all the hundreds of varied and perplexing problems you have had to solve, your solution differed from mine in only two—the Panama tolls and Vera Cruz expedition.

Yours sincerely,   G. S. Macfarland.

ALS (WP, DLC).
[1] Macfarland had talked to Wilson at the White House on September 5.

From Herbert Bruce Brougham

Dear Mr. President: Philadelphia 28th September 1917

Inclosed herewith is a copy of our editorial comment on Colonel House's mission,[1] in which I have tried to interpret your own attitude toward an investigation of the problems that will confront the peace conference.[2] If the comment is wrong in its premises, or if, as is probable, it needs supplementing, should not the time be opportune for a comprehensive statement from you on the subject?

It is still deemed wise to hold in abeyance our plan for an association of ably conducted newspapers, about which you advised me with so much sympathy and candor. Meanwhile, it is my earnest wish that the Ledger should stand in the forefront of enlightened opinion about the war and its issues which are to be tried out in the peace conference.

I feel that we should spare no effort to lend our aid in illuminating and broadening the path of American diplomacy overseas, and in this endeavor we bespeak your support and encouragement.   Very sincerely yours,   H. B. Brougham

TLS (WP, DLC).

¹ The Philadelphia *Public Ledger*, on September 27, had published a dispatch from its Washington correspondent, Lincoln Colcord, which revealed that Wilson had asked House to organize and direct a group to prepare for American participation in a future peace conference. This revelation led to much discussion in the American press in the next few days. See Lawrence E. Gelfand, *The Inquiry: American Preparations for Peace, 1917-1919* (New Haven, Conn., 1963), pp. 39-41.

² This editorial concluded as follows:

"In this spirit the President has asked Colonel House to survey the field of military, naval and political conditions in the countries of our enemies and our friends; to get at the economic, political and emotional state of things in every country, and to tell frankly to Great Britain, Russia, France, Italy and the neutral Powers the things that we are doing and that we intend to do in the war. Moreover, an attempt will be made to lift the heavy curtain of censorship in Germany and Austria-Hungary, in order to spread among their peoples a comprehension of American war aims and potentialities.

"That is the exalted mission with which Colonel House is charged. His reputation for astuteness in American politics is equaled only by the singular confidence which he commands, not only among the leaders of both the great national parties of the United States, but among the leading statesmen of Europe, with most of whom he has come in personal contact, for an honesty of purpose and of promise that is unswerving in its fulfillment. In this mission he will work, as always, simply and without ostentation. He will act informally, unofficially. He has already established in the informal diplomacy of the world a new principle—that of diplomatic honesty." Philadelphia *Public Ledger*, Sept. 28, 1917, clipping (WP, DLC).

About the report on House's "mission," see WW to H. B. Brougham, Sept. 29, 1917, n. 1.

Two Letters from William Bauchop Wilson
to Joseph Patrick Tumulty

My dear Mr. Tumulty: Washington September 28, 1917.

I am in receipt of your letter of the 27th instant, inclosing telegrams received by Senator Poindexter from George H. Walker, suggesting that the President request certain mills to operate on an eight-hour day.¹

I do not believe it would be advisable for the President to make such a request solely upon the strength of Mr. Walker's judgment without knowing more of the inside information upon which Mr. Walker bases his belief than is contained in his telegrams. I concur in the viewpoint that a settlement of the lumbering situation would go a long ways towards adjusting the other labor difficulties in the State of Washington, particularly if it could be adjusted on an eight-hour basic day with time and one-half for overtime. More than six weeks ago we were assured by the Commissioners of Conciliation of the Department of Labor at Seattle that the workmen would accept a settlement in the lumbering industry on a basic work-day of eight hours at the same rate per hour as they had formerly been receiving for ten hours' work, and would work the additional hours required of them to meet the emergency on the basis of time and one-half for overtime. The proposition appealed to me as being eminently fair. I discussed it with Secretary Baker, and at his suggestion prepared a telegram for his signature as Chairman of the Council of National Defense, making a patriotic appeal for the acceptance of the proposition. The telegram was sent, but the employers refused to accede to the appeal.

I would not want the President to be placed in that kind of a position, and suggest that Senator Poindexter be advised that the Wage Adjustment Commission of the Shipping Board, of which Mr. Macy is the Chairman, will start for Seattle on the 3d instant, and that the suggestions contained in Mr. Walker's telegrams will be placed in their hands for consideration. If they become convinced that the action suggested would bring results, I would have no hesitancy in advising that the President make the request suggested.

I am returning the telegrams herewith.

Sincerely yours,   W B Wilson

TLS (WP, DLC).
¹ G. H. Walker to M. Poindexter, Sept. 26, 1917, two T telegrams (WP, DLC).

My dear Mr. Tumulty: Washington September 28, 1917.

I have your letter of the 24th instant, inclosing telegram from Mr. Cal. Wyatt, General Organizer, American Federation of Labor, and Mr. Clem Wessel, Secretary, Steel City Union, relative to the strike at the Jones and Laughlin plants at Pittsburgh, Pa., and note your inquiry for information as to the circumstances surrounding the strike referred to.

Several days ago we detailed Mr. Charles Bendheim as a Commissioner of Conciliation to use the good offices of the Department of Labor in connection with this controversy. Our latest information from him is that twenty-five hundred are involved in the strike at the Jones and Laughlin steel plant at Pittsburgh, which has been in effect since September 15th, and that there is some danger of the strike extending to all of the plants in this section. The demands are for an eight-hour day and an increase in wages. We understand that the company has expressed a willingness to pay the same wages and put in effect the same conditions of employment as others in that vicinity. The State Board of Mediation of Pennsylvania is also cooperating with Mr. Bendheim, and yesterday afternoon Mr. Joseph F. Guffey,[1] who is General Manager of the Philadelphia Company in Pittsburgh, left Washington for Pittsburgh to get in touch with Mr. Bendheim and to assist him in his efforts to secure an amicable adjustment. We shall be very glad to keep you fully informed as to the progress of the negotiations.

I am returning the telegram which you inclosed herewith.

Sincerely yours,   W B Wilson

TLS (WP, DLC).
[1] Joseph Finch Guffey, student at Princeton, 1890-1892.

Sir William Wiseman to Sir Eric Drummond

[New York] Septr. 28, 1917.

PADEREWSKI is about to present to U.S.G. formal request for recognition of POLISH NATIONAL COMMITTEE and states England, France, and Italy have been similarly approached. HOUSE asks whether, in the event of the PRESIDENT recognising it, British will do the same. Also whether you know the views of the French and Italians. President is in favor of recognising it but feels it would be better if the four powers recognise it simultaneously and in similar terms. Please cable about this as HOUSE will discuss the matter with President Wednesday.

T telegram (W. Wiseman Papers, CtY).

From the Diary of Josephus Daniels

1917 Friday 28 September

Cabinet—short session. Mrs. McAdoo presided at woman's meeting of Liberty Loan bonds. The President said she was very nervous, never having done such a thing before. He said to her "Why don't you follow the example of your father? When he does not know anything about what he must attempt, he makes a bluff at it."

To Joseph Patrick Tumulty

Dear Tumulty: [The White House, Sept. 29, 1917]

I know absolutely nothing about this matter,[1] but it is clear to me that it ought to be handled through the Council of National Defense. I would not dare recommend this enormous expenditure, $100,000,000, without knowing very much more about this matter than I do and I think I ought to have the advice of someone who knows before taking any action at all.

The President.

TL (WP, DLC).
[1] A plan to provide $100,000,000 worth of emergency housing for workers engaged on war contracts, proposed by the Section on Housing of the Committee on Labor of the Advisory Commission of the Council of National Defense. The plan was discussed in P. Hiss to F. Morrison, Sept. 28, 1917, enclosed in F. Morrison to WW, Sept. 28, 1917, both TLS (WP, DLC).

To Herbert Bruce Brougham

[The White House]
My dear Mr. Brougham: 29 September, 1917

It was through the very inconsiderate talk of some people who ought to have known better that any public mention was made of my request to Colonel House to prepare all the materials that we would need in discussing any and all questions that might come up in the eventual peace conference which is sure to come at some time or other, and I am afraid the impression has got about that we are contemplating an early conference, as, of course, we are not. I must frankly say that I feel that the best and most patriotic course just now is to say nothing about it at all.

Of course, I do not mean to reflect in the least on your own kind efforts at interpretation. I merely mean that all discussion of peace at this time, so long as the German Government remains so stubbornly insincere and impossible, is unwise.

Cordially and sincerely yours,   Woodrow Wilson

TLS (Letterpress Books, WP, DLC).

From Thomas Staples Martin

Dear Mr. President: Washington, D. C. September 29, 1917.

Your letter has just been handed me. You need not feel any anxiety about the insurance bill. It will certainly be passed before adjournment. The Committee will report it to the Senate on

Saturday. The revenue bill will be reported the same day. The two bills will have priority of consideration and I hope they can be passed with reasonable promptness. My idea is that when these two bills are passed nothing will remain of sufficient importance to compel a continuation of the session. Some small matters may be passed at odd times, but these two important measures you may rest assured will certainly be passed, and soon after that adjournment can be had.

I agree with you that it is of very great importance that members of Congress get to their homes in order to explain the causes and conditions of the war.

Very respectfully,   Thomas S. Martin.

TLS (WP, DLC).

From William Gibbs McAdoo

Dear Mr. President: Washington September 29, 1917.

Representatives of the various foreign powers borrowing from the United States were recently asked to revise, and if possible reduce, their requisitions for loans from this Government. The disappointing result may be thus stated:

1. *Great Britain.* The British Government, instead of reducing its requests for assistance, has renewed urgently its request that the $400,000,000 open account owed to New York bankers be now covered by a loan from the Treasury. They indicate the urgent need of many millions of dollars for purchasing wheat in Canada and cotton in the United States. Furthermore, huge sums are being monthly expended by them for purchasing foreign exchange bills offered in the New York market, which means substantially that they are unable to pay for goods purchased in neutral countries, although they are being entirely relieved as to direct governmental purchases in the United States by the loans regularly made to them. They also indicate for the campaign of 1918 a rate of munition expenditure which will increase rather than decrease the amounts required for such purposes. It is proposed to prepare for weekly discharges of 83,000 tons of projectiles on the west front. This is substantially double the amount that has been expended per week during the recent offensive, which in turn was a far greater expenditure than had ever been known before.

Independently of the pressure from the British Government, there is strong pressure from Ottawa for a large loan to the Canadian Government. It is represented to me that it will be impossible to continue sending the munitions which Canada has heretofore supplied to England unless help is obtained from the United States Treasury.

2. *France.* The French Government reports that it is impossible to reduce now its request for $160,000,000 a month. A previous request for money with which to pay for cotton is temporarily suspended due to a tentative arrangement by which the expenditures of our army in France are made to balance cotton purchases in the United States. There is no indication that the amount requested by this Government will diminish, and, possibly, in conformity with the English plan of huge campaigning in 1918, there may be demands for larger amounts of munitions.

3. *Italy.* Italian requests for funds for October show a considerable increase over the requests for the previous months. They desire $100,000,000, whereas, previously it was $70,000,000, $40,000,000 and $60,000,000 for August, July and June, respectively. In addition to this, they very urgently ask that $25,000,000 be furnished them as a special fund with which to pay a loan made in the United States before we entered the war, and maturing on the fifteenth of October. They appear to be wholly without means to meet this indebtedness, and speak of default if the loan is not renewed or paid by advances from the Treasury.

4. *Russia.* The disturbed situation in Russia and the difficulties of transportation to that seat of war may possibly diminish in the future the demands upon the Treasury. Just now, however, that Government is drawing heavily upon its already established credits, and these will be exhausted at a relatively early date. Additional requests for credits totalling $235,000,000 to January 1st have just been submitted, this figure being in addition to a sum, approximately $140,000,000, for railway material deliverable next year, and for which Mr. Stevens committed our government in an irresponsible but embarrassing proclamation.[1] A special credit ($75,000,000) was established for Russian expenditures *outside* of the United States—this on an urgent telegram from Mr. Root. Other demands of this sort are to be expected.

5. *Belgium.* The Belgian Government, as you will remember, receives regularly $7,500,000 a month to cover the supply of food for its civil population, and has recently been forced to obtain here loans at the rate of about $4,000,000 per month for the maintenance of its army in the field, as both England and France have stopped all supplies purchaseable here for that pur-

[1] About this matter, see RL to WW, Aug. 13, 1917, Vol. 43.

pose. They ask for funds to construct a military railway behind their lines, but this has not been granted.

6. *Cuba*. After having received recommendations from the War and Navy Departments, and your approval, a loan of $15,000,000 has been determined upon for the Cuban Government. It is hoped and believed that this particular government will not increase its demands beyond the figure thus named.

7. *Roumania*. Very urgent demands have come from Roumania through Petrograd, the original sum asked being $20,000,000. We have had some advice from our own representatives in Russia and Roumania indicating that the amount mentioned is extravagantly high. At this moment, Ambassador Francis is still endeavoring to keep the burden of supplying the Roumanian army upon the Russian Government where it seems properly to belong. His attitude, however, may change at any moment; and in the meantime I am put under great pressure by General Scott to make loans to Roumania at once with or without the advice of Mr. Francis. It is not improbable that it would seem wise to offer some aid to the Roumanian Government with the consequent addition to the burdens of the Treasury. Very recent information from British sources indicates that Great Britain and France may possibly join in this subvention, the share of each to be about $5,000,000 per month.

8. *Greece*. An urgent demand has just reached me through the State Department from the Greek Government asking for an immediate credit of $50,000,000 in order that their troops may be mobilized against the Central Powers. This is seconded by requests from the British and French Governments. No wise decision can be reached without further inquiry into the proposed military movements in view.

9. *China*. The State Department presents to me for immediate consideration a proposition that $25,000,000 to $50,000,000 should be at once credited to China, as this country, having declared war against Germany may, if given the necessary funds, be able to assist considerably in the contest; and, furthermore, American influence in China would be much strengthened if the loan were made by our Government to the existing Chinese Government.

It remains to be seen whether any South American country now about to enter the war will join with all the other belligerents in looking to the United States for financial support.

The French Government has accumulated over a million tons of goods in the United States for which no transportation is available. The Russian and Italian Governments have also immense stocks similarly situated. There is constant pressure upon the Shipping Board by foreign representatives to relieve the congestion above mentioned, and that Board is without the necessary information to determine wisely the allocation of shipping to the various governments in question. Their determinations, like those with respect to loans, must be made without due knowledge of the relative importance of the requisitions made upon them.

Enough has been said above to show the enormous and constantly increasing burdens falling upon our Government in connection with the great war. Substantially it may be said that while the European Governments are spending large sums independently of those borrowed from us, yet all the belligerent operations against Germany are now founded upon the obtainment of financial help from the United States.

At the same time that we feel this increased pressure from abroad, our own Departments are entering upon a course of expenditure unparallelled in the history of the world. I have recently obtained estimates from the War and Navy Departments as to their probable actual paying out of money during the next few months. It is indicated that more than a billion dollars per month will be actually checked out in October, November and December, with probable increases thereafter.

As the result of these combined pressures, it appears that we must immediately raise by loans of one sort or another at least $1,250,000,000 every month. Should the financial exhaustion of the European belligerents become more marked, or should it seem wise that military operations should become more active, the demand upon the United States from foreign quarters would correspondingly increase. The rate at which money must be raised may, therefore, be higher even than that rate which is now confronting me, and which is so high that only by the most energetic and careful measures will it be possible to meet these extraordinary demands.

Viewing the whole situation, I feel it my imperative duty to urge that steps substantially on the lines heretofore presented to you should be taken to have a review of the whole scheme of war making. It is possible that such a review would result in the acceptance of the existing European plans, but it seems beyond doubt that some economies will result from a challenge of the whole existing situation, and a correllation of efforts which now seem to be so little correllated. Into such a coordinated study I feel that our own military expenditures should enter.

It seems not improbable that some of our expenditures may

be modified through closer adjustment to the military needs of the allies, and to the exigencies of the Treasury.

I cannot doubt that the vast complex of problems which are suggested in the foregoing statements should be made the subject of study by such an Inter-Ally Council as has already been proposed and agreed to by European governments, with the condition expressed by their representatives that its functioning will be of little value unless American representatives take part in its councils. Being continuously impressed with the lack of coordination in all of the military efforts which are being made by those who are associated in the war against Germany, I, therefore, feel it again my duty to lay this situation before you and to repeat my recommendation that an American representative or representatives should be permitted to be attached in a consultative capacity to the Inter-Ally Council in order that the financial forces of the United States particularly, and by correllation those of other governments associated with us in the war, should be marshalled against our common enemy with the maximum of efficiency. I am profoundly convinced that there is great lack of efficiency in this matter at present. The progress already made by obtaining the consent of the allied governments for the establishment of the Inter-Ally Council justifies me in urging this particular plan as the one to which we should now adhere, and which needs only to be perfected by the addition of American representatives in order that it may be at a very early date set into motion.

In the meantime, I remain, my dear Mr. President,
Cordially yours,   W G McAdoo

TLS (WP, DLC).

From Edward Mandell House

Dear Governor: New York. September 29, 1917.

In talking with Vance McCormick today he told me that his board were about to come to a decision upon embargoes—particularly with Sweden and Norway.

I advised him to do nothing until he had seen you, since it was a matter of such importance that it might mean bringing into the war all of Scandinavia and possibly against the Allies.

I suppose you have read the confidential memorandum[1] prepared by the British War Council and left with you by Lord Reading. No one knows of this in American [America] outside of you, Lord Reading, Wiseman and myself, therefore the English, French and Italians with whom McCormick's board have reached an agreement concerning embargoes, do not know the real situation.

From that memorandum, it would seem that it would be a bad thing for the Allies for any of the nearby neutrals to get into the war, either for or against the Allies and for the reasons expressed therein.   Affectionately yours,   E. M. House

TLS (WP, DLC).
 1 See n. 1 to the Enclosure printed with EMH to WW, Oct. 3, 1917.

From Edward Parker Davis

My Dear Woodrow,   [Philadelphia] Sept. 29 1917

I think so often of you, with pride and affectionate admiration for the great things you are doing for Humanity.

But are you never burdened with a sense of the infinite scope of this great Drama in which you are cast, and also of your finite powers?

Do you not sometimes crave the Infinite? This thought has gone into verse;[1] you will not judge severely its crude expression: you will welcome kindly its intent, and I am happy in knowing that it will remind you of

Affectionately Yours,   E. P. Davis.

ALS (WP, DLC).

 1 "Our little daily life runs on,
   A trickling stream across the sands,
   The little work of childish hands,
   A few faint heart beats come and gone.

   "We dwell in beauty's holy shrine,
   The altar of the burning sun,
   The temple of a life begun,
   The promise of a life divine.

   "We play our little game of chance,
   We strike our little blows of war;
   There, on the heights where spirits are,
   Eternal glory sets a lance
   And charges down the lists of time,
   And routs the lying crew of sense,
   And with the true magnificence
   Uplifts the shining shields sublime
   Of holy truth, and clear-eyed faith,
   And magic youth with steady hand,
   And all the transcendental band
   Who clothe the spirit like a wraith
   Of sunlight on the shining sea,
   Of shimmer from the midnight moon
   Which fades across the waves too soon,
   And brings again my day to me!

   "Oh glimpse of glory, brief and faint!
   Oh grief of little earthly days!

We hear far off the hymn of praise
From souls of warrior and saint,
And stiffen for our daily task,
And sound the drum beat of our hearts,
And tax our courage to impart
A tithe of hope to those who ask.

"And then, in some unlooked for hour,
Again we hear the music, far
On wings of faith from shining star,
The diapason deep of power,
Eternal, infinite, alone,
But strangely sweet and sweetly strange,
And touching all our human range,
The finite spirit's song of home!

"You who stand forth from all the world,
Leader of men and called of God,
Whose way lies over heights where trod
Prophets and seers, whose voices stirred
The tribes of men with trumpet call
Of righteous wrath, whose altar fires
Consumed the dross of men's desires,
And made God's sunshine safe for all!

"You who have stood on heights alone,
And know the loneliness of power,
And listened through the weary hours
To men whose speech was not your own,
For you the undertone remains
Of that great voice which bade you stand,
For you the people's voice commands
The will of God in thrilling strains.

"And you, you cannot be alone,
Your sacred destiny controls;
You dwell with those immortal souls
Who keep the faith, who still fight on,
Who win such love as may atone
For the long constant bitter fight,
Who sing, through all the weary night,
The finite spirit's song of home!

                                    E.P.D. Sept. 29, 1917"

TI MS (WP, DLC).

To Grenville Stanley Macfarland

My dear Macfarland: [The White House] 1 October, 1917

I am rejoiced at the news brought me by your letter of the twenty-eighth, written *en route*. I shall look for changes now in the policy of the paper which will be to the great advantage of the whole nation.

                    Sincerely your friend,   Woodrow Wilson

TLS (Letterpress Books, WP, DLC).

To Joseph Patrick Tumulty

Dear Tumulty: [The White House, Oct. 1, 1917]

Please intimate to the Department of State that I think probably we have compelled these people to do as much as it is fair to compel them to do in the circumstances, and that I think we had better inform them to that effect.[1] The President.

TL (WP, DLC).
[1] A White House memorandum dated Oct. 1, 1917 (T MS, WP, DLC) reveals that Wilson dictated this note in response to a letter from Grenville S. Macfarland to Tumulty of September 7, which was sent to the Department of State. Macfarland had recited the revisions made by the producers in the motion picture, *Patria*, to meet the criticisms of the Department of State and had requested an early decision as to whether these changes were sufficient. Lansing wrote to Macfarland on October 4 that the State Department had no further objection to *Patria* in its present form. R. Lansing to G. S. Macfarland, Oct. 4, 1917, CCL (WP, DLC).

To Mitchell Kennerley[1]

My dear Mr. Kennerley: [The White House] 1 October, 1917

May I not thank you for your courtesy in sending me the little volume, "Woodrow Wilson and the World's Peace," by George D. Herron?[2] I have read it with the deepest appreciation of Mr. Herron's singular insight into all the elements of a complicated situation and into my own motives and purposes.

Cordially and sincerely yours, Woodrow Wilson

TLS (Letterpress Books, WP, DLC).
[1] Publisher of New York.
[2] George Davis Herron, *Woodrow Wilson and the World's Peace* (New York, 1917). This book was a collection of Herron's articles on Wilson, originally published in European periodicals from December 1916 to July 1917.

To Edward Parker Davis

My dear E. P.: [The White House] 1 October, 1917

This is just a line to acknowledge your thoughtfulness in sending me the verses. I shall look forward to reading them (they have just arrived) with keen pleasure when the day's work is over. I can see by the glance I have given them that they do, as you expected, express a very deep longing which I have often felt.

In great haste

Affectionately yours, Woodrow Wilson

TLS (Letterpress Books, WP, DLC).

From Frank Irving Cobb

Dear Mr. President: New York October 1, 1917.

Thank you for the trouble you took in regard to that Cohalan matter; but it is impossible to overestimate the importance of pulling that particular snake's fangs. He is the brains of all this Irish sedition.

It seems to me that the situation in general is excellent and that you have a right to be highly pleased with it.

With sincere regards,   Frank I Cobb.

TLS (WP, DLC).

From Newton Diehl Baker

Dear Mr. President: Washington. October 1, 1917.

I spent several hours at Camp Meade yesterday and think you may be interested in two things I observed.

On Wednesday the 19th of September, the first contingent of drafted men began to appear there. On Saturday of the same week, a band had been organized out of drafted men, equipped with uniforms and instruments and was parading through the camp playing quite acceptably. This I think shows pretty fine zeal on the part of the officers and a very happy response on the part of the men.

A large part of my time yesterday was spent with the conscientious objectors. Out of 18,000 men there appeared up to last night 27 such objectors. One of them had watched the recruits playing football and baseball, and after two days of separation from the life of the place, he withdrew his objection and joined his company. The remaining 26 are still segregated, receiving considerate treatment but living apart from the rest of the camp. I will send you a complete classification of them later. Nine of them are Old Amish; two, New Amish, three, Friends and then a number of them belong to sects of which I had never heard before; one being "A Brother of God"; another a member of "The Assembly of God"; one was a Russian-born Jew who claimed to be an international socialist and who, I think, is simply lazy and obstinate, without the least comprehension of international socialism. For the most part they seem well-disposed, simple-minded young people who have been imprisoned in a narrow environment and really have no comprehension of the world outside of their own rural and peculiar community. Only two of those with whom I talked seemed quite normal mentally.

Of course, it is too soon to speculate on the problem because we do not yet know how large the number will turn out to be either at Camp Meade or elsewhere; but if it gets no worse than it is at Camp Meade, I am pretty sure that no harm will come in allowing these people to stay at the camps, separated from the life of the camp but close enough gradually to come to understand. The effect of that I think quite certainly would be that a substantial number of them would withdraw their objection and make fairly good soldiers.

Respectfully yours,   Newton D. Baker

TLS (WP, DLC).

Edward Nash Hurley to Joseph Patrick Tumulty

Chicago, Illinois, October 1, 1917.

Judge Payne[1] has accepted and will leave here Thursday night with the entire party for Seattle. I am sure we are very fortunate in getting him as he is most kindly disposed towards labor and will be fair and just in cooperating in any way that the labor adjustment board may desire.   Edward N. Hurley.

T telegram (WP, DLC).
[1] John Barton Payne, lawyer and civic leader of Chicago.

Edwin Thomas Meredith[1] to Joseph Patrick Tumulty

Des Moines, Iowa, October 1, 1917

To permit postage rates fixed in revenue bill to become effective simply means destruction of many worthy publications and consequent harm to the country. I cannot express how serious a matter I consider it. I do not believe those outside publishing business realize what it means. To think Coone and Stewart of Post Office Department[2] who never employed a dollars worth of labor or did other than draw salary from the Government have been successful after years of effort in putting this over is disheartening. They have I feel sure misled Mr. Burleson. The amount raised is a paltry one to the Government, but it is in fact blood money because it means the life of many enterprises. Personally can stand it I hope but I know it is a crime against the country.   E. T. Meredith.

T telegram (WP, DLC).
[1] Publisher and editor of the Des Moines, Ia., *Successful Farming*.
[2] John Cornelius Koons, First Assistant Postmaster General, and Joseph Stewart, Special Assistant to the Attorney General, representing the Post Office Department.

To Thomas Watt Gregory, with Enclosure

The White House

My dear Mr. Attorney General: 2 October, 1917

The suggestion of the Secretary of Labor made in the enclosed letter strikes me very favorably and I send it to you in the hope that you will act upon it unless there is some objection that I do not see or know of.

Cordially and faithfully yours,   Woodrow Wilson

TLS (JDR, RG 60, Numerical File, No. 185354/44½, DNA).

E N C L O S U R E

From William Bauchop Wilson

My dear Mr. President: Washington September 29, 1917.

In connection with the Mooney case which you desire the Commission to investigate, for your information may I suggest the wisdom of the Federal Department of Justice retaining the custody and control of Alexander Berkman,[1] at least until after the Commission has had an opportunity of looking into such facts as it may be able to discover concerning the case.

Berkman is a recognized anarchist. He is the same Alexander Berkman who as a young man shot Henry Clay Frick[2] during the Homestead strike in 1892. In all of his associations since that time there has always been the background of that assault, which makes him appear to be the worst type of anarchist that can be held up for the development of public indignation.

There is very general belief among the friends of Mooney that the indictment recently found against Berkman in San Francisco and the requisition papers issued to the Governor of New York by the Governor of California[3] have been secured for the purpose of bringing Berkman on to the scene in California to prejudice the public mind against Mooney. I have as yet no means of knowing how much basis there is for this sentiment. He is now, however, in the custody of the Federal Department of Justice in New York under charges connected with resistence of the draft. The requisition papers cannot be honored, as I understand it, by the Governor of New York unless the Federal authorities first give up their jurisdiction.

I would be very much pleased if you could advise the Attorney General to retain the custody of Berkman for the present or until the Commission can report to you what it finds out about the case.   Faithfully yours,   W B Wilson

TLS (JDR, RG 60, Numerical File, No. 185354/44½, DNA).

1 While Berkman was serving a term of two years in the federal prison at Atlanta for conspiring with Emma Goldman to obstruct the draft law, a grand jury in San Francisco, on July 14, 1917, had indicted him for murder in connection with the bomb explosion during a Preparedness Day parade there a year earlier. Thomas J. Mooney, and Warren K. Billings were already under sentence of death and life imprisonment, respectively, for complicity in the same crime. Berkman had published an anarchist paper, *The Blast*, in San Francisco about the time of the explosion. *New York Times*, July 15, 1917. About the Mooney-Billings case and its ramifications, see WW to W. D. Stephens, May 11, 1917, Vol. 42, and subsequent documents.

Berkman was brought to New York about July 25 to await the outcome of an appeal on his conviction for conspiring to obstruct the draft. He was held in the Tombs prison, and it was reported that, if he was released, he would be rearrested on the murder charges from San Francisco. Also, the Immigration Commissioner, Frederic C. Howe, had notified the assistant United States district attorney that the immigration authorities were ready to give prompt consideration to a proposal to deport Berkman to Russia, whence he had come about thirty years earlier. *New York Times*, July 27 and 29, 1917. Several thousand members of the Bolshevik party, at a mass meeting in Petrograd on September 30, adopted a resolution of protest against the imprisonment and alleged imposition of a death sentence upon Berkman. It was reported that agitators who had recently come from the United States harangued the crowd, which packed a big circus tent. *Ibid.*, Oct. 2, 1917.

2 In 1917, Frick was a director of the United States Steel Corporation and other corporations and a noted art collector. Berkman had served over fourteen years in prison for shooting and stabbing him in 1892.

3 That is, Governors Whitman and Stephens.

To Edwin Thomas Meredith

My dear Mr. Meredith: [The White House] 2 October, 1917

I know that you always speak with such entire sincerity, and I know also that you are so well informed, that I hesitate to form a judgment different from your own in the matter of the new postal rates, but the matter has been so long under investigation and the investigations on the part of representatives of the Government in more than one administration have led so clearly to the conclusions adopted by the Conference Committee of the two Houses in the discussion of the pending revenue bill, that I must believe there are two sides at least to the question and that the conclusions arrived at by these inquiries are worth putting into effect, at any rate to make sure of their results.

Cordially and sincerely yours,   Woodrow Wilson

TLS (Letterpress Books, WP, DLC).

Two Letters to Matthew Hale

My dear Mr. Hale: [The White House] 2 October, 1917

Thank you sincerely for your letter expressing your interest and the interest of all Massachusetts Progressives in the passage of the soldiers' insurance bill.[1] I am confident that the members of both Houses are alive to the importance of this legislation and to the unfortunate effect which a failure to pass it at this session would have, and I have every reason to believe that it will become law before the Congress adjourns. My own interest in it is of the deepest sort.

May I not take advantage of this opportunity to congratulate you upon the public spirit you have shown in accepting the nomination for Lieutenant Governor of Massachusetts tendered you by the Democrats of that state? This action on your part is another evidence of your devotion to the cause of progressive principles in government which all forward-looking men believe to be so vital to the welfare of the nation. It is encouraging to find that the men of Massachusetts who think alike in these matters have joined their forces together in a great common cause and I think the wisdom and necessity for this will become more and more evident throughout the nation as the days go by.

Cordially and sincerely yours,   Woodrow Wilson[2]

TLS (Letterpress Books, WP, DLC).
[1] M. Hale to WW, Oct. 1, 1917, TLS (WP, DLC). Hale had called on Wilson at the White House on October 1.
[2] This letter was read to the state convention of the Democratic party at Faneuil Hall, Boston, on October 6. *Springfield Republican*, Oct. 7, 1917. Hale's Republican opponent for lieutenant governor was the incumbent, Calvin Coolidge, to whom Hale referred as "Calvin the Silent."

Personal.

My dear Mr. Hale: [The White House] 2 October, 1917

I am not at all satisfied that I can give it the best formulation but my idea would be that in order to offset Governor McCall's effort to make capital of his being a "war Governor" a plank something like the following would be advisable:

"The greatest task of its history is at present before the nation and the greatest necessity of its life for the effective display of its unity and patriotism. We, therefore, recognize it as our duty to give the fullest and most ungrudging support to the present national administration in the prosecution of this war and of the policies associated with it, and in order to do that we believe it the duty of every voter to associate himself upon every public occasion that offers with the forces that have indisputably supported the administration from the first. Only in this way can it be made clear on both sides of the water what the purpose and spirit of America is. We cannot make that purpose clear by supporting those who are known on both sides of the water to have been the earnest antagonists and severe critics of the administration at a time when the lines of action seemed to lie too near the question of allegiance or lack of allegiance to America as against all the world."

I hope you will think this comes somewhere near it.[1]

Cordially and sincerely yours,   [Woodrow Wilson]

CCL (WP, DLC).
[1] A paraphrase of the proposed plank was included in the Democratic platform as read to the state convention on October 6 by Frederick William Mansfield, the candidate for governor, who adopted the slogan "Indorse the war government, not the war governor." *Springfield Republican*, Oct. 7, 1917.

To Newton Diehl Baker

My dear Mr. Secretary: The White House 2 October, 1917

Thank you very much for your letter of yesterday about your observations at Camp Meade. I am greatly interested by what you tell me of the conscientious objectors and believe with you that the matter will in part solve itself by the experiences of these men in camp.

Cordially and faithfully yours,   Woodrow Wilson

TLS (N. D. Baker Papers, DLC).

From Franklin Knight Lane

[Denver] October 2, 1917.

I have a wire from my office in Washington saying that a letter had been received from you suggesting in a most complimentary way that I go to Chicago on October 9th to speak before the Iroquois Club, especially to undo certain harm done by two certain Republicans.

I assume you did not know that I was in the Far West and I do not know what reply I should make. I went to New Orleans at the request of McAdoo to speak before a National Underwriters convention; then at the request of the State Council of Defense I went into Oklahoma and Kansas. I have made nine speeches in these states in the last four days. It had been my purpose to return at once from Kansas to Chicago, where I had accepted an invitation tendered by the Sunday Night Club, a large club of young men, to speak in the Auditorium next Sunday night, but in Oklahoma I received a wire from McAdoo asking that I go to Salt Lake City to address an audience in the Tabernacle at a great meeting of 15,000 Mormons, and speak on the way. I at once cancelled my Chicago engagement and sent McAdoo word that I would go and have authorized other Liberty Loan meetings to be fixed at other places, and called conferences of my own people in the Northwest.

I have not seen any Chicago papers, but nothing has appeared out here indicating that conditions were abnormally bad in Chicago. I know that you are the one of supreme faith in the people and I can tell you most directly that the people have supreme faith in you. The ignorant believe in the war because you are for it. Every audience I have addressed has risen to its feet and cheered whenever your name was mentioned. Oklahoma and Kansas, notwithstanding evil reports to the contrary, are loyal, sound and strongly with you. They oversubscribed the last loan and will oversubscribe this one. You have sized up public opinion better than any of us. The very poorest tenant farmers are the only ones who have stirred up trouble, and they belong to an anarchistic society known as The Working Class Union.[1] One farmer came to me at Tulsa and said that his name was Gentry. "I am trying to do my best," he said. "I have six children, four boys and two girls. The boys are in the Army and the girls are Red Cross nurses, and I am saving for a Liberty Bond." The country will give you all the men and all the money you ask for. I hear no criticism of the Administration. I have seen many Republicans who frankly said that they were surprised that things had gone so quickly and well without scandal and so honestly.

I shall do what you wish cheerfully. I have stated my dilemma. I do not like to turn up in Chicago after having cancelled my engagement there, and I think I may be able to do more good talking to people of this country out here than I could do there. But you know best.

I hear from one of my men who has just been there that California is as disaffected as any part of the country but I had not thought of going there because McAdoo and Wilson intend to, I understand.
Franklin K. Lane.

T telegram (WP, DLC).
[1] About this group, see T. D. McKeown to WW, Aug. 11, 1917, Vol. 43.

SACRED TO THE MEMORY OF
ELLEN LOUISE AXSON
BELOVED WIFE OF WOODROW WILSON
BORN 15 MAY 1860 AT SAVANNAH GEORGIA
DIED 6 AUGUST 1914 AT WASHINGTON D.C.

A TRAVELLER BETWEEN LIFE AND DEATH
THE REASON FIRM THE TEMPERATE WILL
ENDURANCE FORESIGHT STRENGTH AND SKILL
A PERFECT WOMAN NOBLY PLANNED
TO WARN TO COMFORT AND COMMAND
AND YET A SPIRIT STILL AND BRIGHT
WITH SOMETHING OF ANGELIC LIGHT

Myrtle Hill Cemetery, Rome, Georgia
Sculpture by Herbert Adams

The Red Cross War Council

Secretary Baker with his civilian staff. Counterclockwise: Benedict Crowell, Frederick Keppel, and Edward R. Stettinius

Major General Peyton C. March

Harry A. Garfield

Edward N. Hurley

Lincoln Steffens

Max Eastman

From Thomas Nelson Page

Confidential

My dear Mr. President: Rome October 2, 1917.

The internal situation in Italy seems to be giving some concern to those responsible for the Government, altho for the present they have the matter pretty well in hand. The failure of the wheat crop this year cut down the yield by about 25% under what it was last year, when also there was a short crop, and this has been used to the utmost possible by both Solialistic [Socialistic] and Clerical propagandists to excite the people against the continuance of the war. As I have recently stated in more than one telegram, the Government here is very solicitous to have grain sent to Italy at the earliest moment possible, and even a moderate quantity sent at once would do much to relieve the situation which is a psychological one as well as a practical one. The Premier at a luncheon yesterday given by the Italo-American League to the American Red Cross Commission, headed by Col. Geo. F. Baker, Jr.,[1] turned to Col. Baker and in my hearing made a very earnest statement of the situation. He had already told me that without a sufficient supply of bread,—which the Italian laborers use in great quantity, and, in fact, live on—Italy could not keep on. This want of sufficient grain has been used with great effect by the pro-peace propagandists, and it looks now as though there would be a fight on the floor of the Chamber, based on this condition.

Nothing would do more at present to help Italy than for us to declare a condition of war with Austria.

I have received today a report from one of our Consuls, a very earnest and clear-minded man, which so clearly expresses the conclusion which I myself have arrived at here in Rome that I am quoting it. He says: "I respectfully suggest that the following conditions in America I have found to be discouraging to Italy:

"(1) The lack of a definite declaration of war by America against Austria, Bulgaria and Turkey;

"(2) The lack of a formal pronouncement in favor of Italy's national aspirations;

"(3) The amazing liberty allowed to newspapers and agitators in America, and the shameless and unrestrained way certain Americans abroad have attacked their own Government.

"I find that the utterances of President Wilson have been profoundly stimulating to Italian citizens of all classes, and that America's reply to the Pope's peace proposals had a very happy effect in discouraging the scuttling propaganda of the pacifists and I believe that a statement from him of sympathetic appreciation of Italy's great achievements in this war and of recognition of her desire to achieve national unity would be of great benefit."

I do not know myself whether you feel that the time has come for this step, but unquestionably Austria is engaged in war against us, in fact if not in name, and I know of nothing which would have so great an effect as would the adoption of the suggestion contained above.

Believe me, my dear Mr. President, always,

Sincerely yours,   Thos. Nelson Page

N.B. The Red Cross Commission here has had a great success and I feel sure that it will accomplish great good. T.N.P.

TLS (WP, DLC).
[1] George Fisher Baker, Jr., a banker and corporation director of New York, currently serving as head of the American Red Cross Commission to Italy, with the rank of lieutenant colonel.

From the Diary of Josephus Daniels

1917 Tuesday 2 October

President thought it would do good if Mrs. Dewey would give out the suppressed chapters of Dewey's book on the German attitude.[1]

[1] The *Autobiography of George Dewey, Admiral of the Navy* (New York, 1913) included a chapter, "A Period of Anxiety," on the friction in 1898 between the then Commodore Dewey and Vice-Admiral Otto von Diederichs, commander of the German naval squadron in Manila Bay. In this chapter, Dewey described various incidents, including his reception on July 10 of Diederichs' flag lieutenant, Paul von Hintze, who had brought a memorandum of German grievances. Dewey wrote: "When I had heard them through I made the most of the occasion by using him as a third person to state candidly and firmly my attitude in a verbal message which he conveyed to his superior so successfully that Vice-Admiral von Died[e]richs was able to understand my point of view. There was no further interference with the blockade or breach of the etiquette which had been established by the common consent of the other foreign commanders. Thus, as I explained to the President, after the war was over, a difference of opinion about international law had been adjusted amicably, without adding to the sum of his worries." Dewey, p. 267. This bland summary does not adequately convey the force of Dewey's remarks as Von Hintze reported them to Diederichs, as follows: "Why, I shall stop each vessel whatever may be her colours! And if she does not stop, I shall fire at her! And that means war, do you know, Sir? And I tell you, if Germany wants war, all right, we are ready. With the English I have not the slightest difficulty, they always communicate with me." Otto von Diederichs, "Darstellung der Vorgänge vor Manila von Mai bis August 1898," *Die Grosse Politik der Europäischen Kabinette, 1871-1914* (Berlin, 40 vols., 1922-27), XV, 62n.
The portions of Dewey's *Autobiography* which related to operations in the Phillippines in 1898 were based on a manuscript prepared under his direction by Commander Nathan Sargent and were entitled "The Preparations at Hong Kong, Battle of Manila Bay, Enforcement of Blockade, and Operations Resulting in the Surrender of Manila." This manuscript, which was approved by

Dewey on November 10, 1904, is in the George Dewey Papers, DLC. Thomas A. Bailey, "Dewey and the Germans at Manila Bay," *American Historical Review,* XLV (Oct. 1939), 59-81. Bailey describes the friction between Dewey and Diederichs and quotes the Dewey-Sargent version of Dewey's admonition to Von Hintze. This version agrees substantially with the German account quoted above. Bailey indicates that Dewey also "sanitized" in various other ways the narrative in his *Autobiography.* The omitted passages do not, however, amount to what Daniels called "suppressed chapters." See also Ronald Spector, *Admiral of the New Empire: The Life and Career of George Dewey* (Baton Rouge, La., 1974), pp. 72-82.

From Robert Lansing

PERSONAL AND CONFIDENTIAL:

My dear Mr. President: Washington October 3, 1917.

The French Ambassador called upon me this afternoon and said that his Government were greatly disturbed over the situation in Russia and that it was proposed to hold an Inter-Allied Conference in Paris as soon as possible to consider what means might be adopted to aid Russia and prevent further disintegration. He said that the date tentatively fixed for the meeting was October 16th and that his Government were most anxious that the United States should be represented at the Conference.

He said further that while he hesitated to speak there was a feeling in Paris that Colonel House would be most acceptable as our representative in order that all the phases of the situation could be fully discussed. I asked him if I should present this suggestion to you and he was doubtful about it as he feared you might not like such a suggestion. I replied to him that I was sure you would understand the hesitation which he felt in presenting it and would myself take the responsibility of submitting it to you.

I further told him that personally I did not think it was possible for Colonel House to go at this time but could not speak with any authority on the subject until I had communicated with you. I also said that I did not wish to commit myself in any way as to the United States being represented at the Conference, as it would be very difficult to find a man properly equipped for such a conference and that all I could do was to lay the matter before you. He said that he hoped, in any event, we could have someone present at the Conference even if that person did not take part as a member.

Personally I think something may be gained by a Conference of this sort as Great Britain, France, Italy and Russia will be represented in any event. We might have an "observer" present but where to find one in Europe at this time I am rather at a loss to say. The only man of real acuteness who understands the Russian situation among our diplomatic representatives seems to me to be Ira Nelson Morris, our Minister to Sweden.

I think this matter should be immediately decided as the situation in Russia is certainly critical and everything should be done that can be done to give stability to the Government there and possibly such a Conference as is suggested would be of material aid.   Faithfully yours,   Robert Lansing.

TLS (WP, DLC).

From Edward Mandell House, with Enclosure

Dear Governor: New York. October 3, 1917.

Here is a despatch which the Foreign Office has sent Sir William in reply to his inquiry as to their exact position concerning the embargo on Sweden.

They want her pushed to the limit, inside of war, but it seems to me that in doing this, it is difficult to know when the limit is reached.

I am sorry about all this publicity in regard to the work you have asked me to do but it was inevitable after Frankfurter told Bullitt of the Ledger. I held the Ledger off for three weeks telling them if they published it, it would be denied at the State Department and they would be placed in an embarrassing position. However, it is better to have it out than to make a mystery of it and to have had it discovered after the organization was under way. I believe they will now drop it if nothing more is said.

The Jews from every tribe have descended in force, and they seem determined to break in with a jimmy if they are not let in.
                    Affectionately yours,   E. M. House
I have been worried about Mrs. Wilson. I hope she is not seriously ill.

TLS (WP, DLC).

E N C L O S U R E

London, October 2, 1917.

No. 16.

We think any demand on Sweden should be put in such a way as not to slam door finally. Swedes ought not to be forced to take an absolute decision, but should be given a chance to put forward reliable proposals. We do not believe Sweden is likely to go to war on German side, but if she did effect might be very serious. We should therefore deal with her by way of bargaining and not by way of ultimatum.

Our attitude with regard to both Sweden and Norway remains as described in memorandum of August 4th.[1] By far the most important blockade measure still open to us would be to cut off import of Swedish iron into Germany, and it is worth running some risk to achieve that or even substantially to diminish amount of import. We believe Sweden to be most anxious to maintain neutrality, and so long as she does so, we believe Norway safe from invasion. It is, however, possible that Germany, rather than submit completely to loss of Swedish ore, which is necessary to her, might declare war on Sweden. Probably, therefore, we may have to be content in the end with a ? materially diminished Swedish export to Germany. But it would seem wise to begin with demand for total prohibition.

Our views on whole naval and military aspects of question are set out in Cabinet Committee Report which I believe Lord Reading showed the President.[2] If only we had a Blockade Council here we could interchange views on each point as it arose, much more completely and satisfactorily than is possible by telegraph. We have submitted detailed proposals to French for their approval as to lines on which acceptance of proposals might eventually proceed, and we hope to let U. S. Government have these soon.

T MS (WP, DLC).

[1] *Memorandum*, Aug. 4, 1917, enclosed in WHP to RL, Aug. 13, 1917, TLS (SDR, RG 59, 600.119/359, DNA).

[2] About this memorandum, see W. Wiseman to E. Drummond, Sept. 20, 1917, n. 1.

From David Lawrence

My dear Mr. President: [Washington] October 3rd, 1917.

The morning papers today represent you as being very much annoyed over the publication of certain reports about Col. House.[1] I have been informed by newspaper men that you particularly disliked my article of yesterday in this connection.[2]

I know you are not given to offhand judgment, so I wonder whether it is not possible that in your haste you merely glanced at the headline in yesterday's Washington Times. The body of the article did not say that you had selected anyone for the Peace Commission, but on the contrary, I specifically dealt with that phase of it in this paragraph:

"What will the personnel of the Peace Commission be? It is safe to say that the President has not crossed that bridge yet * * * * Whether the Colonel will be the head of it is difficult to predict. He has never held office, and the impression that prevails here is that he is disinclined to break his precedent."

My article emphasized that Col. House's commission has nothing immediately to do with peace negotiations, and such names as were mentioned were entirely suggested by me personally as men whom it would be desirable to select to aid in the work of preparing data for peace discussion. Editorial suggestion of this kind I am quite sure it is not your wish to see curtailed.

I really thought I was doing a friendly thing by suggesting men of prominence without regard to party, and without regard to their affiliation with the present Administration.

There has been some criticism in the editorial press concerning the placing in the hands of one man such an important work as that of gathering data for the Peace conference, and my purpose was to show that men of prominence, of all political parties, and every variety of view, would certainly be *consulted*, and a true consensus of opinion thus obtained. I made this suggestion entirely on my own authority, and without committing you, Col. House, or the Government to any specific intention.

I was surprised, therefore, to read in the newspapers that you were disturbed by this story, which, if it does anything, certainly meets a growing criticism which you may or may not have noticed in the editorial press within the last few days.

I cannot believe that what I have heard, that you deprecate editorial discussion of these very important matters, and I am confident either that you were told only about the headlines over the article in question, and did not have time to read it, or that you could not have had in mind the article I wrote.

With best wishes, I am

Sincerely yours,   David Lawrence

TLS (WP, DLC).

¹ For example, the *New York Times*, Oct. 3, 1917, carried the following report from Washington:

"For the first time authoritative information from a high quarter was obtained today with reference to the reported undertaking of Colonel E. M. House of New York, President Wilson's friend and adviser, to gather material for use as a basis of American participation in the peace negotiations that will follow the cessation of hostilities.

"President Wilson is greatly annoyed, it was learned, over the interpretation placed on the work of Colonel House that it is in line with a peace move by the United States. The President was never more determined to go forward with the war. Those close to him testify that he is firm in the intention to keep the United States in the fight until the objects for which this Government and its allies are at war are obtained.

"The President has laid down the dictum that the United States will have no dealings with the German Government until the German people have a greater part in the determination of policies, a part sufficient to enable them to furnish adequate peace guarantees. The Entente Powers have accepted this attitude of the President as their own. No doubt exists in the minds of those best acquainted with the President's disposition that, much as he would like to see the war ended, he would never consent to a cessation of hostilities until he saw in prospect the realization of his fixed purpose to make the world safe for democracy.

"It was denied explicitly and emphatically today in the authoritative quarter mentioned that Colonel House was engaged in preparations that contemplated any peace move by the United States. The explanation was offered that about two years ago reports began to come to this Government from its agencies in Europe with reference to conditions that would confront the trade of the world after the war, and these reports, which continue to be received, are being collated and studied by Colonel House with a view to utilizing them in a practical way when trade conditions must be adjusted after the great conflict is over.

"In the course of these two years many men have come to America with knowledge as to probable trade problems growing out of the war, and the President has asked these men to lay their information and views before Colonel House.

"That Colonel House has called upon Justice Brandeis of the United States Supreme Court to assist him in the work he has undertaken for the President has not been made known to the President, and it is not believed by the highest officials of the Administration.

"The indignation expressed today in authoritative quarters over the effort to make it appear that President Wilson was preparing for a peace move left the impression of sincerity."

2 Lawrence's story appeared in the New York *Evening Post*, Oct. 12, 1917. It stated that Colonel House, who had been requested by Wilson to gather information for the use of the American commission to a future peace conference, would "endeavor to mobilize the minds of the country for his tremendous task." House, Lawrence reported, was expected to ask the counsel of Americans of all varieties of opinion. He would have to keep in constant correspondence with the most eminent citizens of the United States and obtain from them comments and memoranda on special problems with which they were most familiar. Among those to be consulted, Lawrence particularly mentioned Louis D. Brandeis, an authority on the Zionist movement and the Palestinian question; Oscar S. Straus, Henry Morgenthau, and Abram Elkus, who, as former ambassadors to Turkey, were familiar with the situation in the Near East; and Elihu Root and William Howard Taft. However, Lawrence pointed out that governmental officials insisted that the appointment of such a fact-finding commission did not mean that peace negotiations were at hand: "It is still an academic study, but as a measure of preparedness for the many years of peace that, it is hoped, will follow the conclusion of the present war, the Administration feels that it is undertaking none too soon a task very vitally related to the future foreign policy of the United States of America."

To Franklin Knight Lane

[The White House] 4 October, 1917

Of course you ought not to go to Chicago. I had lost sight of where you were to be and am sorry I troubled you. Thank you warmly for your telegram.　　　Woodrow Wilson

T telegram (Letterpress Books, WP, DLC).

To Albert Sidney Burleson

My dear Burleson:　　　[The White House] 4 October, 1917

Thank you for letting me see the enclosed.[1] I have looked over them very carefully. It makes up a tremendous case, of course, against Mr. Hearst, but there is nothing new about that and I am sorry to say there is nothing brought out in these articles which would seem to me to prove that Mr. Hearst had overstepped the bounds of law, outrageous as he has been.

Cordially and faithfully yours,   Woodrow Wilson

TLS (Letterpress Books, WP, DLC).

¹ The enclosures (missing in WP, DLC) were three articles by Samuel Hopkins Adams about William Randolph Hearst, under the general heading "Who's Who Against America." They appeared in the *New York Tribune*, September 16, 23, and 30, 1917. Hearst was described as "the leading spirit of German propaganda in the United States to-day." The headlines referred to him as the "Star-Spangled Shammer" and stated, among other things, that "Behind the pretence of patriotism and the outward flag-flying of his newspapers lies a spirit that speaks subtly with a Prussian accent."

To Joseph Patrick Tumulty

Dear Tumulty: [The White House, c. Oct. 4, 1917]

I don't like the tone of this inquiry.¹ I cannot believe, in the first place, that he is correctly quoting Gompers, to whom I gave no definite assurances but to whom I did say, I believe, that I thought it fair and wise that there should be representatives of labor on all boards dealing with industrial questions in the present crisis. To get into a debate as between Mr. Gompers and the representatives of the Roman Catholic Church, however, would be most indiscreet and unwise, and we particularly cannot just now do anything to discredit Mr. Gompers who is doing such valiant service.   The President.

TL (WP, DLC).

¹ Bernard Iddings Bell to JPT, Sept. 17, 1917, T telegram (WP, DLC). Bell, Dean of St. Paul's Cathedral (Protestant Episcopal) of Fond du Lac, Wisc., had wired as follows: "Samuel Gompers stated in Minneapolis that President had agreed to appoint on all war commissions and boards at least one representative agreeable to American Labor and the American Federation officers in particular. Prominent ecclesiastics say Gompers lies. Please wire facts my expense. Worth attention as matter is creating feeling in ticklish pro-German neighborhood." Tumulty acknowledged receipt of the telegram and said that he would be glad to lay its contents before Wilson at the earliest possible moment. JPT to B. I. Bell, Oct. 4, 1917, TLS (WP, DLC).

From Franklin Delano Roosevelt

Washington.

My dear Mr. President,   Thursday Evening [Oct. 4, 1917]

I am glad to be able to tell you that after weeks of conferences I have come to an agreement with the Presidents of the International Unions in regard to all Atlantic Coast Navy Yard wage rates. We are to give increases which will run about 10% but the important feature is that the Unions agree to the new scale for one year from November 1st next. This will mean much to the harmonious prosecution of the Navy's work.[1]

Very sincerely yours   Franklin D Roosevelt

ALS (WP, DLC).
[1] About this matter, see Frank Freidel, *Franklin D. Roosevelt: The Apprenticeship* (Boston, 1952), pp. 328-32.

From Ignace Jan Paderewski

Chicago, Illinois, October 4, 1917.

Mr. President: The Polish National Department of Chicago has conferred upon me the great honor of addressing you at this momentous hour. The National Department is a federation of all important Polish organizations in the United States, including Polish National Alliance, 130,000 members; Polish Roman Catholic Union, 115,000 members; Polish National Council, over 200,000 members; Association of Polish Clergy in America, 800 members; Polish Falcons Alliance, 25,000 members; Polish Womens Alliance, 25,000 members; Polish Alma Mater, 8,000 members; Association of Poles in America, 8,000; Polish Brotherhood of St Joseph 8,000 members; Polish Union of Buffalo, 15,000 members; Polish Union of Wilkesbarre, 20,000 members; Alliance of Poles in America, Cleveland, 8,000 members; Polish Uniformed Society, 5,000 members; Alliance of Polish Singers, 3,000 members, representing an overwhelming majority, approximately 90 per cent of Polish people living in this country.

A great many of these people are loyal citizens of the United States. Led by a profound sense of gratitude and devotion to their adopted country, stirred by unbounded affection for your exalted person, they are fulfilling the duties imposed upon them by the solemnity of circumstances in a way surpassed by none. Still many others, thousands of whom have joined the Colors, are residents only, residents contributing efficiently by their honest labor to the development and increase of American prosperity.

They are hard working people. Out of over four millions of them not one is a millionaire. But every one is willing to take his humble share in the glorious work of Poland's reestablishment so magnanimously proclaimed by you, Mr. President, in your immortal message of January 27th.[1]

The situation in Poland is more critical than ever. Not only did the suffering of the population reach a degree of almost unbearable intensity, but there is also a menace, a continuously growing and immediate menace of a large Polish army being formed by Central Powers against the Allies, for there are still in the vast occupied territory over a million men available for military service. Besides, the country has had no government of its own, no directing political organization, no representatives recognized by foreign powers. In consequence, various not precisely disinterested individuals have been swarming Allied countries, misinforming authorities, misleading public opinion, misrepresenting Poland. Realizing political and strategic necessity of checking the designs of our common enemy, the French government resolved to form a National Polish army on the Western Front and we have been informed that the United States government would make no objections to recruiting of Polish volunteers in this country. Furthermore, both British and French governments in order to put an end to the nefarious pro-German intrigue agreed to recognize the Polish National Committee recently formed in Paris as official experts on Polish questions and unofficial representatives of the Polish Nation provided that the United States government would recognize it as well. The Polish National Committee, headed by Poland's ablest and strongest statesman, Roman Dmowski, has already received assurances of loyal support and cooperation of an immense majority of Polish people where ever living. The Poles from America sent to the Polish National Committee the following message: Conscious of the importance of our act and the solemnity of the occasion, we have this day unanimously agreed to unite with the National Polish Committee in Paris. We welcome with joy our representation on this Committee in the person of Ignace Jan Paderewski. We pledge our loyal cooperation and acknowledge the political supremacy of your Committee. At the same time we desire to express our conviction that your Committee should embrace representatives of as many Polish political parties as possible, in order to strengthen its authority. We further believe that the collective assurance from the Allied governments that a united independent Poland with access to the sea as one of the objects of the war is essential to the success of the Committee's activities. With assurance of loyalty and fraternal greeting. National Polish Department.

Mr. President, the issue of this gigantic struggle between light and darkness, between right and brutal power depends on you. The fate of peoples and governments is in your hands. The wealth and might of this huge Republic made you the principal leader of consolidated human efforts; the greatness and generosity of your character made you the supreme commander of

God's forces. You are the foster-father of a chiefless land. You are Poland's inspired protector. For many a month the spelling of your name has been the only comfort and joy of a starving nation. For many a month among the ruins of a devastated country millions of people have been feeding on you.

Now on the fourteenth of October the bells of Polish churches of those still remaining will call upon the faithful to join in fervent prayer in memory of the noble hero departed a hundred years ago, Thaddeus Kosciuszko. If on that day the news could reach the country that the Polish National Committee in Paris has been recognized, the Polish National army has been sanctioned by our beloved President Wilson, this would certainly give new strength, new hope and new courage to the stricken Nation which trusts but God and you.

This is the object my people entrusted me to most respectfully lay before you, together with their unanimous offering of veneration and everlasting gratitude.

I beg to remain, Mr. President, your respectful and obedient servant,   I. J. Paderewski.

T telegram (SDR, RG 59, 860c.01/62, DNA).
¹ That is, Wilson's "Peace without Victory" address to the Senate, printed at Jan. 22, 1917, Vol. 40.

From Richard Hathaway Edmonds

My dear Mr. President: Baltimore, Oct. 4, 1917.

I am constantly being reminded by information which comes to me from all parts of the country that there is still need for a great awakening of many of our people as to the realities of the war and the reasons for the war. Comparatively few in this country seem to have understood the deliberate plan of Germany, made many years ago, to enrich itself by war at the expense of other countries—a deliberate plan to make war its business as the foundation for creating industries and commerce. Too many of our people are yet loath to believe, and indeed many absolutely refuse to believe that there is a need for food conservation in order to save the Allies and thus save ourselves. Many say that they would be willing to fight if we were invaded but they do not believe in going to Europe to fight, failing entirely to realize that unless Germany is defeated in Europe we would have to endure in this country the sufferings which Belgium and France have had to bear.

Because of these facts I am moved to ask whether you might not deem it wise in a public statement or speech to cover all of these points somewhat in detail, and then to have the Government print in good form, to be easily readable, your speech, and have it delivered through the post offices of the country to every man and woman in the United States and every boy and girl old enough to read. This would mean its being printed in different languages. It would result in several copies going into nearly every home, but this would strengthen its value and make more certain its being read. There are tens of millions of people in this country who would read and heed a statement of this kind coming from you, who would give but little attention to such statements if made by any one else in the country, or by any Department of the Government. These statements must come direct from you as the President of this country and the world leader at this hour, to command the complete acceptation of the skeptics and of the uninformed. The publication of this statement through the newspapers would not be sufficient. Many people do not read the newspapers carefully, and they would not read in full an adequate presentation if they saw it only in the newspapers, because the newspaper is a thing of today and is gone tomorrow. A pamphlet publication would command their respect and their careful reading.

In the larger towns and cities an arrangement could be made with the letter-carriers for their co-operation in helping to deliver a copy into the hands of every one who ever receives mail through them,—and this would practically include everybody. In the smaller villages and country districts a copy could be given by the postmaster to every one in his community. Special effort should be made to see that it reaches every preacher and teacher in the country with the request that from the pulpit and from the teacher's chair these great truths shall be pressed over and over again upon public attention.

Feeling assured that a comprehensive statement or speech from you covering all of these points, printed and distributed in this way, however big the task, would be of almost infinite value, I am taking the liberty of bringing the matter to your attention, trusting that you may feel it wise to give it favorable consideration.   Very truly yours,   Richard H Edmonds

TLS (WP, DLC).

From Grenville Stanley Macfarland

My dear President Wilson,   Washington, October 4, 1917.

Just a line to thank you most heartily for your consideration in the Patria matter.

I enclose also an editorial in the New York American which may interest you.[1] I wrote it under the new arrangement.

Yours sincerely,   G. S. Macfarland.

ALS (WP, DLC).

[1] "The Triumphant Success of the New Liberty Loan is Necessary for Victory in This Terrible War," *New York American*, Oct. 4, 1917. It stated that the German people "must not be left in doubt by any middling success of this loan that the American people stand behind the President in the determination to fight this war to a finish, unless and until the terms of the President's note to the Pope have been fulfilled by the German people." Also filed with Macfarland's letter is an editorial of October 6: "The German Rulers Will Make a Stupid and Disastrous Mistake if They Refuse to Recognize the President's Reasonable and Generous Terms of Peace."

James H. Brennan to Joseph Patrick Tumulty, with Enclosure

Dear Sir,   [Chicago] Oct. 4 1917

On behalf of the Brothers of the International Electrical Workers and the Committee on the Mooney case I wish to thank you for your kindness and courtescy in arranging an interview with His Excellency last Tuesday afternoon.

Enclosed find report of the committee of our organization assuring the President and Yourself of our appreciation of your kindness.   I beg to remain,   Jas H Brennan.

TLS (WP, DLC).

ENCLOSURE

James H. Brennan to the Members of the International Brotherhood of Electrical Workers

Greeting: [Chicago] October 3, 1917

By instructions of the International Brotherhood of Electrical Workers in convention assembled, the committee created by the Convention to go to Washington to enlist the support of the President in the alleged San Francisco bomb conspiracy, (the Mooney case) we, the committee, desire to report through the kindness and efforts of Brother Richard Fitzgerald, Business Agent of #164, in securing a letter of introduction to Secretary Tumulty we secured an audience with President Wilson. The President assured us of his deep interest in the case and his desire to see that justice was done, and that so far as it lay in his power no effort would be spared to see that the defendants would receive fair play.

The committee was impressed by the courtesy and truly democratic manner in which the President received us. The Cabinet had assembled when we reached the White House but we were immediately received, something out of the ordinary.

We cannot too greatly impress on the members of the International Brotherhood of Electrical Workers the great kindness and courtesy shown your committee by Secretary Joseph Tumulty, who went out of his way to favor us, no ceremony, no conceit of position, but with a frank and friendly reception that shows his conception of the American principle of all men being equal. President Wilson's reception was similar.

We also wish to extend our thanks to Thomas A. Griffin[1] of Jersey City for his assistance and courtesy, and to Brother B. A. O'Leary, Business Agent of #26 who not alone very ably assisted us, but also made our visit very pleasant.

Fraternally yours,   Jas H Brennan.

CCLS (WP, DLC).

[1] Thomas F. A. Griffin, former Democratic assemblyman from Hudson County and an old friend of Wilson and Tumulty.

To Richard Hathaway Edmonds

My dear Mr. Edmonds: [The White House] 5 October, 1917

The suggestion contained in your letter of yesterday has been conveyed to me from a good many quarters and I dare say that an opportunity may arise when it will be well for me to make some such utterance as you outline.

At the same time, I get widely variant accounts of the matter from different parts of the country, or rather it would be more correct to say that from most parts of the country I get the report that the people do very distinctly comprehend what the war is about and are very thoughtfully back of the administration.

All I can say now is that I am watching the situation with the greatest interest and shall be ready to speak at the right time, if I know the right time when it comes.

Sincerely yours,   Woodrow Wilson

TLS (Letterpress Books, WP, DLC).

To Samuel Reading Bertron

My dear Mr. Bertron: [The White House] 5 October, 1917

Your letter of October fourth[1] surprises me. If there is pessimism in the business world, I think that New York must be the single center of it, because I must frankly say I do not get such impressions from any other quarter and I am wondering what can really be at the bottom of it, for there is certainly no substantial reason for any pessimism of any kind that I can see.

I realize the hard case in which the railroads and the public service companies are placed for the time being but that is a problem by itself and I do not understand why the difficulties of the transportation world should spread a feeling of discouragement throughout business circles. I wish you would be kind enough to make a somewhat thorough study and analysis of it and let me have a memorandum.

In haste, with much appreciation,

Sincerely yours, Woodrow Wilson

TLS (Letterpress Books, WP, DLC).
[1] It is missing.

To David Lawrence

Personal.

My dear Lawrence: [The White House] 5 October 1917

My whole feeling is this: I think you newspaper men can have no conception of what fire you are playing with when you discuss peace now at all, in any phase or connection. The Germans have in effect realized their programme of Hamburg to Bagdad, could afford to negotiate as to all the territorial fringes, and, if they could bring about a discussion of peace now, would insist upon discussing it upon terms which would leave them in possession of all that they ever expected to get. It is, therefore, very indiscreet in my judgment and altogether against the national interest to discuss peace from any point of view if the administration is brought in in any way. It is perfectly evident to everyone that what Colonel House is attempting to do neither brings peace nearer nor sets it further off, and it is my stern and serious judgment that the whole matter ought to be let alone.

Sincerely yours, Woodrow Wilson

TLS (Letterpress Books, WP, DLC).

To Franklin Delano Roosevelt

My dear Mr. Roosevelt: The White House 5 October, 1917

Thank you for your kindness in sending me your note of last evening. It cheers me very much and I congratulate you upon the successful conclusion of the negotiations.

Cordially and sincerely yours,   Woodrow Wilson

TLS (F. D. Roosevelt Papers, NHpR).

To Edward Parker Davis

My dear E. P.:   [The White House] 5 October, 1917

I had not read your verses when I wrote you the other day. I have now read them and am deeply moved by them. I did not know the generous and beautiful reference to myself which they contained. I want you to know how much it has touched me and how much it means to me as coming from you.

Affectionately yours,   Woodrow Wilson

TLS (Letterpress Books, WP, DLC).

From Edward Mandell House, with Enclosures

Dear Governor: New York. October 5, 1917.

Here is a very important cable which has just been handed me by Sir William. I am enclosing a suggestion for an answer.

If you approve and will send me a telegram, either in the clear or in cypher, tomorrow I will get it off at once. It is important I think that an immediate response is made for they will wait until they get your mind.

I am also enclosing you a cable which came some days ago and a supplimentary one which came today in reference to a chairman for the Allied Conference. This, too, needs a quick reply and I hope you will be able to answer that also tomorrow so I may include it.

Affectionately yours, E. M. House

TLS (WP, DLC).

ENCLOSURE I

No. 19. Personal and most secret.

Following from Mr. Balfour for Col. House:

Our Ambassador at Madrid[1] has received communication from Spanish Government to the effect that a Spanish diplomatic representative has officially reported German Government would be glad to make a communication to us relative to peace. Spanish Government, while disclaiming any desire to intervene or mediate, enquired whether we would be willing to listen to German suggestion or decline all discussion. We do not think it would be either possible or wise to refuse to listen: though we could not discuss without previous consultation with our co-belligerents. We propose to answer in this sense.

Owing to Russian position decision has not yet been taken whether we should inform our principal Allies of the German suggestion before above reply has been sent or wait till Germany puts forward definite proposals, but I thought I would like the President and you to know exactly how matters stand. In view of importance of preserving complete secrecy I have not spoken of it to any representative of the Allies except the French Ambassador here.

Although time has not yet allowed careful consideration of the German proposal cited in the attached message, it is not improbable that, in view of the continued strong offensive on the Western front, of the extensive preparations under way in the United States, and of conditions in Germany, it signifies a genuine attempt to make peace. On the other hand the Germans may have knowledge of the important plans which the Allies are making for next spring and of the grave decisions of policy and strategy which these entail, and it might be that they would attempt to upset them by insincere proposals intended to take advantage of the delicate Russian situation, to embroil the Allies with the Vatican and to interfere with their projects in connection with Poland.   5/10/'17.

Suggestion as to answer—

I think the proper course is the one you propose to adopt, namely, to tell the Spanish envoy that you could not discuss the matter without consulting your co-belligerents and, as so many insincere offers of peace have already been put out semi-officially, you could not even consult your co-belligerents until a more definite proposal is made.

This is Sir William's personal comment on the cable just rec'd   E.M.H.

[1] Sir Arthur Henry Hardinge.

E N C L O S U R E   I I

MEMORANDUM.   October 5th. 1917.

On September 28th. Balfour cabled Wiseman asking whether he could ascertain the reason why President Wilson was irrevocably opposed to the appointment of an American chairman of the Inter-Allied Council.

To-day, October 5th, the following cable was received by Wiseman from Balfour, marked urgent:

"We should all be very grateful for as prompt an answer as possible to the telegram sent you from Balfour and replied to by you provisionally on Sept. 29th. as to the attitude of the U. S. Administration in the matter of their sending an American Chairman for Inter-Allied Council. We promised to agree to a French Chairman if the American Government adhere to their refusal to send a delegate, but Italians are most anxious Chairman should be British or alternatively American. American Chairman would not be called upon to give casting vote in case of disagreement but in a position to report confidentially to his Government his views on situation in such case. Whole machinery for setting up Council is held up pending reply."

T MSS (WP, DLC).

From Newton Diehl Baker

My dear Mr President: Washington October 5, 1917

In view of what you told me a few days ago you will be interested to know that Brigadier General McLachlan,[1] attache of the British Embassy here, called yesterday upon General Bliss to say that he was directed by the General Staff in London to say that they wished it understood that they urged us to place our whole military strength in France and that they had never advised our undertaking any movement elsewhere.

Perhaps some of the newspaper speculations in this country had been brought to their attention; or it may be an evidence of some division of counsels at home.

Respectfully,   Newton D. Baker

ALS (WP, DLC).
[1] James Douglas McLachlan.

From Thomas Watt Gregory

Dear Mr. President: [Washington] October 5, 1917.

The cases against the anthracite coal, the harvester, and the steel combines will shortly be reached for reargument in the Supreme Court. The question has been raised whether there is any reason connected with the national defense for asking a postponement.

I am clear that there is not. On the contrary, price extortions which have been practiced during the present national emergency are an admonition that there should not only be no slackening but rather new energy in the enforcement of the law against combinations of competitive units by which control of the prices of the necessaries of life is concentrated in a few private hands.

The public rightly expects, moreover, that in view of these extortions this Department will be especially vigilant in the investigation and prosecution of combinations to supress competition. At this moment, for example, complaints charging that the milk producers have combined to fix prices are coming into the Department from various sections of the country. But, if the prosecutions against more powerful combines are suspended, the Government can not in good conscience or with any hope of success proceed against smaller offenders. The fact must be faced, therefore, that the suspension of the prosecutions now pending in the Supreme Court would mean the practical suspension of the law altogether.

I recognize, of course, that should these combinations be adjudged unlawful, the bringing about of a condition in harmony with law might cause some temporary disturbance in their affairs, which would be undesirable in the present circumstances. That point could be easily enough met, however, by adjusting the time limit for compliance with the court's decree.

While I am clear in the views above expressed I feel that under existing conditions I should not act upon them without your approval.   Respectfully,   [T. W. Gregory]

CCL (JDR, RG 60, Subject Classification Files, No. 60-0-25423-567X, DNA).

From Raymond Bartlett Stevens

Dear Mr. President: Washington October 5, 1917.

The Senate passed on October 2, a bill (S. 2916) making the workmen's compensation law of any State apply to the men engaged in the loading and unloading of vessels. This bill has been endorsed by practically all of the State Commissions that are interested in workmen's compensation laws, by the American Federal [Federation] of Labor, and by the International Association of Industrial Accident Boards and Commissions.

The Shipping Board feels that the immediate passage of this bill by the House is a matter of great public interest. The swift dispatch of ships depends primarily upon the longshoremen. It is an occupation in which there are a great many accidents. Furthermore, it is an industry especially liable to strikes and disturbances. The passage of this bill would not only do justice to the men employed, but it would greatly tend to reduce friction and trouble and bring about more continuous labor. As Chairman of the arbitration board created by the Shipping Board to deal with disputes in the longshore business, I have been brought in close touch with the longshoremen. I feel certain the immediate passage of this bill would help the Shipping Board in its important duty of keeping the ships continuously in operation.

I understand that Mr. Webb, who is Chairman of the Judiciary Committee, is not enthusiastic over workmen's compensation laws. However, a suggestion from you on the importance of action on this bill before adjournment, I am sure would secure immediate results. I understand there is no serious opposition to the passage of this bill.   Sincerely,   R. B. Stevens

TLS (WP, DLC).

Sir William Conyngham Greene to the Foreign Office

Sir,   Tokyo. October 5th, 1917.

I asked Viscount Motono,[1] whom I had been inable to visit for some time owing to illness, how the Ishii Mission had been faring in America, and whether it was the case, as had been mentioned in the papers, that it had been attended with success.

Viscount Motono said that the reception which Viscount Ishii had met with had far exceeded expectations. Not only in California, where feeling had been most pronounced in the past, but also in Washington and New York, the attitude of the public had been most gratifying. He attributed this favourable atmosphere to the entry of the United States into the War on the same side as Japan, and to the expansion which this had caused in the psychology of the population, which was now in a better position to estimate what other nations, who had been engaged in the struggle earlier than America, had been doing for the common cause. However that might be, His Excellency said that he felt convinced that the *rapprochement* which was now being brought about between the two peoples and the two Governments would exercize a far reaching influence on their future relations, and especially in China. There, His Excellency said, it had been the practice for interested parties, whether Americans for their own purposes, or Chinese for political intrigues, to try and make mischief, or play off one Power against another; but these tactics would be of no avail once the new understanding between America and Japan had become a *fait accompli*.

In this connection Viscount Motono told me that he had every reason to hope that Viscount Ishii had succeeded in reaching an understanding with the United States Government whereby the latter would recognize Japan's special situation in regard to China, and appreciate Japan's attitude towards that country, which was, as I knew, the disavowal of any intention to interfere with the principle of the open door and equal opportunity for all Powers there. Viscount Motono reminded me of a conversation which we had had a month ago (my telegram No. 525 of September 5th 1917) in which he had told me that he was particularly anxious that Viscount Ishii should disabuse President Wilson's mind of any absurd idea that Japan wanted to "grab" China, and said that he hoped that this suspicion, if it had ever had any real existence, had been laid by Viscount Ishii's declaration. As to the understanding itself, Viscount Motono said that he anticipated that it would be embodied in an Exchange of Notes which had been drafted and would shortly be approved. His Excellency added that he would not fail to give me the earliest intimation of the contents of these Notes for your information, and that they would then be communicated to other interested Governments. In reply to an enquiry of mine the Minister replied that the substance of the Notes would certainly eventually be made public.

Referring to the other subjects which had been taken up by Viscount Ishii with the American Government, Viscount Motono told me that Viscount Ishii had had several frank conversations both with the President and with the Secretary of State on the treatment of Japanese Nationals in the United States, and on other subjects of kindred interest. These discussions had, however, covered too wide a field to be reported upon by telegraph, and Viscount Ishii would only deliver his reports thereon on the return of the Mission to Japan.

In conclusion Viscount Motono explained that the so-called Megata Mission which was about to proceed to America[2] had no connection with the Ishii Mission nor indeed with politics at all. It was the fulfillment of a decision arrived at before the Ishii

Mission had been arranged, and it had no other aim than the study of local financial, industrial and economic conditions in America, with a view to future possible cooperation between America and Japan in the latter country, or in China, or elsewhere. The entry of America into the war had greatly affected business relations between Japan and the United States, and the imposition by the latter of export embargoes on steel and gold, for instance, had produced great disorganization in business circles here. These restrictions might even be succeeded by other drastic prohibitions, and so the Government had decided that it was wisest to lose no time in despatching a Body of able business men to the United States, in order to study the local conditions there and make recommendations in regard to the future.

A report of an interesting speech made by the Prime Minister at a send-off dinner to the Mission last night is annexed.[3]

I have the honour to be, with the highest respect,

Sir, Your most obedient, humble servant,

Conyngham Greene[4]

TLS (FO 371/2954, No. 216197, pp. 114-15, PRO).

[1] Viscount Ichiro Motono, Japanese Minister of Foreign Affairs.

[2] A special Japanese financial mission to the United States, headed by Baron Tanetaro Megata, was received in Washington and New York in November 1917. *New York Times*, Nov. 24, 1917.

[3] Not printed. For a brief account of the speeches by Megata and others at a meeting of the America-Japan Society, in Tokyo, see *ibid.*, Oct. 5, 1917.

[4] C. Greene to the Foreign Office, Oct. 4, 1917, T telegram (FO 115/2245, p. 308, PRO), repeats in compacted form portions of this letter.

Sir Cecil Arthur Spring Rice to Sir Eric Drummond

[Washington, Oct. 5, 1917]

Following from Count Horodyski.

Proclamation of National Polish Department of Chicago signed by its members with Paderewski at their head will be issued October 6th (sic) for recruiting of Polish Army. Secretary of State for War will simultaneously issue a statement in favour of it which will conclude by saying that a united and independent Poland is desire of United States Government.

Counsellor of State Department informed me today that United States Government are ready to recognize at any time Polish National Committee in Paris. Two points remain undecided (a) formula to be employed, (b) method and time to be chosen to make a public announcement simultaneously with His Majesty's Government and French Government.

As to (a) I would suggest that you should telegraph to me care of British Embassy here. Formula which is favoured by United

States Government is that Polish National Committee in Paris is recognized as official expert on Polish question and unofficial representatives of Polish nation.

As to (b) I would suggest that instructions be sent to Sir C. Spring Rice to communicate your wishes officially to United States Government.

I propose that date of public recognition by all Governments should be fixed for October 11th.

I would remind you that the more we get (? United States) bound up in Polish question with a declaration that their desire and aims are a united Poland which implies inclusion of Posen and Dantzig the better it is for the whole cause.

I was semi-officially informed today that President will make a public statement on above lines on October 14th the one hundredth anniversary of death of Kosciuszko.

It is important that you should reply on October 8th as there is a Cabinet meeting on October 9th.

T telegram (FO 371/3001, No. 193261, pp. 490-91, PRO).

A Statement

6 October, 1917

The 65th Congress, now adjourning, deserves the gratitude and appreciation of a people whose will and purpose I believe it has faithfully expressed. One cannot examine the record of its action without being impressed by its completeness, its courage and its full comprehension of a great task. The needs of the Army and the Navy have been met in a way that assures the effectiveness of American arms, and the war-making branch of the Government has been abundantly equipped with the powers that were necessary to make the action of the nation effective.

I believe that it has also in equal degree, and as far as possible in the face of war, safeguarded the rights of the people and kept in mind the considerations of social justice so often obscured in the hasty readjustments of such a crisis.

It seems to me that the work of this remarkable session has not only been done thoroughly but that it has also been done with the utmost despatch possible in the circumstances or consistent with a full consideration of the exceedingly critical matters dealt with. Best of all, it has left no doubt as to the spirit and determination of the country but has affirmed them as loyally and as emphatically as our fine soldiers will affirm them on the firing line.

T MS (C. L. Swem Coll., NjP).

To Robert Lansing

My dear Mr. Secretary: The White House 6 October, 1917

I had not seen the enclosed telegram until it came to me from your department; therefore, I assume my office had, quite properly, referred it to your department.

As you know, I am personally very anxious to recognize the Paris Central Committee as Mr. Paderewski suggests and I would be obliged to you for your advice as to how this can most wisely be done with a view to creating the best impression.

Cordially and sincerely yours,   Woodrow Wilson

P.S. I note that the fourteenth of October is suggested by Mr. Paderewski as an impressive date. W.W.

TLS (SDR, RG 59, 860c.01/61, DNA).

To Frank C. Blied[1]

[The White House] 6 October, 1917

I have today signed the Trading with the Enemy Act.[2] Section nineteen goes into effect ten days from this date. You may rest assured that every effort will be made not to cause inconvenience to publications which loyally seek to conform with the spirit of the law.   Woodrow Wilson.

T telegram (Letterpress Books, WP, DLC).
   [1] Blied, a prominent Roman Catholic, was owner and editor of the *Wisconsin Botschafter*, a Democratic weekly, published in Madison in the German language.
   [2] As president of the Wisconsin German Press Association, Blied had asked Wilson for a week or two of grace to permit small weeklies to make the changes required by Section 19 of the Trading with the Enemy Act. F. C. Blied to WW, Oct. 4, 1917, T telegram (WP, DLC).

From Walter Hines Page

London, October 6, 1917.

7355, Most confidential for the Secretary and the President only.

Mr. Balfour with Lord Hardinge, Under Foreign Secretary, called the Ambassadors of the United States, France, Italy, Russia and Japan,[1] to meet him at noon today. He read us a telegram from the British Ambassador at Madrid saying that the Spanish Foreign Secretary[2] had informed him that the Spanish Government had received a request to inquire whether the British Government would receive from Germany a communication regarding peace. The British Ambassador replied that he could not say, but that he thought the British Government's answer would depend on the contents of the communication and on its source. The Spanish Secretary of State for Foreign Affairs said that the request had come from "a very exalted personage" and that he could not give further particulars. He added that the Spanish Government had no intention of mediating or intervening, but that it thought it proper to transmit the question to the British Government.

Mr. Balfour then gave us each a copy of the British reply which he is sending to the British Ambassador at Madrid. It is as follows:

"His Majesty's Government would be prepared to receive any communication that the German Government may desire to make in relation to peace and to discuss it with their allies.["]

Mr. Balfour went on to explain the indefiniteness of the Spanish Secretary's conversation and expressed his strong suspicion that this move was only an effort to divide the allies. He suspects that Germany hopes to satisfy the United States and Great Britain by a proposition regarding Belgium, to satisfy France by a proposition regarding Alsace-Lorraine, and so all the way around separately dishearten one government after another. He suspects also that Germany will try to induce at l[e]ast some of the allies to meet German representatives in conference without definitely stipulating peace terms beforehand.

Mr. Balfour committed the British Government to the plan of discussing every German proposal with all the Great Powers engaged in war against Germany before answering the correspondence and he assumed that all these Powers would do the same. Balfour requested the utmost secrecy about the whole matter at least till more definite developments.

Still more confidential. The British Foreign Office has had this telegram from the Ambassador at Madrid for a fortnight, Balfour remarked, and that he thought too prompt an answer would be bad diplomacy. I have no doubt that another reason for waiting so long to reply to it was the wish to see the result of the battles in France which Haig has won and that these victories make a reply now more opportune. I have for some time had private and confidential information about this subject and have been informed accurately but through subordinate channels that the Roman Catholic influence in the British Government and the dangerous pacifist and semi-pacifist influences have been making desperate efforts to influence the government to send an answer without informing the allied governments and without committing itself to discuss every move with them. These influences failed and I am certain cannot succeed in any future effort but they are to be reckoned definitely as willing to accept terms that fall short of the President's declarations and the public declarations made by members of the British Government. The Buxton group are the Lafollettes of this Kingdom and the Roman Catholics have been informed by Germany through the Pope.

A part of the British Government in fact made it known to the rest that if any attention were paid to these influences they would expose the whole thing and disrupt the government. The government showed no signs of wavering but the pacifists and the semi-pacifists press who are not openly for peace at any price but who work for a premature and indecisive peace are now better understood here, as are the Roman Catholic influences. By this incident they exposed themselves.

I have strong but not conclusive evidence that the Kaiser sent for Villalobar, Spanish Minister at Brussels, who is an extreme pro-German and an unscrupulous intriguer, and that Villalobar conveyed the message to the Spanish Government. The German Ambassador at Madrid[3] knew nothing till long after it had been delivered. Since the Germans did not use their own diplomatic channel they left themselves free to disavow Villalobar and deny that he had authority from them if the course of events goes awry.   Page

T telegram (SDR, RG 59, 763.7219/8290, DNA).
   [1] That is, Page, Paul Cambon, Marquis Guglielmo Imperiali dei Principi di Francavilla, Constantin Nabokov (Chargé d'Affaires), and Viscount Sutemi Chinda.
   [2] Marquis de Lema.
   [3] Prince Maximilian von Ratibor und Corvey.

From James Cardinal Gibbons

My dear Mr. President: Baltimore. October 6, 1917.

In these days of the gravest problems, which have ever weighed upon our American Government, our thoughts go out to the Chief Executive, warmed by a heartfelt sympathy for the heavy burdens of office which he must bear, and freighted with the unwavering determination of loyal citizens to stand by him in his every effort to bring success to our arms, and to achieve those ideals of justice and humanity which compelled our entrance into the war.[1]

Guided, as we are, by the sublime teachings of Christianity, we have no other course open to us but that of obedience and devotion to our country. Our Divine Lord tells us, "Render to Caesar the things that are Caesar's, and to God the things that are God's," and St. Paul following the steps of his Master says, "Let every soul be subject to the higher powers, for, there is no authority but from God, and those that are, are ordained by God. Therefore he who resisteth the power, resisteth the ordinance of God, and they who resist purchase to themselves condemnation." We wish our people to see, and we are striving to help them to realize, that they owe unswerving loyalty to the rulers whom they have elected to office, and that in doing so they are not acting in a slavish manner, for obedience is not an act of servility we pay to man, but an act of homage we pay to God.

We are working to the end that our countrymen may see the folly and grave disobedience of unjust and ill-tempered criticism of national policies. We are bending our efforts to point out to our fellowmen that they in all probability see the present situation from only one angle, whereas the Government sees it from every viewpoint, and is therefore alone in the position to judge of the expediency of national affairs.

In a word we have been exerting our every effort, and will continue to do so, to persuade all Americans that they can do the greatest good to themselves and their country, by a cheerful and generous performance of their duty, as it is pointed out to them by lawfully constituted authority.

With sentiments of highest esteem, I am,

Very faithfully yours,   J. Card. Gibbons

TLS (WP, DLC).
¹ Cardinal Gibbons was one of many prominent persons who had just organized the League for National Unity, about which see the news report printed at Oct. 8, 1917.

From David Lawrence

PERSONAL

My dear Mr. President: [Washington] October 6, 1917

I am grateful to you for your letter of yesterday and I concur heartily in the point that anything which represents the Administration as desirous of peace now when it, in fact, is not, can only work mischief. As for the Colonel House speculation, while I was not one of those who gave the impression that his mission meant an early peace or that it had anything to do with the time when peace negotiations would begin, nevertheless I feel that all the misunderstanding might have been avoided if the original outgiving on the subject had been clearer or if none had been made at all.

In order that there may be no tie-ing up of the Administration to any peace discussion for the present, I am forwarding in confidence a copy of your letter so that the editorial writers may have the benefit of your point of view. I know how anxious Mr. Villard and Mr Ogden and the others are to assist the national interest particularly because the Evening Post did not, so to speak, vote for war. The Evening Post, however, is not urging a premature peace or commenting on it except when news events justify but is endeavoring to express even in these topsy-turvy days the liberalism it has sincerely felt, as you know, for many years, a task by no means easy in the atmosphere of extreme militarism and intolerance being every day fostered by the hang-them-at-sunrise type leaders who with patriotism on their side are poisoning young as well as old with a kind of opinion that I, for one, fear is going to make it difficult for the United States to see consummated the unselfish peace that we stand for. Because if, as the tendency seems now to be, liberal influences are squelched, there will inevitably be a return to the kind of spirit that has prevailed at peace conferences in the past when even Americans have asked "What are we going to get out of all this sacrifice?" To keep alive and even flaming the fires of liberalism which your own election in 1916 kindled so brightly ought to be the duty of every writer or correspondent who believes as I do that no greater liberal has lived in our generation than yourself but who knows also that all the subordinate officials of the Government are not infused with your spirit and who because they wield power can conceivably build up a public opinion that will affect our whole attitude toward progressivism in national as well as international problems.

Pardon me for the length of this letter. I would like to tell you more of the fears and apprehensions which I hear expressed on all sides by men who like myself believe in the objects of this war as expressed by you on April 2nd and want to see peace not a moment sooner than the attainment of those ideals.

It may interest you to know that I have severed my editorial connection with the Washington Times because of a pressure of work and other reasons. With best wishes, I am,

Cordially yours,   David Lawrence

TLS (WP, DLC).

From Thomas Watt Gregory

Dear Mr. President: Washington, D. C. October 6, 1917.

I have given careful attention to the suggestions in your letter of September 25, 1917, transmitting a broad sheet entitled "The People's Counselor" and apparently issued by Theodore Lundy of Chicago.[1]

The matter contained in this scurrilous sheet does not constitute treason within the meaning of that term as defined by the court decisions. The matter, however, apparently falls within the prohibitions of the espionage act, and I have therefore transmitted it to the United States Attorney at Chicago with a request for immediate investigation and action.

Respectfully,   T. W. Gregory

TLS (WP, DLC).
[1] The Editors have not found the "broad sheet." If *The People's Counselor* was a newspaper, it was short-lived and is not listed in the standard guides and reference works.

From William Gibbs AcAdoo

Bowdle, S. D., October 6, 1917.

Warmest congratulations on the passage of the Soldiers and Sailors Insurance Bill. It is the most liberal and humane measure ever enacted by any nation in favor of its fighting men and their dependent families and is another of the great achievements which have distinguished your leadership of the nation.[1]

W. G. McAdoo.

T telegram (WP, DLC).
[1] An Act to amend "An Act to authorize the establishment of a Bureau of War Risk Insurance in the Treasury Department, approved September 2 1914, and for other purposes," approved October 6, 1917, provided, among other things, for the issuance of life and disability insurance policies of up to $10,000 to officers and enlisted men and women of the military and naval forces of the United States. The Act also provided for a system of allotments and family allowances for enlisted men. 40 *Statutes at Large*, 398-411. Premium rates and other terms and conditions were described in the *Official Bulletin*, I (Oct. 17, 1917), 15.

Arthur James Balfour to Sir William Wiseman

[London] Oct. 6th. '17.
Following from Falsterbo [Balfour] for Brussa [House]:

No. 21. Your telegram No. 12 of Sept. 11th. In view of reports that German Government are making great efforts to capture Zionist movement, question of a message of sympathy with movement from H. M. Government has again been considered by Cabinet. Following formula has been suggested:

"H. M. Government view with favour establishment in Palestine of a national home for Jewish race and will use their best endeavours to facilitate achievement of this object; it being clearly understood that nothing shall be done which may prejudice civil and religious rights of existing non-Jewish communities in Palestine or rights and political status enjoyed in any other country by Jews, who are fully contented with their existing nationality and citizenship."

Before taking any decision Cabinet intend to hear views of some of representative Zionists, but meanwhile they would be grateful if you found it possible to ascertain opinion of Adramyti [Wilson] with regard to formula.

T telegram (W. Wiseman Papers, CtY).

To Edward Mandell House

The White House Oct 7 1917

Referring to your letter of fifth   message suggested satisfactory   also proposed chairmanship   Woodrow Wilson

T telegram (E. M. House Papers, CtY).

From Edward Mandell House

Dear Governor: New York. October 7, 1917.

I did not realize when I wrote you Friday night, asking for two important decisions, that my letter would reach you at an adjournment of Congress.

Of course, I am greatly pleased at your reply which has just come. The matter of the chairmanship will now come through regular channels, and will reach you through Lansing in a few days.

I wish you could know how happy I am that Congress has adjourned after having done your pleasure in so many different measures. What an achievement it is! What a pace you have set for your successors! I wonder if any can ever follow.

Affectionately yours,   E. M. House

TLS (WP, DLC).

Sir William Wiseman to Sir Eric Drummond

[New York] Oct. 7th. '17.

No. 20. MOST SECRET.

Following for Falsterbo [Balfour] from W.W.:

a) Reference your No. 19. of 3d. Adramyti [Wilson] sends you following reply: "I think the proper course is the one which I understand you propose to adopt, namely, to tell the Spanish envoy that you could not discuss the matter without consulting your co-belligerents and as so many insincere offers of peace have already been put out semi-officially you could not even consult your co-belligerents until a more definite proposal is made."

b) Reference your No. 127 of Oct. 3d. Adramyti agrees to the appointment of an American chairman.

T telegram (W. Wiseman Papers, CtY).

A News Report

WILSON SEES END OF WAR ONLY WHEN ENEMY IS BEATEN

[*Oct. 8, 1917*]

Washington, Oct 8.—Agitation for a premature peace was characterized as seditious, and those who attacked the allies of America in the present crisis were declared to be enemies of their country by members of the newly organized League for National Unity, who were received at the White House this afternoon by President Wilson.

The President gave his indorsement to the purposes of the league in an address emphasizing the need of team play by the forces of American thought and opinion. He expressed the belief that American public opinion, although understanding the war's causes and principles, needed guidance to remember that the war should end only when Germany was beaten and Germany's rule of autocracy and might superceded by the ideals of democracy.

This is the issue which the American people should always keep in mind, the President said, in order to avoid being misled into byways of thought and the resultant scattering of the force of public opinion. Talk of early peace before Germany is defeated is one of the evidences of misdirected thought, he suggested, and should not cloud the vision of those who understand that the United States is fighting now for the same ideals of democracy and freedom that have always actuated the nation.

The President gave warning that it should not be forgotten that German success would mean not only prevention of the spread of democracy, but possibly the suppression of that already existing.[1]

Cardinal Gibbons of Baltimore, senior prelate of the Roman Catholic Church in the United States, and Frank Mason North of the Federal Council of the Churches of Christ in America, are Honorary Chairmen of the organization, and its list of officers includes men of prominence in organized labor, industry, and finance. Cardinal Gibbons was not present, but the league has received a letter from him subscribing to its principles, which soon will be published.

The league will have headquarters in New York, and will organize at once for service. On its Executive Committee are William R. Willcox, Chairman of the Republican National Committee, and Vance McCormick, Chairman of the Democratic National Committee. It is understood that the machinery of the Speakers' Bureaus of these great organizations may be used in a nation-wide movement to unite the country behind the Government and spread before the people the many acts by Germany which brought about the war.

The announced purpose of the organization is "to create a medium through which the loyal Americans of all classes, sections, creeds, and parties can give expression to the fundamental purpose of the United States to carry on to a successful conclusion this new war for the independence of America and for the preservation of democratic institutions and the vindication of the basic principles of humanity."

This declaration of principles was adopted:

"In an hour when our nation is fighting for the principles upon which it was founded, in an hour when free institutions and the hopes of humanity are at stake, we hold it the duty of every American to take his place on the firing line of public opinion.

"It is not a time for old prejudices or academic discussion as to past differences. Those who are not now for America are against America.

"Our cause is just. We took up the sword only when international law and ancient rights were set at naught, and when our forbearance had been exhausted by persistent deception and broken pledges.

"Our aims are explicit, our purposes unsoiled by any selfishness. We defend the sanctities of life, the fundamental decencies of civilization. We fight for a just and durable peace and that the rule of reason shall be restored to the community of nations.

"In this crisis the unity of the American people must not be impaired by the voices of dissension of [or?] sedition. Agitation for a premature peace is seditious when its object is to weaken the determination of America to see the war through to a conclusive vindication of the principles for which we have taken arms.

"The war we are waging is a war against war and its sacrifices must not be nullified by any truce or armistice that means no more than a breathing spell for the enemy.

"We believe in the wise purpose of the President not to negotiate a peace with any irresponsible and autocratic dynasty.

"We approve the action of the national Government in dispatching an expeditionary force to the land of Lafayette and Rochambeau. Either we fight the enemy on foreign soil, shoulder to shoulder with comrades in arms, or we fight on our soil, backs against our homes, and alone.

"While this war lasts, the cause of the Allies is our cause, their defeat our defeat, and concert of action and unity in spirit between them and us is essential to final victory. We therefore deprecate the exaggeration of old national prejudices—often stimulated by German propaganda—and nothing is more important than the clear understanding that those who in this crisis attack our present allies, attack America.

"We are organized in the interests of a national accord that rises high above any previous division of party, race, creed and circumstance.

"We believe that this is the critical and fateful hour for America and for civilization. To lose now is to lose for many generations. The peril is great and requires our highest endeavors. If defeat comes to us through any weakness, Germany, whose purposes for world-wide dominion are now revealed, might draw to itself, as a magnet does the filings, the residuum of world power, and this would affect the standing and the independence of America.

"We not only accept but heartily approve the decision reached by the President and Congress of the United States to declare war against the common enemy of the free nations, and as loyal citizens of the United States, we pledge to the President and the Government our undivided support to the very end."

Printed in the *New York Times*, Oct. 9, 1917.
[1] No stenographic report of Wilson's remarks is extant.

To Edward Mandell House

My dear House: The White House 8 October, 1917

At last Mrs. Wilson, while not well I am sorry to say, has thrown off the poison of the grippe which got so deep a hold on her, and my mind is free to take up the important matters we ought to confer about. Any time you name this week would be convenient, if you will come down, and I hope that it may be soon.

With affectionate messages from us all,
Faithfully yours,   Woodrow Wilson

TLS (E. M. House Papers, CtY).

To Thomas Samuel Hawes

[The White House] 8 October, 1917

I have shown your telegram of October sixth to Judge Chambers and your acceptance now of the offer as made by him in his letter of September twenty-eighth addressed to R. B. Coleman, General Manager, on behalf of the employees to reduce their original demands for increase of wages to one-half coupled with the proposal on their part to submit to arbitration their demand for reinstatement of Strickland, will be satisfactory provided the arbitration agreement adheres strictly to that proposal and is in conformity with the Act of Congress commonly known as the Newlands law and that arbitration papers be signed and mailed to Judge Chambers as stated in your telegram. I am pleased with this settlement of the controversy.

Woodrow Wilson.

T telegram (Letterpress Books, WP, DLC).

From John Joseph Pershing

[Chaumont] France
Dear Mr. President: October 8, 1917.

In acknowledging the high honor that you have conferred upon me,[1] I pray that you will accept my most sincere and most humble thanks for this expression of your confidence in me.

I again pledge myself, Mr. President, to serve you and the nation unceasingly and loyally and with all my strength, in the full assurance that, with the aid of Divine Providence, we shall succeed in our righteous cause of saving democracy to the world.

It is inspiring, Mr. President, to feel that our country, under your distinguished guidance, has taken the lead in this great task. The people of the allied nations have faith in you as in no other man.

Please accept my earnest wishes for your continued health and strength.

With high esteem, I remain,

Your most obedient servant,   John J. Pershing.

TLS (WP, DLC).

[1] Wilson had just promoted Pershing to the rank of general.

From Walter Hines Page

London, Oct. 8, 1917.

7363. CONFIDENTIAL for the President and the Secretary only.

My 7355, October 6th. Conversations with members of the Government and especially with intelligence officers who know best what is going on in Germany reveal the following facts and opinions.

The German peace inquiry is regarded as the beginning of the end but the end is hardly expected soon. The prevailing idea is that the army general staff which has all the real authority in Germany realize the impossibility of a military victory and think it wise to yield before the American army fights and with the hope of saving the dynasty and its surpassingly autocratic power. Von Kuhlmann and the financial and manufacturing interests wish to save Germany's economic opportunity after the war, and peace movement will be made chiefly with reference to this. In consideration for giving up Belgium and the French provinces the Germans will demand free access to the markets and credit in allied countries. The European allies will not make such an agreement. They realize that artificial and merely punitive commercial measures cannot be permanent but since German commercial methods were distinctly war measures they will be reluctant to agree to a general commercial peace as a condition of ending the war. Every nation will probably reserve its freedom to act in this matter as best suits its interests. Great Britain, France, Italy and Russia do not wish to open a free door for commercial exploitation again and the case of each differs in degree and kind from every other. Their aim is not mainly punitive but rather defensive.

The German army can yet hold out long before a complete defeat and the feeling here is that it will so hold out and prolong preliminary peace efforts, directed chiefly to preserving German economic opportunity. The European allies will not consent to a peace conference before *hopeful* German terms are specifically and authentically stated.

Another subject that engages British thought is Germany's southeastern ambitions. The British are resolved not to permit a German yielding in the west to cause them to forget or neglect the Berlin to Bagdad German scheme. The Germans obviously wish to but [put] off the western allies by yielding western local interests.

Still another point of increasing importance in all peace thought is the submarine. If Germany be left free to manufacture submarines she may in a short time again attack British and American commerce. No complete antidote to the submarine is expected. It will probably have to be met only by the present methods of defense and attack and a very large submarine fleet could be built in a few years at small cost and could again play havoc with ocean commerce and possibly even carry war to America. Peace conditions must cover this subject.

Since the war began about forty per cent of German submarines commissioned have been captured or destroyed but the percentage of the German losses in the early stages of the war was larger than now and the Germans are believed to have nearly two hundred under [construction]. Abundant convoys carrying depth charges are the best defenses yet tried but these cannot prevent a considerable toll on commerce.

What is here called the Catholic conspiracy exists and is strong throughout Roman Catholic Europe. Rome wishes to preserve Austrian loyalty to the Vatican. Devout Roman Catholics of all nationalities are influenced by the church's wishes even English and French Roman Catholics thus find their loyalty divided between their countries and their church and the resolution of many good men is weakened unconsciously. Cardinal Bourne[1] who thinks himself a good Englishman has made decidedly misleading annotations on the Pope's note which are distributed in the cathedral here.

The British thought of peace conditions therefore includes not only Belgium, Alsace-Lorraine, Servia and Poland, but also the future of the submarines, the Berlin-Bagdad scheme, and the intricate question of commercial and financial relations to Germany after the war.

The British military feeling is a feeling of complete confidence in a probably slow but an absolutely sure victory, but an early peace, though possible, is not expected. A long and devious peace effort by Germany is looked for directed towards dividing the allies and towards insuring German economic post-war opportunity by which the Germans plan to prepare for another and more successful attack on democracy.   Page.

T telegram (SDR, RG 59, 763.72119/10493, DNA).
[1] Francis Cardinal Bourne, Archbishop of Westminster.

From Robert Lansing

Dear Mr. President: Washington October 8, 1917.

I transmit herewith a memorandum prepared by the Division of Latin American Affairs,[1] together with a translation of a letter from President Estrada Cabrera of Guatemala, addressed to the Guatemalan Minister in Washington,[2] and a translation of extracts from two Mexican newspapers relative to the attitude of Mexico towards Guatemala.[3]

I also wish to inform you that the Special Mission, sent to the United States by President Estrada Cabrera, has stated in a memorandum presented to the Department of State that the object of its visit is to confirm the engagement made by the Government of Guatemala to cooperate in the defence of the cause espoused by the United States, and that in order to make its cooperation effective Guatemala must obtain the necessary elements, both as to material as well as to political interests. In this memorandum a very definite request is made, which bears close relationship to the letter of President Estrada Cabrera to Minister Mendez above mentioned. The request reads as follows:

"To forestall conflicts which both Mexico and Salvador severally or jointly might, in accordance with plans already known to the Government of the United States, bring on to Guatemala at her border, the last-named country wishes to feel that it may depend on the United States' mediation to avert them, or its assistance to repel them."

I would be glad to receive your direction as to what reply should be made to these two requests.

Faithfully yours,   Robert Lansing.

TLS (WP, DLC).
[1] J. H. Stabler to RL, Aug. 20, 1917, TLS (SDR, RG 59, 712.14/75, DNA). It described the papers presented on August 20 by the Minister of Guatemala, Joaquín Méndez, which are summarized in the following notes. It also stated that the Division of Latin American Affairs did not believe that it would be possible to give Estrada Cabrera "any further assurances than those already given." These were "to the effect that the United States would give Guatemala every support in the present conflict with Germany, it being understood that President Estrada Cabrera had placed his services at the disposal of the United States."

2 M. Estrada Cabrera to J. Méndez, Aug. 5, 1917, T translation (SDR, RG 59, 712.14/75, DNA). It asserted that, as the enclosed extracts from a Mexican newspaper showed, Mexico was only awaiting "a suitable opportunity" to attack Guatemala, and it instructed Méndez to inform the State Department and, if possible, Wilson.

3 Excerpts from the Mexican newspaper *La Defensa*, July 4, 1917: "Guatemala acting at the request of the Yankees takes a perfidiously aggressive attitude toward our country," and July 15, 1917: "Generals Obregon, Alvarado, Hill, and Pablo Gonzales in arms to repel any aggression against the national sovereignty." Both T MSS in SDR, RG 59, filed with 712.14/75, DNA.

From Newton Diehl Baker, with Enclosure

Dear Mr. President: [Washington, c. Oct. 8, 1917]

This is from our "observer" in London. I asked his opinion and that of the military people in London.[1]

Respectfully,   Newton D. Baker

ALS (WP, DLC).
[1] Baker told Bliss on October 5 that Wilson was "greatly interested in learning the views of military men as to what appears to be the actual effect of the present British drive in Flanders." Bliss accordingly sent a telegram to the United States military attaché in London to request this information. T. H. Bliss to JPT, Oct. 6, 1917, TLS (WP, DLC).

E N C L O S U R E

Cablegram received at the War Department Oct. 8, 1917.

Confidential With reference to your cablegram received October 6th   In my opinion Haigs recent advance has increased the British salient around Ypres to such a degree as to threaten the German lines between Ostend and Lille to the point of now making probable, if the advance is continued a little further, that the Germans may have to withdraw their right wing resting on the sea to a point considerably further to the northeast perhaps evacuate Ostend. Haig now occupies the whole Passchendaele ridge with the exception of the village of same name and some isolated heights north of it, and if he can gain these points the British will hold the last remaining high ground on an advance toward the east and Brussels over the Belgian plain. His left flank will then be protected from Germans attacking from the plain below. This position will not only render the whole present German lines from the Ypres salient to the sea insecure but may also oblige the Germans to straighten their lines to the south of the salient in the direction of Lille, withdrawing upon that city. From Haigs position to-day on heights the city of Bruges 30 miles away is plainly visible. The military effect of such a withdrawing north and south of the Ypres salient is obvious and if withdrawing of the German right can be forced to the point of obliging them to give up the submarine bases at Zee Brugge and perhaps Ostend, the movement will have had a naval effect of much importance in addition to the military advantages gained and will materially shorten the duration of the war. The moral and political effect of the present drive is very marked both sides not only for what has already been accomplished but by reason of the prospective possibilities. The results so far are bound to be very depressing to the morale of the German troops and to German public opinion which the German authorities have for some time found it necessary to stimulate by increasing suggestions of the prospect of an early peace negotiated upon the basis of a military situation greatly to their advantage. Any withdrawing therefore which could not be either concealed or explained away might have a seriously disastrous effect in Germany especially in view of the hardships of the approaching winter. The effect on the Allies and especially on the British is proportionately encouraging and the buoyancy of public feeling in this country is already marked.[1] Slocum.[2]

T telegram (WP, DLC).

[1] Haig's major offensive, which led to the third Battle of Ypres (or Passchendaele), July 31-November 10, 1917, actually failed to achieve its main objectives.

[2] That is. Lt. Col. Stephen L'Hommedieu Slocum, U.S.A., military attaché in London.

From Walter Lippmann

My dear Mr. President: [Washington] October 8, 1917.

No doubt the seriousness of the political situation in New York City has already been called to your attention, and I feel that I must write to you briefly in regard to it. The certain facts appear to be the indisputable superiority of Mitchel to all the other candidates.[1] There are many things he has done that liberal minded people cannot altogether agree with and there are more things that he has said which are hard to bear, but the tone and quality of his administration has been extraordinarily fine. From the point of view of the city itself his defeat would be something like a political disaster.

In the course of his administration he has of course raised a formidable opposition: much of it is ignorant opposition but a good deal of it consists of petty special interests, and his reelection is at the present time exceedingly doubtful.

As you know, he is making the issue turn on the support of the war, shoving all municipal issues into the background. Now it is true that the disaffected elements in the city are all against Mitchel. There will be a very large vote for Hillquit and of course Hearst's influence in New York is powerful. There can be no doubt that in the opposition to Mitchel will be found all the pro-German, anti-British, anti-war sentiment there is in the city. On the other hand it by no means follows that all the loyal sentiment in the city will be found on Mitchel's side. There will be thousands of men who will follow you on the issue of the war who will vote against Mitchel. In fact Mitchel himself admitted to me on Friday that a word of support from you would be worth seventy-five thousand votes to him. The obvious deduction from that is that Mitchel does not monopolize the support of the patriotic groups of the city. This has put those of us who wish to see him elected but who wish to preserve the national morale, in a very distressing position. Important as it is to reelect Mitchel from the point of view of a New Yorker, it is even more important that the vote in November should not be allowed to appear as a test of the country's support of the war. The New York World is the only paper which seems to understand this point.

I should like therefore to put this before you for your consideration. Would it not be possible for you to find some way of saying publicly that the issue in New York was one of good government, putting that issue as strongly as possible and at the same time asserting that the only national issue at stake is the cause of good government. This of course is bound to be a somewhat awkward thing to do, but it does seem important in view of the reaction on the rest of the country and abroad, and that there should be some official record before election making it perfectly clear that the outcome in New York is not to be taken as a test vote. A heavy defeat of Mitchel in the present temper of his campaign would let loose pacifist feeling throughout the country as no other thing would do. I know enough about pacifist feeling to be certain that Mitchel is now identified in their minds with a vigorous military policy. It is therefore highly important that something be done to dissociate the issues.

I am, with very warmest regards,

Yours ever,   [Walter Lippmann]

CCL (W. Lippmann Papers, CtY).

[1] The four principal candidates for election on November 5 as Mayor of New York were the incumbent, John Purroy Mitchel (Fusion and City); John Francis Hylan (Democrat and Progressive); Morris Hillquit (Socialist); and William Mason Bennett (Republican). Mitchel's candidacy had been endorsed by Theodore Roosevelt, Charles Evans Hughes, Henry Morgenthau, and Oscar S. Straus. Roosevelt, on the steps of City Hall, had called for three cheers when Mitchel said: "I will run, and will make the fight against Hearst, Hylan, and the Hohenzollerns." *New York Times* rotogravure, Oct. 7, 1917. See Edwin R. Lewinson, *John Purroy Mitchel, The Boy Mayor of New York* (New York, 1965), pp. 206-47.

From Vira Boarman Whitehouse

Sir: New York Oct. 8th, 1917.

Since you cannot leave your duties and come to New York to help the Woman Suffrage Campaign in this State, I am going to ask if you will receive in Washington a delegation of women who hold important positions in the New York State Woman Suffrage Party, and make a brief statement to us of why you think the people of New York State should vote for woman suffrage—as you have already expressed the hope that they would.

We believe that if you will receive a delegation of this sort, and make a short speech to us, it would receive public attention and give a great stimulus to our campaign.

We hope that you will see your way clear to giving us such support.[1]

Yours respectfully,   Vira Boarman Whitehouse

TLS (WP, DLC).
[1] See Mrs. Whitehouse's address and Wilson's reply, printed at Oct. 25, 1917.

From Samuel Reading Bertron

My dear Mr. President: New York October 8, 1917.

Please rest assured that I should not have communicated with you without previously having a basis for my statements. There is no pessimism in this Country as to the result of the war, nor do I think any substantial doubt as to the successful placing of the Liberty Loan, nor can there be any reasonable doubt as to the soundness of the financial status of this Country, provided the situation is thoughtfully handled.

I have reports from as far west as Denver, as far south as Tennessee and as far north as Maine, showing that the banking institutions, in view of what they claim to be the uncertainties of the future, are unwilling to make commitments except for absolute necessities, and they are especially solicitous as to the outcome of the railway situation and that of the public service companies. The securities of these properties have been heretofore regarded as among the safest investments to be had, and are hence largely held by small holders and savings banks throughout the Country. Many of these companies are now not only having to forego or reduce dividends, but in some cases are finding it almost impossible to renew maturing obligations, and this latter is especially serious, because if their maturing obligations cannot be financed receiverships must follow. One large street railway company in the south has offered as high as 11% for one year, on obligations earning five times their interest, which normally could be placed on a 6% basis, and thus far can interest no bankers in advancing it the necessary funds to avoid failure.

Any financial difficulties throughout the Country are naturally first reflected in New York because co-operation here is required usually by institutions throughout the Country, and I had hoped that the feeling was confined to this section, but this is not the case. Railways and public service companies must be able to get money to go on with their improvements as the public's necessities require, and to do this they must show prosperity. If the bonds of these companies continue to depreciate the effect upon savings banks will be harmful. This situation has been brought about somewhat by the necessities of the Country. The free offerings of Government bonds naturally depreciates the value of all other securities, and to make the latter salable at all in competition, they must show good earnings. This Country is rich enough and prosperous enough to absorb both. We have jumped at one stride into a heavier degree of taxation in some respects than England has reached in three years and the people are naturally startled until they become used to it. With the adjournment of Congress the feeling should improve somewhat, and the announcement of the success of the Liberty Loan will also be helpful to the general sentiment, but a statement from you, pointing out the soundness of the Country and your desire that the needs of all sound business enterprises should be cared for, will be extremely helpful.

If, then, even as a war measure, the Interstate Commerce Commission would promptly permit the railroads to increase their rates, it would be exceedingly helpful, both actually and sentimentally. The Conference Committee of Congress all seemed to realize that the increased taxes on public service companies are especially burdensome as they have no possible means of increasing their revenues as other companies have, and yet are compelled to pay enormous increases for everything purchased, as well as for labor, and hence should have relief. Some of the members thought that such relief could be had when Congress meets again in December.

I am disturbed too about the soft coal situation. While I think the prices named for anthracite coal are entirely fair, this is said not to be true in the case of soft coal. In this instance, the price fixed should be sufficiently high, dependent upon the quality and operating conditions, to encourage every small producer to produce coal to the utmost as the output is essential. Where the large producers make undue profits, they will have to surrender them through the excess profit tax, but above all it is essential that everyone in the business should continue to mine the biggest possible output and hence all must see a fair profit.

Many lines of business are very prosperous and the laboring classes have never been so well off but it is the harmonizing of sentiment throughout the Country and helpfulness where needed which is required to produce confidence and keep our Country where conditions warrant them being, confident and prosperous.

I could go into many details but cannot inflict you with a longer letter.

I find that practically all of the heretofore existing criticisms of the Administration have vanished and there is a general appreciation of the enormous accomplishments that have been effected within the last six months and a willinfness [willingness] to give credit to those who have so ably handled a difficult problem.

With very kind regards, please believe me,

Faithfully yours,   S R Bertron

TLS (WP, DLC).

From William Cox Redfield

My dear Mr. President: Washington October 8th, 1917.

There lies before me a dispatch to the State Department from J. B. Jackson,[1] American Consul at Aleppo, now here, suggesting that the agricultural needs of France are such that we should help them. He says:

"As there are great numbers of volunteers from the American Army who are rejected on account of minor physical disability, but who would be entirely serviceable for this work, it is thought that some two or three hundred thousand or even more if necessary thereof might be utilized therefor, forming an auxilliary branch of our Army."

It is, I suppose, quite impossible to do anything of the kind suggested for our own shortage of labor on our farms is such that I presume we have not the men to spare even if the plan were otherwise feasible. The interest serves, however, to introduce the thought which I wish to present:

Has not the time come when in order to sustain the industrial and agricultural activities behind our armies to the full, we ought not only to mobilize any unused forces of the kind available, but to call upon the womanhood of the country definitely to come forward and do what they can to relieve men for the sterner occupations? To illustrate unused forces, I have a friend who is a draftsman of unusual quality but who is lame. He wishes to work and is well able to work at a task but the organization is such in places where he applies that a lame man is not taken. There must be many men in our country who could do something to the gain of the land and to the uplifting of their own sense of manhood if there were some sort of provision made to provide conditions under which they could work. There are also many places in the country occupied by men which women could well fill. It hardly seems as if in the present pressure men ought to be used to run elevators. For many years past fine tool making in factories in Europe has been in the hands of trained women and the work is nothing like as physically severe as the task of the ordinary domestic servant. If the matter were looked into, I think there are many occupations filled by men in department stores which women could fill just as well. I know there is a movement in this general direction but it seems that it should be accelerated. If the matter were to be definitely taken up as a program, possibly the Women's Committee of the Council of National Defense would be able to start it. I think there are probably many thousand women in this country eager to take a productive part. Ought we not to get at the matter definitely?

I am venturing to send a copy of this to the office of the Secretary of Labor. I am sure you will realize that it is not written in any thought of criticism. Factories and farms are calling for men and in so far as women may be able and willing to do some work suited to them which men now do, it seems as if it is our duty to get a readjustment made.

Yours very truly,   William C. Redfield

TLS (WP, DLC).
¹ Jesse B. Jackson.

Charles Lee Swem to Albert Sidney Burleson, with Enclosure

The White House

My dear Mr. Postmaster General: 8 October, 1917

In connection with the enclosed telegram, the President asks if you will be kind enough to send him a report on the Milwaukee Leader.   Sincerely yours,   Chas. L. Swem

TLS (WP, DLC).

ENCLOSURE

Sir: Milwaukee, Wis., October 4, 1917.

I desire to enter my humble protest against the action of Postal officials in cancelling the mailing privileges of the Milwaukee LEADER. The City of Milwaukee has been one of the most orderly cities of the nation during this war. Its great mass of working people have in this great industrial center cooperated the aid [and aided] in war time production. It has carried out every request made by either the United States Government, Red Cross or other organizations seeking assistance to aid the war without a hitch. Our citizens give their services unselfishly; in some of the districts half of the boys who have been drafted are staunch socialists. It is known that the spirit of the men from Milwaukee upon entering their cantonments was of the highest. We have organized the County Council of Defense whose efficiency has been exceeded by no other council in this country. In all this work we have had the cooperation of all the citizens of all parties and of the entire press. Some 12,000 socialist people of this city have subscribed the funds to make the Milwaukee LEADER possible. They are members of the socialist party who fought against the German military program long before this war started and will fight it if it exists after the war ceases. It is true that the paper stands for peace but this has been one of the fundamental precepts of the socialists of the world and of this country since its foundation. It would not be an unusual action for this Government to prevent articles of a certain nature in a newspaper but to take the stand that the newspaper should not be mailed is singling out only a socialist publication for the condemnation of the Government in this community savors very much of hasty and unwise action. There is no doubt in my mind but that the action of the Government will have the direct opposite effect than what it hopes to accomplish. The citizens of Milwaukee love their Government but by so drastic an action the Government can accomplish nothing but drive a wedge between the people and the Administration. I have faith that if this message comes to your personal attention that you will make a personal investigation in which case you will be convinced that the people of this city will enter into the spirit of assisting the Government during this war in a much lighter spirit if it receives on the part of the Government such fair treatment and protection of rights as are guaranteed to its citizens under the Constitution.   Respectfully submitted,   Daniel W. Hoan[1]

T telegram (WP, DLC).
   [1] Daniel Webster Hoan, Mayor of Milwaukee, a Socialist.

From Herbert Adams

My dear Mr. President: New York. October 8, 1917.

I now have the monument for Mrs. Wilson's grave completed. While your overwhelming duties may make it impossible for you to come to New York to see it before it is set up in place, I assume that you would like to have it seen by some member or members of your family.

The marble cutting has been done at Weehawken, and I should be very glad to go with any of the family to see it there, at any time except the 12th, when we have a meeting of the Commission of Fine Arts in Washington.

With devoted regards, I am

Very sincerely yours,   Herbert Adams

TLS (WP, DLC).

A Memorandum by Robert Lansing

MEMORANDUM of CONFERENCE with VISCOUNT ISHII.
October 8, 1917.

Viscount Ishii called this afternoon and submitted to me a counterdraft of the proposed note relative to a redeclaration of the "Open Door" policy.[1]

After reading the counterdraft I told him I would take it under consideration.

TC MS (R. Lansing Papers, NjP).
   [1] A revision of the draft printed as Enclosure III with RL to WW, Sept. 25, 1917.

Kikujiro Ishii to Robert Lansing[1]

THE SPECIAL MISSION OF JAPAN

Handed me by Viscount Ishii

Changes proposed by	Oct 8/17 RL.
Japanese Govt are	Shown to Prest
shown in pencil.	Oct 9/17 RL.

Added Oct 12/17 certain other changes proposed by Ishii. RL.

Excellency:

I have the honor to communicate herein my understanding of the agreement reached by us in our recent conversations touching the questions of mutual interest to our Governments relating to the Republic of China.

~~Charges have repeatedly been made of late, some accusing the United States and others Japan of seeking to take advantage of present world conditions to acquire political influence or control in China. The Governments of the United States and Japan having always recognized China as a sovereign and independent state resent such accusations as offensive and as wholly unjustified.~~

In order to silence ~~such~~ mischievous reports ~~however~~, that have from time to time been circulated, it is believed by us that a public announcement once more of the desires and intentions shared by our two Governments with regard to China is advisable.

The Governments of the United States and Japan recognize that territorial propinquity creates special relations between countries; and consequently the United States Government recognizes that Japan has special in-
(and influence)
terests in China, particularly in that part to which her possessions are contiguous. (The territorial sovereignty of China, nevertheless, remains unimpaired, and) the Government of the United States has every confidence in the repeated assurances of the Imperial Japanese Government that while
Japan
geographical position gives (*them*) such spe-
(and influence)
cial interests they have no desire to discriminate against the trade of other nations or to disregard the commercial rights heretofore granted by China in treaties with other Powers.

The Governments of the United States and Japan deny that they have any purpose to infringe in any way the independence or ter-

Oct. 8/17 A.

1. Oct. 12/17
2. Proposed
   Oct. 12/17
   to be omitted.
Oct. 20/17
consents to
retain.
3 & 4. Oct.
   12/17.

(and sovereignty)

Oct. 13/17.

ritorial integrity∧of China and they declare furthermore that they always adhere to the principle of the so-called "Open Door," or equal opportunity for commerce and indus-

Oct. 8/17 B

try in China ~~and that they will not take ad-~~ ~~vantage of present conditions to seek special~~ ~~rights or privileges in China which would~~ ~~abridge the rights of the citizens or subjects~~ ~~of other friendly States.~~ Moreover they mu-

Alternative pro-posed by me Oct. 12/17. Leaving out *B* they accept this Oct. 20/17.

tually declare that they are opposed to the acquisition by any (other) government of any special rights or privileges that would

affect the independence or territorial integ-

(and sovereignty)

Oct. 13/17.

rity∧of China or that would deny to the sub-jects or citizens of any country the full en-joyment of equal opportunity in the com-merce and industry of China.

Oct. 8/17. C

~~They furthermore agree to bring this dec-~~ ~~laration to the attention of other interested~~ ~~Governments and invite those Governments~~ ~~to give their adherence to these declarations.~~

I shall be glad to have Your Excellency confirm this understanding of the agreement reached by us.

TC MS (R. Lansing Papers, NjP).

[1] The original document is missing in the files of the State Department. For changes in the draft printed below, compare it with the draft enclosed in RL to WW, Sept. 25, 1917; see also Lansing's memorandum printed at Oct. 10, 1917.

Arthur James Balfour to Sir William Wiseman

[London] Oct. 8th. '17.

No. 25. MOST SECRET. Your telegram No. 20.[1] Following from Falsterbo [Balfour] for Brussa [House]: Adramyti [Wilson] will no doubt have received from Mr. Page full account of interview I had with him and other representatives when our policy was explained.[2] I am not quite clear whether latter is in entire har-mony with Adramyti's views as expressed in his message, though I think it is. If not, and if Adramyti would care to have them, I should be very glad to send him reasons which inspire our action.

T telegram (W. Wiseman Papers, CtY).
¹ W. Wiseman to E. Drummond, Oct. 7, 1917.
² That is, WHP to WW, Oct. 6, 1917, No. 7355.

To James Cardinal Gibbons

The White House

My dear Cardinal Gibbons: 9 October, 1917

May I not express my very deep and sincere appreciation of your letter of October sixth? It has brought me cheer and reassurance, and I want you to know how much I appreciate your own action in consenting to preside over the important and influential group of men and women who have so generously undertaken to support the administration in its efforts to make the whole character and purpose of this war and of the Government of the United States in the prosecution of it clear to the whole people.

With warmest appreciation and cordial regards,

Sincerely yours,   Woodrow Wilson

TLS (Baltimore Cathedral Archives).

To Jouett Shouse

My dear Mr. Shouse: The White House 9 October, 1917

There is of course nothing in our recent correspondence about agricultural matters that I would not be perfectly willing to have made public,¹ but I want to suggest this to you, that it would greatly limit my correspondence with members of the two Houses if I had always to write with a view to the publication of the letter and I am afraid I would have always to have that in mind if I were to create precedents of the sort you suggest in your letter of October eighth. I am sure you will understand and justify my feeling.

Cordially and sincerely yours,   Woodrow Wilson²

TLS (J. Shouse Papers, KyU).
¹ Wilson was replying to J. Shouse to WW, Oct. 8, 1917, TLS (WP, DLC), in which Shouse had requested permission to publish in the *Congressional Record* H. C. Hoover to WW, Aug. 27, 1917, about the possible exemption of farmers from military service.
² Shouse replied on October 10 that, in his previous letter, he had expressed himself awkwardly. He had merely wished to publish Hoover's letter and had not sought to publish any letter by Wilson which had not already been released. J. Shouse to WW, Oct. 10, 1917, TLS (WP, DLC).

From Albert Sidney Burleson

My dear Mr. President: Washington October 9, 1917.

Referring to the case of the "Milwaukee Leader" mentioned in the telegram to you of the 4th instant from Honorable Daniel W. Hoan, Mayor of Milwaukee, I attach hereto a typewritten transcript of the hearing before the Third Assistant Postmaster General on September 22nd, which contains a number of quotations from various issues of this publication, which show the general character of matter published therein.[1] The marked portions on pages 3 to 7, inclusive, are types of the matter carried in various issues of this publication.

Faithfully yours, A. S. Burleson

TLS (WP, DLC).
  [1] This transcript is missing both in WP, DLC, and in the papers relating to the case of the *Milwaukee Leader* in the Post Office Department files in DNA.

From Newton Diehl Baker

My dear Mr. President: Washington. October 9, 1917.

In connection with the following telegram addressed to and received by you dated Spokane, Washington, August 21, 1917,

"Labor Council denounce arrest of twenty six workingmen here Sunday by military authorities as outrage and demand their immediate release and punishment of parties responsible. Demand Colonel Dentler[1] be relieved of command pending investigation. Are demanding of Gompers to call General Strike as protest against Prussianizing America. A. H. Nowaka, Secretary Labor."

and the following telegram from the same place and of the same date addressed to and received by me.

"Labor Council denounces arrest twenty six workingmen here Sunday by military authorities. Demands those responsible be punished and that Colonel Dentler be relieved of his command pending investigation. A. H. Nowaka, Secretary Labor Council."

I have to inform you that I have caused the matter referred to in these telegrams to be investigated by an Inspector under the direction of the Commanding General of the Western Department[2] and that the voluminous and comprehensive report of the Inspector together with the accompanying papers[3] have been carefully reviewed by the Inspector General of the Army[4] whose report of his review reads as follows:

"1. This is the report of an investigation of the arrest by Federal Troops under command of Colonel C. E. Dentler, U. S. Army, of members of the Industrial Workers of the World at Spokane, Washington. Investigation was due to the telegrams sent to the President of the United States and to the Secretary of War by A. H. Nowaka, Secretary of the Labor Council Union, denouncing the arrest of 26 workmen as an outrage, demanding their immediate release and punishment of parties responsible and that Colonel Dentler should be relieved from command pending an investigation.

"2. Investigation was made by Lieut. Colonel C. W. Thomas, Jr.,[5] Inspector General, National Guard, who reached the following conclusions: that the situation was very grave; that the people were wrought up and that there was danger of their taking the law into their own hands; that these men were determined to go to any length to obtain the release of the I.W.W. detained, including those held as alien enemies and draft evaders, irrespective of the law; that the Governor of Washington and the civil authorities felt themselves powerless to handle the situation and so stated; that the Governor of Washington made personal request upon Colonel Dentler in writing and through his personal representative for the use of Federal Troops, and that in his action Colonel Dentler carried out the formal and urgent request of the Governor of Washington and the instructions of the Adjutant General of the Army;[6] that the effect of his action was salutary and effectively saved the situation; that Colonel Dentler through Major Clement Wilkins in cooperation with the U. S. Attorney,[7] is handling the cases and that their disposition of these men was a wise one. He recommends that the disposition of the men arrested at Spokane on August 19 be left in the hands of Colonel Dentler, Governor Lister of Washington and the U. S. Attorney at Spokane and that no further action be taken.

"3. The recommendations of the Inspector have been concurred in by the Commanding General, Western Department, and are also concurred in by this office."

I concur in the above stated recommendations of the Inspector which, as appears above, have been concurred in by the Commanding General of the Western Department and are also concurred in by the Inspector General of the Army.

It is believed that no further action by the War Department is required and I recommend that none be had.

Very sincerely yours,   Newton D. Baker

TLS (WP, DLC).
1 Clarence Eugene Dentler, Colonel, U.S.A.
2 Maj. Gen. Arthur Murray.
3 They are missing.
4 Maj. Gen. John Loomis Chamberlain.
5 He cannot be further identified.
6 That is, Maj. Gen. Henry Pinckney McCain.
7 Francis Arthur Garrecht.

Benjamin Strong to Joseph Patrick Tumulty

New York, October 9, 1917.

Tried to reach you on Saturday and Sunday in endeavor to find if you could hold out any encouragement regarding subject of our conversation in connection with meeting at Carnegie Hall on eighteenth. Have discussed matter with associates here and they think it exceedingly important that this plan be carried out if possible along lines of what is at stake in the war. We all feel this would stimulate the whole country as well as liberty loan organizations to greater effort which is much needed as returns as [are] somewhat discouraging. Have arranged to have committee go over to Washington if you can offer any encouragement, but pressure of work on liberty loan is so great they await word from you before doing so. Will be glad to go over again myself if necessary and you think it advisable. Am anxiously awaiting answer.[1]   Strong.

T telegram (WP, DLC).
1 "Dear Tumulty: I must not do this unless it is absolutely necessary. My own feeling is that there are several more campaigns of this sort to come and that I ought to reserve myself for a later effort in case the subsequent loans should prove more sluggish than this one. The President." WW to JPT, Oct. 9, 1917, TL (WP, DLC). JPT to B. Strong, Oct. 9, 1917, TLS (B. Strong Papers, Federal Reserve Bank of N. Y.-Ar), is a paraphrase of Wilson's letter.

From the Diary of Josephus Daniels

October Tuesday 9 1917

WW told of English sailors who entertained German sailors at banquet. After English petty officer proposed toast to 'is 'ighness the German H'emper[or], he asked the G. if he would not propose health of the English King. Asked twice. No answer. Then up come your H-Emperor, putting his hand down his throat.

Burleson told of gentlemen just back from England who said all the country was ringing with praise of what our destroyers were doing. "When will you be ready?" "I am ready now."[1]

1 Daniels later expanded this account: When the first flotilla of American destroyers arrived at Queenstown, Ireland, to serve with the British anti-

submarine forces, Admiral Sir Lewis Bayly asked Commander Joseph Knefler Taussig, U.S.N., when his ships would be ready to go to sea. The British admiral "naturally supposed that, after a long and stormy voyage, the Americans would ask time for rest and repairs."

" 'We are ready now, sir,' " Commander Taussig replied; " 'that is, as soon as we finish refueling.' "

" 'I will give you four days from the time of arrival,' " the Admiral said. " 'Will that be sufficient?' "

" 'Yes,' " was the answer, " 'that will be more than ample time.' " Josephus Daniels, *The Wilson Era: Years of War and After, 1917-1923* (Chapel Hill, N. C., 1946), p. 74.

To Thomas Watt Gregory

[The White House]

My dear Mr. Attorney General: 10 October, 1917

I have your letter of October fifth about the policy to be pursued in the prosecution of the trust cases now before the Supreme Court and want to say that I entirely approve of the policy therein suggested.

Cordially and faithfully yours,   Woodrow Wilson

TLS (Letterpress Books, WP, DLC).

To Herbert Adams

My dear Mr. Adams: [The White House] 10 October, 1917

Thank you for your letter of October eighth. I find that my daughter, Mrs. McAdoo, is expecting to be in New York on Monday next, the fifteenth, and she has cheerfully undertaken to get in touch with you there and arrange to go with you to see the monument at Weehawken.

I am very glad indeed to hear that it is finished and shall look forward with the greatest interest to its being placed.

Cordially and sincerely yours,   Woodrow Wilson

TLS (Letterpress Books, WP, DLC).

From Robert Lansing, with Enclosures

MOST SECRET AND CONFIDENTIAL:

My dear Mr. President: Washington October 10, 1917.

Baron di Valentino, Secretary of the Italian Embassy,[1] called upon me Monday as the Ambassador was ill, and told me of the substance of a communication from the Papal Secretary of State[2] which he said had been handed to the English Minister at the

Vatican[3] ten days before. I asked him if the Ambassador would be willing to give me a copy of the communication and also the comments of Baron Sonnino on the subject. Yesterday evening he sent to my house the enclosed papers for my *"Personal and Confidential"* information.

I confess I am surprised that the British Government has not given us the text of this document. I think I shall ask the British Ambassador for an explanation.

Will you please, at your convenience, return these papers for my confidential file?   Faithfully yours,   Robert Lansing

[1] Baron Pietro Arone di Valentino, First Secretary of Embassy.
[2] That is, Pietro Cardinal Gasparri.
[3] That is, John Francis Charles, Count de Salis.

E N C L O S U R E   I

Count Macchi di Cellere to Robert Lansing

Personal and confidential.

My dear Mr. Lansing,   Washington, October 9th, 1917.

Baron di Valentino has reported to me your desire to have a free translation of the Papal note handed by the Vatican to the English Minister accredited to the Holy See on September 28th, as well as a paraphrase of the various remarks made by Baron Sonnino on the subject, and cabled to me together with the note.

I take pleasure in complying with your request and beg to enclose copy of both the note and said remarks for your personal and confidential information.

I am, my dear Mr. Lansing,
                    Very sincerely Yours   Macchi di Cellere

TLS (WP, DLC).

E N C L O S U R E   I I

Free translation of the note handed by the Vatican to the English Minister accredited with the Holy See on the 28th of September 1917.

The closing of the Swiss-Italian frontier having prevented the transmission of the diplomatic courier during several days, the Holy See has received with delay the answers of Germany and Austria to the Papal appeal for peace. The undersigned Cardinal

Secretary of State of His Holiness hastens now to send to Your Excellency an authentic copy of that document.

Germany's answer contains an explicit acceptance of the first and second paragraph of the Pope's appeal. Of the other four paragraphs the acceptance is implicit on the face of the various parts of the answer. As concerns the words: "agreeable with the peace manifestation of the Reichstag of July 19th ult." the Holy See has particular and strongly founded reason to believe and proclaim that they must be understood in the sense that Germany accepts the third and fourth paragraph of the Papal appeal.

In Austria's answer the acceptance of the Pope's proposals, including the fifth and sixth paragraph, is even clearer. The answers having been prepared jointly, it seems that there can be no doubt that they complete each other.

It would undoubtedly have been desirable that, in the interest of peace, the answers had been explicit on all single points. It must be recognized however that, even as they are, they leave an open door to an exchange of ideas. If therefore the Governments of the Entente, moved as they are, by the desire to restore peace in the world, do not refuse to enter into negotiations, the Holy See is disposed to lend its assistance to ask for further explanations on the points which may be suggested.

So far as the general disarmament is concerned, it is desired by everybody and is the foundation of peace and prosperity. His Holiness in deference for the warring powers, did not deem proper to indicate in his letter the means to attain and maintain it, thinking it better to leave the question imprejudiced and wait for the favorable occasion to determine it.

But His Holiness thinks that the only practical and easy means to reach this end is the following: by agreement among the civilized nations including non belligerents, compulsory military service is simultaneously suppressed. At the same time an international tribunal of arbitration is instituted for the purpose of defining all international controversies and sanctioning the complete isolation of any nation that might try to re-establish the compulsory military service or should refuse to submit to arbitration any international controversy, or should refuse to submit to the decision of the arbitration tribunal.

Even leaving aside any other consideration, the recent example of England and America prove that the volunteer system furnishes the contingent necessary to the maintenance of public order but does not furnish the enormous armies that are required to carry on a modern war.

Once the compulsory military service is, by common agreement, suppressed and the volunteer system is established in its stead, the general disarmament would follow almost automatically without any perturbation of the public order and with all the consequences regarding the establishment of such permanent peace as is possible in this world and the restoration, in the shortest possible period of the ruined finances of all nations. This without touching on other advantages the importance of which anybody can readily see.

The compulsory military service has been for over a century the cause of many evils. The remedy for such evils lays in the simultaneous and reciprocal suppression of compulsory military service. Once this is suppressed, it could not, even in the present constitution of the Central Empires, be reestablished without a parliamentary law the passing of which is improbable for many reasons, especially in view of the fact that it would require the approval of the people, as has been even recently said in a document or a highly authoritative personage.

Strictly personal and confidential
(Remarks by Baron Sonnino)[1]

It is evident that the Vatican is endeavoring to make itself necessary for eventual peace discussions. This is indicated by the Pope's suggestion to serve as a medium for the transmission of possible peace proposals and counter-proposals, thus trying to gain admission in the Peace Conference. The Central Empires, fully endorsing the Pontiff in this move, are speculating upon the alleged disaffection for the war of some parts of public opinion in the Allied Countries and upon the possibility of breaking up the Entente. At the same time they are endeavoring to start either directly or indirectly peace discussion or at least to give this impression to the various populations, without on the other hand compromising themselves with anything concrete or precise. Thus they hope to produce a certain weakening of the peoples of the Allied countries: weakening which besides having some influence on the morale of the Armies, would make in all events a resumption of hostilities very difficult if not absolutely impossible, however exaggerated the requests of the Central Empires might be. The fact of the beginning of any peace discussion whatsoever with the western allies without any serious pledge being given by the Central Empires for the integrity of Russia would immediately be used in Petrograd to obtain there a separate peace or at least to increase the internal dissensions in Russia and thus paralize her action.

It would therefore be dangerous to encourage all these intrigues by answering now to the Holy See and letting the warring peoples believe that negotiations of some sort are being conducted.

The imprecise and vague references made by Germany in regard to Belgium and to the other fundamental points of any peace, as well as the various speeches lately held in the enemy countries, among the others the one by Czernin in Budapest,[2] show clearly what little foundation there is in the Vatican's assurances that there is in the Central Empires disposition to make serious concessions to the Entente.

An answer to the Holy See or any promise of an answer would irremediably compromise the general situation.

T MS (SDR, RG 59, 763.72119/912½, DNA).
  [1] RLhw.
  [2] At a dinner in Budapest on October 2, Czernin said that Austria-Hungary was prepared for a reasonable peace but would have to reconsider its position if the Allies were unwilling to negotiate one. Wolfgang Steglich, ed., *Der Friedensappell Papst Benedikts XV. vom I. August 1917 und die Mittelmächte* (Wiesbaden, 1970), pp. 400-404.

Benjamin Strong to Joseph Patrick Tumulty

Dear Mr. Tumulty: [New York] October 10, 1917.

Your note of yesterday has just reached me and naturally is disappointing.

It seems to be necessary that I should explain the exact situation in regard to the Liberty Loan, as it will make clear why I have felt so urgently the need for assistance from the President at this time.

The people of this country do not yet realize the issues of the war. The object of the meeting in Carnegie Hall, when Lord Reading is to make an address, is to submit to the people of the country the fact that the issue in this war is constitutional government. The president alone can give the meeting exactly the character and influence desired.

But there are other considerations bearing on the success of the loan which are causing us much anxiety. The burden of taxation to be imposed by the new revenue bill will necessarily be very heavy. It particularly applies to corporations which, while they have made large profits, have at the same time so increased investments in plant and inventory that they must borrow heavily in order to pay their taxes. And to add to the difficulties of a very complicated situation, many of the large railroad systems of the country and the holders of their securities are also beginning to have grave anxiety as to their ability to raise money for absolutely necessary purposes, including refunding, and to make heavy tax payments, during the period that such enormous demands are being made by the Government upon the money markets.

It is no exaggeration to say that the country's money center has developed a desperately gloomy view of the outlook, which is seriously affecting the results of our labor of placing the Government's bonds. I believe this can all be swept away and the last week of our campaign be made a stampede if the President could arrange to make an address in New York and make it one of confidence and reassurance.

It is probably unnecessary for me to state in detail what is being done here to insure stable monetary conditions in the Government's interest. This bank is lending its resources just as freely as may be demanded of it. The banks of the city are taking hundreds of millions of the Government's obligations every week or two in order that temporary financing may be successful pending the bond issue. Sixty seven of the largest New York City banks and trust companies have undertaken to lend generally in the money markets a total of $231,000,000., which amount they will increase if necessary. The firms and institutions represented on the Liberty Loan Committee, of which I am chairman, have just entered into an obligation to purchase up to $100,000,000 of the outstanding 3½% bonds and the new 4% bonds in order that they may not sell below par while the new issue is being placed. Trust companies with total resources of $1,600,000,000. have been brought into the Federal Reserve System. Other things of less importance are being done as needed, but it is nevertheless a fact that a great deal of concern exists in financial circles as to the outlook for the railroads and corporations that must soon be heavy borrowers, and nothing will change this situation so positively as an address by the President.

I also want to point out one important feature of this loan. The minimum of $3,000,000,000. must be greatly exceeded. If this loan is very heavily over-subscribed, succeeding loans will be undertaken with a degree of confidence that will not exist if this one is barely sold and no more. In other words, I believe, to make this loan a success will have a greater effect upon subsequent loans than anything else that can be done, and it is most important that we should not approach the spring, when even larger borrowings must be effected, with a feeling that the financial situation must be rescued, but rather that it does not need rescue.

You will be interested to know that we have now, according to the best estimate, about one hundred thousand people in this district working on the loan. They themselves today need encouragement.

I regret very much feeling the necessity for writing so urgently on this matter, but feel sure that the President realizes that the men who are associated with me in this work are devoting every energy and resource at their command to make the loan a success, and I am convinced that nothing will be so encouraging and contribute so greatly to making their labor a success as the support of the President's well known courage, publicly stated at this time.   Very truly yours,   [Benjamin Strong]

CCL (B. Strong Papers, Federal Reserve Bank of N. Y.-Ar).

Sir William Wiseman to Edward Mandell House, with Enclosure

Dear Mr. House: [New York] October 10, 1917.

I am attaching to this letter a memorandum on the subject of the three councils we have been discussing. Council number one is, of course, already in existence and meets from time to time. The other two councils are not as yet formed, but I understand that your government favors the idea, in principle at any rate. It must be quite clear, however, that the three councils are entirely separate and do not in any way depend on one another. Council number one is the one which was referred to in the letter to the President[1] and is, of course, by far the most important of the three. The British Government, and I am quite sure the French and Italian agree with us, want you to attend council number one as the American representative. We also want American representatives on councils two and three, but I feel very strongly that you ought not to be concerned with the operations of numbers two and three. When we first suggested that you should come to Europe to attend council number one we naturally thought of it as a temporary visit because, of course, this council would not sit for more than a week or so.

The question that occurs to me is whether if you stay permanently you can avoid being overwhelmed with the work of two and three. Council number one is a war council in the most important sense and concerns only a very few men at the very top. The Blockade and Supply Councils concern the heads of all departments, at the same time both these councils are of essential importance and must be conducted smoothly and effectively in order to win the war.

It has been our experience that when you come to questions of policy you cannot separate naval and military operations from supplies, shipping, finance. Each one of these affects the other and they cannot be kept in watertight compartments. I believe that if you will go over and attend the war council and stay in Europe to the end of the war you cannot avoid dealing with all the problems that arise after they have reached a certain point of importance. It would seem to me better to face the situation from the outset and realize that your government is taking a very important step. In my opinion it is no less than shifting the center of gravity of the war from Washington to London and Paris. It would be a bad thing for American prestige to have American representatives in Europe who are not able to give decisions, and apart from that such representatives would not be able to help things along and might as well not be there. From the point of view of carrying on the war most effectively I have no doubt that it would be best to send a permanent American Commission with offices in both London and Paris. The Commission should have both naval and military representatives and members of the commission would be American representatives on all of the three councils we have mentioned. This, in my opinion, is the only practicable and effective way of getting proper cooperation, but there remain the two difficulties to be overcome. In the first place you must contemplate delegating an important part of the authority of the American Government to the Commission; and secondly, you must consider whether, if you go as head of the Commission, it would be possible for you to keep clear of the many vital problems which arise almost daily in the cooperation of the Allies and devote sufficient time to those problems which are really the most important and which you have made your particular study.

Believe me,   Yours very sincerely,   W Wiseman

This was written very hastily & is, I fear, badly expressed but I hope it may serve its purpose.

I cannot help seeing many difficulties in the new proposal. Would it be possible to make your visit appear as of a temporary nature.

If you found it worked out well you could stay on. This might give you the opportunity of returning here for a while if you thought it wiser.   W.

TLS with Hw PS (E. M. House Papers, CtY).
[1] That is, D. Lloyd George to WW, Sept. 3, 1917.

ENCLOSURE

In discussing the question of American representation in Europe three councils have been mentioned at which it is thought the United States ought to be represented. They are as follows:

1. The Allied Council of War.

This council is composed of representatives of the Allied Governments, including naval and military representatives. This council has met before and will meet again whenever it is found necessary. The members of the council have supreme authority from their governments to discuss the political aims of the Allies and the various military objectives which may help to realize these aims. The next meeting of this council is fixed for October 15th in Paris, and the most important matter which will be discussed at this meeting of the council is the military strategy to be employed by the Allies in the coming year as, in modern warfare on as large a scale as the present war, it is necessary to determine the military strategy and lay out plans at least six months before they can come to fruition. It is necessary, therefore, for the Allies to meet within the next few weeks and settle the military plans which they hope to carry out successfully next spring and summer. It was this council which was referred to in the letter which the President received. It would be possible, of course, for American representatives to attend this council and return to Washington when the council had concluded its session. The meeting now fixed for the 15th of October could not be postponed, but it would be quite possible for the meeting to adjourn to a future date in order to await the arrival of the American representatives.

2. The Inter-allied Council.

This council has not been formed, but the subject has been under discussion for some months and was first suggested by Mr. McAdoo. The object of this council would be to regulate supplies amongst the Allies. All requisitions made on behalf of any of the Allied governments for money, munitions of war, food, shipping, coal, etc., would be passed upon by this council. The purpose would be to determine which requisition ought to have priority for the good of the common cause. It is suggested that the council should sit in London but that the section dealing with finance should be located in Paris. This council would, of course, sit permanently until the end of the war.

3. The Joint Embargo or Blockade Council.

This council is not yet in existence but it would be intended to provide effective machinery to carry out joint negotiations with neutral countries. The Exports Board at Washington is already acting informally with the British and French experts. The proposed council would insure that British blockade measures should not clash with the policy of the American Government. The main business of the council would be to regulate supplies to neutral countries. This council would also sit permanently until the end of the war, but would have its headquarters in London.   Wiseman,   Oct. 10, 1917

TS MS (E. M. House Papers, CtY).

A Memorandum by Robert Lansing

MEMORANDUM of Conference with
VISCOUNT ISHII, A.M.
OCTOBER 10, 1917.

On the 8th Viscount Ishii left with me a draft of the proposed note from this Government to Japan, showing in lead pencil the changes desired by his Government in the note. (The document is hereto attached.)

The Viscount called upon me this morning and asked if I had had an opportunity to consider the changes proposed. I told him that I had and that so far as striking out the second paragraph on the first page and making the insertion which he proposed it would be agreeable to this Government.

As to the next change, which appears on the third page of the document,[1] I said that while I admitted the phrase which his Government desired to have eliminated would not materially affect the document, it seemed to me that both Governments were losing a very great opportunity of placing themselves in a generous light before the Allied Powers.

The Viscount replied he realized that, but that there were political reasons at home which he felt embarrassed his Government in accepting the phrase as it stood, especially as the preceding declarations cover the entire ground.

I said to him that while I felt that was so, the direct declaration that neither of the Governments would seek advantage during the war would receive the greatest applause in the Allied countries; that those countries were in difficult financial situations; that they were almost on the verge of bankruptcy; that Japan and the United States were the only countries who could use their resources in the development of China; and that it would be a noble and generous act to say to these countries—

"You have been fighting our battles and we will not take advantage of your condition but will hold your rights sacred and give you every opportunity to recover from this war along commercial and industrial lines in the Far East."

The Viscount replied to this that he was in full accord with me, but in view of his Government's desires he could not commit them to an acceptance of the phrase; but that he would immediately telegraph and explain the advantage of retaining it.

I said to him that of course it might be found politically impossible to concede this request, although it affected both nations equally; that I only saw one other way of making the document complete in case that phrase was rejected and that was to strike out the word "*other*" in the 4th line from the bottom of page 3; and that while I hoped his Government would not feel compelled to reject the clause proposed, especially as it only applied to the present time, it might not be inadvisable to consider the alternative proposal of striking out the word "other."

The Viscount said he would bear this in mind and also communicate with his Government.

We then discussed the matter of better telegraphic communication between Japan and the United States, and I made the suggestion to him that it might be advisable to appoint a joint commission of four to consider the subject, in order that they might work out a general plan of wireless and cable communication which would materially reduce the present rates and expedite the transmission of information.

The Viscount said he would communicate this to his Government at once and that it met with his approval.

I asked him if there had ever been any communication with any of the Allied Powers in regard to the military participation of Japan in the war. He said that almost three years ago the matter had been broached by Great Britain informally but that his Government had pointed out at that time the impossibility of maintaining a force at any considerable distance from Japan. I asked him if there had been any later communications and he said not to his knowledge. I therefore let the matter drop.

He left with the understanding that as soon as he had received a reply from his Government he would see me again.

T MS (SDR, RG 59, 793.94/594½, DNA).
¹ "Oct. 8/17 13."

To Albert Sidney Burleson

My dear Burleson: The White House 11 October, 1917

I am sure you will agree with me that we must act with the utmost caution and liberality in all our censorship, and in connection with it I want you to read the enclosed very thoughtful editorial from the Springfield Republican which is always moderate and always reflects the opinion of the very sort of people whose judgment we would like to have approve what we do.[1]

Cordially and faithfully yours, Woodrow Wilson

TLS (A. S. Burleson Papers, DLC).

[1] It is missing; however, it was "The Washington Censors," an editorial in the *Springfield*, Mass., *Republican*, Oct. 9, 1917. The editorial said that a number of liberal and radical supporters of the war effort were becoming increasingly apprehensive about Burleson's denial of mailing privileges to Socialist publications. The more the Postmaster General suppressed such publications, the editorial said, the more "depressed" would prowar liberals and radicals become. The editorial then concluded: "There would be solid reassurance in this matter if the censorship powers could be practically vested by the president in a special body composed of men whose public reputation for broad and liberal views would guarantee the country against a use of the censorship narrowly bureaucratic or intolerant or stupid. The powers now being exercised by the postal authorities in censoring the press are immensely important and their bearing on the popular support of the war may prove incalculable. The president has placed some of our foremost citizens in other places of high responsibility which the war emergency created; why should not men of national reputation for judgment and insight be given control of the war censorship powers of the post-office department?

"Frankly, neither Postmaster-General Burleson nor any of his subordinates seems to measure up to the job. They do not command public confidence as men exercising such authority should command it."

To Robert Lansing

My dear Mr. Secretary: The White House 11 October, 1917

You know the circumstances of our recent relations with Guatemala so much better than I do that I hesitate to form a judgment upon this matter before receiving an expression of your own views. If you regard President Estrada Cabrera as trustworthy, I think we should go to considerable lengths in expressing our friendship and our wish to serve Guatemala in any further way that may be possible, but I notice that the opinion expressed in the attached memorandum is not favorable to any further assurances to President Cabrera, and so I would be very much obliged for your own advice.

Cordially and sincerely yours, Woodrow Wilson

TLS (SDR, RG 59, 712.14/76, DNA).

To William Cox Redfield

Confidential.

My dear Mr. Secretary: [The White House] 11 October, 1917

The matter to which you call my attention in your letter of October eighth has given me a great deal of thought and a great deal of concern, but I am afraid that the suggestion made by our Consul at Aleppo, Mr. J. B. Jackson, could not wisely be complied with.

It would take a great deal of explaining to our American farmers and others; but more than that, there lies very near the surface in France, I have been told, a very considerable revolutionary feeling and this feeling may easily, it is thought, be stirred by any indication that men or women from other countries are going to take the place of French men and French women in the industrial life of that country. They have no objection, of course, to auxiliary forces of the Army working on the railways behind the lines and doing the things that are obviously connected with the operations and the supply of the armies, but they are intensely jealous of the intrusion of outsiders in the general industrial work of the country.

Cordially and sincerely yours,   [Woodrow Wilson]

CCL (WP, DLC).

To Samuel Reading Bertron

My dear Mr. Bertron: [The White House] 11 October, 1917

Of course, I did not mean to imply in my earlier letter that you were not speaking upon sufficient information. I merely meant to tell you the fact that I did not get such views of the depression in business circles from anywhere but New York, with the possible exception of certain banking circles in Boston. I meant to convey to you that cheering information.

I realize the importance of the matters that you call my attention to and they have caused me a great deal of concern, as well as having absorbed a great deal of my thought and attention. You may be sure I am glad to have them set forth by those who, like yourself, are in direct contact with business matters, and you may also be sure that I want to do everything in my power to help.

Cordially and sincerely yours,   Woodrow Wilson

TLS (Letterpress Books, WP, DLC).

To Joseph Wright Harriman

Personal.

My dear Mr. Harriman: [The White House] 11 October, 1917

Your letter of October eighth[1] presents a very serious picture of affairs. I must frankly say that I cannot believe that the situation looks so dark in most parts of the country, but, of course, I have no pride of opinion in the matter and it is one in which I would not venture to speak with confidence, since no one can thread the complexities of the situation without a very much wider observation and a very much fuller knowledge than I can pretend to.

You will understand that I may very often find it necessary to sign a bill like the tax bill, for example, in which there are items in which my judgment would not at all have concurred but the major features and parts of which seem to me necessary and legitimate. It is not possible for me to veto individual items and I must judge a bill by the large.

I do not see just what sort of statement I could make at present which would convey the reassurance you so much desire, but you may be sure that whatever uncertainties now distress the business world will be removed one by one at the earliest possible moment.

Cordially and sincerely yours,   Woodrow Wilson

TLS (Letterpress Books, WP, DLC).
    [1] It is missing.

To John Singer Sargent

My dear Mr. Sargent: [The White House] 11 October, 1917

Congress has adjourned and my mind turns to the suggestion I made that probably after the adjournment it would be possible for me to sit for the portrait which the Governors of the National Gallery of Ireland so generously desire.[1]

I would be very glad to know your own engagements and whether it would be convenient for you to come down next week or the week after.

I would also like to know, if it is possible for you to answer such a question, how much time it would probably be necessary for me to set aside for the purpose.

With the pleasantest anticipations of knowing you,
    Cordially and sincerely yours,   Woodrow Wilson

TLS (Letterpress Books, WP, DLC).
    [1] WW to J. S. Sargent, July 18, 1917, Vol. 43.

From Newton Diehl Baker

Dear Mr President   Washington October 11, 1917

The enclosed study will interest you. It is long but thorough.[1]

Respectfully   Newton D. Baker

ALS (WP, DLC).

[1] That is, the study referred to in NDB to WW, Sept. 22, 1917 (first letter of that date). Bliss noted that Wilson was receiving proposals from many quarters on how to conduct the war and said that, on September 22, he had instructed Col. P. D. Lochridge, Acting Chief of the War College Division, to have a report prepared for Baker on the best use of American forces. This report should explain the strategy of operating against the Central Powers on the western front instead of from the south. The report was to review the arguments for advancing through Italy, Macedonia, Mesopotamia, Russia, and other areas, and to give reasons why these routes should not be selected. Bliss suggested that the report emphasize the vital importance of the western front: "Manifestly overcoming France is a great objective of the Germans. With France crushed the plight of England and ourselves should be pointed out. While matters are at about a deadlock on the Western Front, a preponderance of two or three million men, which we hope to place there on the side of the Allies in the near future, promises a possibility of success. . . . Consider the effect on the morale of the French and English troops in France if we should announce a policy of pulling out to start a campaign of our own in a distant quarter of the world, where we would find great difficulty in supplying ourselves and to which place it is practically impossible to obtain sufficient transportation for troops at this time. . . . As Germany enjoys the enormous military advantage of interior lines she gains by the dissemination of efforts of the Allies. On the other hand, we gain by combining and cooperating with the strongest forces in the conflict." P. D. Lochridge to Committee Consisting of the Chairmen of the War College Division Committees, Sept. 22, 1917, T MS, with HwS notation by Bliss that this memorandum was a correct résumé of his instructions (WP, DLC).

Lochridge, on September 28, submitted to Bliss a memorandum, "Strategy of the present war," with three enclosures: "Memorandum on a strategic comparison of the Western Front with the Eastern Mediterranean," "Lines of advance against the Central Powers," and "Line of advance through Russia." P. D. Lochridge to T. H. Bliss, Sept. 28, 1917, T MSS (WP, DLC). The four papers amounted to twenty-three single-spaced typewritten pages. The basic memorandum gave these reasons why the United States Army was being sent to France: France was much closer than Russia and could be reached more securely; the need for men was greater in France; the Allies had requested that the main American effort be made there; the United States was already committed to a course of action there; prospects for victory were greatest there; and it was strategically sound to concentrate on the bulk of the enemy's forces. This first memorandum also analyzed other proposed plans of campaign and showed that they presented greater difficulties, both logistical and operational, and poorer prospects for success. Until the situation as to shipping, men, and equipment and the submarine menace had completely changed, Lochridge concluded, the possibility of operating in any of the other suggested theaters did not "warrant serious consideration." The three enclosed memoranda gave military, political, and geographical information to support Lochridge's conclusions.

The Wilson Papers, DLC, also contain some earlier drafts and related studies, as well as a letter drafted for Baker's signature and intended for George E. Chamberlain, Chairman of the Senate Military Affairs Committee. This letter, which was to explain why the United States should not adopt a proposal to send a force to Turkey, incorporated much of the language used in the documents described above. Baker did not sign the letter but instead returned it to Bliss with this note:

"Please send this admirable letter to the President. I do not think it should be sent to Senator Chamberlain. We should not discuss this question in writing with anyone. The possibility of its falling into unauthorized hands is too great.

"The people will simply have to rest in the assurance that the military authorities know their business." NDB to T. H. Bliss, c. Oct. 5, 1917, CC MS (WP, DLC).

From David Lloyd George

[London] Oct. 11th. '17.

No. 27. Please give paraphrase of following message to Brussa [House] from Falsterbo [Balfour]:

Provided, of course, you see no objection, I should be grateful if you felt able to communicate following message from Prime Minister to Adramyti [Wilson]:

I venture to invite your earnest attention to following facts in shipping position. Total world tonnage lost by enemy action first thirty months of war was about four and a half million tons gross. A further four & a quarter million tons was lost in first seven months of intensive submarine campaign. At rate of loss during this campaign and allowing for marine risk losses and for serious damage to vessels not actually sunk, total loss in world tonnage may be taken at about eight million tons gross per annum, this rate being rather more favourable than previous estimate of (eight and a * * * million) tons as result of recent improvement which at the moment is being maintained. Against this Great Britain whose building last year was brought down to some 600.000 tons gross through expenditure of strength in other directions, is making immense efforts to build two and a half million tons (next) year, but it is feared that it will be impossible to realize this programme fully. Allowing for building in rest of world outside America and at present rate of loss this means deficit of at least five and a half million tons gross per annum. Meanwhile, as you know, tonnage, even apart from future losses, is very seriously short of what is needed to meet Allied military and civilian requirements. In (the) spring tonnage must be limiting factor to operations in every sphere. It is important to make it clear now that Great Britain sees no prospect of being able both to continue her own naval and military share in war and to transport in her own ships supplies for forces and for civilian population and also to continue to give as many ships to her Allies as heretofore. At same time needs of France and Italy for food and coal, already great, will, in the spring, be extremely serious. Similarly Russia may want supplies for 1918 White Sea season for which British vessels will not be available. This will be time when America will be faced with great problem of transporting her own armies and supplies. In the circumstances earnestly suggest you should consider whether it is not possible for

America to commence building programme sufficient with building in rest of world to outbuild submarine destruction at present
rate, i.e. programme of say six million tons gross per year. This
means, of course, immense effort, but you will remember that the
reason why it is possible for us to build on this scale is that in
common with our Allies we had to expend our strength on immediate necessities in early stage of war, of increasing armies,
navies and munitions and strength is now committed in these
directions. A much smaller effort directed to shipbuilding would
have enabled us to outbuild submarine destruction even at present rate. It was only in third year of war, however, that merchant
shipping became a factor as vital as armies, navies and munitions. It is at this stage that America, whose industrial and engineering resources are greatest of any country, entered into the
war, and effort required to outbuild submarine destruction, immense as it is, is relatively small compared with the tasks successfully achieved by Allies in other directions. To build six
million tons gross would take about three and a half million tons
of steel, or less than 10% of American output and perhaps half
a million men, majority unskilled. If programme of kind suggested were at once (definitely) taken in hand and pressed vigorously it might, we suggest, have an effect on German hopes
and consequently on German endurance altogether out of proportion to any similar effect even before any large number of
vessels had actually been built. No building programme of the
kind indicated above could, of course, mature soon enough to
provide number of ships which will be demanded next spring,
but knowledge that ships will be available at later dates will make
it possible to work on narrower margins and would materially
assist to get through extremely critical period before the harvests
of next summer. It is true that during last week or two amount
of tonnage destroyed by submarines has materially diminished,
but we cannot yet be sure that this improvement is more than
temporary. It would clearly be very rash to base any permanent
policy or calculations upon it and I cannot therefore too strongly
emphasize most serious danger that relatively much greater expenditure of effort in other directions by all countries at war
with Germany may be nullified and rendered ineffective if effort
in this direction of building ships is inadequate.

America is training a great army. It is of the greatest importance that it should be transported and maintained without
withdrawing so many ships engaged in maintaining present
forces as will subtract as much strength from them as American
army will add.

Owing to secrecy of cipher W. it is important that Prime Minister's message should be adequately paraphrased.

T telegram (W. Wiseman Papers, CtY).

To Joseph Patrick Tumulty, with Enclosure

Dear Tumulty: [The White House, c. Oct. 12, 1917]

I do not think I ought to reply to this letter. I would be obliged if you would acknowledge it and say that it does not seem possible for me to take part in discussions where I am not present to hear both sides. The President.

TL (WP, DLC).

ENCLOSURE

From Frank Coe Barnes[1]

Dear Sir: Schenectady, New York 8 October 1917

The New York State Modern Language Association, an organization of some six hundred teachers in this state, and one of the constituent bodies of the Federation of Modern Language teachers including New England, the Middle States, and the states of the middle West and South, holds its annual convention at Syracuse in Thanksgiving week of this year and the undersigned has been deputed as retiring president of the Association and past chairman of the Federation to ask an expression of opinion from you on the topic named below. We ask also your permission to have your reply read before the convention.

We realize that, with the great duties devolving upon you, it might even under normal conditions be difficult for you to find time to answer us and that in the present great crisis it may be impossible for you to do so, but we also know your deep concern for everything that affects the welfare of the American people and we believe that our problem properly comes under that head, as it deals with the interests of the youth of the land.

This is our question:

There is at present in many quarters a tendency on the part of school boards and some other bodies in charge of educational matters to discontinue or at least discourage the study of the German language in our schools because we are at war with Germany. In view of the great value of this language, both from the cultural and pedagogicol side and from the commercial or so-called practical standpoint, is this movement wise or unwise? From the point of view of the educator and of the merchant has not this language now, and will it not continue to have, regardless of the war and its outcome, the same great worth as a subject of study in our high schools and colleges which it has had in the past?

It is needless to say that even the briefest statement of your views in this connection will be of the greatest help to us and will be most gratefully received.

Assuring you, on behalf of our association, of our earnest sympathy and full support in the great work which you are doing for our country, I am

Most respectfully yours,   F C Barnes

TLS (WP, DLC).
[1] Professor of Modern Languages at Union College.

To Joseph Patrick Tumulty

Dear Tumulty: [The White House, c. Oct. 12, 1917]

I doubt if it would be wise for me to return a personal acknowledgment of these resolutions[1] because they so directly reflect upon the character of a Senator of the United States. Do you not think it would be well for me to delegate to you the acknowledgment along with an expression of my warm appreciation of the patriotic feeling and purpose embodied?   The President.

TL (WP, DLC).
[1] These resolutions by the Wisconsin state and county councils of defense, meeting at Madison, stated that Senator La Follette had hindered the councils, encouraged opposition to the government in its prosecution of the war, and misrepresented the true sentiment of the vast majority of the people of Wisconsin. The councils condemned La Follette's stand as "aiding and abetting the enemy" and demanded his resignation and, if he refused to resign, asked the United States Senate to expel him. State Council of Defense to WW, Oct. 9, 1917, T telegram (WP, DLC).

To Ollie Murray James

[The White House] October 12, 1917

Mrs. Wilson and I extend to you our profound sympathy in your sorrow.[1] God grant you comfort and solace.

Woodrow Wilson

T telegram (Letterpress Books, WP, DLC).
[1] Elizabeth (Mrs. L. H.) James, mother of Senator James, had died on October 12 at her home in Marion, Ky.

From Grenville Stanley Macfarland

My dear President Wilson,   [Washington] October 12, 1917.

I can not help calling to your attention the proclaimed attitude of the Postmaster General toward alleged "seditious" newspapers.[1] I think that I can express my mind to you without personal interest because it appears to be beyond the power of the Postmaster to harm the newspapers with which I am associated even if they should pass his dead line. The denial of the mailing privileges would mean an insignificant loss of circulation in one direction and a huge gain in another.

It strikes me that there is error both in the Postmaster's formula of regulation and in the method of applying it. To say that the government may be criticised freely, but that subserviency to Wall Street or to profiteerers etc. etc. may not be charged, is like telling a child that he may go in swimming but must not go near the water.

Moreover, the application of any general formula seeking to regulate the freedom of opinion expression by a newspaper, is the exercise of a power of the first degree in a democracy—a pregnant, serious, delicate act even toward the humblest publication. It ought not to be an act of technique but of statesmanship in *every case*. It ought not to be in the hands of a man without vision. Surely not in the hands of a subordinate of a subordinate.

You know better than I, that the American people—especially the middle classes and ["]intellectuals," are more nervous about anything that concerns free speech than about anything else. The Columbia College affair is only in its first episode.[2] Watch it develope.

Please, my dear President Wilson, do not let the government, in these critical days, generate and unnecessarily confine a lot of explosive gas, either through the use of a wrong formula or the bungling of a remote and mechanical subordinate.

I trouble you with this long-hand note because I feel this so strongly and have no confidential clerk to whom I can dictate it, here in Washington.   Yours sincerely   G. S. Macfarland

ALS (WP, DLC).

[1] Macfarland enclosed a news account from the *New York Times*, Oct. 10, 1917, under the headline: "Burleson Tells Newspapers What They May Not Say." It described an Executive Order expected to be issued shortly by Wilson to establish various restrictions authorized by the Trading with the Enemy Act. The *Times* also reported that Burleson had said that publications need not fear suppression under the Act unless they transgressed the bounds of legitimate criticism of the President, the administration, the army, the navy, or the conduct of the war. Burleson was quoted as saying the following:

"We shall take great care not to let criticism which is personally or politically offensive to the Administration affect our action. But if newspapers go so far as to impugn the motives of the Government and thus encourage insubordination, they will be dealt with severely.

"For instance, papers may not say that the Government is controlled by Wall Street or munition manufacturers, or any other special interests. Publications of any news calculated to urge the people to violate law would be considered grounds for drastic action. We will not tolerate campaigns against conscription, enlistments, sale of securities, or revenue collections. We will not permit the publication or circulation of anything hampering the war's prosecution or attacking improperly our allies."

Burleson also said that no Socialist paper would be barred from the mails unless it contained treasonable or seditious matter. "The trouble," he added, "is that most Socialist papers do contain this matter."

[2] The trustees of Columbia University, on October 1, had dismissed from the faculty James McKeen Cattell, Professor of Psychology, and Henry Wadsworth Longfellow Dana, Assistant Professor of English, on charges that they had disseminated doctrines tending to encourage a spirit of disloyalty to the United States Government. The trustees referred to letters written in August by Cattell to members of Congress urging them to vote against sending drafted soldiers to Europe. The trustees also referred to Dana's activities as a member of the People's Council. *New York Times*, Oct. 2, 1917. A week later, on October 8, Charles Austin Beard, Professor of Political Science, resigned from the university and gave as his reason that the institution had fallen under the control of a small and active group of trustees, who, although they were "without standing in the world of education," were "reactionary and visionless in politics," and "narrow and mediaeval in religion," had the power to throttle freedom of expression at Columbia University, and had done so. *Ibid.*, Oct. 9, 1917.

From George Creel

Dear Mr. President: Washington, D. C. Oct. 12th, 1917.

With regard to attached,[1] I hope to see you Tuesday. May I ask that nothing be done until then. I am going to New York to-morrow to complete arrangements for the expenditure of $1,000,000. contributed to Russian publicity by Mr. Thompson.[2]

Respectfully, George Creel

TLS (WP, DLC).

[1] It is missing.

[2] William Boyce Thompson, a New York banker and mining investor, was "ostensibly" business manager of the American Red Cross Commission to Russia, with the rank of lieutenant colonel. For accounts of his activities in Russia, see Hermann Hagedorn, *The Magnate: William Boyce Thompson and His Time, 1869-1930* (New York, 1935), pp. 180-251; George F. Kennan, *Russia Leaves the War* (Princeton, N. J., 1956), pp. 52-62; and George Creel, *Rebel at Large* (New York, 1947), pp. 176-77.

A Memorandum by Robert Lansing, with Enclosure

MEMORANDUM of Conference with
VISCOUNT ISHII, October 12, 1917.

Viscount Ishii called upon me this morning by appointment and said that there were two or three suggested changes in the draft of the proposed note to him which he had been instructed to make by his Government, but which he had, at our former interview, thought it needless to do. He had, however, since that time, received direct instructions to suggest the changes and he therefore did so.

(The changes which he suggested appear on the second page of the draft which he submitted to me with corrections on October 8th.)

After examining the changes I said to him that the first and fourth proposals, which include the insertion of the words—"and influence"—we could not accept; that I was afraid of the construction which would be placed upon the word "influence" as meaning political influence; and that not only in this country but in China such an interpretation would cause grave anxiety.

As to the second and third proposals I would be glad to take them into consideration.

Viscount Ishii explained as to the second proposal that it seemed unnecessary, in view of the paragraph at the top of the third page, and that the Japanese people were very sensitive about their purposes being doubted; and the paragraph which he proposed to eliminate gave the impression that it was intended to bind them to something which they promised to do in another part of the note in conjunction with the United States.

I perceived that there was a measure of reason in his position and therefore agreed to take the matter under consideration.

The third proposed change was not suggested by his Government; it was intended not to limit the special influence to the Japanese Government but to make them apply to Japan as a nation. While I said I would take the matter under consideration I felt that there was little reason to object to the proposal.

The Ambassador also submitted to me a draft of a reply to the proposed note which I told him seemed to be entirely acceptable but that I would like to consider it before saying so.

E N C L O S U R E

THE SPECIAL MISSION OF JAPAN

> Handed me by Viscount Ishii,
> Oct. 12/17 RL.

(Draft.)

Sir:

I have the honor to acknowledge the receipt of your note of to-day, communicating to me your understanding of the agreement reached by us in our recent conversations touching the questions of mutual interests to our Governments relating to the Republic of China.

I am happy to be able to confirm to you, under authorization of my Government, the understanding in question set forth in the following terms:—

In order to silence mischievous reports * * * *

I take this opportunity to convey to you, Sir, the assurances of my highest consideration.

TC MSS (R. Lansing Papers, NjP).

Lord Reading to the War Cabinet and Others

Washington, D. C. 12th. October, 1917.

Q. 54. Urgent. *Private* VERY SECRET. From Lord Reading to War Cabinet, Mr. Balfour and Chancellor of Exchequer.

I had long interview today with President and House. We again discussed question of closer co-operation between U. S. and Allies and the desirability of U. S. appointing representatives to sit on the Councils of the Allies. President said that hitherto he had been indisposed to appoint representatives owing to the want of experience of U. S. in the war, but that he would now view favourably an invitation from the Allies that a representative of U. S. should attend the Allies Military Council and also, the Inter-Allied Council dealing with priority of supplies from U. S. to the Allies.

(1) *Military Council.*

President expressed opinion that U. S. representative would not be in position to take very active part in Military Council owing to want of sufficient experience but he thought it would be of advantage for the U. S. to be represented.

(2) *Inter-Allied Council on supplies from U. S.*

President stated that he was prepared to accede to request to appoint U. S. representative and, if the Allies desired it, he would assent to this representative acting as chairman of this Council. I said that it had been, and I believe still was, the wish of the British and Allied Governments that the U. S. representative should preside.

(3) *Inter-Allies Blockade Council.*

President is not favourably disposed to appointment of representative, as he thinks it better that U. S. should keep control of its own exports and should not be regarded as being controlled by agreement with Allies. I think the underlying reason for this view is related to internal politics and that President thinks trouble might possibly be caused if it were thought that the restrictions on exports, and consequently on Traders' operations, were directed from England. It must always be remembered that there is, as explained in previous cables, a body of opinion that regards too close an agreement with England, particularly in trade matters, with some apprehension and even suspicion. The President appeared to have come to a decision in his own mind upon this point, and I therefore suggested that notwithstanding this conclusion he should consider the sending of a representative from the U. S. Board of Exports Control to England for the purpose of conferring with British Blockade Minister and other authorities upon blockade matters without actually being appointed a representative on the Council. President was favourably disposed towards this suggestion. I do not think his decision against representative on the Blockade Council should be regarded as final for all time.

(4) *Procedure*.

I told President that the probable course of procedure would be for the Allied Governments to send instructions without delay to their respective Ambassadors at Washington to tender formal invitation to the President to appoint representatives of U. S. on each of the three Councils.

(5) I took the opportunity of pointing out to President that in some respects the U. S. Departments were proceeding with their programme without regard to the requirements of the Allies and that some more effective control should be devised for the purpose of considering and determining how best to utilise the available resources of the U. S. having regard more particularly to the actual conduct of military operations by the Allied armies in the field. He said he had been considering the means of solving the problem and we discussed possible ways of remedying present situation. I am hopeful that he will take matter in hand immediately as it is urgent. The delay is not owing to any want of goodwill by members of the Administration or to lack of appreciation of urgency. Individually each Minister agrees that a remedy must be found without delay but Ministers are very busy.

T telegram (FO 115/2309, pp. 133-35, PRO).

From the Diary of Josephus Daniels

1917 Friday 12 October

Cabinet—Baker told of fact that most men drafted preferred infantry, small guns & artillery & few quartermaster duty & this showed they wished to fight as much as the men who volunteered. The conscientious objectors are segregated, no harm done them,

& one by one they come out and say they are ready to serve. Heads of churches opposed to fighting are writing urging that these men be put to work and not remain idle. More democratic feeling in the army.

WW talked of conditions abroad & spoke of suggestion that he appoint a commission on reconstruction after the war. He said Jusserand went up in the air when he read W's statement no selfish trade arrangements after the war. Some will wish to have league to prevent Germany trading with the world. This country will have the money & can compel the nations to measure up to our standard or not be given credit. We must impose these American views upon Europe for the good of all. To try to shut up Germany would be to plan to have another war & would be contrary to American views.

Lansing: England should put her Australian ships into carrying wheat to her & France.

Benson to go to France with House & Bliss

Two Letters to Edward Mandell House

My dear House: The White House 13 October, 1917

I find in my pocket the memorandum you gave me about the Zionist movement. I am afraid I did not say to you that I concurred in the formula suggested from the other side. I do, and would be obliged if you would let them know it.

    Cordially and faithfully yours,   Woodrow Wilson

TLS (E. M. House Papers, CtY).

Dear House,   [The White House, c. Oct. 13, 1917]

There is nothing particularly new in this,[1] but you will be interested.   W.W.

ALI (E. M. House Papers, CtY).
[1] A CC of WHP to WW, Oct. 8, 1917, No. 7363.

To Albert Sidney Burleson

My dear Burleson: [The White House] 13 October, 1917

I can't answer this letter of Macfarland's until I know what he is talking about. There are quotations in the letter from what appears to be a statement issued by the Post Office Department. Will you not let me see the statement and tell me also what sort of reassurance ought to be conveyed to Mr. Macfarland? He is a real friend and a real patriot.

Faithfully yours,   [Woodrow Wilson]

CCL (WP, DLC).

To Carrie Clinton Lane Chapman Catt

My dear Mrs. Catt: [The White House] 13 October, 1917

May I not express to you my very deep interest in the campaign in New York for the adoption of woman suffrage, and may I not say that I hope that no voter will be influenced in his decision with regard to this great matter by anything the so-called pickets may have done here in Washington? However justly they may have laid themselves open to serious criticism, their action represents, I am sure, so small a fraction of the women of the country who are urging the adoption of woman suffrage that it would be most unfair and argue a very narrow view to allow their actions to prejudice the cause itself. I am very anxious to see the great State of New York set a great example in this matter.

Cordially and sincerely yours,   Woodrow Wilson

TLS (Letterpress Books, WP, DLC).

To Newton Diehl Baker

My dear Mr. Secretary: The White House 13 October, 1917

Thank you very much for your reply under date of October ninth to my inquiries concerning the action of Colonel Dentler. I believe that the matter has been handled in a proper way.

Cordially and sincerely yours,   Woodrow Wilson

TLS (N. D. Baker Papers, DLC).

From John Singer Sargent

Boston, Mass., October 13, 1917.

Letter received. Will you kindly wire me if it will be convenient to begin sittings Wednesday, October seventeenth. If so, can reach Washington Tuesday night.   Sargent.

T telegram (WP, DLC).

Sir William Wiseman to Sir Eric Drummond

[New York] Octr. 13, 1917.

Very urgent and Very secret, No. 25.

(A). Ever since READING and I arrived in the States, we have been urging that U.S.G. should send fully-empowered representatives to London or Paris to deal at first-hand with the Allied Governments on the most urgent questions which require co-operation.

(B). READING had an interview with the President on this subject soon after arrival, and has discussed it on several occasions with other members of the Administration, while I have very frequently discussed it with HOUSE, who has been in New York. In the meantime invitations and suggestions were received from the French and Italian Commissions, and from various departments of our Government through the Embassy and Northcliffe, requesting the U.S.G. to send representatives on various matters, particularly supplies.

(C). This led to some confusion, and U.S.G. were not quite sure what was wanted or which was the most urgent request. The main suggestions, however, narrowed down to a request for United States representation on the three following Councils:

No. 1. The Inter-Allied War Council, which I understand is meeting on Monday, the 15th., particularly to discuss military plans for this Winter and next Spring, also to consider generally the political situation.

No. 2. An Inter-Allied Council originally proposed by MCADOO as a solution of financial difficulties. This would be a priority council, dealing with finance, supplies[,] shipping, etc., and would sit permanently in London or Paris. All applications for money or supplies from the United States would be dealt with by this Council and priority decided.

No. 3. A joint British-American Blockade or Embargo Council, which would sit in London, and utilise the machinery of our Ministry of Blockade, but in such a way as not to clash with the policy of the American Government.

There were other proposed councils, but these appear to be the most important in the order in which I have placed them.

(D). On October 3rd. I received No. 127 from Phillips,[1] asking for an immediate decision on the question of an American Representative on the Inter-Allied Supply Council.

HOUSE at once wrote fully to the President,[2] and received a telegram in reply that he approved of the appointment of an

American Chairman,[3] which news I communicated at once in my No. 20 of October 7th to you.[4]

It was evident, however, that there was some confusion in the President's mind regarding these various proposed councils, and that personal interviews were necessary in order to get the matter settled clearly. Also READING had received no reply from the President as to American participation in the Allied War Council.

HOUSE therefore went on Tuesday to stay at the White House especially to settle these matters. He returned to New York last night. At his request I also went to Washington.

(E). After several discussions between the President and House, and a meeting with Reading yesterday, the President said that his policy had been not to send American representatives to sit in the councils of the Allies because he felt the United States had not enough experience in the war, but on the information that we had given him he had changed his mind and come to the conclusion that it was necessary for the U. S. to be represented. The difficulty is that there are so few men who could be spared whom he would trust in that capacity. He informed House definitely that he would not send anyone unless House would go, and asked him to proceed to Europe as soon as possible, and stay there as special American representative until the end of the war. House was very much opposed to going at all, because he has devoted all his energies to the subject which interests him most, namely: that of peace terms and the American case for the Peace Conference. You know that the President has officially charged him to prepare the American case. House felt that his work was that of a peace envoy and that he was now being asked to go on a War mission that would deal with war measures and co-operation for war. As foreshadowed in my previous cables, he has tried to get the President to send either BAKER or LANSING, or both. Finally he agreed to accept the mission provided it was clearly understood that it was to be only for the purpose of attending the Inter-Allied War Council, and that he would be able to return to the States immediately that was finished.

(F). If HOUSE goes, the President will probably send a representative of the Treasury, chief of [or] deputy-chief of the Army and Navy Staff, a representative of the Committee dealing with supplies, and a representative of the Embargo Committee. Although House will not officially concern himself with these matters, he will be able to consult with his American colleagues in London on questions of policy and it should then be possible for our Government to arrange for permanent American representation on the Blockade and Supply Councils.

(G). The main difficulty now is the question of dates. There has been such a delay in getting a decision from the President that there must be an adjournment of the Council of the 15th. October for at least a month if House is to attend. READING has intimated that he thinks the necessary adjournment could be made, and it is on this idea that the present plan is based. If the War Council cannot be adjourned to allow for House's arrival, I am afraid the whole question would have to be re-opened again. Stop. Whilst my personal opinion is that the President would still be willing to send House to confer informally with the Allied Chiefs, he might not think it worth sending him if the military plans for the coming year are settled before he arrives, and I am sure House would not go only to discuss co-operation on supplies and finance.

(H). Reading has suggested that the Council of October 15th. should be adjourned to November 15th; that House should leave about the 1st. November, arriving in London about the 10th, as he would require a few days consultation before the Council. It is evident that if this plan is adopted House and his party must immediately make their arrangements for departure; indeed, they are already beginning to do so. If, therefore, this plan is not practicable, and the Council cannot be adjourned, we should be informed without a moment's delay. You will probably cable to Reading, who is in Washington, but I suggest that you should also cable to me in New York as I am living in the same building as House and can get him at any moment, and the President has really left the arrangements in his hands.

(I). If the mission goes, I think we ought to strain every point to send either the "Mauretania" or the "Olympic" to Halifax for them. If [It] would be enormously appreciated not only by the members of the commission but by the President, who is anxious about their safety.

(J). May I ask you on account of HOUSE's position, not to show this cable at any rate in entirely [entirely] to anyone except Balfour. We should remember particularly PAGE's position.

T telegram (W. Wiseman Papers, CtY).

1 C. J. Phillips to W. Wiseman, No. 127, Oct. 3, 1917, T telegram (W. Wiseman Papers, CtY).

2 EMH to WW, Oct. 5, 1917.

3 WW to EMH, Oct. 7, 1917.

4 W. Wiseman to E. Drummond, Oct. 7, 1917.

A Memorandum by Robert Lansing

MEMORANDUM of Conference with
VISCOUNT ISHII, October 13, 1917.

At my request Viscount Ishii came to the Department for a further discussion of the proposed changes in the draft of note which he had made on the 12th.

I told him that I wished to confirm what I had said that the words *"and influence"* appearing in his 1st and 4th proposals were entirely unacceptable and could not be considered; that the change of *"them"* to *"Japan"* was approved; and that the 2nd proposal, striking out the words "The territorial sovereignty of China, nevertheless, remains unimpaired, and—" had received very careful consideration.

I said that I appreciated the possible impression which the words might cause as to Japan's motives and purposes and was of course very desirous to avoid any language which would arouse criticism of his Government at home. I went on to say that possibly the words could be stricken out if the amendment B of October 8th was retained and the word "sovereignty" could be inserted in the phrase "the independence or territorial integrity of China," appearing twice on page 3.

I said the unwillingness of his Government to retain the words of B. of October 8th was a great disappointment to the President and to me and that I could not understand how they could fail to see the tremendous effect it would have on their Allies as well as on Germany. I said to him that certainly his Government did not propose to act contrary to the statement.

He replied, "Certainly not. It is only for the effect upon the people in Japan."

"But," I said, "that objection seems very trivial compared with the psychological value of such a generous announcement to the world. Is your Government willing to state this confidentially in the event that they will not come out openly and do so?"

The Viscount replied that he was convinced that they would do that, but that he appreciated himself the great value of including the statement in the note and was in entire accord with me as to the great influence it would have upon public opinion in the Allied countries and Germany. He said that he ought to say that he was laboring under great disadvantages with his own Government, that they did not consider him wholly loyal because he had been in an opposition cabinet, and that they, therefore, felt that he was not doing all that he might in urging their views.

Ishii spoke with much feeling and said that I must know that his Government's suspicions were groundless.

I replied that his Government were utterly wrong in their judgment as to his course, that he had most faithfully represented Japanese interests, and that no representative of his country had ever created so deep an impression on this Government and the American people as he had or done so much to restore full confidence in the good faith of Japan and the friendship of the Japanese people for America.

We then reverted to the text of the note and I urged the retention of the words in B of October 8th. The Viscount said that he would again take it up with his Government though he was not sanguine of success.

I then spoke of the inclusion of the word "sovereignty" on page 3 and pointed out that the word did not appear except in the phrase which his Government desired stricken out (Proposal 2, Oct. 12th). He said that it seemed to him that "independence" and "sovereignty" meant the same thing; and I was forced to confess that there was force in what he said, but that the President was most desirous to retain the word.

I suggested that possibly the phrase might read "the independence or territorial integrity and sovereignty of China," which would be a direct transference of "territorial sovereignty" from the phrase his Government desired to eliminate. The Viscount seemed favorable to this and said that he would propose it to his Government, but that I must remember that the words "independence and territorial integrity" were taken from the Root-Takahira agreement. I said that I realized that, but that this new agreement was broader in scope and ought not to be limited by previous language unless there was some reason for so doing, and that I felt that it would be more effective to exhibit originality rather than to repeat phrases already uttered.

Reverting to striking out B. of October 8th, I asked him if he had submitted to his Government the alternative suggestion in case it was omitted, namely the omission of "other" in the 4th line from the bottom of page 3. He said that he had not. I said that of course he understood the very consideration of elimination of the sentence depended upon the word "other" going out also.

We then went on to discuss other formulae and I suggested that possibly, in case his Government declined to omit "other," the world "mutually" might be changed to "severally." He did not see the full significance of this, which was to bind the United

States to opposition against special rights and privileges by Japan and *vice versa*. I also said that we might consider the insertion of the words "in the same way" after the word "opposed." I told him that I did not want this last suggestion, which he said pleased him, to be taken as an actual proposal until I had had more time to consider its exact meaning.

The Viscount again spoke of the unpleasant relations existing between him and his Government, that they felt that he should have seen and conferred more frequently with the President, and that they apparently had no conception of the relation existing between an Ambassador and the President in a negotiation of this sort. He said that he realized that their suggestions were out of the question, that when he was Minister of Foreign Affairs he would have been astounded if an Ambassador had asked to negotiate with the Emperor or the Premier, and that he presumed that he would be blamed and his course of action severely criticized. He spoke of this with some emotion and said that, if his Government would only give him a free hand and not consider him disloyal he was sure we would soon reach an agreement for he would assuredly include in the note the sentence which we so much desired and which he also desired.

He left with the understanding that he would communicate with me on hearing from his Government.

TC MS (R. Lansing Papers, NjP).

From the Diary of Colonel House

[New York] October 13, 1917.

I returned from Washington this morning. Gordon came over with me. I have had three or four strenuous days. The White House motor met us and I took Gordon and Louise to their home before going to the White House.

The President was over at the offices, having just finished a Cabinet meeting, and having some engagements which detained him. I sat in Mrs. Wilson's room with her, going over the happenings since we last met in New York. The President came in just before dinner and we had no talk until after we had eaten and gone to his study. He opened the conversation at once by saying that he was not willing that anyone should go abroad to represent him excepting me. "No one in America," and he whimsically added, "or in Europe either, knows my mind and I am not willing to trust them to attempt to interpret it." This was apropos of Lloyd George's request that someone should be sent to represent the United States at the next War Council.

The President knows that both the English and French desire me to come. The French have gone so far as to ask for me formally. The British have done so informally. Some of my recent letters will indicate that I thought it best that someone other than myself should go at this time, because the Central Powers might think it peace propaganda rather than a war measure, my name being so inseparably connected with peace. I suggested Baker or McAdoo, but the President would have none of them. We discussed the matter in detail, and the questions of strategy on each of the fronts. We spoke of the Italian campaign and the campaign in Asia Minor, and the partition or non-partition of Turkey.

The President suggested the making of another speech in which to say that our people must not be deceived by Germany's apparent willingness to give up Belgium and Alsace-Lorraine, for it would leave her impregnable in both Austria and Turkey and her dream of Mittle-Europa would be realized. He thought it important that our people should understand that the evacuation of both Belgium and France were a part of the Allies' program, and not so important a part as to restrict German power for evil in the future.

He thought he should say that Turkey should become effaced, and that the disposition of it should be left to the peace conference. Without advising that I thought it advisable to make such a speech now, I added that if it was made, it should be stated that Turkey must not be partitioned among the belligerents, but must become autonomous in its several parts according to racial lines. He accepted this addenda.

The President was surprised when I told him that the present Government in Russia did not desire the internationalization of the Dardanelles because they were afraid they would have to maintain a large fleet in the Black Sea, and they preferred the Black Sea to remain a Russian sea as at present. He thought this might be met by some form of guarantee, a suggestion, indeed, I have already made to the Russian Ambassador and other Russians with whom I have talked.

I told the President that Burleson desired to be a peace commissioner, in fact, everybody I knew desired to be one. The President replied, "do you think the American people would sustain me in being the only representative from the United States at the conference?" I did not know, and thought it was something to be considered later. There will of necessity be committees at the peace conference and there must be at least three commissioners in order to have representation on these committees, if for nothing else. Then, too, the other nations will have more than one and we should stultify ourselves. I put this idea of being sole representative at the peace conference in the President's mind some two years ago, but conditions then were quite different from those that confront us now. Then we were not in the war, and he would have gone over in quite a different capacity.

The President was tired and retired early in order to have a massage. Mrs. Wilson and I talked for a half hour and we too retired by ten o'clock.

On Wednesday the 10th, I went to the State Department and was with Lansing, Polk, Phillips, Gordon and others until lunch time. The President and I had no conversations at lunch or dinner, but after dinner we went into executive session until ten o'clock. We threshed out the question of my going abroad to represent the United States at the Allied War Council. We discussed whether we should have a representative on the Embargo Board. He strongly objected until I read him a memorandum from Sir William Wiseman which is attached to the record.[1] Wiseman has pointed out the danger of transferring the center of gravity from this country to Europe. He believes this is inevitable if I go abroad to remain as long as the President has in mind, and take with me a military, Naval, and economic staff.

This shook the President because he has no intention of loosening his hold on the situation.

We took up many other matters I had in mind to discuss with him, but all of comparatively minor importance. We discussed his successor, and whether or not he might come from the Cabinet, and whether McAdoo or Baker had the better chance.

On Thursday, the 11th, I had another busy day at the State Department. I also saw Jusserand, Reading, Wiseman, the Attorney General, the Postmaster General, and heaven knows who else.

Practically all the information which the British Foreign Office receives that is of value come[s] to me either directly or through Wiseman or Reading for me. Many of these cables are attached to the record, others I destroy.

I had a long talk with Lansing regarding the organization for the peace conference. He is eager to be in it and I want him to help and will endeavor to arrange it that way. In speaking to the President, however, he told me distinctly that he preferred everything to go to him rather than to the State Department, and he would refer to the State Department what he thought necessary. Later I got him to agree, since I am going to Europe, for Mezes to keep in touch with Lansing, but the President added, "and also with me." I shall arrange this and shall endeavor to give Lansing a larger and larger part. He is fond of detail work and can relieve me of much of that. His ideas are good along certain lines, especially as to technique, for which I have no liking.

On Friday the 12th, it was arranged for Lord Reading and Sir William Wiseman to come to the White House at twelve o'clock for a conference with the President and with me. Wiseman and I concluded afterward that it would be best for him not to come because it might hurt the sensibilities of Reading and Sir Ceceil Spring-Rice as well, therefore the President authorized me to eliminate Wiseman.

Sir William was disturbed at my decision to go to Europe, particularly, if my stay was to be a long one. He thought my influence abroad would be lessened because it would be impossible not to get tangled up with the jealousies and ambitions of the Allies. He thought I would be pulled this way and that, and it would be impossible to satisfy any of them. He also thought Lloyd George was making a distinct effort to use me to further his plans. George is afraid to antagonize the military and naval authorities by proposing a new objective in a field other than the Western Front, and wants to use me for his own purposes.

Reading came at noon and remained for an hour. The interview was uninteresting, as far as I was concerned, because I had talked the subjects out with both, and Reading knew what the President intended to propose, and the President knew what Reading expected. Reading seemed pleased with the President's reception. I walked to the door with him and he asked me to meet him at five o'clock at the British Embassy for a further conference.

At this conference, I definitely decided that I would attend the Allied War Council. Reading was pleased and offered me his house in London. He also offered to cable his Government asking them to send the Mauretania or Olympic to Halifax to take me over. I have made it clear to both the British and French Governments that I wish to go in the simplest way possible. There must be no banquets, no receptions, but merely conferences to transact business as speedily as possible.

At our conference Tuesday night, the President authorized me to see both Baker and Daniels and tell them of our plans and ask them to suggest suitable military and naval officers to accompany me. The President thought General Bliss, Chief of Staff, would be the proper man to represent the Army, to which Baker later readily acquiesced. Baker sent for Bliss while I was at the War Department, and the three of us had some talk upon the subject. When I visited the Navy Department, Daniels suggested Admiral Benson, but I asked him not to make a definite decision until later. Daniels also sent for Benson without telling him the purpose but merely indicating that he desired us to know one another.

After returning to the White House I told the President I had definitely decided it was best for me to go and that we had better make plans accordingly. He was pleased and said he felt confident that I would keep free from entanglements and antagonisms. I expressed confidence that my mission would bring him further prestige rather than lessen that which he already has.

It was agreed that I should come to Washington again before sailing.

1 W. Wiseman to EMH, Oct. 10, 1917.

Arthur James Balfour to Sir William Wiseman

[London] 14 Oct 1917

PRIVATE AND VERY SECRET.

Your tel. of Oct 13.

Please after consultation with Lord Reading convey following message to President whatever way you think best. I am telegraphing separately to Col H.

"I am authorized by French British Governments to express their earnest hope that it will prove possible for your Government to send a representative to Europe to discuss important questions of military and other of vital interest to cobelligerents. We learn with utmost gratification that invitation is likely to be successful and that we hope for invaluable presence at our councils of Colonel House."

T telegram (FO 115/2309, p. 142, PRO).

To Newton Diehl Baker

My dear Baker: The White House 15 October, 1917

The authorities of the Federal Reserve Bank in New York (and many others, for that matter) have been urging me to attend a meeting at Carnegie Hall on the eighteenth of this month, at which they expect to make their chief effort to commend the Liberty Loan to lukewarm and panicky New York.

I am taking the liberty of sending you one of Mr. Strong's letters.[1] He is Governor of the Federal Reserve Bank in New York. I have consulted not only my own judgment but a good many people whose knowledge of the situation is better than mine and my conclusion is that it would not be best for me to go, but I do think that it might be wise for some prominent member of the administration to be present to represent it and to speak. Would you feel that you could go?

I sincerely beg that you will give me the frankest answer and if you think that it is too much of a burden or something which would too seriously interfere with your own work, I want you to say so frankly with the assurance that I would understand and approve your declining; but if you can go, it would be a very great advantage and help. I, therefore, lay the matter frankly before you.　　Cordially and sincerely yours,　Woodrow Wilson

TLS (N. D. Baker Papers, DLC).
[1] Probably B. Strong to JPT, Oct. 10, 1917.

To John Singer Sargent

[The White House] 15 October, 1917

Can sit for you Thursday afternoon. Would be glad if you would get in touch with office as soon as you reach town.
　　　　　　　　　　　　　　　　Woodrow Wilson.

T telegram (Letterpress Books, WP, DLC).

From Joseph Patrick Tumulty, with Enclosure

[The White House] 15th October [1917].

What does the President want Mr. Tumulty to do in this matter?

TL (WP, DLC).

ENCLOSURE

Vira Boarman Whitehouse to Joseph Patrick Tumulty

Dear Mr. Tumulty: New York Oct. 13th, 1917.

Your letter of October 12th has brought rejoicing to the suffrage camp. You say the President asks what would be the best time for the interview we have requested. I would suggest the afternoon of Wednesday, Oct. 24th, Thursday, Oct. 25th, Monday, Oct. 29th or Tuesday, Oct. 30th. Of these dates, the 24th or 25th seem to me preferable, because we would then have time to get the full advantage of any statement the President may make, during the ten days which will then precede Election.

I ask your advice or comment upon the following plan, which has been suggested: That we should take about one hundred or more women to Washington in a special train, that a committee of eight or ten from this number be appointed to wait upon the President and that a short introductory speech should be made to the President about the present situation in regard to suffrage and the work women are called upon to do in this war, and that his answer should be promptly reported by us to the delegation awaiting without.

Of course, we want to arouse the greatest possible public interest in this interview, because we believe it can do more than any one thing to help win our campaign, but if the demonstration I suggest seems too much of a good thing to you, we will be glad to abandon it and bring only a few of the officers of the New York State Woman Suffrage Party to Washington.

Awaiting your reply,
                    Yours sincerely,   Vira Boarman Whitehouse

TLS (WP, DLC).

To Joseph Patrick Tumulty

Dear Tumulty: [The White House, Oct. 15, 1917]

So far as I can see, the twenty-fifth will suit me as well as any other day and I think the plan proposed is a very good one.
                    The President.

TL (WP, DLC).

From Lord Reading

Dear Mr. President,   Washington, D. C. 15th. October, 1917.

I communicated the substance of our recent conversation to my Government and have to-day received a reply which I thought right to bring immediately to your notice.

I am now authorised by the French and British Governments to express their earnest hope that it will prove possible for your Government to send a representative to Europe to discuss important military and other questions of vital interest to cobelligerents. My Government has learnt with the utmost gratification that the invitation is likely to receive your favourable consideration.

The British Ambassador and I waited upon the Secretary of State this morning and conveyed this message to him. I understand that the French Ambassador, as the doyen of the Diplomatic Corps, will without delay, present the formal invitation to the Secretary of State.

My Government is also extremely pleased to learn that it may hope for the invaluable presence of Colonel House as the representative of the United States.

I am, Dear Mr. President,   Yours sincerely,   Reading

CCL (IOR MSS, Eur. F 118/114, India Office Library and Records).

From Edward Mandell House, with Enclosures

Dear Governor: New York. October 15, 1917.

Thank you for sending me Page's cable. He sees but one side of the picture and always the same side.

Wiseman gave me last night his confidential report from a friend in the F. O. and here are some of the things he says. I am enclosing you a copy of a cable which has just come to him from Petrograd which is interesting if true.

Affectionately yours,   E. M. House

TLS (WP, DLC).

E N C L O S U R E   I

The situation in Italy is more threatening. Everyone expects a political crisis when the Chamber re-opens on October 15th. The

Provinces of Genoa, Turin and Milan have been placed in the war zone which is a euphemism for martial law, and there are various other signs that the Government feels the need to use the strong hand, though whether it is strong enough to do so is doubtful.

But grave doubts are expressed as to whether Italy can fight through another winter campaign. A diplomat who has been 20 years in Rome, and is supposed to be the best-informed foreigner there says "Italy will fight through the winter *if it can*." By this he means to imply that she can only continue to fight if she is well supplied with coal and corn. Factories are already idle because of coal. There have been several food riots already; but it seems that these can be laid to the door of bad distribution rather than of actual shortage. Nevertheless, in estimating for next year, to quote the diplomat again: "For every ten Italians there is food for seven. Are the other three going to starve, or will someone outside of Italy feed them? The war has shown that the United Kingdom cannot starve the Central Empires, but that it can starve the Neutrals and Italy." My informant ends up his whole communication thus: "I hope that people in London realize the gravity of the situation. My personal view is that without extensive imports from the United Kingdom and America of food and fuel, there will be serious trouble in Italy in the winter and if serious trouble breaks out there is not organization civil or military, central or local, that can cope with it."

I had a short talk with Scott (of the Manchester Guardian)[1] yesterday. He is getting disgruntled with the Government, says that L-G is letting things slip out of his control both as to administration and policy, that Milner and Curzon sit like two spiders weaving webs and keeping quiet about it, and that George, resting from his gyrations for the moment, gets caught in them, and then, what they say he is to do, does without further thought. He complains that L.-G. will not work, whereas Milner and Curzon do.

He talked to me about W.W.'s* decision that the members of Congress ought to take no part in the Allied Parliamentary Conference. He is very firm in his approval of America keeping out of formal alliances, and definitely asks me to tell you this. He thinks that apart from being much better for her to be able to play a lone hand when she wants to, that *we* may be very glad to be able to say, possibly to France, and probably to Italy: "Yes, we do agree, and as far as we are concerned, we should feel bound to stick to it, but America disagrees. We cannot coerce her, and we cannot neglect her advice either. Nor can you."

*you

1 Charles Prestwich Scott, editor of the Manchester *Guardian* since 1872.

E N C L O S U R E   I I

Petrograd Dated October 10, 1917.

(a) Turkish agent has arrived her[e] via Stockholm sent officially to Russian Government by Turkish opposition. He states that Turkey is ripe for revolution and displacement of Sultan, murder of Enver, and separate peace. He is authorized to offer as follows:

Opening of Dardanelles, destruction Bosphorus forts, autonomy for Mesopotamia and Armenia. He demands guarantee for the retention of Constantinople and present territory in Europe. He reports extreme distress in Turkey. He is seeing leaders of all parties here. If agreement is reached it would be useful to arrange revolt in Bohemia at same time.

(b) Coalition Government formed, but not expected to last more than three weeks when all Russian SOVIET is assembled. BOLSHEVICS have confidence that army will leave (group undecipherable) on 12th. General Staff expect grave trouble. Workmen and Soldier's Council now completely under control of extreme left.

T MSS (WP, DLC).

From the Diary of Josephus Daniels

October Monday 15 1917

Went to see Mrs. Dewey about her giving out for publication D's unpublished chapter telling of actions of Germans at Manila & how Dewey read the riot act to officer who came on board the Olympia. WW thought it might be well to publish. She said the Admiral had decided not to print & if she gave it out now it might provoke controversy and she did not think it would please him.

To Edward Mandell House, with Enclosure

Dear House   [The White House, c. Oct. 16, 1917]

You will read this with interest. *Is* this the latest English view with reference to the neutrals & the war?   W.W.

ALI (E. M. House Papers, CtY).

E N C L O S U R E

London Oct. 13, 1917.

7416. Gunther[1] has been shown a series of telegrams sent since October first by the Foreign Office to Sir C. Spring-Rice outlining imperative demands which the Foreign Office suggests should be made of neutrals. These instructions to Spring-Rice seem to answer the last sentence in your confidential telegram to me, 5575 of October 9, 9 p.m., to the effect that the British Government seem to desire a complete embargo but hesitate "to definitely recommend" such a course.[2] On the contrary the prolongation of the present British embargo is not in the least desired. It was adopted as a temporary measure pending acceptance by the border neutrals of the Allied demands and concessions. It has already cost Great Britain a matter of fifty million pounds sterling not to speak of the adverse effect on exchange.

The British Government are confident that complete demands can now be made without risk of driving any border neutral into the war on the side of Germany. The British have examined into this supposed danger, which did exist earlier in the war, by military, political and economic experts, and they have satisfied themselves that the danger now no longer exists. An Allied victory is now so certain that none of these states if it wished would dare join the enemy. Some of the reasons for this conclusion were set forth in Cecil's memorandum transmitted with my despatch number 6758 of August thirteenth last.[3]

Some of the Scandinavian states are intimating that they might be driven into the enemy's camp. But they have long used this threat against the British and it is natural that they should still use it. They have little else to use. Pending negotiations they continue their profitable exports to Germany which are of great use to the Germans and individual go betweens take energetic advantage of the interval of indecision.

On the other hand these neutrals are becoming weary of our detention of their ships and there are indications that they would really welcome definite demands by us and that they expect them to be severe. The British believe that the neutral representatives will continue to bluff as long as they think they can thereby gain their ends but that when a clear policy is put into effect they will become tractable.

The Russian objection is not regarded here as of the greatest importance. Doubtless it could be met through diplomatic agreement. It is believed that too much deference *can easily be* shown to Russia in such case to the jeopardy of the general cause. Even if retaliatory measures are adopted by Sweden, which is believed unlikely, the disadvantage would be of short duration if we act promptly.

In the matter of Swedish transit the Swedes have played both fast and loose. Spring-Rice can explain the subterfuge of giving through bills lading to Germany but not to Russia on the grounds of the break in transit at Haparanda.   Page.

T telegram (E. M. House Papers, CtY).
1 Franklin Mott Gunther, First Secretary of the American embassy.
2 RL to WHP, Oct. 9, 1917, *FR-WWS 1917*, 2, II, 962.
3 WHP to RL, Aug. 13, 1917, TLS (SDR, RG 59, 600.119/359, DNA).

From Albert Sidney Burleson

My dear Mr. President: Washington October 16, 1917.
I am in receipt of yours of October 13, enclosing letter from Mr. G. S. MacFarland, of date October 12, which I am returning herewith. I do not know to what statement Mr. MacFarland refers. I have in no statement "proclaimed the attitude of the Postmaster General toward alleged 'seditious' newspapers." This is what I have repeatedly said defining the Department's attitude in the enforcement of the Espionage Act and the Trading-with-the Enemy Act:

No one connected with the Government from the President down asks immunity from criticism or even attack, but while this great war is in progress no publication containing or advocating or urging treason, insurrection or forcible resistance to any law of the United States will be tolerated. Included in the forbidden practices are these: "Any matter intended to interfere with the operation or success of the military or naval forces of the United States, or to promote the success of its enemies, incitement to the violation of the draft law, publications intended to cause insubordination, disloyalty, mutiny or refusal of duty in the military or naval forces of the United States, or which is intended to obstruct the recruiting or enlistment service of the United States." These are the things prohibited by the law I am directed to enforce. And also opposition to the sale of United States bonds, or to the collection of authorized revenues, assertions to the effect that the United States declared war for an evil or an insufficient purpose and is but the tool of selfish and designing interests, will be regarded as violations of these laws. These things I have detailed are the practices the traitorous press here have been resorting to, to further the cause of Prussianism in our country.

To quote from a recent editorial in The World: "To avoid all trouble with the postal authorities, therefore, the publisher of an American newspaper, no matter what its language, need only observe a simple rule. He is not to take his inspiration from Berlin and he is to be loyal to the United States."

It is my purpose in the administration of these laws to act with moderation and caution but with firmness and dispatch.

Faithfully yours,   A. S. Burleson

TLS (WP, DLC).

From Edward Mandell House, with Enclosures

Dear Governor: New York. October 16, 1917.

I have a letter from Page which pleases me much. I am sending you an extract from it, which I hope you will let Mrs. Wilson also read.

I will let the British Government know that the formula they suggest as to the Zionist Movement meets with your approval.

I hope you will send Vance McCormick over with me to look into the British methods regarding the embargo. It would please them to have him come, and it could not fail to be of value to us in working out this problem over here.

Affectionately yours,   E. M. House

TLS (WP, DLC).

ENCLOSURE I

Extract from letter of W. H. Page

By far the most important peace plan or utterance is the President's extraordinary answer to the Pope. His flat and convincing refusal to take the word of the present rulers of Germany as of any value has had more effect here than any other utterance and is, so far, the best contribution we have made to the war. The best evidence that I can get shows also that it has had more effect in Germany than anything else that has been said by anybody. That hit the bull's eye with perfect accuracy; and it has been accepted here as *the* war aim and *the* war condition. So far as I can make out it is working in Germany towards peace with more effect than any other deliverance made by anybody. And it steadied the already unshakable resolution here amazingly.

ENCLOSURE II

Cable from Mr. Balfour to E. M. House

London, October 15, 1917.

Am very grateful for your message. I need not say how delighted I am that you are coming here; I feel certain everything can be arranged as you wish. Your visit will give great pleasure to us all, and particularly to me.

T MSS (WP, DLC).

From Carrie Clinton Lane Chapman Catt

My dear Mr. President: New York October 16, 1917.

I thank you most gratefully for your kind letter which quite fills the need in the New York State Suffrage campaign.

The collective mind seems to have moods like an individual and just now it is hunting for excuses which can serve as reasons for failure to move forward.

Most sincerely, Carrie Chapman Catt

TLS (WP, DLC).

Sir William Wiseman to Sir Eric Drummond

[New York] Oct. 16th. '17.

No. 27. Your No. 21 of 6th.[1] Brussa [House] put formula before Adramyti [Wilson] who approves of it, but asks that no mention of his approval shall be made when H.M.G. makes formula public, as he has arranged that American Jews shall then ask him for his approval which he will give publicly here.

T telegram (W. Wiseman Papers, CtY).
[1] A. J. Balfour to W. Wiseman, Oct. 6, 1917.

From the Diary of Josephus Daniels

1917 Tuesday 16 October

Cabinet—Houston brought up the fact that members of missions went about saying that if this or that were not done, the allies would be defeated, & thought they ought to be told not to talk. President said Senator Hitchcock asked "Is there anything hopeful?" having become blue by pessimistic talk. The President said he dissipated his pessimism to some extent. Trying to unload on us burdens they should bear, particularly the enmity of small neutral nations adjoining Germany. Wish us to press embargo without their help & evoke all the odium.

To Vance Criswell McCormick

Confidential.

My dear McCormick: [The White House] 17 October, 1917

Here is a letter from Thomas Nelson Page,[1] our Ambassador at Rome, which I am sure you will read with interest. I know from independent sources that the situation in Italy with regard to the attitude of the people in general is a very critical one and I hope that you may be able to bring the various agencies together which can and will supply these pressing needs in Italy, at any rate in some considerable part.

Will you not be kind enough to return Mr. Page's letter after you have read it?

Cordially and sincerely yours,   Woodrow Wilson

TLS (Letterpress Books, WP, DLC).
[1] T. N. Page to WW, Oct. 2, 1917.

From Edward Mandell House, with Enclosure

Dear Governor: New York. October 17, 1917.

If Page's telegram concerning the embargo of the European neutrals is a fair reflection of the opinion of the British Government, it is a direct contradiction of what they have told us privately. Wiseman is sending a cable outlining the matter and requesting a definite statement as to what they really think desirable.

Lippmann has just been here and is very much disturbed. I have asked him to outline in a letter some of the things he told me, a copy of which I am sending you.

No matter how much we deplore the attitude of the socialists as to the war, yet more harm may easily be done by repression. Between the two courses, it is better to err on the side of leniency.

I have seen for sometime that trouble was brewing and I spoke to Burleson when in Washington. I believe you will have to take the matter largely into your own hands for he could never have a proper understanding of it.

Affectionately yours, E. M. House

TLS (WP, DLC).

E N C L O S U R E

Walter Lippmann to Edward Mandell House

Dear Colonel House,   New York City. October 17 [1917].

At your suggestion I am setting down a few impressions of the effect on morale produced by the Post Office campaign against seditious newspapers.

I find on my return to New York that the radical and liberal groups are in a sullen mood over the government's attitude towards the socialist press. Men like Prof. Dewey, who represent the warmest kind of faith in the war and in the President, have told me that they intend to vote for Hillquit if the Call and the Jewish Daily Forward are excluded from the mails. In the labor movement, apart from those who will support Tammany, the feeling on this issue is at white heat. The position taken by Mr. Burleson is regarded as brutally unreasonable.

So far as I am concerned I have no doctrinaire belief in free speech. In the interest of the war it is necessary to sacrifice some of it. But the point is that the method now being pursued is breaking down the liberal support of the war and is tending to divide the country's articulate opinion into fanatical jingoism and fanatical pacifism.

The thing has worked out about as follows. No one but a man with the President's record of democratic achievement could have united the country as he did last April. It was an utter faith in him, more than anything else which reconciled the humbler people of the country to the war. They accepted conscription because he said it was necessary, and because there were men like Mr. Baker to administer it.

During July and August there was a relaxation, chiefly I think because Washington was too busy to keep the country informed. The President's reply to the Pope completely altered everything however. There has never been a moment since the war began when the country was so thoroughly interested and united. Why even the Masses confessed that it could not oppose a war for such purposes! On the basis of that message no pacifist opposition that amounted to anything could survive. Happily this coincided with the brilliantly successful mobilization of the draft army.

But two forces are at work to destroy this fine national unity. One is the fierce heresy hunting of a portion of the press and the other is the apparent approval of this bitter intolerance on the part of the Post Office. Liberals cannot understand why the government is apparently more apprehensive about what an obscure and discredited little sheet says about Wall Street and munition makers than about Mr. Roosevelt's malicious depreciation of the American army.[1] Suppression of course gives these papers an importance that intrinsically they would never have.

A great government ought to be contemptuously uninterested in such opinion and ought to suppress only military secrets and advice to break the law or evade it. In my opinion the overwhelming number of radicals can be won to the support of the war simply by conserving the spirit of the President's own utterances, and by imaginative administration of the censorship and the necessary suppression of disloyalty.

Censorship in wartime is one of the most delicate tasks that confronts a government. It should never be intrusted to anyone who is not himself tolerant, nor to anyone who is unacquainted with the long record of folly which is the history of suppression.

Sincerely yours,   Walter Lippmann

CCL (E. M. House Papers, CtY).

[1] Roosevelt, in September, had begun to write articles for the Kansas City *Star*; he contributed articles once a week beginning on October 1. His first articles fiercely attacked the War Department for alleged failures and shortcomings. See, particularly, "Broomstick Preparedness" (October 4, 1917) and "Broomstick Apologists" (Oct. 14, 1917).

From Edward Nash Hurley

Dear Mr. President: Washington, D. C. October 17, 1917.

I have some encouraging news regarding the building of ships which I know will prove interesting. I had Lloyds agency make a thorough investigation of the possibilities for the production of steel tonnage. And you will note by the attached statement they estimate that we will produce 3,712,000 deadweight tons of steel during 1918. This is a conservative estimate. In addition to this we have 1,000,000 deadweight tons of wooden ships under contracts which are being built very rapidly. The entire program for six million tons is well under way. In 1916 there were about 520,000 deadweight tons of ships built in this country, and in 1917 there will be turned out about 900,000 tons. As the labor situation in our shipyards at the present time seems most favorable I am hopeful that our goal of six million deadweight tons of shipping for 1918 will be reached.

Very faithfully yours, Edward N. Hurley

Printed in Edward N. Hurley, *The Bridge to France* (Philadelphia, 1927), p. 59.

From Edward Wright Sheldon

My dear Mr. President: [New York] October 17th 1917.

How your body has stood the stupendous burdens which your mind has so commandingly borne these last few months, has been constantly in my thoughts. The question might have involved anxiety, had not I known your Herculean capacity for work. Not since the summer of 1910, when you told me here of the somewhat nebulous political hypothesis which those ambitious and far-sighted statesman propounded for your acceptance, have you been granted anything like an adequate holiday. I am rejoiced by the assurance of those who have recently seen you, that in spite of all these years of incessant and increasing toil, you are as fit physically as a Spartan athlete. I can only hope that their enthusiasm has in it nothing of hyperbole.

The world is following you with admiration. The spirit of this country, notwithstanding exceptional individual lapses, brings profound gratification. The general eagerness to serve, even if only by standing and waiting, is refreshing. In common with the rest, I am doing what I can, in various modest ways. As I wrote you last Spring,[1] I esteem it a privilege to support your leadership, to the utmost of my capacity. I wish that my potentiality of service to the country were greater.

We feel that the new Liberty Loan must and will be a triumphant success. When that is accomplished all our financial and spiritual energies should be directed to preparing for the next bond issue. Such preparation will, I trust, tend to curb somewhat our amazing national extravagance, and to inspire greater readiness for personal sacrifice.

Believe me, with warmest regards,

Yours sincerely, Edward W. Sheldon.

ALS (WP, DLC).
[1] E. W. Sheldon to WW, March 9, 1917, Vol. 41.

Sir William Wiseman to Sir Eric Drummond

[New York] Oct. 17th. '17.

No. 29. With reference to my No. 17 of Sept. 29th.[1] and to your No. 16 of October 2nd.:[2]

The State Department has received a message from Page in which he refers to telegrams sent by F.O. to Spring-Rice since Oct. 1st. in connection with the embargo,[3] and in which Page gives it as his opinion that H.M.G. considers that "complete demands" can and should now be made on border neutrals. By "complete demands" I understand Page to mean the "final pressure" mentioned in my No. 17. Page goes on to say that he understands that H.M.G. have no fear that border neutrals will now join Germany, although they may threaten to do so. Adramyti [Wilson] would like to know if view taken by Page is correct and if you think "complete demands" can now be made. Page's view does not seem to me to be in strict accord with your attitude towards Sweden as set forth in your No. 16. Brussa [House] says Adramyti wants to know which view is correct. He will see him on Friday and would like some expression from you by then.

I have gained impression, which I submit for your consideration, that U.S.G. feels that H.M.G. should not insist too strongly in matter of detained Swedish bags, lest anti-German feeling created in Sweden by previous exposes should be replaced by anti-Allied sentiment.

T telegram (W. Wiseman Papers, CtY).
  [1] W. Wiseman to E. Drummond, No. 17, Sept. 29, 1917, T telegram (W. Wiseman Papers, CtY). Wiseman wrote that Vance McCormick, chairman of the "Embargo Committee," had just told Colonel House that he was about to "put final pressure on SWEDEN and NORWAY to prevent them shipping any supplies to Germany." The Swedes, Wiseman continued, said that this would force them into the war on one side or the other, and the Norwegians said that Germany would invade them. House had warned McCormick not to take any action without consulting the President. Wiseman concluded: "Are you being informed of moves McCORMICK is making, and do you approve? If not, cable at once and HOUSE will take matter up with President."
  [2] It is printed as an Enclosure with EMH to WW, Oct. 3, 1917. This copy omitted the opening sentence: "We are not aware of any recent movements by McCORMICK nor of what exactly is meant by 'final pressure.'"
  [3] WHP to RL, Oct. 13, 1917, printed as an Enclosure with WW to EMH, Oct. 16, 1917.

To Albert Sidney Burleson

My dear Burleson: The White House 18 October, 1917

I am afraid you will be shocked, but I must say that I do not find this hearing very convincing.[1] Some of the things quoted probably cross the line and I have very little doubt that they were all intended to have sinister results, but I must frankly say that I do not think that most of what is quoted ought to be regarded as unmailable. I have read the hearing with some feeling of misgiving as to the impression that was created upon the representatives of the paper which had been summoned, not because I doubt for a moment the purposes or the intelligence or the careful and conscientious methods of the public officials concerned, but because there is a wide margin of judgment here and I think that doubt ought always to be resolved in favor of the utmost freedom of speech.

It does not appear from the hearing what was done. Was the paper, as they so earnestly urged, given another chance?

Cordially and faithfully yours,   Woodrow Wilson

It was not and courts sustained action.[2]

TLS (A. S. Burleson Papers, DLC).
  [1] See ASB to WW, Oct. 9, 1917.
  [2] ASBhw. The Post Office Department was upheld, upon appeal to the Court of Appeals of the District of Columbia, on May 5, 1919. 258 Fed., 282.

To Grenville Stanley Macfarland

My dear Mr. Macfarland: [The White House] 18 October, 1917

Immediately upon receiving your letter of October twelfth, I conferred with the Attorney General[1] who replied on the sixteenth in a letter of which I take the liberty of sending you a copy in order that at any rate part of the impression you have had may be removed.

For I think you have misinterpreted the spirit and purpose of the Postmaster General. I have been keeping in close touch with him and I think that he is as anxious as I am to see that freedom of criticism is permitted up to the limit of putting insuperable obstacles in the way of the Government in the prosecution of the war.   Cordially and sincerely yours.   Woodrow Wilson

TLS (Letterpress Books, WP, DLC).
  [1] Wilson either dictated "the Postmaster General" or else misspoke himself. The Swem shorthand notebooks for October 10-November 19, 1917, are missing in the C. L. Swem Coll., NjP, and there is no copy of a letter from Wilson to Gregory concerning Macfarland's letter in WP, DLC.

From Newton Diehl Baker

(CONFIDENTIAL)

Dear Mr. President: Washington. October 18, 1917.

I have been thinking a good deal about the matter of the convention of the American Federation of Labor.[1] I suppose no one can with safety foretell what will happen there; but it is entirely conceivable that a policy might be adopted with reference to labor conditions throughout the country which, after being approved by a national convention of this kind, would be very inelastic and would embarrass any attempts gradually to adjust relations by composing [differences] between labor and capital.

We are all of us, in one form or another, urging business to associate itself into convenient groups for the increase of production, and the various committees of the Council of National Defense have been a frank recognition of the Government's willingness to see business organized in the Government interest. Personally I should be as willing to see labor organized in the same interest.

I am sending this note only because I know you have under advisement the question as to whether it would be wise for you to go to the convention or to send a message, and I suggest that, in either case, if you think affirmative action by you is wise, it might be well to warn labor not to make an inelastic ultimatum but to leave their accredited representatives free to work out with the Government those just rearrangements which are necessary by reason of war conditions.

                                   Respectfully,   Newton D. Baker

TLS (WP, DLC).
   [1] That is, the national convention of the A. F. of L. Wilson's address to the convention is printed at Nov. 12, 1917.

Robert Lansing to Joseph Patrick Tumulty, with Enclosure

Dear Mr. Tumulty: Washington October 18, 1917.

In obedience to the President's wish, as expressed in your letter to me of the 16th instant, I enclose herewith, for submission to the President, a draft of a proclamation designating Sunday, October 28th, as a day of prayer, pursuant to the request contained in the concurrent resolution adopted by Congress on October 4.

I am, my dear Mr. Tumulty,

                         Sincerely yours,   Robert Lansing

TLS (WP, DLC).

E N C L O S U R E¹

BY THE PRESIDENT OF THE UNITED STATES OF AMERICA.
A PROCLAMATION

Whereas the Congress of the United States, by a concurrent resolution adopted on the fourth day of the present month of October, in view of the entrance of our nation into ⟨a⟩ *the* vast and awful war which *now* afflicts the greater part of the world, has requested ⟨the President to follow the example heretofore established by this country upon becoming engaged in war and⟩ *me* to set apart by official proclamation a day ⟨for prayer for the aid of the Almighty and for the success of our arms⟩ *upon which our people should be called upon to offer concerted prayer to Almighty God for his divine aid in the success of our aims*:

And whereas: It behooves a great free people, nurtured *as we have been* in the eternal principles of justice and *of* right, ⟨obedient⟩ *a nation which has sought* from the earliest days of its existence ⟨as an independent nation⟩ to *be obedient to* the divine teachings which have inspired it⟨s acts and guided it⟩ in the exercise of ⟨the⟩ *its* liberties ⟨which have been vouchsafed to it by the All Powerful⟩, to turn *always* ⟨in time of sore trouble⟩ to the supreme ⟨Deliverer⟩ *Master* and cast themselves *in faith* at His feet, praying for *His* aid and succor in ⟨the⟩ *every* hour of trial, to the end that the great aims to which our fathers dedicated ⟨themselves⟩ *our power as a people* may not perish among men, but be ⟨anew⟩ always asserted and defended *with fresh ardour and devotion* and, through the Divine blessing, ⟨be⟩ set *at last* upon enduring foundations for the benefit of *all* the free peoples of the earth.

Now, therefore, I, Woodrow Wilson, President of the United States, *gladly* responding to the wish expressed by the Congress, do appoint October twenty-eighth, being the last Sunday of the present month, as a day of supplication and prayer for all the people of ⟨this⟩ *the* nation, earnestly ⟨beseeching⟩ *exhorting* all my countrymen to observe the appointed day, according to their several faiths, in solemn ⟨invocation of⟩ *prayer that* God's blessing *may rest* upon the high task which is laid upon us, to the end that the cause for which we give our lives and treasure may triumph and our efforts be blessed with ⟨durable⟩ *high* achievement.

IN WITNESS WHEREOF, I have hereunto set my hand and caused the seal of the United States to be affixed.

DONE at the City of Washington this [blank] day of October in the year of our Lord one thousand nine hundred and seventeen, and of the Independence of the United States of America, the one hundred and forty-second.

By the President: W.W.

Secretary of State.

TI MS (WP, DLC).
¹ Words in angle brackets deleted by Wilson; words in italics added by him. This proclamation was issued on October 19.

To Winthrop More Daniels, with Enclosure

My dear Daniels: The White House 19 October, 1917

I would not send you the enclosed if I did not think it of the utmost importance. It is a memorandum to me from Mr. John Skelton Williams, the Comptroller of the Currency.

I would have preferred to see you personally and talk this matter over, but I know how the newspapers start reports of some kind of "influence" being attempted to which the Commission ought not to yield and therefore I am sending this by the hand of a special messenger.

I can add my testimony to that of Mr. Williams that if the Commission could see its way to making some such statement as he suggests by, let us say, Monday morning, it would have an immensely beneficial influence on the progress of the Loan.

I must admit to having a very profound contempt toward a business world which needs reassurance of this sort, but as you know it does need it and we cannot afford to let any legitimate means go unused which may make this loan an impressive success.

I know that you will understand and sympathize and will feel that I am justified in urging this very seriously. With warmest regard,

Cordially and faithfully yours,   Woodrow Wilson

TLS (Wilson-Daniels Corr., CtY).

ENCLOSURE

MEMORANDUM

October 18, 1917.

By far the most important thing before this country just now is the Second Liberty Loan. For the sake of all that is most dear to us, that must be made a signal and shining success. Our future and the future of civilization depend upon the outcome of this war, and probably the most potential thing that can be done at this moment to shorten the war and bring victory, is for America to give comprehensive and concrete evidence of our enthusiastic determination to win by providing a tremendous over-subscription to the Liberty Loan. Its effect on Germany would be awing.

This, it seems to me, will have a more far reaching effect upon the future of this country than anything else now before us.

The head of our Treasury Department, Secretary McAdoo, is working untiringly, day and night, in trying to bring the people of the country in every section of the land to a realization of this momentous issue, and his splendid efforts are arousing them, and giving results.

But there have been some elements of discouragement recently, and the loan is not going as well as we had hoped. Different excuses are being offered in explanation of this apathy or omission to subscribe.

We are told that those who have cash money but who have other obligations are being frightened by the great shrinkage in values which has taken place in the bond and stock markets, and people of this class say that they will have to hold on to their cash money to protect their loans against further shrinkage in their collateral.

There are others who are NOT BORROWING money, but who have NO CASH, and they say that they can not subscribe without selling securities, and that they cannot sell securities because there is no decent market for them, and that nobody will buy.

There are still others who do not buy Liberty Bonds because market conditions are so unsatisfactory that they fear securities may go lower still, and that the demoralization will spread.

Then there are investors to whom the suggestion has been made that, although they may have no ready money on hand and although they cannot sell their securities, they ought to pledge their high class collateral at banks, borrow the money and invest the proceeds in Liberty Bonds. In reply to such suggestions these security holders say that they would willingly BORROW money from banks to buy Liberty Bonds, but that the banks are now refusing to lend on SECURITIES because they do not know how long the shrinkage may last, and fear when they call their loans, the borrowers may not be able to sell their securities so as to pay them.

I endeavored to throw a little oil on the troubled waters by giving, on Saturday, a statement to the press, stating that National Bank Examiners would exercise a discreet leniency as to requiring banks to mark down the prices of high grade securities under present abnormal conditions. This statement received a favorable reception, and I think will do some good.

I have generally agreed, right along, with the position which the Interstate Commerce Commission has taken in recent years, from time to time, in refusing to raise freight rates, and I also think that the Commission acted wisely in granting the provisional and moderate advances which were made a few months ago, and also in declining to go further at that time, but I cannot fail to see that there have been material changes in the situation since that time, and that a favorable consideration of the subject at this time by the Commission might be productive of important and far reaching results to the country generally, and especially as bearing upon the success of the Liberty Loan.

If I may be pardoned for venturing an opinion, it would be that a horizontal advance, such as the railroads would like to have, of fifteen per cent or twenty per cent has not been shown to be necessary as far as one can judge from the reports of the roads, but it does look as though conditions would warrant the Commission in giving very earnest and special consideration to the advantages which would flow from the granting of SOME general increase NOW, say of not over ten per cent.

An increase of ten per cent would add between $350,000,000 and $400,000,000 to the present net earnings of the railroads, PROVIDED there should be no further increase in the cost of materials, labor and taxes, and it would unquestionably have a profound effect in reestablishing confidence in the securities market. It would favorably affect securities of every kind, and especially would it have a tremendous effect in stimulating subscriptions to the Liberty Bonds.

It may be admitted that the present scale of railroad rates is high enough on the basis of the cost of materials and labor a year ago, but the unprecedented increase in prices which the railroads are now being required to pay for nearly everything they use is not a matter of speculation. The roads cannot get the goods unless they do pay these extortionate prices; and I will say, also, that the prices which are being charged to the railroads, in my judgment, cannot be justified. This is especially true of what the railroads have to buy that is made of steel and iron.

It is obvious, that if our railroads generally are to continue to make both ends meet, one of two things must be done:

First, the prices which they are paying for materials or labor, or both, must be reduced; or,

Second, the roads must be allowed somewhat more profitable

rates in order to live and enjoy even a moderate degree of prosperity.

Can we solve the problem by cutting down the prices of materials and labor in the immediate future?

I do not believe we can do so sufficiently to meet the exigencies of the present situation. There is even now a clamor for a further increase in the price of coal from the two dollar basis, and a good deal of talk of a coal famine. Roads which a year ago were paying eighty-five cents to one dollar for their coal, are now required to pay a minimum of about two dollars. An increase of one dollar a ton on 150 million tons of coal, if the railroads use that amount, means a cutting down of net earnings approximately to the extent of 150 million dollars.

Railroad construction has ceased entirely, but the roads must have a certain tonnage of new rails for necessary repairs, and rails have doubled in the asking price. Fastenings, spikes, bridge material, cross ties and lumber, oils and axle grease, explosives, cars and engines have advanced to prices heretofore unheard of.

The railroads must have these things if they are to continue to operate. In order to get them they have to pay for them unprecedented prices, but still they must have them.

I grant that it would be much better if we could reduce the price of materials and the price of labor to a normal basis, but this cannot be done now. Railroad rates, however, could be advanced, and I believe that the whole country would be benefitted if a moderate advance should be allowed to the roads to meet the present most abnormal situation.

It is true that some railroads are showing not only a large increase in their gross earnings as a result of the war, but they are also, in spite of the high cost, showing some increase in net earnings, although this increase is generally small; other roads are showing a heavy deficit; but even where a slight increase is shown, let us not forget that wear and tear resulting from this increased business probably have not been fully accounted for in reporting net earnings.

If the Interstate Commerce Commission in their wisdom should see fit to supplement the advances which they allowed last Spring, with a further material advance at this time, I think their action would have a most potent effect in reestablishing confidence, in checking the decline of securities, and in justifying, if not in inducing, the banks of the country to be more liberal in their loans.

There are many banks in the country at this time which are really afraid of railroad securities. They stand in dread of more receiverships, and if some of our leading roads should now be forced into receivership, it is hard to see where the trouble would end.

There is the more excuse for this nervousness when we realize that the National Banks themselves own close to five hundred million dollars of railroad bonds—an amount equal to nearly half of their capital. The State Banks, Trust Companies and Savings Banks probably hold at this time approximately a billion and a half dollars additional of railroad securities.

A banker told me a few days ago that he knew of a certain Terminal Company whose bonds were guaranteed by more than six railroad companies, which was trying to raise about 10 or 15 million dollars, and which had been unable to get the money needed, and that the management of this company was seriously considering the question of placing the company in the hands of a receiver as being, perhaps, the best way out of their dilemma, notwithstanding the big guarantees which the corporation enjoyed.

I know of two or three other large railroad systems with an aggregate mileage of probably from twelve to fifteen thousand miles, which at this time may be said to be almost trembling in the balance—their perilous condition can hardly be called a state of equilibrium, as the scales seem even now to be descending. If a substantial increase in rates is granted, these roads can probably be saved. If favorable action is not taken, receiverships may be inevitable.

Are we not now at the parting of the ways? We all know that there has never been a situation in our national history comparable with the present international crisis, and I know of no single step which this Administration could take just at this moment, as we approach the time for the closing of the books on the Liberty Loan, which could be expected to have a more profoundly beneficent, salutary and far reaching effect than would be an announcement that the protection and assistance which is now needed by our railway fabric, will be forthcoming.

It is to be hoped that the Interstate Commerce Commission may reach an early decision on the informal application now pending from the Eastern trunk lines for better rates; but it may be impracticable to issue an order promptly dealing finally and definitely with this rather complex problem—so as to give the relief which is needed not only in the East but elsewhere.

Under such circumstances, would it not be possible for the Commission to make some public announcement to the effect that it has been watching closely the course of events since the issuance of its order of last Spring; that the whole subject has been receiving unremitted attention; that in view of the unprecedented increase in the cost of practically all materials used in railroad operation and in the price of labor and services, it is evident that the roads ought to be permitted to recoup at least a large portion of these inevitable costs by being permitted to charge substantially better rates; and that the Commission will determine as soon as possible how great an increase can consistently be granted, and that it will announce its decision at an early date?

Such an announcement as that would, I believe, give immense relief in financial circles and should create an atmosphere of hopefulness which would tremendously stimulate subscriptions to Liberty Bonds and be of great aid in carrying the aggregate of subscriptions well up to, if not beyond, the five billion dollar mark.

This memorandum is the result of a somewhat careful study and analysis of the present financial situation, an inside knowledge of banking conditions, and is written after consultation with fair minded and well posted men whose opinions are entitled to special weight.

(The magnitude of our railway interests may perhaps be better appreciated when we realize that they represent an investment greater than the total resources of all the National Banks of the country, or, say, approximately eighteen billion dollars ($18,000,000,000).)

T MS (Wilson-Daniels Corr., CtY).

To Thomas Watt Gregory

[The White House]

My dear Mr. Attorney General: 19 October, 1917

Apparently this is a matter with regard to the action of our District Attorney in Oregon.[1]

The treatment of foreign language publications is giving me a great deal of anxiety these days and I would appreciate it very much if you would have this case looked into to see if there is any basis for the complaint made.

Cordially and faithfully yours,   Woodrow Wilson

TLS (Letterpress Books, WP, DLC).
[1] It was a telegram from Albert E. Kern to WW, Oct. 17, 1917. Kern was editor and publisher of the Portland, Ore., *Nachrichten aus dem Nordwesten, und Freie Presse*. A file memorandum states that Kern was protesting against the refusal of the mails to his paper and against an action of the United States district attorney for Oregon, Clarence L. Reames. White House memorandum, Oct. 19, 1917, T MS (WP, DLC).

To Edward Wright Sheldon

My dear Sheldon: The White House 19 October, 1917

It was a very generous thought that prompted you to write your letter of October seventeenth and I thank you for it out of a very full heart. I think you must know how I value your friendship and approval, and such a letter coming from you has brought me deep cheer and encouragement.

I am happy to say that those who have reported to you that I am physically well and fit have spoken the truth. I really never was better in my life, though how it happens I cannot explain. I think it must in part be the stimulation of great duties and the absolute necessity to spend my energies equably throughout the twenty-four hours.

I hope, my dear fellow, that you are keeping well, and it is delightful to think of such a friend in the midst of the financial affairs which mean so much in their right guidance to the prosperity and success of the country.

With warmest regard,
Faithfully and sincerely yours,   Woodrow Wilson

TLS (photostat in RSB Coll., DLC).

From Winthrop More Daniels

My dear Mr. President: Washington October 19, 1917.

Your letter of this date enclosing Comptroller Williams' memorandum came this morning and has had my constant attention ever since.

You do not need to be told how great weight I attach to the memorandum which you think it important to send to me for consideration, nor how desperately eager I am to do my utmost to speed the complete success of the Liberty Loan.

I should, however, be lacking in candor if I failed to say to you that I believe it absolutely impossible to induce the Commission to give the scantiest favorable consideration to Mr. Williams' proposal that we make a public announcement to the effect that the Commission is convinced that rates ought speedily to be substantially increased, say by ten per cent, to allow the carriers to make headway against the larger costs they have been recently confronting.

Moreover, while Mr. Williams' knowledge of the situation and the feeling in banking circles is unquestioned, I am bound to say that our monthly reports from the carriers do not substantiate his assumption that the roads have not, as a general thing, recouped the higher costs prevailing since January 1st last. Moreover, his suggestion that where net earnings show an apparent increase the deterioration of road and equipment probably offset that favorable showing is not borne our [out] by the apparent outlay for maintenance of road and equipment. As a matter of fact, on these two items for the first 7 months they spent over sixty million dollars more than for the same period in 1916.

In the face of the statistical showing to date a pronouncement on our part that we intended to augment revenues, and by the same token, transportation charges, from 350 to 400 million dollars a year could not be justified.

I should qualify the above by stating that in the eastern section of the country,—north of the Ohio and Potomac rivers and east of the Mississippi,—the carriers have made a relatively less favorable showing this calendar year than the roads in the southeast and west of the Mississippi. It may well develop that some additional relief should be accorded in the eastern district.

It seems to me that the Commission might appropriately make a pronouncement of this order: Show exactly how the gross and net revenues to date for the current year compare with 1916; affirm that the showing of earnings completely negatives the pessimism that is so prevalent; and reiterate that, in constant touch as we are with revenues and expenditures, we shall not suffer inadequate revenue to impair the efficiency or the reasonable earning power of the carriers.

More than this I do not believe the Commission would say; and frankly, I must say with all deference to Mr. Williams that more than this it is doubtful whether we ought to say.

I shall immediately send memoranda to each of my colleagues suggesting that we might with propriety do what we can along these lines to forward the complete success of the Liberty Loan.

I must apologize for the detail which I have recited in my reply, because I realize that you are far too busy to be worried by any but considerations of the highest magnitude.

I am, my dear Mr. President, with best regards,

Ever sincerely yours,   Winthrop M. Daniels

TLS (WP, DLC).

From Herbert David Croly

My dear Mr. President: New York City October 19, 1917.

There are certain aspects of the existing relation between the government of the United States and the public opinion of the country in respect to the war which are troubling me very much, and about which I should like to take the liberty of submitting a few considerations to you.

The censorship over public opinion which is now being exercised through the Post Office Department is, I think, really hurting the standing of the war in relation to American public opinion. Take a concrete instance. I know of a very considerable number of men in New York city who voted for you in either 1912 or 1916, or both, and who have never hitherto voted the Socialist ticket, but who in case The New York "Call" and "Vorwaerts" are suppressed will in all probability vote for Mr. Hillquit at the coming municipal election. Their vote in that case will be decided by the fact that it in their opinion is the one way in which they can effectively protest against the suppression of the Socialist press which has been taking place under the cover of war censorship. These men are all men of moderate opinions, high intelligence, who have constituted the best element in your following in the past and who are extremely reluctant now to do anything which will hamper you in the successful prosecution of the war, but they consider that the suppression of these Socialist papers raises an issue of importance scarcely inferior to that of the war itself.

The Post Master General, Mr. Burleson, has announced that all Socialist papers will be denied mailing privileges which state that American participation in the war is part of a capitalist conspiracy for the exploitation of the working classes. The statement is, of course, utterly untrue and sufficiently silly. There is only one course of action which could be taken by the government which would give it any plausibility and that, it seems to me, is precisely the action which is now being taken by the Post Office Department. If the Socialist propaganda is suppressed on the pretext that it hurts the prosecution of the war, the Socialist agitators will have a plain fact on which to base their subsequent agitation. They can then allege that the war is being used for the benefit of the capitalist organizations and for the suppression of its critics, and of course they will not fail to make the most telling use of the argument. Neither can they be effectively hampered in spreading that argument among the wage-earners of the country. They will have no difficulty at all in printing pamphlets by the thousand on small presses and circulating them throughout the country. They are accustomed to this kind of propaganda and really prefer it to propaganda in the open because it is secret, irresponsible, and does not have to bear the test of public criticism. This is what they are doing now, and this is certainly what they will continue to do after their more public means of agitation have been taken away from them.

I would suggest for your consideration that a better method of dealing with this situation could be devised by adapting to it the kind of regulation which has been used in relation to different industrial activities. In dealing with the prices of food and raw material the government has asked for certain large powers which have been granted by Congress, and they have used those powers as a means for negotiating with business men and reaching an agreement which reduces excessive prices without bringing with it the necessity of actual government ownership or operation of the industry. So, in relation to the radical press, would it not be possible to use the power which the government has obtained under the Trading with the Enemy Act in order to negotiate with the Socialist press and persuade them to keep their agitation within certain limits without at the same time forcing them to abandon the kind of agitation which they consider essential to their convictions, and which, just because it is so unreasonable, would in the long run do them more harm than good? There is, I think, no way of preventing the growth of Socialism during the war. In the case of a war of this kind there is bound to be a considerable minority in a diversified population such as the United States which cannot see its necessity and will naturally drift towards the only party which is opposed to the prosecution of the war. There is, I think, no danger that this minority will prove to be of grave embarrassment to the country provided it is not encouraged by what that minority would believe to be persecution. On the other hand, if its organs are suppressed and it is submitted to what looks to it like persecution, the agitation will be increased rather than diminished and will be very much stronger when the war is over than it would otherwise have been.

The policy pursued by the government in relation to public opinion seems to me to incur the danger at the present time of dividing the body of public opinion into two irreconcilable classes. It tends to create on the one hand irreconcilable pacifists and socialists who oppose the war and all its works, and a group of equally irreconcilable pro-war enthusiasts who allow themselves to be possessed by a fighting spirit and who tend to lose all sight of the objects for which America actually went into the war. From what I can learn about conditions west of the Mississippi river such a class division has become well established in that region and is constantly growing in its influence. It has not as yet become so well established in the East, but it is on the increase here, too, and it makes the situation of papers which occupy an intermediate position, such as The New Republic does, extremely difficult. We are constantly being crowded between two extremes. When we try to draw attention to the pacific and constructive purposes which underlie American participation in the war we are accused of being half-hearted, and even of being pro-German, and we necessarily do look half-hearted as compared to the war propagandists who give to the war powers of the government indiscriminate support but who are either indifferent or actually hostile to the purposes for which that power will ultimately be used. The tendency at the present time is to build up a body of public opinion which is either pro-war or anti-war and which has not any intelligent grasp of the way in which the war can be made to serve the purposes which your administration wishes to make it serve. The propagandists connected with the American Security League and the American Defense Society, who are setting themselves up at the present time as the only true arbiters of loyalty and who are gaining a great deal of prestige from that fact, are the very people who will subsequently make the task of realizing the constructive purposes which lie behind American fighting excessively and unnecessarily difficult.

I may add that so far as my personal attitude is concerned there is nothing which I am more anxious to do than to be of some slight service to you in the great work which you are now attempting to accomplish. There is no public object in which I more profoundly believe than the object for which you are waging this war, but just because of the attitude of the government in respect to the censorship, and because the war propaganda is being conducted in such a way that militarists like Mr. Roosevelt are allowed to appropriate it, I have the utmost difficulty in writing about it from week to week without making an appearance of opposing what our government is trying to do. I deeply regret being forced into such a position and that is why I have taken this opportunity of letting you know how the situation looks to me in the hope that perhaps you might be able to do something or say something which will strengthen the position of those who, like myself, believe profoundly both in you and the work which you are trying to do.

Respectfully yours,   Herbert Croly

TLS (WP, DLC).

From Vance Criswell McCormick

Dear Mr. President: Washington Oct. 19th, 1917.

I am returning herewith the letter from Ambassador Thomas Nelson Page enclosed in your letter of October 17th, and which you requested me to return.

I at once took up with Mr. Hoover, Mr. Crosby, and Mr. Hurley, the question as to how we can help Italy, and we expect to reach a conclusion in this matter just as soon as we secure certain necessary information. I hope to be able to report our conclusions in the very near future.

Cordially yours,   Vance C. McCormick

TLS (WP, DLC).

From the Diary of Josephus Daniels

October Friday 19 1917

Went over with Mayo to see President. Mayo told him of message from the King. He told of what he had seen. The President said the English thought we were were [sic] Anglo-Saxons and like themselves. We are very different. He had said one of our troubles was we could understand the English & when they said things against us, we knew it while if F[rance] or G[ermany] did the same we knew nothing about it. He listened to M & hoped some real offensive would come. He was disgusted with the idea of sinking 100 ships to shut up river beyond Heligoland when dynamite could clear the channel.

To Robert Lansing, with Enclosure

Dear Mr. Secretary   [The White House, c. Oct. 20, 1917]

It seems to me that the British are losing their heads in these matters. To do what they here suggest would be stupid folly.

W.W.

ALI (SDR, RG 59, 841.711/2199, DNA).

E N C L O S U R E

London. Oct. 19, 1917.

Urgent and confidential.

My 7471 October 18, 7 p.m.[1] As I have reported the British Government will probably not oppose the surrender of the pouches unopened to the Swedish Minister in deference to your representations and expecially in view of the inclinations of the President, but I have learned from British officials connected with special service that they regard the Swedish Diplomatic pouches as dangerous in the extreme and that the question of withdrawing the courtesy of the immunity of diplomatic pouches from all neutral missions is being considered.

They consider that the pouches in question may well contain matter having to do with German intrigues in Mexico since Germany is now cut off from regular communication with its Legation in Mexico. Please see my telegram 7405 October 12, 11 a.m. on the subject.[2] My number 7277 September 27, 8 p.m.[3] also has a most important bearing on the question and I venture to suggest that the publication of the message it embodied would completely justify the Department's refusal to comply with the Swedish Ministers desires and offset any of the possible ill effects you anticipate.　　　　　　　　　　　　　　Page.

T telegram (SDR, RG 59, 841.711/2199, DNA).
　[1] This telegram is missing in the State Department's files.
　[2] WHP to RL, Oct. 12, 1917, T telegram (SDR, RG 59, 862.20212/862, DNA).
　[3] WHP to RL, Sept. 27, 1917, T telegram (SDR, RG 59, 862.202/20, DNA). This telegram repeated an intercepted telegram from Von Bernstorff to the German Foreign Office dated March 2, 1916. Bernstorff wrote that the embassy's official mails for neutral countries had for some time been sent in part through Swedish official intermediaries "such as couriers, Legation bags, or enclosure in official letters."

To Newton Diehl Baker

My dear Mr. Secretary:　　The White House 20 October, 1917

Thank you for your letter of the eighteenth with its suggestion about the approaching convention of the American Federation of Labor. It is a very wise suggestion and I shall keep it in mind.
　　Cordially and sincerely yours,　Woodrow Wilson

TLS (N. D. Baker Papers, DLC).

To Winthrop More Daniels

My dear Daniels: The White House 20 October, 1917

Thank you very much for your note of yesterday. I am sincerely glad to have new and fuller light thrown on the situation of the railroads. I took it for granted that things were being exaggerated in order to "work" us to some extent, and yet I believe the situation justifies a statement on the part of the Commission and I think the statement you suggest will probably be of the greatest value.

In great haste   Faithfully yours,   Woodrow Wilson

TLS (Wilson-Daniels Corr., CtY).

From Robert Lansing, with Enclosures

Washington

Dear Mr. President,   Saturday evening October 20, 1917.

If it meets with your approval I propose to request Viscount Ishii to file with his note of confirmation completing the exchange a confidential memorandum such as the one here enclosed.

I am hastening this matter as rapidly as possible because it takes him several days to communicate with his Government.

Faithfully yours,   Robert Lansing

ALS (SDR, RG 59, 793.94/594½, DNA).

ENCLOSURE I

MEMORANDUM of Conference
with VISCOUNT ISHII.
October 20, 1917.

Viscount Ishii called at the Department by appointment this morning.

He first said that I probably knew that the Japanese Naval Commissioner had arranged with our naval authorities to take over certain patrol duty in the Pacific now being performed by the SARATOGA in order that the latter might be released for service in the Atlantic, but that his Government desired the arrangement to be confirmed formally through the Department of State. I told him I would communicate at once with the Navy Department and take the necessary steps.

He then said that he had received a communication from his Government and that, rather than vary the language of the Root-

Takahira agreement by inserting the words "and sovereignty" as I had suggested on the 13th, they would consent to retain the phrase "The territorial sovereignty of China, nevertheless, remains unimpaired, and"—(2d proposed amendment of October 12th, page 2). He said further that his Government still insisted on the omission of the declaration on page 3 (October 8, B) but were willing to strike out the word "other" in the fourth line from the bottom.

I told him that I was of course disappointed at the omission of so important a declaration at this time, as I knew the President would be, but that the retention of the clause relating to "sovereignty" and the elimination of the word "other" indicated to me that his Government were desirous of reaching an agreement.

He said that I must know how sincerely he was in favor of the declaration and how he had urged his Government to retain it, but that they seemed to fear domestic criticism, although he seemed to be very vague as to what the criticism would be.

I said that, if the declaration had not been in the draft, it would matter very little, but having been submitted to Japan and rejected it might convey a very wrong impression, that the President felt this very strongly and I hoped they would exchange confidential notes on the subject as I had suggested.

The Viscount replied that he had already presented the suggestion to his Government and that they did not deem it wise to do so. He then produced the paper which is annexed and read to me the argument presented against an exchange of confidential notes. He handed me the paper and I read it again.

When I had finished I told him that I did not consider the arguments very substantial, but that I would like to consider the matter further, and after doing so, I would consult with the President, who I knew would be disappointed that his Government were unwilling to take a course which would remove all possibility of future misunderstanding.

He said that he had hoped to persuade his Government to take one of the two courses which I had suggested, but that he had been unable to do so.

I told him I appreciated the efforts which he had made, that I thought the amendments which he had obtained from his Government had brought the negotiation to an almost successful conclusion, and that I was still hopeful of finding a way which would be satisfactory to both Governments.

I said that I would ask another conference as soon as I could explain the situation to the President.

T MS (SDR, RG 59, 793.94/594½, DNA).

ENCLOSURE II

Confidential Memorandum   *Draft*
to accompany the Reply of   October 20, 1917.
the Japanese Government.

In the preliminary draft note dealing with questions relating to the Republic of China, which arc of mutual interest to Japan and the United States and which, on September 26, 1917, was submitted by the Government of the United States to the Government of Japan for their consideration, there appeared, following the declaration by the two Governments of their adherence to the so-called "Open Door" policy, a further declaration "that they will not take advantage of present conditions to seek special rights and privileges in China which would abridge the rights of the citizens or subjects of other friendly states."

For certain reasons of expediency, which have been orally explained to Government of the United States, the Government of Japan considered it to be unwise to include the above-quoted declaration in the proposed note, and it was, therefore, stricken out by mutual consent.

In order, however, to avoid misconstruction being placed upon this amendment of the note, the Government of Japan desire to affirm that by doing so there was no purpose on their part to assert a contrary principle or policy, and that the elimination of the declaration has no significance whatsoever in determining the terms of the note as finally agreed upon by the two Governments.

RLHw MS (SDR, RG 59, 793.94/594½, DNA).

From Thomas Watt Gregory

Dear Mr. President: Washington, D. C. October 20, 1917.

I am in receipt of yours of the 19th enclosing copy of a telegram sent to you by A. E. Kern, Publisher of the NACHRICHTEN, complaining of the attitude of United States Attorney Reames at Portland, Oregon, toward his paper.

I am having a careful investigation made of the complaint and shall communicate with you further on the subject.

Reames is perhaps the ablest and most efficient district attorney in the far west, if not in the entire west, and I have great confidence in his judgment and patriotism.

         Faithfully yours,   T. W. Gregory

TLS (WP, DLC).

From Grenville Stanley Macfarland

My dear President Wilson: Boston October 20, 1917.

I appreciate very much the courtesy of your reply of the 16th [18th] to my note of the 12th, concerning the attitude of the Postmaster General toward the newspapers and his interpretation of the power given him under the Espionage and Trading-with-the-Enemy Acts.

I wrote to you not so much to get present action from you as to give you a friendly outsider's point of view and to warn you of the danger that the taste of the blood of the helpless little newspapers by the Postmaster General or his subordinates might beget a dangerous appetite for that sort of thing.

I have no doubt that this Administration is freer from the influence of Wall Street and profiteering than any administration since the Civil War, and, perhaps, since any earlier period. I have no doubt of the national disinterestedness of this war. But if the Postmaster General may say that no newspaper may criticize the righteousness of the war, or the disinterestedness of our present government then, if ever a profiteering cabal in power may be waging a rapacious war, when the honor and even the security of the country may depend upon the power of telling the people the truth, the precedent now set might become a serious breach in one of democracy's great bulwarks. Remember the faculty of our forefathers which Burke described as most extraordinary. "Here they anticipate the evil, and judge of the pressure of the grievance by the badness of the principle. They augur misgovernment at a distance; and snuff the approach of tyranny in every tainted breeze."

Your political fortunes illustrate more than the career of any other public man, even Lincoln's, the impotency of newspaper attacks when they seek to stir a majority of the American people against the truth. I do not believe that any man was ever so abused from within and without his party, by religious extremists, by the pro-Germans and the pro-Allies, who would deprive Great Britain and France of the right to buy our ammunition on which their control of the sea gave to them. To use modern miliyary [military] expressions, they subjected you to a direct fire, a cross fire and to an enfilading fire, and they dug mines under your feet. When they exhausted every form of attack tolderated [tolerated] in the public press and platform, they circulated cowardly, underground stories. It was a stream of abuse directed against one man probably never equalled before in American history. Like the Persian miss[i]les at Thermopylae, this storm of abuse seemed actually to shut out the sun from you.

If there is any one man in the world whose public career reveals the saving grace of free speech, it is yours.

Those who want this war to go on until Germany is crushed, no matter how her people democratize and what pledges she is willing to give of repentence and future good behavior, are now in control of nearly all the newspapers and instruments of unofficial terrorism. While you prosecute the war you will have all the help of this sort that you need, and probably more than is good. The Government, without reference to the question of principle, can afford to keep out of the pack which is baying on the heels of the poor little papers and the few men today who are opposing the Government in the rightful prosecution of this war. Most of this abuse came from the very men who today are the most intolerant of any peace that may come before the German people are so far extinguished that they never can contribute anything to our civilization, for that is what making, by force, one country secure from the commercial rivalry of another, means. It is the age old *cassus belli. Censeo, Carthagenem delendam.*

Mr. President, I do not expect you to answer this letter. I did not expect you to answer my letter of August [October] 12th. I quite appreciate that in your position you ought to keep all the doors open, for what may be truly and wisely said today may be untrue or unwise tomorrow. Again I wish to assure you that so far as I know my own mind, I am entirely disinterested in this matter. When you have prosecuted this war to a successful conclusion within the ideals of your reply to the Pope, and have given us public ownership of the railroads and telephone and telegraph companies, you will have made democracy safer both at home and abroad, and will take your place beside Lincoln. How I wish I could make you see, as I think I do, the danger to our democratic republic of the continued private control of our public service corporations.

Yours sincerely,   G. S. Macfarland.

TLS (WP, DLC).

To Robert Lansing, with Enclosures

Dear Mr. Sec'y   [The White House, Oct. 22, 1917]

This seems to me to meet the case and has my approval.

Woodrow Wilson

Rec'd A.M. Oct 22/17   RL

ALI (SDR, RG 59, 793.94/594½, DNA).

E N C L O S U R E   I

MEMORANDUM of Conference
with VISCOUNT ISHII.
October 22, 1917.

The Viscount called at the Department by request and I told
him that the note as finally agreed upon on the 20th was acceptable in itself, but that the President was seriously concerned
over the elimination of the declaration following the one referring
to the "Open Door" policy unless some statement was made in
regard to it. I said that, as I understood that his Government
were opposed to an exchange of confidential notes on the subject, I would suggest that there should accompany the Japanese
reply a memorandum, which I could retain in my confidential
files. I then produced a draft of memorandum such as I had in
mind and read it to him. (A copy of the paper is annexed.)

The Viscount, to whom I handed a copy, read it through very
carefully and said that he would submit it to his Government.

I then handed him the redraft of the note which I had made
on the 20th (of which a copy is annexed).

He spoke of the elimination of the word "other" and asked if
I did not think it well to retain it. I told him "No," and he dropped
the subject.

He asked if the ending of the note would be the same as the
Root-Takahira agreement and I told him that I had not thought
about the matter, but would let him know the next time we met.

E N C L O S U R E   I I

Handed copy to Viscount Ishii
at Conference, Oct. 22/27. RL

CONFIDENTIAL MEMORANDUM To Accompany
the Reply of the Japanese Government.

In the preliminary draft note dealing with questions relating
to the Republic of China, which are of mutual interest to Japan
and the United States and which, on September 26, 1917, was
submitted by the Government of the United States to the Government of Japan for their consideration, there appeared, following the declaration of the two Governments of their adherence
to the so-called "Open Door" policy, a further declaration "that
they will not take advantage of present conditions to seek special

rights and privileges in China which would abridge the rights of the citizens or subjects of other friendly states."

For certain reasons of expediency, which have been orally explained to the Government of the United States, the Government of Japan considered it to be unwise to include the above-quoted declaration in the proposed note, and it was, therefore, stricken out by mutual consent.

In order, however, to avoid misconstruction being placed upon this amendment of the note, the Government of Japan desire to affirm that by doing so there was no purpose on their part to assert a contrary principle or policy, and that the elimination of the declaration has no significance whatsoever in determining the terms of the note as finally agreed upon by the two Governments.

ENCLOSURE III

Handed copy to Viscount Ishii
at conference Oct. 22/17 RL
REDRAFT, OCTOBER 20, 1917.

Excellency:

I have the honor to communicate herein my understanding of the agreement reached by us in our recent conversations touching the questions of mutual interest to our Governments relating to the Republic of China.

In order to silence the mischievous reports that have from time to time been circulated, it is believed by us that a public announcement once more of the desires and intentions shared by our two Governments with regard to China is advisable.

The Governments of the United States and Japan recognize that territorial propinquity creates special relations between countries, and, consequently, the Government of the United States recognizes that Japan has special interests in China, particularly in the part to which her possessions are contiguous.

The territorial sovereignty of China, nevertheless, remains unimpaired and the Government of the United States has every confidence in the repeated assurances of the Imperial Japanese Government that while geographical position gives Japan such special interests they have no desire to discriminate against the trade of other nations or to disregard the commercial rights heretofore granted by China in treaties with other powers.

The Governments of the United States and Japan deny that they have any purpose to infringe in any way the independence or territorial integrity of China and they declare, furthermore, that they always adhere to the principle of the so-called "Open Door" or equal opportunity for commerce and industry in China.

Moreover, they mutually declare that they are opposed to the acquisition by any Government of any special rights or privileges that would affect the independence or territorial integrity of China Change or that would deny to the subjects or citizens of agreed to, the Oct. 31/17 any country (a) full enjoyment of equal opportunity in the commerce and industry of China.

Change   I shall be glad to have your Excellency confirm agreed to, this understanding of the agreements reached by Oct. 31/17 us.

T MSS (SDR, RG 59, 793.94/594½, DNA).

To Herbert David Croly

My dear Mr. Croly: [The White House] 22 October, 1917

I thank you sincerely for your thoughtful and important letter of October nineteenth.

I can assure you that the matter of the censorship has given me as much concern as it has you and after frequent conferences with the Postmaster General I have become convinced that not only have his statements been misunderstood but that he is inclined to be most conservative in the exercise of these great and dangerous powers and that in the one or two instances to which my attention has been called he has sought to act in a very just and conciliatory manner. I hope and believe that as the processes of censorship work out and the results become visible a great part of your apprehension and my own will be relieved.

Cordially and sincerely yours,   Woodrow Wilson

TLS (Letterpress Books, WP, DLC).

To Jean Pierre Husting
and Mary Magdelena Juneau Husting

[The White House] 22 October, 1917

Your son's death has come to me as a great personal grief.[1]
He was one of the most conscientious public servants I have ever
known and had entered upon a career of usefulness to his state
and to the country which was of the highest promise. I grieve
with you with all my heart.   Woodrow Wilson.

T telegram (Letterpress Books, WP, DLC).
   [1] Senator Husting had been killed in a hunting accident on October 21.

From Newton Diehl Baker

CONFIDENTIAL

Dear Mr. President: Washington. October 22, 1917.

Mr. Gompers and five others, comprising the Executive Committee of the American Federation of Labor,[1] called on me today.
They came to repeat and urge a suggestion made sometime ago
to me to the effect that in their judgment it would be an inspiring
thing if you would proclaim to the American people and to the
world in general that the eight-hour day has now become the
accepted basis of industrial employment in this country.

These gentlemen said that the workers in Germany and Austria would be affected by such a declaration, that Labor in this
country, both organized and unorganized, would be stirred and
stimulated by it, and that it would have a tendency to make labor
difficulties in this country impossible during the war.

I pointed out to them that the *maintenance* of existing standards could hardly be interpreted to mean so revolutionary a
change of existing conditions as such a proclamation would
entail; that at once, upon such a statement from you being made
public, all workers at present employed more than eight hours
would feel that they had your authority to demand an eight-hour
day and to enforce their demands, no matter what industry
might be involved or what disorganization might follow from
the unwillingness of their employers to yield the point; that this
was particularly so in the steel industry where relatively very few
of the employees had succeeded in getting the eight-hour day. I
further pointed out the unwisdom of executive legislation on such
a subject, particularly when there was a want of power in the
Executive to enforce such a declaration of opinion. They argued
the matter quite earnestly and asked me whether it would be
possible for them, as a body, to meet you so that they might lay

their views before you. They will be in Washington until Thursday when they leave to attend various meetings throughout the country preliminary to the general convention.

I explained that your engagements are made many days ahead and your time so occupied that it seemed unlikely that your attention could be gotten at this time. I report the matter to you because they will probably ask me whether such a meeting as they desire is possible and also because you may desire to meet them in order to point out to them the unwisdom of action at this time which would tend violently to disturb the labor situation of the country. As a matter of fact, the labor movement is making very rapid progress now and it would be a great pity to cause a reaction by unwise and untimely demands.

Respectfully yours,   Newton D. Baker

TLS (WP, DLC).
    ¹ There were actually eleven members of the Executive Council of the A. F. of L., including Gompers. It is impossible to identify the "five others."

From John Skelton Williams

Confidential.
Dear Mr. President: Washington October 22, 1917.

Since my talk with you on Thursday evening I have had a conference on the subject which I had taken the liberty of bringing before you, with the Attorney General, and I was encouraged to find that he heartily concurred in the views which I had expressed to you and which I had embodied in the memorandum left with you. He realizes fully the seriousness of the situation and the high importance of prompt action. He took steps at once to get in touch with Mr. Anderson,¹ but ascertained that the latter was temporarily out of Washington, and thereupon telegraphed him, urging that he return to the city this morning without fail.

The Attorney General has just called me on the telephone and informs me that Mr. Anderson has returned and that he has had a talk with him.

The Attorney General now tells me that he thinks it important that you should send a message to Mr. Anderson, asking him to call at the White House. He suggests that, if you should feel hesitation about sending for an individual member of the Commission for the discussion of this particular matter, that in view of Mr. Anderson's comprehensive and special knowledge of the whole New England situation you might find it desirable to send for him to ascertain conditions in that particular territory, which are serious from a railroad standpoint (in view of an impending receivership of New England's principal system of railways),[2] and that incidentally the whole situation might be touched upon in your talk to the extent that you may think it desirable.

The Attorney General said he knows Mr. Anderson is anxious to be governed largely by the President's views in this crisis.

I am writing this note in response to the Attorney General's earnest suggestion—made to me after his full talk this morning with Mr. Anderson—that I do so.

I feel it my duty to leave nothing undone that can be done to help insure the success of the Liberty Loan, and therefore trust that you will pardon me for transmitting to you this suggestion, which does seem important.

I sincerely hope that it may be possible for you to act on this suggestion today; the subject is one, I understand, upon which the Commission is at this moment deliberating, and the Attorney General and I both believe that a word from you, as suggested above, would be most helpful.

Respectfully and faithfully yours,   Jno. Skelton Williams

P.S. Subscriptions, formal and informal, to the Liberty Loan thus far reported are less than two billion dollars. This is a long way from the five billion so earnestly desired by all, but I believe it is yet possible to reach the goal.

TLS (WP, DLC).

[1] George Weston Anderson, former United States district attorney for Massachusetts, who had just been appointed to the Interstate Commerce Commission.

[2] That is, the New York, New Haven and Hartford Railroad Co. The *Wall Street Journal*, Sept. 8, 1917, reported that the steady decline in New Haven shares had given rise to rumors of receivership. A sharp decline in net income in the face of record gross income was attributed in large part to extremely costly embargoes. Priority was given to perishable foodstuffs, coal, coke, iron ore, and other war materials. All this disrupted the normal flow of traffic and ran up expenses. The company, according to the *Journal*, was expected to have difficulty in paying $45,000,000 in one-year notes which would come due in May 1918, and it was not clear whether the bankers would be willing to renew them.

New Haven shares dropped on September 11 to a record low of 21½ after a meeting of the directors to arrange for the issue of preferred stock. *New York Times*, Sept. 12, 1917. For detailed information about the New Haven system, see *Poor's Manual of Railroads, 1918* (New York, 1918), pp. 642-719.

From Charles Sumner Hamlin

Dear Mr. President: Washington October 22, 1917.

I have just returned from the West in the Liberty Loan campaign, and tonight I leave for Savannah, Georgia, and spend the rest of the week in the South.

I feel that I ought to tell you that in the West I observed a feeling, quite frequently evidenced, of concern and almost irritability at the presence in this country at Washington and elsewhere of so many prominent Englishmen. The feeling seemed to be that they are too much in evidence and tend to divert the attention of the people from the fact that this is our war as well as that of Great Britain and the other Allies. Some even expressed the view that these gentlemen are lobbying in the interest of Great Britain. Up to the present time the cloud is no larger than a man's hand, but I am fearful that it may grow.

Please do not take the trouble to acknowledge this note. I merely felt it my duty to tell you that this condition exists.

I have not the slightest doubt but that the loan will be handsomely over[sub]scribed.

With best wishes, believe me,

Very sincerely yours,   C S Hamlin

TLS (WP, DLC).

From George Creel

Dear Mr. President: Washington, D. C. Oct. 22nd, 1917.

Mr. Hutchins,[1] First Vice President of the National Bank of Commerce,[2] has consented to go to Russia, without cost to us, to act unofficially in expressing our ideas to the Thompson group. While Thompson has given $1,000,000.00, he is now cabling the State Department to send him $3,000,000.00 a month. I have worked out a complete plan but think it wise to have Mr. Hutchins present when I submit it to you. He can come to Washington tomorrow. May I beg the favor of an appointment?

Respectfully,   George Creel

TLS (WP, DLC).
[1] Robert Grosvenor Hutchins, Jr.
[2] Of New York.

From William Bauchop Wilson

Globe, Ariz., October 22, 1917.

I am happy to be able to report that your commission succeedingnin [succeeded in] sec[u]ring a settlement of the strike difficulties in the Globe-Miami district. This is the most important copper center of the State of Arizona, producing normally twenty one million pounds of copper per month and employing five thousand workmen. The settlement is along lines which assure the maximum output of copper during the period of the war without interrupting by the establishment of practicable machinery for the adjustment of grievances that may arise on the part of the workmen. Result achieved has been made possible through the hearty cooperation of the operators and the leaders of the union. We are now proceeding to Clifton with a view to securing a prompt settlement of the difficulties in the Clifton-Morencie-Metcalf District. W. B. Wilson.

T telegram (WP, DLC).

From Henry Lee Higginson

Dear Mr. President: Boston, October 22, 1917.

Amongst your many duties can you consider the case of the railroads? They are suffering from want of higher rates which, together with increase of wages and materials, have cut off the needed improvements. You know the whole story, but I see the disgust and distress of the investors in railroad shares throughout the land.

Like most houses of our kind, we used to advise the purchase of railroad shares as investments, and used to buy very large quantities of them. Our people did not speculate very much in railroad shares, but they put a great many shares away. It is more than three years since I have asked anybody to buy railroad shares for investment. I see the care and skill with which the Boston & Maine Railroad is run. I have lived on it for the last forty years. The rates are not enough and the service is better than we deserve for the prices which we pay. On the New Haven Road much has been done to make the service better notwithstanding all the adverse circumstances. It is a very valuable property indeed and has had great care and skill during these last three or four years. Mr. Elliott[1] left because it would have killed him, so the doctors said, and he is working for the country in Washington.

But it is the same story all around.

Perhaps there is nothing that you can do, or the contrary may be true. The dislike of the Interstate Commission to allowing railroads to make money (a dislike that one sees in many other people beside that Commission) is inconceivable. If men do not make money they cannot spend it. Our railroad service, which was so wonderful, is behindhand at the present moment and we shall have this autumn insufficient service, and the railroads will have great difficulty in getting money. Already their credit has been much hurt and they must pay higher rates for what they do get.

Of course at the present moment no one is buying anything but Liberty bonds, and it is many weeks, almost months, since we have done much profitable business. Yet, if people were investing in other securities, we should have our share.

I repeat, we cannot advise anybody to buy railroad shares. We have advised many friends and customers to sell their shares, and they have sold them. Many poor people have lost their income on railroad shares because the railroads can pay no dividends, and often they have sold out at a great loss and the shares came to some rich man who has spare capital. I see the funds of many institutions which have relied in part on railroad shares of the highest quality, and I see many men and women of fair and small means who are suffering in the same way.

May I respectfully ask you to forward in some way immediate and wise action by the Interstate Commerce Commission? In my belief it would be a very great blow to our Government and our country if the Government had to take over the railroads, and yet that may become necessary in order to keep the railroads up unless they should be fairly treated. Labor will have its price, and many of the laborers work less as they get more wages. We have to meet that difficulty as we can. But in this age of great trouble, do not let us curtail our means of travel and of exportation of provisions and other goods simply because the railroads cannot provide the necessary cars and engines, tracks, yard room, etc.

With many apologies for troubling you in the matter, I am
Yours very truly, & respectfully   Henry L. Higginson

TLS (WP, DLC).
¹ That is, Howard Elliott, president of the New Haven until April 1917.

From the Diary of Colonel House

The White House, Washington. October 22, 1917.

I came to Washington today on the 11.08. Mezes and David Miller accompanied me. I wanted them to come in order to introduce them to the heads of the Departments in order that they might secure data needed for the peace settlement.

Janet and Gordon met us. I took Janet home in the White House motor, remaining a few minutes to see Louise. I then came to the White House. I had no conversation with the President as it was too near dinner time, and after dinner we went to see "Good Gracious Annabelle"[1] at Belasco's.

[1] This was advertised as "A play of love and laughter," by Clare Kummer, with Lola Fisher, May Vokes, Edwin Nicander, and the entire New York cast.

To The Prime Ministers of Great Britain, France, and Italy

Gentlemen: The White House [Oct. 23, 1917]

I have taken the liberty of commissioning my friend, Mr. Edward M. House, the bearer of this letter, to represent me in the general conference presently to be held by the governments associated in war with the Central Powers, and in any other conferences he may be invited and think it best to take part in, for the purpose of contributing what he can to the clarification of common counsel[,] the concerting of the best possible plans of action, and the establishment of the most effective methods of cooperation. I bespeak for him your generous consideration.

With great respect, and the most earnest hope that our common efforts will lead to an early and decisive victory,

Sincerely Yours,   Woodrow Wilson

WWTLS (E. M. House Papers, CtY).

To The Ambassadors of the United States at London, Paris, and Rome

My dear Friends,   The White House 23 October, 1917.

I am sending Mr. House over to act as my personal representative in the general council presently to be held by the governments associated in war with the Central Powers, and in any other conferences he may be invited and think it best to take part in, for the purpose of clarifying common counsel, concerting the best plans of action, and establishing the most effective means of cooperation, and I would be very much obliged to you if you would be kind enough to cooperate in every way possible with him and the gentlemen who will accompany him, and facilitate in every way the work they will have to do.

With the best wishes and my sincere compliments,

Faithfully Yours,   Woodrow Wilson

WWTLS (E. M. House Papers, CtY).

To John Skelton Williams

My dear Mr. Comptroller: [The White House] 23 October, 1917

I sent your memorandum to Mr. Daniels and I think he would not mind if I asked you to read his reply which I enclose (with the request that you will be kind enough to let me have it again after you have read it). Daniels I have known for a long time and I know that he speaks by the card, and my own impression is that such a statement as he suggests would be itself of the highest value by way of reassuring the country.

Cordially and sincerely yours,   [Woodrow Wilson]

CCL (WP, DLC).

To Winthrop More Daniels

My dear Daniels: The White House 23 October, 1917

I think it would be of the very greatest service to the country if a statement such as you suggest in your letter of October nineteenth, namely, "to show exactly how the gross and net revenues to date for the current year compare with 1916; affirm that the showing of earnings completely negatives the pessimism that is so prevalent; and reiterate that in constant touch as we are with revenues and expenditures we shall not suffer inadequate revenue to impair the efficiency or the reasonable earning power of the carriers," should be made by the Commission and made at once. The announcement this morning of a hastened hearing of the Eastern cases is very valuable. I wonder if the Commission would be willing to add the other?

In haste

Cordially and sincerely yours,   Woodrow Wilson

TLS (Wilson-Daniels Corr., CtY).

To Albert Sidney Burleson

Personal.

My dear Burleson: The White House 23 October, 1917

I think probably it would be wise not to act in the case of "The Call"[1] until after the election in New York City.

I will explain to you later why I make this suggestion.

In haste

Cordially and faithfully yours,   Woodrow Wilson

TLS (A. S. Burleson Papers, DLC).

1 The Post Office Department, on October 8, 1917, had ordered representatives of the New York *Call* to appear in Washington on the following day to show cause why the newspaper should not be denied second-class mailing privileges. No specific charges against the publication were set forth in the notice sent to its offices. Alexander M. Dockery, the Third Assistant Postmaster General, informed the publisher of the *Call* on October 13 that the charges would be made known only at the hearing, which had been postponed to October 15 at the request of the newspaper. At the hearing, the postal authorities charged that the *Call* had published "seditious and disloyal matter." The department, in a public statement on October 25, denied that a decision in regard to the *Call* was being withheld until after the mayoralty election. Rather, the decision had been postponed because the *Call* had not yet filed a brief. The brief was filed on October 26. On about November 13, the department revoked the *Call*'s second-class mailing privileges. *New York Times,* Oct. 9, 14, 16, 26, 27 and Nov. 15, 1917.

To Lucius William Nieman

[The White House] 23 October, 1917

The death of Senator Husting deprives the country of the services of a man of unusual character and of unusual devotion to the true ideals of American loyalty. His death at this time is the more to be mourned on that account. He was one of those who led with unflinching courage in the fight for unselfish and unqualified devotion to the country and for a loyalty upon which no shadow could be cast.   Woodrow Wilson.

T Telegram (Letterpress Books, WP, DLC).

To William Bauchop Wilson

[The White House] 23 October, 1917

My warm appreciation of your telegram of yesterday. It brings heartening news and I congratulate you.

Woodrow Wilson.

T telegram (Letterpress Books, WP, DLC).

From Winthrop More Daniels

My dear Mr. President: Washington October 23, 1917.

Your note of this morning is just at hand.

In the announcement printed in this morning's papers the Commission said, referring to the carriers' suggestion to reopen the Fifteen Per Cent case some 60 days hence:

"If your suggestion is well grounded that further financial relief is needed by the carriers, it is obvious that such relief should be had promptly in order that transportation demands in time of war may be fully met."

The clause quoted, we felt, would be tantamount to the suggestion contained in my letter to you of the 19th instant.

On Saturday a committee of the Commission had a two-hour conference with Comptroller Williams. He urged that the Commission announce its intention of according a ten per cent increase. Such an announcement the Commission felt it impossible and improper to put out. We read to him a statement reciting the revenues, gross and net, for the first eight months of this year as compared with 1915 and 1916. He gave it as his opinion that the statement which we read to him would be of little service and might actually produce an effect opposite to the reassurance it was intended to convey. He urged that the admitted decline in net earnings of eastern carriers as compared with 1916 would be construed as something which we were inclined to minimize. Therefore, in conference yesterday we discarded the statement previously prepared and submitted to Mr. Williams, and issued in its place the letter hastening the reopening of the Fifteen Per Cent case and carrying the statement quoted above. A copy of the letter is transmitted for your perusal if you have time.[1]

I feel reasonably confident that the Commission would regard a supplementary statement as savoring of an anxiety which might be misinterpreted and which you would not desire it to disclose.

I have consulted Commissioner Woolley and may say that he agrees with me in this particular.

With warmest regards,
                    Yours very sincerely,   W. M. Daniels

TLS (WP, DLC).
[1] This enclosure is missing.

From William Lea Chambers

My dear Mr. President: Washington October 23, 1917.

In response to a telephone message to the Executive Offices yesterday, Mr. Tumulty and Mr. Forster both being absent, I was placed in communication with Mr. Hoover who replied that he would get my message to you at the first opportunity. Some thirty minutes later he telephoned me that the matter I desired to present in a brief personal interview you preferred should be presented in written form. I cancelled my midnight train reservations, and succeeded in postponing a conference in New York set for today regarding a serious transportation situation involving the Buffalo-New York switching district, so as to bring the subject in writing to your attention today.

For several weeks past, as my actual engagements in mediation work would permit me the opportunity, I have been conducting negotiations with the Chief Executives of the labor unions, engaged in train operation, with the view to securing an irrefragable agreement that they will not permit a strike order to be issued on any railroad in the United States, with which their organizations have contracts, until after the United States Board of Mediation and Conciliation has had ample opportunity to use its best efforts to bring about an amicable agreement by mediation and conciliation; and, in the event of a failure of such efforts, to secure an agreement from these Executives to submit their controversies to arbitration in accordance with the provisions of the Newlands law. I think I am sufficiently authorized to say that I have already secured the acquiescence of the railroads in this policy, through the Conference Committee of Managers. Your support of the efforts of this Board in the Georgia, Florida & Alabama Railway Company case brought the controversy there to a happy conclusion. While you did not, in precise words, say to the railroad officials in that case that you would take possession of and operate the railroad in case they refused to mediate, and arbitrate if need be, yet you did notify the officials of that railroad, in substance, that the limit of your authority in the premises would be exercised. A word from you now along the same lines, as you know best how to express it, addressed either directly to the Chief Executives of the unions, or, if you prefer it, in a letter addressed to me, which I can exhibit to them, I feel confident will bring my negotiations with them promptly to satisfactory conclusions.

This was the subject I wished yesterday to bring immediately to your attention in a personal interview, and I am at your service on short notice; at any time, it may suit your convenience. I regard this matter as of the highest importance, beyond any work we have in hand, and have arranged a postponement of other pressing demands for my services away from Washington until next Monday in order that I may be here subject to your call. Both Assistant Commissioner Hanger[1] and myself are kept absent from Washington almost continuously and have cases now awaiting us in different parts of the country which will keep us uninterruptedly employed for many weeks.

Very respectfully,   W. L. Chambers

TLS (WP, DLC).

[1] Glossbrenner Wallace William Hanger.

From Arthur Capper

My dear Mr. President: Topeka October 23rd, 1917.

At the risk of appearing presumptuous, I am venturing to make a suggestion relative to exemptions under the second call for troops. I fully appreciate the many difficulties besetting the execution of a matter so delicate and intricate; I realize the impossibility of rendering what will seem to be exact justice to every individual and to every class; but I believe, and I think those charged with the responsibilities of the draft believe, that there is a human side as well as an industrial and *economic* side to the problem presented, and that in the interests of our country due consideration should be given to that phase of the question.

In my official capacity as Governor of one of the commonwealths of the Union, I have been brought face to face with much misery and hardship resulting from the selection of men with wives and young children dependent upon them. My office has been besieged for weeks by young mothers whose homes have been broken up by the drafting of their husbands, leaving the wife and mother not only charged in a large degree with the support of the family, but also with what is of even greater importance its guidance, direction and training at a critical period. Every child has a right to the personal care of a father; the interests of society demand it.

Many of the cases which have been brought to my attention are of young farmers, either tenants or landholders with farms only partially paid for. The burden and responsibility of operating the farm are too heavy for the young wife to assume; the family is not only deprived of its head but our effort to increase agricultural production is also hampered.

Speaking for Kansas I can assure you that the state will cheerfully send to the army its full quota of men, but I respectfully urge that under the second call the rules be made clear and explicit authorizing the exemption of married men with wife and children dependents. The second quota can be filled with single men; the best interest of the nation will, in my opinion, be best served by leaving married men for subsequent calls should such calls be necessary.

With assurance of esteem, I am

Respectfully yours, [Arthur Capper]

CCL (A. Capper Papers, KHi).

From the Diary of Colonel House

October 23, 1917.

The President and I decided this morning that it would be well for me to take over representatives of the Army, Navy, Munitions, Food, Finances, Shipping and Embargo. When he first asked me to go on this trip he wished me to go alone. I had some difficulty in persuading him that I could not possibly confer with the heads of the Allied Governments on matters of policy, and in addition confer with the War, Navy, Treasury, Shipping, Munitions, Food and Embargo Departments of those governments.

It took me the better part of the day seeing my proposed staff, and explaining the purposes of the trip. Admiral Benson has arranged for the transportation. We are to have two cruisers and a destroyer, and we are to be met at the danger zone with four other destroyers. Benson is determined that we shall get across safely if possible, and I have much confidence that he will succeed, since he is to be with us.

Lanier Winslow, who has been in Germany four years, says the safest way for me to go would be to advertise it throughout Germany, and to let them know the ship I was sailing on, illuminating it etc. He thinks I am the last person in the world the Germans wish to destroy, because I am "their best bet for a fair settlement."

I shall not go into details of this busy day. It has been one of hurried conferences; now with the President, and again, with Lansing, Polk and many others.

To Robert Lansing

My dear Mr. Secretary: The White House 24 October, 1917.

I am glad to instruct you to indicate to the French Government and to the other governments associated with us in the war that the Government of the United States accepts the invitation conveyed by the French Ambassador to be represented in the Allied Conference to be held early in November, and that I have designated Mr. Edward M. House to act in that Conference as the representative of the Government of the United States.[1]

Faithfully Yours,   Woodrow Wilson

WWTLS (SDR, RG 59, 763.72 SU/10½, DNA).
    [1] Lansing conveyed this message in RL to J. J. Jusserand, Oct. 24, 1917 (two letters), CCL (SDR, RG 59, 763.72 SU/10½, DNA).

To Winthrop More Daniels

My dear Daniels: The White House 24 October, 1917
Thank you for your note of yesterday, and let me say that I have no doubt that you have done the best thing possible in the circumstances.

Cordially and faithfully yours,   Woodrow Wilson

TLS (Wilson-Daniels Corr., CtY).

From George Creel

My dear Mr. President: Washington, D. C., October 24, 1917.
I am attaching
   (1) A request for the allotment of one million dollars to this Committee for Russian purposes;[1]
   (2) A suggested letter to Mr. Thompson for your signature;
   (3) A letter to Mr. Sisson.[2]

The million is to cover the purchase of motion picture equipment, material, etc., in this country, expenses of people going across, the distribution campaign in Russia, our cable service, and other uses indicated by you in our conversation of yesterday. Every cent will be guarded and accounted for, and it is not my idea that we should make any considerable grant or gift to anyone.

Please do not feel that I have made any mistake in the selection of Mr. Sisson. He is a twenty thousand dollar-a-year executive; he gave up everything to serve his country. He is an organizing genius, a man of the highest ideals, and has more real moral courage than almost anyone I know. It means double work for me to let him go, but he is the only one in whom I have absolute trust. You see, I do not want a man for *display* purposes, but one who will slip in to Russia, see the necessary people, organize the cable, feature, motion picture services, define clearly just what we want and what we do not want, and then slip out again.

I think that every minute counts, and if you approve, and have time to sign these papers, I will send Mr. Sisson to New York tonight to sail at once. In case you wish to see me about these matters, I am holding myself ready to answer a telephone call. Dr. Mott and Mr. McCormick are going to be with me all afternoon.   Respectfully,   George Creel

TLS (WP, DLC).
   [1] This enclosure is missing.
   [2] Edgar Grant Sisson, veteran journalist, at this time Associate Chairman of the Committee on Public Information. The drafts of the letters to Thompson and Sisson are missing.

To George Creel

My dear Creel: The White House 24 October, 1917

I am glad to sign the letters you have suggested and am hurrying them over to you.

In great haste

Cordially and sincerely yours, Woodrow Wilson

TLS (G. Creel Papers, DLC).

To William Boyce Thompson

[The White House]

My dear Colonel Thompson: 24 October, 1917

I had heard already of your helpful interest in Russia's fight for freedom, but not until my talk with Mr. Hutchins today did I fully appreciate the extent of your generosity and the finely practical expression of your sympathy.

It is a great thing at a great time that you have been privileged to do, and I hold it all the more effective in that it is the effort of an individual concerned only with the success of the human struggle. The experience of Europe has made national disinterestedness almost incredible to its peoples, and even the United States, with its demonstrable lack of selfish purpose, cannot go too carefully in the business of helping Russia to help itself.

Mr. Hutchins informs me that you are to remain in Russia as long as you see an opportunity for usefulness. I trust that this is indeed the case, for there is need of some one there to represent unofficially the fraternal interest of America. I am convinced that your whole-heartedness admirably fits you for this important duty, and I hope that you will accept it as another call upon your patriotism. Sincerely yours, [Woodrow Wilson]

CCL (WP, DLC).

To Edgar Grant Sisson

My dear Mr. Sisson: [The White House] 24 October, 1917

Mr. Creel informs me that you are leaving for Russia at once. In our conversation of yesterday I tried to make clear my views as to the nature and extent of any manifestation of our interest in the Russian struggle, and I know that you will be guided by them in everything that you say or do.

We want nothing for ourselves and this very unselfishness carries with it an obligation of open dealing. Wherever the fundamental principles of Russian freedom are at stake, we stand ready to render such aid as lies in our power, but I want this helpfulness based upon request and not upon offer. Guard particularly against any effect of officious intrusion or meddling, and try to express the disinterested friendship that is our sole impulse.

It is a distinct service that you are privileged to render your country and the whole democratic movement, and I know that this will serve at once as reward and inspiration.

Sincerely yours,   [Woodrow Wilson]

CCL (WP, DLC).

From Alexander of Serbia

Salonika,

Very dear and great Friend,   October 24th 1917.

I take the opportunity of my representatives coming to America to send you the expression of the deep gratitude myself and my people feel for the Chief of the great American Republic.

Serbia has been happy to receive numerous and important signs of sympathy from the American Nation long before the United States entered into the war. But the great help which the Serbian people have received from Your countrymen during this war and which my people will never forget was based without any doubt on the principle which You have proclaimed in declaring war on Germany: that the small Nations have the same rights to existence and the same rights to dispose of their destinies as the Great World Powers.

The Serbian Nation which has been fighting for this principle throughout the whole of its new history would have despaired to see it realized—having against it powerful enemies—if States like America, Great Britain and France had not declared themselves for Serbia.

Full of hope henceforth for its national future, since those generous States have taken it in their hands, my Nation joins itself to me to thank You and Your noble People for all the rich material help they have sent us to relieve the miseries of the Serbian soldiers and their families.

Allow me to express the hope that the American Nation, together with its Chief, will continue to show us their goodwill in giving their help to my people in its fight for the Cause of Justice and for the deliverance of its brothers who are expecting with impatience the day when they will be able to proclaim their decision to unite themselves all together in free Serbia.

I avail myself with the greatest pleasure of this opportunity, very dear and great Friend, to send You, with the wishes I am forming for the greatness and the welfare of America, the renewed expression of my highest esteem and my sincerest friendship.   Alexander

HwLS (WP, DLC).

From Vance Criswell McCormick

Dear Mr. President: Washington October 24th, 1917.

In accordance with your suggestion I have been trying to work out some plan whereby we could relieve the situation in Italy. After consultation with the various departments of our Government and the representatives of the Italian Government I discovered the whole trouble was a question of ship tonnage. If a sufficient amount of tonnage was furnished to permit the Italian Government to receive the wheat it has already purchased, as well as coal, I think they would be entirely satisfied for the present.

I hope we can make some special arrangement concerning the shipping, because we could then, through our Embassy in Italy, give some publicity to the aid we are thus rendering which should check the propaganda carried on by the anti-war factions in that country, referred to by Ambassador Page.

I expect to meet the shipping representatives with Mr. Hurley today, and hope we can accomplish something.

                 Cordially yours,   Vance C. McCormick

TLS (WP, DLC).

From the Diary of Colonel House

                                        October 24, 1917.

The President and I had a long talk last night alone. We went over the situation carefully. He again expressed pleasure that I was to represent him, and declared once more that he would not be willing for anyone else to do so.

In the course of the conversation, I expressed the opinion that if such a war as this could be justified at all, its justification would be largely because it had given him a commanding opportunity for unselfish service. The great figures in history, like Alexander, Caesar and Napoleon, had used their power for personal and national aggrandizement, but in the present instance, it should be his purpose to use it for the general good of mankind.

I suggested that the time had come when he might make a statement which would be as important as the announcement he made at Mobile regarding the acquisition of territory by force.[1] Then he laid down the principle that no nation should acquite [acquire] territory without the consent of the governed. Now he should lay down the doctrine that nations should be equally unselfish regarding commerce. There should be complete freedom of commerce upon the seas, no preferential tariffs or transportation rates upon land, making the staple products and raw materials of the world acces[s]ible to all.

The President's eyes glistened and he rose to the argument sympathetically. He asked what I thought of his putting it in his message to Congress this coming December. He argued at some length as to his right to address Congress upon such matters, claiming the Constitution really required him to do so when necessary. I concurred heartily. I thought he was in such a commanding position that he could put through anything that was right and that other governments of the world were in such a precarious plight that they would not dare oppose him. In my opinion, it all came down to a question as to whether he was right and whether what he proposed was actually for the good of all mankind and not merely for a portion of it. To all of this he cordially agreed.

There were two other things to which I called his attention, which I thought should be brought out in the same speech. I thought he should express the idea, an idea which I have so often brought out in the diary recently, i.e. the worst that could happen to Germany herself would be a peace made by her present government; that the only peace that could benefit Germany would be a peace made by a representative government.

I suggested he put in the message a threat that if Germany refused to liberalize her government and continued a menace to the world, the democracies would defend themselves by waging an economic war against her until the German menace had been broken.

The President seemed to approve both suggestions, and, I take it, they will appear sometime soon.

I shall not go into the many other matters we discussed, for my time is limited. We outlined a "letter of marque" for me to use with the Governments of Great Britain, France and Italy. Neither of us knew how it should be addressed, whether to the sovereigns or prime ministers. It was decided to consult the State Department today which I have done. Lansing thinks, since the invitation came to participate in the War Council through the

French Ambassador, Dean of the Diplomatic Corps, that the acceptance should go through the same channel. Therefore, the President wrote a letter to the Secretary of State asking him to inform the French Ambassador that he was pleased to accept the invitation of the Allied Governments to participate in the War Council and that he had commissioned me to represent him. We decided that I should also keep the letter he wrote last night addressed to the Prime Ministers, even though that was not the proper procedure. A copy of this letter is attached, as also is one he has written to our Ambassadors at London, Paris and Rome.

We worked over these letters last night, he taking down in short hand the first text, and afterward re-writing them on his typewriter. This morning he wanted to write a letter and address it to the Kings of Great Britain and Italy and the President of the French Republic instead of the one he had written to the Prime Ministers. I urged him not to bother to do so, declaring that I did not believe it would be necessary for me to show any credentials whatsoever. He then suggested that I have a document making it clear that those accompanying me were under my direction. I thought this too unnecessary. I did not believe there would be any difficulty anywhere. I felt that my relations with those going with me were of such a character that they would readily work under my direction, and yield to any suggestion I might make regarding their activities while abroad.

Sargent continues to paint the portrait of the President. We like it fairly well and are wondering whether he can be induced to make a copy. Mrs. Wilson is especially anxious that this be done. I am afraid, however, that Sargent will be obdurate for he has practictically [practically] given up portrait painting and this canvas is the first for many years. It is to go to Dublin. Sargent gave a blank canvass to the Red Cross and it sold for $50,000.00.

The friendship and affection shown me by the President and Mrs. Wilson touches me deeply. There is no subject too intimate to be discussed before me; there is nothing that can be thought of for my comfort or pleasure that is not urged upon me. In bidding me goodbye, the President again told how deeply appreciative he was of my willingness to represent him at the coming Conference.

After lunch, I went to Janet's and she, Louise and I drove for an hour. They left me at the station where Mezes, Miller and I took the Congressional Limited for New York.

[1] Wilson's address at Mobile, Ala., is printed at Oct. 27, 1913, Vol. 28.

An Address to the President
by Vira Boarman Whitehouse[1]

[Oct. 25, 1917]

Mr. President, Sir: I wish to present to you a delegation representing the New York State Woman Suffrage Party. We thank you most heartily for receiving us. We realize the enormous responsibilities which rest upon you at the present time, and we are certain that you would not allow yourself to be distracted from the consideration of our grave National and International war problems, except for a measure which you recognize as of pressing importance—such as the question of Woman Suffrage.

This measure has, as you know, the endorsement of practically every great industrial and social organization, and of every political party in the country. The Republican and Democratic Parties have declared that it should be decided by State action.

The campaign, which the New York State Woman Suffrage Party is conducting to amend the State Constitution by a referendum to the voters on Election Day, is in accordance with such recommendations.

There has never been a campaign for any cause carried on under such conflicting and confusing conditions, as this campaign of ours.

While the war has brought suffrage to the women of Canada and Russia, the assurance of it to the women of Great Britain, and the promise of it to the women of France, here in America it is used by our opponents as a reason for still longer withholding suffrage from us.

While the change of sentiment in favor of Woman Suffrage in our State is very marked, the issue even now, less than two weeks before Election, is overshadowed by the public interest in the multitudinous details of our entering the war. In consequence many men who are heartily in favor of Woman Suffrage do not yet realize that they are to have an opportunity to vote upon it on Election day.

The confusion is due to the difficulty we have found in carrying on an active campaign, because, while there has never before been so large a number of people on record in the State in favor of any measure as the 1,013,800 women enrolled for Suffrage, these very women, almost without exception, are engrossed in serving their country. They canvass from house to house to sell Liberty Bonds, or to enroll for the Hoover Food Campaign; they work for the Red Cross and raise money for it; they go into the factories and are ready to work in the fields. In fact, Mr. President, they are ready to give—they are now giving—the very support to this country which has led the statesmen of our Allies to declare that the war could not be carried on without such active support on the part of the women.

It is recognized that under these new conditions Woman Suffrage has become not only a question of justice, but one of expediency. Mr. Asquith has declared for it on the grounds of expediency—Lloyd George has said it would be an outrage to withhold it.

Viviani has proclaimed that it is the duty of the men to give women the vote.

Sir Robert Borden in Canada is urging it for the Dominion as a war measure.

This is the experience of our allies who have been in the war almost three years longer than we.

Mr. President, we have come to you as the leader of our country's struggle for Democracy, as the leader of this Government founded on the principles of Democracy, on principles which do not fulfill their meaning as long as women are excluded from the franchise. We have come to you to ask you to send to the voters of New York State a message so urgent and so clear that they, on Election Day, cannot fail as patriotic men to place the women of their State on an equal footing with the women of the Allied Countries, and thus to advance the cause of Democracy at home, as they are ready to fight for it abroad.

T MS (WP, DLC).

1 Wilson received a delegation of approximately 110 members of the New York State Woman Suffrage party at the White House at 2 P.M. on October 25.

A Reply

[Oct. 25, 1917]

Mrs. Whitehouse and ladies: It is with great pleasure that I receive you. I esteem it a privilege to do so. I know the difficulties which you have been laboring under in New York State so clearly set forth by Mrs. Whitehouse, but in my judgment those difficulties cannot be used as an excuse by the leaders of any party or by the voters of any party for neglecting the question which you are pressing upon them. Because, after all, the whole world now is witnessing a struggle between two ideals of government. It is a struggle which goes deeper and touches more of the foundations of the organized life of men than any struggle that has ever taken place before, and no settlement of the questions that lie on the surface can satisfy a situation which requires that the questions which lie underneath and at the foundation should also be settled, and settled right. I am free to say that I think the question of woman suffrage is one of those questions which lie at the foundation.

The world has witnessed a slow political reconstruction, and men have generally been obliged to be satisfied with the slowness of the process. In a sense, it is wholesome that it should be slow, because then it is solid and sure. But I believe that this war is going so to quicken the convictions and the consciousness of mankind with regard to political questions that the speed of reconstruction will be greatly increased. And I believe that, just because we are quickened by the questions of this war, we ought to be quickened to give this question of woman suffrage our immediate consideration.

As one of the spokesmen of a great party, I would be doing nothing less than obeying the mandates of that party if I gave my hearty support to the question of woman suffrage which you represent, but I do not want to speak merely as one of the spokesmen of a party. I want to speak for myself and say that it seems to me that this is the time for the states of this Union to take this action. I perhaps may be touched a little too much by the traditions of our politics, traditions which lay such questions almost entirely upon the states, but I want to see communities declare themselves quickened at this time and show the consequence of the quickening. I think the whole country has appreciated the way in which the women have risen to this great occasion. They not only have done what they have been asked to do, and done it with ardor and efficiency, but they have shown a power to organize for doing things of their own initiative which is quite a different thing and a very much more difficult thing, and I think the whole country has admired the spirit and the capacity and the vision of the women of the United States.

It is almost absurd to say that the country depends upon the women for a large part of the inspiration of its life. That is too obvious to say; but it is now depending upon the women also for suggestions of service, which have been rendered in abundance and with the distinction of originality. I, therefore, am very glad to add my voice to those which are urging the people of the great State of New York to set a great example by voting for woman suffrage. It would be a pleasure if I might utter that advice in their presence. Inasmuch as I am bound too close to my duties here to make that possible, I am glad to have the privilege to ask you to convey that message to them.

It seems to me that this is a time of privilege. All our principles, all our hearts, all our purposes, are being searched; searched not only by our own consciences, but searched by the world, and it is time for the people of the states of this country to show the world in what practical sense they have learned the lessons of democracy—that they are fighting for democracy because they believe in it, and that there is no application of democracy which they do not believe in. I feel, therefore, that I am standing upon the firmest foundations of the age in bidding Godspeed to the cause which you represent and in expressing the ardent hope that the people of New York may realize the great occasion which faces them on election day and may respond to it in noble fashion.[1]

T MS (WP, DLC).
    [1] This statement was printed in full, e.g., in the *New York Times*, Oct. 26, 1917.

A Statement[1]

Oct. 25, 1917.

The *chief part of the* burden of finding food supplies for ⟨the Allies, pending the increase in ships,⟩ *the peoples associated with us in war* falls *for the present* upon the American people, and the drain upon supplies on ⟨this⟩ *such a* scale necessarily affects the prices of our necessaries *of life*.

Our country, *however*, is blessed with an abundance of food-stuffs, and if our people will economize in their use of food ⟨beyond the amounts⟩ , *providently confining themselves to the quantities* required for the maintenance of health and strength; if ⟨we can⟩ *they will* eliminate waste; and if ⟨we⟩ *they* will make use of those commodities of which we have a surplus and thus free for export *a larger proportion of* those required by the world *now* dependent upon us, we shall not only be able to accomplish our obligations to them, but we shall ⟨enable the maintenance of⟩ *obtain and establish* reasonable prices at home. To provide an adequate supply of food *both for our own soldiers on the other side of the seas*, for the civil populations and the armies of the Allies ⟨and our own soldiers abroad⟩ is one of our first and fore-most obligations; for if we are to maintain their constancy in this struggle for the independence of all nations, we must also main-tain their health and strength. The ⟨accomplishment⟩ *solution* of our food problems, *therefore*, is dependent upon the individual service of every man, woman and child in the United States. The great voluntary effort in this direction ⟨initiated⟩ *which has been initiated and organized* by the Food Administration under my direction⟨,⟩ offers an opportunity of service in the war ⟨by⟩ *which is open to* every individual⟨.⟩ , *and by which every individual may serve both his own people and the peoples of the world.*

⟨We will not have accomplished our objectives⟩ *We cannot accomplish our objects in this great war* without ⟨great⟩ sacrifice and devotion, and in no direction can that sacrifice and devotion ⟨to the Nation's interest⟩ be shown more than by each home and public eating place in the country pledging its support to the Food Administration and complying ⟨to⟩ *with* its requests.[2]

T MS (C. L. Swem Coll., NjP).
  [1] The following draft was prepared by Herbert Hoover. Words in angle brackets were deleted by Wilson; words in italics were added by him.
  [2] This appeal was published in the *Official Bulletin*, I (Oct. 29, 1917), 1.

To Harry Augustus Garfield

My dear Garfield: The White House 25 October, 1917

I am sending you this report as bearing very directly upon the matters with which you are dealing.[1]

I would be obliged if after you have extracted from it what you need you would be kind enough to transmit it to Mr. Baruch to guide him in the purchases he is making.

Cordially and faithfully yours,   Woodrow Wilson

TLS (H. A. Garfield Papers, DLC).
  [1] Federal Trade Commission, "Revised Memorandum on Cost of Producing Gasoline and Fuel Oil for Certain Companies Supplying the Navy, June–1917," CC MS (H. A. Garfield Papers, DLC).

To Henry Lee Higginson

My dear Major: [The White House] 25 October, 1917

I am sorry to say I have time for only a line to acknowledge your letter of October twenty-second, but I want to assure you that I have had the interests of the railways very much in my mind, particularly of late, and that I hope from what I have learned that the members of the Interstate Commerce Commission are also sincerely concerned that the railroads should suffer no impairment of efficiency and should be enabled in any way that is within the Commission's power to do their business with efficiency and success.

Cordially and sincerely yours,   Woodrow Wilson

TLS (Letterpress Books, WP, DLC).

To Joseph Patrick Tumulty

Dear Tumulty: [The White House, c. Oct. 25, 1917]

It seems to me to be infernal cheek for this man to ask me this question.[1] I am not in favor of any such game as that proposed or of any public game between Army and Navy teams this season; and a newspaper is certainly not the place for me to express any such official judgment.[2] The President.

TL (WP, DLC).
[1] George McLeod Smith to WW, Oct. 23, 1917, TLS (WP, DLC). Smith, the managing editor of the New York *Evening Sun*, proposed a football game between the United States Military Academy and the United States Naval Academy to be played at the Polo Grounds in New York on November 24 for the benefit of the American Red Cross. He estimated that such a game would raise about $100,000. He added that the *Evening Sun* would be "glad to publish an expression of your opinion on the subject."
[2] For Wilson's final word on this subject, see WW to NDB, Nov. 8, 1917.

From Robert Lansing

My dear Mr. President: Washington October 25, 1917.

I have been thinking over further the matter of credentials for Colonel House and I have come to the conclusion that a simpler way than giving him a certified copy of the letter addressed to the French Ambassador here would be for you to give him a formal designation. I therefore enclose a letter which I would suggest be given him. In view of the regard for formality which prevails among European governments it might be well for me to countersign your letter and place upon it the seal of the Department.

If this course meets with your approval will you please sign the letter and return it to me for transmission to Colonel House—indicating whether or not you approve of the countersigning.

Faithfully yours, Robert Lansing

TLS (WP, DLC).

To Robert Lansing

My dear Mr. Secretary: The White House 25 October, 1917

I am very glad to comply with your suggestion about this letter to House and I would be obliged if you would be kind enough to countersign it and see that it is promptly forwarded to him. I believe he leaves New York on Sunday.

Faithfully yours, Woodrow Wilson

TLS (SDR, RG 59, 763.72 SU/11½, DNA).

To Edward Mandell House[1]

Sir: The White House October 25, 1917.

You are hereby designated to represent the Government of the United States at the Conference to be held by representatives of the Allied Governments in the early part of the month of November, 1917.

I am, Sir,   Your obedient servant   Woodrow Wilson

By the President:
Robert Lansing,
Secretary of State.

TLS (E. M. House Papers, CtY).
  [1] Swem copied Lansing's draft on White House stationery. The seal of the Department of State is affixed just beneath Wilson's signature.

From George Creel

My dear Mr. President: Washington, D. C. October 25, 1917.

It has come to me very directly that the publishers of the Vorwarts, the great Yiddish daily in New York, are boasting of their influence in Washington, even declaring that the White House stands between them and the law. This is nonsense, of course, but I do feel it well to lay the situation before you. In the first days of the European war, the Vorwarts was violently anti-German, but with great suddenness, it swung around and became the most consistent pro-German paper in the country. It is absolutely responsible for the demoralization of the East Side, and is the most dangerous influence that we have to combat. Our investigations force me to believe that Vorwarts is also furnishing the money to maintain the New York Call, the Russky Gollos, and Il Proletario. Russky Gollos is a Russian paper, bitterly complained of by the Russian Ambassador, and Il Proliterio is an Italian paper that has been barred from the mails.

This is merely for your information, and requires no answer.
                                Respectfully,   George Creel

TLS (WP, DLC).

From William Moulton Ingraham

My dear Mr. President: Washington. October 25, 1917.

The Department is in receipt of the following cablegram from Governor-General Harrison at Manila:

"I am requested to transmit the following to the President of the United States: 'The Philippine Legislature deems it a duty incumbent upon it to voice the unequivocal expressions of the loyalty of the people of these islands to the cause of the United States of America in the present war and in this solemn manner to ratify and transmit the same to the American people. We realize that in this war there are being tried in the balance the greatest principles of humanity and right which in future will be the foundation of the stability, peace, and security of all nations, whether they be great or small or belong to one race or the other. Our loyalty to the cause is based on the evident justice of the enforced intervention of the American people in this war in which it has been guided solely by the supreme interest of defending universal democracy and upholding the right of small nations to live in confidence and security under their own governments, safe from the threats and perils of autocracy and imperialism. We firmly believe that the final triumph of democracy, in securing for the world the principle of nationality for the benefit of the small nations, will finally enable our people to attain the ideas for which we have always struggled, namely, our constitution into a free and independent nation with a democratic government of law and order, ready to be another instrument of democracy and universal progress.' Harrision."

Very sincerely,   Wm M Ingraham

TLS (WP, DLC).

From Edward Wright Sheldon

My dear Mr. President: [New York] October 25, 1917.

It gratified keenly to receive your extremely kind letter of October nineteenth. I had not meant to add to your manifold burdens even to the extent of acknowledging my own letter, but you have put me deeply in your debt by the glad confirmation of the news of your excellent health, and by your friendly and generous words. I am very well myself and shall earnestly hope for an unbroken continuance of your physical vigor. It means so much for us and for mankind.

Yours most sincerely,   Edward W. Sheldon.

ALS (WP, DLC).

Samuel Gompers to Joseph Patrick Tumulty

My dear Mr. Tumulty: Washington October 25, 1917

May I trouble you by calling to your attention a letter which I have addressed to the Hon. Newton D. Baker, Secretary of War, and a copy of which you will find here enclosed?[1]

Since writing the letter I have learned that the President has time either Wednesday or Thursday of the coming week which he may be able so to dispose of that he can hear the Committee on Housing, to which reference is made in the letter to Mr. Baker. If you can arrange this for Wednesday, owing to the critical situation, and so advise me, I shall feel under additional obligation.[2]   Sincerely yours,   Saml. Gompers.

TLS (WP, DLC).

[1] S. Gompers to NDB, Oct. 25, 1917, CCL (WP, DLC). Gompers urgently requested interviews with both Baker and Wilson for himself and the other members of the newly established Committee on Housing of the Advisory Commission of the Council of National Defense to discuss the housing situation for workers engaged on war contracts.

[2] Wilson saw Gompers and his committee on October 31.

To Edward Mandell House

Dear House,   The White House. 26 October, 1917.

I think it would be well for you to take this memorandum with you.[1] It is very specific and I think speaks the full truth about the shipping situation. It also shows how seriously we are taking it and trying to solve it. It will serve as an answer to the message you sent me a week or so ago.[2]

I hate to say good-bye. It is an immense comfort to me to have you at hand here for counsel and for friendship. But it is right that you should go. God bless and keep you both! My thoughts will follow you all the weeks through,—and I hope that it will be only weeks that will separate us.

Mrs. Wilson joins in all affectionate messages.

Affectionately Yours,   [blank]

WWTL (E. M. House Papers, CtY).

[1] E. N. Hurley to WW, Oct. 17, 1917.

[2] E. Drummond to W. Wiseman, Oct. 11, 1917.

To William Lea Chambers

My dear Judge Chambers: [The White House] 26 October, 1917

May I not express my very deep and serious interest in your efforts to bring the railroad executives and the brotherhoods engaged in train operation to an agreement that there shall be no interruption in their relations on either side until ample opportunity shall have been afforded the United States Board of Mediation and Conciliation to bring about if possible an amicable agreement, and that in the event of a failure to bring about such an agreement any controversy that may have arisen will be submitted to arbitration in accordance with the provisions of the Newlands law? I take it for granted that your efforts will succeed, because it is inconceivable to me that patriotic men should now for a moment contemplate the interruption of the transportation which is so absolutely necessary to the safety of the nation and to its success in arms, as well as to its whole industrial life; but I wanted, nevertheless, to express my deep personal interest in the matter and to wish you Godspeed. The last thing I should wish to contemplate would be the possibility of being obliged to take any unusual measures to operate the railways, and I have so much confidence that the men you are dealing with will appreciate the patriotic motives underlying your efforts that I shall look forward with assurance to your success.

Cordially and sincerely yours,   Woodrow Wilson

TLS (Letterpress Books, WP, DLC).

To Newton Diehl Baker

My dear Mr. Secretary: [The White House] 26 October, 1917

You will know how to acknowledge for me the enclosed admirable resolutions. I hope that you will have my appreciation expressed in the warmest terms. It would seem as if the people of the Philippine Islands were really awaking to the great opportunities of a new time.

Cordially and faithfully yours,   Woodrow Wilson

TLS (Letterpress Books, WP, DLC).

To Edward Nash Hurley

My dear Hurley: [The White House] 26 October, 1917

Just a line to say that I take it for granted that the allotment of ships proposed to Italy will be acquiesced in by the Shipping Board, but I nevertheless take the liberty of writing to say that in my judgment it is necessary to do something of this sort in order to set matters straight there which might go very wrong indeed if they were not promptly offset.

Cordially and sincerely yours,   [Woodrow Wilson]

CCL (WP, DLC).

From Newton Diehl Baker

Dear Mr. President: Washington. October 26, 1917.

Mr. Frank A. Scott, chairman of the War Industries Board, called on me to-day after the formal acceptance of his resignation, to ask me to convey to you an expression of appreciation on his part of your confidence in him. He asked me whether he should seek an audience with you to pay his formal respects in leaving the Government service, but I assured him that I would convey his message in that regard to you and that you would not misunderstand his not calling in person.

I venture to suggest that he would value very highly a note from you expressing regret at the necessity he is under of separating himself from the public service in which he has been so conspicuously useful and faithful.

Respectfully yours,   Newton D. Baker

TLS (WP, DLC).

From George Creel

Dear Mr. President: Washington, D. C. October 6, 1917.

I am sending, under separate cover, the report just received from Brand Whitlock, and think that you might desire to read it. It is a tremendous thing in my opinion. I plan to divide it into six installments and run it day after day in every newspaper in the United States. Every word of it is front page material.[1]

May I have your authorization for this plan?

Respectfully,   George Creel

TLS (WP, DLC).
[1] The "report" was the one on German atrocities in Belgium which Frank L. Polk had asked Whitlock to write in a dispatch sent to him in mid-August. B. Whitlock to FLP, Aug. 16, 1917, Allan Nevins, ed., *The Letters and Journal of Brand Whitlock* (2 vols., New York and London, 1936), I, 233-34. Whitlock's journal reveals that he was working on the report as late as September 29 (*ibid.*, II, 444-46). This report should not be confused with Whitlock's book on Belgium (about which see WW to RL, Aug. 16, 1917, n. 1, Vol. 43), which he was working on at the same time.

From Harry Augustus Garfield

Dear Mr. President: [Washington] October 26, 1917

It is my understanding that in fixing provisional prices for the sale of coal, it was intended to allow a fair profit to the operators. The public does not desire, nor is it necessary to meet the present emergency, that the coal industry should be asked to make more of a sacrifice than may reasonably be required of all staple industries. Exorbitant profits only have been the subject of concern. It needs no argument to justify Congressional and Executive action against profiteering, when the people of the United States are called upon to make unusual sacrifices.

As a result of the conference held in Washington between the operators and the miners of the Central Field, an agreement was reached on the 6th of October providing, among other things, an increase of wages as follows:

An advance of 10¢ per ton to miners,

Advances ranging from 75¢ to $1.40 per day to laborers,

An advance of 15% for yardage and dead work.

This will result in an increase to miners of 50% and to the best paid laborers of 78% over the wages of April 1, 1914. These increases are not in excess of the advance in cost of living for that period.

It is obvious that these advances in wages must be taken either from the operator or the consumer. On the assumption that the prices fixed yielded a fair profit to the operator, it is clear that if this increase of wages is to fall entirely upon the operators, their profits will no longer be fair, unless the result of the increase bears an insignificant relation to those profits. This question was submitted to me, as Fuel Administrator. It is not possible to estimate the exact effect of the proposed increases upon the prices fixed.

In view of the foregoing consideration, I respectfully recommend that the prices fixed by your proclamation of August 21st and such modification as have been made pursuant to your order of August 23rd appointing a Fuel Administrator, for the sale of bituminous coal at the mines, be uniformly increased in the sum of [blank] cents per ton, subject, however, to the following exceptions:

(1) This increase in prices shall not apply to any coal sold at the mine under an existing contract containing a provision for an increase in the price of coal thereunder in case of an increase in wages paid to miners.

(2) This increase in prices shall not apply in any district in which the operators and miners fail to agree upon a penalty provision, satisfactory to the Fuel Administrator, for the automatic collection of fines in the spirit of the agreement entered into betweeen the operators and miners at Washington, October 6, 1917.

For your information, I attach hereto a copy of the supplemental agreement of October 6, 1917 between the operators and the miners of the Central Competitive Fields composed of Western Pennsylvania, Ohio, Indiana and Illinois.

Respectfully submitted,   [H. A. Garfield]

CCL (H. A. Garfield Papers, DLC).

From the Diary of Josephus Daniels

1917 Friday 26 October

At Cabinet meeting the President spoke of good work I had been doing and of the other members. I took Admiral Browning, of the British Navy,[1] & the President emphasized to him his earnest desire to do something audacious in the line of offense.

Pres. told of Aspinwall, Iowa, where Germans lived. They took no Liberty bonds. Delegation from near-by towns went over, shut up every store, arrested the owner of the town hall because he would not permit its use for a Liberty Loan meeting. WW: What right or authority? None McAdoo thought obstructing the liberty bond campaign.

Burleson told of pro-German papers. When their editors were sent for he asked: Have you printed that Germans dropped bombs on Red Cross hospitals? Have you printed any atrocities practised by Germans? In every case such news had been deleted & they promised it would not occur again.

[1] That is, Vice-Admiral Sir Montague E. Browning.

To George Creel

My dear Creel: The White House 27 October, 1917

Please don't pay any attention to such boasts as you quote from the Vorwarts. This is a thorny business we are handling in the matter of these disloyal newspapers, but I am keeping in close touch with the Postmaster General and I believe the thing is being worked out with some degree of equity and success.

In haste   Faithfully yours,   Woodrow Wilson

TLS (G. Creel Papers, DLC).

To Harry Augustus Garfield

My dear Garfield: The White House 27 October, 1917

Thank you for sending me these. I take pleasure in returning both the order[1] and the letter with my sincere approval.

Cordially and faithfully yours,   Woodrow Wilson

TLS (H. A. Garfield Papers, DLC).
[1] The order provided for an increase of forty-five cents per ton for bituminous coal. *Official Bulletin*, I (Oct. 29, 1917), 2.

To Joseph Patrick Tumulty

Dear Tumulty: [The White House, c. Oct. 27, 1917]

I do not think that this lady is in the condition of mind to discuss this matter,[1] but I would be very much obliged if you would take this letter to Louis Brownlow and find out whether he really knows the conditions at Occoquan, letting him see how very important I deem it to see that there is certainly no sufficient foundation for such statements as Mrs. Kendall makes.

The President.

TL (WP, DLC).
[1] A White House memorandum reveals that he referred to a letter to Tumulty, dated October 23, 1917, from Mrs. Frederick W. Kendall of Hamburg, New York. She protested against the treatment of suffragettes imprisoned at Occoquan.

From Robert Lansing, with Enclosure

PERSONAL AND CONFIDENTIAL:
My dear Mr. President: Washington October 27, 1917.

I had this morning another interview with Viscount Ishii. As you know I submitted to him last Monday a memorandum relative to the important clause which had been stricken out of the note to be sent him. He submitted the matter to his Government and has received a proposed protocol instead of the memorandum suggested by me. I enclose a copy for your consideration. It is my view that this practically covers the ground and of course avoids the idea of suspicion as to Japan's purpose which might have been drawn from the memorandum submitted by us.

This protocol would be signed by the Viscount and myself and retained confidentially, but he informs me that his Government does not feel it would have to be kept as secret as a memorandum such as we proposed.

I would be obliged if you could indicate your wishes as soon as possible as Viscount Ishii is very anxious to set out on his homeward journey.   Faithfully yours,   Robert Lansing.

TLS (WP, DLC).

E N C L O S U R E

The Special Mission of Japan

Protocol.

In the course of the conversations between the Japanese Special Ambassador and the Secretary of State of the United States which have led to the exchange of notes between them dated this day, declaring the policy of the two Governments with regard to China,[1] the question of embodying the following clause in such declaration came up for discussion: "they (the Governments of Japan and the United States) will not take advantage of the present conditions to seek special rights or privileges in China which would abridge the rights of the subjects or citizens of other friendly states."

Upon careful examination of the question, it was agreed that the clause above quoted being superfluous in the relations of the two Governments and liable to create erroneous impression in the minds of the public, should be eliminated from the declaration.

It was, however, well understood that the principle enunciated in the clause which was thus suppressed was in perfect accord with the policy actually pursued by the two Governments in China.

T MS (WP, DLC).

[1] For the text of the notes exchanged by Lansing and Ishii on November 2, 1917, see *FR 1917*, pp. 264-65. See also Burton F. Beers, *Vain Endeavor: Robert Lansing's Attempts to End the American-Japanese Rivalry* (Durham, N. C., 1962), pp. 111-19.

From Edward Mandell House, with Enclosures

Dear Governor: New York. October 27, 1917.

When Mezes was in Washington he saw both Houston and Taussig. I asked him to give me a memorandum of what they said. In view of our conversation concerning your coming message to Congress I am sending this memorandum to you for your information.

I feel very strongly that something should be done at the Peace Conference to end, as far as practicable, trade restrictions. They have been and must continue to be a menace to peace. With tariff barriers broken, with subsidies by common consent eliminated, and with real freedom of the seas both in peace and in time of war, the world could look with confidence to the future.

There should be no monopoly by any nation of raw materials, or the essentials for food and clothing.

You announced in your Mobile speech the doctrine that no territory should ever again be acquired by aggression, and this doctrine is now generally recognized throughout the world. If you can now use your commanding position to bring to the fore this other doctrine which is so fundamental to peace, you will have done more for mankind than any other ruler that has lived.

If you write such a message as we talked of, I hope you will think it well to say that the worst thing that could happen to Germany would be a peace made by a government that was not representative. That such a peace would inevitably lead to economic warfare afterwards—a warfare in which by force of circumstances this Government would be compelled to take part.

I shall think of you and dear Mrs. Wilson constantly while I am away, and I shall put forth the best there is in me to do the things you have intrusted to me. I am sure you know how happy you have made me by giving me this great opportunity to serve.

Will you not remember that one of the highest duties imposed upon you is to care for yourself, for I do not put it too strongly when I say you are the one hope left to this torn and distracted world. Without your leadership God alone knows how long we will wander in the wilderness.

Yours with devotion and affection,   E. M. House

TLS (WP, DLC).

ENCLOSURE I

MEMORANDUM

Taussig says that his commission has in preparation for publication a report (due January 1, 1918, but probably to be delayed a month or more) which would make the recommendations listed below.[1] The report does not deal with colonies or dependencies which are not self-governing, that is, whose tariff laws are drafted by the mother country.

The report will recommend that no effort be made to interfere with the adoption of any tariff policy that may seem best to it by any nation, but that it shall be agreed that the tariff adopted by any nation or self-governing dependency shall apply without discrimination or allowance of special privileges to goods coming from any source whatever; subject, however, to the two following exceptions:

1. Where two jurisdictions have long lines of common frontier, as in the case of Austria and Germany, or of the United States and Canada, that special tariff arrangements may be allowable; and

2. That in cases where traditional or historical relations are peculiar and somewhat unique, as between ourselves and Cuba, or once more, between Germany and Austria, exceptions may also be allowed.

A further item in the recommendation as to our own domestic policy is to be that Congress shall vest in the President the authority to impose punitive duties on specified articles in cases where other nations do not, in ways to be specified in the law, follow out the program indicated above.

¹ See F. W. Taussig to WW, Nov. 8, 1917.

E N C L O S U R E   I I

MEMORANDUM

Houston urged that the stability of the peace to be ultimately concluded would be powerfully furthered if the following provisions should be agreed to and their *continued observation insured*.

1. Universal free trade or abolition of tariffs; this being all but indispensable in "backward" areas (e.g. Asia Minor and Central Africa) and in colonies that do not enjoy self-government in tariff matters.

2. Access to international railways and shipping facilities of *all* freight and passengers without special privilege for nationals of any country, i.e., the regulation of international commerce carriers on lines similar to those adopted by us in the regulation of interstate commerce, and by a body in general similar to our Interstate Commerce Commission.

3. (Less, but very important). No ship or rail subsidies.

4. The putting of international cables and wireless under the Postal Union or some similar international body, so that business intelligence and news may move freely, uncontrolled by special

privilege anywhere. Possibly there should also be international regulation of such news bureaus as Reuter and Wolff.

These provisos he regarded as important in the order of their mention. As to the abolition of tariffs, he pointed out that the revenue from customs in this country constitutes at present a little more than one-tenth of the total revenue from taxes enjoyed by this government. In times of ordinary expenditure revenues derived from other sources than custom duties could be greatly reduced by this country and still meet all the necessities of government; and the same or a similar condition exists in other belligerent countries, and no doubt in a number of neutral countries.

He pointed out further that our present loans to other governments called for an annual interest payment to us of approximately $500,000,000, and that other debts due us abroad would raise our income earnings from such sources to an amount totaling six or seven million to a billion annually. The meeting of these interest obligations by other nations and their nationals would be rendered very difficult if we did not allow them to pay in part in duty free goods, and would be greatly facilitated if they could do so.

He thought that it would not be difficult to make it clear to other governments that the abolition of tariffs would be to their interest; in the first place, and pre-eminently because rivalry among them would be reduced to a rivalry in efficiency, in order to extend and hold profitable markets beyond their borders, and would no longer include the irritating element of unfair discrimination; but also because to each markets would then be opened which have been closed or barred by tariff difficulties and vexations. For instance, if free trade prevailed in the extensive English colonial markets, great possibilities would be opened up to Germany and France. If it prevailed in the French colonies, opportunities would in a similar way be opened up to England and Germany. He recalled that one of the leading French statesmen had recently suggested that the razing of the tariff barriers about the North African colonies of France was advisable, and that his statement did not meet opposition in the French Chamber or French press. He also expressed his opinion that if the abolition of the tariff in this country could be presented to the people as a measure indispensable or highly conducive to the stability and permanence of peace, a sufficient additional force would be added to the sentiment in favor of such a policy that already exists to insure its adoption.

T MS (WP, DLC).

From William Cox Redfield

Personal and *Confidential.*

Dear Mr. President: Washington, D. C., October 27, 1917.

I know what must be your keen interest in the New York City election and, of course, as a voter in that city I am myself deeply concerned about it. I confess that as the situation is today it looks as if we were doomed to four years of Tammany Hall and probably to four unusually bad years even for Tammany. Hyland is a Brooklyn man of a radical, yet of a rather weak type, without experience in large matters, of whom the best that can be said is that he has shown radical tendencies as a county judge with limited jurisdiction yet with a record that is negatively good.

Today I have received a letter from my valued friend, Dr. Charles R. Richards, head of the Cooper Union.[1] In that relation he is in intimate touch with the life of the plainer people of the city. He lives himself in the east side, on Second Avenue.

I have not ventured myself to say a word because of my federal position. I should like to make it plain where I stand—which is, of course, for Mitchel—if you think it wise for me to do so. I wish you felt it in your own power, considering the occasion as a purely non-partisan one, to raise your own voice on behalf of the best administration New York City has had for many a long year. I have been an officer of that city. I know what Tammany standards mean and I look forward with horror to their being reestablished.   Yours very truly,   William C. Redfield

TLS (WP, DLC).
[1] Charles Russell Richards.

From William Lea Chambers

My dear Mr. President: Washington October 27, 1917.

Please let me thank you for your letter of the 26th which quite meets the situation and is particularly opportune in connection with the New York, New Haven & Hartford Railroad case which Mr. Hanger has been mediating for some days past. I have a telegram from him this morning, dated New York, 11:20 last night as follows:

"Situation here serious by reason of the fact that company unwilling to arbitrate one of cases in controversy. Will not be able to meet appointment in Chicago for week at least. Notify Chicago bearing in mind that Illinois Central may claim precedence there."

In reply I have wired him to hold railroad officials in conference until a messenger arrives this evening. I am sending him
the original of your letter and believe a quick agreement to arbitrate will be the result.

With your letter, I propose to have a meeting with the executives of the organizations during the coming week, and if it is
possible for you to give me an appointment for a very brief interview there are a few questions I would like to discuss with you.
I do not think more than a few moments would be required for
the interview.

I have just concluded a very important settlement on the
Atlantic Coast Line Railway, a mediation agreement being signed
yesterday afternoon, and am now engaged on a Baltimore & Ohio
case which I think will result in a mediation settlement.

Very respectfully yours,   W. L. Chambers

TLS (WP, DLC).

From Herbert Bruce Brougham

My dear Mr. Wilson: Philadelphia 27th October 1917

The record of my correspondence with you concerning the
Public Ledger's news of the cession of the Danish West Indies,
which, as you will recall, was voluntarily withheld from publication by us for many weeks,[1] should attest sufficiently to you and
to Mr. Lansing my own attitude toward matters which concern
the State Department. I may add that we have preserved almost
meticulous circumspection with regard to news on other matters
the publication of which might seriously affect American foreign
relations.

You will not wish to believe, I am sure, that my personal attitude toward the prescriptions of the State Department could
suddenly change to one of disrespect and contempt. Yet that
seems to be the impression conveyed to Mr. Lansing in a report
made of Mr. Patchen's telephonic conversation with me on 24th
October, concerning Mr. Bullitt's dispatch which appeared on
that morning in the Public Ledger.[2]

May I say that I knew nothing whatever about this publication until I saw it in our newspaper? This fact I tried to make
clear to Mr. Patchen. When he asked me what possible explanation could be given of its appearance, contrary to the expressed
warning of the State Department previously sent to this office,
both Mr. Patchen and I were laboring under the mistaken assumption that Mr. Spurgeon[3] must have ordered the dispatch to

be printed. I was at pains to tell Mr. Patchen, however, that Mr. Spurgeon was out of town, that I could not venture to speak for him in his absence, but I thought personally that his ordering of the dispatch to be printed (and I knew nothing to the contrary) could only be from his judgment that the information it conveyed would not be of military advantage to the enemy, and that its publication of news responsibly derived was according to the functions of the newspaper and his conception of his duty to his readers. "Please understand," I distinctly reiterated, "that this is only a tentative interpretation which might be put upon it; as I have told you, Mr. Spurgeon is away, and I really do not know what is his view of the case."

I have felt, on account of our very cordial relations, extending over a series of years from your Presidency of Princeton, that this detailed personal explanation is due you. Mr. Spurgeon's letter to Mr. Lansing[4] suffices to show his attitude toward this deplorable incident.   Very sincerely yours,   H. B. Brougham

TLS (WP, DLC).
[1] WW to H. B. Brougham, June 29, 1916, CCL; H. B. Brougham to RL, July 8, 1916, TLS; WW to H. B. Brougham, July 13, 1916, CCL; H. B. Brougham to WW, July 18, 1916, TLS; WW to H. B. Brougham, July 20 and 25, 1916 (two letters), CCL; and H. B. Brougham to WW, July 27, 1916, TLS, all in WP, DLC.
[2] William C. Bullitt, "House to Go to Paris War Conference," Philadelphia *Public Ledger*, Oct. 24, 1917. As the title indicates, Bullitt's chief revelation was that House was to attend the conference of the Allies in Paris in November. He admitted that there had as yet been no official announcement of House's trip and that Lansing refused either to confirm or deny that House was about to leave for France, but he stated that he was "informed on thoroughly trustworthy authority" that House would go. Bullitt further declared that Walter Lippmann was to accompany House as his chief assistant. The great significance of House's participation in the conference, Bullitt wrote, lay in the fact that, during the meeting, "the entire question of war aims" would be "discussed in full."
[3] John J. Spurgeon, executive editor of the Philadelphia *Public Ledger*.
[4] Printed as an Enclosure with RL to JPT, Nov. 6, 1917.

Vira Boarman Whitehouse to Joseph Patrick Tumulty

Dear Mr. Tumulty: New York Oct. 27th, 1917

I have written a letter of thanks to the President,[1] but I keep thinking of how much we owe to you for having obtained for us this interview with the President and for having made all the arrangements in so perfect a manner. Every member of the delegation was delighted with everything, and I must confess to you that I, myself, was pleasantly surprised by the warmth of the President's speech and by the very great and visible effect it has had upon our campaign.

We expect to win and we will know that this occasion has been a large factor in our victory, and we shall know, too, that you deserve a lion's share of our gratitude.

Yours sincerely,   Vira Boarman Whitehouse.

TLS (WP, DLC).
¹ It is missing in WP, DLC.

To Edward Mandell House

The White House. October 28, 1917.

Goodbye   God bless and keep you.   Wilson.

TC telegram (E. M. House Papers, CtY).

From Newton Diehl Baker

My dear Mr. President: Washington. October 28, 1917.

On October 17th you sent me a note, which I herewith return, from Mr. Morgenthau.¹

I have had this suggestion up in various forms and have conferred about it with the Secretary of Agriculture and others. We are clear that it would be difficult to secure any large body of valuably trained agricultural labor to send to France for this purpose. Our own difficulties in that matter are great and the men whom we would send would, of course, be withdrawn from agriculture in this country and have a brief seasonal occupation in France, where they would have to be fed and maintained and where the output of their labor could not possibly be so great as in this country.

An alternative suggestion has occurred to me which may have some value, and I am asking General Bliss to take it up with General Pershing. It would involve the use of such Americans in General Pershing's force as are trained farmers for brief periods of plowing and planting and harvesting, by granting them furlough and assigning them to particular districts in France. Whether or not this can be worked out as a practical thing can only be determined, I fancy, by General Pershing; but I am putting the whole case before General Bliss, who will take it up and endeavor to arrive at some helpful conclusion. Should General Pershing, in cooperation with the French Minister of Agriculture,² believe that he could be helpful in this regard, we might send over some tractors and gang plows to be helpfully used when the planting season arrives.

Respectfully,   Newton D. Baker

TLS (WP, DLC).

1 H. Morgenthau to WW, Oct. 16, 1917, TLS (WP, DLC).
2 Ferdinand David.

From Edward Mandell House, with Enclosure

Dear Governor: New York. October 28, 1917.

I am enclosing you a copy of a letter which has just come from Frazier.

I have heard from many quarters the same story so it is doubtless true. Tardieu, I think, was the last one who spoke to me about it.

It seems that Pershing, knowing Joffre, has been with him much and has counseled with him rather than with Petain. Petain, I am told, is both vain and jealous, but, nevertheless, he is the one Pershing should cooperate with since Joffre has no authority whatsoever.

I shall give Bliss a hint of the trouble and let him try to straighten it out.   Affectionately yours,   E. M. House

TLS (WP, DLC).

E N C L O S U R E

Arthur Hugh Frazier to Edward Mandell House

Dear Mr. House: Paris. October 12, 1917.

A report was brought to me a few days ago by a trustworthy person that M. Painlevé, the Prime Minister and Minister of War had expressed the earnest hope that you might come to France in the near future. It was explained to me that M. Painlevé desired your presence to reconcile differences of opinion between General Pershing and General Pétain; personally I believe that these differences have been greatly exaggerated and will find their own solution.

Nevertheless, in the fourth year of the war, with everyone rather weary of the whole thing, I seem to notice more signs of lack of harmony between the Allies than ever before. As we are the most disinterested nation engaged and as we have the confidence of all the Allies to a greater extent than any other country I believe it is our logical rôle to unite the Allies in concerted action and to act as a general harmonizing influence. You are far better able to judge than I whether it is advisable for you to come to Europe at the present time but I am sure that if you should decide to come now you would find a very warm welcome in France.   Respectfully yours,   Arthur Hugh Frazier.

TCL (N. D. Baker Papers, DLC).

From the Diary of Josephus Daniels

1917 Sunday 28 October

In afternoon had a long talk with Admiral Benson about trip & the big questions before us.

"I have perfect faith that Providence orders our ways in our daily life["] he said. It is beautiful to see a strong & able man with such childlike faith. He goes on that faith. I gave him WW's message & instructions: All possible cooperation but we must be free.

To Newton Diehl Baker

My dear Mr. Secretary: The White House 29 October, 1917

House has sent me the enclosed which I think is of rather serious significance. It seems that General Pershing, having known Marshal Joffre before going to France, has quite naturally been consulting him a great deal and General Petain very little. Petain has been hurt by this, and it would doubtless be very well to have a hint dropped to General Pershing.

In House's letter which accompanied this he says, "I shall give Bliss hint of the trouble and let him try to straighten it out." Perhaps that is the best way.

Cordially and sincerely yours,   Woodrow Wilson

TLS (N. D. Baker Papers, DLC).

To Thomas Watt Gregory

[The White House]

My dear Mr. Attorney General: 29 October, 1917

I dare say we should only be assisting Mr. Hillquit by apparently making him a martyr if the Government should pay any attention to his recent outrageous utterances about the Liberty Loan, but so many people have been disturbed by what he has said that I take the liberty of sending you the enclosed letter[1] and of asking what you have been thinking about the matter.

Cordially and faithfully yours,   Woodrow Wilson

TLS (Letterpress Books, WP, DLC).

¹ It is missing. However, a White House memorandum reveals that it was a letter dated October 25, 1917, from Charles P. Lundquiste of Brooklyn which discussed "utterances of Candidate Hilquit concerning the Liberty Loan."

To William Cox Redfield

Personal.

My dear Mr. Secretary: [The White House] 29 October, 1917

Thank you for having let me see the enclosed letter. I am sorry to say that I cannot take any part in the mayoralty campaign in New York. To tell you the truth, I have lost confidence in Mayor Mitchel of late, for reasons which I hope I may have an opportunity of explaining to you soon. I dare say that from the point of view of those who, like myself, cannot admire him it is Hobson's choice in this respect, and I realize how serious the issues involved are.

Cordially and sincerely yours,   [Woodrow Wilson]

CCL (WP, DLC).

To Frank Augustus Scott

My dear Mr. Scott: [The White House] 29 October, 1917

Thank you for the kind message you sent me through the Secretary of War.

It is with genuine regret on the part of all of us that we see you retire from the important post you have occupied with so much credit to yourself and usefulness to the Government, and I want to send you this line to express my sincere thanks and appreciation and to say how much I hope that your health is not seriously impaired and that it will soon be firmly re-established.

Cordially and sincerely yours,   Woodrow Wilson

TLS (Letterpress Books, WP, DLC).

From Franklin Delano Roosevelt, with Enclosure

Dear Mr. President: Washington. October 29, 1917.

I am very sorry to bother you, but in view of our several talks during the summer I am sending a copy of a memorandum which I have just given to the Secretary. As you probably know, Admiral Mayo reported on his return that the British Admiralty would like "serious consideration" of the Straits of Dover and Scotland to

Norway barriers, and a week or so later we telegraphed Admiral Sims to ask whether the British Admiralty really approved attempting the plan. We received an affirmative reply a few days ago and now our General Board has also approved.

This much has been accomplished in six months, but it is my duty to tell you that if the plan is put into execution with the same speed and method employed in the past other priceless months will be wasted and the success of the plan will be jeopodized [jeopardized]. I can only repeat what I have told the Secretary: Some one person in whom you have confidence should be given the order and the necessary authority to execute the plan without delay, and he, working with an Englishman clothed with the same orders and authority, will succeed if success is possible.

I dislike exaggeration, but it is really true that the elimination of all submarines from the waters between the United States and Europe must of necessity be a vital factor in winning the war.

Faithfully yours,   Franklin D Roosevelt

TLS (WP, DLC).

ENCLOSURE

CONFIDENTIAL   October 29, 1917.

MEMORANDUM FOR THE SECRETARY:

SUBJECT: Proposed measures to close English Channel and North Sea against submarines by mine barrage.

1. This is, of course, nothing more nor less than a resurrection of my proposition, which, with all earnestness possible, I called to the attention of the President, the Secretary of the Navy, the Chief of Operations, the General Board, Admiral Sims (and through the British Admiralty), Admiral de Chair (and through him also the British Admiralty) and Admiral Chocheprat (and through him the French Ministry of Marine) during the months of May and June past.

2. While I have never claimed that the proposed plan was an infallible one, and while, quite properly, I have never attempted to lay down the exact location or the exact type of mines, etc., to be used in the barrage, I did state, and still state, that every consideration of common sense requires that the attempt be made, first in the English Channel and then in the North Sea.

3. But above all, starting when the Balfour and Viviani Missions were here in May, I reiterated the need for haste. I know how unseemly it is to seem to say "I told you so," but it is a literal fact that, while the British Admiralty may be blamed in part,

our own Navy Department is at least largely responsible for failing to consider this proposition seriously during all of these months—May, June, July, August, September and October—which have gone over the dam beyond recall.

4. Now, this is the milk in the cocoanut: The powers that be seem at last willing to take up this proposition seriously. Unless we are willing to throw up our hands and say it is too late, we must admit that the same need for immediate haste exists today as existed last May. We have done altogether too much amiable "consideration" of this matter. If it is to be carried out at all it must be carried out with a different spirit from any of the operations up to now. It will require prompt decision all along the line and an immediate carrying out of the procurement of the materiel—mines and ships.

5. To accomplish the above it should be placed in the hands of one man on our part and one man on the part of the British. These two men should receive orders from their governments, not as to details, but simply orders to carry out the plan. *And most important of all, these men should have all the authority requisite to do this.* This is a bigger matter than sending destroyers abroad or a division of battleships, or building a bunch of new destroyers—it is vital to the winning of the war. Its success cannot be guaranteed. No military or naval operation can be guaranteed. But if it works it will be the biggest single factor in winning the war. I have seen something during the past four and a half years of how our present Navy Department organization works and it so happens that I am also fairly familiar with the way the British Admiralty works. If the suggested plan is carried out solely under the present organizations its chance of success will, in my judgment, be seriously diminished. You need somebody with imagination and authority to make the try.

6. I know you will not mind my sending a copy of this to the President, as I have discussed it with him several times.

Franklin D Roosevelt

CCS MS (WP, DLC).

From Edward Nash Hurley

Dear Mr. President: Washington October 29, 1917.

Regarding the allotment of ships to Italy, the Shipping Board has acted and we are assigning ships for their service. We are putting forth a special effort to be helpful.

Very faithfully yours,   Edward N Hurley

TLS (WP, DLC).

To Newton Diehl Baker

My dear Mr. Secretary: The White House 30 October, 1917

Thank you for your letter of the twenty-eighth about Mr. Morgenthau's suggestion concerning agriculture in France. I entirely agree with your conclusions. I had already written Morgenthau adding this, that several intimations had reached me that there was likely to be very considerable jealousy on the part of the laboring people in France of any attempt to substitute foreign labor for their own.[1]

I think a partial plan such as you yourself suggest would not excite that jealousy, and it may be that General Pershing may find some opportunity for acting upon it.

Always Faithfully yours, Woodrow Wilson

TLS (N. D. Baker Papers, DLC).
[1] WW to H. Morgenthau, Oct. 17, 1917, TLS (Letterpress Books, WP, DLC).

To Joseph Patrick Tumulty, with Enclosure

Dear Tumulty: [The White House, Oct. 30, 1917]

Will you not be kind enough to write Mr. Sinclair a letter saying how much I appreciate the frankness and sincerity and also the generous personal kindness of his letter, and adding this, that I feel convinced that as case follows case in dealings of the Post Office Department with this matter his impression will be very much altered as to the way in which they are being handled? I certainly sympathize with his own principles in this delicate business as stated in his letter.

Please tell him that his suggestion interests me very much and I shall certainly consider the feasibility of acting upon it.

The President.

TL (WP, DLC).

E N C L O S U R E

From Upton Beall Sinclair

Pasadena California

My Dear President Wilson: October 22, 1917.

Recently you said in a public statement that you had been watching with appreciation the activities of those Socialists and labor men who had given their support to the war.[1] Being one of

[1] He referred to Wilson's letter to the American Alliance for Labor and Democracy, WW to S. Gompers, Aug. 31, 1917. Among the leading members of this organization were a number of prowar Socialists.

the group to which you had reference, I am taking the liberty of addressing the most heavily burdened man in the world.

I have supported your policy, though to do so I had to break with the Socialist party, to which I have belonged for sixteen years, and which has meant more to me than I can say. I took the step because I believed that the power of the Prussian military caste must be broken, and that civilization waits until this job has been done. Your reply to the peace letter of the Pope, which came after I had taken my hard decission, was to me a source of inexpressible satisfaction. It was a vindication of my faith in you and in my country. I consider it the greatest sermon ever preached for Democracy, and I believe that it will be judged by posterity as America's greatest contribution to this war.

So, if I come now to plead with you, you will understand that it is as a friend of your house. I am troubled—not by anything you have done, but by some things which your subordinates have done, which seem to me to contradict your appeal for democracy, and to weaken the effect of your message abroad. I believe that I voice the sentiments of millions throughout America, who will give their sincere support to a war for democracy, but who will feel weakened in their enthusiasm if they see any signs that while helping to win democracy abroad, we are losing it at home. What I have reference to is the barring of Socialist papers from the mails, which through a new law is soon to mean their barring from all means of transportation, and their virtual auppression [suppression]. I have seen the Postmaster-General and his subordinates going from one extreme to another, until I can no longer withhold a protest.

In your letter to Max Eastman[2] you state that the line is hard to draw; and I appreciate that. We have an enormous foreign element, in part an enemy element, to which the enemy has been making every sort of treacherous appeal. We have also unintelligent, violent factions; I know, for I have met them in the labor struggles which I have studied at first hand. In the course of this letter I hope to offer practical suggestions; so let me make clear at the outset that I do not believe that unrestricted free speech is possible or desirable in war-time. I recognize that the nation has a duty to protect itself; I agree with you that the only question is where the line is to be drawn. You have had, of necessity, to delegate that task to subordinates; and it is my belief that they have, in the drawing of the line, come much too close to the methods of Autocracy.

Let us set aside, as not included in my appeal, all papers pub-

[2] WW to M. Eastman, Sept. 18, 1917.

lished by aliens, and all papers published in enemy languages; also all papers which incite to acts of treason or rebellion, violence or crime; such papers should be suppressed. I have no word to say for them. My appeal is for papers published by American citizens, who, while obeying the law and advising others to obey the law, desire to agitate to have the law changed; desire to exercise their rights as citizens and free men in a democracy, by criticising the government and advocating changes in its policies. Such men have had their papers barred from the mails, and it has been done with peculiar violence and unreason, suggestive of vindictiveness; that is to say, they have been refused all specifications as to what the government objects to, and all opportunity to conform their utterances to what the government claims is permissible. In the case of the Masses, the procedure was even worse—it can only be described as disgraceful; for the paper first had one issue barred from the mails, and then had its mailing privilege taken away on the ground that it had failed to appear regularly; which is as if a policeman were to knock a man down, and then, because he cried out with pain, arrest him for making a public disturbance.

Mr. President, the value of your letter to the Pope is the message it conveys to the German people, the hope it holds out to them that if they remove from the world the menace of autocracy, they can have immediate peace. But how can we advocate democracy for foreign peoples while we suppress it among our own? What good does it do us to fight for freedom abroad if, in the mean time, we are losing it at home? And do you not see that if such news goes to the pepeople [sic] of Germany, it will entirely stultify the message you have sent them through the Pope? One of the things which the Postmaster-General says no paper may say is that "this government is the tool of Wall Street or the munition makers." Will Mr Burleson permit me to say that the German people say that? And when they read that we are suppressing newspapers, they will say that our government is just the same as theirs, and that our preaching of democracy is just a snare for them. There are plenty of people in America who would like to suppress democracy—cultured and wealthy and influential people; and they have all flocked to support this war— their company must sometimes be embarrassing to a believer in democracy like yourself. I would not suggest that your Postmaster-General is one of these people; he is an old-fashioned Southern democrat, a type that I know well, and I can believe that he is sincere as far as his light goes; but in an interview in the "Public" October 12th he reveals himself a person of such pitiful and childish ignorance concerning modern movements[3] that it is simply a calamity that is [in] this crisis he should be the person to decide what may or may not be uttered by our radical press.

It is a fact that the tendency of every war is to suppress democracy. We know how the French people set out with their revolutionary armies to carry the message of republicanism to the rest of Europe; and how before long they found themselves fighting to subject the rest of Europe to an arrogant autocrat. And my question is this: Is it utterly impossible to conduct a war in a democratic way? Is it impossible to deal with the opponents of war at home with the weapons of democracy, which are reason and fair play, instead of the weapons of autocracy, which are the policeman's club and the jail? I am so convinced of the justice of your war-program, as you have outlined it, that I feel able to defend it with the weapons of Truth; and it is with deep pain that I have seen your aubordinates [subordinates] failing to display a similar confidence in your policies.

For example, Mr. Burleson says that "There can be no campaign against conscription and the draft law." If he means by this that there can be no campaign to advise men to disobey the law, I agree at once. But what if some people wish to campaign for a repeal of the draft law? Under the Constitution they have every right to petition Congress to that effect; yet the Postmaster at St. Louis confiscated thousands of such petitions in the mails; and here in my home city the Peoples' Council, which favors such a constitutional petition, have been forbidden to hold meetings *in a private home*. I know this particular group, and can testify that they are sincere and devoted people, and true democrats. I think they are mistaken about the war; I think I can answer their arguments, and for this very reason I resent the intrusion of violence into the controversy.

I believe there is a way in which we can protect ourselves from false propaganda without so free a use of the policeman's club.

[3] George P. West, "A Talk with Mr. Burleson," New York *Public*, XX (Oct. 12, 1917), 985-87. In his brief interview with West, Burleson had chiefly emphasized his determination to enforce those provisions of the Espionage and Trading with the Enemy Acts which concerned his department. West, by contrast, sought to bring out Burleson's political and social views which, he believed, would influence his enforcement of those laws. According to West, Burleson stated forcefully that Max Eastman was "no better than a traitor" and the content of *The Masses* was "rank treason." Burleson argued that the Wilson administration had done more for labor than any previous one and had "given them all they ought to have." He declared that any laborer who did not rise above the bare subsistence level was deficient in intelligence: "It's the shape of his brain. It's fatality. God Almighty did that, and you can't change it." He insisted that a child of the poorest farmer or factory laborer could get an education and become "a bank director or a railroad president as J. P. Morgan." As for those who failed to improve themselves, Burleson declared: "It's their own fault. This is the freest and finest country God ever made."

The thing to do is to answer it. Let the government establish a bureau of Public Information with a staff of men fully equipped with the facts as to this war, its causes and its purposes; and let the government go to any offending publication and say: "We object to this statement, which is false; we object to this argument, which is based upon false premises and calculated to mislead the public. We offer you the choice, either to be barred from the mails, or to open your columns to an official answer to the objectionable passages, the answer to have reasonable prominence and space."

This would be novel procedure, and I admit that it might excite some derision at the outset; but then, so does every new step in democracy. I contend that it would be an honest and fair way for the community to protect itself; and I contend that it would do more to convince the doubters than any amount of violence. For, as you know Mr President, suppression convinces nobody, and the readers of the "Masses" and the "American Socialist" and the "Call"[4] have not been converted by the Postmaster-General, they have only been made more bitter and more active opponents of the administration. But I know them; I know that while there are some hot-heads and fanatics whom no amount of fact could convince, the vast majority of American Socialists are sincere and honest men, devoted to the truth, and willing to be convinced by reasonable arguments.

In the November issue of Pearson's Magazine appears a letter written to me by a young Jewish workingman in New York. You ought to read that letter, Mr President; it is a letter out of a man's heart, and it will help you to understand what our working people are thinking and feeling. The magazine also publishes my reply, and its own reply to me. The latter contains one statement which I will quote:

"The system of Great Britain has made Ireland irreconcilable; the system of Germany has turned Alsace-Lorraine from French into German, even in sympathy, in little over one generation."[5]

I quote that because it is a typical illustration of statements made by the opponents of this war. However sincerely made, the statement is inconsistent with the facts. But how shall it be answered? Mr Burleson would say by suppressing Pearson's. But this would not convince the readers of Pearson's that the German government was autocratic to the people of Alsace-Lorraine; it would only convince them that the American government is

4 That is, the New York *Call*.
5 "A Socialist and Sinclair," *Pearson's Magazine*, XXXVIII (Nov. 1917), 219-21.

autocratic to the people of America. But let a competent historian take up the challenge and present the facts as to Alsace-Lorraine, duly documented, and he could convince nine out of ten of the readers of Pearson's.

As it happens, I can point to an example of such a historian, and of such writing as I have in mind—William Hard's article in the October "Metropolitan."[6] He is not dealing with Alsace-Lorraine, but with Austria's record with her Bohemian and Slav populations, and Germany's with her Poles; he makes the same inevitable comparison with Ireland, and I believe that any honest person who reads what he has to say will be forever after immune to the false statement that there is no difference between the British and the Prussian systems of government. And by the way, let me suggest an ideal man for the difficult post of Public Defender, the same William Hard. He is a fair man, one of the fairest I know; he is a student and a thinker, a democrat all the way through; he knows this country, its faults as well as its virtues, and he would understand the psychology of the discontented. If we must have a censor, he would make a far better one than the PostMaster-General who is still in that benighted stage where he thinks that Socialism means "dividing up," and that a man is saying something when he remarks—I quote from his interview with George P. West: "Distribute all the wealth in the country with absolute equality, and what would happen within a year? It would all be back in the same hands."

It is hard to draw the line, Mr President, as to the amount of ignorance permitted to a government official; but Mr. Burleson is assuredly on the wrong side of any line that could be drawn by any one.

Yours, in the cause of Democracy,   Upton Sinclair

TLS (WP, DLC).
  [6] William Hard, "The Case of Austria-Hungary," *Metropolitan*, XLVI (Oct. 1917), 23-24, 53-61.

To Albert Sidney Burleson

My dear Burleson: The White House 30 October, 1917

This suggestion has come to me with regard to the disloyal papers, not of course as applying to the cases where they actually break the law, but as applying to cases where they express the opinions which you have rightly objected to but which I doubt whether we have the right to suppress under the terms of the law, or whether it would be wholly wise to attempt to suppress:

It has been suggested that when, for example, they make such statements as that this whole war has been inspired by Wall Street and is being fought in the interest of Wall Street and the money-makers in general, you take this position, that you will deny them the use of the mails unless they open their columns to replies to such statements and give the replies as much prominence as they originally gave the statements themselves; and that for the purpose of carrying out this policy some person or body of persons be employed who could make the replies in explicit and convincing fashion.

What do you think of it?

Faithfully yours,   Woodrow Wilson

TLS (A. S. Burleson Paper, DLC).

To Herbert Bruce Brougham

My dear Mr. Brougham: The White House 30 October, 1917

The impression which you fear the State Department received about the publication of Bullitt's letter had not, as you assumed in your letter of the twenty-seventh, reached me, and I think in any case I would have understood the office['s] relations to the publication.

Of course, the publication itself distressed me very deeply and I cannot believe that a man who would do what Mr. Bullitt did ought to be entrusted with so responsible a position as he occupies here. We can ourselves never trust to his discretion again, and I hope sincerely that the paper will not.

I am very much obliged to you for your kindness in writing, and I am sure that I can count upon your feeling just as I do about matters of this sort.

Cordially and sincerely yours,   Woodrow Wilson

TLS (W. C. Bullitt Papers, CtY).

To Franklin Delano Roosevelt

My dear Mr. Roosevelt: The White House 30 October, 1917

Thank you for your letter of yesterday. I am interesting myself in the matter.   Sincerely yours,   Woodrow Wilson

TLS (F. D. Roosevelt Papers, NHpR).

To Eleanor Smith Kent

My dear Mrs. Kent: [The White House] 30 October, 1917

Your letter of the twenty-ninth brings me news which causes me most genuine grief.[1] I had not heard of your husband's death and the news shocks me very much. It was very generous of you to write to me in the midst of your grief and I appreciate it deeply. I shall always remember "Charlie" Kent with genuine admiration and affection.

With the deepest sympathy,
        Cordially and sincerely yours,   Woodrow Wilson

TLS (Letterpress Books, WP, DLC).
[1] Her letter is missing. Charles William Kent, Wilson's old friend at the University of Virginia, had died on October 5.

From Harry Augustus Garfield, with Enclosure

Dear Mr. President: [Washington] October 30, 1917

A month or more ago, I mentioned to you an article by Mr. Frederic C. Howe which I then understood he would himself send you. He, however, sent it to me and asks that I place it in your hands. As you expressed an interest to see it, I take pleasure in complying with his request.

I am much impressed by the argument Mr. Howe advances. The economic struggle within Western civilization plays a perilously large part in our international relations. I hope you will find an early occasion to present the practical ideal of closer international relations again.

As always, with high regard,
        Faithfully yours,   H. A. Garfield.

TLS (WP, DLC).

E N C L O S U R E

MEMORANDUM FOR THE PRESIDENT SUGGESTING THE ASSEMBLING OF MATERIAL ON THE CLAIMS, INTERESTS AND AMBITIONS OF THE BELLIGERENT POWERS; THE DIPLOMATIC CONTROVERSIES WHICH PRECEDED THE WAR; AND THE PRESENT POLITICAL STATUS AND DEMOCRATIC CLAIMS OF DEPENDENT AND SUBJECT POWERS, ESPECIALLY ABOUT THE MEDITERRANEAN SEA   Submitted by   Frederic C. Howe

I. THE BACKGROUND OF THE EUROPEAN WAR

The negotiations for a permanent and enduring peace at the conclusion of the war will involve the adjustment of controversies that have been before the chancelleries of Europe for a generation. Many of them are very intricate. A knowledge of them can only be gained from scattered sources. Many are closed to us in secret archives or in foreign languages.

Knowledge of these controversies which preceded the war is essential to their correct or permanent settlement. Even to approach an understanding of the mind of the warring powers it is necessary to be familiar with the irritations and conflicts which preceded 1914. We can only understand the ambitions of Germany by a knowledge of the economic, financial and political ambitions of the Empire, and the imperialistic interests in Morocco, Middle Europe, Turkey and Asia Minor. We can only appreciate the psychology of the nation through a knowledge of the tremendous increase in her exports; in the demand for sources of raw material, especially wheat, cotton and iron ore; the growth of her merchant marine; and the activities of her great exploiting banks, like the Deutsche Bank, the Dresdener Bank and others. To understand England it is necessary to appreciate the necessity for protection of her far flung empire; for keeping open her trade routes, especially through the Mediterranean; her colossal investments all over the world; the magnitude of her shipping and industry. Even more important, it is necessary to know the ramifications of her political and economic power in Egypt through the Suez Canal, in Persia and in Asia Minor. The relations of France to Algiers, Tunis and especially Morocco; the investments of her peasants in Russia, Turkey and Asia Minor; and the activities of her investing and exploiting classes afford a key to her interests in the war. Equally important, but far more commonly understood, is the Alsace-Lorraine question, the Polish problem, and the race conflicts of Austro-Hungary and Russia, while the Balkan situation, the race controversies, and the conflict with Turkey are all involved in a permanent, lasting and democratic peace. The ambitions of Italy; how they conflict with those of the Balkan powers; the right of access to the Mediterranean; and especially the status of such water gateways as the Dardanelles, the Straights of Gibraltar, and the Suez and Kiel Canals will all be involved in the discussions at the close of the war.

Only less important are the ambitions and the fears for industry, commerce and investments, for the economic underpinning of the great powers not only at home but in distant lands. For at the outbreak of the war the three great powers of Europe had over-seas investments of approximately $35,000,000,000, one-fourth of which is directly or indirectly involved in the disposition of the territories round about the Mediterranean.

2. PREVIOUS CONFERENCES

Much of the international irritation of Europe during the last generation is traceable to the adjustments of territorial rights and interests by the Berlin conference of 1878; the English, French and Turkish controversies over Egypt; the Algeciras conference over Morocco; and the many diplomatic meetings between England, France, Germany and Russia over the Bagdad Railway and the Near East.

The jealousies and irritations resulting from these conferences were due in large part to three causes:

1. The settlement of the affairs of Europe by representatives only of the ruling houses or classes;

2. The universal indifference to the interests or the fate of weak, dependent and subject races, and the subordination of their rights to the ambitions of the greater powers;

3. The ignorance of some representatives of geographic, ethnic and economic interests which led to very arbitrary divisions of territory and spheres of influence.

It is asserted by some that the Treaty of Berlin has been the mother of almost all of the Balkan wars and diplomatic intrigues of the last generation.

3. THE MOBILIZATION OF MATERIAL

Possibly it is already being done. If not, the assemblage of material and the preparation of a review of the political and economic forces which lie back of the war, together with a bibliography, would be of value to our representatives at the conference. Among the subjects to be covered and the material to be gathered the following occur to me:

(1) A rather brief review of the major controversies centering about Egypt, Morocco, Persia and the Balkan States, with special reference to the developments between 1911 and 1914, which was the period of war preparation by all of the powers.

(2) An analysis of the colonial possessions, spheres of influence, tariff discriminations and privileges, and the exploitation activities of all of the powers during the last generation. This would include the kind, nature and political standing of the concessions in Turkey, Asia Minor, Roumania, Bulgaria; in Tripoli, Tunis, Morocco and Egypt; as well as the inter-relationship of the investing, exploiting and business interests with their respective governments.

The status of foreign claims in China, of Germany in Kiaou-chou, of all of the powers in Southern Africa are part of the story of modern imperialism.

(3) Closely related to the imperialistic and economic claims of the various powers is the status of the Suez Canal, the Dardanelles, the Kiel Canal, and the Straits of Gibraltar, as well as the Bagdad Railway running from the Bosporus to the Persian Gulf.

(4) The conflicting economic interests of Germany and England are colossal. They involve manufacturing and industry, shipping and concessions. And all of the nations have made the interests of these groups a part of their diplomatic policy. They have adopted the closed or the open door. There are discriminating tariffs. There are various active or potential discriminations.

(5) The historical status of Alsace-Lorraine should be stated; of Poland, of the Balkan States, and of the lesser nationalities in Europe. The same is true as to Egypt, Persia, and the North African states which are under the protectorate or control of England, France and Russia.

The whole question of the rights of these states, the political liberties they shall enjoy, and the rights of individual nations or groups of nations to control their industrial life are questions for permanent settlement, if peace is to endure.

(6) Finally, what are the democratic proposals that have been made or are being made to insure world wide security, and with it equality of opportunity, freedom of trade, freedom of the seas, the ending of the closed door, the substitution of joint for exclusive concessions, and the many other monopolistic and nationalistic privileges which have been acquired by force or by diplomacy in recent years.

The peace that will endure is a peace so fundamentally righteous and so basically identified with equal opportunities for industry and liberty that controversies either will not arise or will be open to easy settlement by reference to guiding principles and democratic standards of international relationship.

T MS (H. A. Garfield Papers, DLC).

From the Diary of Josephus Daniels

1917 Tuesday 30 October

WW took up the General Board's & the Admiralty's plan of barrage across North Sea. I told WW it was very difficult, but was the only plan possible to shut off the submarine. It might cut off ½ & that would be important, very costly & very difficult, but all things are possible.

To Harry Augustus Garfield

My dear Garfield: The White House 31 October, 1917
    Thank you for the article by Fred Howe. I shall try to find time to read it, for it covers a matter in which I am greatly interested.
    Does he want it back soon, do you know?
        Cordially and faithfully yours,   Woodrow Wilson

TLS (H. A. Garfield Papers, DLC).

From William Bauchop Wilson

Clifton, Ariz., October 31, 1917.
    I am glad to be able to report a settlement reached by your commission which will result in the prompt resumption of work at the mines in the Clifton-Morenci-Metcalf district which have been idle since the first of July. This means the normal production of about ten millions pounds of copper per month and the employment of over ten thousand men. The speedy settlement here was possible because of the spirit of cooperation with which the commission was met both by the managers and the national as well as the local leaders of the strikers and the patriotic service rendered by Judge Ernest W. Lewis of Arizona.[1] The commission is now proceeding to Bisbee.   W. B. Wilson.

T telegram (WP, DLC).
    [1] Ernest William Lewis, lawyer of Phoenix; associate justice of the Arizona Supreme Court, 1909-1912; at this time a federal commissioner of conciliation in the copper strikes.

From Herbert Bruce Brougham

My dear Mr. Wilson: Philadelphia 31st October 1917
    Whether Mr. Bullitt shall continue to represent us in Washington, which is the question raised in your letter to me of 30th October, depends wholly upon the decision of Mr. Spurgeon and Mr. Curtis. But Mr. Spurgeon informed me he was satisfied that Mr. Bullitt was not aware when he filed his dispatch on the Inter-Allied Conference that its publication was interdicted, and he definitely fixed the responsibility for its appearance upon the

night editors of the Public Ledger, who were fully aware beforehand of the State Department's promulgation of the warning.

Before showing to Mr. Spurgeon your letter to me, therefore, with its stricture upon Mr. Bullitt's continuance in Washington, I venture to ask very earnestly that you call for the statement which Mr. Spurgeon has sent to Mr. Lansing, placing the responsibility for the interdicted publication where, according to his investigation of the facts, it belongs.

May I again assure you of my very deep concern over this incident and the trouble it has given you.

Very sincerely yours,   H. B. Brougham.

TLS (WP, DLC).

From Harry Covington Wheeler

Bisbee, Arizona, October 31, 1917.

Since July twelfth peace, law and order have been enforced in this county and district. This county has been absolutely without disorder. Desiring peace to continue I requested your commission to aid me by limiting I.W.W. witnesses to appear. Many as fifty per day, more than possibly could be heard. This was arbitrarily refused with an admonition that unless all were permitted to return when and as they pleased federal force would be used to compel my subservience as well as the whole local American community. I have advised the commission we including myself would render every aid possible to commission and would see each man wishing to do so would be allowed to appear and testify. However, as repeated threats by I.W.W. have been made Bisbee would be sacked and various persons murdered. I as Sheriff sought assistance and aid of commission to avoid any such possibility. This county over subscribed its bond three times; is giving eight hundred men to the army. We cannot believe the government of the United States will compel us to submit to an organization of disloyal men, seventy per cent foreigners. At this date all here is peaceful. The commission has not yet arrived.

H. C. Wheeler.

T telegram (JDR, RG 60, Numerical File, No. 186813/48, DNA).

David Lloyd George to Lord Reading

[London] 31 Octr. [1917]

Very urgent. no. 4650 Following for Lord Reading before he sees President, from Prime Minister. Begins. Italian situation is serious. Second Italian army appears to be in a state of collapse due to enemy intrigue and propaganda, the men have refused to fight in large numbers and have abandoned most of their guns. Third Italian army is retiring steadily and has saved its artillery but is beginning to be affected by retreat.

Cadorna[1] unexpectedly is hopeful of making a stand on Tagliamento but it is doubtful if this will be possible in which case stand will be made on Piave. For this, French General Staff should arrive in time immediately followed by British.

Last British attack in Flanders was completely successful and has brought our troops (to) outskirts of village of Paschendale. Difficulties owing to mud are still serious and therefore our advances are limited in extent. We did not attempt to take village but will do so shortly.

Submarine losses October not markedly above those for Septr. which was lowest month since intensive campaign began. They are however still heavy and producing serious cumulative effect. Most urgent need of hour is building ships as rapidly as is humanly possible.

T telegram (IOR MSS Eur. F 118/114, India Office Library and Records).
[1] Gen. Luigi Cadorna, commander in chief of the Italian armies.

To Thomas Watt Gregory, with Enclosure

Personal.   [The White House]
My dear Mr. Attorney General: 1 November, 1917

I am sure that you will be interested in this memorandum from the Executive Clerk in my office, Rudolph Forster. If the statements Mr. Hale made to Mr. Forster are indeed true, it is a very serious case of misbehavior on the part of somebody, but I particularly wanted you to note Mr. Hale's offer to submit to investigation of any kind.

Cordially and sincerely yours,   Woodrow Wilson[1]

TLS (Letterpress Books, WP, DLC).
[1] WW to RL, Nov. 1, 1917, TLS (WP, DLC), is the same letter *mutatis mutandis.*

E N C L O S U R E

MEMORANDUM: The White House October 31, 1917.

This morning between 10:00 and 11:00 o'clock William Bayard Hale called me on the telephone and asked if he could see me sometime during the morning. I told him that he could see me at any time he called at the office up until 1:00 o'clock. Following this conversation Mr. Hale, accompanied by his wife,[1] called shortly before 1:00 o'clock and asked if he might talk to me for a few moments privately. Mr. Hale told me that secret service agents were investigating him. He stated that the methods of these agents were rough and brutal in the extreme and that by reason of their methods a situation intolerable to him had been created. He dwelt particularly upon what he termed the efforts of these agents to seduce his stenographer[2]—a young girl of 21 years of age, of a good family, who had been with Mr. and Mrs. Hale for three years, whose family was well-known to Cardinal Farley. Mr. and Mrs. Hale both stated that every effort had been made by a secret service agent[3]—or some one claiming to be such an agent and showing a badge—to intimidate this young girl; that offers of all sorts had been made to her—of jewelry, government bonds, employment under the British government, double salary, threats of fine and imprisonment, threats of personal violence at the point of a revolver, and, worst of all, that attempts had been made to induce this young girl, through the medium of a procuress, to keep assignations for immoral purposes. Mr. Hale stated that the girl under this continued hounding had become hysterical and afraid to leave his house; she had told all these things to Mrs. Hale, and both Mr. and Mrs. Hale felt that the situation was so intolerable that something had to be done.

Mr. Hale stated that attempts had been made to bribe the servants in his apartment; that his telephone conversations had been listened to; his mail opened; and that the private lives of himself and Mrs. Hale had been pried into. Mr. Hale was emphatic in declaring that nothing in his actions justified such conduct. He stated that if the Government suspected him in any way he was perfectly ready and willing to submit to any examination by the Government, to turn over to them his papers, answer any questions they might ask, submit to have his apartment searched, and to give the Government any information which he had; that he had come to Washington for the purpose of answering any questions, and that he would remain here until tomorrow afternoon.

I asked Mr. Hale why he had not gone to see the Attorney

General in this matter rather than come to me. He stated that he did not know the Attorney General and that as he had known me for many years he came to me with the thought that I could let the President know the state of affairs he had outlined. He stated that he was not a criminal; that his work in 1914 and 1915 as the paid manager of a publicity bureau attempting to bring before the people Germany's side of the war was open, above-board, and wellknown; there was no attempt at secrecy; that after that he had been in Berlin as the representative of the Hearst newspapers; that on the day of the declaration of war by the United States he had applied for permission to leave Germany; that he had then gone to Stockholm and from there returned home; that all this was well-known and that there was nothing in his actions to warrant the persecution to which he was being subjected.

Immediately after my talk with Mr. Hale I told Mr. Tumulty of it, and, at his suggestion, have dictated this memorandum for the President.

I attach a note which I have just received from Mr. Hale.[4]

R.F.

TI MS (WP, DLC).
    [1] Olga Unger Hale.
    [2] Theodora Groh.
    [3] A memorandum enclosed in TWG to WGM, Nov. 28, 1917, CCL (JDR, RG 60, Numerical File, No. 44-03-2, DNA), reveals that this person was one J. L. Johnson, who was in fact a member of the Secret Service.
    [4] It is missing, but see Enclosure II printed with WW to R. Forster, Nov. 7, 1917.

To Newton Diehl Baker

My dear Mr. Secretary: The White House 1 November, 1917

I dare say you already have a copy of the enclosed report, but in order to make sure I send you the copy which Mr. Gompers and his committee left with me yesterday[1] and venture to make this request, that you and the Secretary of the Navy and Mr. Hurley will have as early a conference as convenient and join in a recommendation to me of what you think ought to be done and of the way in which you think it ought to be done. I would greatly appreciate this because I feel that the problem is really a very pressing one.

Cordially and sincerely yours,   Woodrow Wilson

TLS (N. D. Baker Papers, DLC).
    [1] See S. Gompers to JPT, Oct. 25, 1917, n. 1.

To William Bauchop Wilson

[The White House] 1 November, 1917

My warmest thanks for your cheering telegram about the Clifton-Morenci-Metcalf settlement. I warmly congratulate you and beg that you will convey to Judge Lewis an expression of my warm appreciation.   Woodrow Wilson.

T telegram (Letterpress Books, WP, DLC).

From Robert Lansing, with Enclosure

My dear Mr. President: Washington November 1, 1917.

I think you will be interested to see a copy which I am sending you of the Declaration of the Executive Council of the American Federation of Labor defining the attitude of the Council regarding a proposed international conference of workmen and socialists from all countries.

The Declaration was sent me by Mr. Gompers himself and it has been given to the Russian Publicity Bureau in New York, now in charge of Mr. Sack,[1] and has been telegraphed to the Ambassador at Petrograd.

Faithfully yours,   Robert Lansing.

TLS (WP, DLC).
[1] Arkady Joseph Sack, head of the Russian Information Bureau in New York. About this organization, see George F. Kennan, *The Decision to Intervene* (Princeton, N. J., 1958), pp. 322-23.

ENCLOSURE

Washington, D. C., October 25, 1917.

The Executive Council of the American Federation of Labor having before it a report made by President Gompers of a conference with Mr. Jacob Baum, who claims to be a courier entrusted with a message from the Executive Committee of the Workmen's and Soldiers' Delegates Council, Department of International Relations of Russia, Vice-President Perham and Secretary Morrison[1] having also reported having conference with Mr. Baum, upon the same subject of his message, and the message being a request for the American Federation of Labor to call or to participate in an international conference of workmen and socialists of all countries, having given the subject matter full consideration, declares as follows:

That we regard it as untimely and inappropriate, conducive to no good result, but on the contrary harmful, to hold an international conference at this time or in the near future with the representatives of all countries, including enemy countries, and we are constrained therefore to decline at this time either to participate in or to call such a conference.

We take occasion to again send fraternal greetings to the people and the Republic of Russia and our earnest wishes for the success and permanency of Russia's democracy. That we all make energetic efforts in our common cause for freedom, justice and democracy in all of the nations of the world.

T MS (WP, DLC).
[1] That is, Henry B. Perham and Frank Morrison.

A Translation of a Memorandum by William Emmanuel Rappard[1]

Valavran, near Geneva [Nov. 1, 1917][2]

An Interview with President Wilson

When the S***s came to my hotel in Washington on Sunday morning, October 28, 1917, to tell me that President Wilson had agreed to receive me in a private audience on the following Thursday, this came to me as a very happy surprise.

I was at once very proud and very ashamed for having obtained this great privilege: proud, because it was so exceptional, and ashamed, because to make sure of getting it, I had resorted to methods which, on any other occasion, I would have deemed unworthy of a republican!

President Wilson is, in fact, the most inaccessible man in the great republic of which he is presently the unchallenged chief. To maintain his state of perfect intellectual and moral equilibrium and to preserve complete mastery of his thought and will,

[1] Professor of Economics at the University of Geneva. He had been an Instructor and Assistant Professor of Economics at Harvard from 1911 to 1913. He later became a widely recognized authority on international organization. He, together with John Syz, a cotton manufacturer of Zurich, and Wilhelm Stämpfli, president of the War Prison Association, were the members of a mission named by the Swiss government to accompany Hans Sulzer, the new Swiss Minister to the United States, to Washington. The mission was primarily concerned with publicizing the needs and difficulties of Switzerland and preparing the way for a trade agreement between Switzerland and the United States. Its members met with prominent and influential Americans in the business world, the press, and the universities. See Heinz K. Meier, *Friendship Under Stress: U.S.-Swiss Relations, 1900-1950* (Bern, 1970), pp. 72-75.
[2] This date is ascribed to this document, which was written later, because, as Rappard says below, it was based upon notes which Rappard took at the interview.

he devotes a large part of his time to relaxation, to family life, and to outdoor sports. He voluntarily isolates himself and flees the empty fatigues and inevitable unpleasantnesses of the world with a persistence which surprises his fellow citizens, all the more because this reserve is hardly in the tradition of the American presidency.

To one such citizen, who once stood in wonder before him and dared to ask if he did not fear losing the necessary contact with public opinion, he gave this revealing reply, reported to me by one of my friends:

"When I wish to know the true sentiment of my country, I lock myself in my study and sink into the depths of my consciousness as a citizen, and there I am sure to find it."

This was the response of a sage, of an intellectual who has a wonderful knowledge of the public spirit of his country because he knows its history well and feels himself to be in perfect harmony with it on all fundamental questions of national policy.

It is in this need of fruitful solitude and in this spiritual awareness of the popular sentiment that we must look for the secret of the extraordinary power that Wilson exercises over the destinies of his country. It is by this intelligent introspection that the great democratic magistrate succeeds in sensing the hidden will of the masses and in following, even while guiding it, the public opinion of a nation to which he belongs with every fiber of his being. It is in this voluntary isolation also, in which this artistic soul takes delight—sensitive and restless as well as intelligent and strong—that it is necessary to look for the explanation of the originality and vigor of his historic messages, whose lofty inspiration and impeccable form strike even his most implacable adversaries.

Happy is the republic whose chief, resolutely refusing to exhaust himself in the daily routine of administrative drudgery, knows how to reserve his energies for the great tasks of government and, from among eloquent and sincere appeals to reason, to the imagination, and to the national will, can recognize the most important tasks which by no means require his personal attention.

But this method of government, whose general advantages are so obvious, presents inconveniences no less evident for the crowd of persons seeking audience! The reader also can understand the joy and pride I felt when, at last, after several weeks of waiting, I saw the order lifted which had inexorably blocked entry to the White House to so many other applicants of greater importance.

I owe this favor especially to the benevolent intercession of several American friends who kindly consented to use their influence to aid my insistence and my importunity. University men for the most part, old colleagues therefore of both the President and of the one so eager to meet him (who on this occasion was serving Switzerland as its very temporary representative), they showed good will, patience, and skill for which I can never be sufficiently grateful. They receive once again an assurance of my heartfelt gratitude, to which I must especially add an expression of my regret and humility for having so greatly abused their friendship, in badgering them and persecuting them so pitilessly with my entreaties!

If I put such a high price on having a private conversation with the President, it was certainly not for giving myself the vain satisfaction of succeeding where so many others had failed. I had hoped to be able to talk to him about Switzerland in a manner and with details that are incompatible with diplomatic convention and with the solemnity of an official audience. The outcome did not disappoint this hope.

President Wilson received me in the simplest and most cordial way imaginable. After a few words on the subject of our mutual friends (whose intervention had led him to receive me), he begged me to tell him the special purpose of my visit.

I tried at first to explain the situation of Switzerland. The density of its population and the structure of its economic organization, added to the nature of its soil, sub-soil, and climate, rendered the country entirely dependent on the foreigner. Only Germany could provide the coal and iron needed for our industrial life. Since the outbreak of the war, only the United States could supply grains to us. I noted how little we worried, from the political standpoint, about this economic dependence on the United States, since we are dealing with a republic which he himself had said has for us "a friendship based on similar principles of life, a similar ideal, and common aspirations."

This declaration, made at the opening of the Soldier's Home which bears his name in Switzerland, I would have wished to hear repeated in more lasting form at the conclusion, then approaching, of the convention by which the United States would assure our material existence. Beyond the fact that including this declaration could have hastened the conclusion of this economic accord,[3] it would also have given it a new moral signifi-

---

[3] The Swiss had for some time been negotiating with the United States for necessary imports of American grains. These negotiations ultimately resulted in a "Memorandum of December 5, 1917, between the War Trade Board and the Swiss Government in Regard to Exports from the United States to Switzerland." It is printed in *FR-WWS 1917*, 2, II, 1185-96. For a detailed

cance and impact. For Switzerland, it would have been beneficial to recall in this way the meaning and value of our principles of republican and democratic federalism especially to certain elements of our own population too inclined to forget them. And, on the other hand, I thought that thus to affirm the actual existence of these principles in the very heart of Europe, in a very old republic of Germanic origin, would have been helpful for the propagation of these principles, for President Wilson, and for all of liberal humanity awaiting with him the salvation of the world.

The President gave my exposition the most alert and critical attention, as was shown by the vivacity of his expression and the questions with which he interrupted me. What I said about the disaffection regarding democracy found among certain Swiss elements seemed to interest him particularly. He remarked that that scarcely surprised him because he had noticed similar symptoms in corresponding elements in the United States.

After I had fully developed my ideas, he looked at me with a shrewd smile, which, by the way, has often surprised those who see him only as a visionary, ignorant of all the vulgarities of practical politics, and he said to me:

"You ask me, sir, for a fine-sounding declaration. But don't you believe that the Swiss people would, instead, respond to some good cargoes of wheat?"

"Mr. President," I hastened to say, "we are too aware of the generous friendship of the United States even to entertain the idea that it could consider letting us die of hunger. But would not a declaration of principle on this subject help to secure for you all the moral benefit of your generosity?"

"Perhaps," he replied, "but the difficulties of tonnage and the necessity not to forget the other neutrals keep me from doing for Switzerland all that my friendship for her inclines me to do."

I naturally refrained from saying a single word contrary to the solidarity which must unite all the small neutral countries of Europe in the present crisis. But I did not fail to observe that our geographical situation, our republican and federal form of government, and our German-language press seemed altogether to constitute in our favor claims for special solicitude.

In this regard I allowed myself to remind President Wilson of a passage in his famous work, *The State*, which had struck me very much: "The Swiss cantons," he wrote some thirty years ago, "being allied to one another, show the world how Germans, French, and Italians, inspired by principles of mutual assistance,

discussion of the complex negotiations and the ambiguous nature of the resulting agreement, see Meier, pp. 75-86.

respect for each other's liberties, and natural tolerance, can together constitute a confederation that is both stable and free."* This conception of the Helvetic state, which was set forth by my interlocutor when he was a young professor of political science— is it not the same as that which he, now President of the most powerful of republics, proposes to realize in the world by the constitution of a league of nations?

This flash back, which the President in no way repudiated, raised the conversation to a level which was particularly dear to him. What struck me above all, as he spoke to me about the international regime of the future, was his tone, which revealed an ardent conviction and a sort of internal exaltation.

"The establishment of a league of nations," he says to me, "is in my view a matter of moral persuasion more than a problem of juridical organization. I have never worked for the formation of a league of peoples with any intention of favoring one group of belligerents at the expense of the other, but only for the benefit of all peaceable humanity. When men of good will, of whatever country, come to understand their true common interests, the most redoubtable obstacles which bar the route to the establishment of a new international order will have been surmounted. That is why my most fervent desire is that this war will bring a peace in which justice is forced on everyone. Then, finally, when we can enter negotiations, it will be with the firm resolve to ask nothing for ourselves and to do all that we can to hinder those who seek anything that would be unjust."

I shall not repeat here all the rest of what President Wilson said to me on this subject. Attentive readers of his various messages will in any case have no trouble in getting his point.

I retain only one point of special interest to our country. Having spoken of the economic war which will inevitably follow the military war, if the latter does not bring a peace of justice and liberty for all, the President did me the honor of asking my opinion on this subject. I took the liberty of saying to him that, in Switzerland, we had joyously welcomed the repudiation of economic warfare, as proclaimed in his famous reply to the Pope. In fact, the establishment of an international league from which America's present adversaries were barred would plunge our country into the most painful difficulty. The project of a league of nations, that is to say, the extension to the world of the fundamental principle of the Helvetic Confederation, would of course be greeted by the Swiss with enthusiastic approbation. On the other hand, a rupture of economic relations with the empire

---

* Woodrow Wilson, *The State*, rev. ed., New York, 1898, p. 301.

which is our neighbor and which has long been both our chief customer and our chief supplier, would be without doubt an utter material impossibility.

Mr. Wilson replied: "I understand that difficulty very well. But, with no offense intended, I can say that Switzerland's attitude in this matter is of no great consequence, even for herself. This is because, whether or not Switzerland becomes a member of the league of nations, none of her neighbors would dream of attacking her. And if, by some misfortune, she became the object of agression by one of them, all the others would come to her aid."

Reassuring as this declaration was from the military point of view, it clearly suggested no solution to the agonizing problem for our country which would arise if a league of nations was formed from which Germany should be excluded.

Toward the end of our conversation, I took the liberty of calling the President's attention to a particular subject which at the moment preoccupied certain elements in Switzerland. The concentration of American troops, in ever greater numbers, not far from our frontier, had led to press commentaries which revealed a certain apprehension. I told my interlocutor about some of them. I recalled to him the example of Italy, which, at the beginning of the war had expressly declared its intention to respect our neutrality, in spite of the fact that she had not been among the number of signatory powers of the treaties of 1815 and was not yet among the number of belligerents. An analogous declaration by the American government, I added, would no doubt allay the worries which had been manifested.

"It never occured to me!"[4] declared the President. "But if such a declaration is really needed to remove distrust of us in Switzerland, I will lose no time in taking it up with the gentlemen of the Department of State."

One recalls that such official assurances were given on this subject to the Federal Council some weeks later by the Chargé d'Affaires of the United States in Bern.[5] Even if these terms were not entirely satisfactory in the light of our traditional doctrine of neutrality, still they should suffice to reassure completely those who, being ignorant of the trends of American policy, might have had any doubts about the aims.

[4] Rappard wrote these words in English and then repeated them in French.
[5] A declaration of respect for Swiss neutrality, the only such declaration to be issued by the United States during the First World War, was given out by the Department of State on November 30. RL to H. R. Wilson, Nov. 30, 1917, FR-WWS 1917, 2, I, 758. See also, Meier, pp. 80-81.

This brief account of my interview with President Wilson**
would be incomplete if I did not say a word about the personal
impression that my interlocutor made on me.

Physically, I was struck by the force and health which radiated
from this body, which an outdoor regimen has preserved, in spite
of his sixty years, with all the appearance of youth and almost
that of adolescence. The vivacity and the penetration of his attention, which becomes somewhat clouded in reverie when,
"thinking aloud," as he said to me, Mr. Wilson spoke of the league
of nations of the future; the energy of his lower jaw and chin;
the frankness and restraint of his gestures; the impeccable clarity of his speech—all this, revealed him as the fulfillment of the
type of the Anglo-Saxon intellectual, in full and free possession
of exceptional moral and cerebral faculties. The weight of crushing responsibilities obviously weighs on his shoulders, but I know
of no man who has given me more strongly the impression of
having the stature to support such responsibilities.

I add that it is a singular good fortune for our country that, in
the present crisis, the head of the great republic overseas should
be a statesman passionately devoted to the cause of democracy
and of liberal federalism, to the cause, in other terms, of the political ideal which produces the common moral grandeur of his
country and of our own.

It is important for all Swiss to be conscious of the fact that
to attack this man, as certain journalists in Switzerland have
done (whom I wish to believe to be foreigners, who have no respect for the facts) is to attack one's own country. He himself is
the defender—the most convinced, the most fervent, and the most
influential—of the principles which lie not only at the base of his
own political system but whose triumph in the world can alone
assure our national future.   William E. Rappard

T MS (J. I. 149 Mission Paris 1919, I-III, William E. Rappard, Swiss Federal
Archives).

** I have sought to render this account as faithfully as possible. I have re-
constituted it with the aid of notes which I took at the very time itself of the
interview, after I had cleared the barrage of journalists who mounted guard at
the gate of the White House.

To Joseph Patrick Tumulty, with Enclosure

Dear Tumulty: [The White House, c. Nov. 2, 1917]

I don't like to answer this letter myself but I would be very
much obliged if you would answer it in the kindest spirit, for I
believe John Spargo is a perfectly sincere and patriotic man.

Please tell him that he is mistaken in supposing that this matter is being handled entirely by the Postmaster General and his subordinates, that I am trying to keep in constant touch with it, and that he will find in the long run that the ban is applied to very few papers indeed, only to those indeed whose offenses against the law are manifest and flagrant. I believe that experience will vindicate us in this matter. Please express my personal appreciation of his letter and its generous tone.[1]   The President.

TL (WP, DLC).
  [1] JPT to J. Spargo, Nov. 3, 1917, TLS (J. Spargo Coll., VtU), is a paraphrase of Wilson's letter.

E N C L O S U R E

From John Spargo

Dear Mr. President: New York November 1, 1917.

  Will you permit me to second the appeal and protest of my friend and colleague, Mr. Upton Sinclair, published in today's newspapers. As you know from the first I have been enthusiastically and loyally supporting your war policy. In common with a very large number of radicals, I have rejoiced to acknowledge your leadership in this great crisis. I know therefore that you will not misunderstand my attitude in the matter of the suppression of the newspapers which fall under the ban of the Post Office censorship. It is quite obvious that there must be some restriction of the press in such times as the present, and equally obvious that it is exceedingly difficult to draw the line with full safety to the national cause and to our democratic traditions and institutions. I have no doubt at all that you desire to preserve to the fullest extent possible our own democratic principles and rights while the struggle for world democracy is going on; but it has been painfully evident to me for some time past that the reactionary methods of the Postal Department are not only wholly at variance with the principles of democracy, but are alienating a great many earnest men and women of whose loyalty there can be no question, but who feel that they must be equally loyal to the fundamental principles of democracy and are therefore forced into a position of more or less active criticism and even opposition to your Administration.

  This I believe to be a very serious matter, Mr. President, and one which well deserves your earnest and prompt consideration. In my own immediate circle of acquaintances, I know scores of such men and women who desire above all things to give you their solid support, but whose resentment at the unwarranted and unnecessary suppression of criticism by the press compels them to be in spite of themselves constant critics of your Administration.

I have believed that the fundamental error lies in permitting censorship of war discussion to reside in the hands of the Postmaster General and his subordinates, men who are entirely out of touch with the great liberal and radical movements of our time. If you could see your way clear to take the censorship so far as it applies to discussions of the principles underlying our participation in the war out of the hands of the Postal Department, and place it in the hands of a small commission in which well known and trusted liberals and radicals predominate, with the understanding that the commission would trust more to moral suasion and intellectual argument than to repressive force, the problem would be largely solved. I am satisfied that it is quite possible to permit a wide range of free discussion, to overcome opposition and remove misunderstanding, and to secure the support of by far the greater number of those liberals and radicals who are now distrustful of our part in the war and more or less active opponents of the Administration.

Will you not, Mr. President, arrange to have a very frank discussion of this matter with a group of leading radicals of various schools with a view to understanding their protest and the difficulties they are experiencing in supporting you in this great crisis.

With assurances of my profound respect and loyal support,
Very respectfully yours,   John Spargo.

TLS (WP, DLC).

From Thomas Watt Gregory

Washington, D. C.
My dear Mr. President: November 2nd, 1917.

You wrote me under date of October, 19th, calling attention to a telegram which you had received from Portland, Oregon, signed "A. E. Kern, The Nachrichten," in which Kern complained that he and his newspaper were being made the subject of persecution at the hands of Mr. Reames, United States Attorney at Oregon and asking for your interference.

A careful investigation of this subject has been made by this Department. The Nachrichten is a proposed weekly to be published in German. In the past Kern has been associated with the

Deutsche Zeitung and the Portland American published by the German Publishing Company of which Kern is principal and controlling owner. The last mentioned newspapers have contained much disloyal matter and this Department, only a few days ago, interned for the period of the war Max Lucke who had been employed on one of these papers and who had contributed much of the disloyal matter.

We have asked the Postmaster General to scrutinize carefully the character of the proposed newspaper, but Lucke's internment will probably do away with most of the trouble.

In my opinion no blame attaches to Mr. Reames in connection with this subject. The decision here to intern Lucke vindicates his judgment.   Respectfully,   T. W. Gregory

TLS (WP, DLC).

From Newton Diehl Baker

My dear Mr. President: Washington. November 2, 1917.

On my return to the office this afternoon, I called General Crozier and asked him whether there are in fact any alien enemies employed in any arsenal in the United States. He tells me there are not; that all employees in our arsenals are brought in through the Civil Service, which limits its nominees to actual citizens of the country.

The Civil Service lists have not recently been quite adequate to supply all the labor we needed, and men have therefore been taken on temporarily, pending their full qualification under the Civil Service, but there has been no abandonment of the rule requiring citizenship. General Crozier advises me that very careful precautions are taken to ensure against the employment of any such non-citizen.

He tells me further that the only place in which we employ persons of German birth are in the Frankford Arsenal in the manufacture of optical instruments, but even in this place, the employees are all naturalized.

                    Respectfully yours,   Newton D. Baker

TLS (WP, DLC).

From Charles Raymond Macauley

My dear Mr. President: New York November second 1917

I have gladly contributed the necessary copies of the motion picture I had the honor to take in Washington in June, 1916 to the National War Council of the Y.M.C.A.

I have been asked to request of you a spoken title to be used with your picture. The accompanying copy of a letter received to-day will fully explain its purpose.[1] Permit me to add, by way of suggestion, that motion picture captions run about thirty or forty words in length.

Very sincerely yours,   C. R. Macauley

TLS (WP, DLC).
[1] Herbert Frederic Rawll to C. R. Macauley, Nov. 2, 1917, TCL (WP, DLC).

Lord Reading to David Lloyd George and Others

Washington. D. C. November 2nd 1917.

Lord Reading would be much obliged if the following could be despatched through [to] the Foreign Office:

VERY SECRET. Following from Lord Reading for Prime Minister, War Cabinet, and Mr Balfour. Q. 82. Your cablegram No. 4650 of 31st. October. Have had long interview with President and I showed him your cablegram. Meanwhile the news had arrived of the taking of a further 60,000 prisoners and hundreds of guns, making 180,000 prisoners and 1500 guns as announced by Berlin. I particularly impressed upon him that we had given every possible assistance in furnishing supplies and that there was no ground for the suggestion that the defeats were due to failure on our part to send supplies. I explained the situation which had arisen just before I left London with regard to the sending of further military support. The President recognised the difficulties of the situation and that there was tendency of Italians to throw blame on us as partial explanation of events. The President informed me that credits had been granted by U. S. Treasury to Italy of $230,000,000 & that every assistance in way of supplies wd be given by U S, and that U. S. were providing ships to carry supplies. President had received information that 70,000 French troops had arrived in Italy but doubted accuracy of numbers. I informed him that our troops had been despatched but I had no news of their arrival.

Your 4654 and 4655 of November 1st unfortunately arrived too late. I did nevertheless raise the question at interview of obtaining assistance of Japanese troops for Russia. President informed me that he had discussed matter with Japanese Envoy Extraordinary and that President had formed definite impression that Japan did not intend to send troops into fighting line. President said he would support any representations we might make. I did not raise the question of sending U. S. troops to Russia, as I was awaiting your cablegram, but I informed President that I was expecting a cablegram from you in answer to information about Russia which I had cabled to you.

I ventured to impress again upon the President the urgency of proceeding with the shipbuilding programme. Of course President fully realises situation. My object was to strengthen Hurley's (chairman of Shipping Board) hand in obtaining any further necessary powers.

President asked whether we had heard rumours of Sweden taking military steps or making preparations therefor. I replied we had heard nothing new except information obtained today that Swedish Government was transferring its balances in U. S. banks into names of various agents.

Your cables 4654 and 4655 arrived two hours later. I paraphrased the two cables and gave document to Lansing with whom I was spending evening and he will produce it to President today when Cabinet meets. I have been very careful not to force the suggestion of U. S. troops being sent to Russia. I have merely suggested that President might consider it and if he thought wise announce to Press that it was being considered. Lansing agreed that in this form it could very properly be put forward. Latest Russian news in Press here scarcely encourages U. S. to send their troops to Russia.

T telegram (IOR MSS Eur. F 118/114, India Office Library and Records).

From the Diary of Josephus Daniels

November Friday 2 1917

Cabinet—WW criticism is that this is rich man's war, & it was reported that sons of rich men were being given places in W[ashington] & others, away from firing line and this ought to be prevented. Mostly in new organizations Lane said he thought this mistake & that rich men's sons were going quicker than others. Cannot be too careful said W.W.

Asked Baker to commandeer guns & hundred million rounds of ammunition belonging to Scandinavian country & then send to Italy. He said he could not approve Ordnance recomm to let explosives go by express.

To Robert Lansing, with Enclosure

My dear Mr. Secretary,   The White House [c. Nov. 3, 1917].

Thank you for this, which I return for your files. Has anything further been heard about the independent organization within the army here referred to? It might eventually save the situation,—and Russia.   Faithfully Yours,   W.W.

WWTLI (SDR, RG 59, 763.72/7947, DNA).

E N C L O S U R E

Handed me by Lord Reading
to show to Pres't Nov 1/17
(9 pm) R L

I received cablegram from the Prime Minister as follows:[1] "With reference to your cablegram of November 1st,[2] raising question of the use of Japanese troops, the view of the British Cabinet is that the Japanese authorities would never assent to such a proposal if made. It may be that the U. S. Administration may have some better means of knowledge, and of course, if they think that the Japanese could be induced to send an Expeditionary Force to Russia we would support them in every way possible. The Cabinet has received an important cablegram from their chief military representative in Russia. It is to the effect that the Q.M.G. in Russia[3] has every reason to anticipate that by the month of January there will be an available Russian Army of at least 400,000 selected men. Many applications are being made to him from various units of the military forces requesting that some steps may be adopted for the purpose of protecting those soldiers in the fighting line who wish to do their duty from the propaganda of the Maximalists.[4] A plan has already been adopted to secure the benefit of this distinct step in advance of the morale. The men themselves have proposed that they should get together all those who wish to continue the fight and thus make separate armies. The whole plan is based upon companies being formed of volunteers who come from the same territorial area or zemstvl.[5]

A number of companies is already in existence. The basis is that the men swear to concern themselves with the war only. The men will be clothed and fed by the zemstvls, who will also take all steps to prevent agitators from getting amongst those soldiers. Cadres are being established on the basis of volunteers from soldiers of other regiments, who may choose their own leaders or officers. The plan is to extend from companies eventually to regiments which will all be based upon the territorial principle. The scheme further is to constitute a volunteer committee for the province composed of all the councils of the zemstvls in the province in order that there may be effective cooperation among the provinces and the councils. It is anticipated that Petrograd will be opposed to the plan, but it is thought that it has now got so strong a hold that it cannot be prevented.

It is clear, in the opinion of this high Russian authority, that it is of the utmost importance that the morale of the Russian troops should be improved, and that there is ground for hoping that an attempt for this purpose will be successful. If the U. S. Administration would consider whether it would be possible for them to raise such a question with the Russian Government of sending U. S. troops to Russia it might be of the greatest value, more especially having regard to the situation in Italy. The British Government does not know whether it would be possible for the U. S. Administration to send troops if the Russian Government were agreeable, or even whether such a scheme could be considered; but the matter is of such importance that we cannot help putting it before you for use if you think right."

T MS (SDR, RG 59, 763.72/7947, DNA).
¹ Actually, two telegrams: D. Lloyd George to Lord Reading, Nos. 4654-4655, Nov. 1, 1917, T telegrams (IOR MSS Eur. F 118/114, India Office Library and Records).
² The Editors have not found this telegram.
³ Gen. Mikhail Konstantinovich Dietrichs.
⁴ That is, the Bolsheviks.
⁵ That is, the zemstvo, a unit of local government in Russia.

To Thomas Watt Gregory

[The White House]

My dear Mr. Attorney General: 3 November, 1917

Here are two telegrams¹ which I am taking the liberty of sending you in order to ask this question: In case the full committee of which Secretary Wilson is chairman should make the same recommendation that Mr. Verner Z. Reed makes in the first of these two telegrams, I would like to know whether I have the authority under existing law to commandeer the plants and operation of the Pacific Telephone and Telegraph Company, as Mr. Reed suggests? I would be very much obliged to you for an opinion on that subject.

    Cordially and faithfully yours,   Woodrow Wilson

TLS (Letterpress Books, WP, DLC).
¹ They are missing, but see TWG to WW, Nov. 9, 1917.

To Harry Augustus Garfield

My dear Garfield: The White House 3 November, 1917

I am returning this article of Howe's with sincere appreciation that you should have let me see it. I have read it all and read it with the greatest interest and profit. Thank you very much.
          Cordially and sincerely yours,   Woodrow Wilson

TLS (H. A. Garfield Papers, DLC).

To Newton Diehl Baker

My dear Mr. Secretary: The White House 3 November, 1917

I am very much gratified by the report conveyed by your letter of yesterday as to the employment of alien enemies. It reassures me very much.

It leaves, however, the big problem of the employment of alien enemies in factories supplying the war-making departments. As to that I wish very much that I had some notion of what ought to be done.   Faithfully yours,   Woodrow Wilson

TLS (N. D. Baker Papers, DLC).

From Franklin Knight Lane

My dear Mr. President: Washington November 3, 1917.

On April 7, 1917, the Council of National Defense adopted a report submitted by the Chairman of the Executive Committee of the Committee on Labor of the Advisory Commission of the Council,[1] urging that no change in existing standards be made during the war by either employers or employees except with the approval of the Council of National Defense. The exact language follows:

"That the Council of National Defense should issue a statement to employers and employees in our industrial plants and transportation systems advising that neither employers nor employees shall endeavor to take advantage of the country's necessities to change existing standards. When economic or other emergencies arise requiring changes of standards, the same should be made only after such proposed changes have been investigated and approved by the Council of National Defense."

On April 21, 1917, the Council approved a modification of the above, making an exception of the standard of living, or wages, from other standards. The exception stated that no change in wages should be sought by employers or employees by strikes or lockouts without giving the established agencies of the Government an opportunity to adjust the difficulties without a stoppage of work. The exact language follows:

"The one other standard that the Council had in mind was the standard of living. It recognizes that the standard of living is indefinite and difficult to determine, because it is in a measure dependent upon the purchasing power of the wages received remaining the same. It believes, however, that no arbitrary change in wages should be sought at this time by either employers or employees through the process of strikes or lockouts without at least giving the established agencies of the Government, the Mediation Board in the transportation service and the Division of Conciliation of the Department of Labor in the other industries, an opportunity to adjust the difficulties without a stoppage of work occurring. While the Council of National Defense does not mean to intimate that under ordinary circumstances the efficiency of workers is the only element that should be taken into consideration in fixing the hours of labor, safety, sanitation, women's work and child labor standards, it is the object that must be attained during the period when the nation's safety is involved. It may therefore be necessary for the Council, as a result of its investigations and experience, to suggest modifications and changes in these standards during that time. It is not the purpose of the Council, however, to undertake to determine the wage rate that will be sufficient to maintain the existing standards of living. That should be referred to the mediation agencies of the Government above referred to or to such other constituted agencies as may exist to the end that such questions may be adjusted in an orderly and equitable manner to avoid the stoppage of industries which are so vital to the interests of the nation at this critical time."

It was hoped that employers and employees, especially organized labor, would live up to the suggestion of the Committee on Labor (Mr. Samuel Gompers, Chairman) of the Advisory Commission of the Council of National Defense.

The facts, as I am reliably informed, are these:

Between April 6, 1917, and October 19, 1917, there occurred upward of 221 strikes in the United States.

The number of workmen directly affected by these strikes was upward of 179,103.

The number of workmen indirectly affected by the strikes of

others was upward of 188,985, making no allowance for the thousands affected by the longshoremen's strikes.

The total number of workmen idle for a time was thus upward of 368,088.

A strike lasting only ten days is a short strike. Assuming that the 221 strikes averaged ten days each, the total idle man days was upward of 3,680,088 between April 6, 1917 and October 19, 1917.

3,680,088 idle man days in terms of 40,000 man days to build a 5,000 ton steel ship is 92 ships aggregating 460,000 tons.

3,680,088 idle man days in terms of one man day per rifle is 3,680,088 rifles.

A producing program which began with the principles of no strikes or lockouts became a program of no strikes without mediation first.

The next step in 221 disputes was no mediation without strikes first, as shown above.

The next step for producing efficiency must be no strikes.

The annual convention of the American Federation of Labor, consisting of international unions, will be held at Buffalo on November 12th. I would urge that about 30 executives of the unions which more directly control essential war production be invited to confer with you prior to that date, to determine on a policy which will prevent the constant interruption of production for war purposes. The Commissioners of Conciliation of the Department of Labor and the President's Commission have a wonderful record of accomplishments for settling strikes after they have occurred. Organized labor should give the Government the opportunity to adjust controversies before strikes occur.

At this conference it could safely be made plain that for the war employers would agree not to object to the peaceable extension of trade unionism; that they would make no efforts to "open" a "closed shop"; that they would submit all controversies concerning standards, including wages and lockouts, to any official body on which they have equal representation with labor, and would abide by its decisions; that they would adhere strictly to health and safety laws and laws concerning woman and child labor; that they would not lower prices now in force for piece work except by Government direction; that if a union in a "closed" shop after due notice was unable to furnish sufficient union workers, any non-union employees taken on would be the first to be dismissed on the contraction of business and the shop restored to its previous "closed" status; that the only barrier in the way of steady production is the unwillingness of the unions to uphold the proposition of settlement before a strike instead of after a strike.

The imminence of the convention seems to me to make some step necessary at this time. I would take the matter up with Secretary Wilson were he here, and have sent a copy of this letter to him. You undoubtedly can put an end to this most serious situation by calling on the international labor leaders to take a stand that will not be so radical as that taken in England[2] and yet will insure to the men good wages and good conditions, and make sure that our industry will not be paralyzed.

Cordially yours,   Franklin K. Lane

TLS (WP, DLC).
[1] Samuel Gompers.
[2] For a good brief discussion of British labor and the war effort, see Ernest Llewellyn Woodward, *Great Britain and the War of 1914-1918* (London and New York, 1967), pp. 468-83.

Three Letters from Newton Diehl Baker

(Confidential)

Dear Mr. President: Washington. November 3, 1917.

Some time ago you directed me to have a conference with the Shipping Board and food controller and the Secretary of the Navy with regard to a better coordination of shipping facilities, present and prospective, and for the making of any recommendations to you which in our judgment would improve the shipping situation.

We had such a meeting, attended by Mr. Hoover, Mr. Hurley, Secretary Daniels and me. General estimates and data were studied dealing with the food situation in our own and allied countries, and the tonnage situation so far as it was understood. No suggestion evolved except that it might become necessary to recommend the commandeering of neutral tonnage in our ports. We were, however, unanimous in the belief that the action should not be taken by the Government of the United States unless it was simultaneously taken by the Governments of Great Britain, France, Italy and as far as possible by all other nations actually involved in war against the Central Powers, or any of them. In other words, we felt that it was not just to ask the United States to relieve the general stringency of tonnage for belligerent use by acting alone in this matter.

In the meantime, it seemed that the data with regard to shipping had not yet been so compiled as to make a clear exhibit of the exact situation. I therefore instructed the Director of the

Council of National Defense[1] to have the statistical division reduce the whole subject of shipping to chart form. That is being done and will be completed in a few days. I think it will be a graphic study which will add much to our knowledge of the whole problem. From present appearances, it seems likely to show that the tonnage difficulty is not so much a shortage of tonnage as it is an intolerable delay in loading and unloading ships, and that, therefore, the greatest relief which can be afforded is to be looked for in measures which will add real dispatch to the forwarding of vessels already available for use. Whether or not this can be relied upon as a solution to the problem, it seems quite certain to add materially to the efficiency of the ships now available.

I will report the result of the study to you at once upon its completion.   Respectfully,   Newton D. Baker

[1] Walter Sherman Gifford.

Information only

Dear Mr. President: Washington. November 3, 1917.

By your direction, I reported back to the persons summoned to confer about the coordination of the facilities of the port of New York and suggested that, in order to put the matter forward, a meeting be held in New York to organize the war board of the port of New York and establish the clearing house needed to reconcile the conflicting interests there. The meeting was called for Saturday morning at 10 o'clock in New York City, and I am now returning from having attended that meeting personally.

The departments of the Government represented were the Treasury, War, Navy, Commerce and the Shipping Board; Mr. Hurley attending in person; the joint New York, New Jersey board attended in a body; the dock commissioner of New York City,[1] and others representing various interests in terminal facilities were there.

The arrangement actually effected is as follows:

The War Board of the Port of New York consists of the Secretary of the Treasury (Chairman), the Secretaries of War, Navy and Commerce, the Chairman of the Shipping Board, the Mayor of New York, and the Chairman of the N. Y., N. J. Port Board.[2] Each of these members is authorized to be represented at any meeting by a person designated by him. Upon matters of major policy, the board can meet in Washington, determine policies to be followed and general rules for the guidance of all concerned.

The executive agency of the Board of the Port of New York is to be Mr. Bush of the Bush Terminal,[3] if he consent to act. This executive agent will have an office, certain clerical help and will attempt to coordinate the various facilities of the port, with the war interest of the Government given all necessary precedence. He will be aided by an executive council, upon which the several Government interests will be represented and also representatives of the lighterage, trucking, railroad, warehousing, and other interests which will be affected by any orders made. It is expected that most questions which arise will be harmoniously adjusted by the executive agent bringing together the representatives of conflicting interests, and that [once] any result has been arrived at, the agency having the power necessary to execute it will be called upon to act.

All present at the meeting believed the plan as completed promising of immediate results and of great future value.

Respectfully,   Newton D. Baker

[1] Robert A. C. Smith.
[2] William Russell Willcox.
[3] Irving Ter Bush, president of the Bush Terminal Co.

Information only.

Personal

Dear Mr. President,   Washington. November 3, 1917.

I have just received a letter from General J. Franklin Bell, who is at Camp Upton, on Long Island,[1] giving me the facts with regard to some of the young drafted men, who were loaned by him to the Liberty Loan Committee of New York.

These boys were largely Jews from the East side of New York. They collected subscriptions aggregating $610,000 practically all in subscriptions of fifty and one hundred dollars each.

General Bell's report continues to the effect that he is informed that these young men made a very favorable impression by their soldierly bearing, earnestness and intelligence; that they went out of their way to impress upon the members of the Advisory Trades Committee the fact that they were entirely satisfied with their treatment at Camp Upton, that the clothing and food were excellent and that any remarks which the people in New York City had heard as to bad treatment came from irresponsible and unintelligent soldiers who were not interested in their work.

I had heard in New York that the East Side Jewish district was an especially nervous center, full of agitation against the draft, and that when these young Jewish boys came home in their uniforms, their families were filled with pride, and a great deal of the unrest and dissatisfaction in the district was changed into an equally strong feeling of enthusiasm and local pride.

The incident seems to me a note-worthy one, and has probably served a very useful purpose in clarifying public feeling in a section of New York City not easily susceptible to direct argument on public questions.

Respectfully yours,   Newton D. Baker

TLS (WP, DLC).
  [1] Maj. Gen. James Franklin Bell, commander of the 77th Division of the National Army.

From Thomas Watt Gregory

Dear Mr. President: Washington, D. C. November 3, 1917.

I am in receipt of yours of October 29th accompanied by a letter addressed to you by Charles P. Lundquiste of 348 Douglas St., Brooklyn, N. Y., and also of Mr. Tumulty's note of October 30th referring to me a wire sent you by Mr. Joseph D. Baucus, all relating to the mayoralty campaign in New York City.

I am impressed with the idea that the Lundquiste letter was written by a crazy man or at least by a person not normal. The Baucus wire is mainly hysterical.

You ask what I think about the Hillquit situation. In his speeches he has been very close to the line a number of times, but, in my judgment, any proceedings against him would enable him to pose as a martyr and would be likely to increase his voting strength. I am having my representatives in New York City watch the situation rather carefully, and if a point is reached where he can be proceeded against it will give me a great deal of pleasure to take that course. Just at present, however, I should regard it as altogether inadvisable unless he said something considerably more disloyal than the utterances so far reported to me.

Faithfully yours,   T. W. Gregory

TLS (WP, DLC).

From George Creel, with Enclosure

My dear Mr. President: [Washington] November 4, 1917.

Do you care to have me get up a statement for you of the new relations existing between the United States and Canada, to be used in the Canadian Press?[1] This has been asked of me.

Do you care to receive a committee representing the Open Forums of the country? These people, in the main, are loyal and it might be a good chance to state your views on free speech and state your views as to where free speech leaves off and disloyalty begins.

We now have 15,000 speakers in the Four Minute Men,[2] a wonderful volunteer organization full of enthusiasm and intelligence. Might I ask you to sign the attached letter, it will be sent to each one as a personal message.

Will it be convenient for me to bring Otto Kahn to see you sometime Thursday.   Respectfully,   George Creel

TLS (WP, DLC).

[1] American newspapers, e.g., the *New York Times*, Oct. 16, 1917, had reported that the government of the Dominion of Canada would be represented in Washington by its own representative. However, Canada did not enter into formal diplomatic relations with the United States until 1927.

[2] About this organization and its work, see Vaughn, *Holding Fast the Inner Lines*, pp. 116-26. The Four Minute Men grew in numbers to 74,500 by the end of 1918, when the organization disbanded.

E N C L O S U R E

TO THE 15,000 FOUR MINUTE MEN OF THE UNITED STATES:

May I not express my very real interest in the vigorous and intelligent work your organization is doing in connection with the Committee on Public Information. It is surely a matter worthy of sincere appreciation that a body of thoughtful citizens, with the hearty cooperation of the managers of moving picture theaters, are engaged in the presentation and discussion of the purposes and measures of these critical days.

Men and nations are at their worst or at their best in any great struggle. The spoken word may light the fires of passion and unreason or it may inspire to highest action and noblest sacrifice a nation of freemen. Upon you Four Minute Men, who are charged with a special duty and enjoy a special privilege in the command of your audiences, will rest in a considerable degree, the task of arousing and informing the great body of our people so that when the record of these days is complete we shall read page for page with the deeds of army and navy the story of unity, the spirit of sacrifice, the unceasing labors, the high courage of the men and women at home who held unbroken the inner lines. My best wishes and continuing interest are with you in your work as part of the reserve officer corps in a nation thrice armed because through your efforts it knows better the justice of its cause and the value of what it defends.

Cordially and sincerely yours,   Woodrow Wilson[1]

TC MS (WP, DLC).
[1] Wilson had this letter typed and sent it to Creel in WW to G. Creel, Nov. 5, 1917, CCL (WP, DLC).

From Thomas Nelson Page

Confidential

My dear Mr. President: Rome, November 4th, 1917

In these days of stress and distress I am sending so many telegrams that I give information on nearly everything that I could give it on in a letter. However, there are certain things which one cannot say completely in a telegram.

I had just written a letter giving fully the situation at the moment of the Cabinet Crisis, about ten days ago, and was engaged on the history of this Crisis and its immediate consequences, when like a bolt out of the blue came the announcement that the enemy had broken through the Italian lines by the passes above Caporetto to the north-east of Cividale and Udine and that something very serious had happened. Since then nothing else has seemed worth relating, except that which has followed this extraordinary and unexpected event.

It was known at once that something very serious had happened, but inasmuch as a similar occurrence had taken place a year and a half ago along the Trentino Front, and as the highly praised Second Army under the distinguished General Capello,[1] who had repulsed the enemy and driven them back in May of last year was on the front in the Frioli region where Caporetto is, it was not doubted that the same thing would occur now. Little news came and what did come came only as rumors and stories which apparently had no authority; but after a few days it was known that a real disaster had occurred and that not only had the enemy broken through and captured Cividale, but that Udine itself was already evacuated, the headquarters being moved to Treviso and later to Padua, and that the entire Second Army had disintegrated, flinging away its arms and declaring for peace, and further that the Third Army which held the Carso and southern Isonzo front was in serious danger of being cut off and captured.

The official communiques contained nothing, except the move-

[1] Gen. Luigi Attilio Capello.

ment of the Armies to the new front on the Tagliamento River, and the retirement or withdrawal of the Third Army in safety; it leaked out however that much more had occurred than this.

It is now known that the men of the Second Army in considerable numbers had been reached by the propaganda which for a euphemism is always spoken of as the Socialistic propaganda, and which was in fact partly Socialistic and partly Clericalistic or Vaticanistic in favor of bringing the war to a close by simply refusing to fight. It is currently stated now that this propaganda had made tremendous headway since the last Papal Note added its weight to the Lenistic-socialistic propaganda which was largely supported, according to report, by German Austrian resources, and that when the first lines of the enemy came forward in the Passes back of Caporetto, they came singing the Socialists' songs and the advanced Italian groups united with them and fraternized until other lines came up. In other places or other portions of the lines, the Italians in those Passes fought with splendid spirit, but were simply overwhelmed and the supporting troops which were sent forward on the rush to help meet the attack were either prevented from getting very far by well organized barrage fire or were swept away by a rush of panic-stricken troops who had found themselves deceived and overwhelmed. The distance by these Passes is only six or eight miles, or possibly as many kilometers, and the whole thing was over in an hour, or a little more, and German forces were pouring into the open country. Certain regiments or parts of the line appear to have fought with the utmost heroism; it is said that three regiments of Bersaglieri[2] were completely extirpated; they are gallant and loyal troops, and I can well believe that they did so. Capello, the General in Command, was, it happened, ill and had been ill for some time. Indeed, everything seemed to favor the Germans Austrians and Bulgarians who were in this attack; for one thing there was a very heavy fog which enabled the enemy to mass sufficient forces without being discovered. So rapid was their eruption into the more open country that the Commander of the Fourth Army Corps of this Army is said to have been surrounded in his headquarters and captured before he knew that any thing had occurred. The information of the enemy appears to have been absolutely complete and detailed; it was reported that they knew exactly where everything was and were able at the first shot to destroy the telephone exchange which related to the whole defensive line. However this may have been, the enemy had at

---

[2] An elite corps of light infantry in the Italian army, first organized in 1836.

least information and was sufficiently organized to seize enough of the line held by the Second Army to cut off all those who stood to their guns, and either captured them or forced them to a precipitate retreat. There undoubtedly was plenty of heroism displayed by elements of this Army, but equally beyond doubt is the fact that the surrender if not betrayal of positions which were believed by the General Staff to be impregnable, led to the complete undoing of the entire Second Army and eventually to the capture of Cividale and Udine followed by the evacuation of the entire region west of the Tagliamento River.

The losses in men and material of every kind is not, and possibly will not be known for a long time. The loss in guns alone is commonly said to have been in the neighbourhood of a thousand and I have heard from an unusually well-informed source that it was over fifteen hundred. Roughly speaking, about one third of the entire equipment of the Italian Armies was in the region which has been evacuated, as immense stores of every kind had been deposited there for use during the coming winter.

Cadorna is said to have known the enemy's plans two days before the attack came. On the very day that it commenced, October 24th, the Minister of War, General Giardino[3] made a speech in the Chamber in which he declared that the country might rely with confidence upon the Army which was loyal and sound to the core and ready to die in its defence. This speech made a great impression and the Chamber by a great vote ordered a large edition to be printed and circulated throughout the country. It transpired later that a large remnant of the Second Army had simply "flung down its tools and gone on strike" and so, General Giardino, who is a first-class man, was left off of the new Cabinet. It is said, and I believe it, that he had a statement from General Cadorna as to the loyalty and power of the Army, and that he simply quoted it; and it is also said, though I do not believe it, that General Cadorna was in Rome when Giardino delivered his speech.

It appears to be believed among those who ought to know, that the present situation will necessitate the withdrawal of the Fourth Army from the Dolomite region and the possible withdrawal, indeed I think the almost certain withdrawal, of the First Army from the Trentino line, as the Germans and Austrians are known to have been massing heavy forces along that sector and, it is also said, intend to make there their principal attack. This will necessitate the falling back to the Adige line by the

---

[3] Lt. Gen. Gaetano Ettore Giardino, at this time second in command of the General Staff.

Italian Forces; it is said however that the Adige line is the strongest defensive line in northern Italy and I hear that Cadorna has given assurances that with the aid of the Allies he feels sure of defeating the German-Austrian Army on the Frioli plains.

My own opinion is, as I have indicated to you in my several telegrams, that it all depends upon Italy herself. If her people gather resolution from this disaster and fight with all their might, they can get sufficient aid from the Allies to make good Cadorna's claim. I have given the dark side of the situation because it is the true side and there is no use in blinking facts. But there is a bright side also.

Deeds of heroism have been shown by elements even in this now disorganized Second Army equal to any known in any war in any time. The withdrawal of the Third Army, even although they must have lost a great many guns—I have heard the number of heavy guns lost placed as high as sixty—was accomplished in a way to make it one of the real feats of this war, and an even greater feat is the quiet way in which the Italian people have up to the present under conditions which must have kept them in a state of inexpressable anguish, have met this disaster and face the hardly less agonizing uncertainties of the future. I believe that Italy will yet show the enemy that she has recovered from this staggering blow and will justify the confidence that has been reposed in the country for which the heroes and the martyrs of the Resorgimento gave up their lives.

No one who has not lived here in Italy during this time can have any idea what a weight the Italian Government and the Italian people have carried in the unseen, ever-felt, unremitting pressure against this war, exercised by an element which can reach at once both body and spirit: Socialist or Vatican whatever it be called, it has never flagged in its determination to prevent Italy and the Allies from realizing that for which they have been fighting. There are many noble Socialists and many noble Clericals, priests and laymen who have been as patriotic as any enrolled in all these great Armies of Freedom, but against them as against the rest of the patriots of Italy has been ever this influence as unseen but as unremitting as the law of gravitation.

I must now close this letter to send by the pouch to England, and I will continue it as the magazine[s] say, or rather the old weekly newspapers used to say, in my next.

Believe me, my dear Mr. President,

Always most sincerely yours,   Thos. Nelson Page

TLS (WP, DLC).

Paul Samuel Reinsch to Robert Lansing

Peking, Nov. 4, 1917.

Japanese Minister has shown me the text of your note to Baron Ishii in which the American Government recognizes the special interest of Japan in China. While I understand that the reasons which prompted this momentous decision are confidential, I have the honor to ask whether at the time of publication of this note you desire me to present to the Chinese officials any explanation of this action which so profoundly affects their interests and which at first sight appears a reversal of American policy in China. Reinsch.

T telegram (WP, DLC).

To Robert Lansing, with Enclosure

My dear Mr. Secretary: The White House 5 November, 1917

I am sorry to say I do not know the full name of the new Prime Minister of Italy.[1] Perhaps it would be possible to ascertain it in your office.

I have just received the enclosed from him, which no doubt you have seen, and I am returning it with the request that you cable through Mr. Page at Rome the following reply:

"May I not thank you very warmly indeed for your generous message to me upon assuming the direction of the Government of Italy, and may I not express to you in return the very deep interest of the people and Government of the United States in the success of the Italian arms and their unshaken faith in the valor and unconquerable power of the great Italian people? The friendship which the people of the United States feel for Italy is not born of the moment. It is of long standing and is full of all the elements of genuine sympathy and admiration. May I not hope that every good fortune and the most substantial success will crown the great efforts you are making to perpetuate the high traditions of your people?   Wilson."

Faithfully yours,   Woodrow Wilson

TLS (SDR, RG 59, 865.002/37, DNA).
[1] Vittorio Emmanuele Orlando, who had assumed the premiership of Italy on October 30, 1917.

E N C L O S U R E[1]

[Nov. 1, 1917] Rome, Italy

I have the honor of informing Your Excellency that I assume the direction of the Government of Italy. I beg Your Excellency to accept my respectful and cordial greetings as a new and fervent message from the Italian people who affirm anew to the great nation of the United States of America the assurances of their lively sympathy and of their ever increasing admiration whilst the coalition of our enemies with an inhuman force attempts the conquest of the sacred soil of our native land and to break the resistence of our spirits on the frontier and in the interior. The Italian people support, with indomitable courage, the hour of adversity thanks to the tried valor of our forces and the powerful support of our Allies and the harmonious discipline of the whole nation. We have unshaken faith in the day in which from one to the other shore of the free ocean the cry of common victory will resound and that day the human race will be able with better destiny to enter on the path which Your Excellency has pointed out to it by words which will remain resplendent in history.   Orlando.

T MS (SDR, RG 59, 865.002/37, DNA).
  [1] V. Orlando to WW, Nov. 1, 1917, T telegram (SDR, RG 59, 865.002/37, DNA).

To George Creel

My dear Creel: The White House 5 November, 1917

I am afraid I don't know exactly what you mean by the "new relations existing between the United States and Canada," but if you have the time and inclination I would be very much obliged to see any statement you might wish to write, because in that way I could best judge of the advisability of attempting any definition of those relations.

I think perhaps it would not be best for me to receive a committee representing the Open Forums of the country. It would be extremely difficult to state correctly and wisely my views about free speech just now, and I think I had better seek a later occasion.

I would be very glad if you would bring Mr. Kahn in to see me at 2:30 on Thursday.[1]

Cordially and faithfully yours,   Woodrow Wilson

TLS (G. Creel Papers, DLC).
  [1] A very brief news item in the *New York Times*, Nov. 9, 1917, stated only

that Kahn visited Wilson at the White House on November 8 and that he "would not discuss his visit except to say that it was for the purpose of talking over the economic condition of the country." The Editors have found no mention of the visit in the O. H. Kahn Papers, NjP.

To Newton Diehl Baker

My dear Mr. Secretary: The White House 5 November, 1917

Thank you warmly for repeating to me the substance of General Bell's report about the young soldiers who collected $610,000 among the Jews of the East Side of New York. Such reports are certainly most heartening and delightful.

Cordially and sincerely yours,   Woodrow Wilson

TLS (N. D. Baker Papers, DLC).

To Thomas Watt Gregory

[The White House]
My dear Mr. Attorney General: 5 November, 1917

I have your letter about Hillquit. I have very little doubt that your judgment is right in the matter.

Cordially and sincerely yours,   Woodrow Wilson

TLS (Letterpress Books, WP, DLC).

To Franklin Knight Lane

My dear Mr. Secretary: [The White House] 5 November, 1917

Thank you sincerely for your letter of November third about the labor situation. I shall take the suggestion it contains under my most serious consideration.

In haste

Cordially and sincerely yours,   Woodrow Wilson

TLS (Letterpress Books, WP, DLC).

To Charles Raymond Macauley

My dear Macauley: [The White House] 5 November, 1917

You have proposed the one thing to me which I particularly do not know how to do. I could perhaps find something that I had said somewhere that would be appropriate, but just deliberately to utter a sentence addressed to nobody in particular and without any consciousness of an audience of any sort is something I have attempted so often in the past and failed at so invariably that I haven't the heart to try it again.

Cordially and sincerely yours,   Woodrow Wilson

TLS (Letterpress Books, WP, DLC).

To Camille Hart Irvine[1]

My dear Mrs. Irvine: [The White House] 5 November, 1917

I am very glad to answer your letter and thank you most warmly for all its generous friendship.[2]

I have no hesitation in saying Doctor Irvine has made the right decision. It is clearly his duty to keep the school going at its highest capacity if he can, and I think that it is the duty of the teachers associated with him to stick to their tasks unless they are manifestly indispensable to the direct work of the war itself. I think it would be a very great detriment to the country to have our higher schools and the colleges interrupted and unnecessarily depleted, particularly at this time.

May I not congratulate you both on the decision you have made and on the work you are doing?

Cordially and sincerely yours,   Woodrow Wilson

TLS (Letterpress Books, WP, DLC).
[1] Mrs. William Mann Irvine, wife of the headmaster of Mercersburg Academy.
[2] Camille H. Irvine to WW, Nov. 1, 1917, ALS (WP, DLC). She wished to know whether certain teachers at Mercersburg who had been called to military service might be deferred so that the work of the school might continue.

From Robert Lansing, with Enclosure

CONFIDENTIAL.

Dear Mr. President: Washington November 5, 1917.

I am sending you enclosed a copy of a secret memorandum which was handed to Mr. Phillips to-day by Mr. Robertson[1] of the British Embassy.

Mr. Robertson said that this memorandum was received by the Embassy on the third instant, and that a further telegram had just been received saying that Count Czernin had sent a further communication to the British to the effect that the German-Austrian advance into Italy had made no change in the proposal contained in the telegram received on the third. The British Embassy seemed to have confidence in the bona fides of Count Czernin's pledge.

With assurances of respect, etc., I am, my dear Mr. President,
Faithfully yours,   Robert Lansing.

TLS (WP, DLC).
[1] Malcolm Arnold Robertson, First Secretary of the British embassy.

ENCLOSURE

November 3, 1917.

SECRET.

An agent has been sent to Switzerland, according to confidential information received by the British Minister at Berne,[1] for the purpose of letting Great Britain know "officieusement" that if she is prepared to enter into "officieuses" conversations on the subject of peace, the Austrian Government would pledge their honour that the matter would be kept secret. Count Czernin would be ready to make an immediate declaration that, in spite of the recent Austrian success against Italy, the integrity of Italian territory as it existed before the war will be guaranteed.

The British Minister at Berne has been instructed to advise his informant that he is convinced that peace can only be discussed by His Majesty's Government with their Allies but that if the Austrian Government have a definite proposal to make, he will forward it. The French, Italian and Russian representatives at Berne will be informed by the British Minister of what has passed.

T MS (WP, DLC).
[1] Sir Horace George Montagu Rumbold.

From Thomas Watt Gregory

Dear Mr. President: Washington, D. C. November 5, 1917.

I am in receipt of your personal note of the first and the accompanying memorandum of Executive Clerk Rudolph Forster in regard to the complaint of Wm. Bayard Hale of New York City.

I am having his charges thoroughly investigated and have directed the Chief of my Bureau of Investigation[1] to proceed to New York and confer with Mr. Hale and his stenographer. I shall spare no effort to get at the bottom of this.

I am reasonably satisfied that no representative of the Department of Justice has been conducting himself improperly in this connection. So far as the Bureau of Investigation of this

Department is concerned, I do not think it has had Mr. Hale under observation or made any special investigation of him, though it has received certain information which indicates that it might be worth while to look into his activities. I am informed that the authorities of the State of New York have been rather vigorously investigating him, and it is possible that one of the State representatives may have committed the acts of which Mr. Hale complains.   Faithfully yours,   T. W. Gregory

TLS (WP, DLC).
¹ That is, Alexander Bruce Bielaski.

Two Letters to Newton Diehl Baker

My dear Mr. Secretary: EN ROUTE¹, 6 November, 1917

Thank you very much for the report of your conference with the Secretary of the Navy and the Chairman of the Shipping Board and Mr. Hoover with regard to the shipping situation. I have very little doubt that the conclusions foreshadowed in your conference are very well sustained.

Cordially and sincerely yours,   Woodrow Wilson

¹ Wilson was on his way to Princeton to vote in the New Jersey state election. He and Mrs. Wilson returned to the White House at 5:30 p.m. on the same day, November 6.

My dear Mr. Secretary: EN ROUTE, 6 November, 1917

Thank you warmly for your attention to the New York Port matter and for your kindness in going over in person to attend the meeting. I am very much interested in the report you make of that meeting in your letter of November third and think with you that it promises to accomplish a great deal.

Cordially and sincerely yours,   Woodrow Wilson

TLS (N. D. Baker Papers, DLC).

From William Bauchop Wilson

Bisbee, Ariz., November 6, 1917.

Your commission found conditions here unlike those prevailing in the other districts. In this camp containing the great properties of the Copper Queen and Calumet and Arizona, with a normal production of seventeen million pounds monthly, we found the actual copper output at present normal, despite the fact that only seventy five per cent of normal number of men were in the mines. This is due to the fact that the companies have been smelting ore from small mines, not drawn upon normally and were also smelting large reserves. We further found that the development work is considerably less than what it was prior to the strike. We therefore found it necessary to work out some plan of settlement which would assure the country the uninterrupted copper production by the district, for the future at least during the period of the war. I am glad to be able to report that your commission has worked out such a plan of settlement covering the entire district which will go into effect at once. As to the deportations of July twelfth and events following which were the outgrowth of the strike last June our report for findings and recommendations thereon will shortly go to you. We are proceeding to San Francisco.   W. B. Wilson.

T telegram (WP, DLC).

From William Bauchop Wilson and Others, with Enclosure

The President: Bisbee, Arizona, November 6, 1917.

The deportations on the 12th of July, last, from the Warren District of Arizona, as well as the practices that followed such deportations, have deeply affected the opinions of laboring men, as well as the general public, throughout the country. These events have even been made the basis of an attempt to affect adversely public opinion among some of the people of the Allies. Their memory still embarrasses the establishment of industrial peace throughout the country for the period of the war, and it is indispensable to obtain and maintain industrial peace if the war is to be brought to the quickest possible successful conclusion and if lives are not to be needlessly sacrificed. The President's Mediation Commission is charged rather with helping to secure peaceful industrial relations for the future than to sit in judgment upon the errors of the past. But it is impossible to make for peace in the future unless the recurrences of such instances as the Bisbee deportations are avoided. The future cannot be safeguarded against such recurrences unless a candid and just statement is made of the facts surrounding the Bisbee deportation and an understanding is had of the conditions which brought it about. Such candor is necessary for the guidance of all in their future conduct. Such candor is also necessary because if the truth be authoritatively set forth, there will be no basis for any misrepresentation of the facts either through ignorance or design.

The President's Mediation Commission has therefore deemed it a duty which it could not avoid to undertake a thorough and impartial consideration of the facts surrounding the deportations of the 12th of July and the practices which have been pursued since the deportation by officials and citizens of Cochise County. After hearing the representatives of the different elements involved in the deportation, both official and private, the President's Mediation Commission makes these findings:

(1) A strike was called in the Warren district on June 26, 1917, to be effective the following day. While undoubtedly the men sincerely felt that several grievances called for rectification by the companies, having regard to the conditions in this district and the Government's need for its copper production, the grievances were not of such a nature as to have justified the strike. Here as elsewhere there was, however, no machinery for the adjustment of difficulties between the companies and the men which provided for the determination of alleged grievances by some authoritative disinterested tribunal in which both the companies and the men had confidence and before which they had an equal opportunity of urging their respective claims. This is a fundamental difficulty in the settlement of grievances that may arise in this district, and here as in the other mining camps in Arizona visited by the President's Mediation Commission a plan has been worked out establishing such machinery whereby in the future, at least during the period of the war, grievances will be settled by an orderly, impartial process, and the resort to strike or lockout will be wholly without foundation.

(2) Many of those who went out did not in fact believe in the justice of the strike, but supported it, as is common among workingmen, because of their general loyalty to the cause represented by the strikers and their refusal to be regarded in their own estimation, as well as in the minds of fellow workers, as "scabs."

(3) Shortly after the strike was called, the Sheriff of the County, through the Governor of Arizona, requested the aid of Federal troops. The request was based on the fact that the state militia had been drafted into the Federal service and the state therefore was without its normal militia protection. Governor Campbell recommended to the Secretary of War that an immediate investigation of the situation at Bisbee be made by a regular army officer, in order to ascertain the need of troops. The Governor's recommendation was followed, and an investigation of

the situation in Bisbee was made by an experienced officer. Such investigation was made on June 30th and again on July 2d, and after both investigations the officer reported that everything was peaceable and that troops were neither needed nor warranted under existing conditions.

(4) That the conditions in Bisbee were in fact peaceful and free from any manifestations of disorder or violence is the testimony of reputable citizens, as well as of officials of the city and county, who are in a position to report accurately and speak without bias.

(5) Early on the morning of July 12th the Sheriff and a large armed force presuming to act as Deputies under the Sheriff's authority, comprising about two thousand men, rounded up 1186 men in the Warren District, put them aboard a train, and carried them to Columbus, New Mexico. The authorities at Columbus refused to permit those in charge of the deportation to leave the men there, and the train carried them back to the desert town of Hermanas, New Mexico, a nearby station. The deportees were wholly without adequate supply of food and water and shelter for two days. At Hermanas the deported men were abandoned by the guards who had brought them and they were left to shift for themselves. The situation was brought to the attention of the War Department, and on July 14th the deportees were escorted by troops to Columbus, New Mexico, where they were maintained by the Government until the middle of September.

(6) According to an army census, of the deported men 199 were native-born Americans, 468 were citizens, 472 were registered under the selective draft law, and 433 were married. Of the foreign-born, over twenty nationalities were represented, including 141 British, 82 Servians, and 179 Slavs. Germans and Austro-Hungarians (other than Slavs) were comparatively few.

(7) The deportation was carried out under the Sheriff of Cochise County. It was formally decided upon at a meeting of citizens on the night of July 11th, participated in by the managers and other officials of the Copper Queen Consolidated Mining Company (Phelps-Dodge Corporation, Copper Queen Division) and the Calumet and Arizona Mining Company. Those who planned and directed the deportation purposely abstained from consulting about their plans either with the United States Attorney in Arizona, or the law officers of the state or county, or their own legal advisers.

(8) In order to carry the plans for the deportation into successful execution, the leaders in the enterprise utilized the local offices of the Bell Telephone Company and exercised or attempt-

ed to exercise a censorship over parts of interstate connections of both the telephone and telegraph lines in order to prevent any knowledge of the deportation reaching the outside world.

(9) The plan for the deportation and its execution are attributable to the belief in the minds of those who engineered it that violence was contemplated by the strikers and sympathizers with the strikers who had come into the district from without, that life and property would be insecure unless such deportation was undertaken, and that the state was without the necessary armed force to prevent such anticipated violence and to safeguard life and property within the district. This belief has no justification in the evidence in support of it presented by the parties who harbored it.

(10) Neither such fear on the part of the leaders of the deportation as to anticipated violence nor evidence justifying such fear was ever communicated to the Governor of the state of Arizona with a view to renewing the request for Federal troops, based upon changing conditions, nor were the Federal authorities in fact ever apprised that a change of conditions had taken place in the district from that found by the investigating army officer to call for or warrant the interposition of Federal troops.

(11) The deportation was wholly illegal and without authority in law either state or Federal.

(12) Following the deportation of the 12th, in the language of Governor Campbell of Arizona, "the constitutional rights of citizens and others have been ignored by processes not provided by law, viz., by Deputy Sheriffs who refused persons admittance into the district and the passing of judgment by a tribunal without legal jurisdiction resulting in further deportations."

(13) Immediately after the first deportation, and until late in August, the function of the local judiciary was usurped by a body which to all intents and purposes was a vigilance committee, having no authority whatever in law. It caused the deportation of large numbers of others. So far as this committee is concerned, its activities were abandoned at the request of the Governor of Arizona late in August.

(14) Among those who were deported from the district and who thereafter were arrested in seeking entrance into it were several who were registered under the selective draft law and sought to return or remain in the district in order to discharge their legal duty of reporting for physical examination under the draft.

These findings of facts make certain recommendations by the President's Mediation Commission inevitable:

1. All illegal practices and the denial of rights safeguarded by the constitution and statutes must at once cease. The right of unimpeded admittance into the Warren District of all who seek entrance into it in a lawful and peaceable manner must be respected. The right of all persons freely to move about in the Warren District or to continue to reside within it must be scrupulously observed except in so far as such right is restricted by the orderly process of the law. To this end we have directed letters to Governor Campbell and Sheriff Wheeler of Cochise County, of which copies, together with Sheriff Wheeler's acknowledgment, are herewith appended. (Appendix A.)[1]

2. In so far as the deportation of July 12th and the events following constitute violations of the laws of Arizona, we join in the recommendation of Governor Campbell that the responsible law officers of the state and county pursue appropriate remedies for the vindication of such laws.

3. In so far as the evidence before the Commission indicates interference with the enforcement of the selective draft law, the facts should be brought to the attention of the Attorney General of the United States. A memorandum for submission to the Attorney General is herewith appended. (Appendix B.)

4. In so far as the evidence before the Commission indicates an interference with interstate lines of communication, the facts should be submitted for appropriate attention by the Interstate Commerce Commission. A memorandum for submission to the Interstate Commerce Commission is herewith appended. (Appendix C.)[2]

5. In so far as deportations such as we have set forth have not yet been made a Federal offense, it is our duty to report to the President the wisdom of recommending to the Congress that such occurrences hereafter be made criminal under the Federal law to the full extent of the constitutional authority of the Federal Government.

Respectfully submitted,

THE PRESIDENT'S MEDIATION COMMISSION,

W B Wilson, Chairman,

J. L. Spangler

E. P. Marsh

J. H. Walker

Felix Frankfurter
Counsel to the Commission.

TLS (WP, DLC).
  [1] It is missing.
  [2] It is also missing.

ENCLOSURE

(APPENDIX B.)

MEMORANDUM AS TO INTERFERENCE WITH
ENFORCEMENT OF SELECTIVE DRAFT LAW.

Both the deportations and the patrolling at Bisbee, Arizona, described in the report to the President, resulted in interference with the operation of the selective draft law. This interference had two phases.

FIRST: Obstructions to compliance with the statute were placed in the way of certain registrants.

SECOND: Evasion of the law was induced in other registrants, and such evasion was rendered easier.

The obstructions to compliance began with the deportation. This forcibly removed a number of registrants into another state, and out of the district in which they were registered and were to be examined. Notice that they would be held up if they attempted to return, and might be wholly excluded or improperly subjected to imprisonment, was served upon these men by the wholesale exclusions from this district, and arrests therein, which followed immediately upon the first deportation and continued for three months thereafter. In a number of cases, men who had received notices to appear for examination under the law, and had returned for this purpose, were detained at the district line, and thereafter within the district, for varying periods, before being permitted to proceed to the place fixed for their examination. The exhibition of the notice which they had received from the draft board was ineffective to protect them from these acts.

Some of the deported registrants who did not return openly stated, at the conclusion of the interstate deportation, that they would not appear in response to any draft call by a nation which permitted such treatment of its prospective soldiers. Some actually did fail to respond. The circumstances contributed not only to an intention of non-compliance, but made it easier to execute that intention.

Freedom from the supervision, as well as the restraints, of their own community and from their everyday mode of life facilitated the breakdown of the barriers which men ordinarily set up for themselves, and which men find set up for them, against criminal actions of this nature.

The President's Mediation Commission is not advised as to whether or not the acts above outlined constitute a sufficient interference with the working of the statute to be in violation thereof. It is able to report, however, that the effects of the deportations and exclusions upon the labor situation in this country have been nationwide and deplorable; that action by the Department of Justice, even though with respect to violations of law incidentally resulting from the deportations, would go far toward removing one of the sources of labor unrest during the war and toward convincing labor that this Government will do its utmost to prevent the recurrence of illegal practices which labor construes as directed against itself.

The Department of Justice can obtain a full statement of the facts from the following sources:

(1) The stenographic minutes of the testimony before this Commission. (The stenographer, E. W. Powers, Court House Building, Phoenix, Arizona, has been instructed to prepare a copy for the Department.)

(2) The local United States Deputy Marshal, Mr. James McDonald, has obtained a list of deported registrants and the statements of several of them.

(3) The army officials in charge of the refugee camp at Columbus, New Mexico, collected statistics and other data and may be otherwise helpful in supplying information.

(4) Some of the deported men are now in the army, probably in the camp at Linda Vista, California.

T MS (JDR, RG 60, Numerical File, No. 186813/50, DNA).

From Newton Diehl Baker

Personal

Dear Mr. President: Washington. November 6, 1917.

General Crowder desires your signature to this in order that he may use it as a foreword to the new Regulations which he is now having printed for the use of the Exemption Boards. I have re-written his original draft, taking out about half the adjectives, but there still remain a good many. I think it will be encouraging to those people who are doing a pretty big job voluntarily, and without compensation for the most part, if they can have some such word of commendation and encouragement from you.[1]

Respectfully yours,   Newton D. Baker

TLS (WP, DLC).
[1] See WW to NDB, Nov. 8, 1917 (first letter of that date).

From the White House Staff

The White House
Memorandum for the President: November 6, 1917.

Mrs. Helen Gard[e]ner called this afternoon to ask if the President would make an appointment to see on Friday, November 9th, Mrs. Carrie Chapman Catt and three or four representative women from New York, Ohio and Indiana concerning a phase of the Suffrage question. Mrs. Gardner stated that the women who had been responsible for the picketing of the White House planned a rather spectacular demonstration for the 10th and that Mrs. Catt was very anxious to see the President before that date. Mrs. Gardner stated that sometime last summer the President had made an appointment to see Mrs. Catt but that the appointment was canceled on account of the pressure upon the President's time with the understanding that another appointment was to be made later.[1]

TL (WP, DLC).
[1] Wilson saw Mrs. Catt and other leaders of the woman suffrage movement at 4:30 P.M. on November 9. The delegation thanked Wilson for his support on the suffrage question in New York and urged the passage of the proposed woman suffrage amendment to the Constitution. Perhaps the best summary of the meeting was made by Mrs. Catt in a statement quoted in several news reports. "The President listened to all we had to say with apparent interest, and asked us many questions," she said. "We stated to him the political situation as viewed by suffragists since the victory in New York. . . . We made clear to him that we believe it is the duty of the nation to grant the Federal amendment now, in order that the women may be saved the expense and long struggle which is involved in the States by the State referendum plan. We are agreed about this and anxious that the Federal amendment should pass the Sixty-fifth Congress. . . . Today we outlined to him the program we have before us, and he said he did not see any reason why we should not carry it out. We asked if he could do anything to assist that campaign, and he gave us renewed assurances of his sincere friendship for our cause. We believe that he is going to do everything that he can do to help us." *New York Times*, Nov. 10, 1917.

From Harry Covington Wheeler

Bisbee, Ariz., Nov. 6, 1917.

In a wire recently sent you,[1] my assumptions based upon communications with him by wire, I did injustice to the Hon. Secretary of Labor W. B. Wilson. I have found Mr. Wilson honorable, courteous intelligently patriotic and fair, indeed have so found the commission as a whole. They leave tomorrow with the good wishes of a still peaceful community.   Harry C. Wheeler

T telegram (WP, DLC).
[1] H. C. Wheeler to WW, Oct. 31, 1917.

Robert Lansing to Joseph Patrick Tumulty, with Enclosure

PERSONAL

My dear Mr. Tumulty: Washington November 6, 1917.

In response to your letter of November 1st enclosing a letter from Mr. H. B. Brougham of the Philadelphia PUBLIC LEDGER, I beg to return his letter, and also a copy of one which I received from Mr. Spurgeon of the LEDGER.

By Mr. Spurgeon's letter you will perceive that the management in Philadelphia assumes the responsibility for the publication of the article which has caused the controversy.

Mr. Bullitt was not present at either of the interviews in which I requested that the subject of the personnel and purposes of the proposed War Conference be not commented upon by the papers. I am personally convinced that Mr. Bullitt is entirely innocent of wrong in the matter, in view of the explanations which we have received. I consider him a man of integrity who would not knowingly violate a confidence.

In view of what has taken place in this matter I think Mr. Bullitt is the safest representative of the PUBLIC LEDGER we could have in the State Department, and, personally, I feel it would be a mistake to go further into the matter—although of course I am ready to do whatever the President wishes.

Very sincerely yours,   Robert Lansing.

TLS (WP, DLC).

E N C L O S U R E

John J. Spurgeon to Robert Lansing

My dear Mr. Secretary: [Philadelphia] October 25, 1917.

THE PUBLIC LEDGER deeply regrets the violation of your request to refrain from discussion of the American Representatives at the coming Paris Convention.

If anything in the telephone conversation had by Mr. Patchin with Mr. Brougham during my absence and reported to you, gives the impression that either the PUBLIC LEDGER or myself is inclined to ignore such requests, I desire to repudiate any such inclination or intention.

I had gone to New Haven to see former President Taft when Mr. Bullitt's despatch arrived, and knew nothing of its publication until I read it in our newspaper. When the despatch was received, our Managing Editor, having in mind your request, queried our News Bureau calling attention to your letter. It was late at night and Mr. Bullitt had retired when we were able to reach him. He replied that he had no instructions from the State Department that the story was prohibited; that he had procured it in a legitimate way, and knew of no reason why it should not be printed. He has explained to me today that he was not aware of your letter of request, as, in the work of moving our Bureau, all office records were packed in boxes. The error, however, really occurred in this office where your letter was a matter of record, and known to all of our responsible Editors.

For this error, I am sincerely sorry. It is our desire to conduct this newspaper in a manner to earn the approval, rather than the censure, of our Government.

Very respectfully yours,   John J. Spurgeon

TCL (WP, DLC).

A Thanksgiving Proclamation[1]

[Nov. 7, 1917]

It has long been the honored custom of our people to turn in the fruitful autumn of the year in praise and thanksgiving to Almighty God for his many blessings and mercies to us as a nation. That custom we can follow now even in the midst of the tragedy of a world shaken by war and immeasurable disaster, in the midst of sorrow and great peril, because even amidst the darkness that has gathered about us we can see the great blessings God has bestowed upon us, blessings that are better than mere peace of mind and prosperity of enterprise.

We have been given the opportunity to serve mankind as we once served ourselves in the great day of our Declaration of Independence, by taking up arms against a tyranny that threatened to master and debase men everywhere and joining with other free peoples in demanding for all the nations of the world what we then demanded and obtained for ourselves. In this day of the revelation of our duty not only to defend our own rights as a nation but to defend also the rights of free men throughout the world, there has been vouchsafed us in full and inspiring measure the resolution and spirit of united action. We have been brought to one mind and purpose. A new vigor of common counsel and common action has been revealed in us. We should especially thank God that in such circumstances, in the midst of the greatest enterprise the spirits of men have ever entered upon, we have, if we but observe a reasonable and practicable economy, abundance with which to supply the needs of those associated with us as well as our own. A new light shines about us. The great duties of a new day awaken a new and greater national spirit in us. We shall never again be divided or wonder what stuff we are made of.

And while we render thanks for these things let us pray Almighty God that in all humbleness of spirit we may look always to Him for guidance; that we may be kept constant in the spirit and purpose of service; that by His grace our minds may be directed and our hands strengthened; and that in His good time liberty and security and peace and the comradeship of a common justice may be vouchsafed all the nations of the earth.

Wherefore, I, Woodrow Wilson, President of the United States of America, do hereby designate Thursday, the twenty-ninth day of November next as a day of thanksgiving and prayer, and invite the people throughout the land to cease upon that day from their ordinary occupations and in their several homes and places of worship to render thanks to God, the great ruler of nations.　　　　　　　　　　　　　　　　Woodrow Wilson

TS MS (WP, DLC).
　¹ There is a WWsh outline and a WWsh draft of the following document in WP, DLC.

To William Bauchop Wilson

[The White House] 7 November, 1917

My sincere thanks for your telegram of November sixth. I deeply appreciate the thoughtful and successful work you are doing and have done.　　　　　　　　　Woodrow Wilson.

T telegram (Letterpress Books, WP, DLC).

To Rudolph Forster, with Enclosures

Dear Forster:　　　　　　　　[The White House, Nov. 7, 1917]

I see no objection to your making an acknowledgment of the receipt of this letter, but I would prefer that you would not say anything about having acquainted me with its contents. Thank you for consulting me.　　　　　　　　The President.

TL (WP, DLC).

E N C L O S U R E   I

From Rudolph Forster

Dear Mr. President: The White House. November 5, 1917.

Shall I make any acknowledgment of this letter from Dr. Hale; and, if so, shall I say that I have advised you of my interview with him?   R.F.

TLI (WP, DLC).

E N C L O S U R E   I I

William Bayard Hale to Rudolph Forster

Dear Mr. Forster: New York November 2, 1917.

Not having heard from you up to three o'clock yesterday afternoon, I returned by the Congressional Limited to New York, where, at my home, 362 Riverside Drive, I continue to be at the service of the Government.

In order to keep my recollection clear and correct, I am setting down, with Mrs. Hale's aid, a brief memorandum of our conversation on Wednesday:

I called by appointment at the White House about half past twelve, in company with Mrs. Hale, and the three of us went to the old Cabinet Room, where we spent three-quarters of an hour together. You were extremely kind to give me so much time, and the attentiveness with which you listened to my story, and the discretion of your replies was precisely what I had expected from a man wise and experienced in such affairs.

I told you that it appeared that I was under scrutiny by the Secret Service. I said that I and my family and our household had been greatly annoyed and troubled by the activities (blundering and coarse as they were) of certain persons operating in New York, claiming, at least, to be Secret Service agents.

I especially narrated, with considerable detail, (though the whole story, with its more unpleasant features, was too long to ask you to listen to) the experience of my secretary, Miss Theodora Groh. I told you that she was a young lady of twenty-one, a Catholic, of good family, highly connected, living at home and doing nothing without the knowledge of her father and mother, who has worked for me for nearly three years, except during my absence in Europe, and who during many months has done her work at our residence. My wife's interest in the matter was, as she told you, centered upon the attempt to bring to bear upon a young woman for whom she has a high regard, an enterprise at bribery and intimidation calculated to endanger her morals.

We narrated to you how Miss Groh had been besieged by a man calling himself variously "Enfield," "Johnson," etc.; how he had pursuaded Miss Groh, under the chaperonage of a female named Thayer, to meet him at restaurants; begged her (unsuccessfully) to drink intoxicants; offered her jewelry; offered her employment—WITH THE BRITISH GOVERNMENT, at a higher salary than she was receiving; offered her a Liberty Bond; and then dramatically flashed what he said was a Secret Service badge; threatened her with fine, imprisonment, or both; referred to his thirty-eight calibre revolver, and finally terrorized the young girl into accepting a small sum of money. The proposition of this gentleman to Miss Groh was to continue in my employ and to accept her small salary from me, while she spied upon me, took notes of my doings and made a daily report, on a typewriter which he was to deliver to her residence. If she divulged to me the fact that she had become a spy, no terrors were too great for her punishment.

I also told you, Mr. Forster, that the apartment house where I live had apparently been filled with spies. The sordid details you may remember, but I prefer not to set them down. I told you how I had been subpoened before the Assistant Attorney General of New York[1] at a late hour one Saturday night in connection with the Bolo Pasha episode,[2] how I had taken oath that I had never seen nor heard of Bolo Pasha until I read his name in the newspaper a few days before I was subpoened, and how the Assistant Attorney General had fully accepted my denial.

I declared to you, upon my honor, that, while it was well-known that I had been for a year literary advisor to a German Information Bureau, with an open public office at 1123 Broadway, in the heart of the City of New York, I had never done anything not fully in accord with my conscience, or by the most extravagant imagination capable of being thought in the slightest degree illegal. I professed my willingness to answer any and all questions that might be proposed to me by any Department of the Administration, but protested that the methods being used by persons describing themselves as Secret Service agents were undemocratic, un-American and intolerable. I told you that among the enquiries made of my young secretary were such irrelevant ones as my personal habits, the particulars of my resignation from the Ministry many years ago, my relations with my wife. I said that I quite understood the relevancy of the investigation of my bank account, which has been conducted; but I remarked that laborious investigations of my personal character and family affairs could easily be interpreted as an attempt to lay the ground for intimidation, rather than for the extraction of information. I told you that all I feared was an attempt to "plant" something on me, in the inevitable failure to justify any truthful charge against me.

I spoke in this line, I believe, for several minutes, but, I hope, with restrained language and without improper insinuations. I remember several times saying that it was my conviction that nobody in Washington, certainly nobody in the neighborhood of the White House, had authorized the persecution to which I and those around me are being subjected; but that I believed that irresponsible and uncouth recruits to the Secret Service had run away with a perfectly-to-be-understood suggestion that an eye might well be kept upon a writer whose sympathies were known at one time (before the war) to have been somewhat pro-German, and interpreted it as a license to go too far.

You, Mr. Forster, were so good as to listen with close attention, and I am sure you have the whole story in mind. Your comments were discreet—as I expected they would be. You asked what I desired; and I replied that I desired nothing except to relieve my mind and put the White House in possession of what I thought should be to it interesting facts regarding the activities of individuals apparently endeavoring to cover with the prestige of the Federal Government methods which I feel sure the President would not approve.

You did ask whether I might not deem it adviseable to call upon the Attorney General. I think I replied that, having delivered my soul at the White House, I felt under no obligation to do anything further; but that I would remain in Washington, probably at the Hotel New Willard for twenty-four hours, at the service of any official of any Department of the Government who might wish to see me. I said that my house and all my papers were at the instant disposition of the Government.

After a stroll through the President's rooms, which Mrs. Hale much enjoyed, we left, not without having assured the reporters at the door that the "little visit" was entirely social and without the slightest significance.

In the afternoon I wrote you from the Hotel Raleigh, that having been unable to secure quarters at the New Willard, I was at the other hotel, and would remain there until two thirty P.M., Thursday, in case anybody wished to question me.

I dislike, my dear Mr. Forster, to add to your burdens; also, I have no inordinate idea of the importance of my personal affairs. But the case may somewhat interest the President.

If our recollection[s] of Wednesday's conversation are inaccurate in any respect, would it be too much trouble for you to correct them?

With kind regards, I am, dear Mr. Secretary,

Faithfully yours,   Wm. Bayard Hale.

TLS (WP, DLC).

[1] The document cited in n. 3 to the Enclosure printed with WW to T. W. Gregory, Nov. 1, 1917, reveals that this was Alfred Le Roy Becker, Second Deputy Attorney General of New York.

[2] Paul Marie Bolo, given the title of Pasha by the former Khedive of Egypt whom he had served as a financial agent in Paris, was a French adventurer who had gained some notoriety after marrying a rich widow in 1905. He was arrested on September 29, 1917, and charged with having conspired to purchase French newspapers with German funds in order to promote pacifist sentiment in France. The plot proved to be international in scope and involved individuals in many countries. Bolo had traveled to the United States during the war and was alleged to have received funds from Count von Bernstorff, to have deposited them with well-known firms such as J. P. Morgan & Co., and to have got into contact with such figures as William Randolph Hearst and William Bayard Hale. Bolo went on trial on February 4, 1918, and was sentenced to death on February 14. Following the denial of his appeals, he was shot on April 17. See the many references to "Bolo Pacha, Paul" in the *New York Times Index* from September 1917 through April 1918.

To Robert Lansing

My dear Mr. Secretary,   The White House. 7 November, 1917.

I hope that the proper reassurances have gone, or will go at once, to Reinsch. There has not only been no change of policy but there has been a distinct gain for China, of course, and I hope that you will be kind enough to send Reinsch such a message as will serve him to put the whole thing in the right light at Peking and throughout China.   Faithfully Yours,   W.W.

WWTLI (WP, DLC).

From Robert Lansing, with Enclosure

My dear Mr. President: Washington November 7, 1917.

I send you herewith a copy of the statement which was sent to Minister Reinsch for his information in connection with the exchange of notes with Japan, of which the text was also telegraphed to him.   Faithfully yours,   Robert Lansing

TLS (WP, DLC).

ENCLOSURE

Washington, November 5, 1917, 4 p.m.

The following notes were exchanged on November 2 between Viscount Ishii and myself: quote (Then follows text of notes)

Your telegrams of November 4, eleven p.m.,[1] and November 5, twelve noon.[2]

You may say to the Foreign Office: quote. The visit of the Imperial Japanese Mission to the United States afforded an opportunity for free and friendly discussion of interests of the United States and Japan in the Orient. By openly proclaiming that the policy of Japan, as regards China, is not one of aggression, and by declaring that there is no intention to take advantage, commercially or industrially, of the special relations to China created by geographical position, the representatives of Japan have cleared the diplomatic atmosphere of the suspicions which had been so carefully spread by German propaganda.

The Governments of the United States and Japan again declare their adherence to the "open door" policy and recommit themselves, as far as these two Governments are concerned, to the maintenance of equal opportunity for and the full enjoyment by the subjects or citizens of any country in the commerce and industry of China. Japanese commercial and industrial enterprises in China manifestly have, on account of the geographical relation of the two countries, a certain advantage over similar enterprises on the part of the citizens or subjects of any other country.

The Governments of the United States and Japan have taken advantage of a favorable opportunity to make an exchange of expressions with respect to their relations with China. This understanding is formally set forth in the notes exchanged and now transmitted. The statements in the notes require no explanation. They not only contain a re-affirmation of the "open door" policy but introduce a principle of non-interference with the sovereignty and territorial integrity of China, which, generally applied, is essential to perpetual international peace, as has been so clearly declared by President Wilson. unquote.

Lansing

TC telegram (WP, DLC).
[1] P. S. Reinsch to RL, Nov. 4, 1917, printed at that date.
[2] "Japanese Legation yesterday handed to the Foreign Office copy of the note to Ishii, stated to have been (signed by?) (yourself?) on November 2. The Foreign Office is making inquiry here. This Legation is in a highly embarrassing position having received no information." P. S. Reinsch to RL, Nov. 5, 1917, *FR 1917*, p. 266.

From Josephus Daniels

Dear Mr. President: Washington. Nov. 7, 1917.

I am sure you will be glad to know that Mr. House and the members of the Commission have arrived safely in England. In view of the sinking yesterday[1] I was greatly relieved and feel sure you will be happy to get this news.

Sincerely   Josephus Daniels

ALS (WP, DLC).
[1] The American auxiliary gunboat *Alcedo*, a converted yacht, was torpedoed and sunk by a German submarine in the war zone on November 5. The news of the attack was received by the Navy Department on November 6. Twenty-one of the ninety-two officers and crew aboard were reported missing. *Alcedo* was the first American naval vessel to be sunk in the war. *New York Times*, Nov. 7 and 8, 1917.

David Rowland Francis to Robert Lansing

Petrograd, November 7, 1917,
Recd. November 10, 4.20 a.m.

1961. Whitehouse,[1] en route to the Embassy this morning, was accidentally met by aid de camp of Kerensky and several (?) latter who told him that he was hurriedly leaving to meet regular troops on the way to Petrograd to support government which would otherwise be deposed. He acknowledged that Bolshevik control city and that government powerless without reliable troops as there are few here of that nature. He said that he expected that the remainder of ministry would be arrested today and told Whitehouse to convey request to me not to recognize Soviet government if such is established in Petrograd as he expected whole affair to be liquidated within five days but this in my judgment depends on number of soldiers who will obey (him?).   Francis.

T telegram (WP, DLC).
[1] Sheldon Whitehouse, Secretary of the embassy in Petrograd.

From Mary Garrett Hay

New York, Nov. 7, 1917.

The New York City Woman Suffrage party thanks you for assisting us to win a splendid victory for democracy in New York City.[1] We feel that your able championship of our cause had great weight with the men of New York and we are proud of a

President who not only defends the principles of democracy abroad but fights for them at home.

Miss Mary Garrett Hay, Chairman of the
New York City Woman Suffrage Party.

T telegram (WP, DLC).
[1] The amendment to the New York state constitution which granted suffrage to women was approved by a statewide majority of approximately 94,000 votes in the general election held on November 6. The majority in favor of the amendment in New York City was about 92,700. *New York Times*, Nov. 7 and 8, 1917.

From Vira Boarman Whitehouse

New York, November 7, 1917.

We the executive board of the New York State Woman Suffrage Party wish once more to thank the President of the United States for his generous and effective help in our fight for democracy and to express our belief that it is largely owing to his aid that the great empire state has set this great example.

Vira Boarman Whitehouse.

T telegram (WP, DLC).

To Newton Diehl Baker, with Enclosure

My dear Mr. Secretary: [The White House] 8 November, 1917

I have taken the liberty of making a few changes of phrasing in the enclosed but they have not altered the sense at all and I have taken pleasure in signing it as General Crowder desired.

Cordially and sincerely yours,   Woodrow Wilson

TLS (Letterpress Books, WP, DLC).

E N C L O S U R E[1]

The White House November 8, 1917.

The task of selecting and mobilizing the first contingent of the National Army is nearing completion. The expedition and accuracy of its accomplishment ⟨can be interpreted only as an inspiring⟩ *were a most gratifying* demonstration of the efficiency of our democratic institutions. The swiftness with which the machinery for its execution ⟨was⟩ *had to be* assembled, *however*, left room for adjustment and improvement. New Regulations putting these improvements into effect are, *therefore*, being published today. There is no change in the essential obligation of men subject to selection ⟨and⟩. The first draft must stand unaffected by the provisions of the new Règulations ⟨which⟩. *They* can be given no retroactive effect.

The time has come for a more perfect organization of our man power. The selective principle must be carried to its logical conclusion. We must make a complete inventory of the qualifications of all registrants in order to determine, as to each man not already selected for duty with the colors, the place in the military, industrial or agricultural ranks of the nation in which his experience and training can best be made to serve the common good. This project involves an inquiry by the Selection Boards into the domestic, industrial and educational qualifications of nearly ten million men.

Members of these Boards have rendered a conspicuous service. The work was done without regard to personal convenience and under a ⟨press⟩ *pressure* of immediate necessity ⟨that⟩ *which* imposed great sacrifices. Yet the services of men trained ⟨in⟩ *by* the experience of the first draft must *of necessity* be retained and the Selection Boards must provide the directing mechanism for the *new* classification. The thing they have done is of scarcely one tenth the magnitude of the thing that remains to ⟨do⟩ *be done*. It is of *great* importance *both* to our military and *to our* economic interests that the classification be carried swiftly and accurately to a conclusion. An estimate of the time necessary for the work ⟨discloses⟩ *leads to the conclusion* that it can be accomplished in sixty days⟨:⟩; but only if this great marshalling of our resources of men is regarded by all as a national war undertaking of such significance as to challenge the attention and compel the assistance of every American.

I call upon all citizens, *therefore*, to assist Local and District Boards by proferring ⟨their⟩ *such* service⟨s⟩ and such material conveniences as they can offer and by appearing before the boards, either upon summons or upon their own initiative, to give such information as ⟨they may have that⟩ will be useful in classifying ⟨any⟩ registrants. I urge men of the legal profession to offer themselves as associate members of the Legal Advisory Boards to be provided in each community for the purpose of advising registrants of their rights and obligations and of assisting them in the preparation of ⟨the⟩ *their* answers to *the* questions which all men subject to draft are required to submit. I ask the ⟨medical profession⟩ *doctors of the country* to identify ⟨itself⟩ *themselves* with the Medical Advisory Boards which are to be constituted in the various districts throughout the United States for the purpose of ⟨accomplishing the⟩ *making a* systematic physical examination of the registrants. It is important *also* that police officials of every grade and class should be informed of their duty under the Selective Service Law and Regulations, to search for persons who do not respond promptly and to serve the summons of Local and District Boards. Newspapers can be of very great assistance in giving wide publicity to the requirements of the Law and Regulations and to the numbers and names of those who are called to present themselves to their Local Boards from day to day. Finally, I ask that during the time hereafter to be specified as marking the sixty day period of *the* classification, all citizens give ⟨their⟩ attention to the task in hand in order that the process may proceed to a conclusion with swiftness and yet with even and ⟨deliberated⟩ *considerate* justice to all.

T MS (WP, DLC).
¹ Words in the following document in angle brackets deleted by Wilson; words in italics added by him.

To Newton Diehl Baker

My dear Baker: The White House 8 November, 1917

I saw in a letter the other day the suggestion that the Army and Navy football teams be allowed to play in New York an exhibition game for the benefit of some one of the war funds. I take it for granted that your judgment is mine in such a matter, that the Army and Navy ought not to be used for that or any similar purpose, but my own judgment goes further. It seems to me that the Army and Navy game ought to be omitted altogether this season. It is largely a social event and would go very much against my own grain, I know. Indeed, I should not feel disposed to attend it.

I need not say that I heartily approve of athletics for both academies, and hope that they will play all they please on their own grounds, but I think it would make a bad impression if they did more than that this year.

            Cordially and faithfully yours,   Woodrow Wilson¹

TLS (N. D. Baker Papers, DLC).
¹ WW to JD, Nov. 8, 1917, TLS (J. Daniels Papers, DLC), is the same letter, *mutatis mutandis*.

To Joseph Patrick Tumulty

Dear Tumulty: [The White House, c. Nov. 8, 1917]

It is out of the question for me to see Mr. Hearst on any business of any kind and I would be very much obliged to you if you would convey that intimation to Mr. Macfarland so that this suggestion might be as if it had never been made.[1]

The President.

TL (WP, DLC).
[1] Macfarland called Tumulty from Boston on November 8 to say that he "hoped the President would give him permission to bring over some day next week Mr. Hearst for a little informal talk." JPT to WW, Nov. 8, 1917, TL (WP, DLC).

To John Singer Sargent

My dear Mr. Sargent: [The White House] 8 November, 1917

Thank you for your kindness in writing us about Mr. Barnard's statue of Lincoln, now that you have seen it.[1] I am very much interested in what you say of it and delighted that the artist is inclined to take your very interesting suggestions about modifying the posture of it. I am reassured, also, that you should think that with the suggested changes made the statue will probably be worthy of the very unusual distinction which is to be conferred upon it.

It was a great pleasure to know you personally, and Mrs. Wilson joins with me in kindest regards.

Cordially and sincerely yours,   Woodrow Wilson

TLS (Letterpress Books, WP, DLC).
[1] J. S. Sargent to WW, Nov. 6, 1917, ALS (WP, DLC). Sargent discussed the very controversial statue of Abraham Lincoln by George Grey Barnard, commissioned by Charles Phelps Taft and his wife, Annie Sinton Taft. It had been unveiled and presented to the city of Cincinnati on March 31, 1917, in a ceremony at which William Howard Taft was the principal speaker. Barnard's statue depicted a tall, awkward, ugly, carelessly dressed, beardless, prepresidential Lincoln, with large feet and with hands folded over his stomach. It created more controversy than any other visual image of Lincoln before or since. The furor expanded to international dimension when it was proposed that a replica of the work be placed near Westminster Abbey to commemorate a century of peace between Great Britain and the United States. The statue was the subject of heated debate in newspapers and magazines. It was condemned by Robert Todd Lincoln and defended by Theodore Roosevelt and George Bernard Shaw. As it turned out, a replica of Augustus Saint-Gaudens' standing Lincoln was placed in the location near Westminster Abbey in 1920, while the replica of Barnard's statue went to a park in Manchester, England, in 1919. For a good summary of the creation of Barnard's statue and the controversy over it, see F. Lauriston Bullard, *Lincoln in Marble and Bronze* (New Brunswick, N. J., 1952), pp. 84-85, 228-41.

Sargent had just seen the statue when he wrote to Wilson and had concluded that the chief reason why the work was so controversial was "the attitude of the arms and hands, that somehow gives the figure the look of a victim awaiting his fate." He told Wilson that he had had a long talk with

Barnard and had found the sculptor disposed to make a "radical change" in the position of the arms and hands and to "modify certain things that had been criticized" about the feet and clothing. In point of fact, no such changes were made, either in the bronze replica sent to Manchester or in a later reproduction for Louisville, Kentucky. Donald Charles Durman, *He Belongs to the Ages: The Statues of Abraham Lincoln* (Ann Arbor, Mich., 1951), pp. 152-56.

To Vira Boarman Whitehouse

[The White House]

My dear Mrs. Whitehouse: 8 November, 1917

I deeply appreciate the telegram which you and the other members of the Executive Board of the New York State Woman Suffrage Party were gracious enough to send me yesterday. It gratifies me very much to think that you believe that it was in part owing to my aid that the great Empire State adopted woman suffrage. It gives me additional pleasure in the result.

Cordially and sincerely yours,   Woodrow Wilson

TLS (Letterpress Books, WP, DLC).

To Mary Garrett Hay

My dear Miss Hay: [The White House] 8 November, 1917

Thank you very warmly for your telegram of November seventh. I am indeed gratified that you think that my championing of the cause of suffrage had great weight with the voters of New York. It gives me the right to rejoice with you in the victory.

Cordially and sincerely yours,   Woodrow Wilson

TLS (Letterpress Books, WP, DLC).

To Josephus Daniels

My dear Daniels: The White House 8 November, 1917

It was kind of you to send me the message about the arrival of House and the members of the Commission. I thank you with all my heart. It was cheering and reassuring news to get.

Cordially and sincerely yours,   Woodrow Wilson

TLS (J. Daniels Papers, DLC).

From Newton Diehl Baker, with Enclosure

My dear Mr. President: Washington. November 8, 1917.

I enclose you a very briefly stated history of the Liberty Airplane Engine. I think you will be interested to glance this over in view of the statements Senator Wadsworth made to you not long ago.[1] Colonel Deeds,[2] who makes this statement, was until recently a civilian, a manufacturer of very large experience, and of uniform success in his private industrial enterprises. His statements, I think, can be taken without question.

The net result of this statement, so far as the eight cylinder engine is concerned, is shown in sections 5, 8 and 9.

Respectfully yours,   Newton D. Baker

Col Deeds has just telephoned me that the latest test developed an actual speed of an airplane with Liberty Engine, of 120 miles per hour, and that they are now sure they will reach 140 miles per hour.

TLS (WP, DLC).

[1] Wilson saw Senator Wadsworth on November 1. There is no record of what was said at the interview. However, Wadsworth probably stated to Wilson his firmly held conviction that the Liberty engine would not fit into any airplane available at that time. James Wolcott Wadsworth, Jr., "Memoir," pp. 210-12, Oral History Research Office, NNC.

[2] Col. Edward Andrew Deeds, manufacturer of Dayton, Ohio, now a member of the Aircraft Production Board.

E N C L O S U R E

CONFIDENTIAL   Washington November 6th, 1917

From: Edward A. Deeds, Colonel, Signal Corps.
To: Chief Signal Officer of the Army.[1]
Subject: Liberty Airplane Engine.

1. The decision to build the Liberty Airplane Engine was largely influenced by the following:

A—The Allies had attempted to build sixty different kinds of engines with unsatisfactory results.

B—The Enemy adopted one type of engine and concentrated upon it with efficient results.

C—There was no reliable engine above 150 H.P. in production in the United States.

D—There was no reliable engine of 350 H.P. in quantity production abroad.

E—To adapt a foreign make of engine to our production methods would take longer than to make a complete new design.

F—The decision to make a Government design would immediately make available for our designers all foreign experience, as well as the experience of the best builders of our own country. This would not be possible if the usual commercial competition methods prevailed.

G—One type of engine would make the repair problem possible, even though the ocean separated the factories from the front.

H—A quantity production could be secured far in excess of what could be possible in any other way.

2. The Liberty Engine was to embody no new, untried elements, but was to combine the latest proven parts and principles. Whether it were a four, six, eight, or twelve cylinder, the component parts were to be interchangeable.

3. The story of how the design was made and an engine produced in twenty eight days is most inspiring, but will be omitted from this statement.

4. Ten experimental engines were ordered—five eight cylinder and five twelve cylinder. At that time 250 H.P. seemed sufficient and the eight cylinder engines were produced first.

5. The eight cylinder engines exceeded specifications in horsepower output, smoothness of operation, and weighed two pounds less than originally calculated. One was sent to Pikes Peak, mounted on a truck, and for four weeks was run at various altitudes with excellant results. With two passengers and a heavy plane, it broke the American altitude record on its second flight.

6. The first twelve cylinder engine was completed August thirteenth. The official fifty hour test was run the week of August twenty-second. The final paragraph from Inspector Reynolds' long, detailed report is quoted:

"A consideration of the data collected, we believe, will show that the fundamental construction is such that very satisfactory service with a long life and a high order of efficiency will be given by this power plant, and that the design has passed from the experimental stage into the field of proven engines."

(signed) *Lynn Reynolds*
A.M.E., Nat. Advis. Com. Aero.,
Acting Insp., Equip. Div. S.C.S.S.L.

7. Both the eight and twelve cylinder, by these tests, have proven their worth.

8. The Commission of experts sent abroad by the Signal Corps reported that the tendency was toward higher horsepowers. In view of these and other reports from abroad, it was decided to take a decisive step in advance and concentrate on the twelve

cylinder engine of higher horse power. This engine gives 365 H.P. at 1500 R.P.M. and 445 H.P. at 1800 R.P.M.

9. Many rumors have been circulated that the eight cylinder engine failed. There is no basis for any such inferences. It was superseded by the twelve for the reason above stated. Here we might add that there have been many rumors circulated, and some unpatriotic publication, tending to discredit the Liberty Engine. Fortunately an engine is not influenced in its performance by rumor or print. Whenever a vital part of an important public program is undertaken with as much vigor as has the Liberty Engine, we may expect attempts to discredit by those who have something to sell or someone to exploit. We are not being deterred by those who prefer to do their "bite" instead of their "bit."

10. Dr. Sabine,[2] who is just back after a year abroad investigating aeronautics, reports:

"The engines and planes as proposed in our program, more nearly anticipates the needs of the allies next Spring than does their own."

11. Our Liberty twelve is flying daily under observation of United States Army Officers, in a DeHaviland Four modified to receive it, at Dayton, Ohio. The plans, engine, and all accessories were built in this country. The results are most satisfactory. Two are flying in boats at Buffalo under the direction of Naval Officials. The speed of one boat was increased from its best previous record with other engines of 78 miles per hour, to 97 miles per hour. The other from a previous record of 86 miles per hour to 104 miles per hour.

12. Another engine will start this week on an endurance test, finally running it to destruction. Two more will again be put through the fifty hour acceptance test this month. Twenty-five are to be delivered by December first, and all will be used for endurance tests and ultimately run to destruction. The fundamentals of the engine are already demonstrated beyond doubt. These unusual tests are for further verification so that if any slight modifications are advisable, they can be immediately incorporated into production.

13. Our contractors are Packard, whose reputation is international; Henry M. Leland,[3] who built the Cadillac—a mechanic without a peer; Marmon of Indianapolis,[4] large manufacturers and experienced in racing cars; Henry Ford, with large resources and the most expert workers of alloy steel in this country; Dusenberg,[5] with an ideal plant and racing car and marine engine

experience; and Trego,[6] an engineer of experience in experimental work on large horsepower airplane engines.

14. The experts from the different contractors meet weekly and interchange ideas and experiences. The best talent this country affords is concentrated co-operatively and patriotically in this important service.

15. Millions of dollars have already been expended in tools and machinery and production will begin in December, rapidly increasing to 2,500 engines in March and 5,000 in May—from that time on it can be increased as the needs demand.

16. Those responsible for the production of Liberty Engines are men of experience in development and production work, and have a full realization of the size of the task imposed

17. Designs are now being developed for a sixteen cylinder, using standard Liberty parts. This is in anticipation of a possible necessity for still greater horse power in single units.

18. A report is in preparation giving a complete history of the Liberty Engine. This statement is made in advance of the official report.   E. A. Deeds.

TS MS (WP, DLC).
[1] Maj. Gen. George Owen Squier.
[2] Wallace Clement Ware Sabine, Hollis Professor of Mathematics and Natural Philosophy at Harvard.
[3] Henry Martyn Leland.
[4] Howard C. Marmon.
[5] Frederick Samuel Duesenberg.
[6] Frank H. Trego.

From Frank William Taussig, with Enclosure

My dear Mr. President: Washington November 8, 1917.

I take the liberty of transmitting herewith a memorandum on the commercial policy of the United States, prepared as the outcome of a conference with Dr. Mezes, of the College of the City of New York. The conference itself was the result of previous correspondence with Colonel House, and led me to state to Dr. Mezes in some detail my own opinions on the attitude which the United States should take in negotiations and understandings relating to our commercial policy. At his request, I formulated my opinions in this memorandum, which was then transmitted to him. Needless to say, it was not for public use.

I should add that this statement represents my individual opinions, not the views of the Tariff Commission. At the same time, I have talked over the matter with my associates and find that their general attitude is not dissimilar from my own.

I have taken the liberty also of sending a copy of the memorandum to the Secretary of State.

Believe me, with high respect and regard,

Sincerely yours,   F. W. Taussig

TLS (WP, DLC).

E N C L O S U R E

MEMORANDUM
on
The Policy to be followed by the U. S. in
international negotiations on commercial policy.

1. The United States should keep free from any economic alliances. We should not join in any retaliatory or punitive commercial arrangements and should not undertake to give special favors to any country or set of countries.

2. The United States should recognize the right of every nation to settle its tariff system on its own principles. We should make no propaganda for protection or for free trade. We should hold ourselves free to settle our own tariff policy as we may think expedient, and recognize the right of other countries to do the same.

3. This recognition of freedom, and attitude of non-interference, should extend to colonial policy also. We hold ourselves free to settle our arrangements with our colonies as we see fit, and we should undertake no interference with other countries concerning their relations with their colonies. If the United States should give favors to other countries as regards goods sent by them to colonies of the United States, the same favors should be extended to other countries on the same terms.

The policy of abstention from interference with colonial relations would, however, not necessarily apply where there are self-governing colonies. Preferential arrangements, for example, between Great Britain on the one hand and such self-governing colonies as Canada and Australia on the other, might possibly give us occasion at least for conference and friendly discussion; whereas the relations of Great Britain with the West Indies and British India, and those of France, Germany and Italy with their own tropical colonies, would be deemed outside the scope of international discussion and negotiation.

4. The United States should make a determined and active effort not to be "frozen out." We should get from every country

the same terms which it gives to other countries. If France or Italy, for example, should make commercial treaties, giving special favors each to the other, the United States should endeavor to secure from France and Italy the same favored treatment. Similarly, if Japan should make a commercial treaty with China, the United States should insist upon having the same advantages as each of these countries gave to the other.

5. Further, the United States should use its efforts to bring about a *general situation* of this kind. We should work for an international policy of the open door,—the same terms for all. Even though the only matter of direct concern to the United States is that this country should secure for itself whatever favors or advantages are granted to others, we should endeavor to discourage preferential and differential tariffs, and discourage economic alliances all around.

6. A general policy of this sort is not necessarily inconsistent with certain limited arrangements for special favors and preferential rates.

a. One exception would arise where there are settled and long-established special political relations between one country and another, such for example, the relations between the United States and Cuba; these justify our present arrangement for a reciprocal preference. A similar exception would presumably be admitted if Germany and Austria made an arrangement for reciprocal concessions to each other.

b. Exceptions might also arise on grounds of geographical propinquity, resting primarily on the convenience of border trade. If for example, the United States should make a reciprocity treaty with Canada, similar to that which was proposed in 1911, the favors granted by the United States to Canada would not necessarily be accorded to all other countries.

Barring exceptions of these kinds, however, the United States should not undertake to secure special favors for herself, and should be willing to give up any special favors she may now have. For example, there is at present an arrangement by which Brazil admits United States goods at specially lowered duties. We should express our willingness to give up this arrangement, and certainly should not insist on its retention.

7. To further this general policy, and more especially to prevent the United States from being "frozen out," this country must have a weapon. It must rely not merely upon diplomatic persuasion and protest, or its own willingness to adopt an open policy. It must have something in the nature of a bargaining tariff; it must put potential retaliation on its program. A weapon

of this sort (bargaining or retaliatory tariff) should be kept in the background, not flourished, not used except in the last extremity. But it should be available.

8. The precise form for such a bargaining tariff needs careful consideration. It may possibly take the form of (a) *lower* duties for those countries which give the United States open door treatment; or (b) *enhanced* duties for those countries which refuse to give the United States open door treatment. Again, it may take the form of, (a) a general provision, of a drag-net sort, by which a supplement of 10, 20 or 25 per cent may be added to existing duties, or a similar horizontal reduction made from existing duties; (b) an enumerated list of articles, with exact duties (extra rates) specified for each of the articles, this list conceivably to be varied and differentiated according to the course of trade between the United States and the particular countries concerned.

These alternatives are receiving the careful attention of the Tariff Commission; but the details are not essential as regards the general policy of *some* bargaining provisions.

9. One thing, however, would seem to be clear; that legislation should be enacted which would put power to apply the weapon in the hands of the President. He should be authorized to put into effect the provisions of the bargaining tariff, without the need of confirmation by the Senate for each separate commercial arrangement. Necessity of confirmation by the Senate has wrecked previous negotiations; it should be obviated for the future.   F. W. Taussig.

T MS (WP, DLC).

Newton Diehl Baker to Josephus Daniels

Personal

My dear Mr. Secretary: Washington. November 8, 1917.

The enclosed memorandum was sent to the President by Mr. Hoover.[1] A copy of it has been sent to Mr. Hurley. The President wants you to read it and he expects to call a conference at his earliest convenience, to be attended by you, Mr. Hurley, and me, with him, so that we can discuss the matter for his information.[2] I have read the memorandum and if you will bring it to the conference with you when the President calls it I will be much obliged to you.   Cordially yours,   Newton D. Baker

TLS (J. Daniels Papers, DLC).
[1] H. C. Hoover to WW, Nov. 5, 1917, TLS (WP, DLC). This was simply a

covering letter for H. C. Hoover to E. N. Hurley, Nov. 5, 1917, CCL, and H. C. Hoover to EMH, Oct. 26 and Nov. 5, 1917, TCL, all in the J. Daniels Papers, DLC. The letter to Hurley called attention to the large quantities of such foodstuffs as sugar, molasses, coffee, and vegetable oils which the United States would have to import during the next twelve months and expressed great apprehension as to whether the necessary shipping would be available. Hoover elaborated on this apprehension in his two letters to House. The one of October 26 suggested that the Allies should draw their food imports as much as possible from sources farther away than the United States in order to ease the strain on shipping and railroad facilities and to preserve the food reserves of the United States in the event that the international food situation became even more critical in future years. In his letter to House of November 5, Hoover went so far as to suggest that it might be wise if the effort to send an American army to France was abandoned in favor of concentrating America's resources on the production for and the transportation of food and munitions to the Allies.

2 The Editors have been unable to discover any information about this conference if, indeed, it did occur.

To Frank William Taussig

My dear Mr. Taussig: [The White House] 9 November, 1917

Thank you sincerely for sending me the memorandum of the outcome of your consultation with Doctor Mezes. I shall value it very highly to my thought on the important subject with which it deals.

      Cordially and sincerely yours,   Woodrow Wilson

TLS (Letterpress Books, WP, DLC).

A Telegram and a Letter from Edward Mandell House

From House—London 9 Nov., P.M.

Russian-Italian situation is a depressing influence and it is fortunate that we arrived at this time in order to encourage our associates. Balfour told me you are informed we could not have come at a more advantageous time. George and military authorities have been absent in Italy but return tomorrow when some preliminary conferences will be held. All members of the commission are doing excellently and are making a fine impression. I think we will be able to put something into the situation which has heretofore been lacking. I am going to Paris just after the middle of next week.

WWhw decode (WP, DLC).

From Edward Mandell House, with Enclosure

Dear Governor,   London. November 9, 1917.

I am enclosing an extraordinary memorandum which Buckler has sent me. I am to see Milner this afternoon and will get directly from him whether or not Buckler has accurately stated his views. If this memorandum should get out it would be the undoing of Milner, therefore I hope you will keep it for your own information.

Our main task for the moment is to keep up the courage of our friends here and in France. I have seen today two members of the French Cabinet who happened to be in London and I have done what I could to steady them.

We are meeting with every courtesy and every source of information has been opened to us. I am told that the Commissioners are making a good impression. They are working steadily and are doing in a day more than such bodies usually do in a week. They all seem amenable to advice and are ready and willing to do the things that I suggest as being necessary.

Page has been delightful and helpful and is doing everything that he can to further our purposes.

                    Affectionately yours,   E. M. House

Milner does not come in time to add to this letter, and the mail now closes.

TLS (WP, DLC).

E N C L O S U R E

William Hepburn Buckler to Edward Mandell House

Strictly Confidential

The following are notes of a conversation with *Lord Milner* held at the house of my sister-in-law (13 Gerald Road)[1] yesterday evening between 10.30 and midnight.

                    London, November 3, 1917.

I asked whether he thought that in anticipation of the peace conference Great Britain and the United States might agree on a form of international constitution—similar to that of the Danube Commission—for districts such as Palestine and Albania, which would need to be placed under some kind of international control.

This might well be done, he said, in the case of Palestine, for

Great Britain and the United States had practically agreed upon treating her as the future "home of the Jewish race," and she would be easy to govern because too poor to be coveted by powerful neighbours.

For Albania he thought that the methods of administration and control would have to be different from those adopted in Palestine because of the bitterness of international rivalries and the lawlessness of the Albanian people. He admitted that it would be an excellent thing if this country and America could agree to lay before the peace conference some detailed scheme of government for both those districts.

Such international administration, however, would be difficult to operate, and ought therefore to be created in as few cases as possible. If Constantinople and the Straits were neutralized, he thought that the Turks should be left at Constantinople, and certain points on the Straits might be guarded by garrisons established under international agreement.

With regard to the Balkans in general he failed to see how the promises which England had made to individual States could possibly be redeemed in full. Serbia, he thought, would be most difficult to restore, even to her pre-1912 boundaries, because Bulgaria was holding and claiming part of that territory. The proposed bestowal upon Serbia of lands now held by Austria-Hungary (i.e. the project of Greater Serbia or Iugo-Slavia) seemed to him chimerical. The collapse of Russia, followed as it now was by that of Italy, made this solution impracticable, since there was now no force capable of detaching from Austria her South-eastern provinces.

Should the war continue for two or three years more, he granted that almost anything was conceivable, but he doubted whether Great Britain and the United States, which are now the only unexhausted powers opposed to Germany, would be willing to continue the fight so long for the sake of Serbian or Rumanian aspirations.

He then asked me the date of Colonel House's arrival. I said I believed it would be early next week. He expressed great pleasure at Colonel House having undertaken this mission, since he was "pro-Ally in heart without being pro-Ally in head" and capable of seeing facts as they are undistorted by his personal sympathies.

He said with great earnestness that he wanted me to repeat to Colonel House and to *nobody* else what he was about to tell me.

"Our diplomacy," he said, "has been in my opinion and still is deplorably weak in its attitude towards our enemies. For the past ten months we have been receiving all kinds of intimation, more or less definite, as to German offers of negotiation. Not only have we taken absolutely no steps to test the sincerity or the extent of these offers, but if anyone however remotely connected with this country is seen so much as talking to anyone however remotely connected with Germany, there is at once an absurd outcry of 'peace trap' and an insinuation that we are about to betray this or that ally. I hope that America will not imitate our timidity. How *are* we ever to know what our enemies will offer, unless we keep our ears open? We ought to listen to every 'peace whisper'—of course on the distinct understanding that all offers must be considered by the Entente as a whole.

"If we see an American making inquiries as to German proposals, depend upon it we shall know quite well that America is not intending to 'cart' us, and we ought to insist that our Allies shall have this same confidence in us."

I reminded him that Briand had lately received peace overtures in Switzerland and that so far from disapproving this action the French had dismissed Ribot for having rejected such overtures as a "trap."

"I think it most important," he said, "that some means be found of keeping in close touch with authoritative German opinion.

"This is all the more necessary since the Italian disaster threatens to prolong the war. Of course we must assume that the military party in Germany is for the time being triumphant, but on the other hand Germany and Austria are suffering acutely and clearly anxious for peace. The appointment of the new Chancellor Hertling,[2] a Bavarian and a Roman Catholic, is a portent showing at least that the Germans are breaking with past traditions. And a government may be the more ready to make a reasonable though inglorious peace when a great success has strengthened its hold on its own people."

He inquired whether the United States had, as he hoped, some means of keeping in touch with Turkey and Bulgaria, for he regretted to say that Great Britain had at present no such facilities. If those countries felt inclined to approach the Entente, he could not see how they were to do it. I replied that I did not know for certain, but was not aware of any channel by which confidential communications could pass to Turkey, nor even to Bulgaria, without the knowledge of Germany or of Austria.

He said he was inclined to wish that in his reply to the Papal Note, the President had not insisted so strongly upon what amounted to a revolution in Germany, that is upon an event almost impossible to bring about during war.

I replied that the President had carefully refrained from saying "no peace with Hohenzollerns," and had merely insisted on
guarantees for civilian and popular control of German policy.
The nature of those guarantees was not specified, and it seemed
to me therefore that, when the Germans sincerely wanted peace,
without domination, it would be easy for them to give such guarantees as would satisfy the President's formula.

Our interview ended with a talk over the Italian situation, and
on examining a map we came to the conclusion that the Italian
army would probably be compelled to retreat as far as the Adige,
thus abandoning Venetia as well as Friuli. Any line of defence
eastward of the Adige could probably be turned by an Austrian
"push" southward through the mountains.

He has no hope that Italy will again be able to molest Austria
during this war.

N.B. The above passages in quotation-marks (pp 3-5) are
not of course a verbatim report, such as a stenographer would
make: but they reproduce in the main Lord M's own phrasology,
and I thus report them because they contain a message to Col.
House.   W.H.B.

CC MS (WP, DLC).
  1 Unidentified.
  2 Georg Friedrich, Count von Hertling, a leader of the Center party and Prime
Minister of Bavaria, had, according to different sources, been appointed
Chancellor by William II on October 25, October 28, or November 1.

From Sidney Edward Mezes, with Enclosure

Dear Mr. President: [New York] November 9, 1917.

I am sending you, by the courtesy of Mr. Gregory, a somewhat
rough preliminary and brief outline of the subjects to be dealt
with in The Inquiry. Much that is to be done on the more delicate
topics will naturally have to await Colonel House's return, or
your own suggestion.

                    Very sincerely yours,   S. E. Mezes.

TLS (WP, DLC).

E N C L O S U R E

A PRELIMINARY BRIEF OUTLINE
OF THE SUBJECTS TO BE DEALT WITH IN THE INQUIRY

I. *Suppressed, Oppressed and Backward Peoples*, etc. (e.g., Poles, Bohemians, Jugo-Slavs, African regions); in each case—
   1. Past and Present: History, Geography, (Races, *Maps*); Government and Politics, Social Status, Economics (business, agriculture), Strategy (chiefly to judge unfounded boundary claims).
   2. Serious Proposals for Future: By whom made (nations, parties, leaders) and why; light thrown on each by data in 1, especially as to whether it would tend to establish a suitable geographic and business unit (with needed access to sea and marlets [markets]) and tend, by constitution or laws (granting independence, autonomy, or civil and cultural rights) to insure sufficient freedom, security, and where feasible, unity.

II. *International Business; Commercial Freedom and Equity.*
   1. Physical bases; past and present operation and regulation; serious proposals analyzed. Straits, Canals, Rivers, Ports, Railways, Cables, Wireless, Aircraft (??).
   2. Tariff Studies; e.g., Universal Free Trade; Most Favored Nation treatment for (practically) all; Revenue Tariffs; Open Door; Fair Access to Raw Materials; "Key" Industries and Materials.
   3. Export of capital; concessions, spheres; facts and serious proposals.

III. *Studies in International Law*
   1. Surveys of positions taken by Important Nations on timely questions; also positions of text writers on them.
   2. Serious proposals for vital changes analytically presented with forward outlook; by whom made and why; e.g., for
      1. Humanizing warfare on land, on sea, in air, (weapons, gasses, mines, submarines, etc.)
      2. The Freedom of the Seas.
   3. Limitation of Armaments on land and sea.
   4. Aid to workers on II above and IV below, and to other workers.

IV. *Analytical Presentation of Serious Proposals* for organizing (giving structure to) a concert of the authority and force of mankind to insure a just and lasting peace.

V. *Restoration*: Data and Estimates, insofar as, and if accessible.

*Summaries of Important Divisions that Belong
Together and General Summary.*

T MS (WP, DLC).

From George Creel, with Enclosure

My dear Mr. President: Washington, D. C. Nov. 9th, 1917.

Dr. Mott is eager for some message from you with which to start up his $35,000.00 [$35,000,000] campaign. I have drawn up attached letter for your approval. He begs to have it by to-morrow, so if you see fit to sign it and will return it this afternoon, I shall send it by special delivery tonight. You will notice that I have incorporated a brief mention of other organizations doing like work.

The militant suffragettes, that is, the Congressional Union, are asking to have an audience with you on Monday, to urge the federal amendment and request immediate release of the pickets.[1] May I advise against such an audience and if you agree with me will you suggest form of refusal. Mrs. Catt and Dr. Shaw speak for equal suffrage in the nation, and the Congressional Union is without standing and deserves no recognition.

Respectfully,   George Creel

TLS (WP, DLC).
[1] Wilson did not see the group at this time.

E N C L O S U R E[1]

My dear Mr. Mott:

In the prosecution of a war against the dominance of militarism and for the protection of our homes, we must make every effort to lighten the burdens of the men who carry our colors and to keep them close to the ideals of the homes for which they are *making the supreme sacrific⟨ing⟩e*. To do this among our own soldiers in camps at home and ⟨in the trenches⟩ abroad and to carry the generous message of an unselfish America to the soldiers and prisoners in France, in Russia, in Italy, ⟨to⟩ *and* do these things without regard to race and creed *or nationality* is to give reality to their faith in our land and in the common cause we defend.

The generous work inaugurated by the Y.M.C.A., the Knights

of Columbus and the Y.M.H.A. is so instinct with the best ⟨of⟩ purposes and already *is* so rich in accomplishment that it should be heartily supported. The special campaign for $35,000,000 which the Y.M.C.A. has inaugurated is of ⟨such⟩ vital importance ⟨in⟩ *to* the work of increasing the contentment and efficiency of our citizen army; is ⟨so⟩ fundamental to making morals the basis of military morale, ⟨that it⟩ *and* should engage the generous support of all our people. I bespeak for it ⟨among our people⟩ *a una-nimity and* a unity of effort⟨s⟩ and *of* gifts, ⟨that⟩ *to speed* this patriotic and practical work ⟨may go⟩ forward to abundant *and complete* success.[2]

T MS (WP, DLC).
    [1] Words in angle brackets in the following document deleted by Wilson; words in italics added by him.
    [2] The emended letter is WW to J. R. Mott, Nov. 9, 1917, TLS (J. R. Mott Coll., CtY-D).

From Thomas Watt Gregory

My dear Mr. President: Washington, D. C. November 9, 1917.

With your letter of November 3 you send me copies of two telegrams, one from Secretary Wilson and one from Mr. Vernon Z. Reed, which concern a proposed commandeering of the plants and properties of the Pacific Telephone and Telegraph Company and of its officials, superintendents, foremen and employees, whether at work or on strike, "to such extent as may be necessary to maintain full efficiency of operation." You ask whether you have authority under existing law to commandeer the plants and operation of this company as Mr. Reed suggests. Speaking from the meagre facts which these telegrams contain, it is my opinion that no such power has been given you by any existing law.

I observe that two things are proposed by Mr. Reed's telegram: first, the commandeering of the plants and properties of the company, and, second, the impressment into the Government service of some or all of its officials, superintendents, foremen and employees—all to the end that a threatened general strike may be averted. While these proposals constitute a single programme, they raise somewhat different legal questions.

In so far as the seizure of the physical properties is concerned, it is clear that the Government, speaking in the large sense, may take them over whenever they are needed for public use upon payment of just compensation. It is in the exercise of this power of eminent domain that Congress has empowered you to use or control any radio station or apparatus (Act of August 13, 1912,

c. 287, sec. 2, 37 Stat. 303); to take possession of any plant or plants which refuse to furnish military supplies at a reasonable price, and manufacture therein through the Ordnance Department such material as may be required (Act of June 3, 1916, c. 134, sec. 120, 39 Stat. 213); to make similar seizure and use of factories making ships or war material for the navy (Act of March 4, 1917, c. 180, 39 Stat. 1193), or ships or materials under the statutory provisions governing the expenditure of the "Emergency Shipping Fund" (Act of June 15, 1917, Public No. 23, 65th Congress); to "take possession and assume control of any system or systems of transportation, or any part thereof, and to utilize the same, to the exclusion as far as may be necessary of all other traffic thereon, for the transfer or transportation of troops, war material and equipment, or for such other purposes connected with the emergency as may be needful or desirable" (Act of August 29, 1916, 39 Stat. 645, c. 418); to requisition foods, feeds, fuels, and other supplies necessary to the support of the army or the maintenance of the navy, or any other public use connected with the common defense, and storage facilities therefor (Act of August 10, 1917, sec. 10, Public No. 41, 65th Congress); to take over when necessary to secure an adequate supply of necessaries for the support of the army or the maintenance of the navy, or for any other public use connected with the common defense, any factory, packing house, oil pipe line, mine or other plant, or any part thereof, in or through which any necessaries are or may be manufactured, produced, prepared or mined (id. sec. 12); to commandeer distilled spirits (id. sec. 16); and to "requisition and take over the plant, business, and all appurtenances thereof" belonging to a producer of or dealer in coal and coke who fails to conform to the requirements of the act (id. sec. 25).

Evidently none of these statutes, which constitute as I believe all the existing legislation of this character, is broad enough to cover the present case. No doubt as Commander-in-Chief of the army and navy you may, in time of war, seize upon those things which are presently necessary to equip, maintain, transport or manoeuvre either arm without waiting for express statutory authority; but the power is an extraordinary one and not to be pressed beyond the emergency which evokes it. So of the power of eminent domain itself; it draws from the necessity of the government, not from mere general convenience; and ceases when the govenmental need has been supplied. In so far as the service now rendered by the Pacific Telephone and Telegraph Company is necessary to the government's purposes, Congress unquestionably could authorize the seizure of the property in order to secure its continuance; but until it has done so I think you can act only in the presence of some truly military emergency.

The case as to the officials, superintendents, foremen and employees is still more difficult, for it involves what is in effect civil conscription. Of course, aside from your power as commander in the actual theatre of war, where you rule by force of arms, you have no power to enforce such involuntary service in the absence of direct legislation. That there may be, however, civil as well as military conscription is witnessed by the various road laws of the States, the power to summon the *posse comitatus*, jury duty, and so forth. But you may recall that by your direction a bill was prepared by my department following the passage of the Adamson Act which made express provision for just what is suggested here, under which the officers, agents, and employees of railroad, telegraph and telephone companies could have been drafted for the operation of their lines in time of actual or threatened war, insurrection or invasion. This bill had as a precedent a somewhat similar act passed January 31, 1862, c. 15, 12 Stat. 334. It was introduced in the Senate, but never got beyond the committee stage. The selective draft act of May 18, 1917, does, it is true, authorize you to raise and maintain by voluntary enlistment or draft as therein provided "special and technical troops"; but it is obvious that neither the letter nor the spirit of this provision adapt it to the case in hand. Since these special and technical troops are to be drafted as the act provides, the field of selection is limited to males between the ages of 21 and 31; and their further designation as troops which are to be embodied into organizations and officered as are other levies under the act makes it plain that they are not intended to be diverted to mere civilian service not directly connected with the operations of war.

Faithfully yours,   T. W. Gregory

TLS (WP, DLC).

From the White House Staff, with Enclosure

The White House.
Memorandum for the President: November 9, 1917.

Dr. McCracken[1] of the Red Cross called this afternoon at the request of Chairman Davison and stated that it was the intention of the Red Cross to make a drive next month for 10,000,000 additional members—the drive to end on Christmas Eve. The Red Cross are very anxious that the President issue some appeal in connection with this effort, and Dr. McCracken has submitted the attached draft. Dr. McCracken stated that it will be necessary to start the printing for this effort very shortly and would like to have something from the President by the first of next week.

TL (WP, DLC).
  [1] Henry Noble MacCracken, President of Vassar College and executive secretary of the national committee for the Christmas membership drive of the American Red Cross.

ENCLOSURE[1]

TO THE PEOPLE OF THE UNITED STATES: November 9, 1917.

Ten million Americans are invited to join the American Red Cross during the week ending with Christmas Eve. The times require that every branch of our great National effort shall be loyally upheld and ⟨the season suggests that the Red Cross should be your agent in loyal expression⟩ *it is peculiarly fitting that at the Christmas season the Red Cross should be the branch through which your willingness to help is expressed.*

You should join the American Red Cross because it alone can carry the ⟨pleasures⟩ *pledges* of Christmas good-will to those who are bearing for us the real burdens of the world war⟨,⟩ both in our own Army and Navy and the nations upon whose territory the issues of the world are being fought out. Your evidence of faith in this work in [is] necessary for ⟨them⟩ *their heartening and cheer.*

You should join the Red Cross because ⟨when allowance is made for work that must be condicted [conducted] on the conditions resembling a run on a bank,⟩ this ⟨unofficial⟩ arm of the National service is steadily and efficiently maintaining its overseas relief in every suffering land, administering our millions wisely and well, and awakening the gratitude of every people.

Our consciences will not let us enjoy the Christmas season if this pledge of support to our cause and the world's weal *is* left ⟨undone⟩ *unfulfilled.* Red Cross membership is the Christmas spirit in terms of action.

President of the American Red Cross.

T MS (WP, DLC).
  [1] Words in angle brackets in the following document deleted by Wilson; words in italics added by him. This appeal, in its emended form, was printed in the *Official Bulletin*, I (Dec. 11, 1917), 1.

Samuel Gompers to Joseph Patrick Tumulty

Buffalo, N. Y., Nov. 9, 1917.

The presence of the President at convention American Federation of Labor and an address by him would be a master stroke at this time. Such a manifestation of solidarity of the people of the United States without regard to class or condition, particularly in view of the chaotic Russian situation would have a wonderfully stabilizing influence. Please telegraph me Statler Hotel, Buffalo, or have the President do so, to-day or tomorrow, Saturday morning early.   Samuel Gompers.

T telegram (WP, DLC).

From the Diary of Josephus Daniels

1917 Friday 9 November

Shall retirement pay for clerks? WW favored. McAdoo thought some insurance measure would follow soldiers and sailors act. Lane said he dropped three old men and all three committed suicide. WW "That is the way out."

W.W. story of Vance[1] trying to induce negro to join Pres. Ch. Said "I don't believe in the doctrine of election." V. said "I do & it is sound["]. Negro "I aint never heard you was a candidate."

Baker: Man loved to be in limelight. Wife wanted him to join Baptist ch. No. Didn't believe in immersion. Why not? Have to stay too long out of public eye.

McAdoo: Shall we lend money to Russia? WW thought we could not yet presume R. would fail—must wait WW pleased, on the whole, with election returns[2] and must pay penalty by receiving Womans delegation today[3]

McAdoo did not think Morgan interests trying to depress markets. Why stocks low? One thing people prefer government bonds.

[1] Governor Zebulon Baird Vance of North Carolina.
[2] Wilson was undoubtedly most pleased by the passage of the woman suffrage amendment in New York at the election held on November 6 (about which see Mary G. Hay to WW, Nov. 7, 1917, n. 1). He was certainly also pleased by the election of John Francis Hylan, a Democrat, as Mayor of New York. In this contest, Hylan received 313,956 votes; Mitchel, 155,497; Hillquit, 145,332; and Bennett, 56,438.
[3] Wilson received Mrs. Catt and her group at 4:30 p.m.

To George Creel, with Enclosure

My dear Creel: The White House 10 November, 1917

Here is a very important letter which I wish you would read and inwardly digest. It seems to me to hit very near the heart of the subject it is concerned with.

Faithfully yours,   Woodrow Wilson

TLS (G. Creel Papers, DLC).

E N C L O S U R E

From Charles Edward Russell

My dear Mr. President: Chicago, Ill. November 7, 1917

I think that it is perfectly clear that the disasters in Italy are a direct result of the situation in Russia. The Germans would never have dared to make this diversion of troops, guns and energy to the Italian front if they had not proved by the Riga drive that they had nothing to fear from the Russian army.

The possible consequences of the drive into Italy I need not dwell upon. Doubtless you have considered them all, including the shadow of an immeasurable catastrophe that looms behind them.

Close observations in Russia last summer convinced me that the Russian army is now nothing but a reflex of the Russian people. There is no other authority. If the Russian army hangs back and does not want to fight any more it is because the Russian people have no heart in the war.

Yet it is perfectly possible to make them have heart in the war, to make them eager for it and to have therefore the Russian army keen and tense for the battle.

The trouble is that at present the average Russian sees nothing in the war that appeals to the soul in him. The war was made by the Czar; that mere fact prejudices the average Russian against it. Then it is something opposed to his dream of universal brotherhood and the instantaneous Republic of the World that came upon him with this Revolution. He has never for a moment laid hold of the fact that this Revolution of his that means so much to him is involved in this war; he never has suspected that if Germany wins the Revolution will be lost. His feeling for democracy and his passion for this Revolution are the strongest springs of action in every typical Russian. It is quite useless to say to him, as some are saying, that Russia ought to fight because of her pledge to the Allies. His reply is ready; it is that Russia of the people made no such pledges; all were made by the Czar. The typical Russian acknowledges no obligation on the part of Russia to the Allies; he only acknowledges the duty of a democrat to fight for democracy.

I write to beg therefore that the education campaign carried on by this country in Russia be carefully directed along these lines. If it is addressed to the Russian's passion for democracy, and if it shows him that his beloved Revolution is in peril, he will be ready to fight with all his strength, and there is no better fighter in the world. The most useful thing would be to film pictures and printed appeals relating the struggle for democracy elsewhere, picturing the heroes of democracy and their sacrifices, and leading up to the present struggle as the final battle in a long conflict, which is exactly what it is. I think it of the utmost importance that anything in the nature of lecturing or badgering the Russians should be strictly avoided. They resent such preachments. The great thing is to appeal to their democratic sense. If that is properly done this winter the Russians will be fighting next spring and fighting as hard as anybody.

It has already occurred to your careful consideration that $5,000,000 expended now on this educational campaign may obviate the expenditure of billions hereafter.

I pray, my dear Mr. President, for your health and strength for the great task that has been laid upon you to save freedom for all mankind. God bless and guide you.

Yours very truly,   [Charles E. Russell]

TCL (G. Creel Papers, DLC).

To Charles Edward Russell

My dear Mr. Russell: The White House 10 November, 1917

I deeply appreciate your letter. It runs along the lines of my own thought, only you speak from knowledge and I have thought by inference, and you may be sure that I will do my best to act along the lines it suggests, though all sorts of work in Russia now is rendered extremely difficult because no one channel connects with any other, apparently.

Cordially and sincerely yours,   Woodrow Wilson

TLS (C. E. Russell Papers, DLC).

To Joseph Patrick Tumulty, with Enclosure

Dear Tumulty: [The White House, c. Nov. 10, 1917]

Don't you think it would be well to have copies of this interesting and satisfactory letter sent to the ladies who telegraphed me yesterday?[1] It seems to me that this is a frank and satisfactory way of dealing with their question, and I should like them to know the facts.   The President.

TL (WP, DLC).
[1] One, which is missing, came from Lillian D. Wald. See JPT to Lillian D. Wald, Nov. 12, 1917. A handwritten note at the top of the Enclosure says: "Copy sent Mrs. Amos Pinchot & Miss L. D. Wald."

E N C L O S U R E

From William Gwynn Gardiner[1]

The President,   Washington November 9, 1917.

Mr. Tumulty has just advised me that the President desires information as to the exact conditions at the District Jail, where the suffragists are now confined.

After a consultation Wednesday with Mr. John Joy Edson, President of the Board of Charities of this city,[2] and Mr. George E. Hamilton, of that Board[3] (this Board having supervision of the District Jail), it was thought advisable to select an eminent physician of wide experience in the supervision and control of such institutions, to visit the District Jail and talk with and examine if necessary Miss Paul and Miss Winslow,[4] the two suffragists now on a hunger-strike. Dr. W. A. White, of the St. Elizabeth's Hospital,[5] therefore went to the Jail on Wednesday afternoon, saw Miss Paul and Miss Winslow, and after an interview with them, advised me that if I would go to the Jail with him on the following morning and talk with these two young women, we might be able to induce them to take food.

I went to the Jail, accompanied by Dr. White, yesterday, and during several hours spent there, we went through the institution, giving special attention to the preparation and cooking of the foodstuff used to supply the inmates. Dr. White expressed the opinion that the quality of the food as well as the service was all that could be expected. We also examined the quarters occupied by the pickets, in the east wing of the Jail. We found everything there in good condition, and Dr. White expressed entire satisfaction with the sanitary condition of the Jail. We were also furnished by the Superintendent of the Jail[6] with menus of the meals served in the last few days, and Dr. White, upon examination of these, expressed approval.

We found in the quarters occupied by the suffragists, windows broken and paint off the walls. We were informed by the matrons in charge that this had been caused by the suffragists striking the walls of their cells with the heels of their shoes; they then threw their shoes through the windows, breaking the glass.

I then went with Dr. White to the Hospital of the Jail, where Miss Paul and Miss Winslow were confined. We spent considerable time with Miss Paul. During the interview Miss Paul stated that the National Woman's Party had received $30,000 since she had been in jail, which she said was evidence of the great number of friends and admirers of the party and their loyalty to it. She also said that she recognized the fact that President Wilson was a friend to the suffragists, but that they had determined upon picketing as a means of bringing the cause before the people of the country and keeping it before them. She stated further that she had decided upon this hunger-strike as a means of compelling those in authority to accede to her demands; that her demands were perfectly simple. She stated her demands thus:

"We are political prisoners and must therefore be treated unlike other prisoners," she said. "We want such food as the suffragists have been accustomed to in their homes. All of the suffragists must be furnished with eggs and milk every day; they must be permitted to have such articles of food and delicacies as they demand sent them by their friends outside of the Jail; they must have plenty of light and air, the daily papers delivered to them, and the right to attend to their work while in the Jail." The right to send out such correspondence as they desired and to receive such as was delivered to the Jail must be given them. She said political prisoners are recognized by other countries, although it required hunger-strikes to force such recognition, therefore hunger-strikes would force such recognition in this country.

Miss Paul said that the food furnished her in the hospital was all that she desired, it being first-class in every respect; but that the food served her and her associates while in the Jail proper was not the kind of food they had been used to and was not such as would keep them well and strong.

Miss Paul gave us to understand that only upon the promise of the proper officials that these demands would be in every respect met and that the promise would be carried out not only in regard to those now in prison, but those who might hereafter be imprisoned for the same cause, would she take her food.

The room in which Miss Paul, as well as the room in which Miss Winslow was confined, was well-lighted, well-ventilated, and perfectly clean. Miss Paul is a very, very frail woman, but seemed quite strong when she undertook to emphasize what she claimed as her rights. Miss Winslow, on the other hand, was apparently a strong, robust woman. There was no evidence of nervousness on the part of either of them; both seemed perfectly calm, but very determined.

After leaving the rooms, a consultation was held with Drs. White and Gannon,[7] and it was the opinion of both that it was necessary to feed the patients by the tube process, using force if necessary. Dr. White stated to me that it was an every-day occurrence at his institution to feed patients in this way and that he had some in his institution now that he had been feeding in this manner for twenty years with no ill effect. The doctors agreed upon the quantity and character of the food to be given. I was advised by Dr. Gannon later in the afternoon that when the patients were informed of the intention of the doctors to compel them to take food, they took the tube through which the food was to be administered and swallowed it willingly, there being no force or persuasion used upon either of them, and that they were now being regularly fed in this manner, with no more than the ordinary discomfort attending such a course of feeding.

We all have in mind the importance of every move in the case and therefore determined to call some physician outside of the regular staff of physicians. Regarding Dr. White as the head of his profession for this purpose, we sought his cooperation and advice. We have also the certificate of Drs. James A. Gannon, the physician to the Jail, Percy D. Hickling and W. M. Barton,[8] who, after visiting the Jail and seeing Miss Paul and Miss Winslow, certified to the necessity and propriety of feeding and by force if necessary.

While the statements emanating from the National Woman's Party have not been correct, Messrs. Hamilton and Edson and I feel that we should not enter into a controversy, but remain silent. I beg to advise you that all of the persons who have dealt in any wise with these suffragists, from the Commissioners down to the guards and matrons, have endeavored in every way consistent with the good order and discipline of the institutions in which they have been confined, to be as considerate of them as possible, but without success, they having beforehand a set purpose and plan to violate every rule of those institutions.[9]

Very respectfully,   W Gwynn Gardiner

TLS (WP, DLC).

1 Washington lawyer and a Commissioner of the District of Columbia.
2 A Washington banker long active in the civic affairs of the District of Columbia, especially in penal reform.
3 George Ernest Hamilton, Dean of the Georgetown University School of Law.
4 That is, Alice Paul and Rose Winslow.
5 William Alanson White, M.D., pioneering psychiatrist and superintendent of St. Elizabeths Hospital, formerly known as the Government Hospital for the Insane.
6 Louis F. Zinkhan.
7 James Alonzo Gannon, M.D., physician of Washington.
8 Daniel Percy Hickling, M.D., Washington physician who specialized in psychiatry and neurology, and Wilfred Mason Barton, M.D., also a physician of Washington.
9 For a radically different account, see Christine Lunardini, "From Equal Suffrage to Equal Rights: The National Woman's Party, 1913-1923" (Ph.D. dissertation, Princeton University, 1981), pp. 245-47. Dr. Lunardini (p. 247) calls the Gardiner report "an interesting piece of fiction."

To William Gwynn Gardiner

My dear Mr. Gardiner: [The White House] 10 November, 1917

Thank you very much for your letter of yesterday about the conditions at the District Jail. I sincerely appreciate the fullness of the information you convey to me. It will be very useful and I must say is very satisfactory.

Cordially and sincerely yours,   Woodrow Wilson

TLS (Letterpress Books, WP, DLC).

From Newton Diehl Baker, with Enclosure

(Personal)

Dear Mr. President: Washington. November 10, 1917.

Sir Stevenson Kent[1] is, I think, known to you. He is a large coal mine owner and operator, and steamship owner and operator. He is in this country chiefly to tell us of English labor conditions. After some weeks in Washington, he made a trip through the cities of the middle west to address chambers of commerce and trades union gatherings. At my request, he has written a very frank account of his impressions. It seems to me so important that I am taking the liberty of inclosing it for your information. His observations in the main confirm my own information. The suggestions, while to some extent perhaps modeled too much upon English experience, certainly contain many suggestions which we may have seriously to consider.

It was because of this situation that I felt especially concerned to have you make the Buffalo trip, if possible. If you were to find yourself able to go there, what you would say would undoubtedly be accepted on both sides as the war duty of the country, and I confess I am more concerned to have industry and capital know what you think they ought to do with regard to labor than to have labor understand its duty. In my own dealing with the industrial problems here, I have found labor more willing to keep step than capital.   Respectfully,   Newton D. Baker

TLS (WP, DLC).
  [1] Sir Stephenson Hamilton Kent, Director-General of the Munitions Labour Supply in the Ministry of Munitions.

E N C L O S U R E

Mr. Secretary Baker.

At your request I report on the impressions that my Mission have received in visiting the various centres that the Council of Defence indicated.

I would wish to emphasise the fact that the suggestions as to action that are contained in this memorandum are but tentatively put forward and I follow with a certain trepidation your request that they should be made.

You will appreciate that I do not, for one moment, claim any sufficient knowledge of conditions and sentiment in your country to lay these suggestions before you except in the most tentative manner.

I beg that you will, therefore, read this document bearing in mind that it is compiled in accordance with your wish and that no special knowledge lies behind the suggested remedies.

It will be within your recollection that my Mission has visited Pittsburgh, Indianapolis, St. Louis, Chicago, Detroit, Cleveland, Buffalo, Boston, Hartford, and has but just arrived at New York. The Mission has met in these various centres such representatives of Capital and Labour as the Councils of Defence may have called together.

We have been given to understand, and it is our impression, that these various bodies have been fully representative of the several interests. The conditions that we have found are, for all practical purposes, common to all districts, though it is, of course, true that the impressions we have gained in the centres vary in degree.

They may be stated as follows:

IMPRESSIONS GAINED FROM LABOUR

On Labour side an attitude of suspicion and hostility to Capital. We have received complaints of victimisation, of profiteering, of the serious increased costs of living and of clothes, and of the wide divergence that exists in earnings in various industries.

Complaint has been made of the impossibility of ascertaining whether the work on which Labour is engaged is Governmental work and should come under the Eight Hours Law; we have been definitely informed that Union Labour has walked the streets at the time that an urgent demand for labour existed on Governmental work, and this from the refusal of employers to employ Union labour.

Complaint has been made of the insufficiency of Labour representation on the State Councils of Defence and generally on Councils and Committees dealing with Labour matters.

In some few instances we have found a complete indifference to the war and absorption in preparation for the struggle that Labour is under the impression must be waged against Capital at some very early date. We have been definitely told that this struggle will be entered upon very soon; and that Labour will no longer tolerate the treatment that is being meted out to it at the present moment.

Complaint has been voiced to us that the Federal Government has done and is doing nothing either to better Labour's condition or to see that justice is rendered to it.

We have been told that women are being substituted for men and the men discharged. We have been told that coloured labour is being imported to take the place of white labour conscripted. That both in regard to the substitution of women and coloured labour the employer is to make a very considerable saving in his wage expenditure, and that Union labour is being victimized in both these connections.

We have also heard complaints that Aliens of Allied Countries, of military age, instead of being recruited for the Army are being employed to the exclusion of native labour and particularly of Union Labour.

At Cleveland at a conference with the heads of the Railway Brotherhoods, I was definitely told that instructions had been given in both the engineering and firemen's brotherhood that the first negro that set foot on a locomotive was to be the signal for the engineer or fireman to quit his job, and that very serious trouble would ensue.

IMPRESSIONS GAINED FROM CAPITAL

On Capital's side it may be said that we have found hostility to a quite unbelievable extent against organized labour. But little thought, and that individually has been given to the problem nor has any attempt been made to bring about a general and material improvement in Capital's relationship with Labour.

We have found almost without exception a firm determination amongst the employers to maintain the conditions of the open shop. I do not think it is an exaggeration to say, speaking generally, that employers in this country attach so much importance to this fact that the winning of the war is almost a secondary consideration to them.

I have no doubt in my mind that to a great number of employers in this country the war is looked upon as a means still further to strengthen employers' position in this respect.

The substitution of women for male labour is being regarded as a means to cheapen production and increase profits and, further, it is being used to victimize organised labour.

The Draft Law would also appear to afford a ready means for this victimisation. I have been given to understand, and on enquiry I find there is a considerable substratum of truth in the charge, that the Tribunal rarely grants exemption to an individual workman unless the employer certifies that the man in question is essential to his business. It is easily understood how readily this will lend itself to the elimination of Union men from establishments.

As an example, the President of the Fireman's Railway Brotherhood informed me that the railways were not claiming exemption for the firemen. The Chairman of the Draft Exemption Board at Cleveland, when I made guarded enquiries, informed me that in his opinion the railways were much to blame in not so doing but that on his own responsibility he had been granting exemptions to a certain number of these men as he felt sure that the railways could not afford to lose this labour and that this labour was essential to transportation work in this country.

GENERAL SUMMARY OF IMPRESSIONS GAINED

As an attempt to summarise the foregoing position, I should be inclined to say that Labour in this country, if reasonably handled, would continue loyally to fulfil its task.

The Labour representatives gave us to understand on innumerable occasions that if Capital would but meet Labour to some degree, it would find Labour only too willing to make a sacrifice and help adjust their relationship.

I cannot recall having met in conference an unreasonable spirit amongst the Labour representatives I have encountered. I should classify them on the whole as a reasonable, intelligent, level-headed lot of men. They all were anxious to control their rank and file and all professed to think that such a control was possible if immediate action were taken to remedy their grievances.

I would wish to lay emphasis on this necessity for immediate action. In their view the accumulation of grievances was rapidly approaching a climax and the general impression I have is that these men, with every wish and anxiety to behave loyally to the executive authority, feel that control will slip from their hands at a very early date unless they can assure the rank and file that the many complaints which they feel they are justified in voicing are to be dealt with at some very early moment.

It should not be forgotten that Capital's refusal to met these leaders of Trade Unionism, or to recognize Trade Unionism, is a position of very considerable danger, from the fact that power may so easily slip from the hands of these responsible men into the hands of the professional agitator, the alien or the I.W.W.

It is, in my view, very necessary that the position of these men should be strengthened at the earliest possible moment and as much as may be possible.

I am sure there is no possibility of Labour and Capital coming together of their own accord. The suspicion and hostility that exists between these two parties is of too long duration and is too acute in form for a rapprochement of their own initiative. It is probably essential that the Federal Government take immediate action to bring these parties together.

PART II
GENERAL POINTS OF IMPORTANCE

To deal with certain general points of importance.

I find that at the moment enticement and auctioneering of labour is a common practice. The enticement to leave their present employment is not confined to the offer of increased wages but has many ingenious variations.

One instance came to my notice of an offer of $10,000 per month to the department in an establishment which gave the best monthly results from the points of view of efficiency and production.

As another example of the conditions now existing I was given to understand in Buffalo that on the completion of the Curtiss plant a further five thousand mechanics would be required. It was expected that two thousand five hundred of them would be forthcoming in Buffalo and that the other two thousand five hundred would be found in other industrial centres.

On the same day I was consulted by a representative from the employers in Rochester who informed me that an erection of a gun-making plant in that town was practically completed and that they would require about two thousand five hundred skilled workers. They thought it probable that they would endeavour to obtain this labour from towns not in their immediate vicinity as they were under the impression that competition so localised might prove too expensive.

On this point I would like to say that failure to control the employers in this respect must lead to the most wide spread unrest and chaos. Auctioneering, while always a vicious system, in war time is of such danger to the State that immediate steps should be taken to end it. It must be plain that the laws of supply and demand apply with as much force to man power as to anything else. The offer of high wages only unsettles labour and will eventually result in drawing labour from employers whose work, while quite essential to the national interest, does not permit of an increase in wages to the same extent as in munition factories, e.g. railways.

I have been informed that nineteen hundred and twelve strikes have taken place in the munitions industry, using the word "munitions" in its broadest sense, since this country's entry into the war, and that the origin of nearly every one of these strikes was an endeavour on the part of organized labour either to obtain recognition of the Union or to better its conditions as to wages or employment.

Whilst it is a fact that the percentage of labour organized in this country is but a small one, it is also a fact that certain of the more highly skilled industrial occupations are to a greater degree organized than this percentage would indicate, e.g. toolmakers.

This fact must not be lost sight of nor must it be forgotten that engineering establishments are wholly dependent upon their tool room hands and that a strike amongst this class of workmen would be a national distaster.

PART III

GOVERNMENTAL ACTION THOUGHT NECESSARY

Before I venture to make concrete suggestions in accordance with your request, I propose to endeavour to set out the action that, in my view, must be taken by the Government at the earliest possible date, if the industrial peace which is so essential to your Nation's continued and full co-operation in the war is to be effective.

I have in mind very clearly the difficulties my Government have encountered and the unrest that is occasioned in the problems I enumerate below.

I would respectfully point out that your Country is but at the beginning of the troubles occasioned by the withdrawal of man power.

The grievances and unrest that at such an early date manifest themselves are occasioned by the withdrawal from its normal occupation of but an infinitessimal part of your man power.

How much more will this grievance be magnified and this unrest manifest itself when a more serious inroad is made on your man power?

Action would appear necessary in regard to

1. The discrimination against and victimisation of Trades Unions and the endeavour of employers to use the accident of war to either maintain, or make, the open shop.

2. Coloured labour being engaged on work that has been in the past looked upon as a white man's job.

3. The dilution of labour; a most delicate matter in that organized labour must see in this operation a most serious menace to their future existence.

4. The substitution of women on man's work.

5. Power to deal drastically with the employer who offers an inducement to labour to leave its present employment and power to regulate and restrict the engagement of labour in any establishment.

6. Compulsory arbitration and the rendering illegal of strikes or lock-outs, together with the power to inflict severe penalties on delinquents.

7. The waiving of restrictive practices for the period of the war and on war work.

8. The limitation of profits.

9. The control of establishments.

10. The Enrolment of Volunteers under a binding obligation to work at any Munitions plant among those whose profits are controlled to which the Government may assign them.

(It is obvious that such body of volunteers is extremely useful in as much as it can be retained on important work or transferred to more important work as desired. In the event of an emergency requirement by the Army it facilitates immediate increased production and further the question of wage does not enter into the transfer of such labour)

11. Power to grant awards of labour in such industries as may be controlled and so meet the increased cost of living

12. The divergencies of earnings as between the essential industries today.

(This should be immediately checked and brought into line; otherwise Labour will be so materially withdrawn from certain essential occupations that their efficiency will be impaired and disaster may arise; or, the Government, itself, will have to bridge over these deficiencies at its own expense, the divergence in question being so wide, that this national expense would neither be justified nor economically sound.)

13. The drastic handling of profiteers in the essentials of life.

ENGLISH EXPERIENCE

It will be within your recollection that, in England, the Munitions of War Act and its subsequent amending acts have endeavoured to deal with the greater part of the problems I set out above.

It will also be within your recollection that in England in the Engineering industry and, for all practical purposes this may be said to cover the greater part of the industrial side of Munitions, wages have been at a practical standstill since this Act was passed.

The British Government, under the terms of this Act definitely limited the profit of the employer in controlling his establishment and the wage of the employee in such establishment on the ground that neither side should profit by the Nation's need.

In so doing, it became its duty to see that Labour, whose wage it had so regulated, was not put to a disadvantage in its living conditions. A Committee on Production was set up whose function it is to weigh evidence placed before it as to the increased cost of living and to grant such awards to Labour affected, as to meet the increased cost of living and so to see that Labour was not put to any disadvantage by the action of the Government.

My Government has delegated to the Labour Departments of the Ministry of Munitions and the Admiralty the administration of this Act and these departments deal with War Labour problems. In my view it would be advantageous that one department should deal with these problems.

In my country these departments are for all practical purposes looked upon as an employer, even when the Labour is not in their direct employ. In the event of a dispute between an employer and his workmen or the department and its direct employees, when the department's endeavour to conciliate fails, the matter is referred to the Ministry of Labour which secures arbitration and so ensures an equitable balance.

PART IV

SUGGESTIONS

Having well considered the foregoing points and at the same time, always asking you to bear in mind that I speak without that intimate knowledge of your country which is essential to the problem, I would suggest that

1. A department be set up to deal with War Labour problems.

2. This department would call together a representative gathering of Capital and Labour.

3. An agreement covering the foregoing (see pages 9 to 11)[1] and certain other minor points should be arrived at in continuous sittings.

The functions of this department would comprise:

1. The appointment of such a number of responsible officers as may be required in industrial centres, to act as the eyes and ears of the department and report the trend of opinion, the possible causes of dissension and generally feel the pulse of Labour.

In war time it is necessary to deal with the possible causes of dissension in their earlier stages. Prevention as [at] such a time is more essential than cure.

2. The decentralisation, to as great an extent as possible, of its functions, direction and final control being retained by the department.

3. The setting up in the various industrial centres of Advisory Committees of Capital and Labour under the Chairmanship of a local officer.

4. The control of dilution and substitution of Labour

5. The exercise of the power to limit non-essential work.

6. The establishment of such a number of employment exchanges throughout the country as may be necessary.

7. The restriction and regulation of the employment of labour.

8. The exercise of the power to control establishments.

9. The regulation of wages to be paid to Union or Non-Union Labour in a Union or Non-Union establishment, and generally: and the making of awards to meet the increased cost of living.

10. The enrolment and transfer of Labour.

11. The establishment of Tribunals on which Labour should have representation with powers of summary jurisdiction over both employers and employed in respect of certain acts to be constituted legal offences, e.g. strikes, lock-outs, absenteeism, etc.

Stephenson Kent 8/11/17

TS MS (WP, DLC).
1 That is, "Part III."

To Newton Diehl Baker

My dear Mr. Secretary: The White House 10 November, 1917

Thank you sincerely for letting me see Sir Stevenson Kent's report. I am going to take the liberty of keeping it until my return from Buffalo.

In haste

Cordially and sincerely yours,   Woodrow Wilson

TLS (N. D. Baker Papers, DLC).

From Josephus Daniels

My dear Mr. President: Washington. November Tenth, 1917

I have your letter of November 8th with regard to the Army and Navy football game and you are correct in assuming that my view is the same as yours—that it ought to be omitted altogether this season. I took the matter up some time ago with Secretary Baker and we notified the teams at Annapolis and West Point that there would be no Army and Navy game this year.

Sincerely yours,   Josephus Daniels

TLS (WP, DLC).

From the Diary of Josephus Daniels

November Saturday 10 1917

Vanguard class (E B Crow)[1] sent meal to me and to the President. I sent to Mrs. Wilson and told her I thought the meal of the Presbyterian class was better than its theology though I would not dare say so to my Presbyterian wife & she would bring down on her head the anathemas if she dared say so to her Presbyterian husband.

Mrs W answered as follows: "We had quite a laugh over your funny note when I read it to the President, and he says he is sure your Presbyterian wife did not see it as you were more considerate of her feelings than I of his. However he is [not] above eating such sainted meal and we shall both enjoy it when we get back from Buffalo. We are starting in ten minutes, so pardon haste"   Faithfully

Edith Bolling Wilson

[1] Edmund Burwell Crow, cashier of the Commercial National Bank of Raleigh, N. C. He was the teacher of the "Vanguard," a Bible study class conducted under the auspices of the First Presbyterian Church of Raleigh.

INDEX

NOTE ON THE INDEX

THE alphabetically arranged analytical table of contents at the front of the volume eliminates duplication, in both contents and index, of references to certain documents, such as letters. Letters are listed in the contents alphabetically by name, and chronologically within each name by page. The subject matter of all letters is, of course, indexed. The Editorial Notes and Wilson's writings are listed in the contents chronologically by page. In addition, the subject matter of both categories is indexed. The index covers all references to books and articles mentioned in text or notes. Footnotes are indexed. Page references to footnotes which place a comma between the page number and "n" cite both text and footnote, thus: "418, n1." On the other hand, absence of the comma indicates reference to the footnote only, thus: "59n1"—the page number denoting where the footnote appears.

The index supplies the fullest known form of names and, for the Wilson and Axson families, relationships as far down as cousins. Persons referred to by nicknames or shortened forms of names can be identified by reference to entries for these forms of the names.

All entries consisting of page numbers only and which refer to concepts, issues, and opinions (such as democracy, the tariff, the money trust, leadership, and labor problems), are references to Wilson's speeches and writings. Page references that follow the symbol Δ in such entries refer to the opinions and comments of others who are identified.

Two cumulative contents-index volumes are now in print: Volume 13, which covers Volumes 1-12, and Volume 26, which covers Volumes 14-25. Volume 39, covering Volumes 27-38, is in preparation.

INDEX